Public Administration in India

Second Edition

Siuli Sarkar
Professor of Political Science and Principal
Lady Brabourne College
Kolkata

PHI Learning Private Limited
Delhi-110092
2018

₹ 425.00

PUBLIC ADMINISTRATION IN INDIA, Second Edition
Siuli Sarkar

ISBN-978-93-87472-91-4 (Print Book)
ISBN-978-93-87472-92-1 (e-Book)

The export rights of this book are vested solely with the publisher.

Second Printing (Second Edition) . . . . . . **June, 2018**

Published by Asoke K. Ghosh, PHI Learning Private Limited, Rimjhim House, 111, Patparganj Industrial Estate, Delhi-110092 and Printed by Raj Press, New Delhi-110012.

To

my husband

ABHIRUP

Contents

Preface ..... *xv*

1. **CONTINUITY AND CHANGE IN INDIAN ADMINISTRATION: A Brief Historical Outline** **1–32**

   1.1 Introduction ***1***
   1.2 Indian Administration: Different Phases ***3***
   - 1.2.1 Ancient Indian Administration ***5***
   - 1.2.2 Rajput Administration ***9***
   - 1.2.3 Sultanate Administration ***9***
   - 1.2.4 Mughal Administration ***10***
   - 1.2.5 British Administration ***16***
   - 1.2.6 Administration after Independence ***19***

   1.3 Post-Independence Administration: Various Features ***20***
   1.4 Changing Role of Indian Administration ***26***

   Questions ***30***
   Notes and References ***31***

2. **THE CIVIL SERVICE IN INDIA** **33–61**

   2.1 Introduction ***33***
   2.2 Structure of Civil Services ***34***
   - 2.2.1 Evolutionary Phase (1947–69) ***35***
   - 2.2.2 Experimental Phase (1970–84) ***36***
   - 2.2.3 Transitional Phase (1985–90) ***37***
   - 2.2.4 Reformist Phase (1991–95) ***37***
   - 2.2.5 Mainstream Phase (1996–Present) ***38***

   2.3 Terms and Conditions of UPSC Jobs ***39***
   - 2.3.1 Direct Recruitment to Civil Services ***40***
   - 2.3.2 Present Scheme of Competitive Examination ***40***

   2.4 Two Agencies or Instruments of Recruitment: Union Public Service Commission and State Public Service Commission ***43***

2.4.1 Union Public Service Commission ***43***
2.4.2 State Public Service Commission ***46***

2.5 Training of Higher Civil Services in India ***50***

2.5.1 Need for Training ***50***
2.5.2 Origin and Development of Training ***50***
2.5.3 Kinds of Training ***51***
2.5.4 Training Institutes ***52***
2.5.5 Shortcomings or Imperfections of Training ***55***

2.6 Some Developments in the Indian Civil Service ***55***

Questions ***59***
Notes and References ***60***

3. ADMINISTRATION AND POLITICS OF INDIA: The Central Picture **62–98**

3.1 Introduction ***62***
3.2 Meaning, Nature, Functions and Role of the Central Secretariat ***63***
3.3 Structure of the Central Secretariat ***64***
3.4 Prime Minister's Secretariat/Office ***70***

3.4.1 Structure ***70***
3.4.2 Functions ***72***
3.4.3 Role of the PMO (1947–Till Date) ***73***

3.5 Cabinet Secretariat ***77***

3.5.1 Role of the Cabinet Secretariat ***78***

3.6 The Cabinet Secretary ***79***
3.7 Union Government ***81***
3.8 President of India ***82***
3.9 Vice-President of India ***85***
3.10 Prime Minister and Council of Ministers ***86***
3.11 Several Ministries ***89***

3.11.1 Ministry of Finance ***89***
3.11.2 Ministry of Home Affairs ***91***
3.11.3 Ministry of External Affairs ***93***

3.12 Cabinet Committees ***95***

Questions ***96***
Notes and References ***97***

4. ADMINISTRATION AND POLITICS OF INDIA: The Provincial (State) Picture **99–119**

4.1 Introduction ***99***
4.2 State Secretariat: Functions and Structure ***100***
4.3 Chief Secretary ***102***

4.3.1 Appointment ***102***
4.3.2 Tenure ***103***
4.3.3 Functions ***103***

4.4 Departments/Directorates *105*

4.4.1 Heads of Departments/Directorates *105*
4.4.2 Functions *106*

4.5 Secretariat and Field Departments in States: Their Mutual Relationship *107*
4.6 Chief Secretary as the Link between Various Components of the State Government *108*
4.7 State Government: The Political Profile *109*
4.8 Governor: The Constitutional Head of the State Government *110*

4.8.1 Legislative Powers *111*
4.8.2 Executive Powers *111*
4.8.3 Financial Powers *112*
4.8.4 Judicial Powers *112*
4.8.5 Discretionary Powers *112*

4.9 Chief Minister: The Real Head of the State Government *115*
4.10 Council of Ministers *117*

Questions *118*
Notes and References *118*

5. DISTRICT ADMINISTRATION: Changing Role of the Collector 120–137

5.1 Introduction *120*
5.2 District Administration: Its Functions *121*
5.3 Organization of District Administration *122*
5.4 Collector: Evolution of His Role in District Administration *124*

5.4.1 Duties of Collector *125*

5.5 Changing Role of Collector *126*
5.6 Manysided Tasks of the Collector *127*

5.6.1 Revenue Collector *128*
5.6.2 District Magistrate *128*
5.6.3 Coordinator between Different Departments of the District *129*
5.6.4 Crisis Administrator *130*
5.6.5 Development Officer *131*

5.7 Collector as the Chief Executive Officer of the Zilla Parishad *132*

5.7.1 Conclusion *133*

Questions *136*
Notes and References *136*

6. LOCAL SELF GOVERNMENT IN INDIA: An Urban Picture 138–179

6.1 Meaning of Local Self Government *138*

6.1.1 Characteristics of Local Self Government ***139***
6.1.2 Success of Local Self Government: Necessary Conditions ***140***

6.2 Local Self Government as an International Concept ***142***

6.2.1 Local Self Governments in Various Parts of the World ***144***

6.3 Local Self Government in India: The General Philosophy ***154***

6.3.1 Local Government and Local Self Government ***155***
6.3.2 Constitutional Status of Local Government in India ***156***

6.4 Urban Local Self Government in India ***157***

6.4.1 Municipal Corporation ***159***

6.4.1.1 Kolkata Municipal Corporation (KMC) ***163***

6.4.2 Municipal Council or Municipality ***167***
6.4.3 Notified Area Committee ***169***
6.4.4 Town Area Committee ***170***
6.4.5 Cantonment Board ***170***
6.4.6 Township ***172***

6.5 Seventy-Fourth Constitutional Amendment ***173***

Questions ***178***
Notes and References ***178***

7. LOCAL SELF GOVERNMENT IN INDIA: A Rural Picture.............180–206

7.1 Introduction ***180***
7.2 Balvantrai Mehta Committee and Asoka Mehta Committee ***181***

7.2.1 Local Self Governmental Changes at the National Level ***183***

7.3 Local Governemnt in Rural India: Various Tiers ***184***

7.3.1 Gram Sabha ***184***
7.3.2 Panchayat or Gram Panchayat ***186***
7.3.3 Panchayat Samiti ***189***
7.3.4 Zilla Parishad ***192***

7.4 The Constitution (73rd Amendment) Act, 1993 ***193***

7.4.1 Drawbacks in Women's Participation in Panchayats: Negative Impact of 73rd Amendment ***195***

7.5 Panchayats in Three Southern States of India ***197***

7.5.1 Andhra Pradesh Panchayati Raj System ***197***
7.5.2 Karnataka Panchayati Raj System ***198***
7.5.3 Kerala Panchayati Raj System ***199***

7.6 West Bengal: A Unique Picture of Panchayats ***201***

Questions ***204***
Notes and References ***205***

8. WOMEN'S PARTICIPATION IN LOCAL SELF GOVERNMENT......207–240

8.1 Introduction *207*
8.2 Women in Society and Politics: The World View *209*
8.3 Movements and Indian Women *211*
8.4 Indian Women and Panchayati Raj Politics: A Pre-Reservation Picture *216*
8.5 Constitutional Provision for the Uplift of Women *219*
8.5.1 81st Amendment Bill *220*
8.6 The Immediate Results: Post-Reservation Picture *224*
8.7 Grass Roots Initiatives: Picture of Indian Panchayats in General *227*
8.7.1 Women's Representation in Second Generation Panchayats: Some Efforts *228*
8.8 Empowerment and Development *229*
8.9 Empowerment of Women: Some Problems and Constraints *230*
8.10 Women's Empowerment: An Optimistic View *232*
8.10.1 Some Recent Views on Women's Empowerment *234*
Questions *236*
Notes and References *237*

9. PLANNING AND PLAN ADMINISTRATION......241–274

9.1 Introduction *241*
9.1.1 Essentials of Planning *242*
9.2 Indian Planning: Aims and Features *244*
9.2.1 Aims or Objectives of Planning *244*
9.2.2 Features of Indian Planning *246*
9.2.3 A Liberal Trend *246*
9.3 Planning Commission *248*
9.3.1 Composition *249*
9.3.2 Functions and Responsibilities *252*
9.3.3 Organization *253*
9.3.4 ARC View on Planning Commission *254*
9.3.5 Evaluation of the Planning Commission *256*
9.3.6 Changing Nature of Planning: NITI Aayog *257*
9.4 National Development Council (NDC) *261*
9.4.1 Composition *262*
9.4.2 Committees of NDC *263*
9.4.3 Functions of the NDC *264*
9.4.4 Evaluation of NDC *265*
9.5 Planning Machinery at the State Level *267*
9.5.1 State Planning Boards *268*

9.6 District Planning *269*

9.6.1 Operational Phases of District Planning *270*
9.6.2 Constitutional Amendment *272*

Questions *273*
Notes and References *273*

10. FINANCIAL ADMINISTRATION 275–301

10.1 Introduction *275*
10.2 Finance Commission *277*
10.3 Parliamentary Committees *284*

10.3.1 Public Accounts Committee (PAC) *285*
10.3.2 Estimates Committee (EC) *288*

10.4 Comptroller and Auditor-General (CAG) *290*
10.5 Election Commission *293*
10.6 Zonal Councils *297*

Questions *299*
Notes and References *300*

11. CITIZENS AND ADMINISTRATION 302–329

11.1 Introduction *302*
11.2 Public Grievances in Various Spheres of Administration *306*
11.3 Methods to Promote Good Relations between Citizens and Administration *309*

11.3.1 Infusing Competence among Government Employees *309*
11.3.2 Need for Administrative Improvements and Reforms *310*
11.3.3 Proper Matching between Expansion of Public Activities and Availability of Resources *310*
11.3.4 Proper Development of Public Relations *310*
11.3.5 Genuine and Well-Equipped Machinery to be Set Up at All Levels to Handle Citizens' Complaints *311*
11.3.6 Enlightened Citizenship *311*

11.4 Scandinavian Influence of Ombudsman *311*
11.5 Indian Efforts since Independence: Series of Lok Pal Bills in India *312*

11.6 Main Features of 1990 Lokpal Bill *315*

11.6.1 Some Recent Developments: Jan Lokpal Bill *316*

11.7 Lokayuktas at the State Level *317*
11.8 Functions of Lokayuktas *319*
11.9 Central Vigilance Commission (CVC) *322*

11.9.1 Vigilance Organization in Ministries/ Departments *323*

11.9.2 Central Bureau of Investigation and the Special Police Establishment *325*
11.10 Vigilance Machinery in States *325*
11.11 Conclusion *326*

Questions *328*
Notes and References *328*

12. COMMUNICATIONS BETWEEN THE PANCHAYATS AND THE MARGINALIZED: A Development Perspective 330–340

12.1 Introduction *330*
12.2 Pattern of Communications within Panchayats *331*
12.3 Pattern of Communications: Panchayats and People *332*
12.4 Shift in the Pattern of Communications since the Second Half of the Last Century *334*
12.5 Unworkable Paradigm of Communication in Rural Bengal *336*
12.6 Remarks on West Bengal *338*
12.7 Rural Marginalised: National Sector *339*

Questions *339*
Notes and References *340*

13. ADMINISTRATIVE REFORMS IN INDIA: Major Committees and Commissions 341–368

13.1 Introduction *341*
13.2 Administrative Reforms in India: Important Committees and Commissions *342*
13.3 The Administrative Reforms Commission (ARC) *347*
13.3.1 Machinery of the Government of India and its Procedure of Work *348*
13.3.2 The Machinery for Planning at all Levels *349*
13.3.3 Centre-State Relations *349*
13.3.4 Financial Administration *349*
13.3.5 Personnel Administration *350*
13.3.6 Economic Administration *351*
13.3.7 Administration at the State Level *351*
13.3.8 Administration at the District Level *352*
13.3.9 Public Sector Undertakings *352*
13.3.10 Redress of Citizens' Grievances *353*
13.3.11 Improvement of the Quality of Membership of the PSC *353*
13.4 The Sarkaria Commission on Centre-State Relations *353*
13.4.1 Appointment of the Commission *353*
13.4.2 Main Contents of the Report of the Sarkaria Commission *354*
13.4.3 Main Issues in Union and State Relations *355*
13.4.4 Main Recommendations of the Sarkaria Commission *356*

13.5 Punchhi Commission (2007) ***360***
13.6 Conclusion ***364***

Questions ***366***
Notes and References ***367***

14. WELFARE ADMINISTRATION 369–408

14.1 Meaning: Historical Background and Constitutional Support ***369***
14.2 Administrative Provision ***371***
14.3 Welfare Administration: A Case Study of a Civil Servant ***372***
14.4 Welfare of Scheduled Castes and Scheduled Tribes ***374***
14.4.1 Machinery for Safeguards of Such Deprived Sections ***374***
14.4.2 Centrally Sponsored Schemes ***375***
14.5 Welfare of Other Backward Classes ***376***
14.6 Welfare of Women ***378***
14.6.1 Welfare of Rural Women ***380***
14.7 Programmes Undertaken Recently for the Welfare of SCs/STs/OBCs and Women ***382***
14.7.1 Welfare of SC/ST/OBCs ***382***
14.7.2 Welfare of Women ***384***
14.8 Argument for Private Sector Reservation ***385***
14.9 Criticism of Reservation ***387***
14.10 Citizen and Social Welfare ***387***
14.10.1 Mahatma Gandhi National Rural Employment Guarantee Act (MGNREGA) ***391***
14.10.2 Sarva Shiksha Abhiyan (SSA) ***396***
14.10.3 National Rural Health Mission (NRHM) ***401***

Questions ***408***
Notes and References ***408***

15. ISSUE AREAS IN INDIAN ADMINISTRATION 409–432

15.1 Introduction ***409***
15.2 Constitutional Framework ***410***
15.3 Personnel Administration ***414***
15.3.1 Bureaucratic System ***415***
15.3.2 Aristocratic System ***415***
15.3.3 Democratic System ***416***
15.3.4 Functions ***416***
15.4 Administration of Law and Order ***417***
15.5 Public Sector Administration ***419***
15.6 Information Technology and Its Impact on Administration ***421***
15.7 Human Rights ***422***

15.8 Globalization and Civil Society *423*
15.9 Gender and Administration *426*

Questions *431*
Notes and References *431*

16. SOME RECENT DEVELOPMENTS IN THE CONCEPT OF ADMINISTRATION 433–449

16.1 Introduction *433*
16.2 Liberalisation and Privatisation *433*
16.3 Governance and Government *438*
16.4 Right to Information *444*
16.4.1 RTI Act (2005) and Intellectual Property Rights *446*
16.4.2 Citizen's Charter *446*

Questions *448*
Notes and References *449*

Name Index* *451–453

Subject Index* *455–460

Preface

In India, even after more than seven decades of Independence, one can still find the existence of heterogeneity in many aspects, which is detrimental to the development of the country. Huge resources are wasted in solving unproductive problems. Public Administration in India, as in many other developing nations, should therefore generate social change to speed up modernization. Keeping in view the social changes, this book takes into account the various administrative structures at the Central, state, district and even the local levels, the roles and functions of these structures, and the significance of various contemporary administrative issues in India.

A strong need was felt to have a standard textbook in the field of Indian administration, putting considerable emphasis on Indian government and politics, civil society and local self-government. This need prompted me to write this book. Most standard textbooks on public administration in India are dated, many of which do not present an all-encompassing and comprehensive account of the recent administrative developments. In this book, a sincere attempt has been made to fill in these gaps.

In the second enlarged edition, the book consists of 16 chapters. Chapter 1 gives a brief historical outline of Indian Administration at different phases—from the Rigvedic period till date. Chapter 2 discusses the structure of Civil Service in our country, the structures and functions of the Union Public Service Commission (UPSC) and the State Public Service Commissions (SPSC), training of civil service officers, etc. Chapters 3 and 4 are on the administration and politics in India, both at the Central and State levels. They describe the meaning, nature, structure and functions of the Central as well as State politico-administrative offices quite elaborately. Chapter 5 focuses on district administration including the changing role of the Collector, and the organizations and functions of various district administrative organizations.

Chapters 6 and 7 concentrate on local self government in India at the urban and rural levels. Along with the local self governmental bodies in India, these chapters also highlight the meaning of local self government, conditions for the success of this institution, and also local governmental organizations existing in USA, UK, France and Japan. Chapter 8 dwells on Indian women's representation in Panchayats during both pre-reservation and post-reservation periods. Chapter 9 discusses the composition and functions of the Planning Commission and National Development Council (NDC), as well as the planning machinery at the state and district levels. Chapter 10 is on Financial Administration in India and it includes a discussion on the composition and functions of the Finance Commission, Parliamentary Committees, the Comptroller and Auditor General (CAG), the Election Commission, and Zonal Councils.

Chapter 11 gives an exposition of the working of the Ombudsman, the institutions of Lokpal, Lokayuktas, Central Vigilance Commission, etc. Chapter 12 describes the patterns of communications between panchayats and the marginalized in a development perspective. Chapter 13 focuses on the Sarkaria Commission, the Administrative Reforms Commission, and their major recommendations along with those of various other committees and commissions in India in the post-independence period. Chapter 14 analyzes the welfare programmes for the scheduled castes, tribes, OBCs and women in India. It also discusses the new schemes of MGNREGA, SSA, NRHM etc. Chapter 15 critically examines the constitutional framework, personnel administration, administration of law and order, public sector administration, Information Technology (IT) and its impact on Indian administration, human rights, the effects of globalization on the civil society and the relation between public administration and gender. Chapter 16 gives a detailed description on three recent issues: public administration in the era of liberalisation and privatisation, governance and government and Right To Information.

I sincerely hope that this book will be an indispensable reading for the students of political science and public administration, both at the undergraduate and postgraduate levels. I believe that it will also meet the requirements of the students preparing for the civil service examinations.

The present edition would not have been possible without the enthusiastic encouragement and active support of the members of my family, friends, students and colleagues. I gratefully recall the constant inspiration I got from my parents late Smt. Sushama Chakravarti (In fact, she was the greatest inspirator of the second edition of this book till her last days) and Sri Nirendranath Chakravarti, my elder brother Krishnarup Chakravarti, my elder sister Sonali Chakravarti Banerjee, my husband Abhirup and my son Agnirup. I also express my gratitude to my ex-student Dr. Payal Bose, presently teaching Political Science at Ramakrishna Sarada Mission Vivekananda Vidyabhavan, Kolkata, for her sincere cooperation and whole-hearted support. Finally, I wish to thank the entire editorial and production team of PHI Learning for their careful processing of the manuscript of the present edition.

Any suggestions for further improvement of the book from the readers are most welcome.

Siuli Sarkar

1 Continuity and Change in Indian Administration
A Brief Historical Outline

1.1 INTRODUCTION

Public administration consists of two words–public and administration. 'Public' includes all the activities carried out directly or indirectly by the administrative apparatus of the government. The word 'administration' has come from the verb 'to administer' which, in turn, is derived from the Latin words *ad* and *ministrare*, meaning 'to serve' or 'to manage'. The dictionary defines administration as 'management of affairs'.

L.D. White defines public administration as a discipline which consists of all those operations having for their purpose the fulfilment or enforcement of public policy.[1]

In the words of Woodrow Wilson, "Public Administration is detailed and systematic application of law. Every application of law is an act of administration."[2]

J.M. Pfiffner observes: "Public administration consists of doing the work of the government, whether it be running an X-ray machine in a health laboratory or coining money in the mint ... administration consists of getting the work of government done by coordinating the efforts of people so that they can work together or accomplish their set tasks. Administration embraces activities which may be highly technical and specialized, as public health and the building of bridges... It also involves managing, directing and supervising the activities of thousands, even millions of workers so that some order and efficiency may result from their efforts..."[3]

On the basis of the above definitions, it may be said that public administration is concerned with the implementation of public policy, as laid down by the competent authority, economically and efficiently for the benefit of the people.

Public administration is the nucleus of development. As early as 1950, the Secretary-General of the United Nations pointed out: "Any systematic effort towards economic development must be preceded by, or coupled with, efforts to make more effective the functioning of governmental machinery."[4] Administration is essential both for developed and developing countries. No system of government can survive without a good system of administration.

In this book, we confine ourselves to the public administrative machinery in India. Since India is a developing country, our primary goal would be to point out the significance of public administration in developing countries. Developing countries are characterized by the following economic features:

- Low Gross National Product (GNP) per capita
- Widespread poverty
- Scarcity of capital
- Rapid population growth and high dependency-burdens
- Low level of productivity
- Technological backwardness
- High level of unemployment
- Greater income inequalities
- Wide gap between urban and rural development
- A negative balance of trade
- A semi-industrial agrarian economy.

Coupled with these economic features, developing countries are characterized by certain typical politico-administrative features. They are as follows:

- Traditional administrative structures
- Introduction of certain new administrative functions
- Outdated processes and procedures to perform functions
- Corrupt practices
- Ill-equipped politico-administrative leadership.

Henderson and Dwivedi in their *Administered Development: The Fifth Decade*[5] have warned the developing countries of poor performance if they do not improve their administrative system. They have further said that the developing nations have a vital stake in orderly functioning of their administrative systems. The time has come for them to opt for accelerated development so as to catch the progress thwarted by their creation of a bunch of rules, regulations, permits and the like, in the past.

In India, even after six decades of independence, one can still find the existence of explicit manifestation of hostile heterogeneity, which is markedly detrimental to development. Huge resources are wasted in order to solve unproductive problems. Public administration in India, as in many other developing nations, should therefore generate social change to inject modernization.

1.2 INDIAN ADMINISTRATION: DIFFERENT PHASES

Before dealing with the various aspects of public administration in India, keeping in view these deficiencies, let us explain the machinery of public administration that existed in our country in ancient days. In this context, we should make a line of distinction between public administration as an academic discipline and public administration as an activity. As an academic discipline, public administration is a century and a decade old. But as an activity, public administration can be traced to the earliest period of human civilization when men started to live in organized societies.[6] The administration of the State in the ancient and medieval periods in both the East and the West was authoritarian, patriarchal and elitist in character. Maintenance of law and order, collection of revenue, etc. were its compulsory functions while welfare activities were purely optional functions. Administrators were small in number, selected entirely at the will of the monarch. The official status of the administrators was no better than the personal servants of the king. The same thing is true of the administration in ancient India also.

The ancient Indian governmental system was established in the Vedic period. This system was in operation till 1000 AD. With the rise and fall of innumerable administrative organizations, the history of Indian administration is gradually developing. Two main features of Indian administration can be noticed in all ages. The *first* is the importance of *village* as the primary unit of administration, and the *second* is the *coordination* between the two opposite trends of *centralization* and *decentralization*. The present Indian administrative system is an advanced version of the ancient Indian administrative system. In fact, the modern public administration in India is composed on the basis of the traditional public administration of our nation.

In ancient India, the power and responsibility to rule the provinces was concentrated in the hands of the ruler. Numerous officers helped him to do this work. According to historian Beni Prasad, centring round the king, there were his close friends as well as a circle of principal officers.[7] In the two Hindu epics of the *Ramayana* and the *Mahabharata*, one can find a mention of administrative officers and their respective Departments. It can also be noticed in *Manu Smriti* and *Sukra Niti*. But the first detailed mention of the offices of the State can be noticed in Kautilya's *Arthasastra*. In the mean time, the administrative system in India was fully developed. In fact, during the reigns of Chandragupta Maurya and his grandson Asoka, the growth of Indian administration had reached its height. Mauryan administrative institutions grew further during the period of the Guptas.

Decentralization had already started in ancient India. For administrative convenience, empires were divided into provinces, provinces were divided into districts, and districts were again divided into certain urban and rural centres. State administration was divided into numerous Departments. Gradually, the number of such Departments increased and their jurisdiction extended significantly.

Regarding administrative principles in ancient India, it may be said that *hierarchy* as a principle was given a positive shape. The seeds of coordination between various Departments could be noticed during that period. During the periods of Chandragupta Maurya and Asoka, observation and inspection were given special importance and prominence. The following Departments existed during that age:

- Palace department
- Army department
- External affairs department
- Revenue department
- Treasury department.

There were many classes among the government officers in ancient India. Three classes of such officers were mentioned in Mauryan administration—city officers, military officers and village officers. Over and above these officers, there were Ministers and advisors. The provincial, district and village officers worked in subordination to the central officers. Altekar has opined that it is doubtful if there existed, like the present classification, all-India services, provincial services and subordinate services. However, '*Mahamatya*' of the Mauryan period and '*Kumaramatya*' of the Gupta period might have belonged to the all-India services. Historian Radhakumud Mukherjee thinks that the King used to appoint officers with the help of his ministers. The King, the Prime Minister and the Priest (*Purohit*) formed, what is known today as, the public service commission.

In ancient India, there existed the organization of a central office where all the government records and documents were kept. One finds the mention of such an office during the Mauryan and Chola periods. The King used to appoint personal Secretary, too. In short, the main function of the central office was to control and inspect provincial and regional governments.

From the historical point of view, however, Indian administration per sé may be studied under the following heads:

- Ancient Indian administration
- Rajput administration
- Sultanate administration
- Mughal administration
- British administration
- Administration after independence.

1.2.1 Ancient Indian Administration

In ancient India, different types of administrative systems were in operation in different periods. The administrative system started during the period of the Indus Valley Civilization. In this period, one can find planned roads and drainage which proves that a kind of municipal government was operating in cities. It looked after the civic demands and made systematic arrangements for the city-dwellers. Again, a single type of houses, a common system of weights and measures and a common script indicate that there was a large empire in the entire area. For convenience, we may divide the period of ancient Indian administration into the following categories:

- Rigvedic period
- Post-Vedic period
- Epic period
- Buddha period
- Mauryan period
- Gupta period.

Rigvedic Period

After the demise of the Indus Valley Civilization, the Rigvedic administrative system started. In this period, the administrative units were known as *Kul*, *'Gram'*, *Vish* and *'Nation'*. In the political system of the Rigvedic period, the smallest unit was the family while the largest unit was the State. The prevalent form of government in this period was monarchical and the office of the King was hereditary. But the Kings were not despotic in nature. In fact, at the time of coronation, they had to take an oath to work in the interest of the people.

Post-Vedic Period

The post-Vedic period was characterized by the rise of powerful kingdom. There was a natural increase in the number of officers assisting the King in the administration. In running the government, the King used to take advice from his Council of Ministers. The Council of Ministers was headed by the *Mukhyamatya*. Just as in the previous period, in the post-Vedic period also *Sabha* and *Samiti* existed as the two prominent institutions to curb the despotism of the King. The judicial administration was also headed by the King who was assisted by other officers.

Epic Period

In the period of the *Ramayana*, the form of government was monarchical. The administrative system of this period was well developed. As a result, most of the people were prosperous and happy. The King was at the apex of the administrative system. There were a number of Ministers and councillors to advise the King in matters of the state and government. During the period of the *Mahabharata*, the State was called 'Saptanghi'. The principal form of government in that period was monarchical. The King set an example of high ideals and performance of one's duties. He was responsible for the welfare of his subjects. To help the King in matters of administration, there were Ministers and officers. Special emphasis was given on merit regarding administrative recruitment.

Buddha Period

The administrative system of the period of Buddha was marked by the existence of 'Mahajanapadas'. Numerous republics could be noticed during this period. Along with these republics, however, there existed four big kingdoms of 'Magadha', 'Avanti', 'Vatsa' and 'Koshala'. In the republics, the real power belonged to the 'sabhas' (councils) which included the common people as well as the elite. The King was the head of the republic. He was elected for a fixed term and was accountable to the council for all his activities.

Mauryan Period

The Mauryan administrative system was characterized by the following features:

1. **The King:** The King was the head of the State and all the powers—executive, legislative, judicial and financial—were vested in him. It was said about the King that his happiness consists in the happiness of his subjects and his welfare lies in the welfare of them. He sacrificed his own interest for the sake of interests of his people. Along with the Council of Ministers, there were a large number of public officials and servants in order to help the King. According to Kautilya's *Arthasastra*, the King was the real life of the State and he was the defender of *Dharma* (virtue). He was expected to be *Dharmik* (i.e., pious and just, not religious in the modern sense). His powers and functions were somewhat curbed by the injunctions of the *Shastras*. He was bound to be grateful, decisive, thinker, fearless and self-controlled. Kautilya's 'ideal King' was to be a conqueror and an expansionist, always busy in expanding the territorial boundaries of his kingdom. But under all circumstances, an unable or incapable King was to be removed at any cost.
2. **Amatya:** Regarding the hierarchical chain, the position of the Amatya was just below that of the King. The Amatya occupied a special position in the Mauryan era. He was one of the topmost public officials. Rankwise, he was somewhat like the present Cabinet Secretary. He was also a special minister. The administrative details were looked after by him. From Kautilya's *Arthasastra*, we come to know the views

of other scholars like Bharadwaj, Vishalaksha, Parashar, etc. regarding the status of the Amatya. According to them, only those persons should be considered to be appointed as Amatyas who were capable, reliable, loyal, scholarly and well-connected. They were highly efficient, intelligent and quick decision-makers. They were entitled to high emoluments, good residence and many other facilities.

Kautilya categorizes all the Ministers, Amatyas and Heads of the Departments into eighteen *Tirthas*.[8] These are:

1. *Mantrin* — Minister/Counsellor
2. *Purohita* — Priest
3. *Senapati* — Commander of the army
4. *Yuvaraja* — Prince
5. *Dauvarika* — Chief of palace attendants
6. *Antarvamsika* — Chief of king's guard
7. *Prasastr* — Magistrate
8. *Samahartr* — Collector-General
9. *Samnidhatr* — Chief Treasurer
10. *Pradestr* — Commissioner
11. *Nayak* — Town guard
12. *Paur* — Chief of the town
13. *Karmanta* — Superintendent of mines
14. *Mantrin parishad Adhyaksha* — Chief of council of ministers
15. *Dandpala* — Officer of the army department
16. *Durgapala* — Guardian of the forts
17. *Antapala* — Officer-in-charge, boundaries
18. *Ativahika* — Officer-in-charge, forests

3. **Janpad:** *Janpad*, the third element of the Mauryan State, includes both territory and the people inhabiting it. Each territory should have well-defined boundaries. It must also have certain natural frontiers like the mountain, river, forest, etc. The overall prosperity of the *Janpad* depended upon the fertility of its land. The dwellers of the *Janpad* used to be industrious, intelligent and loyal, bearing good moral characters.
4. **Forts:** For defence purposes, including external aggressions and internal rebellions, forts were essential. They were well equipped with arms and weapons, food, water and medicines. In maintaining stability and consolidation of States, forts used to play a vital role.
5. **Treasury:** It was the principal basis of the Mauryan State. The finances of the empire were looked after and protected skilfully. Income of the State was derived from taxes like sales

tax, export tax, and village tax. For various expenses, budget was strictly maintained. There was a contingency fund to meet emergency expenses.

6. **Army:** It used to play a key role in the Mauryan State. A good soldier was bound to be loyal, brave, adventurous and well-versed in military sciences. He used to possess the qualities of a *Kshatriya* warrior. The army officers used to possess more qualities of this sort than the ordinary soldiers.
7. **Friends:** The term 'friends' implies a good neighbour State.
8. **Council of ministers:** The Mauryan King or emperor was aided by a Council of Ministers, headed by the Prime Minister. The Prime Minister, known as the *Mahamantrin* or *Mahamatya,* was the most powerful and influential person next to the King. This Council of Ministers comes nearer to the US model than the British model. Ministers were directly accountable to the King, not to any elected body. The King himself appointed the Ministers. Ministers used to be *Kuleen* or of a good family or of a high caste, clever, brave, ambitious, adventurous, patient, popular, well-versed in *Sastras* including *Arthasastra* by Kautilya, loyal and efficient. The King was pleased to consult Ministers individually or collectively. In making higher appointments, the King usually consulted the Council of Ministers or *Mantriparishad.*
9. **Diplomacy:** Diplomacy was considered to be a high quality art. Each King had a Foreign Minister who used to possess special power of policy-making regarding war and peace. Both *Sukraniti* and *Arthasastra* have mentioned various methods of conquests. Kautilya had suggested various methods of diplomacy like espionage, deceit, murder, poisoning and intoxicating. According to him, envoys (*duta*) were of three kinds. The first possessed full ministerial qualifications and were fully entitled to declare war and peace. The second type of envoys possessed ministerial qualifications less by one quarter. The third type possessed ministerial qualifications less by one half. These envoys were mere messengers of royal writs.
10. **Local self government:** In the Hindu state of ancient India administrative power was decentralized. *Puras* (cities) and *Janpadas* had their own administrative system. The village dwellers and city dwellers discharged their own duties. Local affairs were looked after by various kinds of *sabhas* and *samities.* The rural areas had their own system of local administration. Pataliputra (i.e. present Patna) was the capital of Mauryan empire and it had a full-fledged municipal administration.

Gupta Period

The administrative system in the Gupta era was basically monarchical. In running the governmental machinery, the Gupta Kings were assisted by the Council of Ministers. The entire administrative system was divided into certain Departments. Different officers were in charge of the respective Departments. The whole Gupta empire used to be divided into certain provinces which, again, were divided into regions. Regions were further divided into *vishays*. The *gram* (i.e. village) happened to be the smallest administrative unit which was headed by the *gramin* (i.e. the representative of the village). A *gram sabha* (i.e. village council) used to assist the *gramin* the in running the village administration.

1.2.2 Rajput Administration

The monarchical government existed in the administrative system during the Rajput period as well. In a number of administrative activities, the Council of Ministers used to help the King. The State was divided into certain comparatively smaller units. The *prant* was the largest administrative unit during the Rajput period. The controlling power of the ordinary citizens over the village panchayats was much reduced. The main reason behind it was that the Rajput administrative system was principally established on the foundation of the Gupta administration in which the role played by village panchayats was quite insignificant. The old institutions lost their utility and were gradually proceeding towards decay and demise.

1.2.3 Sultanate Administration

The administrative system of the Sultanate period was basically military and the rulers were autocrats. Since it was not possible for any single person to run the State alone, the Sultanate rulers, too, needed help and advice from outside. But the power of the Sultan was undoubtedly most supreme. Political, legal and military powers were concentrated in his hands. He was in charge of judicial administration as well. He could accept advice according to his needs from his advisors.

In the initial stage, the Turkish administration was absolutely military. The country used to be divided into certain regions. There was a principal military administrator in charge of every region. Besides, the King used to be assisted by Ministers. The Chief of these Ministers came to be known as the *Wazir*. He was in charge of the entire administrative system. He had his own Secretariat. Besides, he was aided and assisted by a chain of officers. Next to the *Wazir* was the military head. Apart from these administrators, there were two civil *dewans*. One *dewan* looked after all the religious affairs, religious institutions and the learned persons and the other was in charge of the system of transport and communication. For administrative convenience, the State was divided into a number of *prants*. The heads of the *prants* established certain Departments. Each *prant* was divided into certain *shikos* and each *shiko* was headed by the *shikdar*. Each *shiko* was divided into a number of *sarkars*, each *sarkar* into certain *parganas*, and each *pargana* was further divided into certain villages. The central bureaucrats used to run urban administration. Villages were marked by self-rule, to some extent.

After the end of the Sultanate administration and before the beginning of the Mughal administration, it is necessary to mention the administrative system during the period of Sher Shah. Although Sher Shah was basically the contemporary of the Mughal emperor Humayun; and Babur, Humayun's father, had already established the Mughal empire after the first battle of Panipath in 1526, yet Sher Shah's administrative and revenue system is considered to be the base on which Akbar, the most benevolent emperor of the Mughal era, established his own administration. Sher Shah was an able Afghan ruler and was widely known as a strong organizer and skilful military head. During all his military attacks against Kamran, Humayun's brother, and also against the Rajputs, Sher Shah built up a strong bureaucratic organization. Till his death in 1545, he maintained an unprecedented administrative system in his empire. The Centre was extremely powerful in his empire. He protected the traditional Indian administrative system quite carefully and yet introduced a number of administrative reforms in his land revenue system. The past Turkish administrative system established in North India inspired him in this regard to a great extent. Some historians like Percival Spear think that the Persi administrative system, particularly the Safabid dynasty, of that period was the centre of Sher Shah's inspiration regarding land revenue reforms. Sher Shah's revenue administration was followed entirely by Akbar and his revenue minister Todarmal.

1.2.4 Mughal Administration

A number of biographies of different Mughal emperors including *Ain-i-Akbari, Tujuk-i-Jahangiri, Tarikh-i-Shahjahani* and the written accounts of foreigners like Bernier, Hawkins, Thomas Roe, etc. discuss a lot about the various aspects of the Mughal administration. For convenience, we will discuss some of the fundamental features of the Mughal administration.

Mughal Emperors as Conquerors and Consolidators

It will perhaps not be an exaggeration to say that Indian history during the period between 1526 and 1556 is basically the story of the contest for supremacy between the Mughals and the Afghans. The victory of Akbar in the second battle of Panipat (1556) is considered to be the real beginning of the Mughal empire in India. Akbar himself was a great conqueror and consolidator. Besides, he was an exceptionally wise and intelligent ruler. Soon after winning the royal throne, he became keen on conquests. His career of conquest and expansion continued till the capture of Asirgarh in 1601. He skilfully furnished the best example of Kautilya's hero-king, a *vijigishu*. He was the real founder and protector of such a huge empire as the great Mughal empire. His son Jahangir (also known as Salim), grandson Shah Jahan and great grandson Aurangzeb also continued the policy of expansion of the Mughal empire during their reigns.

Nature of the Mughal Rule

In order to understand the nature of the Mughal rule, one should have a profound knowledge of the nature of the Islamic rule. Islam never dreamt of a society in which the non-Muslims constituted a majority. It believed that the non-Muslims, who were known as *Jimmis*, should have no right as citizens. Islam was so rigid in its outlook that the *Bahais* and the *Quadianis* were considered as non-Muslims. Even the Shias were not considered as the true Muslims. Only the Sunnis were treated to be Muslims by the orthodox section of the community. Such a rigid Islam came in contact with India in the ninth century. Most of the people of India were non-Muslims at that time. They did not want to be converted to the new religion. What is most surprising is that Akbar, the third Mughal emperor, was not an orthodox Muslim ruler. He was extremely liberal towards the Hindus or, for that matter, the non-Muslims. Both Akbar's son Jahangir and grandson Shah Jahan were supporters of religious liberalism. Historian Beni Prasad has described the Mughal State during Jahangir's reign as a "cultured State". However, almost all historians agree that Akbar was much ahead of Jahangir and Shah Jahan if religious liberalism is considered. Fundamentalism became absolutely prominent during the reign of Aurangzeb who himself was an orthodox Sunni Muslim. He once again imposed *jizia* tax upon the Hindus who were relieved of it during Akbar's reign. As a result, the Hindus were extremely dissatisfied with Aurangzeb. The fire of rebellion spread throughout the empire. The seeds of disintegration and downfall of the Mughal empire were sown at that time. In spite of the whole-hearted efforts by Aurangzeb, this demise and downfall could not be arrested.

Emperor

The focal point of the Mughal empire and administration was the emperor. When after the first battle of Panipat (1526) the Mughal empire was established, Babur, the founder of that empire, referred to himself as the *Padshah*. The word *pad* means stability and *shah* means ruler. According to the Muslim code, the emperor should be selected by the people. Persons born in royal families only could claim to be Mughal emperors. It was a regular feature that there was a continuous struggle for the royal throne even during the emperor's reign. In fact, Akbar had to face a rebellion from his eldest son Salim. Aurangzeb, too, ascended the throne after incarcerating his father, the reigning Shah Jahan and killing his elder brother, Dara Shikoh. This dirty practice continued among the later Mughals as well.

The Mughal emperors lived in utter luxury and their life style was magnificent and gorgeous. They enjoyed certain special rights denied to the common people like sitting on the throne, showing their faces every morning to the people, ordering death sentences, organizing elephant fights, hunting tigers and lions, conferring titles and honour, etc. They led busy but well-regulated lives and used to observe heavy schedules daily. It is interesting to point out that the emperor's main interest was supposed to be general welfare of his subjects. According to the *Quoran*, the entire responsibility for people's welfare was vested in the Mughal emperor.

Nobility

The Mughal nobility had two features. *First*, it was a heterogeneous class. The Turks, the Tartars, the Parsees, the Hindus and the Muslims—Indians from all religious communities represented the nobility during the Mughal rule.

Second, it was purely official in nature, not hereditary. The main drawback of the existence of the Mughal nobility was that it prevented the rise of a class that could challenge monarchy and organize revolts against the King.

Mansabdari System

The Mughal administration was military in nature. Each public official had to be enrolled in the army list. As a result, the *Mansabdari* system was created where there were both civilian and military officers. Each government officer could hold a *mansab* (i.e. official appointment of rank and profit). Each *mansabdar* used to supply a given number of troops for the military service. In Akbar's period, there were thirty-three grades of *mansab* ranging from 'commanders of 10' to 'commanders of 10,000'. The Mughal emperor himself used to recruit, promote, suspend or remove these *mansabdars* directly. Each grade carried a definite rate of pay, of which the holder could maintain a quota of horses, elephants, loading animals and carts. The rank was not hereditary. An officer could be given an entirely new responsibility at any moment. Here, one can cite the example of Raja Birbal. He was a good courtier who was sent to fight a war in the north-west, where he died.

Payment to government officers was of two types—cash payment and payment of *jagirs* or land. The *Ain-i-Akbari* by Abul Fazl tells us that the Mughal officers enjoyed inordinately high salaries. Historian Moreland observes that after making deductions for the maintenance of their quota and other incidental expenses, a *Mansabdar* of 5000 received a net monthly salary of at least 18,000 Indian rupees, which undoubtedly was a lot, particularly at the time of Akbar. The general condition of the public jobs was of the same type during the periods of Akbar, Jahangir and Shah Jahan. But it started to deteriorate gradually since the reign of Aurangzeb.

Council of Ministers

The Mughal Ministers were nothing more than mere assistants of the Mughal emperor. The emperor could take the advice of his Ministers, but he was, by no means, bound to take it. The Council remained collectively responsible to the emperor. The number of Ministers was not specified and the Muslim code was silent about their number and mode of appointment including their qualifications. Among the ministers the most important were *Vakils* and *Wazirs*. Both Babur and Humayun appointed *Wazirs*. But as Akbar was a minor while getting the royal throne, his guardian Bairam Khan started to rule the empire as *Vakil-i-Sultanat*. Akbar freed himself of all influences by 1562 and separated the two offices of *Vakil* and *Wazir*. The office of the *Vakil* continued till the time of Shah Jahan, but it gradually lost its glamour and influence. Consequently, the office of the *Wazir* emerged powerful and influential.

Revenue System

The chief features of the revenue system were survey of land and its measurement, classification of land and fixation of rates. Akbar's Revenue Minister Todarmal first attempted a new land revenue system in Gujarat. Lands began to be surveyed with the use of a new measurement known as *Illahi gaz* or yard. Land was divided into four classes on the basis of production. These were *polaj* or land capable of being annually cultivated; *parti*, that is, land kept fallow for some time to recover productive capacity; *chachar* or land that had remained fallow for three to four years; and *banjar*, that is, land which had been uncultivated for five years or more. This revenue system was based on the *rayatwari* system. It was absolutely different from the *zamindari* system introduced in north India by the British rulers.

For convenience of revenue collection and administration, the Mughal empire was divided into *subahs* which were subdivided into *sarkars*. Sarkars were again subdivided into *parganas*. Each *pargana* was a union of several villages. There was an officer, known as the *malguzar,* in charge of revenue collection in each district, who was assisted by a number of officers in this task.

Army

Historians are of different opinions regarding the real strength of the Mughal army. From the *Ain-i-Akbari* by Abul Fazl, we come to know that the Mughal army included 3,86,618 cavalry, 42,13,382 infantry,

1863 elephants, 4200 canons and 4500 ships of various kinds. Perhaps the cavalry (which was founded on the basis of the *Mansabdari* system) was the most valuable asset of the Mughal army. Some soldiers of the cavalry directly participated in the wars, some did not. Those who directly participated used arrows and cannons, swords and sticks. Those who did not participate directly carried out orders, distributed water, wrestled, camped and worked as envoys.

Judicial System

The main aim of the Mughal emperors was to establish an impartial judicial system. The liberal rulers established a standard judiciary for both the Hindus and the Muslims. In his short-term reign, Humayun arranged for the Tabl-Adal or judicial-siren. Jahangir and Shah Jahan were both well known for impartial justice. Akbar was particularly famous for establishing 'justice' in the truest sense of the term. Aurangzeb was an extremely orthodox Sunni Muslim ruler. He wanted to establish *Shariyati* rule throughout his empire. But on a particular day of the week, he used to pay proper heed to the needs and demands of his subjects. During his reign, there was an extensive judicial system at the Centre as well as the provinces. The emperor himself was at the apex of the rural and urban courts. He, as the *Khalifa*, was the focal point of the Mughal judiciary.

Police

In the urban areas, the most important administrative officer was the *Kotpal*. His main duty was to maintain peace and security in the city. *Kotpals* used to perform a number of functions during the Mughal period that included catching thieves, determining prices, carrying out the *qazi's* orders, managing prisons, appointing espionages, collecting information of the neighbouring villages, keeping accounts of the property of the dead or the absconded, banning cow-slaughtering, etc.

Welfare Measures

The basic duty of the Mughal emperors was to generate social and economic welfare for their subjects. As a result, the government introduced a number of welfare measures. The Mughal emperors, the Central Government, the provincial governments, village panchayats in the rural areas and municipal bodies in the urban areas—all were intimately associated with public welfare in the Mughal era. A number of voluntary organizations also were involved in this work. Numerous mosques, maqbaras, monuments, forts, palaces and large buildings were built in that age. A number of highways were made which basically worked as the communicating bridge between various trade-centres and the cities throughout the enormous Mughal empire. Shady trees were planted on both sides of these highways. Wells and tanks, too, were there. Inns and *dharamshalas* were made at regular intervals of these highways. Travellers could take rest in such places. For irrigation facilities, ponds were dug and dams were built. There were hospitals for the treatment of the infant and the old. Public baths were really beautiful. The postal system was highly advanced. Various measures were taken to combat such natural calamities as drought and flood.

Provincial and Local Administration

The huge Mughal empire was divided into a number of *subahs* or *prants* for administrative convenience. The number of these *subahs* used to be changed from time to time. The provinces were divided into certain sarkars (something like modern districts) and the *Sarkars* were divided into certain *Parganas*. These were some of the very important administrative and revenue units. The head of the *Subah* was known as the *Subedar* (also known as *Nazim* in some provinces). There was no regulation fixing the tenure of this office. The *subedar* was responsible for the general supervision, economic prosperity, defence and law and order of the province. He also supervised the administration of justice, helped the *Diwan* in collecting revenue, maintained the provincial forts and recommended appointments and promotions to important positions in the province. The provincial *diwan* was second in line, but not subordinate to the subedar. In fact, he was the latter's rival in provincial administration. The duties of the provincial *diwan* were collection of revenue, keeping financial accounts, allotment and disbursement of the salaries of the provincial officers, managing the *jagirs* of the province, realizing revenue from taxes and appointing the *Amins*, *Kroris* and *Tahsildars* in the provinces with the consent of the high *diwan*.

The *Sadar* of the province was directly appointed by the Centre. He supervised and distributed grants, took charge of promotion of learning by encouraging *Ulema* through stipends and looked after the religious interests in the *Subah*. The *Qazi* was in charge of the judicial department of the *Subah*. In some provinces, the offices of the *Sadar* and the *Qazi* were merged.

The *Bakshi* of the *Subah* was the counterpart of the *Mir Bakshi* at the Centre. Appointed by the Imperial Court, he was in charge of the military establishment of the province. He looked after the recruitment, organization, discipline and efficiency of the provincial army.

Regarding maintenance of law and order in the provinces, the *Faujdar* was the chief assistant of the *Subedar*. There were several *Faujdars* in a province, each in charge of a fixed area called the *faujdari*. He used to protect the tax-payers, punish the lawless and rebels, crush violence and lawless conduct, and reform the troublemakers.

Below the *Parganas*, there were villages called *Mawdah* or *Dih*. In a *Mawdah*, there were small hamlets called *naglah*. Under Shah Jahan, his *Wazir* created another intermediary unit called the *Chakla* between *Sarkar* and *Pargana*. *Chakla* basically included a number of *Parganas*. The *Sarkar*, however, continued to exist.

Three more offices—those of *Amir*, *Bitikchi* and *Khazandar*—deserve mention in local administration. The *Amir* was responsible for the working of the entire Revenue Department of the subdivision and worked under the direct control of the provincial *Diwan*. The *Bitikchi* assisted the *Amir* by doing necessary paperworks that formed the basis of assessment and collection of revenue. The *Khazandar* assisted the *Amir* in receiving money from the cultivators and issuing receipts.

1.2.5 British Administration

The Indian administrative system at present is largely a legacy of the British rule in pre-independence India. To make the Indian political system according to the structure of British parliamentary democracy, the contribution of the British administrative structure in India is immense. For convenience of discussion, we will divide the British administrative system into the following subsections:

East India Company (EIC)

The history of the British rule in India started on 31 December, 1600, when the British Crown granted a group of merchants a monopoly over trade in the East. After the fall of the Mughal empire, the EIC acquired a huge territory i.e. India and exerted immense political power. Together wtih mercantile employees, it employed a large number of civilians as clerks, writers, and the like. At that time the company had two controlling authorities—the Board of Control and the Court of Directors. The Board of Control was a much superior body as it was appointed by the British Parliament, while the members of the Court of Directors were nominated by the proprietors of the Company.[9] The civil service under the Company was divided into two categories: Covenanted civil service, and Uncovenanted civil service.

The first category was reserved only for the English. These civil servants used to serve the Company faithfully and protected the Company by all means.[10] The second category of service included the Indians, the Parsis, the English and the Portuguese. They did not have to sign any covenant with the Company.

Prominent Achievements of the Company Rule

The Regulating Act of 1773 should be regarded as the basis of the structural form of the Government of India. It is also the first statute which recognizes the Company as performing functions other than those of trade.[11] The Act applied mainly to Bengal Presidency. The Company used to appoint a Governor-General and a Council of four members in Bengal. The Governor-General was entitled to control the Presidencies of Madras and Bombay as well. Under this Act of 1773, Warren Hastings was appointed as the Governor-General. During his regime, the civil servants began to extend and expand their trade activities. They changed from "being a brand of commercial adventures and fortune hunters to a public service in the modern sense of the word."[12] The Company changed its status from the merchants to the government. It got the entire responsibility of revenue and maintenance of law and order. These were basically the skeleton functions of a slowly emerging police State.

The Secretariat, which is an important part of modern administration, had its beginning in those early days. The modern Secretariat originally was the office of the factory writers. In Bengal and Madras, there was a Secretary to the Council of the Governor-General and he was helped by five or six junior servants. This structure, created by Hastings, was further advanced by his successor, Lord Cornwallis who introduced a highly liberal system of remuneration, offering the recipient no alternative between poverty and dishonesty.[13] He also separated the customs from the Revenue Department. District officers of his time used to enjoy greater powers than the Collector of yester years.

The period of Lord Wellesley (1799–1805), however, marked a new epoch in the history of the civil services. His contribution to the field of training was immense. He was the first to realize that the functions of the Company were increasing. So, he made quick arrangements for the administrative training of the Company's civil servants. He issued orders for setting up the Fort William College at Calcutta in May, 1800, for training the Company's civil servants. The Fort William College was opened in November, 1800.

The next training institute, The East India College, was set up in England by the orders of the Court of Directors in 1805.

The Charter Act of 1830, together with renewing the Company's charter for a period of twenty years, made some other provisions. The large Presidency of Bengal was divided into two parts those of Bengal and Agra.

The next Act which came into operation was the Charter Act of 1853. This abolished the system of patronage and introduced the system of open competition as a method of recruitment. The entrance examination was to be conducted in London by a Civil Service Commission, which was set up in 1854. The age limit of candidates was 19 to 22 years.

According to the rules of the Macaulay Committee, a chain of administrative reforms started. For this, the British government set up various commissions, committees, boards, study teams, etc. The Report of the commission (The Civil Service Commission set up in 1854) is considered to be the Bible on competitive recruitment and training. It stated categorically that the candidates for senior governmental jobs should be appointed on the basis of a competitive examination that was open to the young men belonging to the age group of 18 to 23 years.

1858 and After

The Sepoy Mutiny of 1857, which eventually took the shape of a mass uprising or rather a people's war, brought about some fundamental changes in Indian administration. First we should mention the Act of 1858 which abolished the Court of Directors and the Board of Control—the two principal wings of the Company. The entire power and authority of the Company including the government, territories and revenues of India were transferred from the Company to the Crown. It authorized the appointment of an Additional Principal Secretary of State for India and also created the Council of India. The 1858 Act did not make any radical changes in the governmental system of India. The Governor-General continued to be equally powerful. Conditions of service in the public sector were to be determined by the Secretary of State. At that time, the administrative system of India had the following characteristics:[14]

1. The decay of the village panchayat system
2. Grouping of provinces without regard to the principles of racial, cultural and linguistic affinities
3. Enormous growth in public expenditure, particularly of military expenditure
4. Insufficient attention to education, public health, irrigation, etc.
5. Neglect of indigenous industry and agriculture, resulting in extreme poverty, often culminating in epidemics and famines
6. Excessive curtails on the political activities of the people like their freedom of speech and movement, freedom of the press, etc.

In 1859, Lord Canning introduced the 'portfolio' system. Under this, the work of the government, divided into several branches, was entrusted to different members of the Governor-General's Council. The main aim of the 'portfolio' system was to weaken the already existing highly centralized bureaucratic system to some extent. The Act of 1861 envisaged that the Finance and Home Departments were to be consulted on matters of finance and internal administration, respectively. This Act initiated the process of decentralization. The Legislative Councils of Bombay and Madras got back some of their lost powers. New councils were set up in other provinces as well.

Lord Ripon was in India from 1880 to 1884. The concept of 'self government' started to be very popular since that period. Gladstone, the liberal Prime Minister of Great Britain, declared at that time that he had failed to provide India with the advantages and blessings of independent institutions. Just after winning the 1880 elections, he sent Lord Ripon to India as the Governor-General. From 1880 to 1884—within this very short span of four years—Ripon introduced a local self governmental system for the rural and urban areas of India. His liberal administrative system, just like his educational system, Ilbert Bill, etc. became extremely popular.

The Aitchison Commission was appointed in 1886–87. The Commission supported the formation of a lower, local civil service to be called the Provincial Civil Service. As a result, as the Commission thought, the local demands would be satisfied. According to its recommendations, three services were established: (i) Imperial Civil Service, (ii) Provincial Civil Service, and (iii) Subordinate Civil Services.

The Indian Councils Act of 1892 enlarged the functions of the Legislative Councils. Though the system of direct elections was not approved, the preliminary process had started.

The Indian Councils Act (popularly known as the Morley Minto Reforms) of 1909 further increased the size of the Legislative Councils.

Next was introduced the Government of India Act, 1919. This Act basically changed the structure of provincial governments. A governmental system known as *Dyarchy* was introduced. Under this scheme, the provincial subjects were divided into two categories—*Reserved* and *Transferred*. All the important subjects like home, police, press, finance etc. were put in the *Reserved Category*. The *Transferred* list included such departments as medicine, health, education, etc.[15] Local self government became a provincial and transferred subject under a responsible Indian Minister.

As the experiment of 'dyarchy' was an utter failure, the British government appointed in 1923 the Royal Commission on the Superior Civil Services in India under the chairmanship of Lord Lee. Under the recommendations of the Lee Commission, the Federal Public Service Commission, consisting of a Chairman and four other members, was appointed. It started working with effect from October 1, 1926.

The Government of India Act (1935) proposed a federal system in place of 'dyarchy'. Along with provincial autonomy, this Act divided the subjects into three lists—Union, State and Concurrent. The Department of Planning was established in 1944, but was abolished in July 1946. After the end of World War II, three separate Departments were made for education, health and agriculture.

It is clear that Indian administration faced several experiments during the period of the British rule. A number of reforms were introduced one after another. The British rulers retained some major characteristic features of the Mughal administrative system. The simultaneous existence of continuity and change became a distinct feature of Indian administration.

1.2.6 Administration after Independence

India achieved independence from the British in 1947. So the administration of independent India is more than 61 years old. One can notice a number of developmental changes in various areas of administration. Simultaneously, a considerable number of negative sides of Indian administration can also be visible. These sides are briefly discussed in the next section.

1.3 POST-INDEPENDENCE ADMINISTRATION: VARIOUS FEATURES

Post-independence administrative system in India was somewhat unique in the sense it contained both the features of traditional Mughal administration, modern British administration and semi-traditional semi-modern indegenous administration of independent India. Hence it resembled, to some extent, the administrative system prevailing in the prismatic society as depicted by Frederic Riggs. The features of Post-independence Indian administration are as follows:

1. **Political instability or non-permanence:** Since independence, India has been experiencing a series of changes in her political scenario. For the first thirty years after independence, i.e. from 1947 to 1977, our national political life had been controlled more or less by the Indian National Congress. Only in 1967, after the fourth Lok Sabha elections, the Congress Party got a thinner majority in the Lok Sabha and it lost to the opposition parties in many States, where the Samyukt Vidhayak Dals (a loose collection of opposition parties) formed the governments. From 1977 to 1980, a combination of all opposition parties under the name of the Janata Party ruled at the Centre. During the period from 1980 to 1989, the Congress Party again came to power to control the national politics. The Janata Dal and the Samajwadi Janata Party reigned at the Centre from 1989 to 1991. Again the Congress Party came to control the national political scenario. The general elections of 1996 witnessed a novel experiment under the leadership of Dewa Gowda. He headed a combination of 13 opposition parties under the name of United Front. But the sudden decision of the Congress Party to withdraw support to the Dewa Gowda government in March 1997 automatically toppled the government at the Centre. The United Front government headed by I.K. Gujral assumed office in April 1997. But Gujral's eight-month old government resigned after the Congress had withdrawn its support. The Bhartiya Janata Party (BJP) ruled at the Centre from 1998 to 2004. After the fourteenth Lok Sabha elections in 2004, the Congress Party again came to power at the Centre. At the provincial level also, the allied parties of the BJP became weak. On the contrary, the allied parties of the Congress became more and more powerful. In the fifteenth Lok Sabha elections held in 2009, the Congress-led United Progessive Alliance (UPA) retained its power at the Centre. The BJP lost the elections quite remarkably. One significant reason behind the magnificient success of the UPA as a number of social scientists believe, was the strong alliance between the Congress and the TMC (Trina Mool Congress).

Narendra Modi led the BJP (Bhartiya Janata Party) in the 2014 general election that gave the party a majority in the Lok Sabha. It was the first time that a single party had achieved a majority in Indian Parliament since 1984. Modi himself was elected to Parliament from Varanasi. Since May 2014 Modi's administration started to gain a shape.

2. **Threat and danger of India turning into an agglomeration of different independent states:** In disobeying the Preamble to the Indian Constitution, there is always a threat to the unity and integrity of the nation from different sides. The fire of violence and unrest becomes predominant over non-violence and peace. Militants are very often active in Jammu & Kashmir and Punjab in the north-west. They have unhesitatingly declared their ideology to create separate and independent States in that region. The north-east is also burning with militancy and demands have quite often been raised by the ULFA (United Liberation Front of Assam) and similar groups like Kamtapuris, GNLF (Gorkha National Liberation Front), etc. for self determination. Nowadays, the Gorkha Janamukti Morcha (headed by Bimal Gurung, Roshan Giri, etc.) demands a separate State of Darjeeling, coming out of the control of the State of West Bengal. In the south also, the LTTE (Liberation Tigers of Tamil Elam) has been continuously creating unrest in Tamil Nadu. Both Jharkhand and Uttarakhand have been created as separate States as a result of such separatist demands. Some activists like Raj Thakre are keen on making Maharashtra only for the Marathis. Thus, it is evident that almost the entire nation of India is in flames. The rule of guns and sticks reigns everywhere.

3. **Failure to maintain law and order:** Just after independence, the ruling Congress Party did a blunder by giving priority to the issue of development over the issue of maintenance of law and order. It is true that development in a poor and backward country like India is vital. But at the same time, it should also be remembered that development here is possible only when there is peace in the atmosphere. While both the Union and State Legislatures are busy making and amending laws, the existing laws are not observed in practice by the people. Muscle power and violence reign in several parts of the nation.

4. **Too much pressure upon administration:** In the past several years since independence, there has been a vast increase in the number of Ministries and Departments of administration. At the time of the transfer of power in 1947,

the work of the government of India was carried out by only 18 Ministries. The Ministries in charge of industrial development, science, technology, commerce, education, social welfare, etc. have undergone remarkable expansion. In 1947, the number of members in the Central Council of Ministers stood at 16. By 1973, this number had gone up to 60 and, in 1987, it went up to 68. The figure had touched to 79 in 2009–14 ministry. In 2014–19 ministry it again has come down to 75. The change in the break-up is like the following:

	2009–14	*2014–19*
Cabinet Ministers	31	26
Ministers of State (Independent charge)	08	13
Ministers of State	40	36

This increase means addition in the number of appointees in charge of various Departments and Ministries. As a result of such a huge increase, the number of Secretariat officers has also risen remarkably. This is shown in Table 1.1:[16]

Table 1.1

Names of the posts	*1973*	*1991*
Secretary/Special Secretary	50	124
Additional Secretary	44	103
Joint Secretary	219	411
Director	124	369
Deputy Secretary	404	525
Under Secretary	617	1124

As a result, a number of problems have been created in the administrative sphere. There has continuously been a tremendous increase in the number of Ministries, Departments, Secretariat officers of the civil services, public undertakings, boards and commissions, advisory bodies, new constitutional or legal bodies, etc. In fact, nobody in our country perhaps rightly knows the exact number of such bodies at any given time.

5. **Administrative categories and political control over administration:** Corresponding with the federal division of legislative and executive responsibilities, there are three broad categories of Indian administration. The Union and State Governments have their own respective administrative personnel called Central services and State services. In addition, Indian federation has a unique cadre of administrative personnel called All-India Services, which are recruited by an

autonomous Constitutional Commission, viz. Union Public Service Commission. Such administrative personnel are trained in central academies of administration and in the field in State Governments to which they are permanently allocated.

These personnel may temporarily serve the Union Government on deputation. In fact, senior most administrative positions in the State as well as Union Governments are held by these officers. They work under the disciplinary jurisdiction of whichever level of government they may be serving for at a particular time. In the case of ultimate disciplinary measure of suspension and dismissal, a reference to the Union Home Ministry is mandatory.

The administration of each category is subject to the political control of the Executive. Civil services can offer whatever advice they consider appropriate; but once a policy decision is made by the political executive, administration is duty-bound to carry it out. The relationship between the administration and the legislature is not direct. It is intermediated through Ministers.

Since the All-India Services are designed to have a centralist mindset and a provincialist cadre-allocation, they were naturally suspected by the non-Congress State Governments when they were initially formed while the Congress still continues to hold the fort at the Centre. There were demands before the Sarkaria Commission on Centre-State Relations for the abolition of All-India Services, which the Commission did not accept.

Side by side, a number of developmental changes in India should be treated as achievements of public administration. The significant achievements of Indian administration are as under:

1. **GDP growth:** The launching of the Five Year Plans since 1951 initiated a process of development to raise the standard of living of the people living in extreme poverty. The growth rate in the Gross Domestic Products (GDP) was 3.61% in 1951–52. In 2005–06, it became 9.6%. In 2006–07, it was 9.4% and in 2007–08, it was 8.7%. The Eleventh Five Year Plan target (2007–08 to 2011–12) regarding GDP growth rate was 9%.
2. **Employment:** During the past two decades, employment has grown at a rate of about 2.2% per annum, which is even less than the population growth. Thus, a serious problem of unemployment and under-employment is created. From the latest data available, it is found that (in the formal sector) 18.01 million people are employed in the public sector while 8.45 million people are employed in the private sector during 2004–05.
3. **Cultivated area of foodgrains:** The total cultivated area of food grains was 118.75 million hectare in 1950–51. In

1960–61, it became 115.60 million hectare. In 1984–85, it went up to 140.90 million hectare. But it went down to 123.50 million hectare in 2006–07. This implies a fall in the area of food grains production and a corresponding rise in the area devoted to commercial crops.

4. **Irrigated area:** The irrigated area went significantly up from 22.6 million hectare in the 50s to 74.3 million hectare by 1989–90. In 2005–06, this figure went up to as under:

   Rice – 24.5 million hectare (56.0% of the total area under rice cultivation)

   Wheat – 23.8 million hectare (89.5% of the total area under wheat cultivation)

5. **Food grains production:** Between 1950–51 and 1988–89, India's food grains production went up from 50.8 million tonnes per annum to 170.2 million tonnes per annum. In 2005–06, it rose as high as 208.6 million tonnes per annum. Milk production also saw a significant increase.

6. **Infant mortality rate:** Though the achievements have been adequate, the gains in terms of quality of life have been slow, as the increasing population continues to erode the net benefits.

   The infant mortality rate has declined to 80 per 1000 by 1990, as compared to 129 per 1000 in 1971. In 2006, it was 56 per 1000 for males, 59 per 1000 for females, and 57 per 1000 for the combined population of India.

7. **Crude birth rate and crude death rate:** The crude birth rate has declined to 29.9 per 1000 by 1990, as compared to 37 per 1000 in 1971. In 2006, it was 23.5 per 1000.

   Similarly, crude death rate has also declined from 22.8 per 1000 in 1951 to 10.9 per 1000 in 1988. In 2006, it was 7.5 per 1000.

8. **Life expectancy:** Life expectancy has sharply risen from a mere 32 years in 1947 to almost double in 2001–06. For males, it is 62.3 years; for females, it is 63.9 years; and for the combined population, it is 63.2 years (2001–05 data).

9. **Rural-urban population:** In 1901, the rural population in India was 89 per cent while the urban population was 11 per cent. In 1991 the figures were 74 per cent and 26 per cent, respectively. In 2001, they were 72.2 per cent and 27.8 per cent, respectively. This increasing urban population has created problems like housing, slums, lack of civic amenities, inadequate living environment, and a higher rate of urban crimes.

10. **Sex ratio:** The number of females for 1000 males declined from 972 in 1901 to 929 in 1991. It slightly rose to 933 per 1000 males in 2001. In the rural areas, there are 946 females per 1000 males, while in the urban areas, there are 900 females per 1000 males.

    The 1991 census results reveal that the percentage of female literates is only 39.42, compared to 29.75 in 1981. The 2001 census results reveal the following data:

	Male	Female	Persons
Rural	71.4	46.7	59.40
Urban	86.7	73.2	80.30
Combined	75.85	54.16	65.38

    The achievement in the attainment of literacy rate is very slow. Besides, the quality of education is deteriorating. There is a need of a good vocational education system to provide employment and cater to the needs of the industry.

    There is lot of unemployment among Indian females. In 2001, 51.7 per cent of the total male population in India were workers (both main and marginal), whereas 25.6 per cent of the total female population in India were workers (both main and marginal).

11. **SC/ST population:** In 2001 census, scheduled caste population in India was 16.2 per cent while scheduled tribe population was 8.2 per cent of the total Indian population. The governments at the Union and State levels are trying their best to improve the status of scheduled castes and tribes, particularly at the rural level. A very large number of people belonging to these castes and tribes still continue to be socially, economically and educationally backward and are struggling at the bottom of the socio-economic pyramid.

12. **Religious composition:** India, in the truest sense of the term, is a religious polyanthus. The 2001 Census Reports reveal the following information:

Hindu	–	80.5 per cent of the total population
Muslim	–	13.4 per cent of the total population
Christian	–	2.3 per cent of the total population
Sikh	–	1.9 per cent of the total population
Others	–	1.9 per cent of the total population

    Law and order situations are likely to get deteriorated centring round several communal issues. Under such circumstances, the administration has to be doubly alert.

13. **Poverty line:** To quote the Eighth Five Year Plan: "The fact remains that after 40 years of planned development, about 200

million are still poor in rural India. In 1987, the rural poverty line in terms of per capita monthly expenditure was Rs. 131.80. The average incidence of rural poverty conceals wide inter-state differences which suggest that greater attention needs to be paid to the regions which have a greater concentration of the rural poor."[17] Though the annual per capita income has been slowly rising over time, a huge number of people are still below the poverty line.

According to the Planning Commission Estimates of 2004–05, 27.09 per cent of the rural population, 23.62 per cent of the urban population and 26.10 per cent of the rural and urban combined population are below the poverty line. 75 per cent of the Indian poor live in rural areas.

14. **Access to safe water:** From 1991 Census Reports, it is revealed that 27 per cent of the Indian population does not have access to safe water. The 2001 Census Reports reveal that the situation has slightly improved where 90 per cent of the urban population, 73 per cent of the rural population and 77.9 per cent of the rural and urban combined population have access to safe water.

Although the above developmental changes are considered to be the achievements of Indian administration, yet a lot more is still to be achieved.

1.4 CHANGING ROLE OF INDIAN ADMINISTRATION

Till 1947, two prominent features of Indian administration which had been steadily emphasized were:

- Law and order and revenue-oriented role of the bureaucracy in colonial India
- The feudalistic and patrimonial role of the bureaucracy in the Princely States integrated with the Indian Union.

The post-independence objectives of the Indian political system were:

- State-led strategy of industrialization
- Development of civic community in rural and urban India.

Public administration in India in this context tried to address, in its own way, the objective of building up a new structure of administration with an emphasis on 'development administration' conceptualized by Edward Weidner as "an action–oriented and goal–oriented administrative system".[18] It was felt to be absolutely essential to establish a bureaucratic apparatus for controlling the expanding scope of the public sector enterprises. Along with public enterprises, about 500 BDOs were appointed in each newly created lowest level of administrative unit of the State. Panchayati raj bodies of elected representatives were also set up.

During the 60s and the 70s of the last century, Indian administration faced newer and newer challenges like drought, flood, growing mass poverty and unemployment. As a result, additional strategies of development were adopted promptly like the Green Revolution during and after the mid-1960s and Poverty Alleviation Programmes since the 1970s. With the assistance from nationalized banks, quite a few poverty alleviation measures were initiated which included Antyodaya, Integrated Rural Development Programme (IRDP), White Revolution (dairy and poultry farming), etc. Thus, during the Nehru and Indira Gandhi eras, both "socialistic" development (conceived mainly as an interventionist State with a strong public sector) and "populistic" 'Garibi Hatao' kind of development (understood mainly in terms of the State's endeavour to drastically reduce the number of population living below the poverty line) were emphasized.[19]

By the end of the 1980s, both the kinds of development administration faced a deep crisis. *Firstly*, public sector undertakings fell prey to overstaffing and irrational use of resources and thus incurred huge losses, while the private sector performed much better.

Secondly, agriculture under private family cultivation showed promising results in spite of inadequate investment by the State.

These two factors, coupled with a severe balance of payment crisis (imbalance between import and export), necessitated remedial action on the part of Indian administration. Neo-liberal economic policies with accent on bureaucratic deregulation, privatization and globalization were introduced since 1991.

In the late 1990s, Kuldeep Mathur described this change in the context of Indian administration quite clearly. To quote him:

"This paradigmatic shift now introduces a fresh challenge to public administration. It tends to reduce the scope of intervention, but at the same time expects a change in the quality of intervention in chosen sectors."[20]

What Mathur implied is that the bureaucratic machinery in the changed situation should not be considered as the only instrument of policy implementation. In the civil society, cooperative endeavours or community based organizations can quite well develop their own capacity of resource management and use. If the State withdraws, the voluntary sector obviously can come forward. In this new administrative environment, as Mathur opines, "the buzz words are bureaucratic accountability, decentralization, participation, and community-based organizations or NGOs."[21]

This changed ambience has given birth to a number of new ideas like New Public Management (NPM), alternative development, sustainable development, good governance, etc. By New Public Management, Prof. Mohit Bhattacharya understands three principal things[22]:

- New Public Management indicates a shift from conventional public policy to the private management norms in terms of cost effectiveness.
- New Public Management believes in clusters instead of pyramids of organizations for the structural framework.
- New Public Management emphasizes flexible and adaptive operational systems rather than rigid planning and traditional bureaucratic hierarchy.

Richard C. Box suggests that administrators and academic experts of public administration in the changed administrative situation are under pressure to practise and theorize State administration differently from the ways and means of conventional wisdom. The new situation is characterized by two prominent features: (i) cost-effectiveness and (ii) autonomy from democratic pressure and oversight. To quote Box:

"New Public Management seeks to separate politics (in the sense of decision making by the people or their representatives) from administration, allowing (or making) managers to manage according to cost-benefit economic rationality, largely free from day-to-day democratic oversight.... Such a separation resembles the old politics-administration dichotomy and Herbert Simon's (1945–1997) description of administrative decisions that are largely 'factual'. In this reformed management setting, the public-private distinction is 'essentially obsolete' and management is generic across sectors...."[23]

The other much-emphasized newer ideas of Indian administration were alternative development, sustainable development, good governance, etc. Alternative development and sustainable development paradigms stress the importance of newer developmental concerns such as equity, quality of life, human development, gender and child justice, protection of environment and ecological balance, etc.[24]

Before understanding the terms like 'governance' and 'good governance', one should properly distinguish between 'government' and 'governance'. The 'government' is conventionally a *structure* while 'governance' is a *process* in which agencies other than government are roped in. Governance, according to scholars, is a conceptual riddle.[25] Semantically, it refers to government-run administration. Given its roots in the concern of the World Bank for recovering 'loans' given to the sub-Saharan African States, it has become integrally linked with the 'neo-liberal' thrust in contemporary global politics. In an interdependent world, governance is also projected as perhaps the most appropriate device to confront and mitigate the challenges of the network society.

'Governance' and 'good governance' become somewhat identical when 'governance' is sought to be defined as "a perception of the good society and the means to attain it: a construction of rationalities and a range of political technologies constantly negotiated among actors in a network."[26]

A recent World Bank publication has identified the following governance indicators: (i) accountability, (ii) political stability, (iii) Government effectiveness, (iv) regulatory quality, (v) rule of law, and (vi) control of corruption. The first two indicators operationalize "the process by which those in authority are selected and replaced." The next two indicators operationalize the quality, competence and independence of the civil service from political pressures and the credibility of Government's commitment to policies. The last two indicators summarize "the respect of citizens and the State for the institutions which govern their interactions."[27]

The shift of emphasis from welfare liberalism to business liberalism in Indian political economy throughout the 1990s requires adjustments on the part of our administrative system. Direct bureaucratic control by Government Departments must be replaced by facilitatory regulation by independent, often semi-judicial, regulatory authorities in various sectors of national and provincial economies, e.g. Central or State Electricity Regulatory Authorities, Telecom Regulatory Authority, Security and Exchange Board of India (SEBI), Competition Commission, Central Intelligence Regulatory Authority (CIRA), etc., all of which have been created under Parliamentary or State Legislative statutes since 1991. Besides, there is a growing emphasis on the necessity that in the changed situation of marketization, public administration must be operated like a business.

Modi's administration (2014–19) has tried to raise foreign direct investment in the Indian economy. It also increased expenditure on infrastructure and reduced expenditure on healthcare and social welfare programmes. By abolishing the Planning Commission, Modi has brought about centralisation of power and tried to make the bureaucracy more and more efficient. From the very beginning of his tenure as the Prime Minister, he has started a high-profile sanitation campaign, and weakened or even abolished environmental and labour laws.

The Modi government launched a crackdown against a number of civil society organisations. In the first year of his administration he ordered the Intelligence Bureau to investigate against tens of thousands of such organisations as, according to the administration, they were slowing economic growth. This led to discontent even within the BJP regarding Modi's style of functioning.

He also repealed 1159 obsolete laws by 2016, against a total of 1301 such laws repealed by previous governments over a span of 64 years. To come closer to the people, Modi started a monthly radio programme titled "Mann Ki Baat" since October, 2014. By ensuring that government services would be available electronically, by building infrastructure to provide high-speed internet access to rural areas, by boosting the manufacture of electronic goods in the country and also by promoting and continuously encouraging digital literacy, the Modi administration has truly launched the digital India programme.

On November 8, 2016 Modi government announced the demonetisation of all ₹500 and ₹1000 banknotes of the Mahatma Gandhi Series. The government claimed that it would curtail the shadow economy and crack down on the illicit and counterfeit cash to fund terrorism as well as illegitimate activities. The sudden announcement of demonetisation and the prolonged cash shortages in weeks after weeks created problems of citizens throughout India leading to a significant disruption in our economy. Initially, the move was backed by several bankers and some international commentators. But it was heavily criticized by members of the opposition parties, leading to debates in both Houses of the Parliament. The move was met with severe protests, litigations and strikes in a number of places across India. It was heavily criticized by prominent economists and world media since it was considered to have reduced India's GDP and industrial production. Yet several well-known bankers like Arundhati Bhattacharya, Chanda Kochhar etc. appreciated the move by Modi administration since, according to them, this would help curb black money. Businessmen like Anand Mahindra (Mahindra Group), Sajjan Jindal (JSW Group), Kunal Bahl (Snapdeal and Free Charge) also liked the move for this, in their consideration, would accelerate e-commerce. Mr. N.R. Narayana Murthy, founder of Infosys, in fact, praised the move.

Goods and Services Tax (GST) was introduced in India on July 1, 2017. Being an indirect tax, GST was applicable throughout India which replaced multiple cascading taxes levied by the Central and State governments. It was introduced as the 101st Constitutional Amendment Act, 2017, following the passage of 122nd Constitutional Amendment Bill. The GST is governed by GST Council, and the Finance Minister of India is the Chairman of the Council. GST replaced a number of indirect taxes with a unified tax. Thus, it is aimed at reshaping India's 2 trillion dollar economy rather dramatically. Under GST, goods and services are taxed at the following rates: 0%, 5%, 12%, 18% and 28%. There is a special rate of 0.25% on rough-precious and semi-precious stones and 3% on gold. Moreover, a cess of 22% or other rates on top of 28% GST applies on a few items like aerated drinks, luxury cars and tobacco products.

Questions

1. Briefly point out the features of Indian administration in its different phases from the Rig Vedic era till 1947.
2. Explain the various features of Indian adminstration from independence till date.
3. Examine the changing role of Indian administration since 1947.
4. Write short notes on:
   (a) Economic and politico-administrative features of the administrative systems of developing countries

(b) Ancient Indian administration
(c) Sultanate administration in India
(d) Mughal administration
(e) British administration in India
(f) Mauryan administration.
(g) Demonetisation.
(h) Mann Ki Baat.
(i) Goods and Services Tax (GST).

Notes and References

1. White, L.D., *Introduction to the Study of Public Administration*, Macmillan, 1955.
2. Wilson, Woodrow, The Study of Administration, *Political Science Quarterly*, 1941.
3. Pfiffner, J.M., *Public Administration*, The Ronald Press Company, New York, 1946.
4. Official Records of the ECOSOC (E/1708), Agenda item 10.
5. Henderson, Keith M. and O.P. Dwivedi, *Administered Development: The Fifth Decade*, 1992.
6. Basu, Rumki, *Public Administration: Concepts and Theories*, 3rd ed., Sterling, 1994.
7. Avasthi and Avasthi, *Public Administration in India*, 9th rev. ed., Lakshmi Narain Agarwal, Agra, 2003.
8. Arora, R.K. and Rajni Goyal, *Indian Public Administration*, Wishwa Prakashan, New Delhi, 2001.
9. See for details, Cooke Taylor, *A Popular History of British India*, Mittal, Delhi, 1987.
10. Mishra, B.B., *The Administrative History of India*, Oxford University Press, New Delhi, 1970.
11. Chesney, George, *Indian Polity*, Metropolitan, New Delhi, 1976.
12. Ghosal cited in Dwarkadas, R., *Role of Higher Civil Service in India*, Bombay, Popular Book Depot, Bombay, 1958.
13. Chesney, George, *op. cit.*
14. Pylee, M.V., *Constitutional Government in India*, Asia, Bombay, 1968.
15. *Ibid.*
16. Avasthi and Avasthi, *op. cit.*
17. Government of India, Eighth Five Year Plan (1992–97), Vol. II, New Delhi, 1992.

18. Weidner, Edward quoted in Bhattacharya, Mohit, *Social Theory and Development Administration*, 3rd ed., Jawahar Publishers & Distributors, New Delhi, 2002.

19. Singh, M.P. and Rekha Saxena, *Indian Politics: Contemporary Issues and Concerns*, Prentice-Hall of India, New Delhi, 2008.

20. Mathur, Kuldeep, Introduction: The Emerging Concerns in Public Administration, in Mathur, Kuldeep (Ed.), *Development Policy and Administration*, Sage, New Delhi, 1998.

21. *Ibid.*

22. Bhattacharya, Mohit, *op. cit.*

23. Box, Richard C., Running Government Like a Business: Implications for Public Administration Theory and Practice, in Chakrabarty, Bidyut and Mohit Bhattacharya (Eds.), *Public Administration: A Reader*, Oxford University Press, New Delhi, 2003.

24. Kothari, Ashish, Environment, Equity, Sustainability: The Essential Links, in Singh, M.P. and Rekha Saxena (Eds), *Ideologies and Institutions in Indian Politics*, Deep and Deep, Delhi, 1998.

25. Chakrabarty, Bidyut, *Reinventing Public Administration: The Indian Experience*, Orient Longman, New Delhi, 2007.

26. *Ibid.*

27. Singh, M.P. and Rekha Saxena (Eds.), *op. cit.*

2 The Civil Service in India

2.1 INTRODUCTION

L.D. White has characterized public administration as the "heart of the problem of modern government." It is indeed no exaggeration to give public administration the status of the "fourth organ of government". In any country, public administration is manned by public or civil services. The term 'civil service' is well defined by Herman Finer as a "professional body of officials, permanent, paid and skilled." It is this great body of men and women that "translates law into action from one end of the country to the other and brings the national government into its daily contacts with the rank and file in the country...."[1]

The duties of the civil service today are many and varied. They include: advice to Ministers on all matters of policy; supervision of all aspects of the government's scientific research, carrying out the social services; numerous routine functions like collecting taxes, keeping accounts, selling postage stamps, etc. Nowadays, the public officials perform various kinds of functions. The first function is the implementation of the government's policies. Secondly, they have semi-legislative and semi-judicial functions. Thirdly, they advise the political executive on policy matters. Fourthly, public relations constitute an important part of the duties of public officials. Again, public officials of certain positions are expected to explain the government policies to the people and to win their cooperation in the implementation of such policies. In India, in the context of parliamentary democracy, the public official is accountable directly to the political executive and indirectly to the Parliament and the people. Many scholars have identified the following major trends that have characterized the civil services in many countries during recent years, with particular reference to India:[2]

- Rapid increase in the number of civil servants
- Increasing diversification of civil services by the recruitment of more and more technicians, specialists and experts
- Change in the traditional concept of civil service neutrality

- Increasing emphasis on professional standards
- Various new tasks of the civil service
- Qualities needed in the civil service in the changed context
- Breakdown of the Weberian model in independent India.

2.2 STRUCTURE OF CIVIL SERVICES

The entire unit of civil services in India may be grouped under two broad categories—Central Services and State Services. The former serves the Central Government while the latter serves various State Governments and Union Territories. Central Services are organized into four Groups–A, B, C and D. The officer class includes Group A and Group B services. Group A comprises All-India and Group A Central Services. Group B comprises basically the class of first-line supervisors. Group C comprises clerical jobs. Group D comprises a large bulk of unskilled employees including *safai* employees, messengers, peons, *daftaris, jamadars*, cyclostyle machine operators, etc. The Sixth Pay Commission in its Report has recommended for the abolition of the Group D category. The existing employees belonging to this category will be given a special training so that they can upgrade themselves to be fit for the lowest strata of the Group C category. Those who will fail to successfully learn the training course will be fixed at a special 'zero pay band' category. Ultimately, the Group D services are planned to be done by outsourcing.

Here we are concerned with Group A and Group B services only, which have been termed Higher Civil Services. The main point of our discussion will be recruitment and training of these Higher Civil Services. We will discuss it principally in the context of post-independence India. But for convenience in understanding the context, the pre-independence recruitment and training may sometimes be discussed.

After independence, sixty two long years have gone. During this period of more than six decades, innumerable changes have come in the Indian administrative system. The civil services themselves have undoubtedly changed their respective roles time and again. Girish Pradhan has divided the post-independence Indian administration, on the basis of the changes in civil services, into five major phases.[3] These are as follows:

1. Evolutionary phase (1947–69)
2. Experimental phase (1970–84)
3. Transitional phase (1985–90)
4. Reformist phase (1991–95)
5. Mainstream phase (1996–Present)

Each phase is discussed in the following sections.

2.2.1 Evolutionary Phase (1947–69)

In its two hundred years' rule, the colonizing power systematically extracted so much wealth from India that the nation became absolutely poor. She did not have sufficient tools and skills to transform her economy into a modern one. Both industry and agriculture were in a state of stagnation and utter backwardness. Lack of education and fanaticism gave birth to a number of communal tensions. Hence, in the post-independence period, the primary task before the civil service was to eradicate these imperfections and thus to make the foundation of a modern administrative system in India. The cornerstone of this was the Constitution of India.[4]

The British rule in India was based on the performance of a few administrators from the Indian Civil Service (ICS). These administrators were known as ICS officers. It is said that when, in 1947, the British left India, they left behind the ICS officers the development work of free India. Hence, all the important posts from the district through the province to the capital started to be occupied by such officers who, in reality, appeared to be all-in-all. These ICS officers were regarded as impartial judges and some of them were actually judges, for they were free to decide whether to remain on the administrative side or to be in the judiciary.

From 1947 to 1969, there appeared a number of evolutions in the civil service in India. Civil services—both the All-India Service and various provincial services—became remarkably matured. In 1949, N. Gopalaswami Ayyangar recommended various suggestions for improving the governmental methods. The Gorwala Report of April 1951 pointed out that a clean, efficient and impartial administrative system was the most fundamental condition for the success of democratic planning. Paul H. Appleby, therefore, emphasized the need for establishing a central office that bears the responsibility of reviewing structures, management and procedures of government. As a result, the Organization and Methods Division was set up in the office of the Cabinet Secretary. Training for the civil service and development of the district administration were categorically emphasized in a report by V.T. Krishnamachari. In another report in 1964, K. Santhanam put special emphasis upon the issue of corruption and its probable remedies.

In the evolutionary phase if the first cornerstone was the making of the Indian Constitution, then obviously the second one would be the whole process of economic planning.[5] This was the period when the provinces were reorganized along linguistic lines. The reorganization of States was completed by the State Reorganization Commission of 1953. After 2002, India consisted of 28 States and 6 Union Territories.

In the 1960s, the bureaucracy was exposed to be absolutely inadequate to deal with the challenges thrown up by the development activities. As a result, the Administrative Reforms Commission (ARC) was set up in January 1966. The ARC was given the tasks to (a) ensure that the highest standards of efficiency and integrity is maintained in the public services, (b) make public administration a suitable instrument for carrying out the socio-economic goals of development, and (c) make the administrative machinery responsive to the people. Thus, the civil service was completely remade after a series of changes in its role. In 1970, the ARC made a number of recommendations and submitted them to the government. With this submission, the evolutionary or first phase (1947–69) of the post-independence civil services in India ended.

2.2.2 Experimental Phase (1970–84)

In the experimental phase, for the first time, it was realized that everything in the administrative structure was not working properly. But it was absolutely unknown how to improve this structure or, in other words, what changes are to be brought about in the structure. The implementation of a large number of changes suggested by the ARC took almost a decade to be completed.[6] All Union Ministries dealing with development were asked to adopt the performance budgeting technique. The Bureau of Public Enterprises—which had been set up in the late 1960s—was considerably strengthened.

In the experimental phase, administration faced challenges from two sides — both externally and internally. The external challenge came when there was an exodus of refugees from former East Pakistan (now Bangladesh). Indian administration boldly met the challenge of refugees. The manner in which the refugee problem was dealt during the period shows the capacity of the Indian bureaucracy under pressure. The national emergency during 1975–76 (which the then Prime Minister Mrs. Indira Gandhi declared in June 1975) was the internal challenge that the Indian civil service faced during the experimental phase. In the Lok Sabha elections of 1977, Mrs. Gandhi was defeated and the Congress Government was dismissed. The rethinking in the administrative sphere that started after the elections of 1977 continued the experimental phase even after. The Chairman of the ARC, Mr. Morarji Desai, became the new Prime Minister of the country. It was thought that civil service reforms would gain momentum. But very soon, within two years only, his government, too, was dismissed. Administrative reforms naturally became much slower.

During the emergency, many leaders were heckled by our bureaucracy. The Shah Commission was highly critical of the role played by the bureaucracy. This had an adverse impact upon the IAS officers. The most important reform during this phase was perhaps the setting up of Departments of Personnel and Administrative Reforms at the provincial levels. Besides, the aspects of training of the civil servants were considerably emphasized.

After the assassination of Mrs. Indira Gandhi in 1984, the experimental phase came to an end. Rajiv Gandhi, the next Prime Minister of India, was gradually becoming impatient with the slow pace of bureaucracy. He emphasized the need for a modern or New York culture in administration in which speedy performance and result orientation were given utmost priority.

2.2.3 Transitional Phase (1985–90)

In January 1985, the newly settled Prime Minister Mr. Rajiv Gandhi declared that the principal aim of administration as well as civil service would be to adjust with the socio-economic changes. This aim implies decentralization of the decision-making process, enforcing accountability, simplification of rules and procedures, prompt service to citizens and speedy creation of a separate Ministry called the Ministry of Programme Implementation (MPI). Annual Action Plans (AAPs) for all Ministries and public enterprises were made as a follow-up. Management By Objectives (MBOs) was introduced during this period.

It was decided that administration would be much more speedy and clientele-oriented. Where there was any scope for inter-ministerial consultation, minimum time limit for policy implementation would have to be prescribed. The technical, specialist or other agencies were asked to state the broad guidelines for implementation, as far as practicable, so that the respective ministries were not involved in a case-by-case clearance. The entire administrative environment was improved and as a result more functional layouts came out and newer and newer administrative equipment were introduced. Voluntary or Non-Governmental Organizations (NGOs) were attempted for the first time to be involved directly in these efficient administrative activities.

Emphasis was given to the need for, and importance of, training to a significant extent. Concrete steps were taken to introduce compulsory training programmes for all civil servants, especially those holding higher posts. A number of State institutes for rural development were established.

During this phase, due to his technical background and young age, Rajiv Gandhi could efficiently introduce a series of changes in administrative affairs. This brought about not only more efficient working of the government, but an opportunity for huge economic growth. This was perhaps the most long-lasting benefit of the transitional phase.

2.2.4 Reformist Phase (1991–95)

Since 1991, the economic reforms were basically characterized by conscious policies of liberalization, privatization and globalization. The reform packages in the sphere of administration were a response to the foreign exchange and fiscal crisis of 1991. The administrative system of this period was marked by an enormous size of the governmental machinery and the consequent growth of employment in government services. The total size of the government, including the Central, State and Local establishments, came to be less than 20 million. The cost of salaries of all government employees in 1991 stood at Rs. 7000 crores for India as a whole.[7]

The public sector employment in India had increased from 4.10 million in 1953 to 18.97 million in 1991. The share of the public sector in the total employment in the organized sector had increased from 58.3 per cent in 1961 to 70.7 per cent in 1991. The share of private sector employment had gone down from 41.7 per cent to 29.3 per cent during the same period.[8]

In this period, the Central Government as well as various State Governments introduced the Voluntary Retirement Scheme (VRS) with a view to allow those who want to seek premature retirement from the government service with a lumpsum of retirement benefits and also to give chances to the relatively younger people to be appointed in the government service.

2.2.5 Mainstream Phase (1996–Present)

From the mainstream phase, it was started to be thought that if the government does not trust its civil service, it would be difficult to expect the civil service to serve the public and to adopt welfare measures for them. A trend is seen to bring all the administrative issues into the open and discuss them freely.[9]

The Ministry of Personnel, Public Grievances and Pensions under the Government of India prepared a document entitled 'An Agenda for Effective and Responsible Administration'. In the document it was said that governance must extend beyond conventional bureaucracies and empower the citizens to involve themselves in public services through autonomously elected local administrative agencies. It was further stated that the public administration and the civil service at all levels were passing through difficult times in terms of the credibility of the civil service before the public, for there was a growing public perception of an unholy alliance between certain elements among politicians and civil servants, on the one hand, and criminals, on the other. As a result, there was an increasing criticism of the low level of honesty, transparency and accessibility among the bureaucrats.[10]

A major result of the Responsive Administration Conference was the adoption of Citizen's Charters and the Right to Information. The newly created unified civil service is characterized by the following features:[11]

1. All the services and cadres are merged into a unified grading structure with equality of opportunity for all who enter the service in any State.

2. All 'classes' among the public personnel have been abolished and replaced by a unified grading structure: a peon at the bottom and a Secretary or Departmental Head at the top. In all, a unified 22-grade pay scale has been introduced, thus doing away with the more than 600 salary scales that were in operation.
3. The unified structure of the civil service enables promotions to higher posts throughout the range of the public service. Vertical movements as well as horizontal movements are introduced side by side.
4. The correct grading of each post is determined by correct job evaluation.

2.3 TERMS AND CONDITIONS OF UPSC JOBS

The following matters constitute the terms and conditions of service of a government employee:

(a) Salary or wage including subsistence allowance during suspension, periodical increments, etc.
(b) Leave, provident fund, gratuity
(c) Promotion, seniority
(d) Superannuation pension
(e) Tenure or termination of service
(f) Transfer, deputation
(g) Disciplinary proceedings.

Article 310 provides that all civil servants of the All-India services or of civil services under the Union shall hold office during the pleasure of the President. The government's right to terminate the services is, however, subject to the restrictions imposed by Article 311(1) and 311(2). Article 310 cannot be invoked independently.

The rules and regulations regarding the various conditions of service are determined by the following Parliamentary Acts:

(a) The Indian Administrative Service (Recruitment) Rules, 1954
(b) The Indian Administrative Service (Regulation of Seniority) Rules, 1954
(c) All India Services (Conduct) Rules, 1954 and 1968
(d) All India Services (Discipline and Appeal) Rules, 1954 and 1969
(e) All India Services (Leave) Rules, 1955
(f) All India Services (Provident Fund) Rules, 1955
(g) All India Services (Study Leave) Regulations, 1960.

2.3.1 Direct Recruitment to Civil Services

Since Independence, the first significant batch of changes for direct recruitment to the All-India and Central Services were introduced in 1979 on the basis of the Report of the Committee on Recruitment Policy and Selection Methods (Kothari Committee). The Committee was appointed in 1974 and it submitted its report in 1976.

The next important changes were brought about after the Satish Chandra Committee, set up in 1988, had made its recommendations. The Committee reported in 1989 and the Government of India decided to implement some of the recommendations with effect from the 1993 examination.

2.3.2 Present Scheme of Competitive Examination

The present scheme of competitive examination is described here.

Any Indian citizen having a university degree and belonging to the age-group of 21–28 is eligible to appear in the competitive examination. For the scheduled caste and scheduled tribe candidates, there is a provision for age-relaxation.

There is a single examination for recruitment to the Indian Administrative Service, Indian Foreign Service, Indian Police Service and Group 'A' (former Class I) Central services. Thus, under the present scheme, all the services are put on the same footing.

The civil service examination basically has two parts—a qualifying preliminary examination (objective type) and the main examination (including both written examination and interview).

The preliminary examination consists of two papers, one in General Studies and the second in an optional subject out of the following subjects:

Agriculture, Botany, Chemistry, Commerce, Economics, Engineering (Civil, Electrical or Mechanical), Geography, Geology, Indian History, Law, Mathematics, Philosophy, Physics, Political Science, Psychology, Sociology and Zoology.

Both the General Studies and optional papers are of objective type. The General Studies paper carries 150 marks and the optional subject paper carries 300 marks. Only those who qualify in the preliminary examination (carrying 450 marks in all) are allowed to appear in the main examination. But the marks obtained in the preliminary examination are not considered in the main examination.

The main examination consists of two parts: written examination and interview. The written examination is a vast one which consists of eight papers, each carrying 300 marks (all conventional essay type). These eight papers are as follows:

1. One Indian language mentioned in the Eighth Schedule of the Constitution (the languages are: Assamese, Bengali, Gujrati,

Hindi, Kannada, Kashmiri, Malayalam, Marathi, Oriya, Punjabi, Sanskrit, Sindhi, Tamil, Telugu and Urdu).

2. English

3. & 4. General Studies

5. & 6. First Optional Subject

7. & 8. Second Optional Subject.

As his optional subjects, a candidate may choose any two subjects from the following 24 subjects:

1. Agriculture
2. Botany
3. Chemistry
4. Civil Engineering
5. Commerce and Accountancy
6. Economics
7. Electrical Engineering
8. Geography
9. Geology
10. History
11. Law
12. Literature in any one of the following 21 languages: Assamese, Bengali, Gujrati, Hindi, Kannada, Kashmiri, Marathi, Malayalam, Oriya, Punjabi, Sanskrit, Sindhi, Tamil, Telugu, Urdu, Arabic, Persian, German, French, Russian and English
13. Management and Public Administration
14. Mathematics
15. Mechanical Engineering
16. Philosophy
17. Physics
18. Sociology
19. Psychology
20. Political Science and International Relations
21. Anthropology
22. Animal Husbandry and Veterinary Science
23. Medical Science
24. Telecommunication Engineering.

It is to be noted that a candidate taking 'Management and Public Administration' is not allowed to take 'Political Science and International Relations'. Although the question papers, both for the preliminary and the main examinations, are set only in English and Hindi, yet candidates can write their papers (other than English and the language papers) either in English or in any language mentioned in the Eighth Schedule to the Indian Constitution.

Only those who qualify in the written part of the main examination are called for interview. This interview is conducted by the UPSC. The marks for interview are 250. The marks obtained in the written part of the main examination and in the interview are added and the final merit list is prepared on the basis of these added marks.

The candidates are allowed three chances for the civil service examination. There is, however, no restriction regarding such chances for the SC and ST candidates.

The allocation of the candidates to different services is made on the basis of their rank in the final merit list as well as their preferences. The Kothari Committee has argued that allocation to the services would become more scientific if this is done after watching the candidate's performance during the period of training and also in the post-training test. So, the Committee recommended in favour of allocating the candidates to the various services after they had completed their training. But this recommendation was not accepted.

The list of successful candidates arranged in order of merit is sent by the Union Public Service Commission to the Ministry of Home Affairs. The first choice of selection is given to the Ministry of External Affairs. After it has chosen the required quota for the Foreign Service, the Home Ministry chooses for the IAS. Then come other Departments in a fixed order. Again, in making the selection, the preferences indicated by the candidates in their application forms are also taken into account.

Such a system of examination has been subject to a great deal of criticism. First, there are doubts regarding the reliability of marks awarded at viva voce (interview). It is pointed out that there is a considerable scope for the elements of chance and luck here. The selection of a candidate depends to a great extent on the passing moods of examiners, differences in the political leanings of the persons at the interview board, differences in the nature of questions asked to different candidates, and so on. It is now open to debate whether a 15–20 minutes' conversation on any matter can really lead to a correct evaluation of the qualities sought for in candidates. As a result, suggesting the replacement of the existing interview system in India by a system of some psychological tests, A.D. Gorwala categorically points out: "The importance of psychological tests must be realized and they must gradually replace the viva voce.... The holding of such tests will, of course, cost more, but if thereby the services get better material,... the extra money will have been well spent."[12]

The system of written examination, too, has been sharply criticized. Pointing out the flaws of the written examination, Gorwala states: "There are also often complaints about the low standard of some of the papers set for optional subjects, and it is felt that candidates taking those subjects have an unfair advantage."[13]

Commenting on the general inadequacy of the system of selection, Appleby remarks: "The criteria by which personnel are selected by the Public Service Commissions are not up-to-date, and examining and appraising techniques are far from modern.... Selection is too much in terms of academic records and appraisals by experienced academic examiners, too little in terms of many other considerations highly important in public administration..."[14]

In December 1978, the Union Government accepted the scheme of examination as recommended by the Kothari Committee. Thus the competitive examination held by the UPSC since 1979 marked a significant departure from the pattern followed till 1979.

In 1988, another Committee, 'Committee to Review the Scheme of the Civil Services Examination', was appointed under the chairmanship of Satish Chandra. This Committee submitted its report in 1989 and a few recommendations of this Committee were accepted and became operative from 1993 examinations.

2.4 TWO AGENCIES OR INSTRUMENTS OF RECRUITMENT: UNION PUBLIC SERVICE COMMISSION AND STATE PUBLIC SERVICE COMMISSION

2.4.1 Union Public Service Commission

The Royal Commission on the Superior Civil Services (popularly known as Lee Commission) made a strong plea in its report of 1924 for the establishment of a public service commission in India. The Report said categorically: "In America a civil service commission has been constituted to control recruitment of the services.... Canada, Australia and South Africa now possess Public or Civil Service Acts, regulating the position and control of the Public Service Commission to which the duty of administering the act is entrusted. It was this need which the framers of the Government of India Act had in mind when they made provision in Section 96-C for the establishment of a Public Service Commission."[15] Section 96-C of the Government of India Act of 1919 provided for the establishment of a Public Service Commission in India.

It has been stated in the 1919 Act that the commission will consist of not more than five members, of whom one shall be a Chairman, appointed by the Secretary of State in Council. Each member shall hold office for five years, and he/she may be reappointed. No member shall be removed from office before the expiry of his/her term, except by order of the Secretary of State in Council. The commission was given such functions as may be assigned to it by the Secretary of State in Council. Following the recommendation of the Lee Commission, a Central Public Service Commission was set up in 1926. Its role was limited to all-India and higher services. Following the recommendations of the Simon

Commission, the Government of India Act, 1935 provided in Section 264 for the establishment of a Federal Public Service Commission. The present Constitution (Article 315) also provides that "there shall be a Public Service Commission for the Union and a Public Service Commission for each State".

Composition

The two main aspects of composition of the Union Public Service Commission (UPSC)—number of members and conditions of service—are determined by the Indian President. In the Constitution of India it has been clearly stated that there shall be six to eight members of the commission. Thus including the Chairman, its strength would be nine. On the advice of the Prime Minister, the President appoints the Chairman and the members of the commission. It is also provided by the Constitution that at least half the members have to be persons who have held office for at least ten years under the Government of India or a State Government. A member can hold office for a term of six years from the date he joins duty or until he attains the age of sixty-five years, whichever is earlier. A member of the UPSC is not eligible for the same appointment for a second term. Nor can he undertake employment simultaneously under the Union or State Government. The Chairman is ineligible for any future employment under the government after his retirement. But other members are entitled to accept the chairmanship of the Union Public Service Commission or of a State Public Service Commission (SPSC).

The conditions of service of members of the UPSC cannot be varied to their disadvantage after appointment. Their salaries and allowances are charged to the consolidated fund of India. A special procedure has been laid down in the Constitution to remove a member from office. Article 317 provides that the Chairman or a member of the commission can be removed from office by the President on the ground of misbehaviour only after the Supreme Court has on enquiry recommended such removal. Pending the enquiry by the court, the President may suspend the member concerned. A member including the Chairman would be deemed guilty of misbehaviour, if he becomes interested in any government contract or agreement or participates by any means in its profit or in any monetary benefit arising from it otherwise than as a member. Article 317 also provides that the President may by order remove the Chairman or any other member from office, if he is proved to be an insolvent or is engaged during the term of office in any paid employment outside the duties of his office or is infirm of body or mind.

Functions

The jurisdiction of the UPSC extends to the public services of the Union Government and the centrally administered territories. Article 320(2) of our Constitution clearly States that if requested by any two or more States, the UPSC should assist them in framing and operating schemes of joint recruitment for any services, for which candidates possessing special qualifications are required. Again, Article 315(4) empowers the commission to agree to serve all or any of the needs of the State. For instance, the UPSC served the needs of the State of Sikkim in this matter till the establishment of the SPSC there.

The functions of the UPSC are embodied in Article 320. Article 321 provides for conferring on the UPSC some additional functions. According to Article 320, the functions of the commission may broadly be divided into two categories: (a) mandatory or administrative and (b) consultative or advisory. Mandatory or administrative functions include the conducting of examinations for appointments to the services of the Union Government. Such examinations may be written or by interview or by both.

The second category of functions, i.e. consultative or advisory functions of the UPSC can be located in the following spheres:

1. Matters relating to methods of recruitment to civil services and civil posts.
2. Principles to be followed in making appointments to civil services and posts and in making promotions and transfers from one service to another.
3. All disciplinary matters affecting a person serving under the Union Government in a civil capacity including memorials or petitions relating to such matters.
4. Any claim by or in respect of any person who is serving or has served under the Union Government in a civil capacity.
5. Any claim or award of a pension in respect of injuries sustained by Union Government servants in the discharge of their official duties.
6. Any other matter which the President may refer to the commission.

Participating in the parliamentary debates regarding the real character of the Union Public Service Commission, Sir Samuel Hoare, the then Secretary of State for India, observed: "...the Public Service Commissions had much better be advisory. Experience goes to show that they are likely to have more influence if they are advisory than if they have mandatory powers."[16]

The relations of the UPSC with different Ministries or Departments of the Union Government are coordinated by the Ministry of Home Affairs. But in its day-to-day work, the UPSC deals directly with the different Ministries or Departments and the various heads of executive Departments.

In terms of Article 323(1), it is the duty of the UPSC to present annually to the President a report containing the annual work done by the commission. This report is placed before the Parliament.

Evaluation of the working of the Union Public Service Commission

The public service commissions are a common feature of almost all democratic governments today. The functions of these commissions fall under three categories:

- Recruitment to civil service
- Promotion, disciplinary cases and appeals against disciplinary actions
- Fixation of classification, salaries, conditions of service, training, etc.

In Britain, the Civil Service Commission is principally bothered with recruitment covering the advertisement of civil service vacancies in the press and career booklets, conduction of examinations and interviews, announcement of the results of competitions, and, after necessary investigation of health and character of successful candidates, issuing certificates indicating that such and such candidates are qualified for permanent appointments. It is true that since 1968, after the recommendations of the Fulton Committee, the Civil Service Commission of Britain has been more closely linked than in the past with training and subsequent career development policy.

In the United States, before World War II, the Civil Service Commission performed operating personnel work. But after the war, and more particularly after 1958, it functions were extended to providing leadership in personnel programmes covering all minute aspects of personnel management. In cooperation with the Bureau of the Budget, in federal personnel administration, it provides leadership. The commission now assists the US President in making top policy decisions and thus it is rightly termed as the "personnel arm of the Chief Executive."

Evaluating the role of our UPSC, C.N. Bhalerao observes: "In carrying out their functions the Public Service Commissions in India face various problems vis-à-vis the executive governments.... In general terms it may be said that the Indian scene reveals a combination of patronage and merit in the public service characteristic of many transitional societies of Asia."[17]

2.4.2 State Public Service Commission

The Royal Commission on the Superior Civil Service (popularly known as the Lee Commission) in its report of 1924 categorically argued in favour of the appointment of public service commissions for the states or provinces of India. Unlike the recommendation to have a Union Public Service Commission, the Lee Commission's recommendation to have State Public Service Commissions was remarkably ignored. Instead, the Union Public Service Commission itself was entrusted with the task of recruitment to the provincial civil service.

But the Government of India Act, 1935, in Section 264, provided for the establishment of a public service commission for each province. When the Act came into operation in April, 1937, provincial public service commissions were set up in many provinces. Articles 315 to 323 of Part XIV of our Constitution provides for a Public Service Commission for each State. In this connection, it should be mentioned that unlike Britain and the USA, where the civil service commissions are mere creations of the respective legislatures, in India the public service commissions have a constitutional basis and consequently are in a much stronger position. Today, each State has its own Public Service Commission. Regarding recruitment to their services, our Union Territories are helped by the UPSC.

Composition

There is no uniformity regarding the number of members constituting different State Public Service Commissions. The large State of Uttar Pradesh (from the point of view of population) has one Chairman and seven other members while the small State of Assam has one Chairman and only two other members. The Chairman and members of the SPSC are appointed by the Governor on the basis of the advice of the Cabinet. The Constitution makes it clear that at least half the number of members have to be persons who have held office for at least ten years under the Government of India or a State Government.

Each member of the SPSC holds office for a term of six years or until the attainment of the age of sixty years, whichever is earlier. The conditions of service of the members are more or less the same as those of the Union Public Service Commission except that their salary varies from State to State. The expenses of the SPSCs are charged on the consolidated fund of the state.

To ensure the independence of the SPSC, the Constitution debars the Chairman and members from reappointment to the same office. They cannot even undertake any further employment under the Union or the State Government except the chairmanship of any SPSC or the chairmanship or membership of the UPSC. Again, Article 317 provides that the Chairman or any member of the SPSC can be removed from office by the order of the President on the ground of misbehaviour only after the Supreme Court has on enquiry recommended such removal. A Chairman or member would be considered guilty of misbehaviour, if he becomes interested in any government contract or agreement or participates in any way in its profit or in any kind of monetary benefit whatsoever. Article 317 also points out that the President may by order remove the Chairman or any other member if he/she is proved to be an insolvent or is engaged during the term of his/her office in any paid employment or is infirm of body or mind.

Functions

Article 320 of our Constitution prescribes the following functions of the SPSC:

1. The SPSC shall conduct examinations for appointment to the State service.
2. If requested by two or more States to assist them in framing and operating schemes of joint recruitment, the SPSC may give its consent. This recruitment is basically meant for services for which candidates possessing special qualifications are required.
3. The SPSC shall perform any other function in respect with services conferred by the State Legislature.
4. The SPSC shall give advice on:
   - (a) matters relating to methods of recruitment to civil services and civil posts;
   - (b) principles to be followed in making appointments to civil services and posts and in making promotions and transfers from one service to another;
   - (c) all disciplinary matters affecting a person serving under the government of the State in a civil capacity including memorials or petitions relating to such matters;
   - (d) any claim by any person, who is serving or has served under the State Government in a civil capacity; and
   - (e) any claim for the award of a pension in respect of injuries sustained by government servants in the discharge of their official duties.

The Governor can make regulations specifying the matters where, either generally or specifically, it will not be necessary for the State Government to consult the SPSC. Thus, some regulations have been made in Maharashtra decreasing the jurisdiction of the SPSC.

Article 321 empowers the State Legislature to extend the powers of the SPSC by making an Act for the purpose. This provision has been utilized by the Maharashtra Government to extend the powers of the Maharashtra SPSC to the staff of the Secretariat of the Maharashtra State Legislature and certain categories of employees of the Mumbai Municipal Corporation.

In Uttar Pradesh also, certain categories of posts under the Nagar Mahapalikas (municipal corporations) and Zilla Parishads have been brought within the purview of the Uttar Pradesh SPSC.

In performing its tasks, the SPSC takes the assistance of various heads of Departments and other government officials. It also employs suitable persons as examiners, supervisors and invigilators at the examinations conducted by it.

The Chief Minister and the Chief Secretary of any State coordinate the relations of the SPSC with various Departments of the State

Government. But in its day-to-day work and statutory responsibilities, it deals directly with the different Departments of the State Government and the various heads of Departments.

According to Article 323, the SPSC submits an annual report on its work to the Governor.

Evaluation of the working of the State Public Service Commission

- In the first place, the functions performed by the SPSC are not very extensive. On the contrary, in Britain or the United States, the SPSC counterparts perform more extensive functions relating to the training of the civil servants and subsequent career development.
- Secondly, some State Governments have removed certain posts from the purview of the SPSC and thus have abused the provision of clause (3) of Article 320.
- Thirdly, in relation to the cases of rejections of the UPSC recommendations by the Union Government, the cases of rejections of the SPSC recommendations by the State Governments are much larger in number.
- Lastly, regarding selection the SPSCs take a very long time. Sometimes, they take a year or even more.

Recommendations of the Administrative Reforms Commission in respect of improving the quality of membership of the UPSC and the SPSCs

The Administrative Reforms Commission (ARC), on the basis of the suggestions made by the study team, made the following recommendations:[18]

1. In making appointments to the SPSC, the Governor should consult the Chairman of the UPSC and the Chairman of the SPSC. (The Chairman of the SPSC may also be consulted regarding the appointment of his own successor.)
2. In making appointments to the UPSC, the Chairman of the UPSC should be consulted. (Regarding the appointment of the his own successor also, he should be consulted.)
3. At least two-thirds of the members of the UPSC should be drawn from among the Chairmen and members of the SPSC.
4. At least one of the members of the SPSC should be from a different State.
5. The minimum academic qualification for membership of any SPSC should be a university degree.
6. A member of the UPSC or SPSC selected from among government officers should have held office under a State Government or the Central Government for at least ten years.

7. Members selected from non-officials should have practised at least for ten years in any of the recognized professions like teaching, law, medicine, engineering, science, technology, accountancy or administration.

2.5 TRAINING OF HIGHER CIVIL SERVICES IN INDIA

This section will basically deal with training of the IAS officers under the following five specific heads:

- Need for training
- Origin and development of training
- Types of training
- Training institutes
- Shortcomings or imperfections of training.

2.5.1 Need for Training

The need for training the civil services was recognized from the very beginning. The army for the first time developed a very good system of training its personnel. Training in the army continues throughout one's career. Such training is both theoretical and practical. Over the years, the army has evolved a detailed system of training for its officers. Training is regarded to be absolutely important since promotions in ranks for the civil services are related to success in such training programmes.

2.5.2 Origin and Development of Training

In the ancient Hindu society, the younger boys were given training in the families of their teachers (*gurugriha*). This was true for those who were keen on specialization. At that time, no regular training institutions as such were grown. Only some individuals specialized in the art constituted some kind of training centres. Training was lifelong, continuous and totally inexpensive. The approach, in short, was training by "doing" and "learning from mistake".

Later, the East India Company made some efforts in this direction. It set up a college at Fort Williams at Calcutta (1800–1806) and later another college named East India College (1809–1857) to train the Company's employees most of whom came from Britain. Halisbury College in this respect was quite well known and its contribution was widely recognized.

After World War II, the entire perspective of administration in India was changed. The public servants in the changed situation were necessitated to be trained to assume new responsibilities in the growing context of development and democratization. In 1954, the Indian Institute of Public Administration (IIPA) was established in

New Delhi on the basis of the Appleby Report of 1953. This institute opened the School of Public Administration in 1958 that started an educational programme leading to the Master's Diploma in Public Administration conferred on the students after one full year of training. The Central and State Government officials of middle rank and college teachers from various parts of the country could take such training. Later, the National Academy of Administration was established at Mussoorie. In 1965, a separate training division was created in the Home Ministry. In the same year, the School of Public Administration was dissolved and the IIPA was turned into a training-cum-research institute. In various provinces of India, a number of schools and academies of administration were established in subsequent years. A major change was brought about in 1970 when a Department of Personnel was created. In March 1985, the new Ministry of Personnel, Public Grievances and Pensions was created. This Ministry had three Departments of which one was that of Personnel and Training.

2.5.3 Kinds of Training

Training given to the IAS officers is basically of two types—in-service training and mid-career training. The in-service training itself can be divided into two categories—pre-1969 training programme and post-1969 sandwich programme which is carried on till now.

Pre-1969 In-Service Training Programme

After being selected as IAS and non-IAS Central Government officers, the candidates are known as probationers who have to take a compulsory training at the National Academy of Administration, Mussoorie. Till 1969, this training programme included a foundational course for six months for all the services (both IAS and non-IAS). After completing this course, the probationers of the services other than the IAS officers leave for their respective training institutes for institutional training. But the IAS probationers stay at the Academy till their training course is completed. The main aim of the foundational course was to acquaint the IAS officers with the constitutional, economic, social and political framework of India, to make them aware of the general principles of public administration as well as governmental activities and to teach them to maintain the general ethics of their profession like objectivity, thoroughness, honesty and integrity.[19] This course was also expected to develop among recruits to different services a feeling of belongingness to common public service and a broadly common outlook.[20] Besides, the candidates were imparted a course of institutional and professional training like riding, diriving, etc.

Post-1969 Sandwich Training Programme

After 1969, a new training programme, commonly known as *sandwich course*, was introduced. Under the new system, the probationer has to complete two spells of training. The foundation course completes after six months. Then the IAS probationers are sent to their respective States or provinces for practical training. This course, known as district training, completes after another year. Then the probationers again go back to the Academy to complete their second part of training. There the administrative problems are more emphatically discussed. Such problems have either been encountered or observed by the probationers in the course of their practical training in their respective States. This second part of training, which is supposed to be "more problem-oriented",[21] lasts for three months.

Each probationer should keep regular contacts with one counsellor at the Academy to whom he writes regularly describing what he studies during practical training, the problems he faces and the idea he gets. The probationer should also prepare reports on various subjects allotted to him by the Academy teachers. The probationer's final evaluation at the Academy depends significantly on such detailed reports.[22]

Before the probationer becomes a full-fledged IAS officer and is sent to the allotted state, he has to pass an examination which is held by the UPSC.

Mid-Career Training

Both the National Academies at Mussoorie and Hyderabad give such training to the civil servants. The Mussoorie Academy runs a six-week refresher course for civil servants having seniority of 10–15 years.

Since 1986, the Hyderabad National Academy has restructured its training courses which now include (a) Level One Management Course of four weeks duration for IPS officers who have completed 6 to 10 years of service, (b) Level Two Management Course of four weeks duration for IPS officers who have completed 11 to 16 years of service, (c) Level Three Management Course of two weeks duration for IPS officers who have completed 17 to 20 years of service, (d) Vertical Interaction Course of one week duration for IPS officers from the rank of SP to that of DGP, (e) Training Administrators Course of four weeks duration for SPs only, (f) Training of Trainers Course of a duration of four weeks each in two phases for DSPs only, and (g) Vertically Integrated Training Programme of one week duration for IAS officers from the rank of Sub-Collector to that of Cabinet Secretary. This training programme is set specifically on the theme of terrorism and violence. The Academy also conducts short-term specialized courses such as One-Week Course on Women in Bureaucracy or a short Two-Week Course for the probationers of India Customs and Central Excise Group-A Service.

2.5.4 Training Institutes

As training institutes, the National Academy of Administration at Mussoorie and the National Academy of Administration at Hyderabad play leading roles. The contribution to training of some other semi-governmental and non-governmental institutes also deserves special mention. Their activities are described below:

1. **IIPA, New Delhi:** On the basis of Appleby's recommendations in his Survey of Indian Administration (1953), the Indian Institute of Public Administration (IIPA), New Delhi was created in 1954. Later, in 1958, the Indian School of Public Administration (ISPA) was founded principally by the Ford Foundation. The school, modelled on the Littauer Centre at Harvard and the Maxwell School at Syracuse, developed an educational-cum-training programme for the civil servants of India. In our country, for the first time, the syllabus of ISPA brought the academic and the administrative officers in close contact. Any IAS officer of the rank of Joint Secretary or his equivalent usually was the chief guest speaker in the weekly seminar of each specialized course of the ISPA. The school organized quite a few special courses on different aspects of public administration. S.R. Maheshwari, a retired professor of Public Administration in the school, gave a list of 63 such courses.

   The ISPA was dissolved in 1968. Today's IIPA is basically a training institute for the Indian Civil Servants. Since 1975, the IIPA has been organizing an Advanced Professional Programme in Public Administration leading to the award of M.Phil degree. It is a nine-month course aiming at training the middle and senior level civil servants. Again, the IIPA organizes many short-term courses as well.
2. **Administrative Staff College, Hyderabad:** On the basis of the recommendation of the All-India Council for Technical Education, the Administrative Staff College (ASC), Hyderabad was established in 1957. This college is patterned on the Administrative Staff College at Henley in Great Britain. The fundamental aim of the ASC, Hyderabad is to bring together senior administrators both from the private and the public sectors and to arrange for a kind of 'get together' by exchanging their ideas and experiences and also by enabling them to assume higher responsibilities.
3. **Institute of Secretariat Training and Management, New Delhi:** The old Central Secretariat Training School, established in 1948, came to be known as the Institute of Secretariat Training and Management since 1971. It is basically a training institute for the lower level of civil servants or Group C staff like section officers, assistant and lower and upper division clerks. The courses offered here include organization and methods, office procedure, financial rules and regulations, etc. These persons, after they complete their training, are posted to different Ministries for practical training. This institute also conducts refresher courses as mid-career training for the employees belonging to Grade C.

4. **National Institute of Rural Development (NIRD), Hyderabad:** Soon after the inauguration of the Community Development Programmes in 1952, the Government of India set up the Central Institute of Study and Research in Community Development at Mussoorie in 1958 to organize research and mid-career training programmes. This institute was shifted to Hyderabad in the mid-seventies under the new name of NIRD.
5. **Other Training Institutes:** Some kind of in-service training is given at the National Academy of Administration at Mussoorie and the Police Academy at Hyderabad. After 1969, the Mussoorie Academy has been a training institute only for the IAS probationers. In 1972, it was named as the Lal Bahadur Shastri Academy. It now conducts a one-year course for the IAS officers prescribed under the rules. It also conducts a foundational course for certain services including the IAS. This course includes the teaching of Economics, History and Indian Culture, Law, Political Concepts and Constitutional Law and Public Administration, Management and Behavioural Sciences. At the end of this course, there is an examination and the marks secured are added to the main recruitment examination.

The IPS officers (probationers) are given more or less a similar training. This was initially arranged at the Central Police Training College at Mount Abu in Rajasthan. During the emergency, it was shifted to Hyderabad. Now it is known as Sardar Vallabhbhai Patel National Police Academy, set up in 1975. The in-serve training imparted to the probationers since 1986 includes two courses: (a) Foundational and (b) Basic. The Foundational Course of a 16 weeks duration is meant for the probationers of Central Services Group A. This course was earlier conducted at the Mussoorie Academy. Now it is conducted at the NPA, Hyderabad and at NADT, Nagpur. The Basic Course is meant for IPS probationers and its duration is eleven and a half months. The syllabus of training includes studies of crime, methods of fighting corruption, fire and emergency relief, etc. Again, training is also conducted in the fields of drill, handling of weapons, etc. After completion of this one-year training, the UPSC holds an examination which the probationer has to pass. After it, he/she becomes a full-fledged IPS officer and is posted as Assistant Superintendent of Police in the State assigned to him earlier.

Training programmes are also arranged for the Central Services Group A. The Indian Foreign Service (IFS) tops the list of Allied Services. In order of merit, the IFS stands next to the IAS and comes just before the IPS. Corresponding to their IAS counterparts, the IFS probationers are also given an intensive training. The training programme for these probationers puts special emphasis on the study of languages.

2.5.5 Shortcomings or Imperfections of Training

The main defect in the training system of Indian civil servants is the absence of a sound and unified policy of training. Training facilities are not equal in all government Departments and are not coordinated in a unified pattern. Class II and subordinate services employees rarely get any opportunity for systematic post-entry training.

Another disturbing fact is that no class relationship exists between training and promotion. Hence, many employees are discouraged to undertake training.

The contents of the training courses, too, are not flawless. According to the critics, they need to be modified with the rapid progress in modern administrative thought and practice as well as the changing socio-economic environment of Indian administration. Both contents and techniques of training should have been more flexible and dynamic, taking into account the changing needs and aspirations of the people.[23]

The levels of attendance in the training courses of IPS officers of senior ranks are not at all satisfactory. Very often the course capacity is not fully utilized. This may be due to factors such as location of the training institute/centre, the officer not being relieved from his posting due to paucity of training reserves or lack of interest. In general, if there is some kind of tension, the IPS officers are not relieved by the State Governments for attending training courses.

In India training of civil servants has been an extremely neglected aspect of personnel administration till recently. In 1968, a training division was established in the Ministry of Home Affairs to deal with training policy and programmes.

As a result of the acceptance of the redefinition of administration, each employee, from a desk worker to a field worker, is labelled as an 'administrator'. Public officials now will have to cope up with such new roles as those of business executives, executors of economic policy, planners, industrial managers, dispensers of social services, etc. Understanding these new jobs as well as acting in accordance with such understanding requires a radical change in the civil servants' outlook, knowledge, skills and orientation.[24]

2.6 SOME DEVELOPMENTS IN THE INDIAN CIVIL SERVICE

Broadly speaking, the Higher Civil Services of India can be divided into two heads—(a) the All India Services and (b) the Central Civil Services (Group A). The recruits are generally selected through any of the rigorous examinations like Civil Services Examination, Engineering Services Examination, Combined Geo-Scientist and Geologist Examination, IES/ISS Examination, Combined Medical Services Examination, Central Armed Police Forces of Union Public Service Commission (UPSC) Examination for Group A posts.

The All India Services constitute the following categories:

- Indian Administrative Service (IAS)
- Indian Foreign Service (IFS)
- Indian Police Service (IPS)

Central Civil Services (Group A) constitute the following categories:

- Border Roads Engineering Service
- Botanical Survey of India
- Central Architects Service
- Central Engineering (Civil) Service
- Central Engineering (Electrical and Mechanical) Service
- Central Engineering Service (Roads)
- Central Health Service
- Central Information Service
- Central Legal Service
- Central Labour Service
- Central Power Engineering Service
- Central Revenues Chemical Service
- Central Secretariat Service
- Central Secretariat Official Language Service
- Central Trade Service
- Central Water Engineering Service
- Company Law Board Service
- Defence Research and Development Service
- Directorate General of Civil Aviation
- Directorate General of Mines Safety
- General Central Service
- Geographical Survey of India
- Indian Archaeological and Heritage Service
- Indian Audits and Accounts Service
- Indian Broadcasting Service
- Indian Corporate Law Service
- Indian Civil Accounts Service
- Indian Cost Accounts Service
- Indian Defence Accounts Service
- Indian Defence Estates Service
- Indian Defence Service of Engineers
- Indian Economic Service
- Indian Engineering Services
- Indian Enterprise Development Service

- Indian Foreign Service
- Indian Frontier Administrative Service
- Indian Information Service
- Indian Meteorological Service
- Indian Ordnance Factories Service
- Indian Ordnance Factories Health Service
- Indian Postal Service
- Indian Posts and Telegraphs Accounts and Finance Service
- Indian Radio Regulatory Service
- Indian Railway Medical Services
- Indian Railway Service of Engineers
- Indian Railway Service of Mechanical Engineers
- Indian Railway Service of Electrical Engineers
- Indian Railway Service of Signal Engineers
- Indian Railway Stores Service
- Indian Railway Accounts Service
- Indian Railway Personnel Service
- Indian Railway Traffic Service
- Indian Revenue Service
- Indian Salt Service
- Indian Skill Development Service
- Indian Statistical Service
- Indian Telecommunication Service
- Indian Trade Service
- Mercantile Marine Training Ship Service
- Railway Protection Board
- Survey of India
- Telegraph Traffic Service
- Zoological Survey of India

Central Group B Services comprise the following:

- Central Secretariat Service
- Armed Forces Headquarters Civil Services
- Income Tax Service
- Indian Foreign Service (General Cadre Grade I and General Cadre Grade II only)
- Indian Posts and Telegraphs Accounts and Finance Service, Group B Telecommunication Wing
- Indian Posts and Telegraphs Accounts and Finance Service, Group B Postal Wing
- Indian Salt Service

- Indian Meteorological Service
- Central Secretariat Official Language Service
- Central Secretariat Stenographers' Service (Grade I, Grade II and Selection Grade Officers only)
- Central Health Service
- Botanical Survey of India
- Geological Survey of India
- Survey of India
- Zoological Survey of India
- Central Electrical Engineering Service
- Central Engineering Service
- Central Power Engineering Service
- Postal Superintendents' Service
- Postmasters' Service
- Railway Board Secretariat Service
- Telecommunication Engineering Service
- Telegraphs Traffic Service
- Central Excise Service
- Customs Appraisers Service
- Customs Preventive Service
- Defence Secretariat Service

State Group B Services fall under the following categories:

- Assistant Registrar Cooperative Societies
- Block Development Officer
- District Employment Officer
- District Food and Supplies Controller/Officer
- District Treasury Officer
- District Welfare Officer
- Excise and Taxation Officer
- Provincial Civil Services, Class II
- Provincial Police Services, Class II
- Tehsildar/Talukdar/Assistant Collector
- Any other Class I/Class II Service notified as per rules by the concerned State, i.e., officers, lecturers, assistant professors, associate professors or Principals of Government Degree Colleges (Class I).

In 2012, a study was released by the Hong Kong-based Political and Economic Risk Consultancy. But, quite alarmingly, Indian bureaucracy was rated by it as the worst in Asia, marked by full of corruption and inefficiency. Such a pathetic civil service was responsible, as the study estimated, for most of the complaints raised by the Indian business executives. A paper prepared in 2012 by the Ministry of Personnel, Public Grievances and Pensions, Government of India, clearly reveals that corruption is present at all levels of Indian civil services and it is 'institutionalised'.[25]

On November 28, 2011, the Department of Personnel and Training of the Ministry of Personnel, Public Grievances and Pensions, Government of India, proposed to create retirement or removal of incompetent, inefficient and unfruitful All India Service Officers after 15 years of their service, instead of tolerating them until they reach the age of retirement. T.S.R. Subramanian, former Cabinet Secretary, welcomed this suggestion with political caution. P.C. Hota, former UPSC Chairman, remarked that the removed officers' service records should be analysed before a decision is taken against them. Accepting the timely proposal, Rule 16(3) of the All India Services (death-cum-retirement benefits) Rules of 1958 was amended on January 31, 2012.[26]

The Supreme Court of India in October 2013 ordered both Government of India and State Governments to ensure fixed tenure to Indian civil servants. The 2006 judgement of the Supreme Court in Prakash Singh Case on police reforms was on similar lines. The judgement was welcomed by our bureaucrats and media, hoping that it would ensure the independence of the bureaucracy.

As many as 72 officers of the Indian Revenue Service were dismissed and another 33 officers of the same service were forced to retire by the Ministry of Finance, Government of India in 2016. They were accused of inefficiency and on disciplinary grounds. In the same year, it was reported that our Government has decided to give power to the mass to seek prosecution of corrupt IAS officers.

To get back the lost glory of the Indian Civil Service, the Civil Service Day is celebrated each year on 21 April. The purpose of such observance is to rededicate and recommit the civil servants of India to the cause of the people. It is observed by all Civil Services. The day gives our civil servants the opportunity to think about future strategies to combat probable challenges in days to come. All civil servants of Central and State Governments are honoured for excellence in public administration by our Prime Minister on the occasion.

In 2015, the Indian Government approved the formation of Indian Skill Development Service. In 2016, the Indian Government approved the formation of Indian Enterprise Development Service. Thus, in Indian civil services, there has of late been a trend of emphasizing the significance of both skill and enterprise.

Questions

1. Briefly discuss the structure of the civil services in India in its various phases.

2. Explain the terms and conditions as well as the process of recruitment regarding the civil services of India.
3. Briefly describe the composition and functions of the UPSC and evaluate its role.
4. Describe the compositon and functions fo the SPSC. Also, evaluate its working.
5. Briefly discuss the process of training of the higher civil services in India.
6. Write short notes on
   (a) Training institutes for civil servants in India
   (b) Composition of the UPSC
   (c) Composition of the SPSC
   (d) Present scheme of competitive examinations in India.
7. Briefly analyse the recent developments in the Indian Civil Service.

Notes and References

1. Ogg, F.A., *English Government and Politics*, Macmillan, New York, 1947.
2. Avasthi and Avasthi, *Public Administration in India*, Laxmi Narain Agarwal, Agra, 2003.
3. Pradhan, Girish, *Civil Service Reform in Independent India: An Overview*, IIPA, No. 4, Oct.–Dec., 2001.
4. Austin, Granville, *The Indian Constitution: Cornerstone of a Nation*, Oxford, 1966.
5. Avasthi and Avasthi, *op. cit.*
6. Pradhan, Girish, *op. cit.*
7. Basu, P.K., *Administrative Reorganization in India: Some Strategic Issues, The Changing Role of Government: Management of Social and Economic Activities*, Commonwealth Secretariat, 1991.
8. Das, S.K., *Civil Service Reform and Structural Adjustment*, Oxford University Press, Delhi, 1998.
9. Banerjee, A.M. and K.A. Chandrasekhar, *Some Issues in Civil Services Reform: Renewing Governance*, Tata McGraw Hill, 1996.
10. *Department of Administrative Reforms and Public Grievances, Agenda for an Effective and Responsive Administration*, New Delhi, Government of India, November, 1996.
11. Maheshwari, S.R., *Indian Administration*, Orient Longman, New Delhi, 2002.
12. Gorwala, A.D., *Report on Public Administration*, 1951.

13. *Ibid.*
14. Appleby, P.H., Report of a Survey.
15. *The Lee Commission Report* (1924) as quoted in *The Organization of the Government of Uttar Pradesh*, Chand & Chand Company, New Delhi, 1970.
16. *Parliamentary Debates (Britain),* Vol. 300, Column 858.
17. Bhalerao, C.N., *Public Service Commissions of India*, Sterling Publishers, Delhi, 1966.
18. *The ARC Report on Personnel Administration*, Government of India, New Delhi, 1969.
19. Krishnamachari, V.T., *Report on Indian and State Administrative Services and Problems of District Administration*, Planning Commission, New Delhi, 1962.
20. Avasthi, A. and S.R. Maheshwari, *Public Administration*, Lakshmi Narain Agarwal, Agra, 1992.
21. *Ibid.*
22. Maheshwari, S.R., *op. cit.*
23. Basu, Rumki, *Public Administration on Concepts and Theories*, 3rd Rev. ed., Sterling Publisher, Delhi, 1994.
24. Chowdhari, L.H., Training for Development, *IJPA*, Vol. XXVI, 1980.
25. Sharma, Aman, "Federal Government Paper Admits Corruption at All Levels in Civil Services", *India Today*, New Delhi, April 14, 2012.
26. *Government of India notification for amending Rule 16(3) of the All India Service (DCRB) Rules, 1958*, Government of India, June 26, 2012.

3 Administration and Politics of India
The Central Picture

3.1 INTRODUCTION

Before dealing with the composition and functions of the Central Secretariat of the present day, it would be worthwhile to have a glimpse into its origin. The Central Secretariat, like quite a few other administrative organizations, is a legacy of the British rule in India.

Before 1756, the President and the Council at Fort William transacted all their business in one single Department with the help of a Secretary and a few assistants. After the 'packets' had reached from England, the Secretary laid them before the council for orders and instructions. When such orders and instructions were issued, they were conveyed to the authorities concerned for execution. Thus, "the Central Secretariat at Fort William in Bengal was designed to furnish the requisite information for the formulation of policy and to carry out the orders of the Company's Government."[1] Later, both Lord Cornwallis and Lord Wellesley contributed towards organizing the Secretariat. In 1919, the famous Montague–Chelmsford reforms were made, which eventually divided the Secretariat functions between the Central and provincial governments. With the outbreak of World War II in 1939, the government had to assume several new functions and burdens. Special officers were appointed to meet the exigencies of the time which led to the rapid expansion of the administrative machinery. The total strength of the Secretariat which was 29 in 1919 increased to 200 during the period of World War II.

Since independence in 1947, the Government of India announced its various welfare programmes leading to a marked increase in the number of offices and Ministries. To cope with the increasing workload, more and more personnel were recruited. This was done by promotion from lower ranks and also through emergency recruitment.[2]

Under the Constitution of India (1950), all executive actions of the Union Government are taken in the name of the President. But the President is a mere formal and constitutional head. There is a Council of Ministers, with the Prime Minister at its head, to aid and advise the President in the exercise of his functions. Thus, the real executive authority is vested in the Cabinet or the summation of Ministers with the Prime Minister, acting as the nucleus. These Ministers obviously cannot perform such huge number of functions and hence they need assistance. Therefore, for purposes of administrative convenience, the Government of India is divided into Ministries and Departments which together constitute what is known as the *Central Secretariat.* Offices, subordinate offices and other field agencies are attached to implement policies enunciated by the Ministers in consultation with the Secretariat.

3.2 MEANING, NATURE, FUNCTIONS AND ROLE OF THE CENTRAL SECRETARIAT

The word 'Secretariat' literally means the office of the Secretary. The Central Government has three essential organs: (a) the Minister, (b) the Secretary and (c) the Executive Head. The most important function of the Minister is to make the policy. The Secretary's duty is to provide necessary materials by which such decisions can be reached and implemented. The Executive Head performs the function of carrying the decisions into effect.

Orders and instructions issued by the Central Secretariat are regarded as the orders of the Government of India. Hence, in the administrative set-up the Central Secretariat occupies a key position. The Central Secretariat is the summation of various Ministries/Departments of the Union Government. Just like the Council of Ministers, the Central Secretariat also works as a single unit with collective responsibility. Secretaries constituting the Central Secretariat are Secretaries to the Union Government as a whole and not to any particular Minister.

The main function of the Central Secretariat is to assist and advise the Ministers regarding the following matters:

- Making and modifying policies from time to time
- Framing laws, rules and regulations
- Formulating sectoral planning and programmes
- Budgeting and controlling expenditure
- Supervising and controlling the execution of policies and programmes by field agencies, and evaluating results
- Coordinating and interpreting policies, assisting other branches of the government and maintaining contacts with State administrators
- Initiating measures to develop greater organizational competence
- Discharging their responsibilities to the Parliament.

Describing the real status of the Central Secretariat, Asok Chanda observes: "The Central Secretariat is ... the principal executive instrument of the Union Government and is responsible for administering the Central subjects, coordinating the activities of national importance and assisting in the formulation of foreign, economic and financial policies."[3] Thus, the Central Secretariat plays two kinds of role simultaneously. On the one hand, it is a policy-making, coordinating and supervisory agency, and, on the other, it is the main executive agency of the government. The Central Secretariat is concerned with every detail of administration. The functions and responsibilities of the Central Secretariat have been rapidly increasing. Naturally its authority has grown too. The superior position of the Central Secretariat is recognized by the fact that the Secretariat personnel are being given higher grades of salaries than their counterparts working in field agencies. In fact, the field officers are entitled to special pay immediately after they join the Central Secretariat. It seems that the prestige of the Central Secretariat has gone up too high.

3.3 STRUCTURE OF THE CENTRAL SECRETARIAT

It is said that the Central Secretariat is the summation of various Ministries and Departments. But the Cabinet Secretariat, which is a Ministry comprising more than one Department, is still known as the Secretariat. In a Ministry, the ultimate charge is allotted to a Minister. This charge may include one or more Departments. Each Department is under the charge of one Secretary. Many large Ministries like agriculture, defence, education, external affairs, finance, home, etc. have more than one Department in their charge.

A Department, on the other hand, is defined as an organizational unit consisting of a secretary. Thus, a Department should be identified with a Secretary's charge and a Ministry should be identified with a Minister's charge.

A Ministry, for the purpose of expediting internal organizational activities, is divided into the following segments. There is an officer in charge of each segment.

Department – Secretary/Additional Secretary/Special Secretary

Wing – Joint Secretary/Additional Secretary

Division – Director/Deputy Secretary

Branch – Under Secretary

Section – Section Officer

The functions and roles played by such officers are briefly described below:

1. **Secretary:** A Secretary is usually the administrative head of a Ministry or a Department. He is the main advisor to the Minister on all matters of policy and administration within his Ministry or

Department. He enjoys complete and undivided responsibility for efficient administration. The Secretary represents his Ministry or Department before the Parliamentary Committee on Public Accounts. He receives weekly summaries describing the nature of cases which have been disposed of by his subordinate officers. Thus, he becomes continuously aware of the working of his Department.

N. Gopalaswami Ayyangar suggested: "A Secretary should not be immersed in files and burdened with routine. It is essential that he should have time to grasp the overall picture, size up the problems facing government in the field allotted to his charge, and think and plan ahead. All these are his proper functions and must be efficiently performed."[4] Thus, the Secretary stands at the topmost point of the departmental authority and draws the highest salary available to any member of the civil service.

2. **Special Secretary:** More than one level of authority has been introduced since 1947 and thus the original hierarchy of administration has been disturbed. This tends to weaken the solidarity, efficiency and effectiveness of a number of administrative posts. The introduction of a new post designated as Special Secretary is a good example of such weakening. As Asok Chanda observes, in 1951 a Special Secretary, enjoying the pay, status and authority of a Secretary, was appointed to the Ministry of Agriculture. This was a unique post where neither the principles on which such a post was created nor its relations with the Permanent Secretary were defined.[5] A Special Secretary was also appointed (with the rank of a Secretary) in charge of the Department of Kashmir Affairs in the Ministry of Home Affairs. It can thus be said that there is no well-defined principle regarding the appointment, rank and pay of a Special Secretary.
3. **Additional Secretary:** Initially, the officer next in hierarchy to the Secretary was the Deputy Secretary. But later, some new levels of Joint, Additional and Special Secretaries were formed. In 1937, the Organization and Procedure Committee referred to these new levels. Almost every committee has recommended either the abolition of these new posts or their drastic reduction in number. However, such newer intermediary ranks have ultimately succeeded. In reality, these posts have been created to reward some senior Joint Secretary by raising both his salary and rank. This new officer has no specified duty or work. Sometimes, he is placed in charge of a Department, doing the work of a Secretary. All other times, he is placed at the head of a 'wing' and performs the functions of a Joint Secretary. Still at other times, he helps the Secretary in a specified field of activity.

In the opinion of Richard Tottenham,[6] there is and should be no difference of functions, but only of pay between a Joint Secretary and an Additional Secretary. In both cases, their real function is to lighten the burden of the Secretary.

However, the Personnel Study Team of the Administrative Reforms Commission (ARC) and the ARC itself suggested the creation of a definite level of Additional Secretary. Thus in the Secretariat hierarchy, the level of Additional Secretary has come to stay. This level provides considerable relief to the Secretary in the Ministries of larger size. As a result, the Secretary can now concentrate on the more important policy matters.

4. **Joint Secretary:** Where the volume of work in a Ministry exceeds the manageable charge of a Secretary, one or more 'wings' may be established within the Ministry. Normally a Joint Secretary takes in charge of each wing. Regarding all business falling under his wing, the Joint Secretary is in charge of maximum measure of independent functioning and responsibility.

   For three main reasons, this post of Joint Secretary was created in the early twenties of the twentieth century. They are as under:

   (a) The functions of some Departments were enhanced so remarkably that it became extremely difficult for one Secretary to deal with all the increased work.
   (b) For one Secretary, it became really difficult to combine separate items of business.
   (c) With the emergence of two Houses of legislature at the Centre in 1920, it was necessary that senior officers should be present in both Houses to assist the members of the legislature in the legislative work.

   Criticising the emergence of the new level of Joint Secretaries between the Secretary and his Deputy Secretaries, N. Gopalaswami Ayyangar has observed: "The interposition of an officer (called joint or additional secretary) between the Secretary and the Deputy Secretary in a Department is prima facie an unsatisfactory arrangement even when it is made for the purpose for which it should normally be made, namely, to relieve the Secretary of a block of work and deal directly with the Minister in respect of that work. Even at its best, I consider the arrangement to be unsatisfactory because the Secretary is not thereby formally relieved of his general (or *de jure*) responsibility while *de facto* responsibility is entrusted to another officer."[7]

5. **Director:** This post is relatively a new addition since it was created in 1960. Mostly to satisfy the ego of certain officers, the post of 'Director' was created. The responsibilities of Director are more or less the same as those of a Deputy Secretary.

6. **Deputy Secretary:** A Deputy Secretary is an officer acting on behalf of the Secretary. He is in charge of the Secretariat division. He remains responsible for the performance of governmental functions within his territorial jurisdiction. He should be able to dispose of the majority of cases coming up to him. On more important cases where the Secretary or the Joint Secretary gives him written or oral orders, the Deputy Secretary uses his discretionary powers in taking such orders. On the whole, the Deputy Secretary occupies a key position in the Central Secretariat.
7. **Under Secretary:** An Under Secretary is in charge of a branch in a Ministry and has full authority regarding the despatch of business and the maintenance of discipline. In the Maxwell Committee Report, the role of the Under Secretary has been clearly mentioned in the following way:[8]

   "The grade of the Under Secretary should ordinarily initiate action on all inward communications, but he should not hesitate even at that stage to bring a receipt immediately to the notice of the Deputy Secretary for any instructions which the latter might wish to give.... More important files he should submit to the Deputy Secretary in such a form that in ordinary course the Deputy Secretary should be enabled to deal with the case quite briefly. Under Secretaries should also attempt to reduce ... the number of files to be formally submitted to the Deputy Secretary...."
8. **Assistant Secretary:** Till our independence in 1947, there was another level below the Under Secretary. This level was known as the *assistant secretary*. These posts were created as a result of the recommendation of the Secretariat Committee of 1919. The Maxwell Report (1937), however, recommended for the abolition of the post. The recommendation was effected after 1947.
9. **Officer on Special Duty (OSD):** It is an old device to accommodate certain persons or to meet an unexpected emergency. But it has appeared to be useful to practising administrators. Certain features inherent in the system are as follows:
   - The designation OSD has a special charm which attracts a lot of persons.
   - The post does not indicate any status. It means any position at a given time depending on the nature and type of work.
   - The government in recent years has been appointing OSDs more easily and frequently than originally envisaged.
   - There is a growing trend towards such officers staying on in their special posts indefinitely. The post is of a temporary nature. It suits both the officer concerned and his boss.

- The post is ideal for training. In the words of S.R. Maheshwari, "the post of OSD ideally tends itself to use as a training post."
- The post has both administrative reason and political reason behind its creation.

10. **Section Officer:** Superintendents, in charge of sections, are known as *section officers*. The section officer basically supervises the work of the staff of his section, but he himself handles the important and intricate cases. He distributes the work among his staff; trains, assists and advises the staff; coordinates the work in his section; ensures prompt and efficient disposal of work in his section; adopts necessary measures for the steady progress of cases; submits arrear statements and other periodical returns in time; maintains the section diary, file register and other documents of the section properly; ensures safeguarding of secret and top secret papers; issues reminders, acknowledgements, etc.; remains responsible for the disposal of routine cases; maintains order and discipline in the section and keeps the section neat and clean.

Apart from the above mentioned officers, this section will describe the functions of the assistants and upper division clerks, on the one hand, and lower division clerks and typists, on the other.

1. **Assistants and Upper Division Clerks:** An assistant usually works under the orders of the section officer. The assistant usually remains responsible for the work entrusted to him by the section officer. He normally examines and puts suitable notes and drafts on cases promptly and submits them quickly to his immediate boss, i.e. the section officer. He maintains his diary properly and keeps papers and files in tidy condition. Some assistants may be selected as more efficient ones who are usually authorized to submit cases directly to the branch officer.

   Upper division clerks perform more or less similar functions as with those of assistants. But they are not ordinarily entitled to deal with 'important' cases as the assistants are:
2. **Lower Division Clerks and Typists:** Such functionaries are normally entrusted with work of a routine nature. These work include registration of papers, maintenance and circulation of other registers, indexing, recording, proof corrections, preparation of arrear statements, supervision of corrections to reference books, typing, submission of routine and simple drafts, etc.

There has been a remarkable increase in recent years in the volume of work in the Central Secretariat. The main reasons behind this increase are:

1. At present, the government has assumed increasing responsibilities for regulating trade and industry, controlling restrictive

practices, nationalization of banking and insurance, promotion of economic development, fostering science and technology, etc.

2. There has also been an increase in the number of public sector undertakings in various fields which, in turn, gives birth to a steady increase in the secretarial work.
3. Again, due to the increasing executive accountability to the legislature and the increasing scrutiny by the standing committees of the Union legislature, there is an increasing need for maintaining proper records of all cases involving financial sanctions.

As a result of all these factors, there has been a remarkable growth in the number of central secretariat posts at various levels.

In this context, it would probably not be totally irrelevant to describe the Union Home Ministry and its expanded Secretariat at present. The Home Ministry is topped by the Home Minister who is of Cabinet rank. He, again, is assisted by two Ministers of State. The division of functions among the Minister and Ministers of State for Home Affairs is decided by the Home Minister. There are certain matters which are disposed of at the level of the Ministers of State. However, all sensitive issues, particularly those of internal security, must reach the Home Minister's level, and sometimes even the Prime Minister's level. The most important issues are discussed at the level of the Political Affairs Committee of the Cabinet and even in the entire Cabinet. In recent years, with serious threats to internal peace and security, the Home Ministry's functioning has assumed special significance. The Ministry of Home Affairs has one Deputy Minister as well. He assists the two Ministers of State and the Home Minister in the performance of their duties. The administrative head of the Ministry is the Home Secretary, who is a senior IAS officer. The Department of Official Languages, though a part of the Ministry of Home Affairs, has a separate Secretary. There are two special Secretaries to assist the Home Secretary in the conduct of official business. Below them are a large number of Joint Secretaries, Directors, Deputy Secretaries and Under Secretaries.

The top-level organization of the Ministry of Home Affairs is given in Figure 3.1. It helps one to understand the size of the secretarial expansion. Regarding the efficiency of the Central Secretariat, the Administrative Reforms Commission has categorically mentioned in its report that the Central Secretariat is busy with performing so many unnecessary functions that, at present, it has been turned into a vast agency without any control imposed on it. As a result, the administrative machinery has been malfunctioning and there is no clear-cut territorial boundary line between the responsibilities of different Departments. For the same reason, the work has become indefinite and there has been unnecessary delay. Besides, the increasing number of officials has resulted in the deteriorating standard of work. Hence, the higher level officers are overburdened with work.[9]

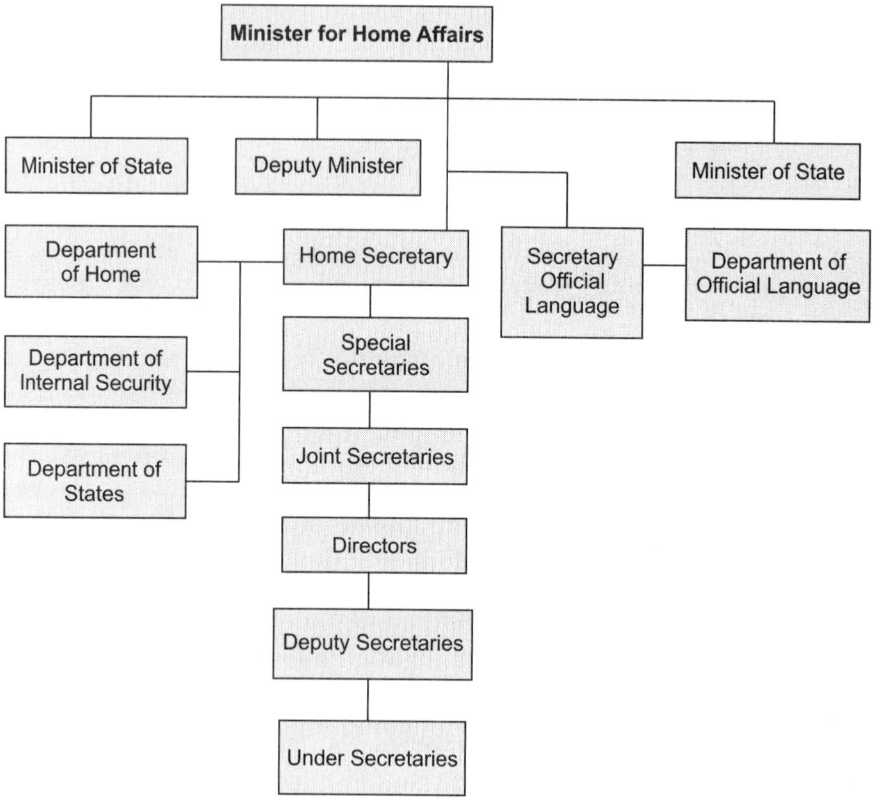

FIGURE 3.1 Structure of the Union Ministry of Home Affairs.

3.4 PRIME MINISTER'S SECRETARIAT/OFFICE

Prime Minister's Secretariat (PMS) was created on August 15, 1947, Since June 1977, it came to be known as the Prime Minister's Office (PMO). The PMS was created basically for the purpose of performing the functions of the Secretary to the Governor-General. The PMS was an extra-constitutional institution having no mention in the Constitution.

The PMO occupies the status of a Department of the Government of India under the Allocation of Business Rules, 1961. Officially, it is a link between the Prime Minister and his Ministers, on the one hand, and the President, Governors, Chief Ministers and Foreign Representatives, on the other. Basically, PMO is concerned with party matters, personal correspondence, complaints from the public, etc.

3.4.1 Structure

At the apex of the Prime Minister's Office (PMO), there is obviously the Prime Minister himself. Just below him is the Principal Secretary to the Prime Minister. The organizational hierarchy of the PMO can be understood from Figure 3.2.

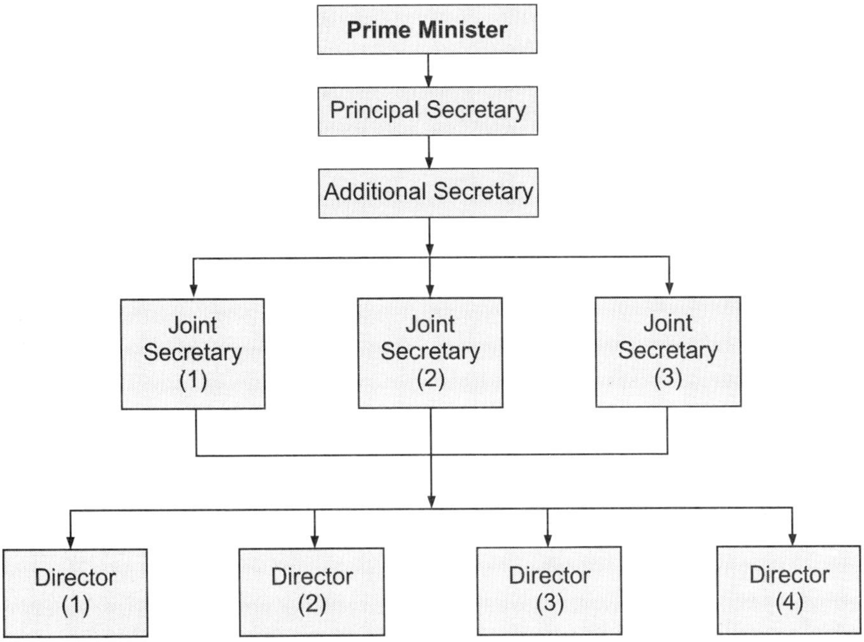

FIGURE 3.2 Hierarchical structure of the PMO in India.

- **Prime Minister:** The principal official of the PMO is undoubtedly the Prime Minister himself. The structural organization of the PMO is determined by him. It is he who decides which person would occupy which position in this hierarchical order.
- **Principal Secretary:** The Principal Secretary to the Prime Minister is the head of the bureaucratic pyramid of the PMO who deals with all governmental files in the office. He is in charge of various matters of the Ministers that the PM asks him to deal with.
- ***Additional Secretary:*** According to the PM's advice, the Additional Secretary normally looks after the personnel and policy matters of the various Ministries.
- ***Joint Secretary (1):*** He is in-charge of Home Affairs, Law and Justice.
- ***Joint Secretary (2):*** He looks after the administrative system of the PMO and the Ministries of Surface Transport, Railways, and Civil Aviation, and Communications.
- ***Joint Secretary (3):*** He handles the various aspects of the Ministries of External Affairs, Defence and Atomic Energy.
  - ♦ **Director (1)** He is an officer on special duty looking after rural development and civil supplies.
  - ♦ **Director (2)** He is in-charge of Home Affairs.

- **Director (3)** Having no specific responsibilities, he acts basically as a trouble-shooter.
- **Director (4)** He is concerned with various matters of the State Governments, particularly those of the North-East.

Below the above mentioned officers, there are several functionaries belonging to Class I, Class II, Class III and Class IV services.

The PMO ensures secretarial assistance to the Prime Minister. It includes the anti-corruption unit and the public wing dealing with grievances.

Which files are to be submitted before the PM and what would be the subject matters of those files–these things depend on the fact whether the PM himself is holding direct charge of the Ministry or whether there is a Cabinet Minister or Minister of State in charge of the Ministry.

In the case of the latter, most matters are looked after by the Cabinet Minister or Minister of State. Only some very important policy issues are received by the PMO. In the case of the former, all matters are submitted to the PMO. The PM has traditionally been the Minister-in-charge of such Departments as Space, Atomic Energy and the Ministry of Personnel, Public Grievances and Pensions. Since the PM is the ex-officio Chairman of the Planning Commission, many valuable files are forwarded to the PMO for his comments and clearance.

Some vital matters that need the Prime Minister's personal attention are as follows:

(a) Important issues relating to defence
(b) Civilian and military decorations where presidential approval is a must
(c) All important policy issues
(d) Appointment proposals of Indian Heads of Missions abroad
(e) All important decisions relating to Cabinet Secretariat
(f) Appointments to the Central Administrative Tribunal, State Administrative Tribunals, UPSC, Election Commission, Commissions attached to various ministries, etc.
(g) All policy matters relating to bureaucratic administration and administrative reforms
(h) Special packages announced by the Prime Minister for the States
(i) All judicial appointments for which presidential approval is necessary.

The Prime Minister's National Relief Fund (PMNRF) and the National Defence Fund (NDF) are operated directly by the PMO.

3.4.2 Functions

The main task of the Secretaries and Directors of the PMO is to help the Prime Minister in the performance of his functions as the governmental head. These officials assist the PM in maintaining links with the President, Union Ministers, Governors, Chief Ministers, representatives of foreign governments in India, etc. On the public side, the Secretariat of the PMO handles various requests or complaints from members of the public addressed to the PM. The jurisdiction of the Secretariat may extend over any subject or activity not specially allotted to any Ministry or Department. It is convenient for the Secretariat to make answers for questions raised in the Parliament on some general subjects not allotted to any particular Ministry. The main functions of the Secretariat of the PMO are as follows:

1. To deal with all references that have to come to the PM
2. To help the PM in the discharge of his overall responsibilities as the Chief Executive.
3. To help the PM to act as the Chairman of the Planning Commission.
4. To help the PM in maintaining relations with the press and the public.
5. To assist the PM in examining cases submitted to him for orders under prescribed rules.

3.4.3 Role of the PMO (1947–Till Date)

Till 1947, the Secretary to the Governor-General assisted the Executive Council of him. It was a small Secretariat which helped the Governor-General. After independence in 1947, the Prime Minister as the Chief Executive set up his own Secretariat known as the Prime Minister's Secretariat (PMS). The role played by the PMS (which since 1977 came to be known as the PMO or Prime Minister's Office) has changed with time. Till the death of our first Prime Minister Jawaharlal Nehru in 1964, the strength as well as the role of the PMS was quite limited. But in power and importance, it was next to the Cabinet Secretariat. Nehru appointed H.V.R. Iyengar, a senior ICS officer, as his principal private Secretary. Being an able officer with a remarkable charismatic personality, he began to attend all Cabinet meetings. This is a tradition being maintained since his time. Following the British model, the post of the Principal Private Secretary was reduced to the rank of Joint Secretary. In 1958–59, Nehru's small Secretariat consisted of 129 persons and the annual Secretariat budget was ₹6,75,000.

During the tenure of our next Prime Minister Lal Bahadur Shastri, the PMS was revitalized and strengthened to a great extent. Shastri appointed L.K. Jha, a senior IAS officer, as his Secretary. His dynamic personality, like that of his predecessor, upheld the status of the Secretariat. It became almost a Department under a full Secretary. The post of Principal Private Secretary was restored to its former status of Secretary. Enhancing the size and status of the Secretariat, Jha gradually appeared to be a Super Secretary.

Indira Gandhi was the next Prime Minister. In the first phase of her tenure, Jha was at the top of the PMS. During this phase, due to her lack of administrative experience, Mrs. Gandhi had to depend on Jha to a significant extent. Mr. Jha was always present at all the meetings between Mrs. Gandhi, on the one hand, and all have officers and foreign delegates, on the other. He even accompanied Mrs. Gandhi in all her foreign tours. He wonderfully played all such roles as an able administrator. He enhanced the size of the Prime Minister's Secretariat remarkably. In 1968–69, the secretarial staff of the PMS included 201 persons of all categories and its annual budget was ₹13.15 lakhs. When Jha was appointed as a member of the Atomic Energy Commission, the status of the Principal Secretary was enhanced even more.

When Jha was appointed the Governor of the Reserve Bank of India, P.N. Haksar became the Secretary to the Prime Minister. For one year, Haksar was known as the Prime Minister's Secretary. After it, he was redesignated as the Principal Secretary which definitely was an even higher rank. During the tenure of Haksar, who proved to be an able and efficient Secretary, the Prime Minister's secretariat became an absolutely independent executive force. Haksar, however, tried his best to prevent Mrs. Gandhi's younger son Sanjay Gandhi from influencing, dominating and dictating the Prime Minister's Secretariat. For doing this, he had to pay a heavy price as he was immediately replaced from the post of the Principal Secretary to that of the Deputy Chairman of the Planning Commission.

P.N. Dhar, who had an academic background, was appointed as the Secretary after Haksar. Initially, he was designated as an advisor. Later, he was redesignated as a Secretary, but was never given the pivotal rank of the Principal Secretary.

After her remarkable victory at the Lok Sabha polls in 1971 and particularly after the declaration of Emergency in June 1975, Mrs. Gandhi wanted to increase the size and importance of her Secretariat. Eventually, the writs of the PMS started to be followed by all Ministers, Departments and executive agencies. By the end of her term, before the victory of the Janata Party, the PMS included 242 persons and its budget was more than ₹30 lakhs. Virtually, her Secretariat used to formulate the national policies while the Cabinet Secretariat was merely its enforcement arm.

After the Lok Sabha elections of March 1977, a radical change was visible in the political as well as administrative system. The Janata Government replaced the Congress Government at the Centre. Morarji Desai, the new Prime Minister, appointed V. Shankar, a retired ICS officer, as the top of the Prime Minister's Office (PMO) and designated him as 'Principal Secretary' on the maximum salary. Remembering the erstwhile state of emergency (1975–77) during the tenure of her predecessor Mrs. Indira Gandhi, Morarji Desai dared not to give the Prime Minister's Secretariat ultimate power. In fact, he transformed the erstwhile Secretariat into a mere office. Hence the Prime Minister's office (PMO), replacing the Prime Minister's Secretariat (PMS), instead of making various policies, was empowered only to actually help the Prime Minister in administrative and other affairs of national importance.

After the Lok Sabha polls of 1980, Mrs. Gandhi came back to power. She remained in power till her assassination on October 31, 1984. During the last phase of her long tenure, the PMO never attained its former position.

After her sudden death in 1984, her elder son Rajiv Gandhi became the new Prime Minister. As Prime Minister, he completed his full term of five years and was defeated at the 1989 polls. During his tenure, the PMO was enhanced both quantitatively and qualitatively and somewhat regained its lost honour. Arun Singh, who was the Minister of State in the PMO and was virtually running the PMO, was transferred to the Ministry of Defence. A hurry was somehow felt to take India to the 21st century. The PMO, too, naturally reflected this quick urge of the then PM for modernization. He relied more on his small group of advisors consisting of top bureaucrats, technocrats and managers rather than on politicians and his cabinet colleagues. Rajiv Gandhi's PMO made a number of innovations in the field of science and technology due to his keen interest in technology. In fact, he dreamt of turning his PMO into something like the US presidential office. Appointing many advisors from his "Dehradun-brigade", he started to give the PMO some extra-constitutional powers and authority.

During the tenure of Chandrasekhar, the PMO became most inactive. As the PMO of a freak government, it was rapidly weakened.

After Rajiv Gandhi's assassination in May 1991, P.V. Narasimha Rao became the Prime Minister of India. He was a different kind of Prime Minister having faith in moderation, mildness, consensus and consultations. He had his political Secretary; but not much was heard of his PMO. A write-up in *India Today* of September 15, 1992, page 51, gives a vivid account of the position of the then Prime Minister, P.V. Narasimha Rao, and his PMO. It said: "Meanwhile, the PMO has made a comeback to the spotlight, though still largely a faceless organization." In the write-up, Rao had been harshly criticized for his over-dependence on Mr. Verma who virtually ran the Ministries in Rao's control and who had full control over the Foreign Investment Promotion Board. The Deve Gowda Government was in power for ten months only. It was a coalition government. The PMO during this period was not a very strong one. I.K. Gujral was even a weaker Prime Minister and his PMO was very inactive.

Atal Behari Vajpayee's PMO was equally weak and inactive. *India Today* of April 20, 1998, pp. 20–21, gives a vivid account of the then position of the PMO. It said that Atalji's secretariat was a good mixture of the old and new, reflecting his cautiousness and priorities. At the top-most position was the Principal Secretary, Brajesh Mishra, an IFS Officer, serving as India's permanent representative to the United Nations. Mishra was the first Principal Secretary who was also a member of the then ruling party and the first non-IAS Officer to occupy that crucial post. Vajpayee chose Pramod Mahajan as his political advisor with Cabinet rank. A senior PMO official compared Mahajan's style with Arun Nehru's–firm and authoritative, having "the ear of the PM". Vajpayee was gradually leaning towards a small group of advisors–the people who used to think like him. T.K.A. Nair, the Secretary in Vajpayee's PMO, was asked to be interested in continuity and not to make sweeping changes. He brought in only one Joint Secretary of his choice–Ashok Saikia, an Assam cadre IAS Officer. He continued to keep the Anti-Corruption Cell set up by Gujral. During Vajpayee's tenure, Mr. Sudheendra Kulkarni was informally working as the Press Secretary.

After the fourteenth Lok Sabha elections in 2004, Mr. Manmohan Singh became our Prime Minister. Just after its formation, Mr. Sanjay Mitra, a senior IAS officer and the then Chairman of the West Bengal State Electricity Board, was included in Manmohan Singh's PMO. T.K.A. Nair, the Principal Secretary to the Prime Minister, had been given an extension, according to sources in the Prime Minister's Office. Mr. Nair was the first official to join Dr. Manmohan Singh's Prime Ministerial staff in May, 2004. He was first named an Officer on Special Duty (OSD) and then, within two days, was redesignated as Principal Secretary to Prime Minister for a three-year period. The decision to extend Mr. Nair's tenure was taken the day after a new Cabinet Secretary was named. The decision put an end to the speculation and uncertainty whether the retiring Cabinet Secretary, B.K. Chaturvedi, would replace Mr. Nair. After the fifteenth Lok Sabha elections in 2009, the basic pattern of the PMO in UPA government did not change much.

In 2014, the BJP Government came to power at the Centre. Mr. Narendra Modi became the Prime Minister of India.* The important officers of his PMO are Shri Nripendra Misra, Shri Ajit Doval, Dr. P.K. Mishra, Shri Bhaskar Khulbe, Shri Tarun Bajaj, Shri Vinay Mohan Kwatra, Dr. T.V. Somanathan, Shri A.K. Sharma, Shri Anurag Jain, Ms. Debashree Mukherjee, Shri Brajendra Navnit, Shri V. Sheshadri etc. The first four among them bear the important offices of Principal Secretary, National Security Adviser, Additional Principal Secretary and Secretary, respectively. The next eight persons act as Joint Secretaries. There is still a long list of significant officers in Modi's PMO assigned to perform a series of functions. Through these dynamic, dedicated and determined officers, Modi seeks to reflect the hope and ambition of our one billion Indians.

* On 26th May, 2014 Narendra Modi took oath as our Prime Minister. He became the first ever Prime Minister of India to be born after Indian independence in 1947.

Whenever a new Prime Minister takes over, there is utter curiosity and anxiety to see how the PMO would be and how it develops further during his tenure. This is more true about the BJP and its allies. Over the years, PMO has grown into a high profile body. Quite often, it has exceeded the powers of the Cabinet Secretariat and actively interfered with the working of various Ministries and Departments. People who constitute the PMO have acquired power and authority of their own in the name of the Prime Minister. Sometimes even the PMO comes to assume much more authority and power than the Prime Minister originally intended.[10]

3.5 CABINET SECRETARIAT

The Cabinet Secretariat is the successor to the Secretariat of the Executive Council of the Viceroy. The success and efficiency of the Cabinet depend, to a significant extent, on the efficiency of the Cabinet Secretariat. Its main function is to prepare the agenda of the Cabinet meeting, to provide information and materials necessary for its laws, and to maintain the records of the discussions and decisions both of the Cabinet and its Committees. Major activities and decisions are informed by the Cabinet Secretariat to the President, the Vice-President and all the Ministries.

The Cabinet Secretariat consists of about 500 posts. The department is organized in three wings–the civil wing, the military wing and the intelligence wing. The main function of the civil wing is to look after the various secretarial work of the Cabinet, its various standing and ad hoc committees. The main task of the military wing is to supervise carefully the work of the meetings of the Defence Committee, National Defence Council, Military Affairs Committee and many other committees associated with defence. The intelligence wing is basically concerned with matters related to the Joint Intelligence Committee of the Cabinet. Apart from these three wings, an additional committee, named Joint Communication Electronics Committee, was created in the Cabinet Secretariat in 1977.

Besides the Cabinet Secretary, there are three other Secretaries in the Cabinet Secretariat. They are the heads of the three above mentioned wings respectively: Coordination (civil), Security (military) and Research and Analysis Wing (RAW). The Secretary, Coordination, prepares the agenda and other important papers for Cabinet meetings. In this work, he is assisted by Additional Secretary, Coordination, Joint Secretary, Coordination, and a Joint Secretary for Joint Interrogation Committee who is usually a senior IPS officer. The Secretary, Security, is also an IPS officer who remains responsible for the security of the Prime Minister and his colleagues. In this work, he is helped by the Director, Special Protection Group who looks after the physical protection of the Prime Minister and his blood relations. The Secretary, RAW, is concerned with external intelligence. As Director General (Security) and also as the head of Special Frontier Force and Aviation Research Centre, he performs some specialized functions.

A significantly important organ of the Cabinet Secretariat emerged in 1988. It is known as the Directorate of Public Grievances, which is basically an independent appellate body of a non-statutory character. The Directorate entertains public grievances against the actions and decisions of some of the Central Government institutions like Public Sector Banks, Life Insurance Corporation, Railways, Post Office, etc.

The rise of the Cabinet Secretariat in India during the last thirty-five to forty years indicates a remarkable concentration of power in the hand of the Prime Minister. The Prime Minister's Secretariat (PMS)/ Prime Minister's Office (PMO) and the Cabinet Secretariat together act as overall supervisory agencies. This centralizing trend, however, accords well with the general structure of the Cabinet form of government. With the advancement of technology, expansion in the scope of the government and the creation of a number of governmental and semi-governmental organizations, it needs to be ensured that Ministers and Secretaries of respective Ministries and Departments do not suffer from any kind of insecurity and loss of responsibility. There should also be some kind of provision of expert assistance to the Cabinet and Cabinet Committees.

During the tenure of Rajiv Gandhi, the influence of the Cabinet Secretariat grew to a significant extent. It was working almost as a 'super Cabinet'.

3.5.1 Role of the Cabinet Secretariat

The first and foremost function of the Cabinet Secretariat is to perform the necessary secretarial work relating to the meeting of the Cabinet and its Committees. Some papers are circulated by the Cabinet Secretariat for the consideration of the Cabinet, and its Committees. Some other papers are circulated by the Cabinet Secretariat to the President, the Vice-President, the members of the Cabinet, Cabinet Committees and Council of Ministers. The papers which are mostly circulated are economic reviews, fortnightly political reports from state governments and centrally administered territorial administrators, monthly summaries from the Ministries or Departments giving a brief account of their activities and decisions, quarterly reports on the economic conditions of both the Centre and the States, review of the five-year plans, reports on agricultural production, reports on prices of food articles, reports on administrative reforms, reports on the working of the industrial and commercial undertakings of the Central Government, brief notes on important matters from Ministries and Departments, any other paper which the Prime Minister may wish to circulate to his Ministers.

In cases where there is a difference of opinions among different Ministries, the Cabinet Secretary tries to resolve such differences and to arrive at agreed or, at least, acceptable decisions. As head of the Cabinet Secretariat, the Cabinet Secretary is responsible for securing coordination and timely action by all Ministries/Departments of the Government of India in all affairs where either the Cabinet, as a whole, or the Prime Minister, in particular, is interested. For this purpose, the Cabinet Secretary can convene meetings of the Secretaries and senior officials, whenever necessary. The Cabinet Secretariat communicates the decisions of the Cabinet and Cabinet Committees to the Ministries and Departments concerned. The Cabinet Secretariat keeps a constant watch on the implementation of various decisions taken by the Secretariat. It also supervises the implementation of decisions taken by the Cabinet and its committees. A monthly statement indicating the progress on the ministerial cases is sent to the Cabinet Secretariat. If it is noticed by the Cabinet Secretariat that the progress is not much satisfactory, then the matter is taken up at a higher level.

Several cases involving the President, the Prime Minister, various Ministries and the Parliament are brought before the Cabinet Secretariat. Some of these cases are as follows:

(a) Cases involving legislation including the issuing of ordinances
(b) Address and messages of the President to the Parliament
(c) Proposals to summon or prorogue the Parliament or dissolve the Lok Sabha
(d) Cases involving negotiations with foreign countries on treaties, agreements, etc.
(e) Proposals for sending delegations of persons abroad in any capacity
(f) Cases involving financial proposals
(g) Cases which a Minister puts to the Cabinet for decision and direction
(h) Proposals to vary or reverse decisions
(i) Proposals to appoint public committees of enquiry and consideration of reports of such committees.

3.6 THE CABINET SECRETARY

In the British administrative system, the Cabinet Secretary is almost at the focal point of the Cabinet. Being the top administrator, he is almost an advisor and conscience-keeper to all officials. Whenever there arises any kind of inter-departmental problem, the British officials come to the Cabinet Secretary to take advice and assistance. Above all, the Cabinet Secretary is the Secretary to the Prime Minister and hence very close to him. The ex-British Prime Minister Wilson has said about the status of the Cabinet Secretary: "... the Permanent Secretary of the Cabinet is also my Permanent Secretary.... He advises me, briefs me, not only for cabinet meetings over which I preside, but on the general running of the government so far as policy is concerned."[11]

He hears all and speaks only when asked for information. He is assisted by many other officials who, in the words of Prof. S.R. Maheshwari, "are all career civil servants working in the Cabinet Secretariat."[12] Today the Cabinet Secretary is a very important official of the Central Government. The Cabinet Secretariat as an office was invented in England in 1916 during the tenure of Lloyd George. Sir Maurice Hankey was the first Cabinet Secretary. In India this office was created in 1950 during the tenure of our first Prime Minister Jawaharlal Nehru. N.R. Pillai was the first Cabinet Secretary of India.

There are some differences between the Cabinet Secretary of India and that of Great Britain. Usually, the seniormost civil servant chosen by the government occupies the office of the Cabinet Secretary. In Britain, the Cabinet Secretary is appointed by selection based on merit. Secondly, in India a civil servant is appointed as Cabinet Secretary at the end of his service career. The average tenure of this post is normally less than three years and in some cases, if it seems necessary, he is given extension. But in Britain, the average tenure of the Cabinet Secretary is about ten years. Maurice Hankey, the first Cabinet Secretary of Britain, occupied this prestigious office for twenty-two years, whereas in India, as it has been pointed out, there have been nine Cabinet Secretaries in twenty-five years.[13]

The study team on reorganization of governmental machinery observes that the Cabinet Secretary should be selected from amongst outstanding secretaries. On selection, he should be appointed for a term of four years. The Deshmukh Study Team had suggested to give the Cabinet Secretary a higher salary than other Secretaries in order to ensure his pre-eminent position. But the Administrative Reforms Commission, however, had thought that inequality in pay-scales might adversely affect the cordial relation between the Cabinet Secretary and other Secretaries. Hence, it did not accept the Team's recommendations. Yet, the Cabinet Secretary draws the maximum salary of an IAS officer. Besides, he draws a special entertainment allowance.

Regarding the functions of the Cabinet Secretary, the Ayyangar Report says that being an administrative officer of the highest rank, the Cabinet Secretary should perform a positive function of securing coordination. The Deshmukh Study Team, however, was not satisfied with the working of the office. It said that there were shortcomings at the apex point, namely, at the point of the Cabinet Secretary, for good management was not adequately forthcoming from that point. Consequently, a sense of helplessness was felt about the senior management of the Union Government. The Deshmukh Study Team has clearly pointed out that the principal reason behind this helplessness is that the Cabinet Secretary has not been allotted a clear-cut role and a strong enough position.

Hence, the Team recommended the following measures to improve the position of the Cabinet Secretary:

(a) The position of the Cabinet Secretary should be recognized clearly in the Government of India Transaction of Business Rules.

(b) Cases involving differences of opinion between two or more Ministers should be reported by the Secretary concerned to the Cabinet Secretary at as early a stage as possible.

(c) The Cabinet Secretary should regularly meet other secretaries.

(d) The Cabinet Secretary should be given a salary which establishes his pre-eminent position vis-à-vis other secretaries.

The role played by the Cabinet Secretary can be well understood from the following remarks of Khera: "The Cabinet Secretary provided the eyes and ears for the Prime Minister to keep in touch with the process of official business in the central government. But he is in no sense the watchdog or invigilator on behalf of the Prime Minister.... The Cabinet Secretary's is a very general staff function, not a line function in relation to the Ministries. His business is to help, not to oversee."[14]

Thus, the Cabinet Secretary, in other words, does not and should not interfere in the working of the Departments. Besides, he does not have any administrative authority in relation to them as each Department has a Secretary of its own. But in reality it happens that he is looked up to provide guidance and consultation to all officials. It appears that he is a sort of advisor and conscience-keeper to all the permanent officials. During the time of interdepartmental difficulties, they come to him for advice and guidance. "He seems to be a man in whom all permanent officials have great confidence...."[15]

The leadership qualities of a civil servant are tested most during his tenure as the Cabinet Secretary, which is indeed a dream-post for every bureaucrat. A Cabinet Secretary by performing his functions plays three important roles as visionary, leader and motivator. But obviously different Cabinet Secretaries such as N.K. Mukherjee, Naresh Chandra, B.G. Deshmukh, T.N. Seshan, S.N. Rajgopal, and Zafar Saifulla have different styles of functioning. This style tends to influence the entire organization of Cabinet Secretariat to a significant extent.

3.7 UNION GOVERNMENT

The ultimate power in a democratic set-up rests with the people. Administration is the executive organ for implementing the policies and programmes of the government as approved by the legislature. It operates within the framework of a set-up of constitutional provisions, laws, rules and conventions developed over the years. In the governance of India, the executive part of the government plays a prominent role. In the present and subsequent sections, an attempt has been made to provide a general idea of the political executive of India at the Union level. It is interesting to see its role in a parliamentary and, at the same time, federal set up of our nation.

A modern executive consists of its political and bureaucratic arms.[16] Since the Indian Constitution seeks to combine parliamentary as well as federal principles of government, the executive here has roles both in parliamentary and federal components of the government. Under the Indian Constitution, the political executive is legally and democratically constituted, and is subject to legislative control and judicial review. Any argument of executive prerogative or privilege in the monarchical tradition of independent India would be highly untenable.

In terms of Indian Constitutional law, executive power is the residue of governmental functions that are neither legislative nor judicial.[17] In certain exigencies, it can be used prior to legislative sanction subject to the Constitution.[18] Broadly speaking, the Constitution includes at least three limitations on the Union executive power:

- Separation of powers between the three major organs of government
- Federal division of powers between the Union and States
- Fundamental rights of citizens.

The federal executive in India is partly elected and partly appointed. It comprises the President, the Vice-President, the Prime Minister and the Council of Ministers and the bureaucracy. Since the powers and functions of the bureaucracy have been elaborately discussed in the previous sections of this chapter, the following sections will deal with the President, the Vice President, the Prime Minister and the Council of Ministers. Roles played by the Ministry of Finance and several other vital Ministries as well as by Cabinet Committee, will be explained in the subsequent sections.

3.8 PRESIDENT OF INDIA

Unlike the US President, the President of India is the head of the State, not the head of the Government. Article 53 of our Constitution reads:

> "The executive powers of the Union shall be vested in the President and shall be exercised by him either directly or through the officers subordinate to him...."

The election of the President of India is held following the principle of 'proportional representation by means of single transferable vote'. Those who have the right to vote in this regard are the Members of Parliament and the Members of (State) Legislative Assemblies. Voting takes place by secret ballot.

To win the presidential election, a candidate must obtain a fixed quota of votes. The quota is determined after excluding the invalid ballot papers by means of the following formula:

$$\text{Electoral Quota} = \frac{\text{Total Number of Valid Votes}}{\text{Number of Candidates} + 1} + 1$$

A voter has to mark his preferences by putting 1, 2, 3, and so on against the names of the candidates given in the ballot paper. After the votes are polled, counting is done. If, a candidate obtains votes more than or equal to the quota, he is declared elected. If at the first count, no candidate gets the quota, the candidate securing least number of votes is eliminated, and his votes are distributed among other candidates according to the voters' second preferences. The process of counting is repeated till any of the remaining candidates obtains the required quota of votes. The candidate finally surviving the process of elimination is thus elected as the Indian President.

Some loopholes in the existing system of Presidential election have been discovered, as a result of which the following recommendations have been prescribed:

(a) The Presidential electoral college should include within its ambit Union Territories, so that it may claim to be more national in character.

(b) Under the existing system, a non-political candidate, even if he is qualified and well-known, cannot be the President of India without sufficient political support.

(c) Under the Presidential and Vice-Presidential Elections (Amendment) Act, 1974, the candidates contesting the presidential election are required to make a security deposit of ₹2500 each. This measure has not proved to be effective.

To be eligible for the election to the Presidency, a person must have the following qualifications:

(a) He must be a citizen of India.

(b) He must have completed the age of 35 years.

(c) He should be qualified to be a member of the Lok Sabha.

(d) He should not hold any office of profit under the National, State or Local Government of India.

The President shall hold office for a term of five years from the date on which he enters upon his office. But he is eligible for re-election to the office of the President. His office may terminate earlier, within his term of five years, in either of the following ways:

- The President may resign his office in writing addressed to the Vice-President of India.

- The President may be removed from the office for violating the Constitution. This is done by applying the procedure of Impeachment (Article 61).

The Constitutional powers of the Indian President may be classified into the following seven types.

1. **Executive Powers:** The President is the head of the Union Executive and Union administration. He has the right to be kept informed by the Prime Minister of all decisions of the Cabinet and of all the administrative affairs.

   He appoints Governors of States, Judges of the Supreme Court and High Courts, the Auditor General of India and many other high officials.

   He also appoints the Prime Minister of India and, with his/her advice, the other Ministers of the Cabinet.

   The President can ask the Council of Ministers to prove its majority in the Lok Sabha.

   He is also the supreme commander of the Armed Forces in India. He has the right to declare a war or to conclude a treaty.

2. **Legislative Powers:** The President is an integral part of the Indian Parliament. He can summon and prorogue both the Houses of the Parliament and dissolve the lower House, i.e. the Lok Sabha.

   He may address either or both Houses of the Parliament. He may also send messages to either or both Houses.

   He nominates a number of members in both Huses.

   No bill can become a law without the assent of the President.

3. **Judicial Powers:** The President appoints the Judges of the Supreme Court and the High Courts. Under Article 72, he has the power to grant pardons. He can even suspend the death sentence of any person.

4. **Financial Powers:** The President causes the annual budget of the Union Government to be laid before the Parliament each year.

5. **Emergency Powers:** The President can proclaim National Emergency (Article 352). If he/she is satisfied that a grave emergency exists whereby the security of the country is threatened by war or external aggression or internal armed rebellion, he may proclaim National Emergency for the whole country.

   Under Article 356, if the President is satisfied that there is a breakdown of the Constitutional machinery in a State, he can proclaim State Emergency for that particular State only.

Under Article 360, if the President is satisfied that a situation has arisen whereby the financial stability of India or of any part of the territory is threatened, he may declare Financial Emergency.

During Emergency the President becomes very powerful and he can even take over the entire administration of the country himself. In short, by declaring an emergency the President can transform the federal Constitution into unitary.

6. **Power of Ordinance:** Under Article 123, except when both Houses of the Parliament are in session, the President may promulgate such Ordinances as the circumstances appear to him to require.
7. **State Powers:** In addition to the appointment of Governors of States, the President has certain other powers relating to the State legislation. Some Bills of the State Legislature require his assent before they become Acts.

   Considering all the above mentioned powers, some think that the Indian President is just a Constitutional head or figure head. In fact, President Rajendra Prasad himself had spoken against giving the President any real power. But Professor D.N. Banerjee had argued in favour of the President, who, according to Banerjee, should act on his own and should not take advice of the Council of Ministers headed by the Prime Minister.

3.9 VICE-PRESIDENT OF INDIA

Article 63 of our Constitution says: "There shall be a Vice-President of India."

Article 66 of the Constitution provides for the procedure of election of the Vice-President. This election is indirect, i.e. he is elected by a specially constituted electoral college consisting of the members of both Houses of Parliament. The election of the Vice-President takes place in accordance with the system of 'proportional representation by means of single transferable vote'. Voting takes place by secret ballot.

Like the President, the Indian Vice-President is also elected for a term of five years. He is, however, eligible for re-election.

The Indian Vice-President shall not be a member of either the Lok Sabha or the Rajya Sabha or a House of the Legislature of any State.

In order to be the Vice-President, a person should have the following qualifications:

(a) He should be a citizen of India.

(b) He must have completed the age of 35 years.

(c) He should be qualified for election as a member of the Council of States.

(d) He should not hold any office of profit under the Union Government or the State Government or the Local Government.

Articles 64 and 65 of our Constitution deal with the powers and functions of the Vice-President. They are as under:

1. The Vice-President of India presides over the meetings of the Second Chamber of the Parliament, i.e. the Rajya Sabha.
2. Occasionally, he represents India in foreign countries.
3. The Vice-President also acts as the President of India in the event of the occurrence of any vacancy in the office of the President.
4. When the President is unable to perform his functions owing to his absence, illness or any other cause, the Vice-President shall perform those functions.

The Vice-President is entitled to such salary, allowances and privileges as determined by the Parliament by law.

Coming next to the President, the Vice-President of India is one of the highest dignitaries in our Constitutional system. Yet no specific function is attached to the office of the Vice-President. Indeed, the makers of our Constitution have made the office of the Vice-President one of dignity, but of little responsibility and prestigious functions.

3.10 PRIME MINISTER AND COUNCIL OF MINISTERS

The Indian Prime Minister is the central figure in our political system. Following the Westminister model existing in Great Britain, the office of the PM of India has emerged as an extremely powerful office. Article 74(1) of our Constitution says: "There shall be a Council of Ministers with the Prime Minister at the head to aid and advise the President..."

In the appointment of the Prime Minister, the President has hardly any choice under normal circumstances. The President normally appoints the leader of the party that enjoys an absolute majority in the Lok Sabha, or a person who is in a position to win the confidence of the majority in that House.

Article 78 of our Constitution specifically mentions the duties of the Prime Minister. His major duties are as follows:

1. To communicate to the President all decisions of the Council of Ministers regarding administration and legislation of India.
2. To furnish such information as the President may call for.
3. To submit for the consideration of the Council of Ministers any matter desired by the President.

The role played by the Prime Minister is briefly discussed below under the following seven broad heads:

1. **As Leader of the Nation:** The Prime Minister becomes the leader of the entire nation, irrespective of caste, creed, religion,

sex, etc. As leader of the nation, he maintains the unity and integrity of the nation and offers leadership at the time of national crisis.

2. **As Leader of the Party or the Coalition of Parties in Power:** As leader of the party, the Prime Minister plays the key role in formulating and popularizing the programmes of the party or the coalition of parties. Since parliamentary government is avowedly a party government, the Prime Minister owes his office to the party support and depends for the tenure of his office on such continued support.
3. **As Leader of the Lok Sabha:** The Prime Minister enjoys the confidence of the House of the People (Lok Sabha). Acting on the advice of the Prime Minister, who is the leader of the House of the People, the President summons, prorogues and dissolves the House. As leader of the Lok Sabha, the Prime Minister takes initiative in making legislation.
4. **As Leader of the Council of Ministers:** Being the leader of the Council of Ministers, the Prime Minister conveys the decisions of the Council to the President. The Government of India today is run by the Prime Minister with the aid and advice of other Ministers. He has unfettered discretion to appoint or dismiss his Ministers as and when required.
5. **As Leader of the Cabinet:** The unity, integrity and efficiency of the whole Cabinet depend largely on the capability, efficiency and leadership of the Prime Minister. He is the person who is principally responsible for the success and failure of the government. As in Great Britain, the Prime Minister of India is also the keystone of the Cabinet arch. Like the British Prime Minister, the Indian Prime Minister, too, is often described as *primus inter pares* meaning the first among equals. In fact, he is something more than the first among equals. Nowadays, the Cabinet as a single unit has been losing its authority and prestige as the final policy-making as well as policy-formulating body with the creation of smaller, minor or core bodies, like the "inner Cabinet", "war Cabinet", "emergency Cabinet", "partial Cabinet", "kitchen Cabinet", "super Cabinet", etc. The Prime Minister is the vital nerve of the Cabinet and is fully free to reshuffle his pack as and when desired.
6. **As Chief Advisor to the President:** Under Article 78 of the Indian Constitution, it is the duty of the Prime Minister to communicate all decisions of the Council of Ministers as well as the Cabinet to the President. Under the law the President appoints the Prime Minister. But anyone, even with a weak knowledge of the working of the Indian Constitution, will admit that in practice it is the Prime Minister who chooses the President.[19]

7. **As Leader of the People:** Today, the Prime Minister is more than a mere leader of the majority party in the Parliament. In reality, he is the leader of the masses and draws his strength from this end. He is elected by the people who vote more for the person than for the party. This is similar to the trend in the United States where the President is directly elected by the people. Modern means of communication, particularly the electronic media, have helped to establish a strong link between the Prime Minister and the people. Media publicity, which the Prime Minister commands and gets, makes the Prime Minister who at the time of general elections goes to the people with the "party platform", and the people expect him to carry out his promises. This has considerably strengthened the office of the Prime Minister, and as no other person in government is in a position to command these resources and opportunities, the Prime Minister stands supreme and unchallenged.

Regarding the position of the Indian Prime Minister, it may be said that he is undoubtedly the most powerful political executive of our country. He has more power and responsibility than the President. The President is the Constitutional head while the Prime Minister is the real head. To be more precise, the President is the Head of the State, while the Prime Minister is the Head of the Government.

The Prime Minister of India is more powerful than his British counterpart. The British Prime Minister cannot determine who will be the King; but the Indian Prime Minister plays an important role in determining who will be the President. The charisma and political ambition of the Prime Minister can undoubtedly enhance his position. The first Indian Prime Minister, Jawaharlal Nehru, by his charisma, personality and efficiency, could greatly increase the dignity and power of the Prime Minister's office. The same thing can be said of his daughter Mrs. Indira Gandhi as the Indian Prime Minister.

The previous Prime Ministers like Lal Bahadur Shastri, Morarji Desai, Charan Singh, V.P. Singh, Chandra Sekhar, A.B. Vajpayee, Deve Gowda and I.K. Gujral enjoyed short tenure as Prime Ministers. They could not make the office of the Prime Minister strong or weak due to the short tenure of their office.

Since 1977, excepting twice in 1980 and 1984, no party in the Lok Sabha elections could secure absolute majority. Hence now we have entered into an age of coalition government. In a coalition government, the Prime Minister is not so strong as he is in a government formed by one party enjoying absolute majority in the Lok Sabha.

The position of the Indian Prime Minister can be understood if we quote one observation of Asquith. What Asquith had said about the British Prime Minister is also equally true about the Indian Prime Minister—"The office of the Prime Minister is what its holder chooses to make it."

3.11 SEVERAL MINISTRIES

In this section, we shall discuss the composition and functions of several important Ministries like the Ministry of Finance, Ministry of Home Affairs and Ministry of External Affairs of the Union Government.

3.11.1 Ministry of Finance

The origin of Ministry of Finance can be traced to 1810 when a separate department of Finance was established in the British Government of India. In 1947, the department of Finance was designated as the Ministry of Finance. It comprised three wings–Expenditure, Economic Affairs and Revenue. In 1949, the Ministry of Finance was organized into two Departments: (i) the Department of Revenue and Expenditure and (ii) the Department of Economic Affairs. The Ministry of Finance has been holding a pivotal place in our Union Government.

Now the Finance Ministry consists of three Departments—Revenue Department, Expenditure Department and Department of Economic Affairs, each under a Secretary. The Ministry of Finance is headed by a senior Minister of the Cabinet rank assisted by three Ministers of State. Finance Secretary is the administrative head of the Ministry of Finance. Each of the three Departments of Finance is headed by the Finance Secretary, assisted by an Additional Secretary, a Joint Secretary, a Director, a Deputy Secretary and some Under Secretaries. The Ministry of Finance draws its officers from the Indian Administrative Service, Indian Audit and Accounts Service, Central Revenue Service, Central Customs and Excise Service and Indian Railway Accounts Service. The middle level positions are filled from the Central Secretariat Service.

The **Revenue Department** is concerned with revenue policy and collection. It deals with matters relating to direct and indirect Union taxes. It exercises this control through the Central Board of Direct Taxes and the Central Board of Excise and Customs. Through the tax laws and their administration, three main objectives are achieved, viz. creation of atmosphere of mutual trust between the tax collector and the tax payer, solution of problems of tax evasion, and reduction of tax arrears, etc.

The **Department of Expenditure** has two divisions—the Civil Expenditure Division and the Defence Expenditure Division. The *Civil Expenditure Division* deals with the scrutiny and sanction of the expenditure of various administrative Ministries. It determines the pay, allowances, leave and other general conditions of service of government employees. It has five branches, namely, Public Finance, Establishment, Cost Accounts, Organization of the Comptroller-General of Accounts, and Staff Inspection. Each of these branches functions under a Joint Secretary and deals with the scrutiny and sanction of a group of administrative Ministers. The *Defence Expenditure Division* deals with the scrutiny and control of defence expenditure. It is headed by an Additional Secretary who is designated as Financial Adviser (Defence). This Division is concerned with the preparation of the Budget of the Defence Departments. It functions internally from within the Ministry of Defence and is treated as one of its branches.

The **Department of Economic Affairs** has six main Divisions, namely, Economic, Banking, Insurance, Budget, Administration and External Finance.

1. **Economic Division:** This is the fundamental wing of the Ministry of Finance. It deals with all economic policy matters affecting the country. Primarily, it has to play an advisory role. Besides, the economic division looks after and monitors the economic performance in the context of the economic situation. It renders advice to the government on policy changes to contain inflation, and increase in the growth. In different domains of economic policy, it renders technical assistance to other Departments and Ministries. The economic division prepares the Annual Economic Survey Report, which is placed before the Parliament as a background document to the Central Budget. This Division maintains proper links with the Reserve Bank of India, the Planning Commission, the Central Statistical Organization and the Economic and Statistical wings of other Ministries.
2. **Banking Division:** It is concerned with the formulation of policies concerning commercial banks and term-lending institutions. However, it does not include the Life Insurance Corporation of India and the Unit Trust of India.
3. **Insurance Division:** It supervises and controls the activities of the nationalized insurance industry–both Life Insurance and General Insurance. Besides, it formulates policies, administers the insurance industry, reviews and monitors the performance of insurance companies and determines the policy conditions of insurance company employees. It also provides acturial advice to Ministers other than Finance, and the State Governments.
4. **Budget Division:** It prepares the Central Budget, submits it to the Parliament and procures the parliamentary sanction.
5. **Administrative division:** It deals with the administrative and vigilance matters concerning the Department and its attached and subordinate offices.
6. **External Finance Division:** It is concerned with matters relating to financial assistance procured by India from sources abroad, viz. the International Monetary Fund, the World Bank, the International Development Association, the Asian Development Bank, the United Nations Development Programme and the Commonwealth Fund for Technical Cooperation.

3.11.2 Ministry of Home Affairs

The origin of the Ministry of Home Affairs can be traced to 1843 when the Secretariat of the Supreme Government was separated from that of the Government of Bengal. It was headed by a Secretary who was a bureaucrat; and it had several branches, namely, General, Revenue, Marine, Legislative and Ecclesiastical. At that time it had to perform functions of heterogeneous nature including personnel matters, internal law and order, political matters, police, jail, explosives, factories, petroleum, education, public works, public health, hospitals, municipalities, local boards, and so on. In the recent past, it was deprived of personnel subject as the same was created into a full-fledged Department in 1970. In 1973, the Department of Administrative Reforms was merged with the Department of Personnel. The Ministry of Home Affairs has been rightly described by Dr. S.R. Maheshwari as the 'mother Ministry' in the Government of India. It is headed by the Minister of Home Affairs, who is a Minister of Cabinet rank.
The functions of the Home Ministry are as follows:

1. India being a country where terrorist and anti-social activities are ever increasing, internal security gains paramount importance and this is what makes the role of the Ministry of Home Affairs so important. The primary responsibility for the maintenance of law and order lies with the States since law and order happens to be a State subject. Yet the Ministry of Home Affairs, as one of the most important Ministries of the Union Government, acts as an advisory body or a coordinating agency. It seeks information from all over India through its various sources, assimilates them and renders advice to the State Governments on the varied problems of internal security. The Ministry keeps a vigilant watch on the law and order situation in India by noting carefully the trends and developments that adversely affect law and order situations in various States of India. Regarding Union Territories, the Ministry holds direct responsibility for law and order.
2. This Ministry also keeps its grip on the communal situations of the country and deploys central forces if such a situation is likely to creep into a volcanic disorder. Likewise, it also has to settle the agitations by industrial workers, students, minorities[20] and many other sections of the population. Civil Defence also falls within its purview.
3. It deals with matters relating to foreigners and foreign citizenship.
4. It conducts census operation after every ten years and is responsible for holding elections to the Parliament and the State Legislatures.
5. It is concerned with the proper maintenance of Centre–State relations and remains responsible for the installation of President's rule in the States.

6. It administers the Indian Police Service and happens to be its cadre-controlling authority. As such, it deals with the appointment to Indian Police Service (IPS), deputation of police officials from States to the Centre, their training, fixation of seniority, pay, etc. and other conditions of service. It also administers other para-military services like Indo-Tibetan Border Police, the Border Security Force, the Central Industrial Security Force, the Assam Rifles and the Central Reserve Police Force.[21]
7. It also exercises control over associated agencies like Intelligence Bureaus, the National Police Academy, the Bureau of Police Research and Development and the Institute of Criminology and Forensic Science.

Since 1985, the Home Ministry has four Departments under it, namely, Department of Internal Security, Department of State, Department of Home and Department of Official Language. The Department of Internal Security deals with matters concerning police, law and order, rehabilitation and resettlement. The Department of State is concerned with relations between the Central Government and the State Governments, inter-State relations and administration of Union Territories. The Department of Home deals with population census, registration of foreigners and rehabilitation of displaced persons. The Department of Official Language implements the provisions of the Official Language Act relating to the use of Hindi as the official language of the Union.

The Ministry of Home Affairs is headed by a senior Minister of Cabinet rank, generally assisted by one or two Ministers of the rank of Minister of State. The level and quantum of such assistance is to be decided by the Prime Minister. Presently, the Home Minister is assisted by a Minister of State and a Deputy Minister.

The administrative head of the Home Department is a senior bureaucrat of IAS cadre known as the Home Secretary. He heads many powerful committees. There are a number of precedents that experience gained as Home Secretary leads to the elevation to the post of Cabinet Secretary. After retirement, quite a few Home Secretaries have been selected as Governors.

The Home Secretary is assisted by Additional Secretaries, Joint Secretaries, Director, Deputy Secretaries and Under Secretaries. The senior positions are invariably held by the IAS and the middle level positions by the Central Secretariat Services.

The Ministry of Home Affairs commands respect since it is known for its uniqueness. Posting in this ministry as such was the envy of the top bureaucracy. However, presently the Department of Economic Affairs under the Ministry of Finance appears to be more allowing for the civil servants as they, in the latter case, can come into the limelight. Still, the importance of the Home Ministry does not stand minimized since the custodians of law and order always have an upper hand.

3.11.3 Ministry of External Affairs

The Foreign Department was established in 1783. Prior to 1947, two separate Departments, namely the External Affairs Department and the Commonwealth Relations Department, existed and conducted India's relations with the foreign countries. Since 1947, the two Departments were merged and a single Department was renamed as Ministry of External Affairs and Commonwealth Relations. In 1949, its nomenclature was again changed to "Ministry of External Affairs". Since 1949, the name has remained unchanged.

The Ministry is headed by a Minister of the rank of a Cabinet Minister. He is assisted by a Minister of State. Till 1964, with a brief break in 1952, the Secretary-General of the United Nations used to be the administrative head of this Ministry. At present, the Foreign Secretary is its administrative head. There are two other Secretaries as well to assist him. They are termed Additional Secretaries–Secretary (External Affairs-I) and Secretary (External Affairs-II)

The Ministry is divided into a number of Divisions. There are two types of such Divisions–Territorial and Functional. Territorial Divisions have been so framed that India's immediate neighbours receive more concentrated attention. Functional Divisions deal with administration, protocol, passport, emigration, external publicity, United Nations conferences, economic affairs and technical assistance, historical research, legal matters and treaties, policy planning and review, personnel, security, communication and civil defence, overseas Indians, finance, coordination, and so on.

The Ministry has an Inspectorate which is to review the scales of allowances and amenities in India's diplomatic missions abroad. An Additional Secretary, known as 'Inspector', heads the Inspectorate.

The Ministry of External Affairs performs the following functions:

1. External Affairs
2. Relations with Foreign States and Commonwealth Countries
3. Affairs dealing with foreign, diplomatic and consular offices, UN offices and UN specialized agencies in India
4. Passports and visas and grant of entry visas for Sri Lankan nationals except missionaries
5. General administration of the Indian Extradition Act (1903) and extra territoriality
6. Extradition of criminals and accused persons from India to foreign and Commonwealth countries and vice versa
7. Preventive Detention in India
8. Emigration from India to overseas countries and the return of emigrates
9. All consular functions, travel arrangements for traders, porters, pilgrims from India to Tibetan regions of China

10. Liaison work with the Education Ministry's cultural scholarship scheme and nomination of private students of Indian origin domiciled abroad to reserved seats in medical and engineering colleges in India
11. Political pensions paid to foreign refugees and descendants of those who rendered services abroad
12. Ceremonial matters concerning foreign and commonwealth visitors and diplomatic and consular representatives
13. Himalayan expeditions and permission to foreigners to travel beyond the Inner Line
14. Coordination and development measures in border areas
15. United Nations specialized agencies and other international conferences
16. Indian Foreign Service
17. External Publicity
18. Political treaties, agreements and conventions with foreign and commonwealth countries
19. Recovery and restoration of abducted persons
20. Evacuation of non-Muslims from Pakistan to India
21. Protection of the rights of minority communities in India and Pakistan
22. Non-Muslim migration from Pakistan and Muslim migration from India
23. Piracies and crimes committed on the seas or in the air, offences against the law of a Nation committed on land or the seas or in the air
24. Offences against laws regarding any of the subjects allotted to this Ministry
25. Hospitality grants of the Government of India
26. Demarcation of the land frontiers of India
27. Border raids and incidents on the border land of India
28. Diplomatic flight clearances for non-scheduled chartered flights of foreign, civil and military aircraft transiting India
29. Matters dealing with the continental shelf, territorial water, contiguous zones, the question of fishery rights in the high seas, and other questions of international law
30. Economic and technical assistance given by India to the Government of Nepal under the Colombo plan for cooperative economic development.

Many other related functions of foreign affairs are performed by this Ministry.

The Ministry of External Affairs is apparently supposed to create a congenial atmosphere for the blossoming of India's friendship with the major powers of the world. It also seeks to cultivate neighbourly relations with the Asiatic countries.

3.12 CABINET COMMITTEES

Cabinet Committees ordinarily are authorized to make final decisions though they are to be communicated to the Cabinet that may review them. The Cabinet under normal circumstances meets once a week. As such it has neither the time nor the ability to tackle all the minor administrative problems. Hence, two types of committees have emerged out—permanent and ad hoc. The Janata Government dismantled superfluous administrative set-up. Hence, in 1977 there were six Cabinet Committees, viz. *Political Affairs Committee, Committee on Economic Affairs, Parliamentary Affairs Committee, Appointment Committee, Committee on Accommodation* and *Informal Group of Ministers on Price Situations*. The number and names of the Cabinet Committees do not remain unchanged. However, some of the Committees—like those of Political Affairs, Economic Affairs, Parliamentary Affairs and Appointments have existed under both Congress and non-Congress governments.

The following permanent Cabinet Committees are of crucial significance:

1. **Political Affairs Committee:** It functions under the chairmanship of the Prime Minister. Its other members are Home, Defence, External Affairs and Finance Ministers. It deals with all crucial matters relating to both internal developments and foreign relations.
2. **Economic Affairs Committee:** It is also chaired by the Prime Minister while the Finance Minister, the Rural Development Minister and the Minister of Industry are its other members. It directs and coordinates governmental activities in the economic field and regulates the working of the national economy.
3. **Committee on Parliamentary Affairs:** The Home Minister is the Chairman of this Committee. Its other members are the Information and Broadcasting Minister, the Minister for Labour, the Law Minister and the Minister for Parliamentary Affairs. The Committee looks after the day-to-day progress of the government business in the Parliament, to secure the smooth passage of legislation. Besides, it determines the Government's attitude to non-official Bills and resolutions coming up before the Parliament.
4. **Appointment Committee:** It functions under the chairmanship of the Prime Minister. The Home Minister and the Ministers concerned are its other members. Its functions revolve round some key appointments.

It takes decisions regarding appointments of the ranks of Deputy Secretary and above, Chairman, Managing Directors and General Managers of State owned Public Corporations, Companies and Enterprises and Governor of the Reserve Bank of India. Besides, it takes decisions regarding all other appointments which are made by the government or which necessitate the approval of the Government of India and which are all salaried appointments.

It also takes decisions on all cases of disagreements between the Department concerned and the Union Public Service Commission regarding any appointment.

Besides the above mentioned *permanent* Cabinet Committees, some *ad-hoc* Cabinet Committees are also set up, for example, to deal with the problems of prices, to review the performance of the Public Undertakings, Export Promotion and Import Substitution, denudation of forests and trees and increase in agricultural prices in view of the increased power rates.

An appraisal of the actual functioning of these Cabinet Committees reveals that by and large they have not proved very effective. In the words of Ashok Chanda: "... the purpose of forming the Cabinet Committees for securing coordination and for reaching quick decisions might also be largely defeated since these committees now include the bulk of the Cabinet Ministers."[22] The opinion of the Administrative Reform Commission (1966–1970) also is not very encouraging. It reported: "Some of the Committees have not met regularly. Several important subjects are not covered by these Committees. Further, they can take up a matter only if it is referred to them by the Minister concerned or by the Cabinet."[23] The ARC suggested that these deficiencies should be eradicated from the working of the Cabinet Committees. Besides, such committees should cover all important areas of Government activity. Also, each Cabinet Committee should meet regularly so that sustained attention is given to various complex problems. Again, the progress of implementation of important policies and programmes may be kept under constant review.[24]

Questions

1. Critically discuss the structure and functions of the Central Secretariat in India.
2. Discuss the role of the PMO from 1947 till date.
3. Explain the functions of the Cabinet Secretary in Indian administrative system.
4. Critically discuss the role played by the President of India.
5. Explain the role played by the Indian Prime Minister and his Cabinet in Indian political system.
6. Examine the functions of key ministries in the Indian politico-administrative system.

7. Write short notes on:
   (a) Vice President
   (b) Ministry of External Affairs
   (c) Cabinet Committees.
   (d) Present structure of the PMO since 2014.

Notes and References

1. Mishra, B.B., *The Central Administration of the East India Company* (1773–1834), Manchester Press, London, 1959.
2. Arora, R.K. and R. Goyal, *Indian Public Administration: Institutions and Issues*, Wishwa Prakashan, 1997.
3. Chanda, Asok, *Indian Administration*, Allen and Unwin, London, 1967.
4. *Report of the Reorganization of the Machinery of Government, 1949 (Ayyangar Report)*, Government of India, New Delhi, 1957.
5. Chanda, Asok, *op. cit.*
6. Tottenham, Richard, *Reports on the Reorganization of Central Government (Two Reports), 1945 and 1946,* Government of India, New Delhi, 1955.
7. Ayyangar Report, *op. cit.*
8. *Maxwell Report or Organization and Procedure (Maxwell) Committee Report,* Government of India, New Delhi, 1937.
9. Maheshwari, S.R., *The Administrative Reforms Commission*, Lakshmi Narain Agarwal, Agra, 1972.
10. Deshmukh, B.G., 'Prime Minister's Office', *IJPA*, New Delhi, July–September, 1997.
11. Broadcasts by the Prime Minister, *The Listener*, London, February 4 and April 6, 1967.
12. Maheshwari, S.R., *Indian Administration*, 4th rev. ed., Orient Longmans, New Delhi, 1989.
13. Khera, S.S., *The Central Executive*, Orient Longman, New Delhi, 1975.
14. *Ibid.*
15. Dwarkadas, R., *Role of Higher Civil Service*, Popular, Bombay, 1958.
16. Singh, M.P. and Rekha Saxena, *Indian Politics: Contemporary Issues and Concerns*, PHI Learning, New Delhi, 2008.
17. *Madhav Rao* v. *Union of India*, AIR 1971, SC 530, paragraphs 94 and 96.

18. *Maganbhai Ishwarbhai Patel* v. *Union of India* (1970), 3, Supreme Court Cases: 400, AIR 1969, SC 783.
19. Avasthi, A. and A.P. Avasthi, *Public Administration in India*, Lakshmi Narain Agarwal, Agra, 2003.
20. Since September 1985, matters concerning the scheduled castes, scheduled tribes, backward classes, communal harmony, etc. have been entrusted to the Ministry of Welfare.
21. These para-military services have been discussed in detail in Chapter 15, Section, 15.4.
22. Chanda, Ashok, *Indian Administration*, George Allen and Unwin, London, 1958.
23. The ARC Report on the Machinery of the Government and its Procedures of Work (1968).
24. *Ibid.*

4 Administration and Politics of India The Provincial (State) Picture

4.1 INTRODUCTION

For the sake of convenience, the administrative structure of the Indian province (State) may be divided into several Departments. A Ministry consists of two or more Departments and a Minister is in-charge of all these Departments. The Minister is the political head of the Department while its administrative head is none other than the Secretary, being a career civil servant. By the expression 'Secretariat' is meant the summation of all the Departments. The State Secretariat, being the place where the Ministers and Secretaries of various Departments have their offices, happens to be located in the State's capital. The State Secretariat is the highest office of the State Government and hence its main executive instrument as well. The State Secretariat, just like its Union counterpart, ensures objectivity, continuity and consistency in the administrative system. It has the power and authority to make rules and principles of procedure for running the governmental machinery smoothly. Hence, in certain cases, the State Secretariat identifies the State Government.

The three essential parts of the State Government are: (a) the Minister, (b) the Secretary, and (c) the Executive Head. The Minister is to make policies and to decide upon them. The Secretary is to look after the implementation of policies and to provide the materials on which policies are decided. The Executive Head is to carry the decisions into effect. The first two functionaries of the State Government—Ministers and Secretaries—are served by the State Secretariat organization which is an aggregation of several administrative Departments of the State. In fact, the State Secretariat works as a single unit with collective responsibility as in the case of the Council of Ministers.

4.2 STATE SECRETARIAT: FUNCTIONS AND STRUCTURE

The Secretariat's principal duty is to help the Ministers in the following matters:

1. Making and changing policies from time to time
2. Framing laws, rules and regulations
3. Formulating sectoral planning and programmes
4. Budgeting and controlling expenditure
5. Supervising the execution of policies and programmes by field agencies and evaluating results
6. Coordinating and implementing policies and thus helping other branches of the State Government
7. Initiating measures to develop greater organizational competence
8. Discharging their responsibilities to the legislature
9. Appointing heads of Departments and consequently establishing their work, salary, leave, etc.
10. Answering Assembly questions.

The Secretariat is divided into a number of administrative Departments. Each Department is basically a hierarchical structure with a small number of officers and the Secretary at the top of the hierarchical chain. There is a wide base of clerical personnel as well. The secretarial hierarchy consists of the Secretary, the Deputy Secretary, the Under Secretary and the Assistant Secretary. There are also Special, Additional and Joint Secretaries in some of the Departments of the State Secretariat. The chair of Deputy Secretary was created principally to relieve the extra burden of the Secretary. The Secretariat officers are subject to the tenure system and are appointed to the Secretariat for a fixed term. The only exception to this system is the Chief Secretary. With a few exceptions, the Secretariat officers are all generalists.

The structure of the State Secretariat is shown in Figure 4.1

The number of Secretariat Departments varies from one State to another. But some of the Departments are common to most of the States. They are as under:

1. General Administration
2. Home
3. Finance
4. Jail
5. Revenue
6. Registration
7. Survey and Settlement
8. Land Reforms

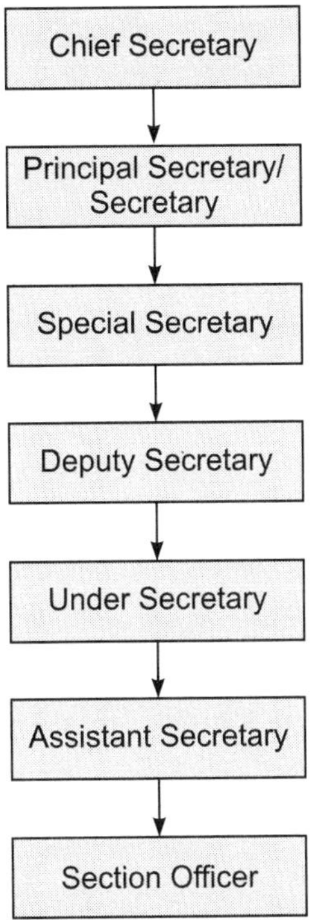

FIGURE 4.1 The Structure of the State Secretariat.

9. Forests
10. Commerce
11. Natural Resources
12. Electricity
13. Agriculture and Food
14. Cooperation
15. Labour and Employment
16. Public Health and Medicine
17. Local Self Government
18. Public Works
19. Education
20. Law
21. Planning and Development
22. Publicity and Information
23. Tribal and Social Welfare
24. Economics and Statistics
25. Housing
26. Rehabilitation

27. Transport
28. Civil Supplies
29. Complaints
30. Irrigation and Power
31. Excise and Taxation
32. Industries
33. Panchayati Raj

4.3 CHIEF SECRETARY

The Chief Secretary is undoubtedly the administrative head of State administration in India. In many ways, he may be described as the State counterpart of the Cabinet Secretary. His role in policy formulation is substantial and so is his supervisory role in the policy implementation apparatus. He is not only the head of the State Secretariat, but, indeed, is in charge of the general administration of the State, which forms part of the portfolio of the Chief Minister himself. Sometimes, his role is described as *primus inter pares* (i.e. first among equals) since he is the Chief of the Secretaries. In fact, he should more rightly be called "the kingpin of the Secretariat". He acts as the focal point of interdepartmental coordination at the officer's level. It is he who provides some sort of leadership to the administrative system of the State. He also acts as the chief liaison between the State Government, on the one hand, and the Union Government and other State Governments, on the other.

Until 1973, the Chief Secretary was not necessarily the senior most civil servant of the State. Certain officers, like the Finance Commissioner in Punjab, were considered senior to the Chief Secretary of the State. In 1973, the post of the Chief Secretary was upgraded and, presently, it is regarded as the most prestigious and influential post in the state civil service structure. It is held by one of the senior most officers of the IAS cadre. His status is equal with that of a Secretary to the Government of India.

4.3.1 Appointment

The Chief Secretary is chosen by the Chief Minister of the State. In doing that, he normally consults the Union Government, though this consultation is not obligatory. Similarly, the Chief Minister may consult the Cabinet or a few Ministers of his Cabinet. But the final decision regarding the appointment of the Chief Secretary is that of the Chief Minister. Three main factors are basically considered by the Chief Minister in this respect. These are as under:

1. **Seniority:** This is a very important criterion and, generally, the choice is restricted to the first four or five IAS officers

according to seniority. Scholars observe that administrators with 20–25 long years of experience in service have generally been appointed as Chief Secretaries.[1]

2. **Service Record, Performance and Merit:** It is also carefully observed whether the incumbent is sufficiently meritorious, possesses the ability to perform functions efficiently and has an excellent service record.
3. **Confidence of the Chief Minister:** This is perhaps the most important factor in the appointment of the Chief Secretary. As the Chief Minister and the Chief Secretary have to work in close association with each other, the latter's personal connection with the Chief Minister is absolutely necessary.

Apart from these factors, different States have evolved different conventions regarding the appointment of the Chief Secretary. For instance, in Andhra Pradesh, it had once been a tradition to appoint the senior most officer as the Chief Secretary.[2] In Rajasthan, on the other hand, on many occasions, a number of senior officers were superseded while selecting the Chief Secretary. Those superseded officers, however, were given equal grade or salary as with the Chief Secretary and were posted outside the secretariat.[3] In Maharashtra, till 1976, the post used to be held by an ICS officer. Only since 1977, an IAS officer has been appointed to this post.[4]

4.3.2 Tenure

There is no fixed tenure for the post of the Chief Secretary. The Administrative Reforms Commission in 1969 had recommended that a Chief Secretary should have a minimum tenure of three to four years.[5] This suggestion has not been accepted primarily because in that case, a Chief Minister may find himself burdened with a Chief Secretary appointed by his predecessor. A Chief Secretary's tenure depends, to a large extent, upon his administrative skill, experience, rapport with the Chief Minister and his ability to take an objective stand on sensitive matters.

4.3.3 Functions

The Chief Secretary performs a lot of functions. The most important among them are as under:

1. He is the principal adviser to the Chief Minister.
2. He controls and supervises the entire State Secretariat.
3. He looks after all other matters for which other secretaries of the State Government are not responsible.
4. Being at the apex of the State Secretariat, he heads a number of committees and is a member of many others.

5. He is the Secretary, by rotation, of the Zonal Council of which the State is a member.
6. He controls the staff who are attached to the Ministers.
7. He is the main channel of communications between his State Government, on the one hand, and the Central Government and other State Governments, on the other.
8. He receives all important and confidential communications from the Central Government and submits them to the Chief Minister.
9. Being head of the State Secretariat, adviser to the Council of Ministers and Chief of the State Civil Service, the Chief Secretary is their mentor and conscience-keeper.

Apart from these functions, the Chief Secretary has three more vital functions to perform. First, he is the Secretary to the State Government in the General Administration Department. This Department is generally concerned with services, protocol and related matters, organizations and methods, elections and census, publicity and tourism, foreigners and passports, emergency, language and Raj Bhawan. Secondly, he is the Secretary to the Cabinet. He prepares the agenda for Cabinet meetings and drafts the minutes of the meetings. In fact, he is in full charge of the business of the Cabinet. Thirdly, he is the Chief of all the Secretaries of the State Secretariat. He presides over a large number of committees and is a member of many other committees. During crises, the Chief Secretary may become a member of any such committee. In fact, crisis administration really utilizes the role of the Chief Secretary as a coordinator. The Rajasthan Administrative Reforms Committee Report categorically states about the actual position of the Chief Secretary in this way: "The Chief Secretary should be in a position to effectively coordinate the work of different Secretariat Departments and ensure that there is a certain degree of uniformity in the policies adopted by the State Government with respect to different Departments."[6]

The committee recommended that all important cases involving adoption of new principles or new schemes should be circulated by the Secretaries of different Departments to the Ministers-in-charge only via the Chief Secretary.

The Study Team of the Central Administrative Reforms Commission in its report has clearly explained the role of the Chief Secretary by mentioning that coordination and discipline of the State Secretariat can be ensured only by strengthening the position of the Chief Secretary, who is to function as the Chief Coordinator under the Chief Minister. Being a senior civil servant of outstanding ability, he should command respect and confidence of all the services in the State. He should usually be the senior most and fittest civil servant whose ability, experience, integrity and impartiality are beyond any question.[7]

4.4 DEPARTMENTS/DIRECTORATES

Governmental policies are to be initiated and formulated which requires decentralization of executive directions. Field agencies need to be established for this purpose. For the smooth performance of functions by the State Secretariat, executive Departments of varying sizes and powers do exist which remain responsible for providing executive directions required for the implementation of policies laid down by the administrative Departments to which they are attached. These executive Departments advise the Secretariat Departments on technical aspects of questions. Below them, the field agencies are found. Financial rules, civil services rules, budget manuals and other codes define the powers of the departmental heads. These rules indicate the category of cases that should go up to the departmental heads for final orders. The orders referred to the government are passed by the Secretary after receiving orders from the Minister-in-charge. The executive Department, observes the Simon Commission, "is an administrative unit, separate from the secretariat, which reaches its apex usually in a single officer like the Inspector General of Police or the Chief Conservator of Forests...."[8] It is seen that each administrative Department of the Secretariat has a corresponding executive Department in the field. But some secretariat Departments (like law) have no field agency.

4.4.1 Heads of Departments/Directorates

Officers who are in-charge of the actual administration of specific services or the execution of projects are placed at the apex of the Departments or directorates. Some of the departmental heads are responsible for the collection of taxes and administration of tax laws. The State Government controls the works of the departmental heads through "administrative Departments" of the Secretariat. The departmental heads enjoy specified financial and administrative powers delegated to them.

The relationship between the Secretary and the Departmental Head is based on the following principles:

1. The primary responsibility of the Secretariat is to make policies while implementing them is the duty of the Department.
2. The Departmental Head is permitted to exercise fullest control over the personnel under him.
3. The Departmental Head is a specialist while the Secretary who supervises his work is a generalist civil servant.
4. Departmental Heads are the executive instruments of the Ministers. But Secretaries are their administrative advisers and assistants.
5. Departmental Heads are the "hands" of the Ministers via whom the latter perform their functions. But Secretaries are Ministers' "ears and eyes" with the help of whom the latter hear and see.

4.4.2 Functions

The following are the major functions of the Departmental Heads:

1. Formulating the Departmental budget within prescribed limits
2. Providing technical advice to the Minister
3. Inspecting the implementation of policies by departmental district staff
4. Allocating grants following governmental rules and regulations
5. Making all appointments, confirmations, postings, transfers and promotions of all subordinate officers including those whose leave are being sanctioned
6. Exercising disciplinary powers over all subordinate officers following governmental rules and regulations
7. Advising the State Public Service Commission regarding promotions and disciplinary actions of and against employees
8. Sanctioning the attendance of officers at conferences other than inter-State or Government of India conferences.

The number of Departmental Heads depends to a large extent upon the number of important subjects executed by the state. The departmental heads are normally called Directors or Commissioners who are helped by Additional Directors, Joint Directors, Deputy Directors and Assistant Directors.

To expedite the Departmental activities, most of the Departments have Divisional Headquarters corresponding to Commissioner's Divisions. Either a Joint Director or a Deputy Director heads each Division. A departmental head as the main head of office has under him officers-in-charge at regional or district levels. In each district, there is a representative of almost each Department. Normally, the departmental head makes the overall superintendence of departmental activities. In a specified number of districts, this supervision is made by the Regional Officer. The Collector or Deputy Commissioner of a district is informed of such activities by the departmental representatives of the district.

The staff of the office is usually appointed from the Department. It implies that they are specialists and technicians. Each Department is headed by a technical officer known as the Registrar or Director or Director-General or Inspector-General or Commissioner or Chief Engineer, etc. Quite often, an IAS officer may be asked to take the charge of such technical departments as agriculture, education, forests, health, sales tax, etc. This hierarchical chain of officers makes the generalist-specialist debate quite prominent at the level of State administration. The whole administrative system from top to bottom is well-knit and hence absolutely centralized. Power is concentrated in the hands of the departmental head and it is exercised through a vast number of officials spread over the whole State.

Since Independence, partly due to the creation of new Departments, there has taken place a large proliferation in the number of Departments as such. There is no common nomenclature for all executive agencies. Their heads are also not designated in any common way. Emoluments, status and roles of the heads of Departments are quite often varied. In the relationship between the Secretariat and the executive Departments, there is no uniformity. Theoretically, Departments are independent regarding their internal working. For this purpose, they have sufficient administrative and financial powers and authority. But as a part of the hierarchical chain, these Departments must submit periodic and/or ad hoc reports of their activities to their immediate superiors. Officers of the State Secretariat may also visit or inspect the departmental offices to examine their activities. In the existing system of State administration, there are disparities between departmental heads and State Secretaries regarding their status, rank and remuneration. The status of the Secretary is considered to be higher than that of the heads of field agencies. The present pattern of service has placed the generalist administrator at a higher position than the professional and technical officer. This is the principal cause of tensions, conflicts and rivalries between the generalists and the specialists. Again, since the reorganization of States in 1956, government offices have been dispersed all over the State, and not in the capital, in particular. In States like Maharashtra, Rajasthan and Uttar Pradesh the headquarters of many executive Departments are located outside the capital. This trend is probably more marked in Madhya Pradesh.

4.5 SECRETARIAT AND FIELD DEPARTMENTS IN STATES: THEIR MUTUAL RELATIONSHIP

The State Government has three basic components, namely, the Ministers, the Secretariat and the Department or Directorate or Inspectorate. It is desirable that functions of these three components should be well defined and that each component should perform its own functions properly and efficiently. Besides, all the components must work in the closest touch with each other. During emergency and crisis, this ideal relationship is disturbed and the Secretariat becomes more and more powerful.

The relation between the Secretariat and the field agencies is a big problem in State administration, which has given birth to much debates, discussions and controversies. A number of committees and commissions have been appointed in recent years to make some recommendations with a view to solving the problem. The suggestions that have been made in this connection are as under:

1. It is observed that powers delegated to various departmental heads are not uniform. It is desirable that there should be uniformity in such powers.

2. The Secretariat must try to see that such delegation of powers is effective at all levels. Besides, delegated powers must be fully exercised. Departmental heads must allow their subordinates to fully exercise the delegated powers. Very often, they do not do so because of the fact that roles of heads of Departments vis-à-vis the field agencies are not properly defined.
3. Another suggestion is made to confer ex-officio Secretariat status on heads or deputy heads of executive agencies.
4. Lastly, a suggestion has been made by the Study Team of the Administrative Reforms Commission on the Machinery of the Government of India. It says that the clear-cut distinction between the Secretariat as the policy-making body and the non-Secretariat organization as the policy-implementing body must be abolished and the administrative Departments in the Secretariat must be connected with the heads of all non-Secretariat organizations.

4.6 CHIEF SECRETARY AS THE LINK BETWEEN VARIOUS COMPONENTS OF THE STATE GOVERNMENT

The success of the Chief Secretary depends upon his link with varied sets of people and institutions which form his work-environment. On the one hand, there are politicians like the Chief Minister, other Ministers, MPs and MLAs while, on the other, there is a whole network of administrative functionaries like Departmental Heads, Divisional Commissioners, Director General of Police, District Collectors and others. The Chief Secretary also has to deal with the public, the media and the service associations. His actual position, therefore, depends upon his sagacity, capacity, charisma and personality in facing the members of his role-set in a decent and efficient way. The Chief Secretary's job, as Mangat Rai observes beautifully, is not a technician's or even a professional's, "he is not a knowledgeable engineer, nor even a first class magistrate, he is part of the process of government and in a democratic republic, part of the human process."[9]

In the Chief Secretary's role-set, the most significant person is perhaps the Chief Minister. It is the trust of the Chief Minister that strengthens the position of the Chief Secretary. The latter has to accept the advice of the former and carry out policies taken by the Council of Ministers headed by the Chief Minister. In fact, the Chief Secretary has to act as an alter ego of the Chief Minister in the administrative sphere.

The Chief Secretary, indeed, has varied functions and responsibilities and some very crucial roles to play in State administration. Though he has enormous authority, dignity, status and influence, yet his personal vision, experience, style of functioning and outlook which help him in discharging his duties most efficiently.

The role played by the Chief Secretary in the State Secretariat can be understood clearly from Figure 4.2.

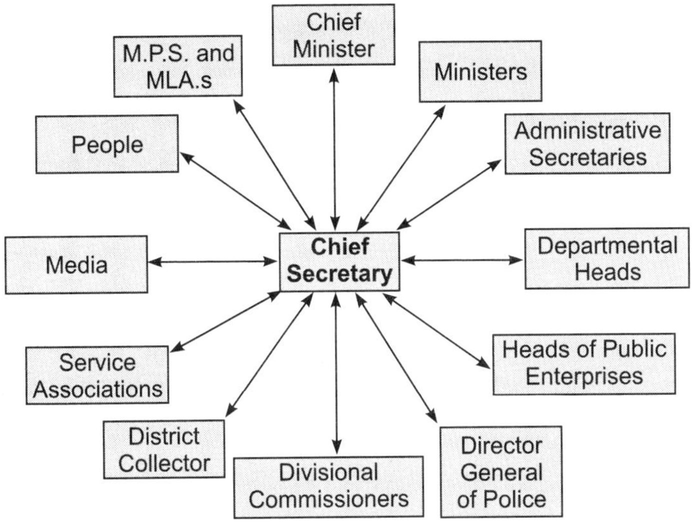

FIGURE 4.2 The Role of the Chief Secretary in the State.

4.7 STATE GOVERNMENT: THE POLITICAL PROFILE

India is a Union of 28 States, six Union Territories and one national Capital Territory of Delhi. Unlike the USA, where federal and State Constitutions and citizenships are dual, the Republic of India is founded on a single Constitution and a unitary citizenship, excepting Jammu and Kashmir which has a Constitution of its own largely conforming to the Constitution of India. Apart from the structure of the Government and some asymmetrical federal features relating to Jammu and Kashmir and the States of Nagaland and Mizoram, and some other tribally predominant States in the Northeast and inlands, as well as the emergency provisions of the Constitution providing for central takeover of State administration for a limited period under specified conditions with parliamentary approval, the Indian federal Constitution is based on symmetrical legal provisions. By and large, both the Union and State Governments function under a uniform Constitution that envisages responsible and representative Governments at Union and State levels and even at the local level.

Like the Union level, the structure of government at the State level, too, is basically based on the parliamentary principle of government within a federal pattern of relationship among governments at various levels. Myron Weiner has rightly pointed out that since the Indian States are generally so large as to be comparable with several European nation-states, they offer a rare opportunity of comparisons in terms of their political and economic performance almost like a quasi-experimental research design.[10] Thus, if some States are politically more stable and others unstable or vulnerable to central intervention, or if some States economically perform better and others fair badly, these differentials cannot be attributed to different systems of laws and Constitutions. They must be explained in terms of sociological and political factors or good and bad leadership.

4.8 GOVERNOR: THE CONSTITUTIONAL HEAD OF THE STATE GOVERNMENT

Broadly speaking, the pattern of government at the State level happens to be the same as that for the Union. The Head of the State, like his counterpart at the Centre, is a mere Constitutional or ornamental ruler who basically acts on the advice of the Council of Ministers (headed by the Chief Minister), the latter enjoying majority in the lower House of State Legislature. The Constitutional head of the State Government is known as the Governor.

A proposal in the Constituent Assembly that the Governor be directly elected by the people of the State was rejected on the ground that complications might arise if both the Governor and the Chief Minister were elected heads. The former might not like to accept the nominal headship if the verdict of the people had been obtained. Another proposal to elect the Governor by the Legislative Assembly of the State was dropped, apprehending that the Governor would be a mere tool in the hands of a single party or a coalition of parties forming a majority. Hence, keeping in view the intentions of the founding fathers of the Constitution to opt for a Parliamentary set up, it was decided that the Governor might not be elected directly or indirectly. Instead, he should be appointed by the President for a period of five years. A common Governor may be appointed for two or more States including some Union Territories. He holds office during the pleasure of the President. Hence, he can be recalled by the President at any time. He is transferable from one State to another and can tender resignation.

Regarding his qualifications, a Governor must be a citizen of India. He must be 35 years of age or above. He must not hold any office of profit. He cannot be a member of either House of Parliament or a House of the State Legislature.

He is entitled to such emoluments, allowances and privileges as may be determined by the Parliament. These are not to be varied to his disadvantage, during the tenure of his office. He is entitled to have a free residence and a few other perks.

The powers of the Governor of a State, as D.D. Basu observes, are analogous to those of the President excepting that the Governor has no diplomatic, military or emergency powers.[11] Broadly speaking, his powers can be divided into the following categories:

1. Legislative
2. Executive
3. Financial
4. Judicial
5. Discretionary.

4.8.1 Legislative Powers

Though the Governor is not a member of either House of the State Legislature, yet he exercises various legislative powers which are as under:

1. He summons each House of the State Legislature.
2. He may prorogue each House and can dissolve only the lower House of the State Legislature, i.e. the Legislative Assembly.
3. He addresses each House at the commencement of the first session of each year and the first session after each General Election.
4. Bills passed by the State Legislature are sent to him for his formal consent. He can return the Bill for reconsideration of the House.
5. He can reserve certain Bills for the assent of the President.
6. He nominates 1/6 of the members of the Legislative Council (if the State Legislature is bicameral) from among the persons who have practical experience in Literature, Art, Science, Social service, etc.
7. He nominates some members of the Anglo-Indian Community if the latter is inadequately represented in the House.
8. On the advice of the Election Commission, he decides questions arising about the disqualification of any member of either House.
9. He issues ordinances during the recess of the legislature if some eventuality crops up.
10. He may also send messages to the Legislature on a Bill pending in the Legislature.
11. He can get the State Assembly suspended while recommending to the President the taking over of the State administration by the latter.

4.8.2 Executive Powers

The following executive powers are vested in the Governor:

1. His executive powers extend to the matters in the State list. Subject to the executive authority of the President, he can make laws on the subjects in the Concurrent list as well.

2. He frames rules for the transaction of business of the Government of the State and for its allocation among the Ministers.
3. He can seek information from the Chief Minister and it is the duty of the Chief Minister as well to keep him informed.
4. He may instruct the Chief Minister to submit any individual Minister's decision for the consideration of the Council of Ministers.
5. He appoints the Chief Minister and on his advice the other Ministers.
6. He appoints the Advocate General, the Chairman of the State Public Service Commission, and many other members.
7. For the appointment of the judges of the State High Court, the Governor is consulted.
8. He acts as the Chancellor of State Universities.

4.8.3 Financial Powers

The following are some of the financial powers of the Governor:

1. No Money Bill can be introduced in the State Legislature except on his recommendations.
2. He can make advances out of the Contingency Fund which is at his disposal to meet unforeseen expenditure.
3. No demand for grant can be made except on his recommendation.
4. He can ask for supplementary, additional or excess grants from the State Legislature.
5. It is he who sees that the annual financial statement of the State budget is placed before the Legislature and passed by it.
6. Amendments concerning financial matters cannot be moved except on the recommendations of the Governor.

4.8.4 Judicial Powers

The following judicial powers are exercised by the Governor:

1. He decides on matters concerning appointments, postings and promotion of district judges and other judicial officers.
2. He can or cannot grant pardon to persons convicted by the courts of law or remitting or commuting their sentence.

4.8.5 Discretionary Powers

There are certain powers regarding which he does not act on the advice of the Council of Ministers. They are termed *discretionary powers* of the Governor. They are as under:

1. The Governor of Assam possesses the discretionary power of administering the tribal areas of the State.
2. If a Governor is appointed as the Administrator of an adjoining Union Territory by the President of India, he has to exercise his functions independently.
3. The Governor of Nagaland possesses vast and discretionary powers to combat violent activities of hostile Nagas.
4. The Governor may independently appraise the breakdown of Constitutional machinery in the State and may submit his report to the President with his recommendations.
5. He may reserve any Bill for the consideration of the President after it has been passed by the State Legislature on the ground that it may conflict with a law or policy of the Union Government.
6. In certain important matters, he has to seek the advice of the President before promulgating an ordinance. The Ministers do not come in the picture at all.
7. In the event of a conflict between the Union and the State Governments on a matter relating to their respective competence in the exercise of executive authority, the Governor can use his discretion.
8. The Governor may permit intimation of legal proceedings against the ex or present Chief Minister involved in a scandal.
9. In a coalition of political parties aspiring to form a Government, the Governor may exercise his discretionary power by choosing one of the leaders of coalition partners for the office of Chief Ministership. After 1967, when the era of coalition governments ushered in the State Politics, Governors often made use of such a power.
10. Under certain circumstances like the Ministry losing majority in the legislature on account of defections, but keen to retain power, it advises the Governor to prorogue the Assembly to save itself from the censure motion. The Opposition, on the other hand, may approach the Governor to dismiss the Ministry as it does not retain the confidence of the majority. In such a ticklish situation, the Governor can exercise his discretion regarding the dismissal of the ministry.
11. Under normal circumstances, the Legislative Assembly is dissolved by the Governor only on the completion of its tenure. Yet, if the electorate appeal to the Governor in a Parliamentary set up to take necessary steps so that a situation of political instability can be ended, such a dissolution of the Legislative Assembly is possible before the completion of its tenure. The Governor may not be advised by the CM to dissolve or not to

dissolve the Legislative Assembly. But in the interest of the State concerned, he may act according to his discretion.

12. He has discretion to seek information from the Chief Minister regarding any administrative or legislative matter of the State. Dr. B.R. Ambedkar remarked: "... It is to enable the Governor to discharge his functions in respect of a good and pure administration that we propose to give the power to call for any information."[12]

An appraisal of these discretionary powers reveals that though there is no specific mention about most of these powers in the Constitution, yet they are inherent in a particular situation. The provision regarding discretionary powers of the Governor is couched in general terms. Article 163(2) states: "If any question arises whether any matter is or is not a matter in respect of which the Governor is, by or under this Constitution, required to act in his discretion, the decision of the Governor in his discretion is final, and the validity of anything done by the Governor shall not be called in question on the ground that he ought or ought not to have acted in his discretion." This Article empowers the Governor to be the master of the situation. His discretionary power has been made unchallengeable.

During an emergency rule as per the Article 353, the Governor can override the advice of the Council of Ministers, if specifically permitted by the Indian President only.

In a contingency situation such as President's Rule, the Governor has virtually no rule or powers, unless specifically permitted by the Indian President under Articles 160, 356 and 357. Usually the Governor is not permitted to take any decision on his own without the advice of the State Cabinet when an elected Government is in charge under the provisions of Part VI of our Constitution. Only to Jammu and Kashmir, the Governor's Rule is applicable. It is often used synonymous with President's Rule in other States of India.

In January 2014, the Central Bureau of Investigation (CBI) approached the Union Law Ministry under the UPA Government to record statements of Mr. M.K. Narayanan, the (then) West Bengal Governor and Mr. B.V. Wanchoo, the (then) Goa Governor. The statements were regarded to be of utmost importance as Mr. Narayanan was the National Security Adviser and Mr. Wanchoo was the Chief of Special Protection Group at the time of signing a contract with Agusta Westland, an Italian helicopter designing and manufacturing company. But the UPA was defeated in 2014 general election and the BJP Government was formed. With the permission of the newly formed Central Government, the (then) Governor of West Bengal, Mr. Narayanan was the first ever Governor to be questioned by the police in a criminal case. Mr. Narayanan was questioned by the CBI since he was a "witness" in the ₹3600 crore Indian helicopter bribery scandal in 2013. In the same case the (then) Goa Governor Mr. Wanchoo was also questioned by the CBI. Similarly, the Governor of Arunachal Pradesh, who was appointed by the ruling party at the Centre, was sacked by the President of India after the Supreme Court had ruled against his unconstitutional acts. These events happen to give a strong message to the State Governors that they, by seeking protection from the Centre, should not commit unjust and illegal acts.

4.9 CHIEF MINISTER: THE REAL HEAD OF THE STATE GOVERNMENT

The Chief Minister at the State Government is analogous to the Prime Minister at the Union Government. Like the Prime Minister, the Chief Minister is the real executive head of the State Government. Article 164 provides that the Chief Minister is to be appointed by the Governor. On the advice of the Chief Minister, the Governor appoints other Ministers of the State Government. Generally, the leader of the majority party is called by the Governor to constitute the Council of Ministers. If a particular party enjoys a clear-cut majority, the Governor is not left with any choice. In a coalition also, an accepted leader of the parties is to be called to act as the Chief Minister. The Constitution remains silent as to whether the Chief Minister should be a member of the lower House only.

Like his replica at the Centre, the Chief Minister has been described as the "keystone of the Cabinet arch", "a moon among the lesser stars", "the sun around whom Ministers revolve like planets", etc. At the State level, his powers are numerous and authority unquestionable. Following are his powers and functions:

1. **Formation of the Council of Ministers:** The Chief Minister has been rightly described as the creator, preserver and destroyer of the Council of Ministers. On the advice of the Chief Minister, all the other Ministers of the State Government are appointed by the Governor. It is a privilege of the Chief Minister to select a team of his own choice. The Governor may suggest a name, but he cannot insist on the inclusion or exclusion of a name. On the advice of the Chief Minister, the Governor can as well drop a Minister and can even dismiss the entire Council of Ministers. In fact, the Chief Minister's own resignation means resignation of the entire ministry.
2. **Allocation of Portfolios:** The Chief Minister, after constituting his team of Ministers, allocates portfolios to his colleagues. He can reallocate portfolios as well. Of course, while allocating portfolios, particularly Home and Finance, he has to see the importance of the individual concerned and his relation to the Party as well as the Chief Minister himself.
3. **Chairmanship of the Cabinet:** The Chief Minister acts as the Chairman of the Cabinet. He convenes and presides over its

meetings. These meetings are generally attended by the entire Cabinet. The Ministers of State also can attend such meetings.

4. **Power of Coordination:** He coordinates the policies and working of all the Ministers. He exercises general supervision over the Council of Ministers and is consulted by the Ministers in case of conflict between two or more of them. He, as the chief coordinator, is supposed to bring about harmony and elicit cooperation from all the Ministers.
5. **Liasion between the Governor and the Council of Ministers:** According to Article 167 of our Constitution, the Chief Minister acts as the communicating channel between the Governor and the Council of Ministers. Likewise, the Governor can seek any information from the Council of Ministers through the Chief Minister. If the Governor so requires, he can submit to the Council of Ministers any matter on which a decision had been taken by an individual Minister.
6. **Leader of the House:** The Chief Minister, being the leader of the House, is the chief spokesman of it. He helps to maintain discipline in the House. He supports any Minister who gets bogged down on the floor of the House while defending his Department. His statements are supposed to be valuable. He can advise the Governor to dissolve the House though such advice can be rejected by the latter. The Speaker of the House consults the Chief Minister before fixing up any agenda for the House.
7. **Patronage:** Top official appointments, viz. Advocate General and members of State Public Service Commission are made by the Governor, yet, in actual practice, they are all the nominees of the Chief Minister.
8. **Leadership of the Party:** The Chief Minister is the leader of the majority party before elections and after victory at the election results. As the leader of the majority party, he issues whips and sees that they are strictly followed by the party members.

An appraisal of all the above mentioned powers of the Chief Minister reveals that he holds a pivotal position in the State Government. He is central to the formation of the Council of Ministers and central to its death. He is more a Captain of the team of Ministers and not its boss. However, he is bound by the dictates of the High Command. To what extent he is assertive and can bring round the High Command to his point of view depends, to a significantly large extent, on his personality, calibre, social tangibility and his closeness with the rest of his colleagues. A popular leader, commanding dynamic personality and equipped with administrative skill, being modest as well as non-corrupt, is likely to govern the State more vigorously and, comparatively speaking, more independently. Even the High Command, too, will not like to ignore his point of view or turn down his recommendations.

4.10 COUNCIL OF MINISTERS

Article 164 of our Constitution provides that the Governor shall appoint the Chief Minister and, on the advice of the Chief Minister, the Council of Ministers. In actual practice, the Governor can recommend names for inclusion in the Ministry, but cannot insist on getting anyone included. It is the Chief Minister who finalizes the list of Ministers.

The Council of Ministers is composed of Cabinet Ministers, Ministers of State, Deputy Ministers and Parliamentary Secretaries. However, the Cabinet Ministers head the Departments generally. The size of the Council is determined by the Chief Minister. There has been a tendency to have oversized ministries in order to give representation to various shades of opinion. The Administrative Reforms Commission suggested: "Taking a broad view of the needs of the administration in different States, we consider that big States like Uttar Pradesh, Bihar, Madhya Pradesh and Maharashtra may have about 20 persons in the Council of Ministers. The middle sized States like Madras, Mysore and Andhra Pradesh may have 14 to 18 Ministers and the small states like Kerala, Haryana and Punjab 8 to 12."[13]

The Ministers individually and collectively remain responsible to the State Legislative Assembly. Article 164(2) states: "The Council of Ministers shall be collectively responsible to the Legislative Assembly of the State." The Ministers work unitedly as a team. "All for one and one for all" policy works in the functioning of the Council of Ministers. No Minister can dissociate himself from the collective decision of the Council. The Council remains in power so long as it commands the confidence of the legislature. If a no-confidence motion is ever passed, the Council of Ministers has to tender resignation.

The following are the functions of the Council of Ministers:

1. To maintain law and order and ensure security of life and property of the people in the State.
2. To formulate the policies of the State and implement them effectively.
3. To decide the legislative programme of the Legislative Assembly and sponsor all important Bills.
4. To control the financial policy and decide the tax structure for the public welfare of the State.
5. To chalk out programmes and schemes for the socio-economic changes of the State.
6. To make important appointments of Heads of Departments.
7. To discuss disputes with other States.

8. To advise the Governor on the appointment of judges of the High Court.
9. To consider the State's share of work in the Five Year Plans.
10. To frame proposal for incurring expenditure out of State reserves.

Examining the above mentioned powers of the Council of Ministers, it is clearly revealed that the Ministers are the guides and masters of the State Legislature. Besides, they are the formulators and executors of different State policies. However, the State Legislature still enjoys the right of passing a vote of 'no-confidence' against a ministry. The Ministers are also subject to severe criticism during the question hour in the State Legislature. Besides, the tight grip of the Party High Command and that of the party executive at the State level are effective checks on it. The individual Ministers cannot bypass the Chief Minister unless they are least bothered with retaining their ministerial status.

Questions

1. Examine the functions of the Chief Secretary in the State Secretariat.
2. Discuss the role played by the Governor of the Indian state. Is The only the Constitutional head of the State Government? Explain.
3. Explain the roles played by the Chief Minister and his Council of Ministers in the Indian state.
4. Write short notes on:
   (a) Relations between Departments and Directorates
   (b) Discretionary powers of the Governor
   (c) Council of Ministers of the State Government.
5. Discuss the discretionary powers of the Governor in the light of some recent developments.

Notes and References

1. Sogani, Meena, *The Chief Secretary in India*, Associated, New Delhi, 1984.
2. Muttalib, M.A. and M.A. Aleem, Andhra Pradesh, in A.P. Padhi (Ed.), *State Administration in India*, Vol. I, Uppal, New Delhi, 1988.
3. Arora, R.K. and R. Goyal, *Indian Public Administration*, 2nd rev. ed., Wishwa Prakashan, New Delhi, 1997.
4. Murti, V.S., Maharashtra, in A.P. Padhi (Ed.), *State Administration in India*, Vol. I, Uppal, New Delhi, 1988.

5. Government of India, Administrative Reforms Commission (ARC), *Report on State Administration*, New Delhi, 1968.
6. *Report of the Administrative Reforms Committee*, Rajasthan, 1963.
7. *Report of the Study Team (Administrative Reforms Commission) on the State Level Administration*, New Delhi, 1968.
8. *Report of the Indian Statutory Commission*, Vol. I, 1930.
9. Rai, E.N. Mangat, *Commitment My Style: Career in the Indian Civil Service*, Vikas, New Delhi, 1973.
10. Weiner, Myron (Ed.), *State Politics in India*, Princeton University Press, Princeton, 1966. (The Introduction)
11. Basu, D.D., *Commentaries on the Constitution of India*, Vol. II.
12. *Constituent Assembly Debates*, Vol. VIII, p. 545.
13. Quoted by Maheshwari, S.R. in *The Administrative Reforms Commission*, 1970, pp. 86–87.

5 District Administration Changing Role of the Collector

5.1 INTRODUCTION

The district is the basic territorial unit of administration in India. According to the Chamber's Dictionary, a district is "a subdivision of a division". It may be defined as "a sufficiently large territory with an overall unity, governed by common historical, geographical, social and economic conditions."[1] The size of a district varies from State to State. In Tamil Nadu, for example, this size is large whereas in Uttar Pradesh, it is small. The average size of a district, from the point of view of administration, should be around 40,000 square miles.

The district, as accepted universally, is the key unit of State Government in India at present. In fact, it has always existed as the unit of administration throughout the long administrative history of our country. The Mauryas, for instance, had divided their huge dominion into provinces which were subdivided into districts known as *ahors*, *vishays* and *pradesas*. During Ashok's period, *pradeshikas* were officers charged with the welfare of *pradeshas* or districts. Similarly, under the Guptas, their extensive kingdom was divided into provinces which were again subdivided into *vishays* or *mandalas*—something like districts. The Mughal emperors, too, for running the administrative machinery smoothly, divided their vast empire into provinces or *subahs* which, in turn, were subdivided into districts or *sarkars*. The *sarkar* was the counterpart of the modern Indian district and the term is significant as it means "government in its total manifestation". The British rulers gave pride of place to the district as the basic unit of administration. During the British period, the district virtually became a kind of sub-capital in the political as well as administrative sense. In independent India also, the district continues to retain its position as the pivot of administrative and governmental structure in Indian States. Governmental policies are translated into practice at this level. From this level, the demands of local people are communicated to the

State Government. A big and complex governmental machinery is in operation at the district level. By its accomplishments at this level, one can measure the extent of success of the governmental plans, policies, programmes and projects. Every village or town in India is a part of a district. The district is truly a unit of administration with which almost every citizen comes into contact.

There are various types of districts in India:

1. Rural districts are the average districts.
2. There are some urban and semi-urban districts where the local administration concentrates more on urban problems.
3. In Bihar and West Bengal, there are many industrial districts found heavily round the industrial belts.
4. There are many backward districts where local people are totally deprived of any kind of opportunity and advantage.
5. Lastly, some Indian districts are labelled as 'hilly districts' where the pattern of living differs from that of the rest of Indian districts.

But most Indian districts constitute the mixture of these different types.

5.2 DISTRICT ADMINISTRATION: ITS FUNCTIONS

District administration implies the management of the task of government so far as it lies within an area legally recognized as a district. Most of the State Government Departments outside the Secretariat have external or field services located in the district. In some cases, the Union Government also has its field agencies located at the district level. The sum total of the activities of these Departments and some other Departments associated with Union governmental affairs together constitute what is commonly known as the district administrative machinery. S.S. Khera wisely observed: "District administration is the total functioning of government in a district; that total and complex organization of the management of public affairs at work, dynamic and not static in the territory of a geographically demarcated district ... District administration includes all the agencies of government, the individual officials and functionaries, public servants ... all institutions for the management of public affairs in the district, all the bodies corporate such as the panchayats of different kinds ... all advisory bodies associated with the administration".[2]

The immense functions of district administration can be classified into six broad categories which are: (a) regulatory, (b) developmental, (c) functions of local bodies, (d) conducting elections, (e) emergency and (f) residuary.

Of these, regulatory and developmental functions are perhaps the most important functions of district administration. *Regulatory functions* include the maintenance of law and order, control of crime and administration of justice. Regulatory functions also cover land administration including the assessment and collection of land revenue, collection of such other taxes as sales tax, forest and excise tax, income tax, etc. Controlling, regulating and distributing food and civil supplies, too, come under regulatory functions of district administration.

By *developmental functions*, we mean basically such functions like agricultural production, cooperation, animal husbandry, fisheries, and welfare activities like public health, education, social welfare, etc.

Functions of local bodies are concerned with the administration of urban and rural local bodies. Constitution and running of Zilla Parishads (rural) and District Boards, Municipal Corporations and Municipalities (urban) are the local body functions of district administration.

An election-conducting function concerns the holding of elections to the Parliament, the State Legislature and local bodies.

By *emergency functions*, we mean the activities of district administration during emergency situations and natural calamities like flood, drought, etc.

The *residuary functions* of district administration do not consist of executive works done that have neither been precisely defined nor is there a specific government representative in the district to perform such functions. The Collector, as the chief representative of the State Government in the district, has to discharge all such duties including issuing, renewal, suspension and cancellation of arm licences, enforcement of special Acts, campaigns for small savings, duties related to publicity and public relations, protocol duties, etc.

5.3 ORGANIZATION OF DISTRICT ADMINISTRATION

In the earlier days, the Collector/Deputy Commissioner had to perform all six types of functions stated before. With the introduction of local self government institutions and the gradual setting up of technical departments, these functions tended to be shared by many instead of one. As a result, in place of unity of commands, there emerged multiplicity of commands. This change in the performance of district administrative functions became more and more prominent since the Government of India Acts (1919, 1935). In fact, nowadays, as the Central Administration Reforms Commission observes, only the regulatory functions are to be performed by the Collector and the developmental functions are left with the panchayati raj institutions. The enormous size of functions along with the multiplicity of commands has led to the emergence of the district as a kind of sub-capital where district headquarters of various technical departments are located. The names of such Departments and the designations of officers heading those Departments vary from State to State. But a more or less representative list is given below:

	Name of Department	*Designation of the District Head*
1.	Agriculture	District Agriculture Officer/Assistant Director of Agriculture
2.	Backward Classes/ Harijan Welfare	Backward Classes Welfare Officer/ Harijan Welfare Officer
3.	Cooperatives	Assistant/Deputy Registrar of Co-operative Societies
4.	Education	District Education Officer/Inspector of Schools
5.	Employment	District Employment Officer
6.	Excise	District Excise Officer/Superintendent of Excise
7.	Forest	Divisional/District Forest Officer
8.	Health and Family Planning	District Health Officer
9.	Industries	District Industries Officer/Assistant Director of Industries
10.	Jails	Superintendent of Jails
11.	Judiciary	District and Sessions Judge
12.	Labour	Assistant Labour Commissioner/ District Labour Officer
13.	Medicine	District Medical Officer/Civil Surgeon
14.	Panchayats/Panchayats and Social Services	District Panchayat Officer
15.	Planning	District Planning Officer
16.	Police	Superintendent of Police
17.	Publicity/Information	District Publicity Officer/Assistant Director of Publicity
18.	Public Works	Executive Engineer
19.	Registration	Collector
20.	Revenue and General Administration	Collector
21.	Sales Tax	District Sales Tax Officer
22.	Statistics	District Statistics Officer
23.	Treasury and Accounts	District Accounts Officer/District Treasury Officer
24.	Veterinary and Animal Husbandry	Assistant Director of Veterinary Services/District Veterinary Officer

5.4 COLLECTOR: EVOLUTION OF HIS ROLE IN DISTRICT ADMINISTRATION

The collector or Deputy Commissioner or District Officer is the linchpin of district administration. He is at the apex of the district. He is known as Collector in some of the States like Rajasthan and Madhya Pradesh and Deputy Commissioner in other States like Punjab and Haryana. In some other States like West Bengal, he is termed District Magistrate as well. Being the head of district administration, the Collector occupies a unique position in the entire administrative system of India. The institution of Collector came into existence during the days of the East India Company and since then, it has enjoyed a place of pride in the district. Under the British rule, the district was the basis of administration and the Collector, as the head of the district, played a key role in the administrative set-up. On the framework of this fundamental administrative unit, civil, criminal and political jurisdictions were built. The pattern of district administration in India is based on the ancient Indian system of territorial organization which provided various areawise levels of administration like divisional, subdivisional, etc.[3]

Mughal rulers also followed the system of territorial administration, when the British East India Company appeared on the scene. The office of the "Collector of Revenue" was created under the East India Company in 1772.[4]

In 1787, the administration of revenue, civil justice and magistracy was united in the office of the District Collector. Thus, he became an extremely powerful civil servant running the executive machinery in the district. After the 1857 revolt, the Bengal system of district administration was modified and the pattern of integrated field administration, adopted in other parts of the nation, was also introduced in Bengal. The District Collector of this period became the symbol of imperial rule. In fact, the Collector was not merely the representative of the government. He was rather the government or *sarkar* himself. Paternalism and authoritarianism were the two characteristic features of the system of collector raj. Various factors like the growth of rapid means of communication, the spread of education, the freedom of the press, the introduction of local self governmental institutions, etc. had an impact upon the authority and power of the Collector.

The introduction of provincial autonomy in April, 1937 gave birth to an enlarged sphere of activity of the Collector. Till 1937, the Collector concentrated on public order, impartial administration of justice, prompt collection of revenue and the correct maintenance of land records. But by 1939, his sphere of activities included rural development, cooperative movement and the village panchayats. The Second World War (1939–1945) added a new dimension to the functions and duties of the District Collector and imposed some additional responsibilities upon his shoulders. After independence in 1947, several newer problems were created and the burden of all such additional problems fell principally on the already over-burdened shoulders of the Collector.

Since 1947, the introduction of the community development programme, introduction of the panchayati raj and the acceptance of the concept of "welfare State" have radically changed the duties of the Collector. From the maintenance of law and order and the collection of revenue, the major emphasis has now shifted to the development of human and material resources and the eradication of poverty. Under these altered circumstances, the Collector cannot afford to keep a distance from the people and is rather primarily expected to work with the people and for the people. A Collector now has to spend a lot of time in listening to the grievances of the people. To the socio-cultural life of the district, he is expected to contribute a lot. Thus, he is no longer the sole "eyes and ears" of government as was the case under the British rule. He acts as an instrument of executing governmental policies, programmes, plans and projects formulated largely by the ruling political party at the State level. With his expanding responsibilities and a gross change from regulatory to developmental functions, the Collector gradually has become the most harassed and hard-pressed of all government employees. Yet, he is regarded as the backbone of district administration in India.

5.4.1 Duties of Collector

The Collector is the key person of district administration. He is normally a member of the Indian Administrative Service. As the Collector, he is directly responsible to the Divisional Commissioner and through him to the State Government. His main duties are as follows:

1. He maintains law and order in the district.
2. He collects land revenue and other taxes promptly and fairly.
3. He directs and fulfils the development plans with which the country's destiny is interrelated.
4. He performs various regulatory functions of the government like rationing of food, purchase of agricultural products, regulating the movement of commodities, etc.
5. He takes immediate actions in case of disaster, natural calamity and any other emergency.
6. He carries on development activities of the government.
7. He acts as a kind of buffer between citizens and administration, protecting one against the possible harassment by the other.
8. In order to maximize the number of officers in his district and to keep his office efficient, he keeps friendly relations with governmental officials at the district level.

According to the *Imperial Gazetteer of India*, a Collector of strong and sympathetic character with the gift of insight may gain the strongest hold over the affections and imagination of the peasantry and tales of his sagacity will be told in the remotest corners of the village many years after his name has ceased to be borne on the civil list of the province.[5] The position of the Collector remains the same even today depending upon his dynamism and his approach to the citizens.

5.5 CHANGING ROLE OF COLLECTOR

Being born in pre-independence India, the institution of District Collector still remains one of the most glorious and honoured institution. The dignified office, view some scholars,[6] "admirably survived the historic role of change from an alien regime to a national one." The democratic set up of India, vigorous attempts at decentralization, increasing developmental responsibilities, rise of public awareness and increasing freedom of public opinion are some of the crucial reasons behind the multifarious role of the Collector.

Belonging to the Indian Administrative Service and appointed under the Land Revenue Code, the Collector is vested with powers under the various Central and State laws. He is appointed to a district in a State in accordance with the existing scheme of IAS. IAS direct recruits are posted as Collectors in their twenties or thirties whereas the promoters to the IAS from the State civil services occupy this position generally in their fifties.

Unlike their British forefathers, who considered themselves as uncrowned sovereigns of an empire, the Collectors in the post-independence period are much more enthusiastic with a bright vision for the welfare of the respective district-dwellers. Besides, the social background of this institution has also undergone a significant change. While the earlier Collectors belonged to the upper strata of society, the newer ones belong more and more to the middle and even low income groups[7] due to the spread of education and reservation of seats. Hence, these newer Collectors are expected to have a greater degree of sympathy and understanding for the underprivileged sections. The ultimate power of the Indian bureaucracy is thus controlled by such social forces as the changing socio-economic background of Collectors.[8]

The introduction of the Constitution of independent India weakened the position of the Collector to a significant extent. Article 50 of our Constitution separates the judiciary from the executive. Whereas in pre-independence India, the Collectors exercised both executive and judicial powers, in post-independence India separate judicial officers began to be appointed in the districts. As a result, Collectors nowadays no longer hold the same judicial authority as their forefathers did in the British period.

The emergence of a number of technical Departments like labour, agriculture, cooperatives, etc. along with a host of executive officers who man these Departments has resulted in the drastic reduction of the

Collector's power and authority. Some of these technical Departments are headed by specialists and are relatively independent of the Collector.

The developmental role of the Collector has also been reduced sharply as a result of the introduction of democratic decentralization in the form of Panchayati Raj. The Zilla Parishads, the uppermost tier of the three-tier Panchayati Raj System, have emerged at the district level as separate centres of power, largely independent of the Collector. In some States like West Bengal, where 'red' panchayats are the real strength of the ruling CPI(M) party, the power of the Zilla Parishad has curtailed the powers of the District Collector drastically since the eighties of the twentieth century.[9] Political parties have become an important channel of communication between the people and the government. In many States of India, Collectors find themselves totally alienated on several occasions when a number of sensitive decisions, affecting the common district dwellers, are taken largely by political parties.

Many other factors like the overburdened position of the Collector, his loss of contacts with the masses, frequent breakdown of law and order situation in the district, unmanageably large size of some districts, problems of coordination with the police, the revenue department and the technical departments–all together or individually contribute to the reduction of the Collector's original power.

Though his influence is shrinking, yet his area of activity is still vast. He is undoubtedly the most important functionary at the apex of the district administration. As Dwarka Das points out: "The position of the Collector has remained a classic example of unclassified, unconsolidated, diffused responsibility that seems to be one of the marked features of the Indian administrative system."[10] In fact, even after losing his powers to some extent, his responsibility is not reduced. This is somewhat reflected in the observation of Paul H. Appleby: "He (the Collector) was in earlier days and is now somewhat in theory or in most nostalgic yearning more or less responsible for everything done by the government within his geographical area."[11]

In a democratic political set-up like India's, the role-content may change. No institution at present can be an exact replica of what it was originally. Today, in the perspective of public welfare as the governmental objective in general, in spite of the reduction of the Collector's powers, he still remains the general manager of the business of the State government at the district level. His functions vary in relative importance and in scale from one State to another and even from one season to another in the same State or district. [12]

5.6 MANYSIDED TASKS OF THE COLLECTOR

In this section, we discuss the multifarious tasks of the District Collector as the Revenue Collector, District Magistrate, Coordinator of various Departments at the district level, Crisis Administrator and Development Officer.

5.6.1 Revenue Collector

The traditional and the foremost task of the Collector is to assess and collect land revenue as the head of revenue administration of the district. S.S. Khera and H. Rai point out two principles in this regard[13]– the first is that revenue which is assessed must be collected in full, strictly avoiding any tendency to relax and the second one is timely collection of the dues. The second principle is stressed particularly because, in case of lapse, collection becomes more and more difficult.

Taxes due to the government may be of several types like irrigation dues, income-tax dues, agricultural dues, canal dues, various kinds of loans, etc. The collection of sales tax arrears is another responsibility of the Collector. Excise duties on various commodities like drugs, petrol, liquor, etc. are levied by the District Excise Officer, working under the Collector.

Agricultural loans are distributed by the Collector and his staff. Relief works are to be taken up on a very extensive scale in case of famine or flood when land revenue rents may be suspended.[14]

The Collector is also responsible for land acquisition. Due to many developmental projects, housing schemes, etc., land has to be acquired for public purposes. Under the Indian Treasure Trove Act, the Collector has to report to the State Government about the discovery of a treasure, its nature, value, etc.[15]

The Collector is responsible for general supervision, physical verification, checking, certifying and communicating to the Accountant General of the exact balances as found to exist at his inspection. Again, as the revenue officer of the district, he prepares and maintains land records. A revision of such records is also demanded from him. He hears appeals in the revenue cases against orders of the lower courts. In order to perform such vast revenue functions, the Collector has a huge staff to assist him.

5.6.2 District Magistrate

The magisterial function of the Collector is also of immense. As the District Magistrate, the Collector is responsible for the maintenance of law and order within the territorial boundary of the district. Socio-political and communal tensions along with terrorism, smuggling and several other offences have added to his burdens.

As District Magistrate, the Collector has to communicate continuously with the police, the judiciary and the jails. In the district, the police force is kept under the control and supervision of the District Magistrate. Khera points out clearly that when the District Magistrate, however junior he may be, is present, he assumes charge of the situation and the police must follow his orders. It is the District Magistrate (DM) who must order to fire or to use force and the District Superintendent of Police (SP), who is under the control of the District Magistrate, must act according to such order. In the seventies of the last century, a debate was raised relating to the relationship between the SP and the DM. An attempt was made to reconcile the general supervision of the SP by the DM with the essential freedom required by the SP in his day-to-day working. The root of this debate can be traced back to the last quarter of the 19th century, when the Collector was regarded to be the all-in-all in the district and when in the Police Manual the SP was described as a mere assistant of the DM. The Indian Police Commission during 1902–1905 asked the DM not to interfere in matters of departmental management and discipline of the police.[16] In modern times also, tensions can be generated when supervision could be misinterpreted as interference. Since 1978, in the metropolitan cities like Kolkata, Mumbai, Delhi, etc., the responsibility for law and order vests with the Police Commissioner, and the District Magistrate has nothing to say in this regard.

In communicating with the judiciary, the DM faces certain problems. Article 50 of our Constitution, as has been stated already, separates the judiciary from the executive. As a result of this separation, the whole range of judicial proceedings is now the sole responsibility of the judiciary under the control of the State High Court. The DM now acts as an agent of the judiciary. The execution of writs is usually done through the magisterial element of the district administration. Under the scheme of separation, the DM does not inspect trial registers and case records.

Regarding his communications with jails, the DM is in a controlling position. He usually controls the district jail. He can visit the jail from time to time to see that everything goes well. He deals with such issues as granting of superior classes to prisoners, premature release of prisoners, mercy petitions by prisoners, etc. When a condemned prisoner is executed, the DM is normally present because he has to sign the necessary certificates.

5.6.3 Coordinator Between Different Departments of the District

Previously, the Collector used to act as the coordinator of all important official activities in the district. Since Independence, this coordinating function of the Collector began to be weakened as a result of the gradual setting up of many technical Departments, at the district level, headed by specialists. After the birth and evolution of Such departments as public health, public works, agriculture, irrigation, education and cooperation, the question which started to be raised is: Can and should the Collector be made responsible for coordinating the activities of all these Departments into a single whole? These Departments, though work within the district, are not under the direct supervision of the Collector. In administrative and technical regards, they are rather responsible to their respective heads of Departments in the State Secretariat. These Departments have their own developmental activities that they conduct on their own without being interfered by the Collector. This has resulted in the gradual weakening of the Collector's role as a coordinating agency.

But on this role, the success of the district planning depends to a significant extent. Hence, a strong need is felt to strengthen his role in this respect. If various Departments in the district work at cross purposes, then the very spirit of district development is adversely affected. Under these circumstances, the coordinating role of the Collector becomes more and more vital. In October 1965, the then Prime Minister Lal Bahadur Shastri remarked that the Collector should treat himself as a commander who would organize the activities of all the Departments working dedicatingly as soldiers on the battle front. The Collector should try to achieve the target that must be clearly laid down.[17]

To play this coordinating role properly, the Collector should regularly hold meetings of the officers posted at the various Departments of the district. He should remove bottlenecks within Departments by strongly controlling them, bring out unity among Departments, achieve the trust of each Department and allow breathing space to each.

5.6.4 Crisis Administrator

During crises, the Collector can get an opportunity to play his real role—the role which emerges out of his vibrant consciousness and inner potentialities. Crises, as O'Malley observes, "cannot be met by the rule of thumb procedure which is ascribed to a routine-ridden bureaucracy but call for and bring out the higher qualities of leadership and resource."[18] During crises, as T.N. Chaturvedi warns, work of the Collector should not be done out of a sense of compensation, but of duty. As a result, he may go beyond the written boundaries when crises occur. Crisis administration is not an old and outdated interpretation of rules and regulations. Instead, it is a vibrant and ever-dynamic response to any unforeseen contingency.[19] During emergencies caused by natural calamities like floods, famines, droughts, cyclones, etc. or man-made crises such as riots, fire, blasts, etc., it is the Collector who holds a broad umbrella over the entire district. For instance, during a communal riot, loot, murder and fire are the usual scenes. Temples and mosques are attacked. At that time, it is the Collector's duty to see that the police arrive on time, fire brigades are called, hospitals are alerted and the panicky public put at ease. Similarly, during floods, he has to arrange rescue operations, take measures to control epidemics, call for the army for supply of food and drinking water. Under the

Defence of India Rules, the Collector can exercise several powers during external attacks.[20] The Collector's role as the crisis administrator was emphasized by Woodruff as well.[21]

5.6.5 Development Officer

After the introduction of development planning in India, the role of the Collector as Development Officer became more and more prominent. Rural development, i.e. all-round development of the dwellers of the rural sector is considered to be an essential characteristic feature of a welfare State. On the basis of this consideration since 1952, with the introduction of the Community Development Programme, a number of programmes were launched for the benefit of the poorest of the poor in the rural areas of India. In the sixties of the twentieth century, several rural developmental schemes were started. Such schemes were specifically related to health, education, employment, improvement of housing conditions and programmes for rural youth, women and children. A number of area development programmes like DDP, DPAP, TDP, CAD, etc. became important during the seventies of the twentieth century. Eradication of poverty and improvement of the living standard of the rural poor were the two basic objectives of such programmes.

In performing these functions of economic development, the Collector's role is not that advisory, but rather of a Development Officer. His leadership quality is particularly emphasized. It may be noted in this context that the situation is not the same all over India. For example, in Gujarat and Maharashtra all development activities have been transferred to the District Development Officer who, also, is an IAS officer. In these States, the Collector's role in developing rural areas is not vital. But in Rajasthan, all development activities are the primary responsibility of the Collector. In fact, the Rajasthan Panchayat Samiti and Zilla Parishad Act, 1959, has given some responsibilities of district development upon the shoulders of the Collector who plays the role of the District Development Officer as well.

The Collector, being the Development Officer, is the ex officio Chairman of the District Rural Development Agency (DRDA), which is basically an agency responsible for the implementation of rural development programmes. Under a broad framework of Integrated Rural Development Programme (IRDP), a number of schemes are implemented by the DRDA. There are area-based schemes like the Desert Development Programme and the Drought Prone Area Programme. Again, there are individual beneficiary schemes like Training the Rural Youth for Self Employment (TRYSE), National Rural Employment Programme (NREP) and National Rural Employment Generating Programme (NREGP), aiming at providing more employment to the rural youth. Some schemes like Development of Women and Children in Rural Areas (DWCRA) aim at rural women's and children's welfare. Finally, there are such schemes as the Samagra Gram Vikas Programme which aim at the overall development of the rural sector of India.

The Collector plays his developmental roles in his capacity as the head of the District Industries Centre, Chairman of the City Monitoring Committee, Chairman of the district-level Bankers Coordination Committee, etc. He is actively involved in implementing 20-Point programme. For the speedy settlement of land and revenue disputes, the government launches revenue campaigns with which the Collector is closely associated. By developmental roles, all such functions are meant.

5.7 COLLECTOR AS THE CHIEF EXECUTIVE OFFICER OF THE ZILLA PARISHAD

The Chief Executive Officer (CEO) of the highest tier of the panchayati raj institution in India, namely, the Zilla Parishad, is the administrative head of the body. Normally, this post is occupied by the Collector. In this respect, he is endowed with a vast array of powers and responsibilities. He may be regarded as the pivot around which the entire administrative system of the Zilla Parishad revolves.

Viewing his specific powers and duties in this capacity, the role of the CEO can be divided into certain categories. These are:

1. CEO as the person enjoying the power related to Zilla Parishad meetings
2. CEO as the chief archivist of the Zilla Parishad and as one exercising power over development and coordination at the district level
3. CEO as the person possessing financial power of the Zilla Parishad
4. CEO as the person supervising the financial aspects of the Panchayat Samitis under his Zilla Parishad.

First, we discuss the role of a CEO who enjoys powers related to Zilla Parishad meetings. In this capacity, he prepares the agenda for the meetings along with suitable notes on various items. He is responsible for taking actions on decisions arrived at the meetings. He keeps the *Sabhadhipati* aware of the progress, problems and difficulties of various departmental activities in the district as well as the blocks under the district. Again, he is authorized to attend all the meetings of the Zilla Parishad. In case he cannot attend, he must depute the Secretary of the Zilla Parishad to attend the meetings. He may also attend the meetings of the Permanent Committees of the Parishad as far as possible.

Next, we explain the role of a CEO as the chief archivist of the Parishad and as one who enjoys huge power related to the development and coordination at the district level. Each correspondence of the Parishad is signed by the CEO. It is under his custody where the records of the Parishad are kept. He issues necessary directives to the district level officers for the execution of schemes formulated by the Zilla Parishad and its Permanent Committees. He also obtains progress reports from the district level officers about the execution of such schemes. Again, he submits the same to the Parishad and its Permanent Committees. The CEO of this category has also to secure coordination between the Zilla Parishad, its Permanent Committees and other governmental Departments at the district level relating to planning and execution of schemes.

Now the role of the CEO possessing financial power of the Zilla Parishad is explained. The CEO of this category maintains the proper accounts of the Parishad. He prepares the quarterly reports of expenditure of the Parishad and submits these reports to the Finance Permanent Committee. In all matters relating to budget, grants, financial contributions, loans, etc., the CEO is responsible to the Zilla Parishad and its Permanent Committees through the *Sabhadhipati*. In order to prepare the budget of the Parishad, the CEO collects necessary figures of the probable receipts and expenditure of the Parishad. For this purpose, he can consult various State level officers and State plan budgets. He also draws up a draft budget with explanatory notes. The draft budget along with the recommendations of the Finance permanent Committee is placed before the Parishad.

Finally, the role played by the CEO supervising the financial aspects of the Panchayat Samitis under his Zilla Parishad is discussed. The CEO of this category has some significant functions regarding the budget of the Panchayat Samiti. At least two months in advance of the date prescribed for the preparation of the Samiti budget, the CEO of the Parishad puts up before the Finance Permanent Committee the proposals indicating the resources which the Parishad can send to the Panchayat Samiti during the budget year. The CEO also inspects the offices and works of the Panchayat Samitis and the institutions managed by these Samitis. While the Permanent Committees want to examine any record of the Zilla Parishad, the CEO of the Parishad, with prior permission of the Sabhadhipati, has to supply such records to the Panchayat Samiti concerned.

These, in short, are the powers vested in the CEO of the Zilla Parishad.

5.7.1 Conclusion

A successful CEO of the Zilla Parishad must possess the following qualities in order to perform his functions efficiently:

1. He must be able to understand the basic needs of the people living in his district. He must be able to speak the language which the district dwellers speak.
2. He should possess some amount of imagination and drive.
3. He must be honest and dedicated while performing his functions.

In West Bengal, the CEO of the Zilla Parishad is, by all means, a generalist executive officer. But this is not a healthy practice. The generalist officer does not usually develop a sense of responsibility and attachment to the institution of the Zilla Parishad since he builds up his career elsewhere. This is very much damaging for the institution itself. On the other hand, there are such people at the Zilla Parishad as its elected members who do not have adequate administrative skill. Hence, the institution of the Zilla Parishad suffers from a dilemma in the sense the elected members, though having adequate attachment, lack administrative knowledge and techniques. The officials, on the contrary, in spite of having adequate skill, have developed no sense of attachment.

In Rajasthan and some other States of India, in order to avoid such problems, a separate panchayati raj service is made available where the career prospects of the persons manning the panchayati raj institutions are directly interwoven with the rise and growth of the Zilla Parishad. Hence, Henry Maddick has unambiguously pointed out that a separate local self government service at the all-India level is necessary.[22] Such a service will be able (a) to draw talents on a national level, (b) to offer higher status, (c) to offer better salary and (d) to provide reasonable scope for prospects.

Finally, it would be interesting to recall one categorization of the Indian Zilla Parishads as suggested by Maddick in one of his earlier and quite well-known works (1966) on the panchayati raj in India.[23] It is presented below:

1. Strong Zilla Parishads can be found in the State of Maharashtra.
2. Zilla Parishads as mere advisory bodies are found in the States of Assam, Tamil Nadu, Karnataka, Orissa, Punjab, Haryana and Rajasthan.
3. Zilla Parishads, belonging to the 'compromise' category, can be found in the States of Gujarat, Andhra Pradesh and Uttar Pradesh. These Parishads are more powerful compared to the second category and less powerful compared to the first one.
4. A special category is made for the Zilla Parishads in the States of Madhya Pradesh, Bihar and West Bengal. Although the Zilla Parishads in these States are considered to have 'special features', they would fall in category 2. In West Bengal, there are four tiers of Local Self Government instead of the usual three.[24]

However, the Parishads in these States are operating with minor variations. In Maharashtra, the Parisad is very strong, overshadowing the Panchayat Samiti. In Gujarat though the Zilla Panchayat (i.e. the Panchayat at the district level) is powerful, the Taluk Panchayat (i.e. the Panchayat at the block level) fares relatively better compared with its counterpart in Maharashtra. In Tamil Nadu, Punjab and Rajasthan, the district-level panchayat body has merely 'advisory' functions. In West Bengal, along with Andhra Pradesh, Bihar, Himachal Pradesh and Uttar Pradesh, the district-level panchayat body is less powerful than that in category 1, but more powerful than that in category 2.[25]

In short, the District Collector's major functions at present are the following:

- Maintenance of Land records, collection of Land revenue and related matters
- Land acquisition
- Control over extraction of Minor Minerals and collection of royalty for Minor Minerals
- Local Self Government
- Resettlement of project affected persons during disaster management and during riots or external aggression
- Town Planning
- Elections
- Entertainments
- Civil Supplies
- Land reforms
- Poverty alleviation
- Law and Order, supervision of police and jails, supervision of subordinate executive magistracy, hearing cases under the preventive section of the Criminal Procedure Code, certification to execute capital punishments.

Even though the District Collector's office has undergone a sea change since its inception, he still holds a major significance in the Centre–State relations as well as the multifarious developments at the local levels.

Since the District Collector is supposed to be appointed by the State Government from the Indian Administrative Service, one should remember that he is a Union or Central officer and all his career progression and service-related issues as well as grudges and grievances are to be handled by the Central Government. It has been arranged in such a way that the District Collector can perform all his functions in a neutral and unbiased manner, without any fear or hesitation, regarding his duties and responsibilities and implementation of all his welfare or developmental policies of both the Centre as well as the State in the respective district where he has been assigned to.

Although his career and service matters are primarily dealt with by the Centre, and he in his career-graph eventually proceeds from the state to the centre, yet he has to prove his worth initially at the state level and at this level he has to work under the guidance and supervision of the state government. Hence, a wise coordination between the Central level and the State level is necessary to be designed by the District Collector for the proper implementation of Central as well as State schemes and policies at the district.

Scholars opine that even though a number of changes, regarding the role played by the District Collector, have taken place over time, he has continued to be the principal chief executive officer and representative of the State government at the district level. In this context one may quote B. Sivaraman: "The role of the Collector and the emphasis on the type of work he has to do at a certain period of history have changed from time to time. But all along he has been the head of administration in the district and he has been the representative of government at that level."[26]

Questions

1. Discuss the changing role of the District Collector.
2. Explain critically the manysided tasks of the District Collector.
3. Write short notes on:
   (a) CEO of the Zilla Parishad
   (b) Types of Indian Zill Parishads
   (c) Types of Indian districts
   (d) Major functions of district administration.
4. What are the functions presently expected from the Collector of Indian district?

Notes and References

1. Sastri, K.N.V., *Principles of District Administration in India.*
2. Khera, S.S., *District Administration in India*, Asia Publishing House, New Delhi, 1964.
3. Majumdar, R.C. (Ed.), The *History and Culture of the Indian People*, Vol. II, Bhartiya Vidya Bhawan, Bombay, 1953.
4. Ghoshal, A.K., *Civil Services in India Under the East India Company*, University of Calcutta, Calcutta, 1944.
5. *The Imperial Gazetteer of India*, Vol. IV, 1909.
6. Eames, Edwin and Parmatma Saran, *District Administration in India*, Vikas, Delhi, 1989.
7. Arora, Ramesh K. and Rajni Goyal, *Indian Public Administration: Institutions and Issues*, Wishwa Prakashan, New Delhi, 1997.
8. Kukkar, Jagdish, The Changing Role of the District Collector in India, in Avasthi, A. and Ramesh K. Arora (Eds.), *Bureaucracy and Development: Indian Perspectives*, Associated Publishing House, New Delhi, 1978.
9. This is discussed in detail.in the last section of the present chapter.
10. Das, Dwarka, *Role of Higher Civil Service in India*, Popular, Bombay, 1958.

11. *Ibid.*
12. Maheshwari, S.R., *State Governments in India*, MacMillan, New Delhi, 1979.
13. Khera, S.S., *op. cit.* Also see Rai, Haridwar, The Changing Role of the District Collector in Chaturvedi, T.N. and R.B. Jain (Eds.), *District Administration*, I.I.P.A., New Delhi, 1980.
14. Shukla, J.D., *State and District Administration in India*, I.I.P.A., New Delhi, 1976.
15. Sharma, Sudesh K., Reorganization of District Administration in India: A Plea for Structural Reforms, in Arora, Ramesh K. (Ed.), *Administrative Change in India*, Aalekh, Jaipur, 1974.
16. Roy, N.C., *The Civil Service in India*, Calcutta: Firma K.L. Mukhopadhyay, 1960.
17. Cited in Dave, P.K., The Collector: Today and Tomorrow, in Chaturvedi, T.N. and R.B. Jain (Eds.), *District Administration*, I.I.P.A., New Delhi, 1980.
18. O'Malley, L.S.S., *The Indian Civil Service (1601–1930)*, John Murray, London, 1934.
19. Chaturvedi, T.N., Crisis Administration, in Chaturvedi, T.N. and R.B. Jain (Eds.), *District Administration*, I.I.P.A., New Delhi, 1980.
20. Ojha, B.S., Role of the Deputy Commissioner in Emergency, in Chaturvedi, T.N. and R.B. Jain (Eds.), *District Administration*, I.I.P.A, New Delhi, 1980; for the same view also see, Srivastava, I.C., The Battle Cry, in Mukerji, M. and R.K. Arora (Eds.), *The Collectors Recollect*, R.B.S.A., Jaipur, 1987.
21. Woodruff, Philip, *The Guardians*, Jonanath Cape, London, 1959.
22. Maddick, Henry, *Panchayati Raj: A Study of Rural Local Government in India*, Longman, London, 1970.
23. Maddick, Henry, *Democracy, Decentralization and Development*, Asia Publishing House, Bombay, 1966.
24. As a result of the West Bengal Panchayat Act of 1957 and the West Bengal Zilla Parishads Act of 1963, a four-tier system of panchayati raj was introduced in West Bengal: (a) Anchal Panchayat, (b) Gram Panchayat, (c) Anchalik Parishad and (d) Zilla Parishad. Then after the 1973 Act, there are three tiers of panchayati raj in West Bengal, namely Gram, Panchayat, Panchayat Samiti and Zilla Parishad.
25. Shiviah, M., K.V. Narayana Rao, L.S.N. Murty and G. Mallikarjuniah, *Panchayati Raj: An Analytical Survey*, National Institute of Community Development, Hyderabad, 1976.
26. Sivaraman, B., "The Collector of the Seventies", *The Indian Journal of Public Administration*, Vol. XI, No. 3, July–September, 1965.

6 Local Self Government in India An Urban Picture

6.1 MEANING OF LOCAL SELF GOVERNMENT

In the present-day world, local self government is considered to be the bottommost part of the five-tier system of government. The supranational agency like the United Nations, being purely voluntary in nature and laying down a code of conduct regarding the relations between the sovereign Nation States, is situated at the apex. The second tier, composed of the regional groupings like the European Union, the Oil and Petroleum Exporting Countries (OPEC), the South Asian Association of Regional Cooperation (SAARC) etc., falls just below the first tier. The third tier comprises governments of individual national states working within their own constitutional boundaries. The governments of constituent units known as States or provinces form the fourth tier. The fifth and the bottommost tier is the local self government.

The local government's jurisdiction is limited to a specific area. Its functions relate to the provision of civic amenities to the population living within its jurisdiction. It lacks the legislative powers. Its powers to raise finances are defined in the Constitutional Amendment Bills. A local government normally functions within the provisions of the statute by which it has been created. It is subordinate to the State or provincial government in the sense it is controlled and supervised by the latter. Under certain circumstances, the State Government can even suspend or dissolve a local government. But fresh elections must be held within six months.

The establishment of the institution of local self government, based on decentralization of powers, has been viewed for a long time as the means by which the State can be made more responsive and more adaptive to the local needs. The system of local self government ensures mass political participation in the decision making process by extending democracy to the grass-roots level. Thus, local self government is considered to be the training ground for democracy.

The popular philosophy of democratic decentralization finds its practical application through the institutions of local self government. Democratic decentralization is democratic in the sense that the source from which power is decentralized has its democratic basis and the body to which power flows is also democratically organized. The local self governmental institutions associate the people with local administration. They recognize the people's right to initiate and execute the policy-decisions in an autonomous way. Local self government is a legalized institutional system where people are allowed to govern via their elected representatives. Such a government has its organization power and authority. But it has to function within the framework of State administration.

6.1.1 Characteristics of Local Self Government

Local self government as an institution is characterized by the following features:

1. **Legal Background:** Local self governments have strong legal support in the sense they are the products of Acts and Statutes. The legislature enacts the Acts which make the statutory provisions for the establishment of local bodies. The composition, functions and powers, sources of revenue and the modus operandi of the local self governmental bodies are clearly specified by such Acts.
2. **Corporate Body:** Any local self governmental institution is a corporate body having perpetual succession and a common seal. Being a corporate body, it can sue and can be sued.
3. **Autonomous Institution:** Any local self governmental institution enjoys the status of autonomy within the limits specified by such legislative Act which creates the institution originally. As a result of such autonomy, the local self governmental body can perform its day-to-day functions independent of (State) governmental control and interference. Within its stipulated legal framework, the local body can even formulate policies. But it can, by no means, cross the boundaries set by the law.
4. **Absence of Sovereignty:** No local self governmental body is sovereign. It should be remembered in this context that sovereignty is an attribute of the State only and no association, organization or body within the State can possess this. Thus, local self governmental institutions are all non-sovereign bodies.
5. **Little Government:** A local body functions within a limited territory with limited power in the style of a government. It

has territorial jurisdiction, managing organization, powers and authority, elected representatives, etc. like that of a little government.

6. **Financial Power:** The local self governmental body is empowered to raise funds by imposing tax, levy, toll, etc. which are all provided by the Acts. But the fund raised by the local body is not sufficient to meet its demands. Hence, the local self governmental bodies have to depend a lot on the financial assistance extended to them by the State and the Central Governments.
7. **Democracy in Decision Making:** The local bodies are popular forums that associate people with the process of local administration. In making local policies and also in implementing them, local people have every right to participate. A local body resembles some kind of direct democracy.
8. **Multifarious Activities:** The local bodies are associated with many-folded activities and supposed to perform multi-purpose functions. Local problems of various dimensions such as water supply, roads, drainage, sports, etc. are sought to be solved by these bodies.
9. **Absence of Separation of Powers:** In local bodies, all three functions of the government–the executive, the legislative and judicial–are mixed up together. No kind of separation of powers, in the true sense of the term, is visible in case of local bodies.
10. **Grass-roots Democracy:** Among local bodies, democracy exists at the grass-roots level. The concept of local self government is deeply associated with the teachings of Gandhiji who seriously urged for spreading democracy down to the grass-roots level. Thus, local self government is the other name of grass roots democracy.

In a broad sense, local self government means decentralization of power to the local bodies elected by the local people to meet local needs. Some opine, local self government is the unit that associates the people with local administration and recognizes the people's right to initiate and execute the policy decisions in an autonomous way. It is a legalized institutional system of elected people who are allowed to administer the local needs. Thus, one can define the local self government as an institution for the management of services and regulatory functions of a specified locality by locally elected representatives with sufficient power of policy making and administration under statutory obligation and supervision.

6.1.2 Success of Local Self Government: Necessary Conditions

Each institution requires certain conditions for its survival and success.

The institution of local self government is no exception in this regard. Each local self governmental body can achieve its targeted success, subject to the fulfilment of certain conditions discussed below

1. Local self governments are supposed to provide civic amenities by performing multi-dimensional functions to fulfil the aspirations of the local people. But the financial resources of these institutions are significantly limited. The resources that they are capable to mobilize fall far short of their actual requirements. Hence for the financial support, the local self governmental bodies have to depend upon both the Central and the State Governments to a large extent. Such a situation is certainly not conducive to the success of any local body.
2. If the working of local self governments suffers seriously by the storms of politics, the success can never be achieved by them. According to many critics, local self governments are the breeding ground of politics. The role of 'unclean politics' in the elections and functioning of local self governments cannot by any means be denied. A major condition for the success of local self government rests on the assumption that politics should not be allowed to spoil the working of the local self government. Now, in reality, the local self government cannot be made totally free from politics. In that case, it must be seen that healthy politics must prevail to assure the conditions necessary for the success of the local self government.
3. Excessive and unnecessary governmental control is an obstacle to the success of the local self government. Such a control over the local self governmental institutions may be of three principal kinds–control over broad policy, control over finance, and control over day-to-day administration. The grass-roots level governments are required to function under the broad framework of policies made by the State Government. Financially too, as has been mentioned already, these bodies have to depend upon both the Central and the State governments. Thus, local bodies are almost bound to function under the governmental control over policy and finance. Hence, if they are not allowed by the upper level governments to function independently in their day-to-day administrative activities, they can never achieve the targeted success.
4. Corruption is seen to be a major obstruction for the success of the local self government. In the developing countries like India, charges of corruption against local self government institutions are the most common features of local administration. If local bodies are found corrupt, hopes, aspirations and expectations of the common people are absolutely crushed. Hence, the existence of corruption-free local self government in a necessary condition for the success of local self government.

5. Last but not least, in order to achieve success, the local self government's healthy functioning should be absolutely free from bureaucratic interference. There is a growing tendency among the bureaucrats to poke their long noses into the daily affairs of local governmental bodies in the name of control over policy and finance. By being too much perfectionists in rules, procedures and norms, the State level bureaucrats indulge in undue delay and unreasonable rigidity. All these appear as significant obstacles to the progress and success of the local self government. If we do not want to replace the 'Lok Raj' or 'People's Raj' by 'Official Raj' or 'Bureaucratic Raj', then excessive and undue bureaucratic interference must, by all means, be eliminated.

6.2 LOCAL SELF GOVERNMENT AS AN INTERNATIONAL CONCEPT

Local self government is indispensable for the daily life of the citizens in a democratic set up. So far as the daily civil life of the citizens and their collective living are concerned, local self government is much more important than higher level governments. The educative importance of the local self government has been highlighted by the scholars. Tocqueville has commented that the local bodies are the pillars of a nation. They are of the same importance to the citizens as the primary schools are to the students. The institutions of local self government are the training ground of democracy. It teaches the people primary knowledge about the use of the franchise and the working of the representative miniature government. John Stuart Mill rightly observes that the local governments provide political education at the grass roots level. Mill opines that there are local problems and local interests common to all its inhabitants. So, it is proper that every locality should have its local body to serve the local interests and solve the local problems. The road to build a good nation, comprising conscious, capable and experienced citizens in public life, lies through the local self government. In shaping a national life, the contribution made by local bodies deserves special mention. The experiences of Switzerland, Great Britain and the United States show that the local institutions play a significant role in stirring up the interests of the common people, who are otherwise indifferent towards the activities of the government.

Liberal political philosophers like J.S. Mill and Lord Bryce consider 'democracy' and 'local self government' synonymous. Hence, their approach to local self government is called *democratic approach*. Democracy becomes meaningful only when democratic forms and contents are extended down to the grass roots level. Local self government is grass roots democracy as it is the extension of democracy to the bottom.

Democracy means more and more power to the people. No form of institution, other than the institution of local self government, has yet been invented through which power flows in the direction of the people. Local self government, in the form of an institutional network spread over the country, assures power to the people irrespective of race, religion, place of birth and caste.

Democracy is essentially related to the principle of decentralization of power from the central to the local areas. The institution of local self government makes the decentralization of power a reality. Under the scheme of decentralization, political and economic powers and various governmental functions are divided between the government at the top and the various local bodies at the bottom. Local self government is based on the proposition that the political authority originates from the people, exercised by the people for catering to the needs of the people. This is what democracy means–government of the people, by the people and for the people.

MacIver observes that democracy is primarily a way of determining who will govern and, broadly, to what ends. From this point of view, freedom of choice is the principal basis of democracy. The local body also determines who shall govern and to what ends. Hence, freedom of choice is present in both democracy and local self government.

J.S. Mill views that democracy means people's participation in the access to power. If this is really attained, the gulf between the government and the governed disappears and the rule of the popular rights is established. This notion of democracy is fulfilled through the institutions of local self government, for there hardly exists any gulf between the local self government and the people locally governed. Democracy rests on public opinion. It is difficult in a big government to ascertain public opinion. But the local self government, being confined in a small area, is formed and guided by the trends of public opinion.

The activities of the local self government are numerous. Indeed, there has been an impressive increase in the functions of local self government throughout the world. In the daily life of a citizen, the local self government is today much more important than the State Government or the Central Government. In fact, their functions are likely to continually increase in future as well. William Robson therefore remarks that "Local authorities have greater opportunities today than ever before. If the powers of the Central Government are increasing, so are the powers of the local councils".[1]

Local government serves as an admirable training ground for the politicians to function at the State and central levels. It provides an outlet for competent and public spirited persons of the locality to render social service to the community. Lord Bryce has therefore pointed out: "It is enough to observe that the countries in which democratic government has most attracted the interest of the people and drawn from their ranks have been Switzerland and the United States, especially those northern and western states in which rural local government has been most developed. These examples justify the maxim that the best school of democracy and the best guarantee for its success, is the practice of local self government".[2]

Finally, local self government contributes to the strength and richness of democracy by promoting diversification of political experience and also by setting itself up as yet another centre of creative activity through democratic action. Jenks points out: "In countries where the organs of local government are under the thumb of the central authority, although the efficiency of administration may be great, the political character of the people will be unsatisfactory;... with the result of instability and corruption in the central government. On the other hand, a country of strong local government may be slow to move, and blundering in its methods, but it will be a country of steady progress, and of political stability and honesty."[3]

One should also mention the weaknesses which arise from the local government. Local government may degenerate into a narrow-minded, selfish and ignorant institution. Because of its small size, it may not attract competent and public spirited persons and thus it gradually becomes sluggish and inefficient. J.S. Mill long ago pointed out: "The greatest imperfection of popular local institutions, and the chief cause of the failure which has often attended them, is the low calibre of the men by whom they are almost always carried on."[4]

6.2.1 Local Self Governments in Various Parts of the World

In this subsection, we discuss the basic patterns of local self governments existing in the USA, UK, France and Japan. From this discussion, a more or less total global picture of the local government may emerge.

American Local Government

The United States has a federal structure with division of powers between the national (federal) and the State Governments. Local government is a State subject. Each State has established its own system of local government depending upon history, culture and experience. Hence, the nomenclature, organization (structure) and functions of different units of local government in the USA differ from State to State. Thus, the American system of local government is primarily characterized by heterogeneity instead of homogeneity.

Another feature of the US local government is a considerably high degree of autonomy enjoyed by the units. The US local government units are comparatively more autonomous than their British counterparts.

At present the US local government consists of the following units:

1. County
2. City (Municipality)
3. Town and township
4. Special district.

Each State of the USA is divided into a number of countries. Each county is subdivided into a number of cities and towns or townships. Again, there are some special districts dealing with particular functions. At present, there are about 3,000 countries, 18,000 cities, 17,000 towns and townships and 40,000 special districts.[5] Let us discuss the organization and functions of each of these units in brief.

1. **County:** Territorially, the largest unit of local government in the USA is the county, which serves as the agency of the State Government. Counties are both administrative subdivisions of the State and units of local government. The organization and functions of these counties differ from State to State and in some States from county to county.

   Each county has a governing body known as County Board/Board of Commissioners/Board of Supervisors/County Court/Police Jury, etc. The governing body consists of four to fifty members elected directly for a period of two to four years. The governing body has a Chairman elected by its members. The Chairman acts as the presiding officer. The governing body, considered to be the nucleus of the county, exercises rule-making and some administrative powers. Besides, the county has a large number of officials called Sheriff, Coroner, Attorney, Auditor, Recorder, Surveyor, Treasurer, Assessor, School Superintendent, Judge and Clerk. These officials are elected directly by the people, normally for a term of two years, and exercise their administrative powers independent of the governing body.

   Generally, each county performs the following functions:

   (a) Law enforcement
   (b) Administration of justice
   (c) Roads and highways
   (d) Public welfare and public utilities
   (e) Agriculture and cooperative extension
   (f) Education
   (g) Health and sanitation
   (h) Planning and zoning

2. **City:** A city is a unit of urban local self government and is incorporated as a municipality. It is compared with a British borough. It has a Charter, defining its organization and functions. The Charter is granted to a US city by the State Legislature either under a special Act or under general laws.

Again, a city can make its own Charter under the municipal home rule.

On the basis of the relations between the executive and the legislative organs, the city governments can be classified into the following three forms:

(a) ***Mayor-Council Plan:*** This is the oldest and the most popular form of city government in the USA. More than half of the US cities use this form of local government. Under this form, a Mayor is elected directly and independently to act as the Chief Executive Officer of the city. The City Council is elected separately to serve as a legislative body. Depending on the position of the Mayor in the system of city government, this form is subdivided into two further forms or plans, namely, Strong-Mayor Plan and Weak-Mayor Plan.

Under the Strong-Mayor plan, the Mayor has complete executive authority by virtue of which he controls the entire administration of the city. Besides, he appoints and removes the heads of Departments irrespective of the approval of the City Council, i.e. the legislative body. He can veto an ordinance passed by the City Council. He also has strong powers regarding the preparation of the city budget. From this, it is clear that the Strong-Mayor Plan widens the scope for executive supremacy over the legislature.

Under the Weak-Mayor plan, the Mayor has limited executive authority by virtue of which he has no control over the city administration. The heads of Departments are elected directly by the people instead of the Mayor. In appointment and removal, too, the Mayor has limited powers. The City Council single-handedly appoints various officials. The veto power of the Mayor can also be overridden by a special majority of the Council. The City Council directly participates in the preparation of the budget and in a number of administrative matters. Thus, the Weak-Mayor plan encourages openly the legislative dominance over the executive.

(b) ***Commission Plan:*** Under this form of city government, the executive as well as the legislative authority is concentrated in a single body known as the *Commission*. This is a kind of governing body consisting of three to nine members called *Commissioners*. They are directly elected by the people for a period of two to six years. The Commissioners have dual responsibility–collective and individual. Collectively, they serve as the City Council (i.e. the legislative body) by virtue of which they determine the policies, pass the ordinances and control the finance. Individually, they act as heads of the administrative Departments of the city government like public works, finance, public safety, etc. The Commissioners choose a person from among themselves as a Mayor to serve as the Chief Executive. The Mayor, under this plan, is a mere ceremonial leader and a titular head of the city government.

(c) ***City-Manager Plan:*** This is also known as the *Council-Manager Plan.* Under this form of city government, there is a Council consisting of five to seven members who are directly elected for a period of two to four years. This elected Council serves as the legislative body of the city government. The Council elects a Mayor from among its members. He acts as the presiding officer of the Council and is the ceremonial head of the city government, having no executive powers or functions.

The Council appoints a professional administrator, called the City Manager, to act as the chief administrator of the city government. He remains responsible to the Council and holds office during its pleasure. While carrying out the ordinances and policies of the Council, the Manager basically acts as an agent of it. He can perform his administrative functions quite independently. It is the City Manager who appoints and removes the heads of the Departments, makes the budget of the city government and presents it before the Council.

Thus, the City-Manager Plan of city government provides for an executive who has less power than his counterpart in the Strong-Mayor Plan system but more power than that in the Weak-Mayor Plan system. On the whole, it provides for a strong Council and a weak Mayor.

3. **Town and Township:** While counties are subdivided into cities in the urban areas, the former are subdivided into towns and townships in the rural and semi-urban areas.

The governing body of the town is called the *Town Meeting*, which consists of all the eligible voters of the town. It usually meets once a year and elects a Board of chosen men and other official functionaries to carry out the functions of local administration. 'Direct democracy' as an administrative principle can be located to operate in these towns.

The governing body of township in known as the Board of Supervisors or Board of Trustees or Board of Auditors or Advisory Board. It is a small elected body composed of about three members. It passes ordinances, budgets and appoints some officials to carry out the functions of local administration.

4. **Special District:** Special district is a unit of the US local government which provides a specialized machinery to carry

out a specified function and permits a high degree of flexibility in local government. Such districts cut across the jurisdiction of the regular units of local government–county, city, town, and so on. They exist throughout the United States covering both rural and urban areas.

Special districts (or single purpose districts) are created for education, sanitation, soil conservation, water, fire protection, recreation, housing, flood control, etc. They are created as quasi-municipal organizations under the State law with the consent of the people of the districts.

School districts, meant for the maintenance of schools, are the oldest and still the most numerous of these special districts.

Special districts are governed by small boards which are normally elective but can also be appointive. It has taxing and bonding authority.

British Local Government

The British Constitution provides for a unitary State where all governmental powers are vested in the single, supreme Central Government. For administrative convenience, it can create or abolish the units of the British local government. Thus, in Great Britain the local government units derive their authority from the Central Government. The statutes of the British Parliament are the major source of their authority, the other sources being the common law of England and the judicial interpretations.

The present system of local government was established in England in 1974 by the Local Government Act, 1972. The Act has created a two-tier system for the metropolitan areas (Conurbations) and a three-tier system for the remainder (mixed urban and rural areas). The conurbations are divided into six metropolitan counties. Each metropolitan county is divided into some metropolitan districts. The total number of metropolitan districts is thirty-six. Similarly, the mixed urban and rural areas are divided into thirty-nine non-metropolitan counties. These non-metropolitan counties are further subdivided into 296 non-metropolitan districts.[6] Again, each non-metropolitan district is divided into parishes or towns. There is no difference between the parishes and the towns except that the Chairmen of towns are called Mayors.

The system of local government in and around London is always different from that in other parts of England. The London Government Act of 1963 established the present structure in 1965. Under the Act of 1963, Greater London became a clearly defined local government area for the first time. Within this area there are the city of London and thirty-two London Boroughs. The Corporation of the city of London acts through three courts, namely, the Court of Common Council, the Court of Aldermen and the Court of Common Hall. Of these, the Court of Common Council is the real governing body and enjoys both legislative and executive powers.

The overall picture of the present pattern of local government existing in England is given in he following chart.

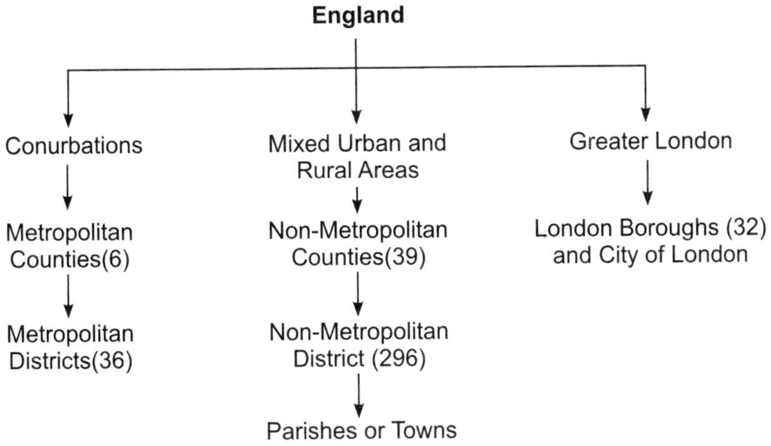

Some other features of the British system of local government are as under:

1. All the units of the British local government (county, district, parish, town) have councils which, acting as both executive and legislative organs of the local government, are the real governing bodies.
2. All members of county councils and district councils are directly elected for a period of four years. The number of members in a council varies between 40 and 100.
3. Not each parish has a council of its own. Parishes with 200 or more electorates have parish councils. A parish council consists of at least five members.
4. Legally, each council is a single public corporation. Hence, it is collectively responsible for taking and implementing decisions.
5. The Presiding Officer of the council is known as its Chairman. He is the ceremonial head of the local authority.
6. Local authorities perform two categories of functions—mandatory and permissive. These authorities operate through committees which supervise administration on behalf of the council.
7. The Local Government Act of 1974 has established the local ombudsmen (on the basis of Scandinavian influence) known as *Commissioner for Local Administration*. They investigate into complaints of maladministration, made by citizens through local councillors.
8. Before the reorganization of the local government structure in Great Britain in 1974, there were six different types of local bodies. They were: County, county borough, urban district, rural

district and parish. On the basis of the recommendations made by the Maud Commission (1967) and the Bains Committee (1972), the British system of local government was reorganized.

French Local Government

Muttalib has excellently summarized the contrasting features of the British and the French systems of local government. According to him, the British pattern is characterized by decentralization, legislative dominance, committee system, multi-purpose activity and voluntary citizen participation. The French pattern, on the other hand, is known for centralization, chain of command, hierarchical structure, executive domination and legislative subordination.

Like its British counterpart, the French Constitution, too, provides for a unitary State where all the governmental powers are vested in the supreme Central Government. For administrative convenience, it can create or abolish the units of local government.

The most important feature of the French local government is the existence of a high degree of centralization. In France, everything is centralized and local government units are controlled by the Central Government through the Minister of Interior, who is the ultimate authority regarding local government. The units of local government are the agencies of Central Government for the purpose of local administration.

Another feature of the French local government is its marked uniformity in organization and functions. Throughout France, the same elective council, the Prefects, Sub-Prefects and Mayors, the same laws and police, the same educational system can be located.

In France there are four kinds of local government units. They are:

1. **Department:** The Department is the largest unit of local government which occupies the topmost place in the local government hierarchy. The Departments broadly correspond to the English counties. But, the area under Departments is double the area under counties. On the basis of population, wealth and political importance, Departments are classified into the following four classes:
   (a) Horse class or special class departments
   (b) First class departments
   (c) Second class departments
   (d) Third class departments

   Each department has a General Council as its legislative wing. It consists of councillors elected directly by the people for a period of six years. The number of councillors varies from Department to Department, the maximum being 67 and the minimum being 17. The Council elects its own President for a term of one year. He acts as the Presiding Officer of the Council. The Council also has a standing committee known as the *Departmental Commission.*

The executive head of the Department is the Prefect, who is appointed by the President of France on the recommendation of the Minister of Interior. The Prefect also acts as a local agent of the Central Government. As an executive head of the Department, he carries out the resolutions and policies of the General Council. As a representative of the Central Government, he has to implement its laws and orders within his Department. Thus, he occupies a dual position.

2. **Arrondisement:** Every department is divided into three or four arrondisements. It is a purely administrative subdivision having no elected council. Hence, it is not a real unit of local government. Its primary function is to reduce and ease the administrative burden on the Department. It is headed by a Sub-Prefect who acts as an agent of the Prefect of a Department. Like Departments, arrondisement are also classified into four classes–Horse Class, First Class, Second Class and Third Class.
3. **Canton:** Each arrondisement is further subdivided into nine cantons. Like an arrondisement, a canton is also a purely administrative subdivision, lacking an elected council and hence, not a real unit of local government. It is a territorial unit mainly for the administration of Army and Judiciary. It also serves as a ward for the election of the General Council of departments. One Councillor is elected from each canton to the departmental council.
4. **Commune:** A commune is the smallest unit of local government in France and stands at the bottom of the hierarchy of local government. In French, the term 'commune' implies not only a subdivision of a canton, but also the government of a city, town, village or township. Unlike the former three units of the French local government, the commune has a historical background and it existed even before the French Revolution of 1789. All the communes in France are governed by the same municipal code.

Each commune has a Municipal Council as its legislative body. It consists of councillors elected directly by the people for a period of six years. The number of councillors varies from commune to commune, the maximum being 37 and the minimum being 11. The Council elects its own Chairman known as Mayor for a period of six years. Brian Chapman observes that the French Mayor has considerably greater personal prestige and personal power than his English counterpart. He is the administrative head of the commune, a prominent local political figure and, in some respects, a State official. According to Chapman, the French Mayor is a figure in local administration whose status may be compared to that of a German Burgomaster, but not to that of an English Mayor.

After studying all the four units of local government, it may be concluded that for the purpose of convenience, the whole area of France is divided into a number of Departments. Each department is further subdivided into a number of arrondisements. Each arrondisement is again subdivided into a number of cantons. Each canton is finally subdivided into communes. The arrondisements and cantons are created only for administrative conveniences and are not the real units of local government. Only Departments and communes are the two real units of local government and administration.

Japanese Local Government

Like democracy, the philosophy of decentralization, the principle of local autonomy and the concept of local self government were introduced in Japan after the Second World War.

The organization, powers and functions of the local government institutions in Japan are determined by the Constitution and the Local Autonomy Law, enacted by the Diet (i.e. the Japanese Legislature) in 1947.

The Japanese Constitution has prominently introduced the principle of local autonomy and has granted extensive rights of self government to the local institutions. It makes the following provisions in this respect:

1. The regulations concerning organization and operation of local bodies shall be fixed by law according to the principle of local autonomy.
2. The local bodies will establish assemblies as their legislative organs.
3. The chief executive officers of all local bodies, the members of their assemblies and such other local officials as determined by law shall be elected by direct popular vote within their communities.
4. Local bodies shall have the right to manage their own property, affairs and administration.
5. A special law, applicable only to one local body, cannot be enacted by the Diet without the consent of the majority of the voters of the local area concerned.

The Local Autonomy Law of 1947 supplements the constitutional provisions and contains, along with many others, the following two important provisions:

1. It takes away the legal power of the Central Government to control the prefectural governments. Similarly, it deprives the prefectural governments of their power to control the municipalities.
2. It provides for the exercise of initiative and recall by the voters of the local bodies. In other words, it provides for the operation

of direct democracy at the local level. Till then, such a thing was unknown in Japan.

At present, Japan has the following units of local government: **Prefecture, City, Town,** and **Village.**

For the purpose of local administration, the whole area of Japan is divided into forty-six prefectures. Each prefecture is subdivided into cities, towns and villages.

1. **Prefectural Government:** The prefectural government consists of a Governor and an Assembly. The Governor is the Chief Executive of a prefecture. He is elected by the local people for a term of four years. He can be removed by the Prime Minister of Japan or by an adverse vote of the Assembly or by a recall election by the local electorate. The Governor has complete control over local administration and local finance, including the preparation of the budget. He can issue ordinances without reference to the Assembly. He also has veto power over the Assembly. He can dissolve the Assembly as well.

   The Assembly is a Single-House legislature. Its strength depends on the local population and ranges approximately between 40 and 120. Its members are elected by the local electorate for a term of four years. It elects its own Chairman and functions through committees. It has the power of approving the prefectural budget. It can override the veto power of the Governor by a special two-thirds majority. Finally, it can pass a vote of no-confidence against the Governor.

2. **Municipal Government:** The local governments of the cities, towns and villages are known as the *municipalities.* Each municipality has a Mayor and a Council. The Mayor is the Chief Executive of a municipality. He is elected by the local people for a term of four years. He can be removed by the Governor of the prefecture or by an adverse vote of the Council or by a recall election by the local electorate. He has complete control over local administration and local finance, including the preparation of the budget. He can issue ordinances without reference to the Council. He has both the veto power over the Council and the power to dissolve the Council.

The Council is a Single-House legislature. Its strength depends on the local population and ranges approximately between 12 and 48. Its members are elected by the local people for a term of four years. It elects its own Chairman and functions through committees. It passes bye-laws and approves the municipal budget. It can override the veto power of the Mayor by a special two-thirds majority. Finally, it can pass a vote of no-confidence against the Mayor.

Thus, the institutional arrangement in the municipal government is the same as in the case of the prefectural government. Again, the

Mayor-Council relationship in the municipality is just like the Governor–Assembly relationship in the prefecture. In short, these arrangements show that the American Presidential system has been followed at the local level administration in Japan. The local political chief in Japan is modelled on the American system of executive elected directly by the people.

In Japan, the local Chief Executives (Governor and Mayor) have a dual role. They serve both the Central Government in national affairs and the local governments in local affairs.

Finally, the Central Government civil service and the local government civil service are separate and distinct in Japan. The local government recruits its own officials who remain in it throughout their career. Like the national public services, the local public services are also divided into two principal categories: (a) regular service and (b) special service.

6.3 LOCAL SELF GOVERNMENT IN INDIA: THE GENERAL PHILOSOPHY

The concept of local self government is not new in India or for the people of India. In ancient days, there hardly existed any town in the sense they exist at present. But from time immemorial, the rural self governments, popularly known as *panchayats*, existed in different parts of India. These village institutions exercised power in almost all the spheres of rural life—agriculture, handicraft and cottage industries, education, religion, justice and many other socio-economic issues. Since the Vedic period, such rural governments used to function for regulating local social life.

But local government in its present form owes its origin to the British rule in India. An introduction of local government may be said to have been made in 1687, when a Municipal Corporation was established in Chennai. The Chater Act of 1793 introduced municipal administration in the Presidency towns of Kolkata and Mumbai. In 1870, Lord Mayo's resolution advocated decentralization of power and formation of municipal governments. Lord Ripon made local government self-governing in 1882. His philosophy of local government was not so easily implemented in India. Yet, Lord Ripon is remembered as the father of local self government in India with immense respects.

In the field of local government, the Government of India Act (1919) marked an era of new interest and activity. The Bengal Municipal Act was passed in 1932 with a view to establishing municipal bodies in the towns. With the growing strength of the national movement, the Government of India Act (1935) was passed and consequently the local governments became constituent parts of the State Government.

In 1947, India achieved independence and from that period, a new era was introduced in the history of local government in India.

Jawaharlal Nehru, the first Prime Minister of independent India, while inaugurating the conference of the Ministers on local self government of the various States (provinces) in 1948, remarked: *Local self government is and must be the basis of any true system of democracy. We have got rather into the habit of thinking of democracy at the top and not so much below. Democracy at the top may not be a success unless you build on this foundation from below.*

The national leaders of our freedom movement fought for achieving self government. They also realized that self government could have no meaning in a vast land like India unless local self governments were established. In other words, if self government was to be made a reality, it must start from the grass roots level. Self government assumes special significance in the context of the actualization of local self government. Decentralization of power is the essence of democracy. This can be achieved only through the functioning of the institutions of local self government. Hence, from the point of view of devolution of power, the importance of local governments can, by no means, be overlooked.

As a member of a big State Government or a bigger Central Government, the citizen has a tendency to behave like passive on-lookers. But due to the existence of the local self government institutions, his urge for civic duties and responsibilities may be stimulated. Thus, local bodies may boost up the personal zeal and sense of duty of the citizen. Democracy cannot succeed without the direct and indirect participation on the part of the people in the governmental process. For the realization of democratic principles, local self governments are very much needed in which people's active participation in formulating policies is remarkably noticed. Thus, the institution of local self government strengthens the foundation of democracy. If all governmental decisions are taken centrally, the people living in the remotest corner of the village will remain absolutely unaware of the many-sided activities of the government. As a result, political apathy among these people is likely to be developed which indirectly helps the bureaucracy to become more and more powerful. Hence, the 'Bureaucratic Raj' may be replaced by the 'People's Raj' by establishing local self government institutions.

6.3.1 Local Government and Local Self Government

It is interesting to see whether the spirit of local government is on any consideration different from that of local self government. In India, local government is popularly known as *local self government*. The latter term originated when the country was under British administration and did not enjoy any self government either at the central or State levels. When a distinct decision was taken by the British Government to associate Indians with administering local affairs, it meant a kind of self government for the people. Lord Ripon's resolution enunciated the following principles which were to inform and guide the local self government in India:

1. Local bodies should have mostly elected non-governmental members and Chairmen.
2. The State control over local bodies should be indirect rather than direct.
3. The local bodies must be endowed with adequate financial resources to carry out their functions.
4. Local self government personnel should operate under the administrative control by the local bodies.
5. The resolution of 1882 should be interpreted by the provincial governments according to the local conditions prevalent in the provinces.

In this context, Surendra Nath Banerjea's comment in 1982 may be recalled. He said: "I regard the concession of local self government is the prelude, the precursor of national (may I venture to hope?) of imperial self-government."[7] This resolution led to the passage of new Acts in various provinces.

It is interesting to find that today the term 'self government' has lost its significance since, as a result of independence, the country enjoys self government both at the central and State levels. Hence, in the Indian Constitution the term used is 'local government'. Again, as there are local bodies like the New Delhi Municipal Committee which are not representative in character, the use of the term 'local self government' will not be entirely correct. The term 'self-government', as scholars opine, may appear embarrassing as well, for it has around itself a ring of virtue, which it is unnecessary to claim and, on occasions, difficult to justify.[8] The term 'local government', being amoral in nature, is therefore preferred to virtue-embodied 'local self government' in the context of post-1947 Indian administration.

6.3.2 Constitutional Status of Local Government in India

The Indian Constitution nowhere defines 'local government'. By local government, the Seventh Schedule (List II, item 5) means the Constitution and powers of municipal corporations, improvement trusts, district boards, mining settlement authorities and other local authorities for the purpose of local self government and village administration. But this illustrates only the types of local bodies existing during the enactment of the Constitution. Besides, this illustration places both the nominated bodies and the elected ones on the same footing, which is simply unacceptable.

Thus viewed, local government in India till 1993 rested on the discretion of the States. Thus, it lacked a right to exist in its own right. The 73rd Constitutional Amendment Act (1993) removed these lacunas. Article 243 of the Constitution defines gram sabha, panchayat, zilla parishad, etc. It refers to the powers of the gram sabha, constitution of panchayats, reservation of seats, duration of panchayats, constitution of Finance Commission, audits and accounts of panchayats, etc. The Constitution has now another schedule, namely the Eleventh Schedule. Part IX of our Constitution, added in 1992, covers structural, organizational, functional and financial aspects of the panchayati raj. The State Legislatures have been empowered to enact laws:

1. to authorize a panchayat to levy, collect and appropriate certain types of taxes, duties, tolls and fees;
2. to assign to a panchayat certain types of taxes, duties, tolls levied and collected by the State Government;
3. to provide for making grants-in-aid to the panchayats from the Consolidated Fund of the States; and
4. to provide for the constitution of such funds for panchayats for crediting all money received by panchayats and also withdrawal of such money from there.

Local self government in India—both rural and urban—achieves the constitutional status since 1993 when the 73rd and 74th Constitutional Amendment Acts were passed (1992) and became operative within a year. This is a unique feature in India since most countries are content with their systems of local governments being governed by statutory laws. India is the fifth country in the world to have enshrined the local government in its Constitution itself, the other countries being Germany, Japan, Brazil and Nigeria. The constitutional recognition of local governments in Germany and Japan was forced on them by the Allied Powers. One must also note that the Draft European Charter of Local Self Government (1982) prepared for the adoption by the member States of the Council of Europe provides for adequate legal protection.

6.4 URBAN LOCAL SELF GOVERNMENT IN INDIA

Urbanization in India is by no means an entirely new or abrupt occurrence. The trend towards urbanization has been evident for a fairly long time which is clear from Table 6.1 enumerating the urban and the rural population of the country since 1901.

Table 6.1 Percentage of Rural and Urban Population

	1901	*1911*	*1921*	*1931*	*1941*	*1951*	*1961*	*1971*	*1981*	*1991*	*2001*
Urban	11	10.40	11.2	12.0	13.9	17.3	18.0	19.9	23.34	25.72	27.8
Rural	89	89.60	88.8	88.0	86.1	82.7	82.0	80.1	76.27	74.28	72.2

This growing trend of urbanization is an inevitable outcome of industrialization, to which we are firmly committed, and also of the general neglect of rural areas. The role and significance of the urban government, as a result, is bound to increase. Urbanization is an integral part of the process of development as it is conceived today. Industrialization and urbanization have become inseparable. Just as a result of the growth of agriculture, villages are developed, so also industry encourages the growth of towns.

Urbanization stands for and strengthens a system of economy that is absolutely different from that prevalent in the villages. A shift from rural to urban society brings about changes not only in the economic structure but also in the social and cultural set-up. The vastness of a city may create a feeling of psychological insecurity. A number of migrators are not biologically or temperamentally fit to bear the stresses and strains of the city. A city offers facilities for education, literacy, occupation, cultural activities, etc. On the other hand, it creates problems to a large number of neourbanites–persons who have recently migrated to the city, bringing with them their rural culture and outlook. All these demand safe and sympathetic handling of the urbanites by the urban local government.

Urban local government in India includes *municipal corporations, municipalities* and *nagar panchayats*. Existing *notified area committees* and *town area committees* have now become the nagar panchayats. In order to be labelled as an urban area, the following criteria have been laid down in the 1991 census:

1. All stuatory towns, i.e. all places with a *corporation, municipality, cantonment, township, notified area committee, town area committee*, etc.
2. All other places which meet the following criteria:
   (a) a minimum population of 5,000
   (b) 75 per cent of the male working population engaged in non-agricultural activity
   (c) a density of population of at least 400 per sq. km.

The number of urban local governments has been increasing in India as a result of an enormous increase in urban and suburban population. The various forms of urban local governmental bodies in India at present are:

1. Municipal corporations
2. Municipal councils or municipalities
3. Notified area committees
4. Town area committees
5. Cantonment boards
6. Townships

The last four categories now fall under the broad category of Nagar Panchayats (as a result of the 74th Constitutional Amendment Act).

The above categories are being described in the following sections.

6.4.1 Municipal Corporation

The municipal corporation is the topmost body of the urban local government, not in the sense that it exercises control over other forms of urban government. Unlike rural local government, urban local government in India is not hierarchical. The municipal corporation as an urban local body is more respectable and enjoys a greater extent of autonomy than other forms of urban local government.

A municipal corporation is set up under a special statute passed by the State Legislature. If it is to be set up in the Union Territory, the special statute is to be passed by the Union Parliament. Bombay, Madras and Calcutta corporations owe their existence to a special legislation. But municipal corporations in KAVAL towns[9] in Uttar Pradesh and GIRJ towns[10] in Madhya Pradesh have been set up under the UP Mahapalika Adhiniyam, 1959, and the MP Municipal Corporation Act, 1956, respectively.

The oldest municipal corporations in the country, namely Bombay, Madras and Calcutta corporations, had been conferred immunity from supersession, for the legislation did not provide for their dissolution. The municipal corporations set up subsequently, however, do not enjoy protection from dissolution. Thus, from the point of view of State control and supervision, the latter are not significantly different from other forms of local self government.

Although municipal corporations in India vary both in population and revenue, they all share some characteristics in common, which are as follows:

1. A corporation is set up only by a statute passed by the State Legislative Assembly.
2. A corporation normally follows the principle of separation of deliberative (legislative) from executive functions.
3. The Mayor is the head of the corporation and holds office for a fixed period of time. The office of the Mayor is ceremonial in nature.
4. The State Government retains powers of control and supervision over the corporation and subsequently it can even take over the administration of the corporation.

Functions of the municipal corporations all over India can be divided into two broad categories: (a) obligatory functions and (b) discretionary functions.

Obligatory functions

1. Supply of wholesome water and construction and maintenance of waterworks
2. Supply of electricity
3. Road transport services

4. Construction, maintenance, naming and numbering of public streets
5. Lighting, watering and cleansing of public streets and other public places
6. Scavenging, removal and disposal of filth and rubbish
7. Construction, maintenance and cleansing of drains and drainage works and of public latrines, urinals, etc.
8. Securing or removal of dangerous buildings and places
9. Removal of obstructions and projections in or upon streets and other public places
10. Establishment and maintenance of hospitals, maternity and child welfare centres
11. Measures for prevention and checking of dangerous diseases
12. Vaccination and inoculation
13. Registration of births and deaths
14. Regulation of places for the disposal of the dead and provision of places for this purpose
15. Provision of primary education
16. Maintenance of fire brigade
17. Publication of annual reports and returns on administration of the corporation
18. Control and regulation of eating places and eatables.

Discretionary functions

1. Construction of public parks, gardens, libraries, museums, theatres, *akharas* (gyms) and stadiums.
2. Public housing
3. Planting and taking care of trees on roadsides and elsewhere
4. Relief of destitute and disabled persons
5. Destruction or detention of ownerless dogs or stray pigs or detention of animals causing nuisance
6. Playing of music for people
7. Civic reception of VIPs
8. Registration of marriages
9. Survey of buildings and lands
10. Organization and management of fairs and exhibitions.

Sources of income

Sources of income of municipal corporations may be grouped under two heads: (a) tax revenue and (b) non-tax revenue. The non-tax revenue includes fees and fines as well as grants and contributions from the government.

Generally speaking, a corporation is empowered to levy the following taxes:

1. Property tax
2. Tax on vehicles and animals
3. Theatre tax
4. Tax on advertisements (other than newspapers)
5. Profession tax
6. Education tax
7. Entertainment tax
8. Tax on consumption and sale of electricity
9. Betterment tax on increase in urban land values caused by the execution of any development or improvement work.

Again, tax on deeds of transfer of any immovable property is collected by the State Government, and the amount collected within the area under the jurisdiction of a corporation is transferred to it.

Council

Although the council is only a part of the municipal corporation, yet the term 'corporation' has almost become a substitute for council. This is broadly indicative of the pervasive character of the council. The council is basically the local legislative assembly, articulating popular wish that is transformed into the law of the town.

The council comprises members, called *councillors*, who are elected on adult franchise for a term varying from three to five years. For purposes of election, the town is divided into as many wards as there are number of seats in the council. A term of three years for the council is considered by many to be rather short. As the council is the legislative assembly of the corporation, it must have a reasonably long tenure so as to be able to implement its policies and to produce their impact. Again, elections held at short intervals tend to keep alive political feuds and may thus obstruct the way of smooth functioning of civil administration. Therefore, the life of the council of the corporation should be fixed at five years, which is also the life of the State Legislative Assembly and the Parliament.

Mayor

The Mayor of the corporation is the first citizen of the city. He presides over the meetings of the council of the corporation. He is elected by the councillors including aldermen from among themselves for a term of one year, which is renewable. In KAVAL towns, the Mayor need not be a member of the council. The Mayor exercises administrative control over the secretariat of the council. In some cities like Delhi, he has access to all records of the corporation and can ask for information from the

Municipal Commissioner on any matter connected with the municipal administration of the city. Again, there are some statutes which specifically empower him to direct, in cases of emergency, execution or stoppage of any work or any act.

Those who are in favour of strengthening of the office of the Mayor view that the Mayor should emerge as the leader of a self-governing, self-respecting community. With this view in mind, the following suggestions are being made:

1. The term of the Mayor should be made co-terminous with that of the council. Provision should also be made for his removal from office by a special majority vote of the council.
2. The Mayor should be consulted by the State Government in the appointment of the Corporation Commissioner.
3. The character-roll of the Commissioner should be written by the Mayor.
4. All official correspondence between the corporation and the State Government should be conducted through the Mayor.
5. The Mayor should be assigned a place next below that of the Speaker of the State Legislative Assembly.
6. The Mayor along with the Chairman of the various committees should constitute an appellate tribunal to hear appeals against the decisions of the Municipal Commissioner.

Municipal Commissioner

The Municipal Commissioner is the Chief Executive Officer of the corporation. He discharges all the duties imposed upon him under the Act and, in times of emergency, may take any action he thinks necessary. The institution of Commissioner is based on the philosophy of keeping policy-making function separate from its administration. The Commissioner is a professional, high-ranking administrator, and he is appointed by the State Government to administer the city. However, he gets his salary from the corporation. The Commissioner has been a regular civil servant who is appointed for a fixed term ranging from three to five years. He is appointed by the State Government in consultation with the Mayor and, at some places, in consultation with the State Public Service Corporation. The Commissioner may be withdrawn at any time. He is normally a senior member of superior civil service–from IAS.

The Commissioner's appointment vesting in the State Government has been the subject of endless heated controversy in India. William A. Robson denounces such a system of civic administration. He writes: "The regime in Bombay provides for executive power to be concentrated in the Municipal Commissioner, an official appointed by the State Government.... We cannot regard Bombay as fulfilling the essential conditions to qualify as a self-governing city;.... In Calcutta a similar system is in existence.... It is a disturbing fact.... How comes it that in these vast metropolitan cities...the democratic spirit burns at so low an ebb that the aspiration to govern itself...has not been achieved?... without successful self-government in the local sphere, a country is unlikely to attain a satisfactory level of self-government at the national level."[11]

The responsibility for the preparation of the corporation budget rests with the Commissioner. Fresh tax proposals are in practice initiated only by him. Besides, after the budget has been voted by the council, the Commissioner has to come to the standing committees to transfer amounts from one minor head to another within the budget grant.

The Commissioner is also the Chief Executive Officer of the corporation. He has the power to speak at the meetings of the council and in its committees without the right to vote. All municipal employees are subject to his supervision and control, although in matters of appointment, promotion and discipline, he shares his authority with the council and its standing committees. This practice weakens the position of the Commissioner vis-à-vis the municipal personnel.

6.4.1.1 Kolkata Municipal Corporation (KMC)

Kolkata Municipal Corporation or KMC, which was formerly known as Calcutta Municipal Corporation or CMC, is principally responsible for the civic infrastructure and overall administration of the capital city of West Bengal, namely Kolkata. It administers an area of 200.71 square kilometres.[12] Its main aim, which is clearly inscribed on its emblem in Bengali script, is *Puroshree Bibardhan*, meaning to enhance the beauty of this city. Mr. Sovan Chatterjee, as the present Mayor of Kolkata, is at the apex of the KMC.

The KMC is a very old body—almost a century and a half years old, for it was established in the year 1876. The Calcutta Municipal Act of 1923 was passed under the guidance of Surendranath Banerjee, the first Minister of Local Self Government in Bengal. This Act made provision for the enfranchisement of women and the annual election of a Mayor. Accordingly, the first Mayor of KMC was Chittaranjan Das while Niyaz Ahamed was his Chief Executive Officer. Later, Jatindra Mohan Sengupta, Bidhan Chandra Roy, Nalini Ranjan Sarkar, Abul Kasem Fazlul Haque etc. became Mayors of this body. Mr. Sovan Chatterjee is the present Mayor of two consecutive terms, viz., 2010–15 and 2015–20.

The city of Kolkata is divided into 144 administrative wards which are grouped into 15 boroughs. Each of the wards has an elected Councilor to the KMC. Each borough has a committee, known as Borough Committee, that consists of the Councilors elected from the respective wards of the boroughs. Through these Borough Committees the KMC performs a number of functions like maintenance of government-aided schools, hospitals and municipal markets properly, dealing with urban planning, road maintenance etc. The KMC, as the highest body of civic administration, performs its functions through the Mayor-in-Council that consists of a Mayor, a Deputy Mayor (who is supposed to assist the Mayor) and ten other elected members of KMC (who also follow the Deputy Mayor in assisting the Mayor). The person who is usually responsible and answerable for the overall functioning of the KMC is the Mayor who is always an elected person, having a tenure of five years. He may serve more than one full term, as willed by the Chief Minister of the State or as determined by the Party.

The jurisdiction of the KMC covers the area of Kolkata district that is fully covered by the Kolkata Police. But the KMC includes an adjacent area as well. In fact, four administrative definitions of the city of Kolkata are available which are as under:

1. Kolkata District
2. The Kolkata Police area and the Kolkata Municipal area (which together constitute the city of Kolkata or "Kolkata City".
3. "Greater Kolkata", which adds to the KMC area a few other areas quite adjacent to it.
4. The Kolkata Metropolitan area.

The area within which the KMC functions also has the following authorities involved in administration:

- The KMC itself
- The Kolkata Collector
- The Kolkata Police
- The DM of South 24 Parganas district

"City" in relation to Kolkata is not an official term. When this term is used, it usually refers to the KMC area.

According to KMC website, erstwhile Joka I and Joka II Gram Panchayats were added to the municipal limits of Kolkata. As a result of such additions, the KMC area has been increased to 200.71 square kilometres or 77.49 square miles. However, Kolkata Police area and KMC area were declared to be coterminous in 2011. Kolkata Postal District extends up to Barrackpur in the North, Barasat in the East, Joka in the South, Baruipur in the South–East and Batanagar in the South–West. Thus, Kolkata Postal area is bigger than the KMC area.

*According to Section 29 of the KMC Act, the KMC has the following obligatory functions:

1. Supply of drinking water in the KMC area
2. Cleaning and removal of filth, rubbish and other obnoxious matters

* Broadly speaking, the functions of the KMC can be divided into two categories: (a) Obligatory and (b) Discretionary.

3. Laying and maintaining Public Streets
4. Providing public lighting
5. Providing sewerage and drainage in the KMC area
6. Naming and numbering of streets and premises
7. Planting of trees on roadsides and elsewhere
8. Laying out or maintaining public parks, gardens or recreation grounds
9. Health and welfare functions
10. Regulation of trade through licensing
11. Providing municipal markets and slaughter-houses
12. Maintaining heritage monuments
13. Record keeping and maintaining statistics
14. Providing by itself or by an agency, means of supply of water for fire-fighting.

According to Section 30 of the KMC Act, the KMC has the following discretionary functions:

1. Furtherance of education
2. Establishment and maintenance of libraries, museums, zoological collections
3. Survey of buildings and lands
4. Providing music and entertainment in public places or public resorts
5. Organisation and management of fairs and exhibitions
6. Acquisition of movable and immovable property for purpose mentioned before
7. Construction of rest house, poor house, infirmaries, children homes, house of deaf and dumb and disabled persons
8. Construction and maintenance of cattle ponds
9. Purchase, construction and maintenance of house for KMC employees
10. Welfare of KMC employees
11. Establishment and maintenance of hospitals and dispensaries
12. Provision of swimming pools, bathing places and other institutions for improvement of community health
13. Construction and maintenance of warehouses, garage sheds and cattle biers
14. Provision of housing accommodation for inhabitants
15. Taking any measure to promote public safety, health and sanitation.

From these 14 obligatory and 15 discretionary functions of the KMC, it is evident that the body provides the following fundamental services to its inhabitants:

- Water Works and Water Supply
- Drainage and Sewerage
- Street Lighting and Electricals
- Roads and Pathways
- Parks and Gardens
- Land Use Control and Building
- Solid Waste Management
- Preventive and Curative Health Care
- Town Planning and Architecture
- Survey and Record
- Municipal Markets
- Improvement of Slums
- Primary Education
- Information and Public Relations

The Calcutta Municipal Corporation Act 1980 came into force in January, 1984. It extended the boundaries of Calcutta by including the Municipalities of South Suburban, Garden Reach and Jadavpur within Calcutta. The number of wards of the Corporation was increased from 100 to 141. The provisions relating to *Bustees* or slums were modified.

In 1984 a major amendment was introduced to remove certain procedural difficulties in the matters of assessment and valuation of lands and buildings, recovery of taxes, etc. Most important amendment was the introduction of "Mayor-in-Council", with all the attributes of the Cabinet form of Government. In the sphere of Municipal administration of India this was undoubtedly a unique step.

The objective of the new Act was basically to make the Corporation more efficient and effective. As a result of the change in the Municipal authority, there appeared three clear authorities, namely:

- The Corporation
- The Mayor-in-Council, and
- The Mayor

The number of wards become 141 with same number of elected Councillors. But after amalgamation of Joka I and Joka II Gram Panchayats, the number of wards under the KMC became 144 with same number of elected Councillors.

The Mayor and the Chairman would be elected by the members who would hold office for 5 years.

The Act of 1980 formed the framework of the modern Corporation with the Municipal Commissioner as the Principal Executive Officer, subject to the control and supervision of the Mayor as the Chief Executive Officer. The Municipal Commissioner is assisted by a group of senior civil officers comprising Joint Municipal Commissioners, Deputy

Municipal Commissioners, Chief Engineers, Controller of Municipal Finance and Accounts, Chief Municipal Auditor and Municipal Secretary.

The 74th Constitutional Amendment, 1992 makes provision for appropriate and adequate representation of all elements of society. It provided reservation of seats for the scheduled castes and tribes and also for women. The same Amendment enabled the State Legislatures to endow the CMC with the power to draw up plans for economic development and social justice. The CMC was also given the prestigious responsibility to plan for economic development and also for improvement, upgradation and promotion of the social, cultural, educational and aesthetic aspects of life for the citizens residing in the city.

The city of Calcutta was renamed as that of Kolkata in 2001 and subsequently the Corporation also changed its name from Calcutta Municipal Corporation (CMC) to Kolkata Municipal Corporation (KMC).

6.4.2 Municipal Council or Municipality

The municipal council kind of urban local government in India is meant exclusively for cities where the provision for civic amenities to the city dwellers becomes pressing but, at the same time, the civic problems have not grown too complex which need to be handled by a municipal corporation.

The functions of municipal committees are generally classified as *obligatory* and *discretionary*.

Obligatory functions are those which must be performed by the municipal council and failure to perform any of these functions will ultimately result in its dissolution. The main obligatory functions of municipal councils are as follows:

1. Supply of pure and wholesome water
2. Construction and maintenance of public streets
3. Lighting and watering public streets
4. Cleansing public streets, places and sewers
5. Regulation of offensive, dangerous or obnoxious trades, callings or practices
6. Maintenance or support of public hospitals
7. Establishment and maintenance of primary schools
8. Registration of births and deaths
9. Removing obstructions and projections in public streets, bridges and other public places
10. Naming streets and numbering houses.

Discretionary functions are those which are not compulsory but may be taken up depending upon the financial resources of the municipality. The major discretionary functions of municipal councils are as under:

1. Laying out of areas
2. Securing or removing dangerous buildings or places
3. Construction and maintenance of public parks, gardens, libraries, museums, rest houses, leper homes, orphanages and rescue homes for women, etc.
4. Planting and maintenance of roadside and other trees
5. Housing for low income groups
6. Making a survey
7. Organizing public receptions, public exhibitions, public entertainment, etc.
8. Provision of transport facilities within the municipality
9. Promotion of welfare of municipal employees
10. Providing music for the people.

It may be noted that the functions of a municipality and those of a municipal corporation are more or less identical.

The sources of municipal revenue are: (a) municipal taxes, (b) fees and rates, (c) income from municipal enterprises and property, and (d) grants and contributions from the Central and State Governments. The principal sources of municipal income are:

1. Property tax
2. Profession tax
3. Octroi
4. Animal and vehicle tax
5. Entertainment tax
6. Water tax
7. Lighting tax
8. Latrines and drainage tax
9. Grants from Central and State Governments.

The municipal council is the people's assembly and makes laws, known as bye-laws, within the framework of the municipal Act, for the civic governance of the city or town. It comprises councillors elected on adult suffrage. There is generally a provision for reservation of seats for scheduled castes and women. The size of the council varies from State to State and, since it is primarily related to the population of the city, it differs from city to city within the same State. The municipal Act prescribes both the maximum and minimum numbers of councillors. The tenure of the municipal council varies from three to five years, although the recent trend is in favour of a term of four or even five years. The Rural-Urban Relationship Committee has considered three years "to be too short a period" and recommended a term of five years.

From among its councillors, the municipal council elects a President whose term is co-terminous with that of the council itself. There have been two methods of electing the President. He may either be elected by the councillors or by the people at large. While the corporation form of local government is based on the philosophy of separation between deliberative (legislative) and executive functions, the municipal council form of urban local government was modelled differently and was founded on the fusion of these two types of functions. Thus, in sharp contrast with the ceremonial office of the corporation Mayor, the President of the municipal council is vested with both executive and deliberative authority. As a result, he is the head of the executive as well as the deliberative wing of the municipality. He presides over and regulates the council meetings, exercises control over the financial, administrative and personnel matters, and addresses the State Government on municipal matters. In many States he is empowered, in case of emergency, to direct or suspend the execution of any work. In Orissa, he is authorized to take disciplinary action (including the right to dismiss) against the municipal personnel. In Gujarat, he acts as the appellate authority hearing appeals against the orders of the executive officer pertaining to disciplinary action against the employees. In West Bengal, he exercises supervisory control over all municipal matters, except those delegated to the executive officer. In many other states like Uttar Pradesh, Andhra Pradesh, Rajasthan and Jammu and Kashmir, the President and the executive officer both share the power of appointment of the staff.

The municipal Act provides for the setting up of a standing committee and other committees to assist the municipality in performing its functions efficiently. What has been said about the committees of corporations holds good in the case of the committees of the municipalities as well. There is also a provision for the council appointing as members of any committee those persons who are not councillors but who possess special qualifications for serving on such committees, or who represent an authority or interest.

6.4.3 Notified Area Committee

Notified area committees, numbering more than 200, are existing in Bihar, Gujarat, Haryana, Madhya Pradesh, Karnataka, Punjab, Jammu and Kashmir, Uttar Pradesh and Himachal Pradesh. A notified area committee is created for an area which does not yet fulfil all the conditions laid down as necessary for the constitution of a municipality but which otherwise is considered important. It is also constituted for a newly developing town. The formation of this committee is notified by the State Government in the government Gazette. Hence, it is called *notified area committee*. The committee functions within the framework of the municipal Act of the State; but only such provisions of the municipal Act apply to it as are notified in the government Gazette. The State Government may also entrust to it powers exercisable under any other Act. The notified area committee enjoys all the powers of the municipal council; but unlike the council, its members, including the Chairman, are nominated by the State Government. Thus, it is an absolutely nominated body.

6.4.4 Town Area Committee

Over 385 in number and meant for small towns, the town area committees have been created in Assam, Kerala, Madhya Pradesh, Uttar Pradesh, West Bengal, Jammu and Kashmir and Himachal Pradesh. This form of urban local government is significantly noticed in Uttar Pradesh which alone accounts for eighty per cent of the total number of town areas committees in our country. Town area committees are governed by separate Acts passed by the State Government. But in Assam, they function under the provisions of the Assam Municipal Act, 1956. The District Collector has been given greater control and powers of supervision over a town area committee. Members of the town area committee are elected or nominated by the State Government, or partly elected and partly nominated. The town area committee is assigned a limited number of functions like street lighting, drainage, conservancy, etc.

The fate of the town area committee kind of urban local government is today in a state of flux, due to the establishment of the panchayati raj institutions in rural India. There is a noticeable trend in favour of making town area committees a part of the rural government. Gujarat has set up nagar panchayats and Karnataka and Tamil Nadu town panchayats, in place of town area committees.

6.4.5 Cantonment Board

Cantonment board of urban government is, indeed, unique and, with the exception of Pakistan and Bangladesh, without parallel in the world. The cantonments are centrally administered areas, being placed under the direct administrative control of the Ministry of Defence in the Central Government in sharp contrast with other forms of local government which are under the control of the State Government. The areas covered under cantonments were acquired in different ways: (a) under treaties with the princes, (b) through downright purchase and (c) by conquest. The two important features of this form of urban local government are: (a) the strong control of the military and the Ministry of Defence over the municipal administration of the cantonment and (b) the severely restricted role allowed to the elective element.

The existing cantonments in India have been grouped into three classes:

1. Class I cantonments in which the civil population exceeds 10,000.

2. Class II cantonments in which the civil population is between 2,500 and 10,000.
3. Class III cantonments in which the civil population is less than 2,500.

The cantonment board (Class I) consists of the following members:

1. The officer commanding the station
2. A first class Magistrate nominated by the District Collector.
3. Health officer in the cantonment
4. Executive engineer in the cantonment
5. Four military officers nominated by the officer commanding the station
6. Seven members elected by the people.

Thus, it is seen that the ratio between the nominated members and the elected ones is 8:7.

The functions entrusted to the cantonment board are classified into obligatory and discretionary.

Obligatory functions

1. Lighting streets and other public places
2. Watering streets and other public places
3. Cleansing streets, drains and other public places
4. Regulating offensive or dangerous trades, callings and practices
5. Removing on the ground of public safety, health or convenience, undesirable obstructions and projections in streets and other places
6. Securing or removing dangerous buildings and places
7. Maintaining and regulating places for the disposal of the dead
8. Constructing and maintaining streets, culverts, markets, slaughter houses, drainage works, drains and sewerage works
9. Planting and maintaining trees on roadsides
10. Supply of pure and wholesome water
11. Registering births and deaths
12. Public vaccination and establishment of public hospitals
13. Establishment of primary schools
14. Protection against fire.

Discretionary functions

1. Construction of public works, tanks, wells, etc.
2. Reclaiming unhealthy localities
3. Taking census
4. Making a survey

5. Relief measures on occurrence of local epidemics
6. Provision of electricity
7. Provision of public transport system.

The income of the cantonment board may be grouped under (a) tax revenue and (b) non-tax revenue. The taxation power of the board is analogous to that of any other ordinary municipality.

There are some changes which aim at strengthening the position of the elective element of the board including its Vice-President. The changes are as under:

1. Parity had been introduced in the strength of the elected and nominated members in all Class I and Class II cantonment boards. Class III cantonment boards have only one elected and one nominated members each.
2. The powers of the civil area committee with regard to control over buildings, boundary walls, issue of trade licenses, etc. have been enlarged.
3. The assessment committee dealing with assessment of house tax has a majority of the elected members.
4. The Vice-President of the board presides over the meeting of the board during the absence of the officer commanding the station.

The cantonment form of urban government, observes S.R. Maheshwari in *Local Government in India,* has come under severe attack from many quarters. As most cantonments are located alongside big cities, the existence of two forms of local government in such proximity is considered by many as unnecessary, wasteful and confusing. Many critics would not feel satisfied with any reform short of its complete amalgamation with a municipal corporation or a municipality. The Rural-Urban Relationship Committee, for example, voiced an opinion and a hope that "the continued existence of cantonments as separate entities is anomalous and they will, in the long run, become part of the neighbouring municipal bodies."[13]

6.4.6 Township

The townships have been established in India either in rural areas or in areas adjacent to existing towns. The Rural-Urban Relationship Committee classified them into three categories: (a) single industry townships like Rourkela, Bhilai and Jamshedpur; (b) townships having an industrial complex such as Durgapur; and (c) small townships like Heavy Electricals Ltd., near the city of Bhopal.

Townships have certain common features which are as under:

1. These townships, unlike other cities, are entirely planned.
2. They all maintain civic services like water, electricity, roads, sewage, etc. and other facilities like medical, educational,

shopping, clubs, community centres, auditoriums, playgrounds and parks, which are of a sufficiently high level.

3. These services and facilities have been financed by the industry.
4. A township has a variety of employment and other opportunities to offer to the people.
5. A township gives birth to a rapid but unsystematic development of the adjoining area, establishing growing interdependence between the two. Thus, very soon satellite townships are developed around the main township. Jamshedpur, for example, has led to the emergence of the towns of Jugsalai and Adityapur.
6. The company township has been resisting attempts at the merger of the adjoining areas with itself as it fears that such a merger would add to the financial and administrative burden of the industry, thereby adversely affecting the interests of the industry.

The township form of local government is treated as a normal administrative task of the company. Public undertakings have set up elaborate organizations for the administration of their townships. Certain undertakings (like Hindustan Steel, Hindustan Machine Tools, etc.) have appointed town administrators assisted by departmental head for allotment, maintenance, horticulture, etc. Some (like Fertilizer Corporation of India, Heavy Electricals, etc.) have appointed administrative officers or estate officers, assisted by engineers and other staff.[14]

The township administration came under the examination of the Rural-Urban Relationship Committee. It expressed its belief that in the long run, the company townships, now functioning as estates, would have to form part of the democratic set-up. It has also recommended that the residents of a small township in close proximity to a major city like Bangalore or Bhopal have been deprived of any participation in the civic administration of their township.

6.5 SEVENTY-FOURTH CONSTITUTIONAL AMENDMENT

When the Narasimha Rao government took charge in 1991, it introduced a Constitution Amendment Bill pertaining to municipalities in the Lok Sabha on 16 September 1991. With a few modifications, it was essentially based on the 65th Amendment Bill. It was passed by both the Houses in December 1992. The Bill has since then been ratified by a resolution of at least half the number of State Legislatures. It received the assent of the President on 20 April 1993 and was published in the Gazette on the same day as the Constitution 74th Amendment Act, 1992.

So far, in the urban areas of India, six principal types of local government existed, namely Municipal Corporations, Municipal

Councils or Municipalities, Notified Area Committees, Town Area Committees, Cantonment Boards and Townships. As a result of the 74th Constitutional Amendment Act, the last four categories now fall under the broad category of Nagar Panchayats. Now the three principal types of local government in urban India are: Municipal Corporations, Municipal Councils or Municipalities and Nagar Panchayats. At present, there are more or less 3600 Municipal Corporations in India. The number of Municipal Councils and Nagar Panchayats in all is around 70,000.[15]

Nagar Panchayats exist in semi-urban, semi-rural areas. These areas have basically rural character; but they have adopted the urban features gradually through a number of years. This type of local government works for both rural and urban population. In a number of States, Nagar Panchayats exist quite successfully.

There are Municipal Councils or Municipalities for the small urban areas or suburbs. But the size of the Municipalities and consequently the size of the population covered by them vary from State to State. This is determined entirely by the government of the state concerned.

The township of some urban areas has such a big size that a number of big industries are developed there. In such large urban areas, Municipal Corporations instead of Municipalities exist.

All States amended the municipalities and corporation Acts in 1994 to give effect to the 74th Constitution Amendment Act. Some State Governments have further amended the laws from time to time to meet the emerging political, legal and administrative problems. The status of municipal legislation in some of the Indian States is as follows:

Andhra Pradesh

There were two municipal laws in the State prior to the 74th Constitution Amendment. They were:

1. Andhra Pradesh Municipalities Act, 1965
2. Hyderabad Municipal Corporations Act, 1955 (governing Hyderabad, Vishakhapatnam and Vijayawada Municipal Corporations).

In accordance with the 74th Constitution Amendment, two Acts were passed: (a) Andhra Pradesh Municipal Act, 1994 and (b) Andhra Pradesh Municipal (Second Amendment) Act, 1994. Both the Acts became effective from June 1994.

Again, a new Act—Andhra Pradesh Municipal Corporations Act, 1994—was passed in the same year. It became effective from July 1994.

Gujarat

Before the 74th Constitution Amendment, there were the following two main municipal laws in Gujarat:

1. Gujarat Municipalities Act, 1963
2. Bombay Provincial Municipal Corporation Act, 1949.

Remaining more or less consistent with the 74th Constitution Amendment, the two above laws were amended in the State, as (a) Gujarat Municipalities (Amendments) Act, 1993 and (b) Bombay Provincial Municipal Corporations (Gujarat Second Amendment) Act, 1993. Both the amended Acts were effective from August, 1993.

Haryana

Prior to the 74th Constitution Amendment, there was only one municipal Act in Haryana, viz. the Haryana Municipal Act, 1973. After 1992, this Act was amended as Haryana Municipal (Amendment) Act, 1994. A new Act was also enacted—the Haryana Municipal Corporations Act, 1994. Both these Acts became effective from May 1994.

Karnataka

There were the following two municipal Acts in the State prior to the 74th Constitution Amendment:

1. Karnataka Municipalities Act, 1964
2. Karnataka Municipal Corporations Act, 1976, governing all the municipal corporations in Karnataka.

These two Acts were amended in 1994 to give effect to the 74th Constitution Amendment in 1994. The amended Acts were: (a) The Karnataka Municipalities (Amendment) Act, 1994 and (b) The Karnataka Municipal Corporations (Amendment) Act, 1994.

Both the above Acts became effective from June 1994.

Kerala

Prior to the 74th Constitution Amendment, there were two municipal Acts in Kerala. They were:

1. Kerala Municipalities Act, 1960
2. Kerala Municipal Corporations Act, 1961.

In conformity with the 74th Constitution Amendment, these two Acts were united and a new Act—Kerala Municipality Act, 1994—was enacted. The new Act became effective from June 1994.

Madhya Pradesh

Two municipal Acts—Madhya Pradesh Municipal Corporation Act, 1956 and Madhya Pradesh Municipalities Act, 1961—existed in Madhya Pradesh prior to the 74th Constitution Amendment. In accordance with the provisions of the 74th Constitution Amendment, these two Acts were amended as (a) Madhya Pradesh Municipal Corporation (Amendment) Act, 1994 and (b) Madhya Pradesh Municipalities (Amendment) Act, 1994. These two Acts became effective from May 1994.

Maharashtra

Just before the constitutional amendment in 1994, there were the following four municipal Acts in Maharasthra:

1. Bombay Municipal Corporation Act, 1888
2. City of Nagpur Corporation Act, 1948
3. Bombay Provincial Municipal Corporation Act, 1949
4. Maharashtra Municipal Councils, Nagar Panchayats and Industrial Township Act, 1965.

These four Acts were combined and in accordance with the 74th Constitution Amendment, a new Act—Maharashtra Municipal Corporations and Municipal Councils (Amendment) Act, 1994—was passed. This Act became effective from May 1994.

Punjab

Prior to the 74th Constitution Amendment, there were the following two municipal Acts in Punjab:

1. Punjab Municipal Act, 1911
2. Punjab Municipal Corporation Act, 1976.

These two Acts were amended to give effect to the provisions of the 74th Constitution Amendment. The new amended Acts are:

1. Punjab Municipal (Amendment) Act, 1994
2. Punjab Municipal Corporation (Amendment) Act, 1994.

These two amended Acts became effective from May 1994. In 1999, these two Acts were combined to form one unified Act—The Punjab Municipal Act, 1999.

Rajasthan

Prior to the Constitutional Amendment (1994), there was only one municipal Act in Rajasthan, viz. The Rajasthan Municipalities Act, 1959. In accordance with the provisions of the 74th Constitution Amendment, the said Act was amended as the Rajasthan Municipalities (Second Amendment) Act, 1994, which became effective from May 1994.

Tamil Nadu

Till the 74th Constitution Amendment, the following four municipal Acts existed in Tamil Nadu:

1. Tamil Nadu District Municipalities Act, 1920
2. Madras City Municipal Corporation Act, 1919
3. Madurai City Municipal Corporation Act, 1971
4. Coimbatore City Municipal Corporation Act, 1981.

Keeping in mind the provisions of the 74th Constitution Amendment, the abovementioned four Acts were amended as the following two Acts: (a) Tamil Nadu District Municipalities (Amendment) Act, 1994 and (b) Tamil Nadu Municipal Corporation Laws (Amendment and Special Provision) Act, 1994.

In addition, three more new Acts related to municipal administration were enacted:

1. Tiruchirapalli City Municipal Corporation Act, 1994
2. Tirunelveli City Municipal Corporation Act, 1994
3. Salem City Municipal Corporation Act, 1994.

All the amended Acts came into effect from June 1994.

Later, a combined new municipal Act covering all aspects of urban governance was enacted. It was named as Tamil Nadu Urban Local Bodies Act, 1998, which replaced all the existing municipal laws of Tamil Nadu. This Act of 1998 became effective from August 2000.

Uttar Pradesh

The following three municipal Acts were effective in Uttar Pradesh immediately before the 74th Constitution Amendment:

1. United Provinces Municipalities Act, 1916
2. Uttar Pradesh Municipal Corporation Act, 1959
3. United Provinces Town Area Act, 1916.

Consistent with the 74th Constitution Amendment, one new Act–the Uttar Pradesh Local Self-Government Laws (Amendment) Act, 1994–was passed by the State Legislature. It came into force from May 1994.

West Bengal

Prior to the 74th Constitution Amendment, there were seven major municipal Acts in West Bengal. These were as under:

1. Calcutta Municipal Corporation Act, 1980
2. Howrah Municipal Corporation Act, 1980
3. Siliguri Municipal Corporation Act, 1990
4. Asansol Municipal Corporation Act, 1990
5. Chandernagore Municipal Act, 1955
6. Chandernagore Municipal Corporation Act, 1990
7. West Bengal Municipal Act, 1993.

The first six Acts were combined and amended as one unified Act–The West Bengal Municipal Corporation Laws (3rd Amendment) Act, 1994.

The seventh Act—West Bengal Municipal Act, 1993–was amended as the West Bengal Municipal Amendment Act, 1994. These amended Acts became effective from July 1994. Again, consistent with the 74th

Constitution Amendment, three new Acts were enacted that were as under:

1. Durgapur Municipal Corporation Act, 1994, which came into effect from October 1996.
2. West Bengal District Planning Committee Act, 1994, which was made effective from May 1994.
3. West Bengal Metropolitan Planning Committee Act, 1994, which became effective from June 1994.

The 74th Constitution Amendment Act introduces a new part, namely, Part IX A, in the Constitution. This part deals with issues relating to municipalities such as their structure and composition, reservation of seats, elections, powers and functions of the urban local bodies, their finances and some miscellaneous provisions. The 74th Constitution Amendment Act thus gives a constitutional status to the municipalities. The provisions of the Act apply to the States (as we have seen just now) as well as the Union Territories.

Questions

1. What is meant by local self government? What are its characteristic features? What are the necessary conditions for the success of the local self government?
2. What are the broad features of the British/US/French/Japanese local self government?
3. What are the major urban local self government institutions in India?
4. Discuss the various types of functions performed by the Municipal Corporation in India.
5. Write short notes on:
   (a) Mayor of Municipal Corporation
   (b) Municipal Commissioner
   (c) Cantonment Board
   (d) Township
   (e) 74th Constitutional Amendment.
6. Write a note on the Kolkata Municipal Corporation.

Notes and References

1. *Encyclopaedia of the Social Sciences*, Vol. IX–X, p. 584.
2. Bryce, James, *Modern Democracies*, Macmillan, New York, 1921.
3. Jenks, Edward, *An Outline of English Local Government,* Methuen & Co., London, 1925.

4. Mill, J.S., *Representative Government*, Everyman's Library Edition, London, 1957.
5. Laxmikanth, M., *Public Administration*, Tata McGraw-Hill, New Delhi, 2002.
6. *Ibid.*
7. Banerjea, Babu Surendranath, G.A. Nateson and Co., Madras, as cited in Bhattacharya, Mohit and Utpal Roy, *Indian Government and Politics*, Book Syndicate, Calcutta, August 1999.
8. Maheshwari, S.R., *Local Government in India*, Lakshmi Narain Agarwal, Agra, 2004.
9. 'KAVAL towns'—this phrase refers to Kanpur, Agra, Varanasi, Allahabad and Lucknow.
10. 'GIRJ towns'—this phrase refers to Gwalior, Indore, Raipur and Jabalpur.
11. Robson, William A., *Great Cities of the World*, George Allen and Unwin, London, 1954.
12. *Mayors of Kolkata*, KMC, May 8, 2015.
13. *Report of the Rural-Urban Relationship Committee,* Vol. I.
14. *Committee on Public Undertakings (Third Lok Sabha): Eighth Report on Townships and Factory Buildings of Public Undertakings,* Lok Sabha Secretariat, New Delhi, 1965.
15. Maheshwari, S.R., *op. cit.*

7 Local Self Government in India A Rural Picture

7.1 INTRODUCTION

Democratic decentralization is the main philosophy upon which the edifice of the Indian panchayati raj system stands. No democratic system can survive unless it takes some positive measures to satisfy the basic requirements of the little rural community through the local efforts of the people who are directly concerned. When local decisions are being taken locally, a sense of pride in one's own community and a sense of responsibility in public mind are increasingly developed.

In order to understand the philosophy of "democratic decentralization' as the base of the local self government in rural India, one should analyze the two terms 'democracy' and 'decentralization', respectively. Usually, 'democracy' implies the rule of the people, by the people and for the people. It means a belief in the benefits that can ensue from involving the polity at the lowest of levels in the process of their own governance. This is essentially the western concept of democracy which surely is regarded to be a positive step towards the introduction of universal adult suffrage. But according to the socialist thinkers, true democracy can never be established only through the introduction of universal adult suffrage. What really needed is people's active and direct participation in the political and socio-economic affairs of the State.[1] Lenin expounded democracy on a 'scientific'[2] level viewing it in the context of social relations. Lenin believed that so long as there are different social classes, there can be no pure democracy. What seemed to be really important to him was the actual participation in the management of the State by the majority of the population. Politics without masses is 'adventurous politics'.[3] Hence, the essence of democracy is administration by the grass-roots population.

On the other hand, 'decentralization' means dispersal of authority among a number of individuals or units. When the central authority in any complex and large-scale organization divests itself of certain powers which are subsequently given to the local units of the same organization and these units, as a result, become autonomous, organizational decentralization takes place. In the words of L.D. White, "The progress of transfer of administrative authority from a lower to a higher level of government is called 'centralization', the converse 'decentralization'".[4]

The combination of these two principles—democracy and decentralization—in the context of rural India means active participation of the Indian ruralites in the administration of their own areas. When the State operated as a mere polis state, the notion of popular participation in rural development had a narrow connotation. But with the emergence of the concepts like welfarism, socialism etc., the State has come to inspire and institutionalize a large number of activities covering the lives of its citizens. Thus, the conventional dichotomy between the State and its citizens was replaced by a relationship of complementarity. Popular participation in the decision-making process, having an autonomous character, came to be advocated as an important tenet of democratic decentralization. It would be wrong to combine popular participation to the western political ideology alone. Today both socialist and western philosophies advocate the need for politics to incorporate the individual as a political force.[5]

The most important context of popular participation in rural India, as identified in the plan document, was the Community Development Programme (CDP). Its specific operational mechanism was the establishment of (a) the village panchayat bodies and (b) the cooperatives. Community Development Programme thought of associating people with the following three stages—those of plan formulation, plan implementation and plan evaluation.

But unfortunately, by the end of the first plan period (1951–52 to 1955–56), it became evident that the disparity between the rich and the poor in rural India was increasing. The poor started thinking themselves to be helpless, and this thought alienated them from the ongoing process of planning. As a result, in the Second Plan Document (1956–57 to 1960–61) the anxious framers of this plan clearly pointed out that the benefits of economic development must first be available to the relatively less privileged classes of society, and that there should be a progressive reduction in the concentration of income, wealth and power.

7.2 BALVANTRAI MEHTA COMMITTEE AND ASOKA MEHTA COMMITTEE

Under these circumstances, the Government of India constituted a Committee—popularly known as the Balvantrai Mehta Committee—in 1957. The study teams made by the Committee visited all-over India and finally came to the conclusion that the failure of the Community

Development Programme might be attributed to the fact that it was basically a programme which was sponsored, directed, implemented and even financed by the bureaucrats who, not being elected, were not responsible to the people and even tried to maintain some sort of distance from the people. Hence, people could not get any chance to associate themselves with the planning process. Besides, the Balvantrai Mehta Committee also suggested that in order to introduce popular participation in the planning process, the establishment of democratic decentralization was a must. The committee envisaged five broad principles relating to the concept of democratic decentralization which are:

1. There should be a three-tier structure of interlinked local self governmental bodies from the village to the district level, the Gram Panchayats operating at the village level, the Panchayat Samitis operating at the block level, and the Zilla Parishads operating at the district level.
2. There should be a genuine transfer of power to these bodies to enable them to discharge their responsibilities.
3. Adequate resources should be transferred to these bodies for their effective performance of functions.
4. All welfare and developmental schemes and programmes up to the district level should be channeled through these bodies only.
5. The panchayati raj system should facilitate further devolution of power and responsibility in future.

Gradually, even after following the measures prescribed in the Balvantrai Mehta Committee Report, the functioning of the panchayati raj system in India had unfolded certain difficulties like over bureaucratization, financial non-viability, concentration of benefits in a few persons only, etc. These shortcomings led some political thinkers to remark that it was not inappropriate to say that "... India is on the way to having a strong rural administration but no rural government."[6]

Under these circumstances, the Central Government in December 1977 appointed another Committee on panchayati raj institutions under the chairmanship of Asoka Mehta. The Asoka Mehta Committee submitted its Report in August 1978.

The most significant recommendation of the Committee was for creating a two-tiered system of the panchayati raj—instead of the usual three-tiered system. It regarded the revenue district as the first point of decentralization below the state Level. The Zilla Parishad, according to the Report of the Committee, should be the executive body below which there is to be a Mandal Panchayat constituted by grouping a number of villages.

The Asoka Mehta Committee in its Report also fovoured open participation of political parties in panchayati raj affairs. This was a somewhat pragmatic and desirable recommendation, because the political parties serve as the principal channel of communication between the people and their rulers and the latter also become accountable to the mass while being directly involved in the panchayati raj affairs.

Thus, these two Committees—the Balvantrai Mehta Committee and the Asoka Mehta Committee—are regarded to be two cornerstones in the history of the local self government in India. While the first Committee shaped the existing pattern of the panchyati raj institutions in India, the second one tried to revitalize them according to the changing situations.

7.2.1 Local Self Governmental Changes at the National Level

In the mean time, some local self governmental changes took place at the national level. The Rajiv Gandhi Government constituted a committee under the chairmanship of L.M. Singhvi to prepare a concept paper on panchyats. The Committee observed that "the institutions of panchayats have become moribund...." The committee further felt that the panchayat institutions in India should be viewed "as institutions of self-government which would naturally facilitate participation of the people in the process of planning and development flowing from and as a part of the concept of self-government.

Thus, while the Balvantrai Mehta Committee had favoured non-political panchayats and the Asoka Mehta Committee stood for political panchayats, the L.M. Singhvi Committee strongly pleaded for constitutionalization of panchayats. Again, while the first two committees had largely conceived panchayat bodies primarily as instruments of rural development, the third committee emphasized the need for developing panchayat bodies primarily as units of self-government."[7]

This was followed by the introduction of the controversial Constitution (64th Amendment) Bill in the Lok Sabha on May 15, 1989, by the late Rajiv Gandhi, the then Prime Minister of India. The Bill provided for the establishment of three-tier panchayats, filling up of all seats in panchayats by direct elections, reservation of seats in panchayats for women, scheduled castes and scheduled tribes, fixed tenure of five years for panchayats, etc. The Bill failed to become an Act as it could not get the required support in the Rajya Sabha. It raised a lot of controversy. The (then) ruling party hailed it as the Magna Carta of democratic decentralization. The opposition parties launched severe attacks on the Bill arguing that it was the destroyer of the very foundation of the federal polity and a surreptitious attempt to forge a direct link between the Centre and the localities by side-tracking the State Government.

The Constitution (73rd Amendment) Act, 1993, is a revised version of the earlier Bill. It is an improvement on the previous one in the sense that some of the provisions such as dismissal of panchayats by the Governors have been deleted.

This Constitutional Amendment has brought about what may be called the "third generation panchayats in India."[8] Many States have by now amended their respective legislations to bring them in conformity with the requirement of the Constitutional Amendment. It is noteworthy that States like Karnataka and Kerala which, along with those of West Bengal and Andhra Pradesh, were able to install the "second-generation panchayats",[9] have later taken backward steps. Bureaucracy is being reinstated in both the States. In Karnataka, the elections to the panchayat bodies were postponed on weak grounds. The Minister-in-charge of panchayats resigned taking upon himself the moral responsibility for not being able to hold elections on time.

7.3 LOCAL GOVERNEMNT IN RURAL INDIA: VARIOUS TIERS

In this section, a general profile of the local government existing in the rural sector of India including the various tiers of the government is sought to be clarified.

7.3.1 Gram Sabha

Gram sabha is the bottommost level institution of the panchayati raj system. It is through the gram sabha that a local self governmental representative is made accountable to the villagers. As the Indian Constitution says: "A gram sabha may exercise such powers and perform such functions at the village level as the legislature of a state may, by law, provide."

Gram sabha is an organ of direct democracy. Its members are all adult residents of the village. It is not made up of the representatives of the people. All States invariably provide for the institution of gram sabha; but functions entrusted to the body vary from State to State.

Gram sabha's members include all the voters whose names are inserted in the electroral roll in States like Uttar Pradesh, West Bengal, Maharashtra, Madhya Pradesh, Andhra Pradesh, Gujarat, Punjab, etc. But States like Rajasthan, Bihar and Karnataka confer membership of the gram sabha to all their residents. The membership of the gram sabha varies from State to State, ranging from 250 to 5000.

Gram sabhas in West Bengal and Madhya Pradesh meet once a year, those in Andhra Pradesh, Gujarat, Maharashtra, Rajasthan, Uttar Pradesh, Karnataka and Kerala meet twice a year, those in Tamil Nadu meet thrice a year, and those in Bihar and Assam meet four times a year.

Functions prescribed for gram sabhas may vary from State to State. Table 7.1 shows precise functions given to the gram sabhas of the respective States.

Table 7.1 Functions of the Gram Sabha in Different States

	Functions	***States***
1.	To examine annual statement of accounts and audit report	Andhra Pradesh, Gujarat, Haryana, Karnataka, Madhya Pradesh, Punjab, Rajasthan
2.	To discuss the report of the last year	Andhra Pradesh, Bihar, Gujarat, Karnatak, Madhya Pradesh, Rajasthan
3.	To review the programme of work for the year or any new programme	Andhra Pradesh, Bihar, Gujarat, Karnataka, Madhya Pradesh, Rajasthan, Punjab
4.	To consider proposals for new taxation or for enhancement of existing taxes	Andhra Pradesh, Bihar
5.	To select schemes, beneficiaries and locations	Andhra Pradesh, Bihar, Karnataka, Kerala, Punjab, Rajasthan, Tamil Nadu, Uttar Pradesh
6.	To mobilize voluntary labours and contributions for community welfare programmes	Bihar, Karnataka, Kerala, Punjab, Rajasthan, Uttar Pradesh and West Bengal
7.	To undertake programme for adult education and family welfare	Bihar, Karnataka, Kerala, Punjab, Rajasthan, Uttar Pradesh
8.	To seek clarifications from the Mukhia and members of gram panchayat about any activity, scheme, income or expenditure	Bihar, Punjab, Rajasthan
9.	To examine audit notes and replies	Bihar
10.	To scrutinize the completed work and all types of activities of the gram panchayat	Haryana and Kerala

On the question of the relationship between a gram sabha and a gram panchayat, two broad views exist. One view is that gram sabha is the parent body and gram panchayat is its executive committee. There is another view that both these bodies should operate as two separate entities and should function independently of each other.

Gram sabhas, regarding their functioning, suffer from several weaknesses after the 73rd Constitution Amendment (1993). These are:

- Gram sabhas are not taken seriously both by panchayats and by people. They are treated as mere advisory or suggestive bodies.
- Gram sabhas are expected to carry out important functions like consideration of the accounts of gram panchayat audit reports, and so on. But in reality, they hardly perform such functions.

Gram sabhas have not altogether been a glaring success in India. Yet, it has the potential to emerge as a powerful forum for participatory democracy.

7.3.2 Panchayat or Gram Panchayat

The panchayat is said to be the executive committee of the gram sabha. It is known by a variety of names. It is called the *panchayat* in Andhra Pradesh, Tamil Nadu, Maharashtra and Rajasthan, the *gram panchayat* in Bihar, Madhya Pradesh, Orissa, Punjab and West Bengal, and the *gaon panchayat* in Assam, Gujarat and Uttar Pradesh. A panchayat generally caters to a population of about 2000. Such a small population, particularly in the context of the widespread illiteracy in the rural sector of India, may not ensure leadership of the required type.

Members of the panchayat are known as *panchas* and are elected by the gram sabha by secret ballot in all the States except Assam, Jammu and Kashmir and Uttar Pradesh. For the purpose of election, the entire gram sabha area is divided into territorial wards, each ward electing one panch–the exception being Assam, Jammu and Kashmir, Haryana and Punjab. In Bihar, the gram panchayat consists of around nine members including the President (known as the Mukhiya), out of which four are directly elected and the remaining four are nominated by its President. In Assam, the local member of the block level body who is directly elected by the gram sabha is also an ex-officio member of the gaon panchayat.

The Presiding Officer of the panchayat is known by a variety of names—he is called *sarpanch* in Andhra Pradesh, Gujarat, Jammu and Kashmir, Madhya Pradesh, Maharashtra, Orissa, Punjab and Rajasthan; *president* in Assam; Kerala and Tamil Nadu; *pradhan* in Uttar Pradesh; *mukhia* in Bihar and Orissa; and *adhyaksha/pradhan* in West Bengal.

The tenure of the panchayat in various States varies from three to five years. In Bihar, three classes of panchayats exist, viz. *prathama varga* gram panchayat, *dwitiya varga* gram panchayat and *tritiya varga* gram panchayat. The term of office varies with the class under which a particular panchayat falls. It is three years in the case of *tritiya varga* gram panchayat, four years in the case of *dwitiya varga* gram panchayat and five years for *prathama varga* gram panchayat.

The functions of a gram panchayat are usually classified into two broad categories: *obligatory* and *discretionary*. The principal *obligatory functions,* i.e. the functions which the panchayat must perform, are as under:

1. Construction, repair and maintenance of public wells, ponds and tanks and supply of water for domestic use
2. Construction and maintenance of sources of water for bathing, washing and for drinking by cattle and to maintain its purity

3. Construction and maintenance of public streets, latrines, drains, gram panchayat roads, culverts, bridges, etc.
4. Lighting of village streets and other public places
5. Cleaning of public roads, drains, tanks and wells and other public places
6. Sanitation, conservancy and prevention of nuisance
7. Regulating places for the disposal of dead bodies, carcasses and other offensive materials including unclaimed corpses
8. Removal of obstructions and projections in public streets or places and in sites not being private property
9. Development of agriculture
10. Promotion of cottage industry
11. Promotion of cooperatives
12. Management of cattle ponds and maintenance of cattle related records
13. Improvement of cattle and their breeding and the general care of the livestock
14. Earmarking places for dumping refuse
15. Preparation of compost manure
16. Construction and maintenance of minor irrigation works
17. Registration of births, deaths and marriages
18. Maintenance of gram panchayat property
19. Inoculation, vaccination and enforcement of other preventive measures against contagious diseases
20. Prevention of fire
21. Regulation and control over shows, shops, eating and other entertainment houses, vendors of drinks, sweetmeats, fruit, milk, etc.
22. Destruction of stray and mad dogs
23. Measures to prevent damage to crops and cattle
24. Regulating the construction of latrines, urinals, drains, water closets, etc.
25. Control over offensive trades
26. Establishment, management and regulation of public markets
27. Management of public land and of village sites
28. Collection of land revenue
29. Help in the census operations
30. Arrangement and distribution of improved seeds
31. Promotion of social education
32. Organizing village volunteer force
33. Collection and maintenance of statistics

34. Regulation of sale and preservation of meat
35. Maintenance of public buildings, some ancient and historical monuments
36. Organizing voluntary labour
37. Assistance in the implementation of land reforms schemes
38. Making arrangements for cooperative management of lands
39. Maintenance of maternity homes.

The *discretionary functions,* i.e. the functions which the gram panchayat may or may not perform, are as under:

1. Planting and nursing of trees on roadsides and other places
2. Construction and maintenance of rest houses, public ghats, etc.
3. Construction and maintenance of playgrounds, clubs, gyms, libraries, parks, etc.
4. Construction and maintenance of slaughter houses
5. Relief of distress
6. Running of community centres
7. Reclaiming unhealthy localities
8. Looking after public health and safety
9. Management and control of public ferries, agricultural and industrial shows and public festivals
10. Promotion of cooperative farming
11. Establishment of granaries
12. Regulation of farming pigs within panchayat limits
13. Removal of weeds
14. Helping in the preparation of national register
15. Promotion of social and moral welfare like eradication of corruption, removal of untouchability, etc.
16. Construction and maintenance of houses for the conservancy staff of the panchayat.

To perform these elaborate functions, the gram panchayat has been given certain sources of revenue. These are:

1. Tax on buildings
2. Lighting tax
3. Tax on profession or trade
4. Tax for private latrines
5. Tax on animals and vehicles
6. Fees on registration of animals sold within the area of the panchayat.

In addition to these compulsory taxes, the panchayat can also levy some other taxes with the previous approval of the zilla parishad.

The principal imperfections of the panchayats, as pointed out by the Study Team on Panchayati Raj (1964) appointed by the Rajasthan Government (which hold equally good for other states also), are as under:

1. Lack of financial resources
2. Lack of secretarial assistance
3. Lack of adequate powers
4. Lack of cooperation from revenue and police agencies
5. Lack of guidance and supervision
6. Apathy on the part of panchas
7. Group factions and cliques in the rural life
8. Complexity of panchayat rules and procedures
9. Lack of timely action against defaulters
10. Proximity of the panchayat samiti
11. Overriding influence of the sarpanch.

This Committee, however, had suggested some measures, in turn. They are:

1. Financial resources of the panchayats should be enlarged.
2. Powers and functions of the panchayats should be more clearly explained.
3. Efficient and regular secretarial assistance should be provided to the panchayats.
4. Rules and procedures should be simple to understand and easy to observe.
5. Cooperation from the revenue and police agencies must be ensured.
6. Mistakes and irregularities should be prevented from occurring.
7. Strict and deterrent action should be taken against defaulters, regardless of whether they are civil servants or persons with some political backing.
8. The sarpanch should be relieved of the duty of maintaining accounts and handling cash.
9. The gram sabha should be made active and should play an effective role.
10. A vigorous effort should be made to educate the mass.

7.3.3 Panchayat Samiti

Just above the tier of gram panchayat (or panchayat) stands the panchayat samiti. The nomenclature of this rural local governmental body is not the same in all the States. It is called *panchayat samiti* in Andhra Pradesh, Bihar, Maharashtra, Orissa, Rajasthan and West Bengal; *kshetra samiti* in Uttar Pradesh; *anchalik panchayat* in Assam;

taluk panchayat in Gujarat; *janapada panchayat* in Madhya Pradesh; *taluk development board* in Karnataka; and *panchayat union council* in Tamil Nadu. Its term varies from three to five years. The panchayat samiti's term is generally co-terminous with that of the panchayat.

There is no uniformity in constituting a panchayat samiti in different States. Broadly speaking, a panchayat samiti consists of elected (non-official) and official members. The sarpanchas of the panchayats in the samiti are made ex-officio members of the panchayat samiti. Members of the State Legislature and of Parliament who have been elected from the area covered under the panchayat samiti are also members, but without the right to vote and are, therefore, called associate members. Again, there is a provision for co-opting a specified number of women and persons from scheduled castes and scheduled tribes as members of the samiti in all the States. Some States provide representation to the cooperative societies operating in the area as well as to persons who possess experience in public administration, public life and rural development.

The President of the panchayat samiti, who is called *president* in Andhra Pradesh, Assam, Gujarat, Madhya Pradesh and Karnataka; *Sabhapati* in West Bengal; *chairman* in Tamil Nadu, Maharashtra, Orissa and Punjab; *pramukha* in Bihar and Uttar Pradesh and *pradhan* in Rajasthan, is at present elected by members of the panchayat samiti in all the States except Rajasthan. In Rajasthan, the President of the panchayat samiti is elected by an electoral college comprising all members of the panchayat samiti and all panchas of the gram and nagar panchayats falling within the area. He can be removed from his office by a vote of no-confidence passed by a special majority of the panchayat samiti.

The office of the President of the panchayat samiti is of utmost importance in the set-up. It is the President who convenes panchayat samiti meetings and presides over them. He exercizes administrative control over the block development officer, who happens to be the EO of the samiti, for the purpose of implementing resolutions of the panchayat samiti or its standing committees.

The functions of the panchayat samiti may be classified into two broad areas:

- Provision of civic amenities
- Fulfilment of development functions.

The first category comprises the following functions:

1. Construction and upkeep of roads within the jurisdiction of the samiti but other than purely gram panchayat roads
2. Supply of drinking water
3. Opening of drains and soakage pits
4. Establishment of primary health centres and maternity centres
5. Provision of medical and health services

6. Provision of primary and basic schools, adult literacy and education centres
7. Assistance to village roads which serve as feeders
8. Establishment and popularization of libraries
9. Establishment of youth organizations, mahila mandals, farmers' clubs, etc.
10. Encouragement for physical and cultural activities.

The following may be considered to be a representative list of functions which fall within the development programme:

1. Execution of all programmes under community development
2. Multiplication and distribution of improved seeds
3. Procurement, distribution and popularization of improved manure and fertilizers
4. Reclamation of land and conservation of soil
5. Providing credit for agricultural purposes
6. Providing irrigation facilities
7. Planting of trees and growing of cillage forests
8. Introducing improved breed of cattle, sheep and poultry
9. Introducing improved fodder
10. Prevention and cure of disease among cattle
11. Dairying and milk supply
12. Opening and development of cooperative societies in various fields
13. Development of cottage, village and small-scale industries
14. Establishment and maintenance of production-cum-training centres.

Usually, a panchayat samiti has the following sources of income available to it:

1. Proceeds of taxes and fees which a panchayat samiti may levy
2. Share of local cess and share of the land revenue received from the zilla parishad
3. Grants from the State Government
4. Loans from the State Government
5. Income from leases granted by the panchayat samiti to public ferries, fairs, etc.
6. Ad hoc grants from or through the zilla parishad
7. Donations and contributions
8. Funds from schemes transferred by the government to the panchayat samiti as an agency for execution.

7.3.4 Zilla Parishad

A zilla parishad constitutes the apex in the panchayati raj system of rural local government in India. As the name itself signifies, the zilla parishad is a rural local government body operating at the district level in all the Indian States except Assam and Tamil Nadu. But States like Haryana, Madhya Pradesh, Karnataka and Orissa have of late abolished the body of zilla parishad, thus changing the traditional three-tiered structure of the panchayati raj into an unknown two-tiered one. In Assam, the apex body has been established at the subdivisional level, making the territorial jurisdiction of the body smaller than that of a district.

The nomenclature is not the same in all the States. It is called *zilla parishad* in Andhra Pradesh, Bihar, Gujarat, Maharashtra, Punjab, Rajasthan, Uttar Pradesh and West Bengal; *mohkuma parishad* in Assam; and *district development council* in Tamil Nadu.

Broadly speaking, a zilla parishad consists of the following members:

- Presidents of panchayat samitis in the district
- All members of Parliament, representing constituencies falling within the district
- All members of the State Legislature returned from constituencies within the district
- A representative of cooperative society, usually the President of the district cooperative society
- Certain specified number of scheduled castes and scheduled tribes
- Some coopted members having some experience in administration, public life or rural development.

The zilla parishad has a membership varying between forty and sixty.

Most States deny representation to urban local government in the zilla parishad, apparently believing that the urban and the rural areas are so completely different and so differently constituted. A zilla parishad is an apex organization and has been made responsible for development of the district as a whole, which must include towns and cities having urban forms of local government. There are continuous interactions between towns and the adjoining villages and these must be monitored and reflected in administrative actions. Urban local governments in the district must be represented in the zilla parishad to enable it to function in a comprehensive, intelligent and meaningful way.

The tenure of the parishad members is dependent upon the original tenure of the organizations to which these members are elected.

The President of the zilla parishad is elected by its members from among themselves. He is called *chairman* in Andhra Pradesh, Tamil Nadu and Punjab; *sabhadhipati* in West Bengal; *president* in Assam, Gujarat and Maharashtra; *adhyaksha* in Bihar and Uttar Pradesh; and *pramukh* in Rajasthan. He presides over the zilla parishad meetings and conducts their proceedings. He inspects the lower tiers of the panchayati raj system and submits inspection report to the zilla parishad. He writes his opinion on the work of the Secretary to the zilla parishad, which is appended with his confidential report.[10]

The functions of the zilla parishad vary from State to State. Broadly speaking, in most States (except Maharashtra and Gujarat) the zilla parishad functions as a supervisory and coordinating body, the pivotal role being reserved for the panchayat samiti. In Maharashtra and Gujarat, on the other hand, the zilla parishad is an executive organization, the panchayat samiti being merely its agent and appendage. These, broadly, are the two models of zilla parishad in the country. The non-Maharashtra model of zilla parishad has been assigned the following functions:

1. It examines and approves the budget of the panchayat samitis.
2. It issues directions to panchayat samitis for performing their functions efficiently.
3. It coordinates development plans prepared by the panchayat samitis. It also coordinates the inter-block activities.
4. It advises the State Government on all matters relating to the development of the district.
5. It distributes State-allocated funds to the panchayat samitis in the district.
6. It informs the District Collector and the Divisional Commissioner about irregularities committed by the panchayats and panchayat samitis in the district.
7. It collects statistics relating to the activities of local authorities in the district.
8. It advises the State Government regarding the allocation of work to be made among panchayats and panchayat samitis in the district.
9. It exercises such powers and performs such functions as may be conferred by the State Government.

In Maharashtra and Gujarat, the zilla parishad has been entrusted with executive functions in fields like agriculture, animal husbandry, forests, social welfare, education, public health, communications, cottage and village industries, housing and community development. The panchayat samiti acts as a mere agent of the zilla parishad in performing all the above functions.

7.4 THE CONSTITUTION (73rd AMENDMENT) ACT, 1993

The 73rd Constitutional Amendment has heralded a new era for the *panchayati raj* in India. With this, the panchayati raj institutions have been provided additional legitimacy and vitality. This Constitutional Amendment has brought about what may be called the *third generation panchayats* in India.

The Union Government's efforts to encourage the participation by the weaker sections and the downtrodden such as the members of the scheduled castes, scheduled tribes and women are indeed commendable. But one should appreciate that change cannot be brought about overnight. This stratum of society which has been exploited for ages cannot at once break free of all the shackles of illiteracy, poverty and tradition. According to the Eighth Five Year Plan, out of all the rural families in India, about 30 per cent are matriarchal. Yet, most women are uneducated, have little or no property of their own and live in an out-and-out tradition-bound society. In such a case, the politically powerful can make them contest elections for their own political gains. Hence, the provision in the 73rd Amendment Act would be really fruitful only if women and members of the scheduled castes and tribes were given proper training in the working of politico-administrative institutions.

Development in all sectors cannot be possible unless the sources of revenue of the panchayati raj bodies are strengthened and these bodies are induced to make themselves financially self-sufficient. Finance Commissions are being set up under the new provisions with a view to providing more and more finances to the panchayats. The Gujarat Panchayati Act, 1993 has already made efforts in this direction. It states that 50 per cent of the village (land) revenue would be utilized for the welfare of the village and out of the remaining 50 per cent, 7.5 per cent would be kept for the backward classes and another 7.5 per cent would be given to panchayats that are doing commendable work.

A hopeful feature of the 73rd Amendment is that as against the Rajiv Gandhi model proposed vide the 64th Constitutional Amendment, the 73rd Amendment goes a step further. The 64th Amendment stipulated that panchayati raj elections would be conducted by the Chief Election Commissioner. The 73rd Amendment provides for an Election Commission for each State for the conduct of such elections. Some States have accordingly appointed such officials.

The 73rd Amendment also provides that *gram sabhas* would be constituted at the village level, thereby giving them a constitutional status.

The Amendment (1993), however, has clearly laid down that elections to the panchayati raj institutions would be held every five years. This is quite a positive step because such elections have repeatedly been postponed in the past in many States due to several reasons.

As a result of the 73rd Amendment Act, more powers and functions can now be devolved upon panchayats, if the State Legislatures so decide. And yet, the role of the bureaucracy in decentralized development cannot be ignored. Therefore, a new equation will have to be arrived at between the bureaucracy and the panchayati raj institutions. The earlier relation of dichotomy between the two was going to be replaced by that of complementarity.

It needs to be emphasized that the functions allotted to the panchayats ought to be real. Though the Eleventh Schedule of the Constitution contains 29 items which can be handed over to the village panchayats, it has been left for each State to decide. Past experience teaches us that arrangements for flow of funds and technical support are more important than a mere increase in the number of functions, even where the functions are assigned to the panchayat bodies.

Finally, elections to the panchayati raj institutions would be fought on a party basis. Hence, the villages could well turn into battlefields in the struggle for power. However, as scholars point out, if the political parties can play a positive role by helping the process of educating the ignorant villagers, studying and offering solutions to their problems, creating a spirit of community and launching a campaign against social evils in the villages, they can undoubtedly modernize rural India and draw the ruralites into the mainstream national politics.[11]

Admitting that the panchayati raj institutions in India are weak and assuming that it will not be smooth sailing for them even after the 73rd Amendment, they do have an important role to play in India's development. Till date, the panchayat bodies have several achievements to their credit. They have enhanced political consciousness among the ruralites and initiated a process of democratic seed-drilling in the Indian soil. Perhaps, the most progressive State in the post-73rd Constitutional Amendment Act is Madhya Pradesh, where the devolution of powers to the panchayati raj institutions has been made in a significantly large number of functional areas. It is in Madhya Pradesh where the *gram sabhas* are meeting four times a year, while in most other States, the institution has yet to experience a systematic revival.

7.4.1 Drawbacks in Women's Participation in Panchayats: Negative Impact of 73rd Amendment

In spite of reservation of seats for women in panchayat bodies, 73rd Amendment to the Indian Constitution in reality has failed to ensure effective participation of women in such bodies due to the misuse and manipulation by the local power-brokers. Also, women's utter ignorance of their rights and procedures, their potentials and abilities and their powers and responsibilities have kept them far behind the local bodies. Hence, researchers have opined that it is quite doubtful if only an increase in the number of reserved seats for women in panchayat bodies is at all able to increase women's real participation and consequently their empowerment. Unless and until some constructive structural changes are brought about to educate and enlighten rural women and make them more politically aware and hence active, nothing much can be achieved. Women representatives are very often constrained by family or even social barriers and are obstructed from participating actively and meaningfully. When they attend large meetings along with a number of male participants, as it has been observed in a number of surveys, they cannot speak freely and cannot even place their demands or raise effective questions. Thus, women representatives receive very little attention and respect. In fact, on most occasions women members are invited only to complete the quorum. Further, as J.C. Johari very rightfully mentions, the officials are found to pay heed to the demands placed by upper class women representatives depriving the needs of peasant women members. Thus, the local bureaucracy tends to systematically nullify the rights of 'lower' class women.[12]

Ms. Sumitra Ahlawat in her paper titled "Impact of the 73rd Amendment of the Indian Constitution on Women Empowerment: An Analytical Study"[13] has clearly mentioned that a situation has undoubtedly been created by the family, community and the State (represented by officials) in which elected women representatives are facing quite a few constraints while playing their roles and discharging their functions in the panchayat bodies. In addition, women representatives have some individual weaknesses as well. They are as under:

- Illiteracy or poor educational levels of the majority of women elected members
- Female representatives overburdened with family responsibilities
- Women's too much shyness and introversion due to the lack of their communication skills
- Poor socio-economic background of women and their poor capacity-building
- Women representatives being totally dominated by male members of their families or male leaders of similar caste groups or similar communities
- Indifferent attitudes of officials to female members' needs and demands
- Female members being misguided by the local bureaucracy
- Apprehension of a total absence of confidence on female representatives by other elected members of the panchayat bodies
- Too much pressure on female members from political parties which have vested interests in the gender reservation in panchayats
- Female representatives being continuously branded as 'incompetent' by common villagers
- Undue interference by husbands of women representatives, considering women as mere puppets

- Widespread use of corruption among male members and local bureaucrats (officials).

Thus, it is clear that 73rd Amendment to our Constitution should not be treated as a magic-wand by which rural women will be empowered overnight. Women's empowerment and enlightenment should be seen as a process that involves sincerity, earnestness and capacity as well as capability on the part of both men and women. It is an altogether challenging task in rural India since due to immense illiteracy rural women even today feel that they are subordinate to their husbands and even to their sons and consequently are totally afraid of taking decisions independently.

7.5 PANCHAYATS IN THREE SOUTHERN STATES OF INDIA

Since the installation of the Janata Party Government at the Centre in 1977, the panchayats in West Bengal and three other States, namely, Andhra Pradesh, Karnataka and Kerala, received huge political attention and were drastically revived. In West Bengal, along with these three States, as has already been pointed out, came into being what may be called the "second generation panchayats".

In the present section, an attempt has been made to review the structure of the panchayats existing in three above mentioned southern States of India.

7.5.1 Andhra Pradesh Panchayati Raj System

Andhra Pradesh is one of the pioneering States of India in introducing a three-tier structure of panchayati raj. It was introduced in the State as early as on November 1, 1959 as per the recommendations of the 1957 study team. The system had a good start, but unfortunately the initial enthusiasm shown for this programme did not last long.

Under the earlier system, the panchayat samitis were entrusted with the responsibility of implementation of all rural development programmes. They were initially started with a lot of hope that they would promote comprehensive rural development programmes in the fields of agriculture, irrigation, animal husbandry, cooperation, communication and industry. But in course of time, these hopes were belied. Lack of coordination among the different agencies, unwieldy management, excessive importance to power and prestige at the cost of service to the people, and weak financial base contributed to this deterioration. Another important reason for the decline of the panchayati raj institutions here was that the development activities, instead of flowing through the panchayati raj institutions, were channelized through parallel agencies like Small Farmers Development Agency, Drought Prone Areas Programmes (now called District Rural

Development Agency), Integrated Tribal Development Agency, etc. The developmental activities were not brought within the purview of the panchayat samitis and the zilla parishads.[14]

The Telugu Desham Party (TDP) Government, which assumed office in 1983, realized that the development activities and welfare programmes had not taken place adequately in the three-tiered panchayati raj system. Initially, the TDP Government had no special emphasis on the panchayati raj. But in its annual convention in May 1984, the ruling party took the decision to bring about changes in the moribund panchayati raj system formally established in Andhra Pradesh in 1959. Thus, the 1984 manifesto spoke of the panchayati raj in unambiguous terms. It said that TDP would work for a directly elected district administrative system forming a third tier in the country's federal polity.

The TDP took Asoka Mehta Committee's recommendation of the two-tier system seriously, but slightly modified it to include village panchayats also. With a view to restructuring the panchayati raj set-up, the TDP Government brought in a new legislation known as *Andhra Pradesh Mandal Praja Parishads, Zilla Praja Parishads and Zilla Pronalika Abhivrudhi Mandals Act,* 1986, by replacing the *Andhra PradeshPanchayat Samitis, Zilla Parishads Act,* 1959. This new Act came into force on January 15, 1987. Elections were held in March 1987 to Mandal Praja Parishad and Zilla Praja Parishad based on the 1986 Act. This election was held on party lines and evoked great popular enthusiasm throughout the State.[15]

Thus, in Andhra Pradesh it is a three-tier local governmental system with gram panchayats at the village level, mandal praja parishads at the block level and zilla praja parishads at the district level. The Presidents of the mandal praja parishads and zilla praja parishads are elected directly by the registered voters in the mandals and zillas on party basis. To provide opportunities for all the communities and backward classes, a reservation of 15 per cent is made for the scheduled castes, 6 per cent for the scheduled tribes and 20 per cent for the backward classes. A provision of 9 per cent reservations is also made for women Presidents of Mandal Praja Parishads.

From this, it is clear that there is much similarity in the composition between the three-tier systems of local self government in West Bengal and Andhra Pradesh. One major difference between the two systems is that unlike in West Bengal, in Andhra Pradesh, apart from the zilla parishad, there is another tier of local self government at the district level, zilla pranalika and abhivrudhi mandal. Secondly, unlike in West Bengal gram panchayats, in elections to the Andhra Pradesh gram panchayat, members are not contested along political parties.

7.5.2 Karnataka Panchayati Raj System

Karnataka came into the panchayati raj map of India in 1956 when *the Karnataka Village Panchayats and Local Boards Act,* 1956, was passed. There was no serious effort to confer real powers and resources to the panchayati raj institutions. The Kandaji Basappa Committee recommended a suitable structure for the State in 1963 and consequently, the Bill for a three-tier structure of local self government was introduced in 1964. Nothing remarkable in this respect happened till 1983 owing to the lack of political will. The Hegde Government installed in 1983 displayed real political will for genuine democratic decentralization. *The Karnataka Zilla Parishads, Taluk Panchayat Samitis, Mandal Panchayats and Nyaya Panchayats Act,* 1983, based on the recommendations of the Asoka Mehta Committee, was enacted.

Under the new system, the mandal panchayat, covering a group of villages, is the first elected tier of the system. The size of its membership varies from 11 to 19. Twenty-five per cent of the membership is earmarked for women and 18 per cent for scheduled castes and scheduled tribes. It is entrusted with all civic functions, powers and responsibilities for development and welfare programmes.

The taluk panchayat is a nominated body comprising ex-officio members—all Presidents of each of the Mandals in a taluk, all MLAs/ MLCs representing any part of the taluk, members of the zilla parishad representing any part of the taluk, Presidents of the taluk level cooperative societies, and five co-opted members belonging to scheduled castes, tribes, backward classes and women. The MLA representing the major part of the taluk is the Chairman of the taluk panchayat samiti.

The zilla parishad is the second directly elected tier in Karnataka. One member for every 28,000 of the population is elected to the zilla parishad. MPs and MLAs, whose constituencies cover the district or part thereof, are members of the zilla parishad. Here, too, there is a provision for reservation of seats for the scheduled castes and tribes.

The zilla parishads in Karnataka are definitely less powerful than those in West Bengal regarding their relations to the lower level panchayats. It should be kept in mind that the plans and budgets formulated at the mandal panchayats in Karnataka cannot be altered by the zilla Parishads. Unlike the West Bengal zilla parishads, the zilla parishads in Karnataka have no controlling power over the mandal panchayats.

In Karnataka, elections to zilla parishads and mandal panchayats based on the new Act of 1983 were held in January 1987. These elections were held on party lines for the first time. Karnataka also, like Andhra Pradesh and West Bengal, encountered opposition to elections on party lines. But the Janata Party stood the ground by asking: "If political parties are indispensable for parliamentary democracy, is it not important that they must take roots in the villages through the nursery of local bodies' elections on party lines?"[16]

7.5.3 Kerala Panchayati Raj System

Kerala came under the panchayati raj system in 1960 when *the Kerala*

Panchayat Act was passed. An attempt was made in 1964 to restructure the Kerala panchayati system through *the Kerala Panchayat Union Council and Zilla Parishad Bill.* The Bill provided for a scheme of panchayati raj on the lines of the recommendations of the Balwant Rai Mehta Study Team. But the Bill could not be pursued owing to the resignation of the ministry.

During the second term of Chief Ministership of E.M.S. Namboodiripad, the *Kerala Panchayati Raj Bill* was introduced in the legislature in 1967. The Bill provided for a two-tier system of local self government–gram panchayats at the village level and zilla parishads at the district level. But the Bill lapsed as the Assembly was dissolved.

During the Chief Ministership of Mr. A.K. Anthony, *the Kerala District Administration Bill* was introduced in the Legislative Assembly in 1978. The Bill was passed in 1979 and received Presidential assent in 1980 during the Chief Ministership of Mr. E.K. Nayanar.[17] *The Kerala District Administration Act*, just like *the Kerala Panchayati Raj Bill* (1967), envisages a two-tier system of democratic decentralization—Panchayats at the village level and district councils at the district level. The Left coalition led by Mr. Nayanar attempted to implement the legislation. But it could not go far as it lost power to the coalition led by Mr. K. Karunakaran in 1984. The Left Democratic Front (LDF) led by Mr. Nayanar again came to power in 1987. This time, the Nayanar Government appointed a special adviser to review the original legislation.

The special adviser recommended the retention of the village panchayats to be brought under the control and supervision of the district councils. According to him, the village panchayats will be headed by the Presidents. The Executive Officer of the village panchayat—to be redesignated as Secretary—will function under the President's control and supervision. This control of the elected non-officials over the non-elected officials is in line with the provision of the other second generation panchayats existing in West Bengal, Andhra Pradesh and Karnataka. The special adviser also suggested for the setting up of a taluk samiti at the taluk (Block) level which would be made more powerful in course of time.

Some of these recommendations were accepted and some rejected. But things changed after the Karunakaran Ministry was installed in the State. The said government has tried to weaken the district council. Now, the post of the Secretary of the Council is held by the Deputy Collector instead of the District Collector.

Again, under the Act, there was a provision for the appointment of the Finance Commission. But the Karunakaran government has left it to the sweet will of the State. It has done so just to make the district council more dependent on the State Government for finance in the absence of any Finance Commission. It is clear that the Karunakaran

Government in Kerala tried to wrest the control of the district councils from the Left who had captured 13 district councils by 1993.

But, unfortunately, there has again been a revival of the bureaucracy in the Kerala panchayati raj system since 1994. *The Kerala Panchayati Raj Bill,* 1994, proposes in effect to centralize power in the hands of officials at the State level, instead of decentralizing it among the people, as has been intended all along since panchayati raj institutions were accepted as the foundation for political and economic decentralization in India. This is an astonishing distortion of the ideals that have guided this country since Mahatma Gandhi began to lead the freedom movement.

The Commissioner, proposed to be appointed under the panchayati raj system, should really have no powers beyond scrutinizing the technical aspects of the budgets presented by individual panchayats. Instead, under the proposed Bill, he has not only powers to add and delete items to and from these budgets, but is also authorized to intervene in the day-to-day functioning of the panchayats. The bureaucracy, represented by the Commissioner at the State level and by Deputy Commissioner at the District level, has in effect crucial veto powers which even can reduce the panchayati raj to a tragic comedy.[18]

7.6 WEST BENGAL: A UNIQUE PICTURE OF PANCHAYATS

In the case of West Bengal, the panchayati raj picture is somewhat different. Here, the Left Front controls both the State (since 1977) and the Local Self Governments (since 1978). With the abolition of the erstwhile gram panchayats in 1978, the total number of elected panchayat leaders has come down, but the number of rural leaders under the new panchayati system still remains formidable. All these rural leaders have been quite conscious of enjoying "powers" which they did not have before. The large number of grass roots leaders in the rural society of West Bengal acts as a strong force against the century-old dominance of the bureaucrats in the administration of Bengal as well as of India.[19]

From 1978 to 1985, the work of the panchayats in West Bengal remained principally the local implementation of State policy and of programmes that came from the State or Central Governments. But on the basis of the experience gained during this period, the Left Front Government decided to decentralize the planning responsibilities downwards through the panchayati framework in the rural areas.

Before 1978, the panchayats did not possess an explicit planning function. Since 1978 they began to be consulted more. But even then, they were not located within a formally constituted planning structure with an explicit planning function of their own. Planning below the State level was a disjointed and somewhat uncoordinated affair. As a result of the introduction of direct party based elections to all three tiers of panchayats and also of the end of "rock departmentalism",[20] the powers of the panchayats were gradually increased. The end of "rock departmentalism" implied that the powers and positions of the bureaucrats were cut short in relation to the elected panchayat members.

After 1978, it was found in West Bengal that all the non-elected elements of the panchayats, i.e. the officials had faced a political climate which brought decentralization of power and wide popular participation in decision-making. The officials, as representatives of vested interests, were opposed to any such change. Their erstwhile lack of empathy with the poor ruralites now began to be considered as something going against the spirit of "popular democracy".

Unlike most of the other States of India, where in spite of the existence of the panchayat bodies the electorate is effectively excluded from the process of governance, in West Bengal, the case is somewhat different. This happened primarily due to the electoral victory of the CPI(M) in the State Assembly Elections in 1977. Rural development and a transformation of the agrarian social relations became the central plank of the CPI(M)'s political strategy. Mr. Benoy Chowdhury, the (then) Land Minister and longtime peasant leader, was responsible from the outset for prioritizing and formulating the agrarian programme of the CPI(M) party. In fact, it is under his leadership that the revitalization of local panchayats including the changed status of the officials has been materialized.

The newly established Left Front Government entrusted a number of important tasks under its agrarian programme to the newly established panchayat bodies. Some of the most important agrarian programmes included Operation Barga, i.e., the identification and redistribution of lands held above the land ceiling, various developmental programmes including the Integrated Rural Development Programme (IRDP), the Food for Work Programme, and later the National Rural Employment Programme (NREP) and Rural Landless Employment Guarantee Programme (RLEGP).

Since the installation of the Left Front Government, seven panchayati raj elections were held in West Bengal. On June 4, 1978, the first panchayat elections took place in the State during the beginning of the ministry of the Left Front Government. It should be kept in mind that democratic decentralization in West Bengal till 1977 was a mere slogan since most of the panchayati raj bodies were superseded or left in a moribund condition. The last time rural people participated in panchayat elections was in 1958–1959, when representatives were elected to the lowest tier (constituted of the erstwhile gram panchayats that had little powers). The subsequent elections to the other tiers of the erstwhile structure were all indirect. The panchayat elections of 1978 marked a definite watershed in the evolution of the panchayati raj institutions in West Bengal. As the elections were held almost after two decades of the moribund existence of the panchayati raj bodies, these elections evoked tremendous public response as was evident from the voting turn-out which was as high as 70 per cent. In 1978 elections, 3242 gram panchayats, 324 panchayat samitis and 15 zilla parishads came into being. 46836 seats in the gram panchayats, 8467 seats in the panchayat samitis and 648 seats in the zilla parishads were created.[21]

In 1983, the next panchayat elections were held. As a result, 3305 gram panchayats, 339 panchayat samitis and 15 zilla parishads came into being. 46050 seats in the gram panchayats, 8664 seats in the panchayat samitis and 678 seats in the zilla parishads were created.[22]

In 1988, the next panchayat elections took place in which 52473 seats in the gram panchayats, 9116 seats in the panchayat samitis and 657 seats in the zilla parishads were created.[23]

The next panchayat elections took place in June 1993. As a result, 60965 gram panchayat seats, 9446 panchayat samiti seats and 655 zilla parishad seats were created.[24]

The next panchayat elections took place in May 1998. As a result, 49199 gram panchayat seats, 8515 panchayat samiti seats and 716 zilla parishad seats were created.[25]

The sixth panchayat elections were held in May 2003. After the elections, 49140 gram panchayat seats, 8500 panchayat samiti seats and 713 zilla parishad seats were made.[26]

The seventh panchayat elections were held in May 2008, as a result of which 3220 gram panchayats, 329 panchayat samitis and 17 zilla parishads[27] were formed. The number of seats in the three tiers is not yet available. But what is most remarkable is that there is a clearly visible crack in the 'red fort' of the panchayats in West Bengal. Critics opine that this may largely be due to the Left Front Government's rapid economic policy of industrialization and consequent land-acquisition which, to a large extent, may have a negative impact upon the millions of poor agriculture-dependent ruralites in West Bengal. Data show that while in the 2003 panchayati raj elections in West Bengal, Left Front's share was 2303 (71.5%) regarding gram panchayats, 284 (86.32%) regarding panchayat samitis and 15 (88.23%) regarding zilla parishads, in the 2008 elections, the numbers are merely 1597 (49.59%), 189 (69.38%) and 13 (76.47%) for the gram panchayats, panchayat samitis and zilla parishads, respectively.

While discussing the evolutionary pattern of the panchayats in West Bengal, one should take note of the fact that in this State panchayats bear not only the stories of incessant success and victory, they also reveal events of maladministration and many other failures.

It is pointed out by some scholars[28] that panchayats in West Bengal have been reduced to a mere implementing agency for routine programmes of rural governance and development. The panchayats here have fallen prey to all the assorted maladies that go with bureaucracy.

There is also the danger of panchayats becoming a 'den' of nepotism and casteism.[29] This political perspective of the panchayati raj in West Bengal is important particularly when panchayats are constituted on the basis of political elections in West Bengal. These political panchayats as self-governing institutions, as observed by some authors, may become "political monsters".[30]

In a study made by Nirmal Mukherjee and D. Bandyopadhyay, the authors have shown that of the total vested agricultural land of 1249177.76 acres only 716916.22 acres had been distributed till 1981. Between December 1981 and September 1992, a total of only 94031 acres of vested agricultural land was distributed. It is observed that of such a rate it will take almost thirty years more to distribute the remaining vested land.[31]

In a working paper (2007) entitled "Industrialisation: Which Way Now?" Prof. Amit Bhaduri and Ms. Medha Patkar have pointed out that it is absolutely shocking that only 14 per cent of the money allotted in the poorest district of Purulia for employment guarantee was spent until December, 2006, more than half the money of employment guarantee provided by the Centre remained unspent in the State of West Bengal, and not more than 16 days of employment could be provided, while the legal and financial provision allows for 100 days.

Critics like Prof. Abhirup Sarkar feel that the politicization of development has an inherent limitation as it helps institutionalize the spoil system which includes the grant of favour in cash and kind to party workers, supporters and even sympathizers.[32] In rural areas the political panchayats give the vulnerable majority (lacking any well-defined property rights within the formal legal framework) some kind of protection and, in return, get their support at the time of elections.

In this context, an important question needs to be addressed. Can a party in power which is based on the principle of 'democratic centralism' allow space for 'democratic decentralization' at the panchayat level? One should point out that this inherent contradiction between 'democratic centralism', as the political ideology of the ruling CPI(M) party in West Bengal, and 'democratic decentralization', as the philosophy of the party programme, may be one of the reasons that the panchayats have now been reduced to "mere developmental agencies instead of developing as autonomous local self-governments."[33]

Questions

1. What are the various tiers of local self government in rural India? What functions are performed by them?
2. Discuss critically the 73rd Constitutional Amendment Act, 1993.
3. Make a comparative study of the panchayati raj systems existing in Andhra Pradesh, Karnataka and Kerala.

4. Critically discuss the unique features of the panchayati raj system in West Bengal.
5. Write short-notes on:
   (a) Zilla Parishads
   (b) Panchayat Samitis
   (c) Gram Panchayats
   (d) Gram Sabha
   (e) 73rd Constitutional Amendment Act.
6. Discuss the drawbacks in women's participation in Indian panchayats.

Notes and References

1. Lenin, V.I., *The State and Revolution*, Progress Publishers, Moscow, 1972.
2. Varlamov, K., *Socialist Management: The Leninist Concept*, Progress Publishers, Moscow, 1977.
3. Lenin, V.I., *Collected Works*, Vol. XX.
4. White, L.D., *Introduction to the Study of Public Administration*, 4th ed., Macmillan, New York, 1958.
5. Webster, Neil, *Panchayati Raj and the Decentralization of Development Planning in West Bengal*, K.P. Bagchi and Company, Calcutta 1992.
6. Avasthi, A. and S. Maheshwari, *Public Administration*, The Premier Press, Agra, 1985.
7. *Kurukshetra*, February, 1986.
8. *Revitalization of Panchayats: The West Bengal Experience*, State Institute of Panchayats, Govt. of West Bengal, Kalyani, Nadia. (The document has been prepared by Prof. Prabhat Datta.)
9. Datta, Prabhat, *The Second Generation Panchayats in India*, Calcutta Book House Private Limited, Calcutta, 1993.
10. The confidential report of the Secretary to the zilla parishad is written by the District Collector who happens to be the Executive Officer of the parishad.
11. Prabhat Datta's essay in Arora, Ramesh K. and Rakesh Hooja (Eds.), *Administration of Rural Development: Indian and Comparative Perspectives*, Arihant, Jaipur, 1995.
12. Johari, J.C., *Indian Government and Politics*, Vishal Publications, 2001.
13. Ahlawat, Sumitra, "Impact of the 73rd Amendment of the Indian Constitution on Women Empowerment: An Analytical Study", *International Journal of Enhanced Research in Educational Development*, Vol. I, Issue 3, April 2013.

14. Rao, K. Ramachandra, Panchayat Perestroika in Andhra Pradesh, in Thakur, Devendra and Shivesh Nandan Singh (Eds.), *District Planning and Panchayati Raj*, Deep and Deep Publications, New Delhi, 1991.
15. Mathew, George, Panchayati Raj—The Second Phase in Thakur, Devendra and Shivesh Nandan Singh (Eds.), *District Planning and Panchayati Raj*, Deep & Deep Publications, New Delhi, 1991.
16. *Ibid.*
17. Biju, M.R. and J.N. Pandya, Democratic Decentralization in an Indian State: Kerala, *Indian Journal of Political Science*, July–September, 1991.
18. Letters to Editor. Kerala Panchayati Raj Bill, *Economic and Political Weekly*, Vol. XXIX, No. 14, April 2, 1994.
19. Mukhopadhyay, Asok K., *The Panchayat Administration in West Bengal*, The World Press Private Limited, Calcutta, 1991.
20. *The Minhas Report*, 1973, coined the term for the first time.
21. Datta, Prabhat, *op cit.*
22. Datta, Prabhat, *op cit.*
23. *Panchayati Raj*, Directorate of Panchayats, Government of West Bengal, Special Election Number, June–August, 1988.
24. *Mainstream*, June 26, 1993.
25. *Pashchimbanga Panchayat Nirbachan, 1998: Tathya O. Samiksha*, Bharater Communist Party (Marxbaadee), Pashchimbanga Rajya Committee, December, 1998.
26. *Pashchimbanga Shashtha Panchayat Nirbachan, 2003: Tathya O. Samiksha,* Bharater Communist Party (Marxbaadee), Pashchimbanga Rajya Committee, May, 2004.
27. *Anandabazaar Patrika,* May 23, 2008.
28. Bhattacharya, Dipankar, New Challenges for Bengal Left: Panchayat Poll Pointers, *Economic and Political Weekly,* Vol. XXVIII, Nos. 29 and and 30, July 17–24, 1993.
29. Krishna, Sudhir, Panchayati Raj, *Economic and Political Weekly,* September 25, 1993.
30. Acharya, Poromesh, Elusive New Horizons: Panchayats in West Bengal, *Economic and Political Weekly,* Vol. XXIX, No. 5, Jan. 29, 1994.
31. Mukherjee, Nirmal and D. Bandyopadhyay, *New Horizons for West Bengal's Panchayats,* The Government of West Bengal, Development of Panchayats, October 1993.
32. Sarkar, Abhirup, Political Economy of West Bengal: A Puzzle and a Hypothesis, *Economic and Political Weekly*, Vol. XLI, No. 4, January 28, 2006.
33. Acharya, Poromesh, *op. cit.*

8 Women's Participation in Local Self Government

8.1 INTRODUCTION

A number of studies on political participation have shown that women in general are less participative in politics than men. It is usually argued, to explain this, that women are less educated and hence less informed of political issues; less attentive to different points of view and hence are less interested in politics—all in relation to men. Such an explanation, however, would be oversimplification of the fact. The lack of participation by women in the political process cannot simply be attributed to their nature, which is said to be basically conservative. In fact, one should also take into consideration the factors of political resources and political interest in order to understand the gender-bias in political participation and also the reasons for the consequent under-representation of women in the political process. As a social group, women still possess fewer political resources than men. They have to be engaged in constant battles against a number of social, economic and political obstacles even today.

Under normal circumstances, women lack the political efficacy associated with political participation. Political efficacy is basically the extent to which an individual feels that his or her political participation will be meaningful. The fact that women are less likely to have such a meaning can have many reasons. One of the reasons may probably be the childhood socialization of girls to the view that both interest and activity in politics go more with males than females. Again, women's interest in formal politics is very often crushed by childbearing, raising the kids, home-making responsibilities, and so on. Besides, women, who are not employed outside home, may be said to have less interest in politics, to acquire less politically relevant information, to be less likely to perceive the consequences of various political events, and to be less likely to develop the skill necessary for successful political activism.

This may, more or less, be equally true for women employed outside home.

In the more industrially developed or economically advanced nations, negative attitudes among males persist towards women as candidates for elective office. Hence, women very often face difficulties in obtaining the political party and interest group organizational as well as financial support which is necessary for electoral candidates.

It is universally accepted that education, employment, health care and other facilities for women should follow one another in a meaningful way. But the social milieu is hardly conducive to moving towards an environment of substantive equality for women with men in all spheres of life. It is evident from the UNDP Human Development Reports that women are discriminated against males everywhere—home, workplace or in the community—and are consistently deprived of their share in decision-making in organizations. The picture is not much brighter even in the western countries. The fact remains that constitutional or legal equality may be conducive but not necessarily leads to substantive equality of women regarding decision making.

Poor and inegalitarian work conditions, illiteracy and lack of job skills, low nutrition and high morbidity among women contribute to the overall poverty and poor health record of women all over the world, particularly in the Third World countries like India. Besides, cuts in public and social sector spending on education, health care and child care after the global advent of liberalization policies particularly damage the conditions of women because of their dual responsibility as wage-earners and house-keepers. As in health conditions, a gender gap is clearly visible in education as well. In India, the adult literacy rate for women stands at 39 per cent, compared to 64.3 per cent for men. The combined primary, secondary and tertiary gross enrolment ratio for girls stands at 54.9 per cent, compared to 79.5 per cent for boys.[1]

Malnutrition remains the most serious problem for women in India and throughout South Asia. Their calorie intake is still well below the minimum daily requirement, particularly in the rural areas. The reasons behind malnutrition in women may be attributed to shortage of food supply, strain of child bearing and unequal distribution of food within the household between boys/men and girls/women where boys/men receive more nutritious food than girls/women since the former are considered to be more valuable to the family. Women in the household eat last and least and, in most of the time, the left-over. Thus, over 60 per cent of women in India are anaemic. This sharply reduces their energy and productivity at home and outside.

It is true that this gender gap in health, education and political participation is gradually decreasing. Though slowly, women in different parts of the world are tending to shed their traditional role and entering the diverse spheres of life, opening different windows in their minds. Movements for women empowerment in different parts of the world are playing prominent roles. But there is a lot yet to be achieved by. women.

8.2 WOMEN IN SOCIETY AND POLITICS: THE WORLD VIEW

The statement—men are the masters of the world of politics—applies to all 'mainstream' societies. In almost all political bodies, from the smallest rural organizations to the central legislatures, men predominate. Even in the USA, people are more likely to accept rather a black man than a white woman as their President. Moreover, the South Asian countries, which are well known for their female Presidents and Prime Ministers, never had more than 10 per cent of women in their Parliaments. Any explanation of the internal working mechanisms of political associations would indicate the influence of inherent patriarchal beliefs. Consideration of mass support all the more strengthens the prevalent ideology.

Great Britain, among all the European countries, has the longest history of democracy. But it has fewer women in Parliament than most other European Union members–only France, Greece and Portugal had lower figures in 1994. Almost sixty years after women gained the right to vote and after a second round of feminist movements, in 1990, women's representation in the British Parliament was only 6 per cent. Again, such responsible positions as Ministers, judges and government boards still claim a disproportionately small number of women in terms of the percentage of women visible in the public sphere. Although women are now gradually entering the various avenues of politics, the rate of entry is still negligible. This conspicuous alienation of women from high political ranks is not very difficult to understand. Of course, no direct method of exclusion is visible. But often a high post requires long experience, long apprenticeship, long-distance travel, and so on. Needless to say that all these are male centric indices. The secret selection procedure, too, goes against the recruitment of women. The efforts to mobilize women within the Labour Party considerably changed the situation in the 1990s. After this, all the major political parties in Great Britain tried to reserve seats for women. This increase in the number of women in politics forced the government to consider women's rights issue more seriously.

A reference should be made to Scandinavian countries that have relatively larger representation in the political organizations. By 1984, women had gained 15 per cent of parliamentary seats in Iceland, 26 per cent in Norway and Denmark, 28 per cent in Sweden and 31 per cent in Finland. The advance in this respect was sustained in Norway, which by 1985 had achieved the 'world record': 34 per cent of its National Assembly seats were held by women and women comprised 40.5 per cent of the membership of county councils. It is argued that the increased female representation is based on three main principles:

1. That it is unjust that women are under-represented on decision-making bodies.
2. That valuable human resources are wasted when half the population is not involved in politics.
3. That in politics women will employ a different set of values and pursue different interests from men.

But the actual gains for women in Scandinavian Parliaments have stemmed from such structural factors as the system of proportional representation instead of a purely majoritarian system and initiatives like quota-based reforms.

Compared to the picture of women's representation in political posts in the West and North European countries and the United States of America, in Latin America, Asia and the African nations, i.e. the so-called 'Third World', the picture is widely different. Not only the prolonged history of colonial domination but also the dynamics of internal polities, religion, caste differentiation and a summation of various other factors have given women's issues in these countries quite a different dimension. After the formal ending of colonial domination, many of the Third World countries adopted a policy of 'development'. But this development has certainly not been uniform for all the countries. Again, overall economic development has not necessarily meant equal access for men and women to the benefits of it. Sometimes, development has only strengthened the control of men over resources, causing the gender gap to remain the same or even to widen.

It can also be argued that the sway of the patriarchal ideology is stronger among the upper classes than the lower. Amartya Sen and Jean Dreze's research[2] shows that in India, from 1901 onwards, the male-female ratio was steadily going against women and this ratio was more unfavourable for the upper classes. Veronika Bennholdt Tomsen, a German feminist researcher, argues that the marginalization of women in the Third World does not owe its origin to the traditional patriarchal system. On the contrary, as she opines, it is much more a result of the modern process of development. She explains that the notion of 'housewife', with which we are so familiar today, is basically a nineteenth century Western European concept. This concept through its social acceptance led to the process of what Tomsen describes as 'domestication' or 'house-wifisation'.[3] She further opines that from the very moment money and commodity economy had started to be prominent, women started rotating towards the sphere of less and even unpaid jobs.

In an analysis of Indian rural women in the 1970s, Maria Mies shows that wherever agriculture rapidly expanded creating new social wealth or where modern consumer items such as films, television or alcohol became preponderant, violence against women took on a monstrous magnitude.[4]

In 1991, women constituted 5.2 per cent of the membership of the Lok Sabha and 9.8 per cent of the membership of the Rajya Sabha. This was lower than the preceding 1989 Parliament. The election results in 1996 showed a further decline in women's representation, and in the 1999 election, 8.8 per cent of parliamentarians were women. While this is certainly a worrying trend, the question remains whether greater participation actually indicates possibilities of change for the better since women in general have a tendency to be dominated or influenced by men–no matter whether they are highly placed politically or not. In 1988, the National Perspective Plan for women suggested that a 30 per cent quota for women should be introduced at all levels of elective bodies. Women's groups insisted on restructing this reservation to village panchayat bodies to encourage grass roots participation of women in politics. The consensus around this demand led to the adoption of the 73rd and 74th amendments to the Constitution in 1993. In 1995, there was a revival of the issue of quota, focussing mainly on Parliament. The Bill for the reservation of seats for women that was placed before the eleventh Parliament in 1997 faced opposition from many quarters. Women's groups were primarily accused of the possibility of privileging the elite women only. Thirty-nine women representatives of the 1991–1996 Indian Parliament were mostly middle class, professional women with little or no links with the broader women's movement at all. Among them, a significant section accessed politics through their families. Since there are no "women's only" constituencies, women MPs are not accountable to women alone. All women MPs have made it clear that they are party women first and the party whip can rarely be flouted. All these factors limit the potential of these women MPs to represent the interests of Indian women over a wide range of issues. Again, this is equally applicable to the predominantly muted presence of Indian women at the village panchayat level. An additional reason of it is the lack of literacy among rural women. Thus, a greater or lesser representation of women in high politics is not the most important criterion to assess the status of women in India. What really needs to be introduced is the concrete presence of values, defining, conditioning and limiting the nature of women's existence in the social, political and economic life of the nation.[5]

8.3 MOVEMENTS AND INDIAN WOMEN

Although Indian women in general are less participative in politics than men, yet they have significantly been found to provide leadership in quite a few social and political movements in India.

The Tebhaga movement (1946–1947 and 1948–1949), for instance, was a major peasant upheaval in Bengal (and later in West Bengal) in the 20th century. It was largely led by women. It failed after tremendous sacrifices by sharecroppers and their allies, the landless labourers and petty artisans. But it left a deep impression in the peasantry psyche. Even after a generation, the deprived peasantry nursed a grievance against the establishment. Hence, when Operation Barga was launched, the question was: how to motivate and inspire sharecroppers to come in large numbers to record their names? Apart from the participatory methodology adopted for the purpose of recording their names, it was thought desirable to project this operation as the culminating stage of their Tebhaga struggle to get a two-thirds share of the crop. As the Land Reforms Commissioner of West Bengal, Mr. Debabrata Bandyopadhyay had published two anthologies, titled *From Tebhaga to Operation Barga* and *From Santhal Rebellion to Operation Barga*. For the release of the first book, the village Khanpur in West Dinajpur district was chosen, where on February 20, 1947, 22 persons including a number of women were killed in police firing. A meeting was organized under a big banyan tree near which most of the bodies of the victims fell. The book, however, was going to be released in late 1979. Syed Mansoor Habibullah, the then speaker of the West Bengal Assembly, who was also a former President of the Provincial Kisan Sabha, and Benoy Chaudhury, the then Land Reforms Minister of West Bengal, were present along with a couple of activist leaders of the Tebhaga movement. There was a very large gathering of the village poor at the meeting. As the meeting progressed, an elderly lady, slightly lame, wanted to meet the Minister to give him something. Mr. Bandyopadhyay took her to the Minister. The lady then untied a corner of her sari and produced five empty bullet shells of .303 rifles which she had collected from the field after the firing was over and the police had left. Her father had died of bullet injury. She was in the forefront when a bullet had grazed her skin making her slightly lame.[6] While handing over the empty shells, she told the Minister that she was happy because what her father died for was being realized that day. The Minister took her to the podium and requested her to repeat what she had told him. The Minister then showed the empty shells to the audience. There was a thunderous response from the crowd.

While Tebhaga movement was basically a political movement, in a number of 'new social movements' including women's movements and ecological movements, Indian women's concerns and participation are relatively recent. Both have come to a head in the 1970s and gathered momentum by the 1980s onwards. In social practice since at least the medieval times, women have been subjected to abject male and social domination. Due to lack of enforcement, even equal inheritance right and alimony in case of divorce enjoyed by women in the traditional Muslim personal law and reformed Hindu personal law remain a set of paper rights only. A uniform civil code for all religious communities is envisaged in the Directive Principles of State Policy in the Constitution. But this constitutional goal, too, remains unrealized.

Development process benefits men and women differentially, both in agriculture and industry. Everywhere men outnumber women in work force, in the industrial sector even more strongly. In almost all sectors, women are generally paid less for the same work, are less mobile, and are losing control over physical assets, education, jobs, promotional avenues and technology. Particularly in our country, women are a declining gender in number as well. To alter the biased scales of justice, some kind of cultural revolution is perhaps necessary. It is important to recognize that sex is only a biological fact, but gender inequality is a conscious construction by society and hence should be radically altered. As Kapur and Cossman[7] observe:

> *"Familial ideology constructs the family as the basic and sacred unit in society, and women's role as wives and mothers as natural and immutable. This vision of the ... women's role ... appears ... beyond question. [It] ... continues to limit law's ability to deliver on its promise of equality for women."*

Despite the active participation of women in the freedom movement of India in its Gandhi–Nehru phase, their representation in the political organizations and processes has failed to go beyond tokenism even in the 1990s. In 1974, the Committee on the Status of Women in India in its Report *Towards Equality* had remarked that the declining trend in the number of women legislators is the result of the reluctance of political parties to sponsor women candidates. It had categorically stated:

"The parties would continue to pay lip service to the cause of women's progress and the policy of 'tokenism' by having a few women in the legislative and executive wings of government whose minority and dependent status offer serious obstacles of their acting as spokesmen for women's rights and opportunities."[8]

Yet, the Committee did not recommend reservation for women in the Parliament or State Legislatures for the following reasons:

1. Women's cause has always been supported by all progressive elements, men as well as women.
2. Separate constituencies for women would narrow their outlook.
3. Their interests as such cannot be isolated from economic, social and political interests of groups, strata and classes in the society.
4. System of special representation for women may precipitate similar demands from various other communities and thus threaten national integration.
5. The privilege of reservation, once granted for women, is difficult to withdraw.
6. Women must compete as equals with men since independence.
7. The minority argument is not applicable to women as they are not a community, they are a category.

However, the Committee recommended the establishment of statutory Women's Panchayats at the village level to ensure greater participation by women in the political process. These Women's Panchayats should run not as parallel organizations to the Gram Panchayats, but as an integral part of the Panchayati Raj structure, with autonomy and resources of their own for the management and administration of welfare and development programmes for women and children.

The 1990s have witnessed the 33 per cent reservation for women in Panchayati Raj institutions. Women's organizations and political leaders of all political parties are fighting for similar reservation for women in the Parliament and State Legislatures.

A recent amendment Bill with this objective was largely supported by people launching the women's movement for their reservation. But some segments of the movement were also worried about the following:

- That the quotas could form a ceiling rather than a minimum to be improved upon.
- That women candidates might be dominated because of their dependence on male party leaders.
- That reservation will treat women like a homogenous group, which increases the likelihood that the 'biwi brigade' of the educated, upper class, upper caste women will be elected, particularly because the Bill does not provide for sub-quotas of OBCs.[9]

India Development Report, 1997, contains nothing on women's development. In 1970, females per 100 males in primary schools were only 60, while their percentage dropped to 39 in secondary schools. In 1995, as many as 62 per cent of females were illiterate compared to 35 per cent of males. Maternal mortality rate (per 1,00,000 live births) in 1989–1995 was as high as 437. Beginning with the Sixth Plan (1980–1985), there was a separate chapter on the concern for women's development for the first time emphasizing health, education and employment. The Eighth Plan (1992–1997) mentioned the concept of empowerment of women and the Tenth Plan elaborated a strategy for this in terms of equal access to basic human services, economic self-reliance and gender justice.[10]

Thus, women's movements, to a large extent, were movements launched by women for their own empowerment via broader representation in political bodies. In that sense, they were political movements. Women took part in many environmental movements as well. The Chipko Movement was perhaps the first organized environmental movement in India, principally carried out by tribal women and children of North India. It was a movement for forest conservation where local tribal women encircled the trees like their own children, refusing the loggers of the contractors to cut trees. The word *chipko* means to hug or to cling to. This was initiated by women when all non-violent legal actions had failed to protect trees. The movement started at the end of the 1960s and the beginning of the 1970s. The Chipko Movement was so intensified that even the then Prime Minister of India finally declared that not a single tree in the region of UP would be touched for the next fifteen years. This movement is an example of the most successful women's struggle to conserve forest. It taught the women of the other parts of the globe the need for biodiversity and to reduce consumption of the forest.

Similarly, Narmada Bachao Andolan (NBA) was basically a women's environmental movement led by Ms. Medha Patkar, a noted environmentalist and a follower of Baba Amte, the latter being Gandhi's disciple and a noted social worker. Narmada is a very important river of south-west India. In Narmada Valley, the ancient civilization and culture were grown up by the Bhils and the Gondas, who were the oldest races of Indian civilization. Two large dam reservoirs were planned to be constructed over the river Narmada in Gujarat and Madhya Pradesh, respectively. Medha Patkar and her followers inspected the villages which, in their opinion, would be affected most adversely by this project. After surveying the project, Medha noticed some inherent flaws in the project:

1. The total cost to materialize the project was very high, and it would not bring any profit.
2. More than one million villagers would be badly affected by the project.
3. By affecting plants and animals, the project would hamper the ecological balance.

Many organizations protested against this project and they all started a mass movement under the leadership of Ms. Patkar. This movement, known popularly as the Narmada Bachao Andolan, was a famous women's movement for the protection of the environment. In September, 1989, 50,000 people gathered in Harsud Valley and raised their voice to ban the project. The major arguments of the movement were:

1. The government estimate to generate 1450 MW of electricity was a false estimate. According to the NBA, the total amount of electricity generated will not exceed 50 MW.
2. It will not contribute to the irrigation facility.
3. As against the government prediction, the NBA predicted that flood might be checked in one area while many more areas would be flooded.
4. NBA estimated that the local loss would exceed ₹ 40,000 crores.
5. One million people will become homeless and will lose agricultural land.

Women have also been found in recent times to make strong protest movements against the rising prices of essential commodities in Maharashtra and Gujarat. The call for "Total Revolution" by J.P. Narayan pushed the women to involve themselves in the movement of Nava Nirman. The Self Employed Women's Association (SEWA) gives opportunities to women to project themselves in every walk of life. SEWA's unforgettable role to arouse political, social and economic consciousness among the female hawkers of Ahmedabad deserves special praise. By providing short-term loans, the SEWA helps the female unorganized sector throughout India. In the eighties of the last century, women's movements were more organized. Women started taking parts in various organizational and political activities, such as demand for a separate State of Uttarakhand, agitations against Bhopal Gas Tragedy, etc.

Very recently, in 2006 in West Bengal, women took a leading role in the mass agitation against the Left Front Government's policy of agricultural land acquisition with a view to speed up industrialization in the State. In Nandigram of East Midnapore district and in Singur of Hughly district, the women of the families of landholding classes constructed barricades against the police with the domestic articles like broom, knife, stick, umbrella, bricks, and so on. On March 14, 2007, a number of rural women and children of Nandigram were either fatally injured or dead in an open confrontation with the police and also with the CPI(M) cadres. In Singur, Ms. Tapasi Malick was raped and murdered in December, 2006. As a result of mass agitation, in these two places led principally by women, industrialization could not even be started in West Bengal.

8.4 INDIAN WOMEN AND PANCHAYATI RAJ POLITICS: A PRE-RESERVATION PICTURE

The State machinery of India, from the very beginning, has tried to establish gender equality in many ways. In Part III (Fundamental Rights) of our Constitution, equality of citizens irrespective of sexes has been established in unequivocal terms. Yet, the Committee on the Status of Women in India (CSWI), after conducting an extensive review of the situation of women in India in 1974, found in its report entitled *Towards Equality* that the constitutional guarantee of equality had "remained an unrealized dream" for the vast majority of Indian women.[11] It has been observed that neither the norms nor the institutions were in a place that would enable women to fulfil the multiple roles that they were expected to play.

Subsequently, a National Policy on Education was undertaken which envisaged a positive interventionist role for education in the empowerment of women. The National Perspective Plan for Women was implemented in 1988. The National Commission for Women was set up in 1992. All such efforts were intended to improve the existing situation regarding the status of women.

The local self government has been embodied as an 'aspiration' in the Constitution of India in 1950. The power to implement it was devolved to States. The first generation panchayats following the Balwantrai Mehta Committee Report had a chequered career. The second generation panchayats, which were created as a follow-up of the Asoka Mehta Committee, had no better fate, with the minor exceptions of West Bengal and Karnataka.

In West Bengal, elections to the local bodies were held at regular intervals. Considerable quantity of power was devolved to these elected bodies. But the panchayat bodies in West Bengal, just like those in the rest of India, reflect utterly poor representation of women. Professor Sonali Chakravarti Banerjee explains it in the following way: "In modern India, women came to public life first through the freedom movement and then through the chances offered by universal franchise and other modernising socio-political forces. In the process, India has received a few nationally important women leaders, though the egalitarian spirit has hardly percolated down to the grass roots levels. In this sense, therefore, the study of the gender composition of Panchayati leadership is also a study of the interplay between tradition and modernity in a changing rural society."[12] Her study confirms the singularly strong sexist bias prevalent in the three-tier Panchayati Raj in India during the pre-reservation period. It is, indeed, remarkable that there has not been a single woman leader in the Hugli Zilla Parishad since its inception (1978) till 1988. All the Sabhadhipatis and Sahakari Sabhadhipatis have only been males since 1978. Thus, the Zilla Parishad leadership has been a male monopoly sector in the absolute sense of the term. Even among the ordinary elected members, there have been very few women. In 1978, no woman was elected to the Zilla Parishad, while in 1983 and 1988, the number of elected female members was 3 and 1, respectively.[13]

Chakravarti Banerjee's study (2002) reveals that this gross under-representation of women is equally pronounced at the Panchayat Samiti level also. In 1983, there was no woman in the leadership positions in any of the Panchayat Samitis. All the Sabhapatis and Sahakari Sabhapatis in the 18 Panchayat Samitis of the Hugli district were males only. In 1988, out of 582 Panchayat Samiti seats, only 3 went to women. Thus, women claimed only 0.5 per cent of the total number of Panchayat Samiti seats. No wonder that their share in the leadership positions came to a naught.

The position of women had rather improved at the Gram Panchayat level in later years. In 1978, there were 8 elected women out of the 2887 elected Gram Panchayat members in the district. No woman was made either Pradhan or Upa-Pradhan in any of the Gram Panchayats in the first panchayat election (1978). In 1983 also, there was no woman

Pradhan or Upa-Pradhan in the district of Hugli. In 1988, however, the total number of elected women members in Gram Panchayat tier came upto 24 (out of a total of 3437 seats). Out of these 24 elected women again, one was elected as Pradhan and three as Upa-Pradhans.[14]

Broadly speaking, the data presented above establish the absolute marginalization of women in the Panchayati Raj before the formula of reservation was imposed from above.

Such a finding regarding the gender bias of the Panchayati Raj organization in the pre-reservation phase confirms similar findings obtained by other studies in this and allied fields. Studies of traditional rural societies have almost everywhere noted the inherent male biases of the social organizations.[15] In the specific case of the Panchayati Raj in India, scholars have detected the same gender bias at every level. A case study conducted in the 1950s in the Jaunpur district of Uttar Pradesh during the local body elections there found that "... it was a male-dominated election of the forty-nine candidates who ran for office and not a single one was a woman. In interview after interview, the women voiced surprise at the notion of voting in any other way than the husband or the male family head or in a way contrary to his wishes or directions. The women were prevailingly aware of the rivalry of A and B and of the stand of their families in respect to these two office seekers. But they were usually uninformed about the contests for panchayat membership in the district and confused about the identities of the candidates. When they were asked for whom they would vote, a common answer was that they would be told what to do by the senior males of the family when the time came".[16]

In a subsequent study conducted in Rajasthan in the 1970s, Bhargava also found the political arena to be a domain of male sex. Bhargava did not find any elected woman at the village Panchayat level or at the Zilla Parishad level, though he could find one elected member in one Panchayat Samiti. He rightly concluded that "in the rural areas when a woman enters into politics, she is taken as an exception."[17]

Again, in a relatively recent study conducted in the Telengana region of Andhra Pradesh, V. Lalini also found the role of women in panchayats to be totally marginal. Out of a total number of 288 panchayat leaders under study, Lalini identified 29 women with elected position in the Panchayat institutions.[18]

In sharp contrast to most other regions of India, the Bengal society in the nineteenth century witnessed several social reform movements for the emancipation of women. But in spite of such an enlightened tradition, however, the male bias of the culture remained pronounced. While identifying the "dominant elite" of the towns and villages of Bengal at the beginning of the twentieth century, Broomfield referred to them as "the Bhadralok, literally ... the gentlemen", as opposed to the ladies.[19] The freedom movement gave birth to some remarkable women freedom fighters, but it was mostly the middle class urban women who came to the forefront during this period and the rural traditions were kept in tact.

In an article by Sushil K. Dey, an architect of the Community Development Programme in West Bengal, one can find perhaps the first concrete reference to a female leader in the rural self government of our province. Dey referred to one village called Sukna, where an aboriginal woman of middle age emerged to leadership when she kept the men on a job of restoring a derelict pond by threatening a strike of all housewives if they left it for other attraction. She has been wise and prominent in village councils since then.[20]

After the panchayat elections in 1978, the Government of West Bengal studied the working of the Gram Panchayats in 1980 and found that "all the elected members of the Gram Panchayats excepting a few happen to be male."[21] G.K. Lieten (1992) devoted considerable amount of attention to the gender issue in panchayats and noted the quasi-complete absence of women in the Panchayati Raj organizations in the State. Out of the 480 candidates for Gram Panchayat and Panchayat Samiti elections in the area under his study, as many as 478 were males. Lieten even observed that many political leaders and candidates did not seem to be aware of the necessity to induce women into all spheres of public life as one of the means of eliminating the gender discrimination.[22] Neil Webster (1992) was equally emphatic in denouncing the gender discrimination in West Bengal Panchayats. He noted that women have largely failed to gain representation in Panchayats because of the social structure and cultural practices against any woman candidate.[23] The semi-official Mukarji–Bandyopadhyay Report (1993) also observed that "largely because of societal constraints, there are very few women in the Panchayats at present, and even fewer in key positions. Women's representation is less than one per cent of the total elected Panchayat members."[24]

8.5 CONSTITUTIONAL PROVISION FOR THE UPLIFT OF WOMEN

The Indian Constitution specifically provides for the protection of the rights of the women. The Constitution-makers knew that within the given socio-cultural order, it might not be possible for women to get gender justice. They suggested special provisions for women on the lines of other weaker sections of society, especially in the Fundamental Rights and the Directive Principles of State Policy of the Indian Constitution. Various important Articles have accordingly been introduced to provide protective discrimination and to promote and protect the interests of the new protagonist–the women.

Article 10 of our Constitution ensures equality of women and their equal protection before the law. Articles 14 and 15 guarantee a life of dignity without discriminating against women on the basis of religion, race, sex, belief, faith or worship. Article 15(1) prohibits discrimination on grounds of religion, sex, caste, birth and a number of other factors. Article 15(3) categorically States: "Nothing in this Article shall prevent the State from making any special provision for women and children." Article 16 focuses on the specific subject of equality in public employment. Article 16(1) seeks to guarantee equality of opportunity in such employment. Article 16(2) prohibits discrimination in public employment on grounds of religion, race or sex.

In this context, it will be relevant to see what Article 40 of our Constitution states:

"The State shall take steps to organize village panchayats and endow them with such powers and authority as may be necessary to enable them to function as units of self-government."

To achieve this aim, the 73rd Amendment has been introduced to the Constitution of India to ensure the representation of women in the various statutory bodies of local self government. All the States adopted the new panchayat legislation by 23rd April, 1994.

The provisions of the 73rd Amendment Act are as under:

- Not less than one-third of the seats have been reserved for women (including that of SCs and STs) and these may be allotted by rotation to different constituencies of a panchayat.
- In proportion to the population of SCs and STs in an area, seats have been reserved for SCs and STs. There is reservation for women in these seats allotted to SCs and STs. Not less than one-third of the total number of seats may be reserved for women.
- Not less than one-third of the total number of seats for the offices of the chairpersons of each level have been reserved for women. This will be rotated among different panchayats at each tier–Gram Panchayat, Panchayat Samiti and Zilla Parishad.
- There are certain general features, which could be taken advantage of by women, such as direct elections for membership and Sarpanch (President) posts, at the grass roots (Gram Panchayat) as well as the intermediate (Panchayat Samiti) levels.
- It has been left to the different States to provide for reservation for membership as chairperson to those hailing from backward classes, if they choose so.

8.5.1 81st Amendment Bill

Another important endeavour in the direction of women's upliftment is the 81st Amendment Bill for 33 per cent women's reservation in Parliament and State Legislatures. It was introduced for the first time in 1996 in the Lok Sabha. After much debates, the Bill was referred to a Select Committee. The passage of this Constitutional Amendment

Bill [Article 330(A)], however, has been deferred again and again. The main objection is the exclusion of reservation for women in minority and the backward groups, specially the OBCs. Some important features of the 81st Constitution Amendment Bill are as under:

- 33 per cent seats to be reserved for women in the Lok Sabha and State assemblies.
- One-third of these seats to be reserved for SC/ST women.
- Bill not to be applied to States/Union Territories, where seats reserved for SC/STs is less than three.

India's search for the goal towards gender equality and gender justice began with the establishment of the Central Social Welfare Board in 1953. The concept of a national machinery for women's uplift has been evolving ever since. A Department of Women and Child Development was set up in 1985 under the Ministry of Human Resource Development. Besides several Constitutional and legal measures, the State has also initiated several schemes and programmes at the micro-level such as the *Development of Women and Children in Rural Areas, Integrated Child Development Services, Mid-day Meals, Education for the Girl Child and Micro-credit,* specially targeted at the marginalized women.

The advocates of women's movements all over the world are moving towards the understanding that the demands for women's rights, namely equality of participation, opportunity and agency in all spheres of life, should be directed primarily to institutions that constitute the structure of society and set the agenda of women's lives.[25]

The National Perspective Plan for Women's Development–1988–2000 had been formulated in 1988. "The Shramshakti Report" also appeared in the same year. By an Act of Parliament, The National Commission for Women came into effect in 1990 to investigate and examine all matters relating to the safeguards provided to women under the Constitution and other laws.

In view of her commitment to various international conventions, India designed a National Policy for Empowerment of Women in 1996. The Policy categorically stipulates that:

- Human rights and fundamental freedom for women on equal basis with men need to be ensured.
- All forms of violence against women–physical, mental, domestic or social–need to be eliminated.
- No discrimination would be allowed in law or practice against women.
- All forms of discrimination against and violation of the rights of girl child would be eliminated by undertaking strong steps including punitive ones.
- Synergy of development measures would be designed for holistic empowerment of women.

- Women's active participation in the decision-making is to be ensured.
- Policies, programmes and systems would be established in order to ensure mainstreaming of women's perspective.
- Gender sensitization programmes would be conducted on regular basis for all sections of society.
- Media should be used to portray a positive image of women.
- For eradication of poverty and provision for women's basic needs, several programmes should be initiated in order to (a) alleviate poverty, (b) provide food security, (c) arrange housing and shelter, (d) provide equal education, (e) formulate a holistic approach to women's health, (f) formulate macro-economic and social policies by institutionalizing women's participation in economic development, and (g) arrange support services like child care facility, etc. to enable women to participate effectively in developmental processes and to provide special attention to the needs of women in providing safe drinking water, sewage disposal and sanitation.
- Women's perspective would be reflected in the policies and programmes for eco-system management.
- Diversity of women's situation is to be acknowledged and special programmes need to be made available for women in the disadvantaged group.
- Budgetary provision is to be enhanced in the programmes related to women.
- Non-Governmental Organizations are to be involved in the formulation and implementation of all policies and programmes affecting the women.
- Gender development indices would be developed by the government.
- Desegregated gender studies would be collected, compiled and published regularly.
- International, regional and sub-regional cooperation for the empowerment of women will be strongly encouraged.

The National Policy for Empowerment of Women (1996) has suggested elaborate strategies and action plans to actualize the prescribed goals. It has an action plan to be initiated at the grass roots, district/sub-district, State and national levels. For the State and national levels, the policy suggests that there would be Councils for giving broad policy advice, guidance and directions. It also suggests that all the Central and State Ministries would have the gender component in their action plans. It suggests elaborate action for the Executive and Legislature in all the areas related to physical, social, cultural, economic and livelihood security of women.

The National Policy States that at "the grass roots, women will be organized into self-help groups at the Anganwari level. These women's groups will be helped to institutionalize themselves into registered societies and to federate at the block/town level. Such societies will bring about synergistic implementation of all the social and economic development programmes by drawing resources made available through government and non-government channels, including banks and financial institutions; and by establishing a close interface with the panchayats/ municipalities."

The *National Commission for Women (NCW),* which was basically a statutory body, was constituted by the government in January 1991. It was constituted with a specific mandate to study and monitor all matters relating to the constitutional and legal safeguards provided for women; to review the existing legislation to suggest amendments wherever necessary; and to look into complaints involving deprivation of the rights of women. Similar Commissions have also been set up in nine States. The NCW has taken up a number of activities, some of which are as under:

- Setting up of 11 expert committees to tender advice on various women's issues
- Conducting pariwarik lok adalats
- Making complaints and pre-litigation cells
- Creating legal awareness
- Welfare of women prisoners and under trials
- Action of issues of women and children.

In order to coordinate and integrate components of all sectoral programmes and to facilitate their convergence to empower women, Indira Mahila Yojana (IMY) was launched as a strategy on August 20, 1995. It proposed to bring out a mechanism by which there could be a systematic coordination and a meaningful integration of various programmes of different sectors to meet women's needs and to ensure that women's interests were taken care of and provided for under each scheme. It was proposed that the mechanism would be operated at the district level as a sub-plan for women to percolate down to the village level appropriately through the Indira Mahila Kendras (IMKs) at village level and Indira Mahila Block Kendras (IMBKs) at block level. The ultimate objective of Indira Mahila Yojana is to empower women by ensuring their direct access to resources through a sustained process of mobilization and convergence of all the ongoing sectoral programmes. The IMY is sought to be operated as a central sponsored scheme. The three basic constituents of IMY are as follows:

- Convergence of inter-sectoral services
- Income generation activities
- Sustained process of education/awareness generation.

Under the proposed convergence of inter-sectoral services, IMY will provide the umbrella cover and all sectoral programmes aimed at women's welfare, including non-formal education, training, formal primary education, skill development, health, family welfare programmes and other minimum needs programmes like drinking water, sanitation, housing roads, electrification, etc. would converge at the village level as per the needs, demands and requirements articulated by the IMY. Income generation activities include creation of employment opportunities through group-dynamics and participation in a broad range of economic activities suited to the local requirements. Under a sustained process of education/awareness generation, the IMY seeks to create a general awareness among women through ensuring information specific to the equality of social status, legal rights, like those of property and inheritance, constitutional safeguards and on different development programmes or issues concerning women.

8.6 THE IMMEDIATE RESULTS: POST-RESERVATION PICTURE

With the compulsory 33 per cent reservation of seats for women in the panchayati raj system, the formal participatory aspect has rather been fulfilled. But questions may still be raised as to whether this 'participation' is really meaningful to the concerned women or whether this 'participation' has anything to do with women's 'empowerment' in the truest sense of the term. Some such questions may partially be answered and some general observations may be made with reference to some empirical studies made particularly in West Bengal and their analyses.

Raghav Chattopadhyay and Esther Duflo (2004) have carried out a study of 166 Gram Panchayats in the district of Birbhum in West Bengal.[26] Their study has focused specifically on the effect of reservation of seats for women in the Gram Panchayats, both as ordinary members and Panchayat Pradhans. It has tried to find out the patterns of participation in Gram Panchayats and village meetings, depending upon cross-sectional comparisons between villages with and without reserved seats.

Maitreesh Ghatak and Maitreya Ghatak (2002) have conducted a study focusing on the attendance at Gram Sansad meetings in a sample of 20 panchayat constituencies located in 14 Gram Panchayats in three different districts of West Bengal–24 Parganas (North), 24 Parganas (South) and South Dinajpur.[27]

Another study, which may be referred to in this context, was made by Prabhat Datta and Chandan Datta (1999) in one block in the district of Birbhum to examine women's participation in West Bengal panchayats empirically.[28]

Again, Pranab Bardhan and Dilip Mookherjee (2004) have undertaken another study specifically on the perception, role and problems faced by women panchayat members in all the districts of West Bengal.[29]

Biswanath Chakraborty has made study on people's participation in local governance in two Gram Panchayats of West Bengal–Mirzapur–Bankipur Gram Panchayat in Singur Block of Hugli district and Maynaguri Gram Panchayat in Maynaguri Block of Jalpaiguri district–during the period between January, 2001 and December, 2003.[30] Among various aspects of popular participation, Chakraborty has examined women's participation in Gram Sansad and Gram Sabha meetings, as well. Chakraborty has made another study (2007), focusing on the Gram Panchayats of 24–Parganas (South), in which, among other things, women's participation, success and empowerment have been measured.

On the basis of another study made by Pranab Bardhan, Sandip Mitra, Dilip Mookherjee and Abhirup Sarkar on the panchayat activities of all the districts of West Bengal except Darjeeling during 2003–2005, the authors have come to the conclusion of a very poor representation of women in the panchayat bodies of West Bengal. Regarding their attendance in the meetings of the Gram Sabha, their participation in the form of raising voice in such meetings and their contribution to political campaigns, their role is markedly insignificant compared to that of their male counterparts and regarding all the above criteria, there is a clear male bias.[31] In a more recent study such authors as Bardhan, Mookherjee and M.L. Parra Torrado have found the effects of reservation for women chairpersons of local government for a specific West Bengal district, suggesting that the effects of reservation are highly context-specific. Reservations for women, as the authors find, are not accompanied by improvements of the vulnerable groups within the villages.[32]

The post-reservation picture in UP, regarding female representation in Panchayats, is no better than that in West Bengal. A study of three villages from Meerut district in UP made by S. Pai cautions that unless reservations are accompanied by female literacy, independent voting rights and the consequent change in the women's status in society, women will continue to act as mere puppet representatives at the hands of the male members of their household.[33]

The relevant findings of all the above mentioned studies on the question of women's participation in local self government may be summarized as under:

- Prior to reservation (73rd Amendment, 1993), when representation of women was not mandatory, women were significantly under-represented.[34]
- This picture changed significantly with the introduction of the policy of reservation of seats in panchayats for women candidates. The gender profile of the Gram Panchayat members and Pradhans consequently underwent a sharp change.

- Women members significantly belong to the youth (18–39 years of age). Hence, there is a probability of future women leadership coming out of these first generation women panchayat members.
- Chakraborty's study (2007) establishes the fact that increased participation of women leads to increased success rates of a large number of programmes, of which the Pulse Polio Immunization Programme may specifically be mentioned.
- It may be questioned whether women's capacity of taking decisions in panchayat institutions was really enhanced with reservation. But their social status was unquestionably uplifted. The improved position of women in the familial decision-making process was significantly noticed.
- With respect to the question of attending Gram Sabha and Gram Sansad meetings, the participation rate of women is significantly low. Although it is reasonably low (12 per cent) overall, yet for women it is even lower–only 9 per cent (Ghatak and Ghatak). This is more or less consistent with the Gram Sabha and Gram Sansad attendance rate as reported by Chakraborty (2001–2003) and the Gram Sabha attendance rate as reported by Chattopadhyay and Duflo (2004). Again, there is a significant tendency for the attendees to be associated with one of the main political parties, with a strong bias in favour of the dominant party in the constituency. On an average, two-thirds of the constituencies were secured by the Left Front and a similar proportion of attendees reported a political affiliation with any of the Left parties. In constituencies where a non-Left Front candidate had secured the seat, the attendance rate of Left Front–affiliated voters was less than one-third uniformly. Hence those voters that were affiliated with the Opposition tended to stay away from such meetings disproportionately (Ghatak and Ghatak, 2002).
- Chattopadhyay and Duflo observe that reservation of Pradhan positions for women meant a remarkably prominent statistical shift in allocation of public expenditure for Gram Panchayats. In Gram Panchayats where the offices of Pradhans are reserved for women candidates, expenditure on drinking water facilities has been increased by 7 per cent, on road maintenance by 39 per cent, while that on informal education centres has been decreased by about 20 per cent. Priority-wise, the two highest items, according to women's consideration, were drinking water and road improvement (31 per cent each), while irrigation and education were among the two lowest items (4 per cent and 6 per cent respectively). On the contrary, the items according to men's consideration consisted of road improvement (25 per cent), irrigation (20 per cent), drinking water (17 per cent) and education (12 per cent).

- Bardhan–Mookherjee study (2004) finds that the provision of benefits of the system has been markedly uneven. Women, SC/ST members and those not politically affiliated with the party in power in the local area still participate in panchayats at low levels. Yet, seat reservations for minorities including women have helped to alleviate this imbalance. Another study by Bardhan et al. (2003–2005) also draws the same conclusion regarding women's position in the panchayat bodies in West Bengal.

8.7 GRASS ROOTS INITIATIVES: PICTURE OF INDIAN PANCHAYATS IN GENERAL

Women in India form the core of the marginalized groups, irrespective of their caste, class, ethnicity and nationality. The process of empowerment for the marginalized women is not simply a statutory provision which is to be given from above. Rather, it is a process to be reactivated with initiatives from below. The process of empowerment aims to demolish the subordinate position of women. It wants to immediately transform the existing social norms which legitimize the structure of subordination of women. Whether the contemporary development discourse would provide the required space for creating an alternative structure and identity of the women from the marginalized groups in the society is a crucial question. What they really need is not a strategy for co-option and integration, but alternative and autonomous avenues for grass roots mobilization that would create and sustain a new collective identity.[35]

Since the introduction of reservation, both intensive and extensive experimentation in grass roots initiatives were undertaken by the Panchayati Raj Institutions in rural India. Various studies conducted throughout India arrive at the following observations regarding women's position in rural self government:

- Representation of women in the panchayat bodies has increased significantly (since the 33 per cent reservation has been made mandatory). In some States like Karnataka, the rate of participation has gone up to 43 per cent.
- Women's participation in the meetings of the panchayati raj bodies has also increased in spite of resistance from conservative forces. On a number of occasions, women are no longer passive participants in the activities of panchayat bodies.
- Though, initially, decisions made by women panchayat functionaries were being widely influenced by pressure from the male members of their families, women are no longer puppet like entities in the panchayats at present. They rather exhibit their independent leadership (Singha Roy, 2001).[36]
- Women have shown greater efficiency and transparency in running the public affairs in panchayats (Mathew, 2003).[37]

8.7.1 Women's Representation in Second Generation Panchayats: Some Efforts

One of the most crucial factors in the leadership structure of the second generation panchayats (i.e. panchayats existing in Andhra Pradesh, Karnataka, Kerala and West Bengal) is the representation of women. Hence, there is reservation of seats in all the second generation panchayats. The demand for reservation of seats for women was forcefully presented in the National Perspective Plan (1988). The Rajiv Gandhi Government, which brought forth the 69th Constitution Amendment Bill in the Parliament in 1986, went a step further by suggesting that 30 per cent of the seats in the panchayats had to be reserved for women. However, the Karnataka legislation provided for 25 per cent reservation of seats, while the Andhra Pradesh legislation made provision for 9 per cent reservation, and the Kerala District Councils Act reserved 30 per cent of the seats in the district councils for women. Of the second generation panchayats, West Bengal had lagged behind for some time. After the 73rd Constitution Amendment (1993), the State Government amended the panchayat legislation for the reservation of 33.33 per cent seats for women in the panchayat bodies. It is, however, interesting to note that besides Kerala, the performance of other Indian States in this respect is not remarkable. While in States like Andhra Pradesh, there are legal flaws, the election results in Karnataka show that women in panchayats come from the richer section of the community and do not really participate in panchayat activities.

Manikyamba studied the social background and role of women presiding officers in the mandal praja parishad in Andhra Pradesh during 1989–1990.[38] This is an interesting study made just before the introduction of the 73rd Amendment. The study reveals that 38.9 and 22.2 per cent of the women Presidents belong to two dominant communities–Reddy and Kappu, respectively. Of women Presidents, 66.7 and 33.3 per cent belong to rich and middle income group families. Besides, 33 per cent of the women Presidents operate with the active help and advice of their husbands. The question may thus be raised as to whether such female leadership can really play any significant role in promoting the cause of the poor women.

It is in Kerala where the situation regarding women's representation in panchayat bodies is qualitatively different. The Kerala legislation provides for 30 per cent reservation of seats for women in the district councils. The election results show that 35 per cent of the members are women and of them 13 per cent are landless.

This shows that reservation by itself does not serve the purpose. It is not an end in itself, but a means to an end. The purpose of women's reservation in the grass roots institutions will be achieved if the environment of the institutions undergoes necessary changes. For rural India, as observes a scholar,[39] it is land reforms which can pave the road for real participation by those women whose participation can add a new dimension to the panchayati raj in India.

8.8 EMPOWERMENT AND DEVELOPMENT

Women's participation in the panchayats is sought to be widened with a view to developing the socio-economic conditions of women. But in relating participation directly to development, there are several problems. A number of questions gradually surround us, as one scholar[40] points out,–how do we view 'development'? What exactly is meant by 'development'? Whose 'development' are we talking about? Likewise, is 'participation' a flat concept? How many forms can political participation take? And finally, can we think and talk about 'women'? Who are these women? Do they constitute any homogeneous unit? These various questions cannot be answered quite easily.

The word 'development' has a typical economic component. It has several synonyms like growth, expansion, etc. which are said to have an overtly economic flavour. Thus, development can be equated with the growth of gross national product or per capita income, increase in the price-index, a booming market, a rise in the points of share market, and so on. All these reflect an economic growth, which again is measured mostly in terms of an increase in a person's real income, his/her daily consumption, and so on.

Following Sen's (2000)[41] famous argument, development may be viewed as the process of expanding real freedoms that people enjoy. In order to increase real freedoms, growth of GNP or increase in per capita income is, of course, necessary. But freedoms depend to a large extent on other determinants like social and economic arrangements, e.g. facilities for education and health care; political and civil rights, e.g. liberty to participate in debates and discussions, etc. This, again, requires a great amount of economic advancement, industrialization, increase in personal income, etc. But these are not all. Development requires removal of poverty as well as tyranny; poor economic opportunities as well as systemic social deprivation; neglect of public facilities as well as religious intolerance; press censorship as well as overactivity of the repressive State.

In recent years, the issues of development and empowerment of women have acquired immense significance. Over the last five decades, the thrust of development has been shifted to the marginalized in India. From the concern of 'growth with stability' during the 1950s, the focus has been shifted since the 1970s to 'growth with social justice'.

In the context of globalization and new economic order, the concept of 'development with empowerment' represents a new coinage, re-orienting the pre-existing social development paradigm towards a process of sharing of power. First of all, there is the necessity to comprehend these dimensions in order to comprehend the nature of deprivation and marginalization of women in society. The question of empowerment of women must also take into account the given socio-economic and political conditions of the society in which women are situated.

Those who have the socio-economic and political power are those who control the knowledge and material resources, and also the ideology. Hence, the process of gaining control over the self, ideology as well as material and knowledge resources, which determine power, may be termed empowerment (Battiwala, 1993).[42] As empowerment deals with power, from the perspective of the marginalized groups, it challenges the power structures of subordination. Empowerment is concerned, as Sen and Grown (1988) observe, with the transformation of the structure of subordination.[43] It implies a process of redistribution of power within and between families or societies. It also implies a process which aims at social equality, that can be achieved only by disempowering some structures, systems and institutions. To Sharma (1992), empowerment means a specific focus on the disadvantaged sections of the society. It aims at changing the nature and direction of the systemic forces which marginalize them.[44] The processes of demolition of the pre-existing structure of subordination and redistribution of power are not automatic. These involve participatory approaches that enable people to emancipate themselves (Kronenburg, 1986),[45] a process of creation of new knowledge (Collins, 1990),[46] a process of conscientization (Freire, 1972),[47] and new identity formation. Hence, empowerment should be viewed not as an end in itself, but as a means to an end, a strategy to bring liberation from all types of domination.

8.9 EMPOWERMENT OF WOMEN: SOME PROBLEMS AND CONSTRAINTS

The rosy picture regarding women's participation in the Panchayati Raj Institutions is not without problems and inherent constraints.

In the first place, over the last fifty years or so, the governmental structure of our State has remained more or less the same with a considerable continuity with the colonial past. Though a number of policies have been formulated and reformulated for the empowerment of women, the agencies for the implementation of the policies have remained unchanged. Hence, there have not been much qualitative changes in the status of women belonging to the marginalized groups of society. Immediately after independence, the women of the marginalized groups have faced the forces of modernity. They have been victimized both because of being women and because of being members of the oppressed sections of society. The various social ills like poverty, unemployment, non-recognition of work, low wages, illiteracy, ignorance, ill-health and the absence of basic amenities of life have been cruelly heaped on them.

Secondly, many steps in the empowerment of women have been taken in India and many more are still required. The constitutional and non-constitutional initiatives have been many, but these have been stricken with various loopholes. The National Policy for Empowerment of Women says very little on grass roots mobilization and resources for the betterment of women. The panchayat bodies are not free from the clutches of the traditional bureaucratic control. The local power lobby also uses its manipulative tactics to retain its influence. It provides ready base for the integration of local labour and some other productive resources with the national and global forces to maximize its own class interests. It still maintains its domination in society. Only through sustained grass roots mobilization, the rising gender consciousness at the grass roots can encounter these forces like local power lobby.

Thirdly, instances of caste and gender-based atrocities can be cited from many States of India. In Madhya Pradesh, for instance, the aftermath of elections to the panchayats, held in the beginning of the twenty-first century in four of its districts viz. Raigarh, Chhatatpur, Raisen and East Nimar, saw ugly abuses of authority. The incidents of a lady Sarpanch being paraded naked, another lady Sarpanch being gang-raped, an Up-Sarpanch being tortured, and a dalit panchayat member being beaten up, have come into limelight.[48]

Fourthly, the implementation of several Acts of Parliament pertaining to the protection of women has been thoroughly ineffective. The Suppression of Immoral Traffic in Women and Girls, 1956, has not been able to arrest the problem of trafficking and prevent the exploitation of women. The Indecent Representation of Women (Prohibition) Act, 1986, has not been systematically enforced. The National Commission of Women Act (1990), which empowers the National Commission of Women to investigate, examine and review all matters relating to safeguards provided for women under the Constitution and other relevant laws, is not satisfactory according to the National Commission of Women. The Commission feels that it should have the power to prosecute and summarily decide on cases of violation of gender justice. Again, there should be commissions for women at State and district levels as well.

Fifthly, studies conducted in various parts of the country bring forth the gender insensitivity of the grass roots workers, illiteracy, lack of training of the marginalized women at the grass roots and the prevailing ideology of patriarchy and gender segregation. These factors have contributed towards the process of marginalization of women who belong to the more deprived sections of society. Again, there are several financial and infrastructural constraints in women's empowerment in panchayat bodies. Attitudes of administrators towards the gender question, which have been Stated to be traditional and stereotyped, are also considered to be an inherent problem in women's empowerment.

As a result of all such flaws, the formal political participation of women in India is a mere 7 per cent. The social agenda hidden in the demand for political representation of women and the larger struggle for equal opportunities continue to pose a challenge to the institutions of democracy.[49]

8.10 WOMEN'S EMPOWERMENT: AN OPTIMISTIC VIEW

It is widely discussed throughout India that women's representation continues to be only token even if the legal stipulations have developed during the first four decades of independence. In this section, we concentrate on a paper (1999) by Nirmala Buch entitled "Women's Experience in New Panchayats: The Emerging Leadership of Rural Women", based principally on a study made in Madhya Pradesh, Rajasthan and UP. It is the follow-up of the 73rd Constitutional Amendment, which is the main focus of the study, documenting the profile, experience, impact and other perceptions about the women in panchayats. Buch has clearly stated that the 73rd Constitutional Amendment has given a new direction for women's representation in panchayats by guaranteeing a critical base of one-third representation which has not been possible so far in other political institutions. In her study, Buch has looked at women's experience in their new political role as panchayat leaders, problems of participation, support of families, communities and other social collectives. She has also tried to see whether this new presence and experience have any empowering effect. Buch and her associates took up the study with no assumptions and to really find out what was happening. She tried not to arrive at simplistic conclusions regarding women, their families, the community and all the social collectives, and the role of the State and the real focus of various interventions.

Buch clearly asserts that the results of her study are encouraging. A number of myths about these women are exploded which can help us to avoid simplistic generalizations about rural Indian women's disinterest in politics, passivity and non-participation in local political institutions, proxyism by their male kins and women's universal political connectivity and belonging only to well-off sections if entering panchayats.

Buch has also tried to see if the formal change made by the 73rd Constitutional Amendment adequately addresses this marginality. Can women's numerical presence transform these structures and make them more receptive to women's needs and concerns? If 33 per cent reservation rules the Panchayati Raj in India, will the system of reservation not defeat the intentions of the amendment? From the study, however, hopes have been expressed that the process of empowerment of women in panchayats would enable them to re-examine their lives, recognize the sources and structures of power and of their own subordination, and initiate action to challenge the existing ideologies as well as structures and institutions. Women would move, as it is hoped from the study, from positions of silence to gaining voice. We may see their transformation from uneducated, unquestioning persons to questioning individuals, who may value their own knowledge and sense of rationality. They may change from having restricted mobility and right to move about only if escorted by men, to gaining much greater autonomy and mobility attending meetings, going to public offices without male escorts and, most significantly, from politically passive persons to significantly conscious and active agents in the political process.

But it is being said that "Women have come into politics as proxy candidates and continue to be manipulated by powerful patriarchal elites. A report on eight short State studies in early 1995 stated that many women were proxy candidates, they were not able to make their presence felt at meetings, were ill informed about procedures and functions of panchayats...." (ISST:1995). Buch's observation is that this is perhaps too quick a conclusion within a year or less of panchayat elections. She adds that such a report significantly contrasts with the experience of her first male research assistant's first visit to meet one of the village panchayat women chairpersons in the predominantly tribal district of Jhabua in Madhya Pradesh. Her leadership, command, confidence and clarity in dealing with the panchayat secretary and with the research assistant himself amazed him. As he put it, this illiterate tribal woman could stand up against any one in her leadership qualities. It is proved, as Buch opines hopefully, that the reservations have provided an opportunity for women's entry into a non-traditional space and a possibility for erosion of traditional gender, caste, class roles and hierarchy. About one and a half decades in the panchayat bodies is too short a period to have a major shift in the dominant patriarchal structures. Hence, one should only hope to see beginnings of the process and the direction of change. He sees it in their awareness and knowledge, confidence and aspiration levels, their perceptions of self, status, recognition, participation and leadership in panchayats and outside. One may believe that in the case of this long marginalized group, these small beginnings are giant steps and have a big potential in future.

We find people eager to believe any negative observations or statements that can be made about these women's performance in panchayats. Hence the new descriptions of proxy, namesake members, sarpanch pati, pradhan pati (husbands doing their work), etc. Is it the insecurity or threat perceived by the patriarchal structures of the rural society or the inability on the part of the haves to see emerging leadership of women from the marginalized group? Buch observes that perhaps it is both.

Women in panchayats have to consider the impact of their outside interaction on their marriage. The male elected officials do not have to consider this aspect of conflict at all. In the field work, as Buch states, women gave illustrations of this concern and their success or inadequacy. A highly educated District Panchayat Chairperson in UP, married in an extremely conservative, upper caste family, expressed how in the neighbouring district the woman chairperson was first motivated and encouraged by her politician husband to contest for the post, but later he had become her biggest opponent and she was facing the challenge in her political role as well as in her marriage. She explained how she had herself learnt a lesson from this and balanced the two roles without compromising on the basics. She also explained how with her performance, she was being offered the candidature for the Parliament and how she negotiated for refusing it. A tribal village panchayat woman chairperson expressed how men do not really want women to come up in politics since they are afraid that they would share in the political power which they are holding almost exclusively, how the women's public role was changing and how men were gradually, though sometimes reluctantly, conceding this change.

Buch in her study has quite distinctly noted that this conflict was more at the district and block levels with comparatively more educated, economically better-off representatives. At the village level and particularly among the socially, economically and educational weaker sections, there was more sharing and support on the part of husbands and in-laws.

There are a number of myths, expresses Buch, about women and their participation in governance in India, particularly when the question relates to rural women who have low literacy rates and numerous social restrictions and other socio-economic handicaps. Buch and her associates have identified at least four such myths about women's participation in the rural local self governing institutions of panchayats:

- Women's passivity and disinterest in political institutions
- Only the well-to-do, upper strata women will come through reservations
- Only privileged kins-women of powerful politicians will enter these institutions to keep the seats for them
- Women who have entered the panchayats are only proxy and namesake members. They do not participate in panchayat activities.

That these are only myths and not the reality can be revealed from the conclusions that Buch and her associates have arrived at.[50]

8.10.1 Some Recent Views on Women's Empowerment

Lori Beaman et al.,[51] whose study on political reservation for women in panchayats is confined to five states of India, namely, West Bengal,

Rajasthan, Kerala, Andhra Pradesh and Karnataka, opine that female leaders increase female participation. The result of their study is intriguing and suggests that political reservation may have implications for female (and possibly male) turnout. Women panchayat leaders tend to increase investment in drinking water infrastructure. Moreover, when there are female panchayat leaders, there are significant effects on the availability of public goods, but quite insignificant effects on the quality of public goods like water, education, transport, fair price shop, public health facilities etc. This study was in many ways supported by the results of the study of Chattopadhyay and Duflo[52] long back. These two researchers observe that reservation of Pradhan positions for women meant a remarkably prominent statistical shift in allocation of public expenditure for Gram Panchayats. Priority-wise, the two highest items of public expenditure, according to women's consideration, were drinking water and road-construction, while irrigation and education were among the two lowest items.

Santosh Kumar and Nishith Prakash[53] in their study have sought to answer two very important questions: (a) Does women reservation in Bihar panchayats lead to improved health outcomes? (b) Specifically, do districts of Bihar with more female leaders perform better compared to districts of Bihar with fewer female leaders? The first panchayat election was held in Bihar in 2001, after a long gap of 23 years. Fifty per cent of seats are reserved for women since 2006 Bihar panchayat elections. It was found that during the period 2001–07, the number of mothers who had received any antenatal care had increased by 23.2 per cent. The number of mothers during the same period who had antenatal check-ups in the first trimester had increased by 3.1 per cent. The number of mothers who had three or more antenatal care had increased by 10.6 per cent. The number of mothers who had at least one tetanus injection during their pregnancy had increased by 21.3 per cent. The number of mothers whose blood pressure had been checked had increased by 5.4 per cent. The number of mothers who had full antenatal check-up had increased by 0.5 per cent. The number of institutional deliveries had increased by 12.3 per cent. The number of child birth at home had decreased by 12.7 per cent. During the same period, children of 12–23 months who had received BCG vaccine had increased by 7.7 per cent. But children of the same age who had received three doses of DPT vaccine had decreased by 3.6 per cent. On the whole, with reservation of female panchayat seats, as the authors have found, Bihar has made substantial progress in health in the last decade, particularly in maternal health. However, quite a few health indicators are still less than the national average. Child health, particularly vaccination, is still a matter of great concern and hence should be taken proper care of.

Lakshmi Iyer et al.[54] have found that an increase in female representation in local government induces a large and significant rise in documented crimes against women in India. Their evidence suggests that this increase is good news as it indicates greater reporting rather than greater incidence of such crimes. Social scientists like Hirschman[55] have strongly recognised the importance of voice for the survival and success of any organisation. A very pertinent question is raised by Iyer et al.: are the benefits to the women maximised by being represented in more influential positions at higher levels of governance, or by large scale representation at lower levels? The authors opine that it is not obvious whether the impact of female district council chairpersons will be undoubtedly larger or smaller than that of female district council members and sub-district level representatives. If district council chairpersons have a greater degree of influence on local police, their impact upon crime may be larger. On the other hand, if the greater proximity of village level leaders to both the police and the victims is a major factor, then having a female district council chairperson might not have much additional impact. On the whole, the authors observe that having female representation at the local government level means strong, positive and significant effects on 'reporting of crimes' by women. It also means greater responsiveness of law enforcement officials to crimes against women. The authors observe that crime against women and under-reporting of such crime is a problem in both developing and developed countries. Encouraging victims to report such crimes is a crucial first step, both in understanding the magnitude of the problem and in ensuring justice.

All such studies indicate that women's reservation in panchayats without providing a considerable level of education for them would fail to produce desirable results. On the other hand, reservation combined with educated female leaders can significantly improve the level of education and consequently the quality of life of the villagers, in general, and the female villagers, in particular.

Questions

1. Critically discuss women's role in launching Indian movements.
2. What kind of role did Indian women play in panchayati raj politics in the pre-reservation era?
3. Discuss the Constitutional provisions for the uplift of Indian women.
4. What kind of changes could be seen regarding women's participation in panchayat politics in the post-reservation era?
5. Write short notes on:
   (a) Major schemes for women's empowerment
   (b) World view of women in politics.
6. Discuss critically some recent views on women's empowerment.

Notes and References

1. Basu, Rumki, The Theory and Politics of Women's Empowerment—Indian Context, *The West Bengal Political Science Review*, Vol. X, No. 2, July–December, 2007.
2. Dreze, Jean and Amartya Sen, *India: Economic Development and Social Opportunity*, Oxford University Press, Delhi, 1995.
3. Mies, Maria and V.B. Tomsen, *The Subsistence Perspective: Beyond the Globalized Economy*, Zed Books, London, 1999.
4. Mies, Maria, *Patriarchy and Accumulation on a World Scale*, Zed Books, London, 1986.
5. Sen, Simonti, Gender and Politics, in Chakraborty, Satyabrata (Ed.) *Political Sociology*, Macmillan India, New Delhi, 2005.
6. Bandyopadhyay, D., *Land, Labour and Governance*, Worldview Publications, Kolkata, 2007.
7. Kapur, Ratna and Brenda Cossman, *Subversive Sites: Feminist Engagements with Law in India*, Sage Publications, New Delhi, 1996.
8. Government of India, Ministry of Social and Women's Welfare, New Delhi, *Towards Equality: Report on the Status of Women*, 1974, Chapter 7.
9. Kishwar, Madhu and Nivedita Menon, cited in Amrita Basu, Gender and Governance: Concepts and Contexts, in Nussbaum, Martha et al., *Essays on Gender and Governance*, UNDP and Macmillan, New Delhi, 2005.
10. Verma, Meera, Women's Movement in India, in *Essays on Indian Government and Politics: A Continuing Review*, Verma, Meera et al. (Eds.), Jawahar Publishers and Distributors, New Delhi, 2004.
11. The report has been discussed more elaborately in Section 8.3 of this chapter.
12. Chakravarti Banerjee, Sonali, *Social Background of Panchayat Leaders in West Bengal*, Dasgupta and Co., Kolkata, 2002.
13. See
    (i) *Panchayat Barsha Parikrama*, Hugli Zilla Parishad, 1980,
    (ii) *Tristar Panchayat Parikrama*, Hugli Zilla Parishad, 1983 and
    (iii) *Smaranika*, Hugli Zilla Parishad, 1988.
14. Information collected from District Panchayat Officer, Hugli.
15. Veblen, Thorstein, *The Theory of the Leisure Class*, Vikas Publishing House, New Delhi, 1974 (Indian Edition).

    For a Marxian interpretation about the status of women in different epochs, see Engels, F., *The Origin of the Family,*

Private Property and the State, Progress Publishers, Moscow, 1977 edition.

16. Opler, Morris Edward, Factors of Tradition and Change in a Local Election in Rural India, in Park and Tinker (Ed.), *Leadership and Political Institutions in India*, Princeton University Press, Princeton, New Jersey, 1959.
17. Bhargava, B.S., *Grass Roots Leadership: A Study of Leadership in Panchayati Raj Elections*, Ashish Publishing House, New Delhi, 1979.
18. Lalini, V., *Rural Leadership in India: A Study of Emerging Trends in Democratic* vs. *Authoritarian Rural Leadership*, Gian Publishing House, New Delhi, 1991.
19. Broomfield, J.H., *Elite Conflict in a Plural Society: Twentieth Century Bengal*, University of California Press, Berkeley and Los Angeles, 1968.
20. Dey, Sushil, K., Community Projects in Action in India, in Park and Tinker (Eds.), *op. cit.*
21. *The Gram Panchayats in West Bengal and Their Activities: Survey and Evaluation*, Government of West Bengal, 1980.
22. Lieten, G.K., *Continuity and Change in Rural West Bengal*, Sage Publications, New Delhi, 1992.
23. Webster, Neil, *Panchayati Raj and the Decentralisation of Development Planning in West Bengal*, K.P. Bagchi and Company, Calcutta, 1992.
24. Mukarji, Nirmal and D. Bandyopadhyay, *New Horizons for West Bengal's Panchayats: A Report for the Government of West Bengal*, Department of Panchayats, 1993.
25. Sridharan, Indhrani, Practicing Human Rights: A Feminist Perspective, in Chiranjivi, J. Nirmal (Ed.), *Human Rights in India: Historical, Social and Political Perspectives*, Oxford University Press, New Delhi, 2000.
26. Chattopadhyay, R. and E. Duflo, Impact of Reservation in Panchayati Raj: Evidence from a Nationwide Randomised Experiment, *Economic and Political Weekly*, February 28, 2004.
27. Ghatak, M. and M. Ghatak, Recent Reforms in the Panchayat System in West Bengal: Towards Greater Participatory Governance?, *Economic and Political Weekly*, January 5, 2002.
28. Datta, Prabhat and Chandan Datta, *Women Panchayat Members in West Bengal: An Empirical Study*, A Monograph from the Society for Participatory Research in Asia, 1999.
29. Bardhan, P. and D. Mookherjee, Poverty Alleviation Efforts of Panchayats in West Bengal, *Economic and Political Weekly*, February 28, 2004.

30. Chakraborty, Biswanath, Democratic Centralization: People's Participation in Local Governance, Proceedings of UGC Sponsored Seminar on Development and Participation, May, 2007.

31. Bardhan, Pranab, Sandip Mitra, Dilip Mookherjee and Abhirup Sarkar, Local Democracy and Clientelism: Implications for Political Stability in Rural West Bengal, *Economic and Political Weekly*, February 28, 2009.

32. Bardhan, Pranab, Dilip Mookherjee and Monica L. Parra Torrado, Impact of Political Reservations in West Bengal Local Governments on Public Service Provision, Working Paper, University of California, Berkeley, 2008.

33. Pai, S., Pradhanis in New Panchayats: Field Notes from Meerut District, *Economic and Political Weekly*, May 2, 1998.

34. See Section 8.4 of this chapter.

35. Singha Roy, Debal K., Women, Society and the State: Some Reflections on the State's Approach towards Women's Empowerment in Society, in Dhameja, Alka (Ed.), *Contemporary Debates in Public Administration*, Prentice-Hall of India, New Delhi, 2003.

36. Singha Roy, Debal K., Criticalities of Grass roots Mobilization, in Singha Roy, Debal K. (Ed.), *Social Development and Empowerment of the Marginalized: Perspectives and Strategies*, Sage Publications, New Delhi, 2001.

37. Mathew, G., Panchayati Raj Institutions and Human Rights in India, *Economic and Political Weekly*, Vol. 38, No. 2, 2003.

38. Manikyamba, P., Women Presiding Officers at the Tertiary Political Levels: Patterns of Induction and Challenges in Performance, *Journal of Rural Development*, Vol. 9, No. 6, 1990.

39. Datta, Prabhat, *The Second Generation Panchayats in India*, Calcutta Book House, Kolkata, 1992.

40. Basu, Rajasri, Gender, Development, Participation and Local Self Government, Proceedings of UGC Sponsored Seminar on Development and Participation, May, 2007.

41. Sen, Amartya, *Development as Freedom*, Oxford University Press, 2000.

42. Batliwala, S., *Empowerment of Women in South Asia: Concepts and Practices*, ASSBAF and FAO Freedom from Hunger Campaign, Action and Development, New Delhi, 1993.

43. Sen, Gita and Caren Grown, *Development, Crises and Alternative Visions: Third World Women's Perspectives*, Earthscan Publications, London, 1988.

44. Sharma, K., Grass-root Organizations and Women's Empowerment: Some Issues in Contemporary Debates, *Samya Shakti*, Vol. 6, 1992.
45. Kronenburg, J., *Empowerment of the Poor: A Comparative Analysis of Two Development Endeavours in Kenya*, Kninlijk Institute, Voor De Tropan, Amsterdam, 1986.
46. Collins, O.H., *Black Feminist Thought: Knowledge Consciousness and Politics of Empowerment*, Routledge, London, 1990.
47. Freire, Paulo, *Pedagogy of the Oppressed*, Penguin Books, Middlesex, 1972.
48. Mathew, G., *op. cit.*
49. Sharma, K., *Power* vs. *Representation*, *Occasional Paper No. 28*, Centre for Women and Development Studies (CWDS), New Delhi, 1999.
50. See Section 8.10.
51. Beaman, Lori, Esther Duflo, Rohini Pande and Petia Topalova, "Political Reservation and Substantive Representation: Evidence from Indian Village Councils", *Indian Policy Forum 7*, 2010–11.
52. Chattopadhyay, R. and E. Duflo, *op. cit.*
53. Kumar, Santosh, Nishith Prakash, "Women Reservation in Bihar and Children's Health Outcomes", *Bihar Growth Week*, Patna, Dec. 15, 2011.
54. Iyer, Lakshmi, Anandi Mani, Prachi Mishra, and Petia Topalova, "The Power of Political Voice: Women's Political Representation and Crime in India", *Working Paper*, Harvard Business School, July 29, 2011.
55. Hirschman, Albert, *Exit, Voice and Loyalty: Responses to Decline in Firms, Organizations and States*, Harvard University Press, Cambridge, MA, 1970.

9 Planning and Plan Administration

9.1 INTRODUCTION

When chaos is created, planning brings about order and introduces rationality in the decision-making process, reducing random and haphazard activities. Planning makes the personnel of the enterprise conscious of the objectives of it and thus encourages their involvement and participation. By promoting internal coordination and thus making integrated and coordinated efforts within an enterprise, planning generates economy and efficiency. No wonder, planning is considered by Terry to be the foundation of the most successful action of an enterprise.

A plan is a predetermined course of action that is firmly based on the nature and extent of socio-economic problems, from which priority goals are derived. Planning, instead of being a guess work, is a conscious determination and projection of a course of action for the future.

Henri Fayol views a plan of action to be a kind of future picture wherein proximate events are outlined with some distinctness while remote events appear progressively less distinct.

A comprehensive definition of planning has been given by Cyril L. Hudson. According to Hudson, to plan is to produce a scheme for future action, to bring about specified results at a specified cost in a specified period of time. It is a deliberate attempt to influence, exploit, bring about and control the nature, direction, extent, speed and effects of change.

Planning for national development is considered to be an essential means for accelerating the growth in the developing countries.[1] It is a major instrument in the service of the basic values and objectives cherished by a community.[2] It provides the economic sinews, the social motivation, and the method for harnessing the scarce economic resources to achieve the desired objectives. The essential elements of a development plan are as follows:

- Enunciating the objectives and targets to be achieved
- Laying down methods to attain these targets
- Providing a time schedule in which these developments will take place.[3]

When we plan for development, it may be termed *development planning*. In one of the United Nations publications, it is reported that development planning relates to a technologically-determined manipulation of policy measures and instruments devised so as to stimulate the actors of the socio-economic scene to act in the way most conducive to the achievement of the national socio-economic development objectives and goals.[4] T.T. Thahane defines it as a process of organizing national economic and social effort for the promotion of achievement of clearly defined national development goals.[5]

Development planning has assumed a role of far-reaching importance in accelerating socio-economic development in the developing and underdeveloped countries. Steady economic progress and modernization of the economy can be attained only through development planning.

9.1.1 Essentials of Planning

In order to make planning effective and successful, the following are essentials:

- Need of qualitative information
- A holistic approach
- Suitable planning methodologies.

Need of qualitative information

It is better to collect less information of sufficient reliability than to collect a mass of data of unsatisfactory quality for scientific and effective planning. Where there is a lack of statistical information, efforts should be made to collect data through properly designed sample surveys. It would not be advisable to wait until complete data are available before starting the planning process.

Holistic approach

There is a need to integrate the social and economic component of development in a plan. A high growth rate of the national product cannot in itself be the ultimate objective of a dynamic society. It is now generally realized that economic growth should be a means towards the eradication of hunger, illiteracy, disease and reduction of existing socio-economic inequalities. The consequences of growth without development are too painful to be ignored.[6] The correlation between economic growth and social development has tended to be low in Asian, African and Latin American countries. In a relatively recent study, this relationship has been critically examined.[7] As Max Millikan had said:

"There is a growing recognition that economic growth alone will not automatically bring with it all the virtues of modernization."[8]

In other words, there is a realization that development is a social as well as an economic process. Because of this intimate relationship, it is very difficult to isolate social development from the economic context. It is a modern trend in which economic planning gives way to socio-economic planning which involves planning for the social goals, with economic development as means rather than an end.[9]

Thus, there is a clear indication of the needs for knitting together social and economic components of development plans.

Suitable planning methodologies

Methodologies of planning should be refined to suit the social, political and economic environment existing in the country. There is enough room for innovation of approaches. Any approach, which may have been successful in some countries, should not be blindly adopted by the administrators. They should find out the methodologies most appropriate in the environment existing in their own countries. The required methods of planning are as under:

1. *Planning to meet the needs of the people:* Planning should be based on the needs of the population. A population base is absolutely necessary for objective planning and evaluation. A planner can formulate a practical plan only if he is familiar with internal problems as well as external forces in the community and in the country as a whole.
2. *Cost-benefit analyses:* All measures of productivity and efficiency should be analyzed in terms of the cost and development of the available and potential resources.
3. *People's participation:* Planning should, by all means, encourage people's participation. People should form an integral part of the planning process. V. Subramaniam writes, "A people's plan cannot be a people's plan unless it has an inbuilt flexibility so that adjustment and mid-term corrections are possible in the light of several factors and circumstances which come to the fore during the implementation of the programme."[10] Thus, there is a need to involve the local people in their own welfare so that their interests are paid proper heed .
4. *Effective relationship between planning and research:* There is a need for constant interaction between researchers and planners. Both planning and research activities are called for at all stages of programme development and implementation, and at each stage planning and research should be mutually supportive. Even at the initial stage of any programme, when it is merely planned, researchers and evaluators should be equally involved.

9.2 INDIAN PLANNING: AIMS AND FEATURES

Even before Independence, the long-term impact and significance of planning was recognized in India. Various ideological perspectives were taken into consideration while eminent individuals and institutions made serious efforts at plan-formulation. Some vital plans like the Bombay Plan, the People's Plan and Gandhian Plan were discussed in the politico-economic circles. The Congress Party had taken initiative in appointing a high level committee to give a blueprint for national planning. At the governmental level also, some initiative was taken when, in 1944, a full-fledged Planning and Development Department was created in the government. But World War II and the growing instability following it could not create the environment for any systematic adoption of planning as an instrument of economic development. Only after India had attained independence, the subject of planning was again seriously thought of.

9.2.1 Aims or Objectives of Planning

The Mahalanobis model of planning, clearly reflected in the Second Five Year Plan document, has continued to influence the philosophy and strategies of successive plans. Ideally, this model should be termed "Nehru-Mahalanobis" model, since it also reflected Nehru's concerns and initiatives. Sukhomoy Chakravarti reveals a less-known fact that Jawaharlal Nehru, the then Prime Minister and Chairman of the Planning Commission, had played a crucial role in drafting the Third Five Year Plan.[11]

The early phase of economic development in post-independence India was marked by government control and intervention in a wide range of economic activities. The model was set by the Soviet experience of planning. The success of the Soviet economy during the thirties and forties of the twentieth century inspired Pandit Jawaharlal Nehru, the first Prime Minister of independent India, to experiment with a socialist model of development. The free market, albeit with a lot of governmental control, was allowed to function side by side. What emerged as a result was christened *a mixed economy*.

The main architect of this early phase of economic planning was Professor Prasanta Mahalanobis whose Second Five Year Plan (1956–1961) model set the basic framework of economic development. The underlying causes of structural backwardness were perceived as follows:

First, the basic constraint on development was seen as being an acute deficiency of material capital, which prevented the introduction of more productive technologies.

Second, the limitation on the speed of capital accumulation was seen to lie in the low capacity to save.

The two, taken together, implied that the primary importance should be given to capital formation and building up of basic and heavy industries like steel.

The Nehru-Mahalanobis strategy is markedly characterized by the following two features:

1. The task of building up basic and heavy industries, it was decided, had to be taken up by the State. If savings were to be substantially raised from a low initial level of around 5 per cent in 1950 to 20 per cent in 1975, the productive capacity of the capital goods sector would have to grow at an accelerated rate to transform the increased savings into investment.
2. At least temporarily, Indian planners ignored international trade as a major source of growth. On the one hand, it was thought that elasticity of export demand was low and no significant increase in export earnings in the short run could be expected. On the other hand, important restrictions were imposed to protect the domestic industries from foreign competition. It was believed that in order to develop the domestic industrial capacity base, such protection was necessary. The argument advanced in favour of protection was the familiar infant industry argument based on economies of scale and externalities.

The development of a heavy capital goods base over a period of time would lead to the diversification of the export basket including machinery and equipment. Increase in employment would be met by pursuing less capital intensive methods of production. In this context, Professor Mahalanobis also mentioned the role of handicrafts, of small scale and village industries, etc. in providing employment.

On the whole, Indian planning, ever since its inception almost six decades ago, has attempted to meet the following objectives of multi-faceted development:

- Securing a significant increase in national income
- Accelerating the planned rate of investment to enhance the proportion of actual investment to national income
- Mitigating the inequalities of income and wealth and regulating the concentration of economic power
- Increasing the quantum of employment for the maximum possible utilization of manpower
- Promoting development in agricultural, industrial and other sectors and striving to achieve inter-sectoral development
- Expediting the development of relatively backward regions and promoting balanced regional development
- Reducing poverty progressively by providing food, work and productivity to the people living below the poverty-line
- Modernizing the economy through institutional innovation, technological advancement and production diversification.[12]

9.2.2 Features of Indian Planning

Till the Seventh Five Year Plan period (1985–1990), i.e. before the phase of liberalization started, Indian planning had some well-defined features. These may be summed up as under:

- Indian planning has basically been comprehensive in scope, involving most of the economy.
- Indian planning has been democratic in orientation with significantly high scope for popular participation.
- Set within a democratic framework, Indian planning has been substantially bureaucratized where administrators have played crucial roles in formulating and implementing plans.
- The principal focus of Indian planning has been on the public sector.
- Indian planning has made the governmental and semi-governmental institutions as promoters and regulators of the Indian economy.
- According to some scholars,[13] the planning system of India during the pre-liberalization phase has almost been like that of democratic centralism of Leninist Russia in which the democratic institutions at the lower level have freedom and opportunity to discuss the requirements of planning at their respective levels, and yet, because of their dependence for resources on the higher level institutions, major policy decisions have always been taken by the Centre.
- Periodwise, Indian planning is both long-range (five yearly) and short-range (annual).

9.2.3 A Liberal Trend

From the end of the Seventh Plan period (1985–1990), the government was markedly inclined towards the policy of economic liberalization. In the Eighth Plan period (1992–1997), the Planning Commission appeared to play a completely new role. A new perspective of Indian planning was marked by entitling the Eighth Five-Year Plan as "a vehicle of development and change". It was categorically stated: "... without doubt the Eighth Plan is a milestone in the great task of nation building."[14] In the words of Mr. Pranab Mukherjee, the erstwhile Deputy Chairman of the Planning Commission, we have to draw the pattern of the Eighth Five Year Plan in the new socio-economic perspective of the world when at every moment we have to face the challenges of free market and competition and that we have to start and continue the tasks of economic reforms and framework-formation in view of the new challenges and crises. Under these changed circumstances, as Mukherjee has observed, we cannot afford to remain alienated from the advanced market economy and, on the contrary, we have rather to proceed carefully and utilize all new opportunities in the interest of the poor and the oppressed. From a highly centralized planning system, we are gradually moving towards indicative planning. It was said that after considering the priorities regarding aims, we have to achieve our aspirations by reducing the problems and complexities as far as possible. The revised role of the Planning Commission was clearly stated in the following manner:

"The Planning Commission will play an integrative role and help in the development of a holistic approach to the policy formation in critical areas of development... Planning Commission will play a system change role and provide internal consultancy for developing better systems."[15]

It was also mentioned that the Planning Commission will play the role of a mediator. On the one hand, it will have a plain and simple role regarding questions like how to accept changes in a smooth way or how to increase national production and efficiency, etc. On the other, it will take some new initiatives regarding monetary distribution. Proper growth and efficient utilization of wealth should be the two major goals of the Planning Commission and, if required, the Commission may build up new well-conducted organizations to take their help while achieving its goals. "In the process of development people must operate and the government must cooperate." The main task of the Commission should be to help and inspire both the government and the people in order to maintain the new speed of action.

It may be said that in the initial phase of liberalization, intensified after 1991, the features of Indian planning have been modified to some extent. The Planning Commission, in its annual reports of 1992–1993 and 1993–1994, has used the term 'indicative' planning for the prospective Indian planning system. Basically, there are two types of planning: (a) indicative planning and (b) compulsive planning. In the first type, the government, by raising its hand just like the traffic police, only gives the direction of any plan. All the vital works of planning, right from designing the main pattern of the plan down to every detail of its implementation, are undertaken by the private sector. In the second type of planning, it is the government which initiates as well as controls all aspects of the plan and the private sector does not have to do anything. In the economically advanced countries like Japan and France, where at the same time a liberal-democratic political system persists, one can find indicative planning. On the contrary, the best example of a country where compulsive planning can be found is perhaps the communist Soviet Union (before its transformation into Russia). It may be said that before 1991–1992, Indian planning basically followed the Soviet model. After the adoption of the policy of economic liberalization, Indian planning has tended to follow the Japanese and the French models in certain respects. As a result, privatization was also welcomed to a great extent.

In the changed perspective, a number of scholars have raised the question that when the present politicians and economic planners of India have maintained a great distance from the Nehruvian policy of socialism and have welcomed capitalism and free market economy to such an extent, whether the planned economy or the Planning Commission, as such, can have any necessity to exist. Professor Bhabatosh Dutta has cleary stated his grudges in this regard and said that the Planning Commission in its initial phase was so extensive in its aims, objectives and activities that since the late seventies of the twentieth century started its degradation and degeneration. It received no honour as a specialist organization. All the crucial decisions started to be taken by the government only, dishonouring the advice of the Commission. More important was that the government, without thinking of the proper implementation of planning, started to attack the Planning Commission and its policies.[16] In the late 1980s, the government declared its increasing dependence on market economy by dismissing planning. Planning, finally, was not dismissed but since the post-1990 period, governmental rights and restraints were significantly reduced regarding industrial policies.

Some scholars[17] have observed that indicative planning of India in the foreseeable future cannot be expected to be patterned after the indicative planning of the western nations. It is unthinkable that in an environment of scarcity, poverty, unemployment and regional imbalances, the role of the nation, in the near future, can be significantly reduced. Thus, the Indian economy is likely to continue as a mixed economy, though the combination of the components that make it 'mixed' may vary during different phases in future.

9.3 PLANNING COMMISSION

The origin of Indian planning perhaps started with the formulation by M. Visvesvaraya of a ten-year plan in 1933 with the target of doubling the national income of India. In 1938, the Indian National Congress took the initiative in setting up of a National Planning Committee with Jawaharlal Nehru as its Chairman. In 1941, a Committee for Planning was appointed which, after a span of two years, was replaced by the Executive Council in which the Governor-General himself became the Chairman. In 1944, a separate Planning and Development Department was established. In the same year, some leading industrialists of India prepared a plan for economic development, entitled the Bombay Plan under the inspiration, direction and assistance of the Planning Department. A number of development schemes were prepared by the Central and Provincial governments, designed to be undertaken at the end of World War II. During the end of 1946, the Advisory Planning Board (established by the government) reviewed the problems of planning. The Board suggested to set up a Planning Commission, directly responsible to the Cabinet and concentrating its entire attention continuously to all the aspects of development. Its suggestion was accepted by the national government and subsequently on March 15, 1950, the Planning Commission was established by a resolution of the Government of India.

9.3.1 Composition

The structure or composition of the Planning Commission has been changed on several occasions since its birth. From the very beginning, the Prime Minister has been its Chairman. In 1951, the Minister of Irrigation and Power became the first full-time Deputy Chairman of the Commission. Till 1953, he was the member and Deputy Chairman of the Planning Commission. During that time, it was decided that there should be a full-fledged Minister of Planning, who would principally act as the spokesman of the Commission. He would be answerable to the Parliament about the Commission's work. In addition to the Finance Minister and the Minister of Planning, some other Union Ministers have also been appointed from time to time as members of the Planning Commission. The Finance Minister and the Minister of Planning are ex officio members of the Commission. In March 1973, the number of ex-officio members of the Commission was four.

In 1977, the Janata Party restructured the composition of the Planning Commission. Besides its full-time members, the Finance Minister, the Defence Minister and the Home Minister were added to the Commission as its part-time members. In 1980, Mrs. Gandhi, after coming to power again, restructured the Planning Commission. Under Rajiv Gandhi, the Commission consisted of a Chairman and eight members including the Deputy Chairman. On February 1, 1994, the National Front Government changed the membership of the Commission to nine. The United Front Government again changed the structure of the Commission and in 1997, its membership was increased to thirteen. Since its inception, many eminent persons from various fields and disciplines have been appointed as Deputy Chairman of the Commission, viz. V.T. Krishnamachari, Ashok Mehta, D.R. Gadgil, Raj Krishna, Pranab Mukherjee, K.C. Pant, etc.

The following portfolios are generally distributed among the members of the Planning Commission:

1. General planning and social services
2. Finance
3. Industries
4. Education and health
5. International trade and development
6. Irrigation and power
7. Social labour

8. Agriculture
9. Administration and transport
10. Natural resources.

Three main parts of the Planning Commission are as under:

1. **Programme Advisors:** They possess the status of Additional Secretaries of the government. They look after the finances, public cooperation and administration, connected with plan implementation, and advise the Planning Commission according to their observations. Regarding field study, progress and implementation of various schemes and projects, the Planning Commission is assisted by programme advisors.
2. **General Secretariat:** It has five major branches, namely (a) administrative branch, (b) general branch, O&M branch and accounts branch, (c) general coordination branch, (d) plan coordination branch, and (e) information and publicity branch.
3. **Technical Divisions:** These divisions study every aspect of the entire plan in detail and decide which schemes and projects should be incorporated in the plan. They also deal with the aspect of research when the technical matters of the plan are examined. These divisions are also responsible for the completion of various projects and schemes of the plan.

   Technical Divisions include the following seventeen divisions. The functions of each division are described in short so that one can have a rough idea of how the Planning Commission works.

   (a) ***Economic, finance and resources division:*** This division is concerned with the overall aspects of planning and assessment of resources. It scrutinizes the size, objectives, priorities and economic policies of each plan. For the financing of the plan, all available resources are sought to be assessed by it.

   (b) ***Education division:*** It deals with the physical, general, technical, rural and women's education and advises the Planning Commission according to its observations. It is also concerned with the National Cadet Corps, Social Service Camps, Student and Youth Camps, Development of Hindi and regional languages, Central Assistance to States for Educational Purposes, National Academies, etc.

   (c) ***Food and agriculture division:*** This division of the Planning Commission is concerned with increasing production, Grow More Food Schemes, Community Development and Extension Service, etc. It also deals with agricultural labour, agricultural marketing, soil conservation, fisheries and forests, etc.

   (d) ***Health division:*** All works associated with health are undertaken by this division. It collects various statistical data relating to health so that it can guide the Planning Commission and the government properly. The reports and advice of various bodies and panels connected with health are also examined by this division.

(e) *Housing division:* This division is concerned with town and country planning and house building. It continuously gets in touch with the Ministries of Works, Housing and Supply, Community Development, Home Affairs, Labour, etc.

(f) *Industry and mineral division:* This division is responsible for the development of heavy and cottage industries and utilization of minerals. It is therefore closely connected with the Ministries of Commerce, Industry, Steel, Mines, Fuel and other technical organizations.

(g) *Irrigation and power division:* This division studies the various methods of improving irrigation facilities and thus creating more and more electricity in India. It also examines carefully various schemes of flood control.

(h) *Labour reforms division:* This division carefully studies all problems relating to labour and employment. It tries to resolve various conflicts between labour and capital by providing useful suggestions for harmonizing labour-capital relations and removing unemployment.

(i) *Programmes administrative division:* This division coordinates the plans of the Centre and States. It prepares regular reports about the progress of the plan.

(j) *Perspective planning division:* This division deals with the prospects of the long-term development of agriculture, resources of power, rise in employment opportunities, etc.

(k) *Public cooperation division:* While implementing the plans, people's cooperation is needed. This division concerns itself with increasing such cooperation; and its proposals and suggestions are paid proper heed to by both the Union and State Governments.

(l) *Resources and scientific rsearch division:* This division deals with scientific research for the development purposes. It takes information of all such researches taking place in India and abroad. This division keeps close contact with various scientific research centres, laboratories, universities and other research organizations.

(m) *Statistics and surveys division:* This division basically does all the statistical works regarding the plan and sends the data to the Planning Commission. For doing this, the division collects the essential data about the progress and implementation of the plan through States' Statistical Bureaus as well as various statistical agencies of the Centre.

(n) *Social welfare division:* This division deals with the various measures which should be taken by the government for the welfare of the backward classes like Harijans and backward castes and tribes. Hence, it keeps close contact with various organizations like Central Social Welfare Board, States' Social Welfare Departments, etc.

(o) *Transport and communications division:* This division makes a specially thorough study regarding the problems of transport and communications. It suggests the Planning Commission various measures to solve such problems as well.

(p) *Village and small industries division:* Coir industries, village industries, silk and sericulture, normal khadi and Ambar khadi, handloom and powerloom constitutes small industries. This section of the Planning Commission carefully studies the problems faced by such industries.

(q) *Management and development administration division:* It looks after the problems of management and development of administration, and suggests measures to the government.

If one thoroughly studies the composition of the Planning Commission, one can understand the close association of the Prime Minister with the Commission. The Administrative Reforms Commission in its interim report on the Machinery for Planning (April, 1967) questioned the necessity of continuing the Prime Minister as the Chairman of the Commission. Its observation was that the Prime Minister should be intimately associated with the Commission activities, without being the Chairman of it. He should preside over the meetings of the Commission whenever he attends such meetings.[18] But on the argument that it is necessary for the coordination and smooth running of the government, this recommendation of the ARC has not been accepted and the Prime Minister continues to act as its Chairman.

9.3.2 Functions and Responsibilities

The role played by the Planning Commission can be assessed by explaining the following functions:

- *Assessing and augmenting resources:* The Commission makes an assessment of the material, capital and human resources of the country, including the technical personnel, and explores all the possibilities of augmenting those resources which are found to be deficient in relation to India's requirements.
- *Plan formulation:* The Planning Commission shoulders the responsibility of formulating plans for the most effective and balanced utilization of the national resources.

- *Defining stages of implementation:* On a priority basis, the Commission defines all the stages at which the plans should be carried out. The Commission also proposes the allocation of resources for the due completion of each stage.
- *Indicating requisites of plan execution:* The Planning Commission indicates factors behind economic recession, and determines the conditions which should be established for the successful execution of plans.
- *Determining execution machinery:* The Commission determines the nature of machinery needed for ensuring successful implementation of each stage of the plan from a holistic perspective.
- *Appraisal:* The Planning Commission evaluates, from time to time, the progress achieved in the implementation of the plan. On the basis of this evaluation, it recommends the necessary adjustments in policy implementation.
- *Advice:* The Planning Commission makes appropriate recommendations for a more effective and efficient formulation, execution and evaluation of socio-economic plans. When the Central and the State Governments make any specific reference to the Commission, the latter may render suitable advice, too.

Speaking in more specific terms, its functions are as under:

- Assessment of resources
- Priorities in allocation of resources
- Problem of planning
- Formulation of the development plans of Central and State Governments
- Planning of industrial development
- Appraisal of the progress achieved in the implementation of the plan.

The principal function of the Commission is to prepare a National Plan, meaning a Five Year Plan broken down into several annual plans. This is its major responsibility and only the Planning Commission can carry it out.[19] In short, the Planning Commission aims at (a) promoting a rapid rise in the standard of living of the people by efficient exploitation of the national resources, (b) increasing production and (c) providing opportunities to all for employment in the service of the country. The Commission, however, is not bothered with how the plans will be implemented, since that is primarily looked after by the various State Governments of the country.

9.3.3 Organization

The organization of the Planning Commission has undergone a series of changes since its inauguration in 1950. It was proposed that there would be Under Secretaries in charge of the Administration and Coordination Branches that would perform the house-keeping functions of the Commission. The main work of the Commission should be organized through Divisions, which may be categorized in the following way:

1. *General planning division:* It includes units that would be concerned with a comprehensive study of the country as a whole.
2. *Special planning division:* It includes units which are concerned with the study of particular sectors of social and economic development.
3. *Programme administration division:* It is composed of units which are concerned with the formulation and implementation of detailed programmes, specially in the States.

Thus, it may be said that the Planning Commission is organized in such a manner that its expert character is easily reflected. In the words of S.R. Maheshwari, the internal organization of the Commission is built around two hierarchies–administrative and technical. The administrative hierarchy is headed by the Secretary of the Planning Commission, controlling a number of subordinates including Joint Secretaries, Deputy Secretaries, Under Secretaries, and other staff. The technical hierarchy begins with Advisers, each of whom is of the rank of Additional Joint Secretary. Under each Adviser comes the Chief who, again, is assisted by Directors, Joint Directors and other staff. The Advisers are usually experts, such as economists, engineers, statisticians, etc. although some of the Advisers may also be drawn from a generalist administrative service like the IAS. The majority of the experts are economists. The Planning Commission is at present the single largest employer of the Indian Economic Service.

The main functional unit of the Commission is the Division. There are 25 Divisions which are responsible for scrutinizing and analyzing various schemes and projects of the plan; conducting technical studies and research; preparing study materials and reports; following up on plan projects, etc. Besides, the Commission has within it the Programme Evaluation Organization and the Computer Services Division.

9.3.4 ARC View on Planning Commission

The Administrative Reforms Commission is of the opinion that in order to be recognized as a professional body, the Planning Commission must be free from political control as much as possible. The ARC suggested that even the Prime Minister should cease to be its Chairman, although he and the Finance Minister should remain closely associated with the actual working of the Commission. The ARC is of the opinion that taking advantage of the Prime Minister's chairmanship, the Planning Commission has "steadily added to its functions and personnel and has stepped into the area of the executive authority" of the Central and State Governments. Thus, it was quite reasonably regarded by the public as a "parallel Cabinet" or even a "super Cabinet". But the ARC categorically favoured the Prime Minister's close association with the Planning Commission in the following way:

"We recommend that this intimate association should be secured without formally making the Prime Minister the Chairman of the Commission. He should be kept informed from time to time of the important decisions taken by the Commission. Whenever a meeting of the Commission is to be held, copies of the agenda and the connected papers should be sent to him. He may attend the meetings of the Commission, express his views and participate in the discussions. He may also summon a meeting of the Commission and address it. He will preside over the meetings of the Commission when he attends it."[20]

The ARC has also clearly viewed that if the Ministers were members, the Commission's capacity to make vital evaluation of plan-implementation by the executive would be much affected.

The Government of India did not fully accept the ARC's view. It was decided by the government that the Prime Minister and the Finance Minister would continue to be the Chairman and member, respectively, of the Planning Commission, while the rest of the Ministers may not be appointed as members. In reality, however, this governmental decision has been violated on most of the occasions and three to four Ministers continue to be the members of the Planning Commission.

The general feeling of the Government of India appears to support the following viewpoints:

- The chairmanship of the Prime Minister bestows on the Planning Commission a legitimacy and authority that would be respected by all the Union Ministers and the State Governments.
- The Prime Minister's and other Union Ministers' presence in the Planning Commission facilitates a close relation between the Union Government and the Commission.
- The presence of the Prime Minister and other Union Ministers makes the Commission's decisions more pragmatic and practical.
- Since planning is a political activity, in an environment of scarcity of resources, the broader governmental issues cannot be divorced from the authoritative allocation of values.

Regarding the membership of the Planning Commission, the ARC had recommended that its number of members should not exceed seven. Out of these, two could be part-time members, though not necessarily so. One of the full-time members should be appointed as Chairman. The Government of India agreed with the ARC view that the Planning Commission should be a compact body. But it did not favour the adoption of any rigid approach regarding the number of its members.

Again, it did not accept the recommendation of appointing any part-time members to the Commission.

The Union Government's totally flexible approach to the issue of membership of the Planning Commission has led to the following practices:

- The Deputy Chairman of the Commission has sometimes been a whole-time member, while at other times, part-time.
- The Finance Minister and two to three other members have been part-time members.
- The number of whole-time expert members has varied from four to seven.

9.3.5 Evaluation of the Planning Commission

Originally, the Planning Commission had high aims and lofty objectives. But, in reality, all the aims and objectives have not yet been achieved. In 1951–1952, the total investment in the First Five Year Plan was of the order of only 2000 crores. In the Eighth Plan (1992–1997), it stands almost eight lakh crores. In this context, it is legitimate to ask what have we got in return. We may quote Vasant Sathe's book[21] since his observation of the whole exercise is shared by many eminent economists, social scientists and administrators. His strong observation may be broken into the following three parts:

- A comparison of Indian economy with the economies of other countries
- The uneven growth of the Indian economy leading to the concentration of wealth in a few hands, thereby sharpening the edge of economic inequality in India
- The creation of black money in the Indian economy and the havoc it has been causing to the economy.

In the words of Sathe: "The fact that after 52 years of independence, India is at the bottom of the list in terms of its share in world trade, which is 0.4 per cent with one of the lowest per capita incomes, is a sad commentary on our performance." He then gives comparative figures. "Even if we like to compare ourselves with a highly populated and large country like China, it is clear that in many areas of infrastructure they are far ahead of us." Sathe informs us that in almost all areas of importance like power, steel, irrigation, transport, we stand nowhere in comparison. Regarding concentration of wealth, he remarks: "It is true that a small section of our population, which is less than 10 per cent, has achieved levels of a comparatively better life. Among them, a much smaller section, about 1 to 2 per cent, enjoys highly affluent levels of income, ..." Regarding the creation of black money in the Indian economy, Sathe's observation is as under:

"... more than ₹50,000 crores of income annually escapes the net of government tax assessment. This does not include the income and wealth generated through smuggling and other illegal activities like drug trafficking. All this unaccounted money is controlled by a very few people. It is this fundamental reality which is responsible for the economic stagnation as well as the situation of stagnation which is prevailing today."

But since the end of the Seventh Five Year Plan period (1985–1990), a liberal economic policy tends to dominate the Planning Commission which obviously reflects in its policy.[22]

9.3.6 Changing Nature of Planning: NITI Aayog

After a long span of 65 years from 1950 to the end of 2014 the Planning Commission seemed to have lost its utility due to the changing nature of the concept of planning itself. The answer to the significant question—why the Planning Commission appeared to be rather replaceable?—is beautifully given by Jayanta Kumar Dab in his paper "From Planning Commission to NITI Aayog: End of Nehruvian Legacy Challenges Ahead"[23] in the following way:

"However expensive and expansive a building may be, it gets old and dilapidated with the passage of time, with the plaster peeling off and the roof on the verge of carving in, endangering the lives beneath it. The same was the case with the Planning Commission or *Yojana Aayog*, the prestigious institution that stood tall amid all policy-making institutions for a long period of 65 years. Indeed, the Planning Commission was the brainchild of Pandit Jawaharlal Nehru, and it was the descendant of the National Planning Committee that Subhas Chandra Bose had set up at the suggestion of Meghnad Saha when he was the Congress President in 1938. Nehru was made its President. Two subsequent plan proposals were floated, one the Bombay plan prepared by the city's industrialists and the People's Plan modelled after the Soviet Plan by M.N. Roy ... independent India adopted a formal model of planning by establishing the Planning Commission on March 15, 1950 with the Prime Minister as its Chairman .... Despite the economic liberalisation in 1991, the Planning Commission continued, but since 1997 there was the realisation that planning ought to be indicative in nature".

Later when the BJP Government came to power at the Centre in May, 2014 after the sixteenth Lok Sabha elections, headed by Mr. Narendra Modi as the Prime Minister, it started thinking seriously regarding replacing the Planning Commission. In line with the BJP Government's new economic approach of a less government and a more decentralised planning, the *NITI Aayog* with a new structure and policy has replaced the old Planning Commission which has been an old witness of a series of successes and failures of its own and consequently the Indian economy. It was indeed a long demand and expectation of the people of India to replace the Planning Commission with a new institution that would be far more relevant and responsive to the contemporary economic conditions of the Country. BJP Government, however, was not the only Government to find the irrelevance of the Planning Commission. For a long time economists and politicians had started questioning its necessity. Once Rajiv Gandhi had called the members of the Planning Commission 'a bunch of jokers'. But he did not bring about any concrete changes in the body. But, former Prime Minister and ex-officio Chairman of the body Mr. Manmohan Singh as well as its Deputy Chairman Mr. K.C. Pant tried to make certain changes. In 2009, Mr. Singh, feeling the loss of relevance of the Planning Commission in the contemporary needs of the Country, asked its members to change the body to be more relevant and timely. In the next year, Mr. Arun Maira, a former member of the Planning Commission and the Head of the Boston Consulting Group in India, recommended a series of changes in the structure, functions, role and resources of the body. His principal argument was that the Indian economy was shifting from a highly centralised planning structure towards indicative planning, and hence the Commission's role should also be modified accordingly.

Parallelly, it should also be kept in mind that when Mr. Narendra Modi was the Chief Minister of Gujarat, a leading industrial state of our Country, he would very often criticise the role of the Commission for its high-handedness in disbursing grants to the states. His criticism was strongly supported by the Chief Ministers of the Opposition-ruled states. Hence, no wonder, after being the Prime Minister, Modi brought about a total change in the entire concept of planning. On May 29, 2014, the Independent Evaluation Office submitted an assessment report to Prime Minister Modi with the recommendation to replace the Planning Commission with a 'control commission'. On August 13, 2014, the Union Cabinet decided to replace the Planning Commission with a diluted version of the National Advisory Council (NAC) of India. On January 1, 2015 a unanimous Union Cabinet resolution was passed to replace the Planning Commission with the newly formed NITI Aayog. On January 1, 2015 when the NITI Aayog was formally established to replace the Planning Commission, Modi announced publicly:

"Through the NITI Aayog, we bid farewell to a *'one-size-fits-all'* approach towards development. The body celebrates India's diversity and plurality. The *Aayog* will foster a spirit of 'cooperative federalism' with the sole principle of developing a pro-people, pro-active and participative development agenda stressing on empowerment and equality". On the necessity of the creation of this new body, Finance Minister, Mr. Arun Jaitley observed: "The 65-year-old Planning Commission had become a redundant organisation. It was relevant in a command economy structure, but not any longer. India is a diversified country and its states are in various phases of economic development along with their own strengths and weaknesses. In this context, a 'one-size-fits-all' approach to economic planning is obsolete. It cannot make India competitive in today's global economy."

Hence, *NITI Aayog* or the Commission equivalent to the National Institution for Transforming India is a Government of India policy think-tank established by the BJP Government to replace the Planning Commission marked by a rigorously centralised top-down model of economy. The principal objective behind the formation of the NITI Aayog is to promote and strengthen Indian state governments' active participation and involvement with the economic policy making process of the Country. The Central Government announced the formation of the NITI Aayog on January 1, 2015 and its first meeting was held on February 8, 2015.

The objectives of the NITI Aayog have been specified by the Press Information Bureau, Government of India, in the following way:

(a) To evolve a shared vision of national development priorities, sectors and strategies with the active involvement of States in the light of national objectives. The vision of the NITI Aayog will then provide a framework of 'national agenda' for the Prime Minister and the Chief Ministers to provide impetus to.

(b) To foster cooperative federalism through structured support initiatives and mechanisms with the States on a continuous basis, recognising that strong states make a strong nation.

(c) To develop mechanisms to formulate credible plans at the village level and aggregate these progressively at higher levels of government.

(d) To ensure, on areas that are specifically referred to it, that the interests of national security are incorporated in economic strategy and policy.

(e) To pay special attention to the sections of our society that may be at risk of not benefitting adequately from economic progress.

(f) To design strategic and long-term policy and programme frameworks and initiatives, and monitor their progress and their efficacy. The lessons learnt through monitoring and feedback will be used for making innovative improvements, including necessary mid-course corrections.

(g) To provide advice and encourage partnerships between key stakeholders and national and international like-minded Think Tanks, as well as educational and policy research institutions.

(h) To create a knowledge, innovation and entrepreneurial support system through a collaborative community of national and international experts, practitioners and other partners.

(i) To offer a platform for resolution of inter-sectoral and inter-departmental issues in order to accelerate the implementation of the development agenda.

(j) To maintain a state-of-the-art Resource Centre, be a repository of research on good governance and best practices in sustainable and equitable development as well as help their dissemination to stake-holders.

(k) To actively monitor and evaluate the implementation of programmes and initiatives, including the identification of the needed resources so as to strengthen the probability of success and scope of delivery.

(l) To focus on technology upgradation and capacity building for implementation of programmes and initiatives.

(m) To undertake other activities as may be necessary in order to further the execution of the national development agenda, and the objectives mentioned above.

Thus, NITI Aayog is supposed to perform the above-mentioned functions.

The NITI Aayog is comprised of the following members:

1. Prime Minister of India as the Chairperson.
2. A Governing Council composed of Chief Ministers of all States and Union Territories with Lieutenant Governor of Andaman and Nicobar Islands.
3. Regional Councils composed of Chief Ministers of States and Lieutenant Governors of Union Territories.
4. Full-time organisational framework composed of a Vice-Chairperson, three full-time members, two part-time members (from leading universities, research organisations and other relevant institutions in an ex-officio capacity), four ex-officio members of the Union Council of Ministers, a Chief Executive Officer (with the rank of Secretary to the Government of India) who looks after administration, and a secretariat.
5. Experts and specialists from various fields, including Prime Minister Mr. Modi as the Chairperson. This Expert Committee also consists of:

   (a) **Vice Chairperson:** Arvind Panagariya

   (b) **Ex-Officio Members:** Rajnath Singh, Arun Jaitley, Suresh Prabhu and Radha Mohan Singh

   (c) **Special Invitees:** Nitin Gadkari, Smriti Zubin Irani and Thawar Chand Gehlot

   (d) **Full-time Members:** Bibek Debroy (economist), V.K. Saraswat (former DRDO Chief) and Ramesh Chand (Agriculture Expert)

   (e) **Chief Executive Officer:** Amitabh Kant

   (f) **Governing Council:** All Chief Ministers of States and Lieutenant Governors of Union Territories

NITI Aayog is different from the Planning Commission on the following parameters:

- **Financial Right:** The Planning Commission used to enjoy full financial power to allocate funds to different Ministries as well as to the State Governments.

  But, the NITI Aayog is primarily an advisory body or a think-tank. It does not possess the powers to allocate funds which might be vested in the Finance Ministry.
- **Full-time Members:** The Planning Commission had quite a few full-time members. For example, the last Commission had as many as eight such members.

  But, the NITI Aayog has fewer number of full-time members than the Planning Commission.
- **States' role:** In the Planning Commission, the States had virtually no role to play. States' role was limited to the National Development Council and annual interaction during plan meetings.

  But, in NITI Aayog, State Governments are expected to play a clearly more significant role than they did in the Planning Commission.
- **Appointment of Member Secretary:** In Planning Commission Secretaries or Member Secretaries used to be appointed through the usual process.

  But, in NITI Aayog, Member Secretary is known as the CEO, who is appointed by the Prime Minister.
- **Provision for Part-time Members:** In the Planning Commission there was no provision for Part-time Members.

  But, in NITI Aayog, there is the provision for a number of Part-time Members, depending upon the need of the time.

9.4 NATIONAL DEVELOPMENT COUNCIL (NDC)

A strong need was felt for a long time since Indian independence for the creation of a body consisting of the Central Government representatives, the constituent units of a federal union and others equally interested and qualified for the job. The draft outline of the First Five Year Plan (July 1951) had expressed the need for such a body as the NDC. The Government of India accepted the proposal, as a result of which the NDC was bron on August 6, 1952. Such an organization was set up to strengthen and mobilize the efforts and resources of our nation in support of the Five Year Plans, to promote common economic policies in all vital spheres, and to ensure the balanced and rapid development of all parts of the country.

The root of such an organization can be found way back in 1946. The Planning Advisory Board, under the chairmanship of K.C. Neogi, had recommended the setting up of an advisory organization which would include representatives of the provinces, princely States and other interests. The Planning Commission in the initial days of its inception had recognized the potential utility of such a coordinating body. The Commission had stressed that in a vast country like India, there was a positive need for a body like the NDC that could facilitate periodical evaluation of planning and its various facets by the Prime Minister and the Chief Ministers of States.

The NDC is undoubtedly one of the key organizations of the planning system in India. It symbolizes the federal approach to planning and it is the instrument for ensuring that the planning system adopts a truly national perspective. The NDC has experienced numerous ups and downs in its fortunes. Its status has been determined by the prevailing political climate and the support provided to it by the government in power at the Centre and the effectiveness of the pressures exerted by the State Governments. The continuing presence of the NDC in the apex policy structure has always been felt.

In October 1967, on the recommendation of the Administrative Reforms Commission, the NDC was reconstituted.

9.4.1 Composition

From its birth, NDC is basically a body composed of top level representatives of the Central as well as the State Governments along with the members of the Planning Commission. The issue of reorganization of NDC was taken up by the Administrative Reforms Commission (ARC) in 1967. According to the recommendations of the ARC, the NDC should be recomposed of the following:

1. The Prime Minister
2. The Deputy Prime Minister, if any
3. The Union Ministers of
   - (a) Finance
   - (b) Food and agriculture
   - (c) Industrial development and company affairs
   - (d) Commerce
   - (e) Railways
   - (f) Transport and shipping
   - (g) Education
   - (h) Labour, employment and rehabilitation
   - (i) Home affairs
   - (j) Irrigation and power
4. The Chief Ministers of all States
5. The members of the Planning Commission.

It was also recommended by the ARC that the Prime Minister should continue as the Chairman of the NDC, while the Secretary of the Planning Commission should act as its Secretary.

With a few modifications of the recommendations of the ARC, the NDC is now recomposed of:

- The Prime Minister
- All Union Cabinet Ministers
- All Chief Ministers of States
- All representatives of the Union Territories
- Members of the Planning Commission.

In October, 1967 the NDC was reconstituted in such a way.

9.4.2 Committees of NDC

Following the 43rd NDC meeting held in 1992–1993, six committees of the NDC were set up, with a view to creating an on-going mechanism for assessing the situation in critical priority areas. The NDC committees are as follows:

- Committee on population
- Committee on micro-level planning
- Committee on austerity
- Committee on employment
- Committee on literacy
- Committee on medical education

Committee on population

The committee on population is supposed to:

(a) review the social and demographic dimensions relevant to the formulation of the National Population Policy,

(b) suggest a mechanism for securing commitment and support of the leadership at all levels for implementing population control programmes,

(c) identify intervention strategies for population control on a holistic basis,

(d) promote people's participation in population programmes,

(e) outline comprehensive policies for women's welfare,

(f) recommend appropriate measures in family welfare programmes, and

(g) recommend suitable mechanisms for continuous review of the implementation of National Population Policy and the associated intervention strategies.

Committee on micro-level planning

The committee on micro-level planning has the following functions:

(a) To define the scope and content of micro-level or sub-State level planning

(b) To delineate the procedures and to envisage steps for making micro-level planning operationally effective and meaningful

(c) To suggest pragmatic ways for the involvement of people at the grass roots level.

Committee on austerity

The committee on austerity identifies the causes of growth of total State Government expenditure and suggests areas where the economy can be effected in establishment expenditure, non-establishment expenditure, subsidies, interest component of State expenditure, etc.

Committee on employment

The committee on employment examines the employment situation in rural and urban areas and among the educated, the uneducated and women. It is also supposed to explain the efficacy of social employment programmes in employment generation and suggest suitable strategies for expanding productive employment opportunities in various sectors.

Committee on literacy

The committee on literacy is set up to do the following:

(a) To review the progress of National Literacy Mission

(b) To seek for the cooperation of the panchayati raj institutions

(c) To integrate the literacy movement with child care, child development, women's economic empowerment, etc.

(d) To provide post-literacy programmes or continuous literacy programmes for literates, neo-literates and women.

Committee on medical education

The committee on medical education recommends measures for ensuring the availability of medical, dental and para-professional manpower. It also suggests measures for expanding education in these areas in both public and private sectors.

9.4.3 Functions of the NDC

On the basis of the recommendations of the ARC in October 1967, the functions of the NDC were redefined to include the following:

- Prescription of guidelines for the formulation of the National Plan

- Assessment of resources for the plan.
- Consideration of the National Plan as formulated by the Planning Commission.
- Consideration of important questions of socio-economic policy affecting national development
- Periodical review of the working of the National Plan
- Recommendation of measures necessary for achieving the broader aims and targets of the National Plan
- Securing active cooperation and participation of the people in implementing various projects associated with the National Plan
- Improving the efficiency of the administrative services
- Ensuring the fullest development of the less advanced regions and sections of the community
- Building up of resources for national development, through sacrifice by all citizens.

It was thought that the NDC would make its recommendations to the Central and State Governments. From its birth, it has been playing its role as a high power consultative body in which the frame of the Five Year Plans, the important problems of the Indian economy and a number of future economic policies have been discussed and solutions arrived at. Thus, apart from the National Plan, the NDC continuously concerns itself with problems like food, land reforms, etc. The first and foremost function of the NDC is to act as a kind of bridge between the Union Government, the Planning Commission and the State Governments. It helps to coordinate not only between policies and programmes of plans but also between various other aspects of national importance. Besides, it provides a good forum for discussion and full and free exchange of views. Lastly, it acts as a device for sharing of responsibility between States and the Union.

9.4.4 Evaluation of NDC

There is a general feeling that the impact of the NDC on the planning process has not been insignificant, though its role could have been much more effective than what it has actually been. While making an overall appraisal, it may be said that the NDC has been successfully functioning as a useful bridge between the Union Government and the Planning Commission, on the one hand, and the State Governments, on the other. In spite of not being a constitutional body, its role has remained respectable over the years. V.T. Krishnamachari observes that the NDC provides a forum in which the Union Ministers and Chief Ministers of States discuss the plans at important stages in their formulation. Plans, before they are presented to the Parliament and State Legislatures, are approved at the meetings of the NDC. The

NDC also considers socio-economic policies affecting the country from a national point of view so that, where necessary, uniformity may be secured. Thus on matters of national importance, the NDC can promote collective thinking and joint action.

But several drawbacks can also be pointed out in the working of the NDC. *In the first place*, from 1952 onwards, the NDC meetings have not been held on a regular basis. In fact, during a few financial years, no NDC meeting was held at all. The ARC has also been critical of this practice of the NDC and has rightfully stressed that the NDC should meet more regularly. In reply, it may be said that the initiative of calling an NDC meeting lies with the Planning Commission of which the Prime Minister happens to be the Chairperson. So, for this the NDC cannot and should not be blamed.

Secondly, some States have complained on several occasions that they do not find adequate time for presenting their own problems and difficulties before the NDC. A reason behind this limitation is said to be the fact that in the Indian planning process, uniformity and commonality, rather than diversity and divergence, have been valued much more.

Thirdly, critics have opined that the meetings of the NDC bear an imprint of partisanship. Chief Ministers of States belonging to the party in power at the Centre generally toe the line of the Union Government while Chief Ministers belonging to the opposition parties are generally critical of the draft plan designed by the Planning Commission.

Fourthly, the NDC is criticized on the ground that it does not evaluate the implementation of Five Year plans and Annual plans on a continuing basis. Though this function is performed by the Planning Commission, yet the task of evaluation also happens to be the first formally defined function of the NDC.

Last but not least, there are persons who view the growing powers of the Council as a growing danger to the privileges of the Central and State Cabinets. They charge that the NDC, by functioning as a virtual super-Cabinet, tends to usurp authority. Thus, Brecher writes in the biography of Jawaharlal Nehru that the NDC was established as a supreme administrative and advisory body on Indian planning, but since its birth the NDC along with its Standing Committee has virtually relegated the Planning Commission to the status of a research arm. Mr. A.P. Jain, ex-Food Minister, charged the NDC for sometimes approving too high targets of production even without the prior consultations of the Ministry concerned. In Jain's opinion, the Council is incompetent, both by law and by the nature of its composition, to take high-level national decisions.

The only defence that can be given to the NDC from the above points of criticism is that it is neither a constitutional nor a statutory body. It is rather a high-ranking policy-making body and how much effect is to be given to its recommendations is to be decided by the Cabinets only.

The Sarkaria Commission opines that the NDC has not been able to act as an effective instrument for developing consensus on the national policies. At the same time, it is observed by the Commission that the NDC has successfully acted as a forum for informal consultation between Central and State Governments on a number of critical economic issues. The Commission, however, has recommended that the NDC should be made more effective, so that it emerges as the supreme institution, at the political level for the Centre-State planning relations. It has also recommended that the NDC should be renamed and reconstituted as 'National Economic and Development Council' (NEDC)–under provisions of Article 263 of our Constitution. It has also suggested for the creation of a Standing Committee of the NEDC, consisting of the Prime Minister, Finance Minister, Deputy Chairman of the Planning Commission, Governor of the Reserve Bank of India and six Chief Ministers, one from each zone, selected by rotation or consensus.[24]

There is a strong need that a "national agenda" should be evolved for a holistic growth of Indian economy, to which the NDC can contribute significantly. In the absence of such a "national agenda", no all-encompassing approach to planning can take place.

9.5 PLANNING MACHINERY AT THE STATE LEVEL

In a federation, a close coordination between Central and State Governments in the sphere of development policy and administration is essential for a balanced and rapid socio-economic development. The responsibility for undertaking planned development through systematic formulation, implementation and evaluation of plans is the responsibility of both the Centre and the States. As the Centre has the Planning Commission, States have Planning Departments. State Planning Department is politically headed either by the Chief Minister or a senior Cabinet Minister. At the administrative level, it is generally the Chief Secretary who heads the State Planning Department. The State Planning Department keeps close contact with the Planning Commission as well as various Ministeries and Departments of the State Government for the preparation of the development plans for the whole State. Since the State Planning Department continues to be the core unit for the formulation, implementation and evaluation of the State's annual as well as five year plans, there has been much emphasis on enhancing its efficiency and effectiveness.

In 1972, the Planning Commission had recommended to the States that their planning Departments should be made more competent by setting up in them the following units:

- Perspective planning unit
- Monitoring plan formulation and evaluation unit
- Project appraisal unit.

- Regional district planning unit
- Plan coordination unit
- Manpower and employment unit.

Since the central financial assistance was available for the purpose of State planning Departments, most States have availed themselves of this facility and strengthened their planning machinery. There is no uniformity in the structural configuration of the planning Departments at the inter-State level, although a kind of functional uniformity prevails in this sphere.

9.5.1 State Planning Boards

In each State, there is a State Planning Board in order to prepare the draft State plan. It prepares the draft by consultations among the experts, Ministers and other decision-makers, as well as by seeking the views and demands of various organizations within the State.

The ARC had outlined the following functions of the State Planning Board in each State:

- To make an assessment of the State resources and formulate plans for the most effective and balanced utilization of these resources.
- To determine plan priorities of the State within the framework of the priorities of the National Plan.
- To assist the district authorities in formulating their development plans within the sphere in which such planning is considered to be useful and feasible, and to coordinate these plans with the State plans.
- To identify factors which tend to retard the economic and social development of the State and determine the set of conditions for successful implementation of the plan.
- To review the progress of implementation of the plan programmes and recommend such adjustments in policies and measures as the review may indicate.

Except in a few States, the State Planning Boards have, however, yet to establish their role in a meaningful manner. They lack adequate expertise and creativity. Their position as the "think tanks" of the government on socio-economic problems has yet to be proved. *The Tribune* has rightly remarked:

"In most States, the Planning Boards, like several 'autonomous' Corporations, have been made sanctuaries for disgruntled, defeated or troublesome politicians who tend to treat plan funds as discretionary grants. Sinecures were deemed necessary to ensure the political support of such politicians in the struggle for ministerial survival amidst recurring toppling drives. Inevitably, such political accommodation has led to the minimum involvement of economic experts who alone should comprise State Planning Boards. It is time the pollution of planning through politics was ended."

Below the State level, the District Planning has been instituted through democratic decentralized planning to plan for the district.

9.6 DISTRICT PLANNING

When the question of planning for a district arises, the traditional approaches to macro or micro level planning may not be entirely helpful. Besides integrating sectoral priorities and sectoral demands, argues Rakesh Hooja, "the integration effort should also keep in mind the social background of the particular area and the various diversities (custom-wise, skillwise, income-wise and the like) of the various groups which form the population of the area."[25] This can possibly be only through a genuine decentralization of the planning process. The sense of participation and involvement of the people of a district in district planning may be phenomenal. It becomes evident from V.K.R.V. Rao's one of the speeches in April 1973:

"The whole *raison d'etre* of district planning rests not only on technical grounds but also on the involvement and participation of the people of the district. What is meant by grass roots planning is that it is not only technically more efficient but also operationally more efficient because of the psychology it creates of a movement for development and social and economic change because of popular participation."[26] Thus, district planning is most likely to enhance the sense of responsibility, dignity and responsiveness among all who are involved in the formulation and implementation of such planning. Hence, district planning is considered to be an effective instrument for strengthening the structure and spirit of democracy in India.

The Working Group on District Planning of the Planning Commission had remarked that decentralization through district planning enables a better perception of local needs, makes better-informed decision-making possible, gives people a better voice in decisions regarding their own welfare, achieves better integration among programmes, ensures effective popular participation, develops local resources and improves productivity. Obviously, the nature of multi-level planning in India has always emphasized sub-State level planning. Within this framework, the preference has generally been for 'district' planning in India.

The principal reasons for selecting a district as a unit for sub-State level planning may be summed up as under:[27]

(a) A district, rather than any other middle level regional unit, is relatively closer to the local population.

(b) A district is large enough to serve as a viable planning unit.

(c) Because of historical reasons, a district has a settled pattern of administration with internal consistency and administrative relationships.

(d) Panchayati raj institutions have been broadly centred round the district boundaries.

(e) Most information relating to revenue, land records, irrigation works, development loaning, housing, roads, electrification, social services, etc. is organized on a district to district basis.

(f) District planning can become a useful instrument for coordination, consistency and rational spatial planning.

(g) Some planning infrastructure already exists at the district level. At the sub-district level, on the other hand, a viable skill-base for planning is scarce.

(h) Local pressure groups cannot be kept within reasonable limits except at the district level.

(i) People's awareness of the administrative process in a district is high because of their long-term association with district administration.

The most comprehensive effort regarding district planning has been made by the Working Group on District Planning of the Planning Commission, headed by C.H. Hanumantha Rao, which, after a long period of deliberation, reported in 1984. Its main findings and suggestions are pointed out below:

- State level district planning unit
- Integrated approach of area planning
- Coordinated devolution of activities
- Organizational integration
- Expanded role and extended responsibilities
- Spatial planning ensuring justice for the weaker sections
- Comprehensive planning covering tentative cost and benefits of each project
- District share defined according to population, area and level of development
- Simple and rigorous methodology adopted for district planning
- Resource management
- Manpower planning and management
- Representative body of district planning
- Collector as chief coordinator for district planning and development
- Chief planning officer next to chief coordinator
- District planning divided into three operational phases.

9.6.1 Operational Phases of District Planning

The Hanumantha Rao Group has suggested a gradual stage-wise approach to the implementation of its recommendations stated just now.[28]

The first stage, known as the *stage of initiation,* would involve the following:

- Defining the scope of district planning and district sector schemes
- Disaggregating plan funds to district
- Formulating criteria for inter-district allocation of plan funds
- Strengthening plan capability at district level
- Establishing horizontal monitoring machinery at the district level and linking it vertically with monitoring mechanisms at the higher levels
- Setting up district planning board/council/committee with popular representation
- Establishing planning procedures for five year plans and annual plans.

The second stage, i.e. the *stage of limited decentralization*, would involve the following:

- Bringing limited sectors of activity within the purview of district planning
- Introducing the concept of free fund and encouraging limited localism in district planning
- Improving multi-level resource allocation for development budgeting
- Delegating extensive powers to the district level
- Streamlining procedures for dovetailing district plans into the State plan.

The third and the final stage, i.e. the *stage of full decentralization*, would involve the following:

- Enlarging localism to cover decision-making in all district sector activities
- Introducing administrative reforms to delegate all decision-making powers at the district level
- Encouraging a high level of popular participation
- Encouraging local initiatives by adopting a budgetary practice
- Making the functionaries of development departments accountable to the district planning body
- Preparing district perspective plans
- Improving and empowering local self governments at the district level
- Evolving healthy relations between the political executive and the bureaucracy.

The Working Group hoped that the final stage of implementation would be completed by 2000 AD. The Group had allowed considerable flexibility to the various States to implement its recommendations.

9.6.2 Constitutional Amendment

Article 243 ZD of our Constitution, included as a result of the 74th Constitutional Amendment Act, States clearly that in every State a District Planning Committee (DPC) shall be constituted in each district to consolidate the plans prepared by the Panchayat and the Municipalities in the district concerned and to prepare a draft development plan for the district as a whole.

The composition of the DPC will be according to the law passed by the State Legislature, which will also mention the way to fill up the committee seats. But four-fifths members of the DPC shall be elected from amongst the elected members of the Panchayats at the district level and of the municipalities in the district in proportion to the ratio of rural-urban population in the district. The State law will determine the functions of the DPC relating to district planning and the manner of choosing its Chairperson.

The DPC, while preparing the draft development plan, will keep in mind the matters of common interest between the Panchayats and the Municipalities including spatial planning, sharing of water and other natural resources, the integrated development of infrastructure and environmental conservation, the extent and type of available financial and other resources, consulting such institutions and organizations that may be specified by the order of the Governor. After the draft development plan is prepared and after it is passed by the Committee of the Chairpersons of the DPC, it will be forwarded to the State Government for incorporation in the State plan.

The 74th Constitutional Amendment Act covers the following aspects of district planning:

(a) It has envisaged the DPC to be representative of the structure of district population.

(b) It has specified the broad objectives of the District Planning Committee and yet has permitted the State and district level flexibility in the definition of their functions.

(c) It has allowed freedom to the States to prescribe the manner of the election of the Chairperson of the DPC.

(d) It has provided for a consultative process in the drafting of the district plans and schemes.

(e) It has prescribed for integration between the district and the State plans.

Thus, for the first time in India, a constitutional planning body has been created and that too at the district level. This obviously is an encouraging opportunity for Indian districts.

Questions

1. Discuss the composition and functions of the Planning Commission/NDC of India.
2. Discuss the planning machinery at the State level of India.
3. Write short notes on:
   (a) District planning
   (b) NDC
   (c) Features/aims of Indian Planning.
4. Write a note on NITI Aayog.

Notes and References

1. Government of India, *The Planning Process*, Planning Commission, New Delhi, 1963.
2. Government of India, *op. cit.,* 1975.
3. Government of India, Administrative Reforms Commission, Report of the Study Team, *Machinery for Planning, 1967*, Delhi, Manager of Publications, 1968.
4. United Nations, *Proceedings of the International Seminar on Organization and Administration of Development Planning Agencies*, U.N. Publication Sales No. E, 74.II HL, Vol. I.
5. Thahane, T.T., Planning for Development, in John Barrat and others (Eds.), *Accelerated Development in Southern Africa*, Macmillan, London, 1974.
6. Salvadore, Sehiave-Campo and Hans W. Sorger, *Perspectives of Economic Development*, Houghton Mifflin & Co., Boston, 1900.
7. Iran, Adelman and Cuntlia T. Morries, *Society, Politics and Economic Development*, N.V. John Hoptrus Press, 1967.
8. Milikan, Max, A Strategy for Development, UN Centre for Social and Economic Information, *Executive Briefing Paper*, I, New York, 1970.
9. WHO, *Public Health Papers*, Interrelationship between Health Programmes and Socio-Economic Development, Geneva, 1973.
10. Subramaniam, V., The Citizen and Planning, *Indian Journal of Public Administration*, July–September, 1975.
11. Chakravarti, Sukhomoy, *Development Planning: The Indian Experience*, Oxford University Press, New Delhi, 1987.
12. Agarwal, A.N., *Indian Economy*, Wiley Eastern, New Delhi, 1994. Also see, Dhingra, Ishwar C., *The Indian Economy: Resource Planning, Development and Problems*, Sultan Chand and Sons, New Delhi, 1994.

13. Arora, R.K. and Rajni Goyal, *Indian Public Administration: Institutions and Issues*, Wishwa Prakashan, New Delhi, 1997.
14. Editorial, *Yojana*, August 15, 1992, p. 3.
15. *Ibid.*, p. 7.
16. Datta, Bhabatosh, *Bharater Arthik Unnayan* (in Bengali), Ananda Publishers, Kolkata, 1984.
17. Arora, R.K. and Rajni Goyal, *op. cit.*
18. *ARC Interim Report on the Machinery for Planning*, New Delhi, Government of India, 1967.
19. Maheshwari, S.R., *Indian Administration*, Orient Longman, New Delhi, 1995.
20. Maheshwari, S.R., *The Administrative Reforms Commission*, Lakshmi Narain Agarwal, Agra, 1972.
21. Sathe, Vasant, *National Government, Agenda for a New India*, UBS Publishers, New Delhi, 1991.
22. It has sufficiently been discussed in Section 9.2, subsection 'A Liberal Trend', of the present chapter.
23. *Mainstream*, Vol. IV, No. 26, New Delhi, June 18, 2016.
24. *Commission on Centre-State Relations (Sarkaria Commission) Report, Part I*, Government of India, New Delhi, 1988.
25. Hooja, Rakesh, Decentralized Planning and the Hanumantha Rao Report, in Kaushik, Asha (Ed.), *Democratic Concerns: The Indian Experience: Essays in Honour of Professor Iqbal Narain,* Vol. II, Aalekh, Jaipur, 1994.
26. *Ibid.*
27. Inamdar, N.R., District Governor, in V.A. Pai Panandiker (Ed.), *Third Survey of Research in Public Administration*, 1997.
28. Hooja, Rakesh and B. Yerram Raju (Eds.), *Decentralized Planning in a Multilevel Framework,* Rawat, Jaipur, 1993.

10 Financial Administration

10.1 INTRODUCTION

Administration and finance are two inseparable terms like a body and its shadow. All administrative activities involve expenditure of some kind. Without finance, the administrative machinery becomes inoperative. No wonder, Kautilya had reminded: "All undertakings depend upon finance. Hence, foremost attention shall be paid to the treasury."[1] On the contrary, finance, too, has to depend upon administration. To be specific, all financial transactions and expenditure, in order to be documented properly, should be administered or executed by efficient means.

The term *financial administration* is used in a broad sense to include all the processes involved in collecting, budgeting, appropriating and expending public money. It also includes auditing income, expenditures, receipts and disbursements and accounting for funds needed to be expended on public services. Thus, financial administration touches the very basis of the socio-economic welfare of the people.

Financial administration is a dynamic process that consists in an on-going chain of operations, performed by the following agencies:

- The Executive, which needs funds
- The Legislature, which alone can grant funds
- The Finance Commission
- The Parliamentary Committees
- The Audit Department

1. **Executive:** The Executive branch of government formulates the annual programme of its work and informs the Legislature of the annual financial needs of the government. The responsibility of formulating the annual budget falls upon the Executive. Financial policies are controlled by the Legislature while the Executive basically formulates and implements the policies of expenditure.

2. **Legislature:** The legislative branch of government in a democratic political system exercise the most crucial control over public finances. In administering the financial affairs of a government, the most important fact is that the Legislature concentrates all powers regarding the raising and spending of public funds. "It is the body which determines what money shall be raised and, in general terms, at least expended."[2] As the fund-raising and fund-granting authority, the Legislature has the power to levy, abolish, increase or decrease any tax. It has the final authority to sanction money for expenditure. Following the British financial system, the Executive in India, too, demands money from the Legislature by presenting the budget while the Legislature grants it.
3. **Finance Commission:** The Finance Commission in India is a unique constitutional body that came into existence in 1950. Although such a Commission is typical of a federal form of government, yet one cannot find similar constitutional institutions even in such federations as the USA, Canada and Australia. Realizing some inevitable federal fiscal imbalances, some constitutional and extra-constitutional provisions are made to provide for financial transfers from the National Government to the State Governments. In India such transfers have been institutionalized by creating a Constitutional Finance Commission under Article 280. The Commission is expected to review the financial needs of the States and to recommend the quantum of resources and their overall distribution among the States.
4. **Parliamentary Committees:** The two financial committees of the Legislature, known as the *Public Accounts Committee* and *Estimates Committee,* exercise financial control on behalf of the legislature. The Public Accounts Committee examines the appropriation accounts in the light of the audit report of the Comptroller and Auditor-General. It draws the attention of the Legislature to any financial irregularity which might have occurred and makes suggestions for preventing them in future.

   The Estimates Committee is a parliamentary instrument which was set up with the primary aim of scrutinizing the estimates included in the budget and making positive suggestions to introduce economy in government expenditure.
5. **Audit Department:** A very important agency for financial control is the Audit Department. After the money has been spent, the entire expenditure is subjected to the 'searchlight' of an independent audit, in order to make sure the legality and propriety of the entire expenditure. Parliamentary approval of taxation and expenditure is almost meaningless if effective arrangements are not devised to know whether parliamentary

behests have been complied with or not. Independent audit is the device to know this. The Comptroller and Auditor-General sees whether the money spent accords with the purposes for which grants were made in the Appropriation Act. It also sees that the amount of expenditure does not exceed what has already been sanctioned.

10.2 FINANCE COMMISSION

The Finance Commission has been aptly described as an institutional innovation of far-reaching importance in the working of the Indian federal system.[3] Despite the elaborate provisions for the division of financial resources between the Union and the States as laid down in the Indian Constitution, the Constitution-makers could realize that the adjustment of federal-State financial relations is a recurring problem and that no distribution could be satisfactory for all the times and under all circumstances. The allocation of revenue to the units of a federation is always a complicated problem and it becomes particularly complicated in a developing economy like India, in view of the fact that the development of social services is primarily the responsibility of the States.

The Constitution-makers, consequently, took into account the possibility of the States lacking adequate finances to cope effectively with their responsibilities and laid down provisions for the devolution of revenues through the transfer of a part of the proceeds of certain Union taxes to the States and also through Union grants-in-aid of the revenues to the States. Our Constitution provides for obligatory as well as permissive sharing of the Union revenues by the States. In order to ensure that this form of Union assistance to the States does not lead to the demise of the State's autonomy, the Constitution provides that the revenues and grants-in-aid shall be made on the basis of the recommendations of an independent agency, which is to be termed *Finance Commission*.

Article 280 of the Indian Constitution provides for the constitution of a Finance Commission by the President every five years. The Constitution does not, however, specify the qualifications and experience of the persons who should be appointed to the Commission. This is in marked contrast with the Union Public Service Commission, where it is specifically indicated that at least 50 per cent of the members should be from the Union and/or State services. But no such reference is made to the nature of the background of the Chairman and ordinary members of the Finance Commission in the Constitution. Article 280 only States that the Finance Commission has to comprise a Chairman and four members and the Parliament is authorized to determine by law the qualifications of the members of the Finance Commission and methods of their selection. All the appointments are made by the President.

Hence, the Parliament has enacted The Finance Commission Act, 1951, which prescribes under Section (3) that the Chairman shall be selected from among the persons who have had experience in public affairs, and the other four members shall be selected from amongst (a) a High Court Judge or one qualified to be appointed to the post; (b) a person having special knowledge of the government finances and accounts; (c) a person having wide experience in financial matters and administration; and (d) a person having special knowledge of economics.

The gap between the two commissions is generally of 5 years. But in practice, however, the commissions have been appointed earlier than the constitutionally stipulated term.

Under the Constitution, the basis for sharing of divisible taxes by the Centre and the States and the principles governing grants-in-aid to the States have to be decided by the Finance Commission every five years. The President can refer to the Commission any other matter in the interest of sound finance. The recommendations of the Finance Commission along with an explanatory memorandum as to the action taken by the government on them are laid before each House of Parliament. Principally, with a view to reduce the vertical as well as horizontal federal fiscal imbalances, the Finance commission is set up which is expected to recommend the financial transfers from the Union Government to the States.[4] It is interesting to know that although the name and the constitution of the Finance Commission originated and evolved in post-independence times, its features (such as, an expert body to enquire into the budgetary position of the Union and the States, to render expert advice on the approach and principles to be formed for the distribution of the divisible pool of revenue between the Union and the States and also amongst the States, and to suggest the specific period during which they are to be in force) owe their origin to the Indian Financial Enquiry Committee of 1936, headed by Otto Niemeyer and the approach and methodology that he adopted during that time.[5] From the Ninth Finance Commission onwards, there has been a general tendency in India on the part of the Financial Commissions to adopt a normative approach, instead of the outdated gap-filling approach that has been evolved by Sir Otto Niemeyer, in assessing the receipts and expenditures of the revenue account of the States and the Centre.

The Finance Commission was originally supposed to be a quasi-arbitral body which function would be to do justice between the Centre and the States.[6] The Commission happens to be the most important body to regulate, coordinate and integrate the finances of the Union Government as well as the State Government.[7]

The Finance Commission is an advisory body and, legally speaking, the President is not bound to act according to its recommendations. It was at the same time recognized by the framers of our Constitution that the creation of such a body in a federal set-up would have little meaning if its recommendations were not to be accepted by the

President, except where considerations of overriding importance justified deviation therefrom. Thus, H.N. Kunzru, a member of the Constituent Assembly, expressed the hope that a convention would grow up that the government should normally accept the recommendations of the Finance Commission. That this hope has been fulfilled to a large extent is clear from the functioning of the Finance Commissions so far.

The terms of reference of the Finance Commission relate to the following:

- The distribution between the Union and the States of the net proceeds of taxes which are to be divided between them under the chapter of financial provisions and the allocation between the States of the respective shares of each of such proceeds.
- The principles that should govern the grants-in-aid of the revenues of the States out of the Consolidated Fund of India.
- Any other matter referred to the Commission by the President in the interests of sound finance.

The establishment of this unique institution may aptly be described as India's original contribution to the theory and practice of federalism since nothing like this was to be found in any other federation. Still, it bears some resemblance to the Commonwealth Grants Commission of Australia which was the precursor of the Finance Commission in India, for it came up as a sequel to the report of a study undertaken by B.K. Nehru and B.P. Adarkar[8] on deputation of the Government of India to Australia in 1946 to study its federal fiscal system and to recommend its relevance to India. However, scholars like Thimmaih think that the two commissions are significantly different from each other, both in terms of their stature and scope of their competence.

So far, fourteen Finance Commissions have been appointed and their recommendations have been placed. The first Finance Commission (1951–1953) made three important recommendations which were accepted by the Government. The recommendations are as follows:

1. Fifty-five per cent of the net proceeds of income tax shall be assigned by the Union to the States and that it should be distributed among them under the terms prescribed by the Commission.
2. The government should accept the principles laid down by the Commission for its guidance in the matter of making general grants-in-aid to the States which require financial assistance.
3. Specific sums as recommended should be given to certain States like West Bengal, Punjab and Assam for five years (1952–1957).

The second Finance Commission (1956–1957) made two major recommendations which were largely accepted by the Union Government. The recommendations are as follows:

1. The States should be given sufficient resources to enable them to meet both their plan and non-plan expenditure.

2. The basic and developmental needs of the States should be considered together and not separately.

The third Finance Commission (1960–1961) recommended the enhancement of the income of the State Governments. Its recommendations were largely accepted by the Union Government.

The fourth Finance Commission (1964–1965) looked with sympathy at the financial problems faced by the States and made important recommendations which were accepted by the Union Government. These recommendations, however, came into force from 1st April, 1966.

The fifth Finance Commission (1968–1969) recommended that the States' share of income tax should be raised to 75 per cent and of Union excise duties to 20 per cent.

The sixth Finance Commission (1972–1973), for the first time, was required to go into the question of the debt position of the States and their non-plan capital gap.

The seventh Finance Commission (1977–1978) was appointed in relation to the next five years beginning in 1979.

The eighth Finance Commission (1982–1984) recommended granting money to the States. But its recommendations could not be implemented by the Union Government on the ground of financial difficulties and late receipt of the Commission's Report.

The ninth Finance Commission (1987–1989) was unique at least for three major reasons. *First*, it took more than two years to consider and examine the financial problems facing the States. *Second*, it submitted two reports. The Commission submitted its first report for 1989–1990 on 29th July, 1988. It submitted its second report, covering the five-year period, commencing on April 1, 1990, on 18 December, 1989. *Third*, the Commission vividly examined the financial problems involved in Centre-State relations and made far-reaching recommendations most of which were accepted by the Union Government. Its main recommendations are given below:

1. Enhancement in the share of the States in income tax and excise duties.
2. Liberal grants-in-aid of revenues of certain States under Article 275(1) of the Constitution towards meeting their non-plan revenue gap as assessed by the Finance Commission for five years (1990–1995).
3. Regarding debt relief, the Finance Commission's recommendations included elongation of maturity period of future central loans for State plans from 15 years to 20 years with 50 per cent loans enjoying a grace period of five years, consolidation of such loans advanced during 1984–1989 and its rescheduling to 15 years with relief in repayment ranging from 5 per cent to 10 per cent, write-off of certain central loans, moratorium of two years (1990–1992) on payment of principal and payment of interest in respect of special loans granted to Punjab.

4. For financing relief expenditure, the Commission recommended replacement of the existing system of margin money by the Calamity Relief Fund for each State to which the Centre should contribute 75 per cent in the form of non-plan grant and the balance of 25 per cent should be contributed by the State Government.

The tenth Finance Commission (1993–1995) decided the basis for sharing of the divisible taxes by the Centre and the States and the principles governing grants-in-aid. Besides, the Commission took into account certain other aspects. Its report covered the period beginning April 1, 1993 and its tenure lasted till November 1995. The main areas of concern of the tenth Finance Commission are as follows:

- Balancing the revenue budget both at the Centre and in the States, and at the same time, generating surplus for capital investment and reducing fiscal deficit.
- Examining the resource adequacy at the Centre to meet expenditures on civil administration, defence, border security, debt-servicing and other committed liabilities
- The issue of capital maintenance expenditure on Plan Schemes, the norms for fixing specified amounts and the manner of monitoring them
- The requirements of States for modernization of administration including computerization of land records
- The revenue resources of the States for the five-year plan period (1995–2000) on the basis of 1993–1994 levels of taxation
- Changes in the principles governing the distribution of the net proceeds of the additional excise duties in any financial year in replacement of the sales tax levied formerly by the State Governments
- Reasonable returns on investment in the various State projects and enterprises and the scope for better fiscal management
- The debt-position of the States as on March 31, 1994 and various corrective measures, keeping in view the financial needs of the Centre
- The existing scheme of Calamity Relief Fund.

The eleventh Finance Commission Report was submitted in 2000. Richer States led by Andhra Pradesh Chief Minister N. Chandrababu Naidu (TDP) met the then Prime Minister Mr. A.B. Vajpayee and expressed some dissatisfaction with its recommendations. Finance Commission reports have consistently given greater weightage to backwardness and population in deciding federal fiscal transfers to States. Although the weightage of economic performance has been increased in recent Finance Commission reports, poorer States still get proportionately more than richer States. Any drastic change in the pattern of transfer is likely to increase regional economic disparities.

The twelfth Finance Commission Report was submitted in 2005. It has recommended an increase in the share of States in the total divisible pool of federal resources from the existing 29.5 per cent to 30.5 per cent. This slight gain to the States may be cancelled out because of the neo-liberal economic policies that have put a strain on Union as well as State finances. In a view from the perspective of States on the twelfth Finance Commission Report, V. Sridhar has commented: Although the Constitution prescribed that the main task of the Finance Commission is to perform its role as an agency for setting the modalities for the transfer of resources from the Centre to the States, the terms of reference of the Twelfth Finance Commission were expanded by asking it to suggest "a plan by which the (State) Governments, collectively and severally, may bring about a restructuring of the public finances, restoring budgetary balance, achieving macro-economic stability and debt reduction along with equitable growth." In specific terms, there were fears that this was, apart from being a violation of the principles of federalism, an attempt by the Centre to straitjacket the States in the liberal reform mode with all its harsh implications for the already financially beleaguered States.[9]

In conclusion, it may be Stated that a paradigmatic shift in economic policies and Union-State relations due to growing federalization of the Indian polity has occurred since the 1990s. Economic liberalization has augmented the autonomy of the State Governments. Federalization has accentuated the tendency towards both political and economic regionalism. This is reflected in the eleventh and twelfth Finance Commission Reports. On the whole, the appointment of the Finance Commission and the submission of its report have ceased to evoke much public attention in India. This is not due to the public's gross indifference to the unintelligible financial matters deliberated upon by the Finance Commissions, but mainly because of the known conservatism of all the past Finance Commissions. In spite of the superficial innovation in the methodology of some of the Commissions, the substantial part of their reports does not show any distinct departure from the methods of the past Finance Commissions.[10]

The thirteenth Finance Commission was set up in 2007 under the chairmanship of Dr. Vijay L. Kelkar. Its operational duration was 2010–15. Major recommendations of the thirteenth Finance Commission were as under:

- The share of states in the net proceeds of the shareable Central taxes should be 32 per cent. This is 1.5 per cent points higher than the recommendation of twelfth Finance Commission.
- Revenue deficit to be progressively reduced and eliminated, followed by revenue surplus by 2013–14.
- Fiscal deficit to be reduced to 3 per cent of the GDP by 2014–15.
- A target of 68 per cent of GDP for the combined debt of Centre and states.

- The Medium Term Fiscal Plan (MTFP) should be reformed and made the statement of commitment rather than a statement of intent.
- FRBM Act needs to be amended to mention the nature of shocks which shall require targets relaxation.
- Both the Centre and states should conclude 'Grand Bargain' to implement the model Goods and Services Act. To incentivise the states, the Finance Commission recommended a sanction of the grant of ₹500 billion.
- Initiatives to reduce the number of Central Sponsored Schemes (CSS) and to restore the predominance of formula-based plan grants.
- States need to address the problem of losses in the power sector in a time-bound manner.

The fourteenth Finance Commission was set up in 2013 under the chairmanship of Dr. Y.V. Reddy. Its operational duration is 2015–20. Its major recommendations are as under:

- The share of states in the net proceeds of the shareable Central taxes should be 42 per cent. This is 10 percentage points higher than the recommendation of the thirteenth Finance Commission.
- Revenue deficit to be progressively reduced and eliminated.
- Fiscal deficit to be reduced to 3 per cent of the GDP by 2017–18.
- A target of 62 per cent of GDP for the combined debt of Centre and states.
- The Medium Term Fiscal Plan (MTFP) should be reformed and made the statement of commitment rather than a statement of intent.
- FRBM Act needs to be amended to mention the nature of shocks which shall require targets relaxation.
- Both the Centre and states should conclude 'Grand Bargain' to implement the model Goods and Services Act.
- Initiatives to reduce the number of Central Sponsored Schemes (CSS) and to restore the predominance of formula-based plan grants.
- States need to address the problem of losses in the power sector in a time-bound manner.

Thus, it seems that the recommendations of both the thirteenth Finance Commission and the fourteenth Finance Commission were almost similar with each other. It is, however, alleged that the Planning Commission had usurped the functions of the Finance Commission and had reduced the latter as merely a body empowered to recommend grants to states on revenue account only (Article 275 of the Indian Constitution). But after the formation of NITI Aayog on January 1,

2015, which has come to replace the Planning Commission (that was neither a constitutional nor a statutory body), the Finance Commission is sought to be empowered with its original task of distribution of revenues to the states.

10.3 PARLIAMENTARY COMMITTEES

In this section we discuss the importance of the Parliamentary Committees as such, and two major Parliamentary Committees, namely, Public Accounts Committee (PAC) and Estimates Committee (EC).

Parliamentary Committees are the backbone of parliamentary power and autonomy. The Parliament being a large body is usually ill-organized for effective parliamentary work. The real parliamentary work relating to scrutiny of legislative and Constitution amendment bills and control of the executive and administration gets done in Parliamentary Committees rather than in the whole House. Being all-party bodies, Parliamentary Committees are different from the Council of Ministers or the Cabinet, which is exclusively a majority-party body or a ruling coalition body.

The effectiveness of the parliamentary control of the Executive depends on the quality of the work of the Parliamentary Committees. Since March 1993, the Parliament has established what are called Ministry-based specialized standing committees for detailed scrutiny of expenditure, administration and government policy. This reform set up Ministry-based committees in place of omnibus committees shadowing a large variety of Ministries. Established under Rule 331C, the members of the committees are nominated by the Rajya Sabha Chairman and the Lok Sabha Speaker and their Chairmen are appointed by the Speaker. The membership of the committees is renewed every year. Each of these committees includes 45 members (30 from the Lok Sabha and 15 from the Rajya Sabha). Party representation in the committees proportionately mirrors the party composition of the Parliament.

It should be noted that these committees are instruments of the Parliament, not of the Government. The role of such committees is advisory, but vitally important in terms of presenting an alternative thinking of the Parliament, which is independent of the thinking of the Cabinet. Good quality committee work can enrich the quality of governance by various means. As Subhash Kashyap aptly remarks:

"Without weakening the parliamentary system, the concept of departmentally related standing select committees provides to Parliament sharper and more effective surveillance tools, restore the balance between parliament's legislative and deliberative functions and its role as a representational body, and above all, save valuable parliamentary time to the mutual advantage of both Parliament and Government."[11]

A recent study of the new committee system of the Parliament suggests that the committees have mostly given attention on the demands for grants relating to the Ministries they oversee. The study also expresses concern at the poor attendance of members in committee meetings–the average range being only 35 to 40 per cent.[12]

Another study remarks that Parliamentary Committees in India, unlike the Congressional Committees in the United States, are mostly ad hoc select committees that are disbanded after a bill's passage. The result is that the most significant work on legislation is done by the relevant Ministry or Department as to the substance and the Ministry of Law and Justice as to the form.[13]

The Parliamentary Committees did not find a mention in the proceedings of the Constituent Assembly, for the makers of the Indian Constitution took them for granted and left it to the House to make provisions for them under their rules of procedure.[14] Accordingly, the Parliament has created numerous ad hoc and standing committees, the prominent of the former type includes the select committees and joint committees. Of the standing committees, More[15] gives a five-fold categorization:

1. Committees to inquire like the Committee on Petitions and the Committee on Privileges
2. Committees to scrutinize like the Committee on Government Assurances and the Committee on Subordinate Legislation
3. Committees of an administrative character relating to the business of the House like the Committee on the Absence of Members
4. Committees dealing with the provisions of facilities to members like the General Purpose Committee and the House Committee
5. The Financial Committees such as the Public Accounts Committee, the Estimates Committee and the Committee on Public Undertakings.

In the following section we discuss the first two Financial Committees.

10.3.1 Public Accounts Committee (PAC)

The institution of PAC set up in 1922 has continued ever since. The Committee became a truly Parliamentary Committee in the post-independence period when two substantial changes took place in its structure and functions: *first*, increasing its membership to twenty-two, seven members of the Rajya Sabha are also made the members of the Committee, and *second*, the Comptroller and Auditor General (CAG) is made an adjunct of the PAC to facilitate the streamlining of its functioning.

The members of the PAC are elected by the Parliament every year from among its members according to the principle of proportional representation by means of the single transferable vote to enable all parties secure due representation on it. The term of office of the members is only one year; but by convention members are re-elected for another year. The Chairman of the PAC is appointed by the Speaker from amongst the members of the PAC. Till 1966–1967, the Chairman belonged to the ruling party. Since then, a member of the Opposition is nominated as the Chairman. In the case of a tie, the Chairman has a casting vote. The quorum for a meeting is four members.

Article 308 of the Rules of Procedure and Conduct of Business in Lok Sabha (1977 edition) lays down the functions of the PAC, which are as follows:

1. To examine the accounts showing the appropriation of sums granted by the Parliament for the expenditure of the Government of India, the annual finance account of the Central Government and such other accounts laid before the House as the PAC may think fit. It does so by examining the annual report of the CAG submitted to the Parliament. While doing so, the Committee has to ensure that:
   (a) the money shown in the accounts as having been disbursed was legally available for an applicable to the service or purpose to which they have been applied or charged;
   (b) the expenditure conforms to the authority which governs it; and
   (c) every reappropriation has been made in accordance with the provisions made under rules framed by a competent authority.
2. To examine the statement of accounts showing the income and expenditure of State corporations, trading and manufacturing schemes, concerns and projects together with the balance sheets and statements of profit and loss accounts which the President may have required to be prepared or are prepared under the provisions of the statutory rules regulating the financing of a particular corporation, trading or manufacturing scheme or concern or project and the report of the CAG on it.
3. To examine the statement of accounts showing the income and expenditure of autonomous and semi-autonomous bodies, the audit of which may be conducted by the CAG, either under the direction of the President or by a statute of Parliament.
4. To consider the report of the CAG in cases where the President may have required him to conduct an audit of any receipts or to examine the accounts of stores and stocks.
5. To examine if any money has been spent on any service during a financial year in excess of the amount granted by the House for that purpose. This will be done with reference to the facts of each case and the circumstances leading to such an excess. The PAC is free to make such recommendation as it deems fit.

On the whole, the main function of the PAC is to examine the report of the CAG submitted every year to the President, who causes it to be laid before the Lok Sabha which in turn refers it to this Committee. The PAC scrutinizes this report with the assistance of the CAG who is not a member of the PAC but attends the meetings of the PAC on invitation and intervenes to clarify the points as well as to assist the PAC generally. The position of the PAC is slightly different in the United Kingdom where the Secretaries appear before the Committee in their capacity as Accounting Officers.[16]

The PAC examines mainly the accounts showing the appropriation of sums granted by the House for the expenditure of the Government of India in order to ascertain whether the money has been spent as authorized by Parliament and for the purpose for which it was granted.[17]

Over the years, the PAC has established its sound credentials as the watchdog of the public finances through an efficient and impeccable track record of inducing a sense of responsibility and precision in the officials in spending the public money. The PAC's impression in the minds of the officials remains one of reminding them of their responsibilities towards the people of the country, whose money they are supposed to utilize with due care.

Two main criticisms against the working of the PAC are made. *First,* it is said that the Committee's work is in the nature of a post mortem examination of accounts. *Second*, a reading of the Committee's reports shows that similar complaints of official neglect, apathy and default are repeated year after year.

As against such criticism, it has to be remembered first that the non-party character of the PAC has come to be accepted and, secondly, that the PAC is assisted by the Finance Ministry and the CAG and such assistance helps in the implementation of its recommendations. In the words of Asok Chanda: "Over a period of years, the committee has entirely fulfilled the expectation that it should develop into a powerful force in the control of public expenditure. It may be claimed that the traditions established and conventions developed by the Public Accounts Committee conform to the highest traditions of a parliamentary democracy."[18]

The very existence of the PAC introduces the element of deterrence in the minds of the officials to desist from probable wastage and wrong appropriation of the precious public resources. Again, the method of functioning of the Committee brings the officials into contact with the Parliamentarians. Moreover, as W.H. Morris–Jones has observed, the work of the PAC serves to bring the officials and politicians together and to train both–the officials in the task of responsiveness to public opinion while the politicians in the task of constructive criticism[19]—in order to achieve the twin purposes of ensuring efficiency and economy in the spending of the public money.

10.3.2 Estimates Committee (EC)

In order to assert the monopoly of the Lower House (i.e. the Lok Sabha) on the financial matters of the government, the Estimates Committee was created in 1950 by the Lok Sabha. Basically, its purpose was to provide for an adequate control over the grants made to the government and the actual appropriation thereof. Replacing the then Standing Finance Committee and consisting of the members drawn exclusively from the Lok Sabha, it is called "the House in miniature as it represents the parties and groups in the Lok Sabha more or less in proportion to their representation in the House."[20]

The first Estimates Committee (EC) in the post-independence era was elected on April 10, 1950. The old standing committee continued for a while but disappeared after the general elections of 1952. Initially, it consisted of 25 members, including the Chairman. In 1956–1957, its membership was increased to 30. It was done with a view to facilitating the constitution of sub-committees and study groups of the committee which were expected to undertake extensive examination of the estimates. The members of the EC are elected from the Lok Sabha only, from amongst the members, according to the principle of proportional representation by means of a single transferable vote. Thus, the Rajya Sabha has absolutely no representation on the EC.

The tenure of a member of the EC is one year, but a practice was initiated in 1956–1957 that, as far as possible, one-third of the members of the EC may be retired annually. This provides the succeeding committee the benefit of continuity of procedures and norms. The EC is normally elected in June and begins its work in July and continues to meet, as far as possible, during the off-session periods.

Thus, broadly speaking, the EC is an instrument of Parliament set up with the primary aim of scrutinizing the estimates included in the budget and to make positive suggestions to introduce economy in government expenditure. Within this broad objective, the primary functions of the EC are as follows:

- To report what economies and improvements in organizational efficiency or administrative reforms, consistent with the policy underlying the estimates, may be affected.
- To suggest alternative policies in order to promote further efficiency and economy in administration.
- To examine whether the money is well laid out within the limits of the policy implied in the estimates.
- To suggest the form in which the estimates shall be presented to the Parliament.

The EC is not concerned with the estimates of most public undertakings, as they were entrusted to the Committee on Public Undertakings in 1964.

The EC is not required to consider all the estimates of different Departments on an annual basis. Its approach is selective. At the beginning of each financial year, it makes a selection of a few Ministries and, in each Ministry, a few subjects are selected to be examined during the year under review. This is done on the British pattern.

It should be pointed out that voting of grants in the Lok Sabha does not depend on the EC having submitted its report. In other words, it is not incumbent on the EC to examine the entire estimates of any one year. The EC is concerned with the estimates only after they have been presented to the House. Rules also enable the EC to continue its examination of the estimates from time to time throughout the financial year. It keeps reporting to the House as the work proceeds. This provision implies that the EC has no role to play in the framing of estimates. It cannot also disallow any expenditure. It is only an advisory body, the duty of which is to examine these estimates after they are passed and also to suggest economies in expenditure. But during the year under review and in future, its suggestions can serve as important guidelines.

Regarding governmental policies, the EC, just after it was set up in 1950, could not interfere with such policies. In fact, the Committee had complained that its power not to examine the policies ultimately curtailed the usefulness of the EC. Hence, the function of suggesting alternative policies was added to the Committee's role description in order to bring about efficiency and economy of the EC.

The EC can also comment on the organizational aspects, functioning and proceedings of various Ministries and Departments and suggest measures by which greater economy could be introduced in administration. In this respect, the second report of the EC was an eye opener. It was entitled the "Reorganization of the Secretariat and Departments of Government of India." It undertook a detailed scrutiny of the establishment of the Central Secretariat and suggested several measures regarding the amalgamation of units, procedures of work, salaries of officials, etc.

The EC also examines the classification and form of accounts presented to the Lok Sabha. The Secretariat of the EC undertakes an examination of the estimates as soon as they are presented to the House to ensure that the classification of the heads of items under 'charged and voted' has been done properly. Where they come across any discrepancies, they bring it to the notice of the Chairman of the Committee who takes up the matter for further consideration with the Finance Minister. While undertaking this work, it is concerned only with the 'headings' of the expenditure and does not go into the economy factor.

Conventionally, though the reports of the Committee are not discussed in the House, its recommendations are regarded as directions to the government which ordinarily accepts them, signifying the position of the Committee as a powerful force not to be ignored.[21]

The nature of the role played by the EC is clearly summed up by Asok Chanda in the following way:

"While the Committee refrains even now from openly criticizing the policy implicit in the estimates, its examination does often indirectly reflect on the manner in which a particular policy has been evolved or is being implemented. There has also been considerable improvement in the organization of the Committee and in its technique, which has better equipped it to fulfil its responsibilities. Even though it works within the limitations inherent in a democratic form of government, its contributions are tending to become more and more effective in economizing national expenditure."[22]

In their endeavour to fulfil the aspirations of the House, the members of the EC invite official as well as non-official experts, if a technical matter comes up for discussion and the members find themselves in a helpless situation.[23] Yet, sometimes, the EC is criticized for not being able to see the wood for the trees. The members of the EC, as pointed out by W.H. Morris–Jones, are supposed to look for possible economies, but they have in fact been happy to rule out the faint line between economy and efficiency. Further, they have not hesitated to recommend in the name of efficiency, large administrative reforms and even reorientation of policy.

10.4 COMPTROLLER AND AUDITOR-GENERAL (CAG)

It is the function of the Parliament not only to vote grants of public expenditure but also to ensure that the grants made by it are spent legally, regularly, faithfully and efficiently. It has also to be ensured that the money has been spent for the purpose and manner in which it was intended. With this end in view, our Constitution has provided for the Office of the Comptroller and Auditor-General (CAG) who examines the annual accounts and submits a report on it to the Parliament every year. This report is examined in detail by the Public Accounts Committee of the Parliament.

The institution of the CAG constitutes one of the pillars on which depends the proper and efficient functioning of the governmental machinery in India. Drawn from the system of financial accountability prevalent in the British period, the office of the CAG is meant to introduce the uniformity of government accounts, on the one hand, and to carry out the responsibility of conducting independent audit, on the other. The institution of the CAG owes its lineage to the Indian Audit and Accounts Department created for the first time in 1753.[24] Due to its criticality in ensuring the sanctity, efficiency and effectiveness of the government accounts in India, the office of the CAG was accorded a prominent place in our Constitution.

The CAG is appointed by the President under the provision of Article 148 of the Indian Constitution. The Parliament in 1953 enacted the Comptroller and Auditor–General's (Conditions of Service) Act which was amended in 1971. He holds office for 6 years or up to the age of 65 years, whichever is earlier. Thus, he has been equated with a judge of the Supreme Court. On retirement, he is entitled to receive an annual pension. To enable him to discharge his duties with independence and fearlessness, he is not given any re-employment under the Government after his retirement. The appointment of Asok Chanda in 1960 as the Chairman of the Third Finance Commission gave birth to considerable public controversy over the matter.[25] His salary, allowances and pension are, however, charged upon the Consolidated Fund of India, and cannot be varied to his disadvantage during his term of office. He does not hold office at the pleasure of the President, unlike other civil servants and can be removed from office only on an address from both Houses of Parliament on the grounds of "proved misbehaviour" or "incapacity". Thus, his conditions of service are, on the whole, equivalent to a senior member of the IAS, holding the rank of a Secretary.

The principal powers and functions of the CAG are as follows:

1. To audit the accounts of the Union Government, the State Governments and the Governments of the Union Territories, having legislative assemblies in so far as the expenditure from the Consolidated Fund is concerned.
2. To audit and report on all expenditure from the Contingency Funds and Public Accounts of the Union and the States.
3. To audit and report on all trading, manufacturing, profit and loss accounts, etc. kept by any Department of the Union or State.
4. To audit and report (after the passing of the 1971 Act) on receipts of expenditure of (a) all bodies and authorities "substantially financed" from the Union or State revenues, (b) government companies, and (c) other corporations or bodies, when so required by laws.

It should be mentioned in this context that prior to the amendment made in 1976 separating audit from accounts and decentralization of the accounts of various Ministries and Departments, the CAG used to compile the accounts of the Union and State Governments.

For performing his duties efficiently, the CAG has access to all books of accounts, stores, offices, treasuries, etc. on the accounts of which he is to report. He presents these reports annually to the President or the Governor, as the case may be, who causes them to be laid before each House of Parliament or the State Assembly.

Owing to the nature and significance of the functions of the institution of CAG, independence and functional autonomy of the office become necessary. Hence, elaborate provisions have been made in our Constitution to ensure the independence of the CAG. A significant provision in this regard is the cumbersome procedure of his removal from office. So far, no overt or covert attempt has been made by the government to either question or fetter the independence and functional autonomy of the office, even at such times when the report of the CAG on the Bofors issue was proving fatal for the then government, which could have successfully gone for initiating the process of removing the CAG from the office.[26]

As the highest audit officer, the CAG's duty is to uphold the Constitution and the Parliamentary legislation in the sphere of financial administration. The CAG is now the chief auditor and is responsible for auditing all expenditures from the revenues of the Central or the State Governments in and outside India and ascertaining whether money shown in the accounts as having been disbursed was legally available for and applicable to the service or the purpose to which it has been applied and whether the expenditure conforms to the authority governing it. Asok Chanda, himself being the incumbent of this high office, described in his book the functions of the CAG. His functions are not merely to ensure that the appropriations made by the Parliament have not been exceeded without a supplementary vote or that the expenditure conforms to rules, but also to satisfy himself, on behalf of Parliament, as to its "wisdom, faithfulness and economy."[27] Chanda gave a new dimension to auditing and it was in this sense that T.N. Chaturvedi, the retired CAG, created a controversy and public debate by exposing the errors in the Bofors transaction in his audit report. The duties of the CAG regarding the audit of receipts are limited and need to be exposed. The receipts from income tax, wealth tax, expenditure tax, estate duty, excise and land revenue are excluded from the scope of his audit. It is a good sign that the income tax receipts are being progressively brought under his purview.

It is important to note the objections raised by Paul Appleby, the noted American scholar, while evaluating the role of the CAG in the Indian political system. Branding Indian audit as a highly pedestrian function with a narrow perspective and very limited utility, he held the CAG accountable for a much prevalent and crippling reluctance on the part of the government officials to take decisions and act decisively. This scathing criticism of Appleby regarding the office of the CAG was not accepted by the Indian scholars like Asok Chanda who held the view:

"In all recognized democracies, audit is not just tolerated as a necessary evil but is also looked upon as a valued ally which brings to notice procedural and technical irregularities and lapses on the part of individuals, whether they be errors of judgment, negligence or acts and intents of dishonesty."[28]

Thus, challenging the attack mounted by Appleby, the system of audit as well as the office of the CAG has remained one of the most useful functions performed for the purpose of seeing that the expenses voted by the Parliament are utilized for the same purpose and with full care for efficiency, economy and effectiveness.

But the flow of criticism does not stop here. D.D. Basu, criticizing the functions of the CAG, points out: "Though the designation of his office indicates that he is to function both as Comptroller and Auditor, our Comptroller and Auditor–General is so far exercising the functions only of an Auditor ... . He has no such control over the issue of money from the Consolidated Fund and many Departments are authorized to draw money by issuing cheques without specific authority from the Comptroller and Auditor–General, who is concerned only at the audit stage when the expenditure has taken place."[29]

10.5 ELECTION COMMISSION

As every election involves huge monetary expenditure, in the chapter on financial administration, the composition and functions of the Election Commission—a free and fair electoral machinery–should be included.

Through popular elections, governmental authority is established with legitimacy, and peaceful and orderly transfer of authority to new leaders can be ensured. A good electoral system is thus absolutely necessary for the existence of a genuine representative government. The absence of general confidence in the verdict of the ballot box may destroy the faith of the public in any democratic system. Much depends on how the system operates in practice, and whether elections are conducted efficiently and impartially by competent and honest administrators free from political bias.[30]

The purity, fairness and freedom of election can be ensured only if the electoral administration, the basic foundation of democracy, is placed beyond the reach of party politics. For conducting elections, the architects of the Indian Constitution attached the highest significance to an independent electoral machinery. For this, it was absolutely necessary that an independent Election Commission with its vast paraphernalia should be set up in India. Such a Commission should ensure free and fair elections of the popular representatives at all levels. Principally, with the idea of fulfilling this long-cherished desire, the Election Commission of India was set up under Article 324. The Article says:

"The superintendence, direction and control of the electoral rolls for, and the conduct of all elections to Parliament and to the Legislature of every State and of elections to the offices of President and Vice-President held under this Constitution, including the appointment of election tribunals for the decision of the doubts and disputes arising out of or in connection with election to Parliament and to the Legislatures of the States, shall be vested in a Commission."

"Article 324", as Dr. Ambedkar pointed out, "proposed to centralise the election machinery in the hands of a single commission, to be assisted by regional Commissioners, working under the supervision, direction and control of the Election Commission and not under the control of the State Governor as envisaged earlier."[31] It was no doubt a significant shift. Electoral administration was attempted to be centralized in order "to prevent injustice being done by the provincial governments to people other than those who belonged to the provinces racially, linguistically and culturally."[32]

Regarding the composition of the Election Commission, Article 324 categorically mentions:

"The Election Commission shall consist of the Chief Election Commissioner and such number of other Election Commissioners, if any, as the President may from time to time fix and the appointment of the Chief Election Commissioner and other Election Commissioners shall, subject to the provisions of any law made on that behalf by Parliament, be made by the President."

Initially, the Election Commission consisted of only the Chief Election Commissioner (CEC), with the issue of appointment of other Election Commissioners (ECs) not finding favour with either the government of the day or the incumbent CEC, though a number of committees on the electoral reforms in India had recommended the expansion of the Election Commission.[33]

At present, the Election Commission consists of the CEC and two ECs, who are appointed by the President. Our Constitution neither lays down any specific qualifications or eligibility conditions for the appointment to the post of either CEC or the ECs nor stipulates any set procedure of their appointments. Though most of the persons appointed to the offices of the CEC and ECs belong to the cadres of elite Indian Administrative Service (IAS), a few people have indeed been appointed from outside the cadres of government service. In such a situation, the constitutional expectation from the Election Commission is that it should function in an independent way without any fear or favour. In order to fortify the independent status and autonomous functioning of the Election Commission, the Constitution has laid down under Article 324(5) that the CEC shall not be removed from his office except in like manner and on the like grounds as a judge of the Supreme Court, and the conditions of service to the CEC shall not be varied to his disadvantage during his tenure. Regarding the removal from office of other ECs, though there are constitutional provisions for their removal on the recommendations of the CEC, there still exists certain degree of uncertainty over the procedure of such removal as the niceties of the issue are being argued in the Supreme Court in the case of the Election Commissioner Navin Chawla.

Of the four pillars of the Indian Constitution, the Election Commission is definitely one. On it depends the integrity of election, which, truly, is the oxygen of democracy. To ensure free, fair and impartial elections, the Constitution of India establishes the Election Commission, a body autonomous in character and free from political or executive influence. The Commission, being an all-India body, has jurisdiction over elections to Parliament, State Legislatures, offices of the President and Vice-President. The reason for having an all-India body to supervise and conduct elections is that some States have a mixed population, as there are native people. A State Government could discriminate against outsiders by so managing things as to exclude them from the electoral rolls and thus deprive them of their right to vote, which is a basic right in a democracy. In order to prevent injustice being done to any section of the population, it was thought best to have one central body which would be free from local influences and have control over the entire electoral machinery in India. Hence, the birth of the Election Commission.

The functions of the Election Commission have been provided for under Article 324(1) which includes "the superintendence, direction and control of the preparation of the electoral rolls for, and the conduct of, all elections to Parliament and to the Legislature of every State and of elections to the offices of President and Vice-President." Such indicative functions of the Election Commission boil down to include the whole gamut of the electoral process including:

"Preparation, maintenance and revision of electoral rolls, the notifications, scrutiny, withdrawals and polling, registration of and recognition to political parties, allotment of election symbols, the appointment of a Chief Electoral Officer (a State Government Official) for each State, and Electoral Registration Officers and Returning Officers and Assistant Officers for each Assembly and parliamentary constituency, and the receiving of election petitions and the appointment of Election Tribunals to consider such petitions."[34]

To ensure the smooth discharge of functions by the Election Commission, it has been authorized to exercise a number of powers regarding the preparation for and conduct of elections. Two such powers are as follows:

First, the Commission is empowered to send the requisition for the number and category of government functionaries including the personnel of the security forces, required for the preparation and actual conduct of the elections bestowed on the Commission. The Union and the State Governments are clearly directed to ensure that the requirements of the Election Commission are readily available on priority basis as any dereliction of duty in this regard would be considered to be the violation of the Constitutional provisions.

Secondly, the Election Commission is also empowered to initiate disciplinary action against the delinquent officials for a dereliction of duty if it finds any deficiency on the part of these officials at the time of conducting elections.

Since its inception with the inauguration of the Constitution of India in 1950, the Election Commission has been functioning successfully. If the conduct of free and fair elections at periodic intervals is regarded to be the essence of democracy, the successful functioning of the electoral machinery must be construed to lie at the heart of the system. On such counts, the Election Commission of India has come out with flying colours. The difference between a true democracy and a farcical democracy lies in the sanctity of free and fair elections in the system. In this regard, the credit needs to be given to the Election Commission of India since it ensures that India remains the leading light among the prime and successful democratic systems of the world.

But very recently, the brightness of this light is significantly reduced since the Centre is faced with an unparalleled situation after the Chief Election Commissioner N. Gopalaswami had recommended to the President that his colleague, Navin Chawla, be sacked for alleged "partisanship". The President has forwarded the letter to the Prime Minister. A unique situation has arisen in the political sphere of India because for the first time in the country a Chief Election Commissioner has sought the removal of an Election Commissioner.

Gopalaswami's action surprised the political establishment which questioned its timing, i.e. just ahead of the 15th general election of the Lok Sabha (2009).[35] Chawla, however, ruled out his resignation and said that he could not see any reason for it. Asked what he would do next, the Election Commissioner said: "We have to conduct the general election and must continue to work in that direction." Gopalaswami retires on April 20, 2009 and is unlikely to be able to oversee the entire exercise. Chawla, the next in seniority on the three-member panel, is supposed to succeed Gopalaswami.

The Centre is expected to react to Gopalaswami's recommendation. Our Foreign Minister Mr. Pranab Mukherjee said that the issue would be examined and the government's response would be made available in due course. Regarding the issue, the reaction of the ruling party, i.e. the Congress, and the opposition, i.e., the BJP, differs from each other remarkably. The Congress refused to comment on the Chief Election Commissioner's recommendation for his colleague's removal, saying it would not like to "politicise" constitutional offices. On the contrary, the BJP went all out to push for Navin Chawla's dismissal. BJP general secretary Arun Jaitley said that Election Commissioner Chawla should not continue to be a part of preparations for the general election. In a news conference, Jaitley categorically remarked:

> "If there are reasons to believe that a person suffers from political bias, he is unfit to be a member of the Election Commission. His continuation as a member will subvert the holding of free and fair elections."

On the other hand, Congress general secretary Digvijay Singh said: "We have always opposed the BJP's attempts to politicise the offices of constitutional authorities. No party can react to media reports especially concerning such a sensitive issue; we don't know what the content of the letter is."[36]

The entire controversy goes back to March 2006 when L.K. Advani approached the President seeking Chawla's removal. The BJP levelled a series of allegations, ranging from linking him to Emergency's excesses to his close association with Sonia Gandhi. When nothing came of the petition, the BJP approached Gopalaswami in January 2008. However, the Chief Election Commissioner has said that his recommendation is based on his own assessment of Chawla's conduct in office.

Under such circumstances, the case would rest basically on two factors:

- The legal and constitutional opaqueness of whether the recommendation is binding, since experts are divided;
- That under the Constitution, the President does not act on his own, but on the advice of the Council of Ministers.

The Election Commission had tried to improve election procedures by the introduction of Electronic Voting Machines or EVMs. It was launched with the thought that these would certainly reduce malpractices and improve the efficiency and accuracy in the process of elections. It was first introduced on an experimental basis in 1982 in the Kerala Legislative Assembly Elections. The Election Commission in February 1998 launched a website of its own to provide accurate information, management, administration and instant results of elections. In 1993, Electors' Photo Identity Cards (EPICs) started to be issued to prevent electoral fraud. By 2004 Lok Sabha elections, the EPICs became absolutely compulsory. Yet, in certain areas ration cards also continued to be allowed for election purposes under certain specific circumstances. In 1998, the Election Commission decided to launch a programme for the computerisation of the electoral rolls. The VVPAT or Voter Verified Paper Audit Trail was introduced in eight Lok Sabha constituencies in the 2014 Lok Sabha Elections. This appeared to be quite a mentionable achievement of the Election Commission of India. However, the VVPAT system with EVMs was first used in a by-poll in September 2013 in Noksen (an Assembly constituency) of Nagaland. Since September 2013 VVPAT started to be used widely in a number of elections throughout the Country.

In the last Lok Sabha Elections (2014) NOTA or None of The Above was added as an option on the EVMs. The specific symbol for NOTA, a ballot paper with a black cross across it, was first introduced on September 18, 2015. The symbol of NOTA has been designed by the National Institute of Design, Ahmedabad.[37]

10.6 ZONAL COUNCILS

To uphold the spirit of federalism in our country, Zonal Councils have been set up in each of the five zones of India–Northern, Southern, Eastern, Western and Central. Just like the Governors' Conference in the United States, Zonal Councils have been created in India, vide Part III of the States Reorganization Act, 1956, for solving problems having an inter-State character. The Northern Zonal Council covers the States of Haryana, Himachal Pradesh, Jammu and Kashmir, Punjab, Rajasthan and also the National Capital Territory of Delhi and the Union Territory of Chandigarh. The Southern Zonal Council covers the States of Andhra Pradesh, Karnataka, Kerala and Tamil Nadu and the Union Territory of Pondicherry. The Eastern Zonal Council includes the States of Bihar, Jharkhand, Orissa, Sikkim and West Bengal. The Western Zonal Council comprises the States of Goa, Maharashtra and Gujarat and the Union Territories of Daman and Diu and Dadra and Nagar Haveli. The Central Zonal council includes the States of Chhattisgarh, Uttarakhand, Uttar Pradesh and Madhya Pradesh. These Zonal Councils have principally been formed to promote inter-State cooperation and coordination.

The seven North-Eastern States, i.e. (i) Assam, (ii) Arunachal Pradesh, (iii) Manipur, (iv) Tripura, (v) Mizoram, (vi) Meghalaya and (vii) Nagaland are not included in the Zonal Councils and their special problems are looked after by the North Eastern Council, set up under the North Eastern Council Act, 1972.

The Chairman of each Zonal Council in India is the Union Home Minister ex officio. The Chief Ministers of the States included in the zone act as the Vice-Chairman on a rotational basis for a year. In the performance of its functions efficiently and effectively, each Zonal Council can have some persons as Advisors to assist the Council. Such Advisors, who are not empowered to vote at any Council meeting, include one person nominated by the Planning Commission, the Chief Secretary of the Government of each State in the zone, and the Development Commissioner of each State. The Zonal Councils, however, are all empowered to appoint Committees of its members and advisors.

Each Zonal Council has a secretariat staff consisting of a Secretary, a Joint Secretary and such other officers as the Chairman of the Council may consider it necessary to appoint. The Chief Secretaries of the States represented in the Council act as Secretaries of the Council by rotation and hold office for one year at a time. The office for each zone is located at such place within the zone as is determined by the Council. All the administrative expenses of the office, including the salaries and allowances of the secretariat staff other than those of the Secretary, are borne by the Central Government out of the money provided by the Parliament for the purpose.

The Zonal Council meets in the States concerned by rotation and at such time as the Chairman of the Council may fix. The meetings of the Council are presided by the Chairman, or in his absence the Vice-Chairman, or in the absence of both, any member chosen by the members present from among themselves. At such meetings all questions are usually decided by a majority of the votes of the members present. In the case of a tie, the Chairman or the Presiding Officer has a second or casting vote. The proceedings of each meeting are forwarded to the Central Government as well as to each State Government concerned.

While discussing the role played by the Zonal Council, we must make it clear that the Council is not an executive body. It is merely an advisory body which can only discuss matters of common interest and forward its recommendations to the Centre and the States concerned. It should also be mentioned that Section 22(1) of the States Reorganization Act, 1956, authorizes the holding of joint meetings of Zonal Councils if deemed necessary. The objective of the joint meetings was to provide a forum for closer cooperation among States and Union Territories, on the one hand, and the Centre and the States, on the other, regarding the common problems arising in different regions in the fields of socio-economic planning, water disputes, inter-State transport, development projects, border disputes, problems related to linguistic minorities, etc. The principal role of the Zonal Councils is to carry out the programmes of the Centre in a given policy developed in the nation's capital. Thus, such Councils discuss the ways and means of implementing the central policy in matters like food conservation, water conservation, etc.

Two points of criticism have been raised against the Zonal Councils. First, it was feared originally that Zonal Councils might prove to be the proverbial "fifth wheel in the administrative coach", acting as an obstacle to speedy and efficient administration. This fear has proved to be unreasonable, for the Zonal Councils have not constituted another level in the traditional hierarchical pattern.[38] Second, the Zonal Councils have been regarded as only an extension of central authority, for they are financed by the Central Government. The Joint Secretary of the Zonal Council is virtually the resident agent of the Central Government in the zone, having administrative control over the Secretariat of the Council. This is criticized to affect the spirit of federalism. The critics opine that in order to make federalism effective, it was necessary to have decentralized administration and provide a platform for consultation among the States and Union Territories themselves.

Questions

1. Discuss the composition of and the role played by the Finance Commission in India.
2. Evaluate the roles played by the Parliamentary Committees in Indian administration.
3. Examine critically the functions of the Election Commission of India.
4. Write short notes on:

(a) PAC	(b) EC	(c) CAG
(d) Zonal Councils	(e) NOTA	(f) EVMs

Notes and References

1. Kautilya, *Arthashastra*, Raghuveer Printing Press, Mysore, 1956.
2. Willoughly, W.F., *Principles of Public Administration*, Brookings Institution, Washington, 1927.
3. Bombwall, K.R., The Finance Commission and the Union–State Relations in India, in T.N. Chaturvedi (Ed.), *Financial Administration*, IIPA, New Delhi, 1986.
4. An important study on these aspects of the federal finances is Thimmaih, G., *Studies in Federal Finances*, Padma Prakashan, Bangalore, 1973 (Ch. II).
5. Rao, G.A., *Finance Commissions in India*, Deep and Deep Publications, New Delhi, 1992.
6. Rao, B.N., *Indian Constitution in the Making*, Orient Longman, Madras, 1960.
7. Mishra, B.R., *Economic Aspects of the Indian Constitution*, Orient Longman, Calcutta, 1958.
8. Report on the *Australian System of Federal Finances and Its Applicability to Indian Constitution*, Government of India, 1947.
9. Sridhar, V., Short-Changing the States, *Front line*, April 8, 2005. Also see, Rao, M. Govinda and Nirvikar Singh, *Political Economy of Federalism in India*, Oxford University Press, New Delhi, 2005.
10. Chakrabarty, Bidyut and Rajendra Kumar Pandey, *Indian Government and Politics*, Sage Publications, New Delhi, 2008.
11. Kashyap, S.C., New Parliamentary Initiative: Subject-Based Standing Committees of Parliament, *Economic and Political Weekly*, Bombay, October 6, 1990.
12. Shastri, Sandeep, Parliamentary Committees in India, and Legislative Control over Administration, in Mehra, A.K. and G.W. Kueck (Eds.), *The Indian Parliament: A Comparative Perspective*, Konark, Delhi (as cited in Singh, M.P. and Rekha Saxena, *Indian Politics: Contemporary Issues and Concerns*, Prentice-Hall of India, New Delhi, 2008).
13. Agarwal, Arun, The Indian Parliament, in Kapur, Devesh and Pratap Bhanu Mehta (Eds.), *Public Institutions in India: Performance and Design*, Oxford University Press, New Delhi, 2005.
14. Kashyap, S.C., *Our Parliament*, National Book Trust, New Delhi, 1992.
15. More, S.S., *Practice and Procedure of Indian Parliament*, cited in Kapur, A.C. and K.K. Mishra, *Select Constitutions*, S. Chand and Co., New Delhi, 2001.

16. Chanda, Asok, *Indian Administration*, George Allen & Unwin Ltd., London, 1961.
17. Kashyap, S.C., *op. cit.*
18. Chanda, Asok, *op. cit.*
19. Morris-Jones, W.H., *Parliament in India*, Longmans Green, London, 1957.
20. Sinha, R.K., The Estimates Committee, in Shakdhar S.L., (Ed.), *The Constitution and Parliament in India*, National Publishing House, New Delhi, 1967.
21. Morris-Jones, W.H., *op. cit.*
22. Chanda, Asok, *op. cit.*
23. Jena, B.B., *Parliamentary Committee in India*, Scientific Book, Calcutta, 1966.
24. Arora, Ramesh K. and Rajni Goyal, *Indian Public Administration: Institutions and Issues*, 2nd rev. ed., Wishwa Prakashan, New Delhi, 1997.
25. Chanda, Asok, *op. cit.*
26. Chakrabarty, Bidyut and Rajendra Kumar Pandey, *op. cit.*
27. Chanda, Asok, *op. cit.*
28. Chanda, Asok, *op. cit.*
29. Basu, D.D., *Introduction to the Constitution of India*, 1991 edition, Prentice-Hall of India, New Delhi.
30. Bhalla, R.P., Electoral Mechanism in India, in Virendra Grover (Ed.), *Political System in India*, Vol. 6, New Delhi, 1998.
31. *Constituent Assembly Debates*, Vol. VII, 15 June, 1949.
32. Shiva Rao, B., *The Framing of India's Constitution*, New Delhi, 1968.
33. Bhalla, R.P., Electoral Mechanism in India (1951–1971), *Indian Journal of Political Science*, No. 33, January–March, 1972.
34. Yadav, Sushma, Election Commission and Electoral Process, in M.P. Singh and Himanshu Roy (Eds.), *Indian Political System*, Jnanda Prakashan, New Delhi, 1998.
35. *The Hindu*, January 31, 2009.
36. *The Telegraph*, February 1, 2009.
37. Jain Bharti, "'None of the Above' option on EVMs to carry its own symbol from Bihar polls", *The Times of India*, September 18, 2015.
38. Maheshwari, S.R., *Indian Administration*, Orient Longman Limited, New Delhi, 1989.

11 Citizens and Administration

11.1 INTRODUCTION

The principal aim of government in a civilized, and more specifically in a democratic, set-up has ever been the happiness, contentment and general welfare of the people who are governed by it. In fact, the strength and tenure of a government depend upon the prosperity of the people, and the security and stability of democracy are determined by their satisfaction. In almost all political systems, there has always been the crucial problem of the average citizen at the cutting edge of administration, being absolutely deprived of the service and treatment to which he is entitled. It is more or less known to all that one of the gravest problems in public administration is how to make the official at the bottom most layer of administrative hierarchy responsive, sympathetic, honest and courteous in his dealings with the citizens and how to enforce such a responsible attitude on his part.

'Mismanagement' and 'corruption' seem to have their root in this colonial system of State and bureaucracy, rather than their natural evolution through a process where the citizen demands for 'accountability' and the ruler for 'adjustments'.[1] Governance or good governance ensures that corruption is minimized, that views of minorities are taken into account and that the voices of the most vulnerable in society are heard in decision-making. It is also responsive to the present and future needs of the society. Such a governance is articulated by the UNDP in terms of the following eight fundamental characteristics:

- Participatory
- Consensus-oriented
- Accountable
- Transparent
- Responsive
- Effective and efficient
- Equitable and inclusive
- Follows the rule of law.[2]

Citizens and administration are so closely related to each other that the existence of one without the other is almost inconceivable in a civilized society. This harmonious relationship depends upon the sincerity, earnestness and cooperation between the two. To quote Robson, "The achievement of good relations between the government and the public is a matter which does not by any means depend solely on the conduct of civil servants and politicians. It depends equally on the attitude of citizens, groups, corporations, associations of all kinds and, indeed, of all unofficial bodies to public authorities. If we want public servants to behave well towards us, we must behave well towards them."[3] Robson clarifies that citizens normally tend to assume that public administrators for their part will always behave well. But if politicians and civil servants are continuously held in low esteem, if abuse and criticism is poured continuously on them and if loose and unconstructive allegations are made about their incompetence, dishonesty, laziness and indifference to the public interests, then officials will fail to develop or display qualities of integrity, industry and public spirit.

On the contrary, if the relation between citizens and administration is good and healthy, it may bring about the following[4]:

- Encourage people's participation in the administrative process–a *sine qua non* for development and modernization.
- Kindle the potential energy of the citizens into kinetic energy to accelerate development.
- Supplement the efforts of the Government in the conduct of its affairs.
- Strengthen the values of democracy in the minds and spirit of the people.
- Enlist respect in the Constitution that is rooted in popular sovereignty.
- Develop bonds of friendship and goodwill between citizens and administration.
- Avoid social unrest, tensions, violence and other social upheavals which have become the order of the day.

Administration should never be viewed as something alienated from people and their needs. It should rather be regarded to be the means by which these needs are met. The administrator, who thinks of his organization as something apart from the society, is not likely to recognize significant problems of the citizens of that society.

The Administrative Reforms Commission (ARC) has also observed in this context: "If, in the prosperity of the people, lies the strength of a government, it is in their contentment that lies the security and stability of democracy."[5]

P.S. Appu, a retired IAS officer, perceives that the All India Services functioned well in India for some two and a half decades after Independence. The decline and debasement of the civil service started around 1973–1974 at the Centre.[6] Bureaucratic degeneration here coincides with the rising temperature of the increasing intensity of inter-party competition and extra-parliamentary mass movement in the politics of independent India. It is pointed out that perhaps the most serious decline in administrative morale occurred during the national Emergency imposed by the then Prime Minister Indira Gandhi in 1975–1977, when she made a call for "committed bureaucracy"—to the ideology of the party in power which under the circumstances seemed to undermine bureaucratic neutrality and commitment to constitutional values. Later in the 1990s, politico-bureaucratic corruption and criminalization of the political process reached an alarming height. Appu described the situation in the following way:

"All over the country Chief Ministers became prisoners in the hands of conflicting political parties and groups. To survive in office they were obliged to placate numerous petty politicians. The new breed of Ministers with tenuous tenures was ever on the lookout for pliable bureaucrats. There was no shortage of unprincipled opportunists in the bureaucracy. Before long a large number of civil servants aligned themselves with particular Ministers and became active collaborators leading to disastrous consequences."[7]

Appu, however, establishes his faith in the retention and rejuvenation of All India Services for three main reasons. First, even in their weakened State, the All-India Services have offered some resistance to the arbitrary actions of cynical politicians. Second, the experience of the Gujarat Riots of 2002 reminds us the neutrality of the police force where the superintendents of police in Kutch, Bhavnagar, Banaskantha and Bharuch took firm actions against the Hindu fanatics and gangsters. Third, the President and the Supreme Court being distant authorities, the civil and police administration, abiding by the Constitution, tend to enable millions of citizens to enjoy the rights guaranteed under the Constitution.

The problem of bureaucratic corruption today has become so pervasive and the failure of administrative vigilance so markedly prominent that only judicial activism on this front appears to solve the problem to some extent. In July 1993, the Government of India established a committee at the administrative level headed by the then Home Secretary N.N. Vohra to take stock of all available information about the activities of Crime Syndicate/Mafia organizations which had developed links with and were being protected by government functionaries and political personalities. The Report, submitted in October 1993, made the following remarks:

"CBI has reported that all over India crime syndicates have become a law unto themselves. Even in the smaller towns and rural areas, musclemen have become the order of the day. Hired assassins have become a part of these organizations. The nexus between the criminal gangs, police, bureaucracy and politicians has come out clearly in various parts of the country. The existing criminal justice system, which was essentially designed to deal with the individual offences/crimes, is unable to deal with the activities of the Mafia: the provision of law in regard to economic offences are weak; there are insurmountable legal difficulties in attaching/confiscating the property acquired through Mafia activities."[8]

The Corruption Perception Index 2002 of Transparency International, Berlin, ranked India at the 73rd position among 102 countries, with Finland as the least corrupt and Bangladesh the most corrupt.[9] To quote N. Vittal, a former Central Vigilance Commissioner:

"There is a close relationship between the bureaucracy, the political leadership, the citizens, the business community and perhaps even the criminals, ... Trying to eliminate corruption in one sector of bureaucracy alone is not going to be effective. After all, tackling corruption is like tackling an epidemic. It is not possible to quarantine one section alone."[10]

Jayprakash Narayan, the socialist-turned Gandhian leader, who led a massive anti-corruption and anti-authoritarian extra-parliamentary mass movement in the first half of the 1970s, described politics as the *gangotri* of corruption in India. The Herculean cleansing of the Augean stables of politics must take place at the source. A neo-feudal rent-seeking political and administrative class in India for transfers and postings still survives the dismantling of the Permit–Licence–Quota Raj even in the new millennium. It is an anachronism that must go.[11]

The naked publicization of bureaucratic corruption has resulted in a distressing decline in the public image of bureaucracy. The National Election Study (NES), 1996, conducted by the Centre for the Study of Developing Societies, has shown that the civil and police bureaucracy ranked at the lowest two positions in an index of popular trust in institutions. Out of a maximum score of 100, bureaucracy secured 27 and police 28, trailing far behind the Election Commission of India and the judiciary.[12]

The National Commission to Review the Working of the Constitution (NCRWC) in its Report (2002) has made a number of recommendations for administrative changes with a view to minimizing corruption. It recommends legally instituted accountability of public servants for their *mala fide* acts of omissions and commissions and their liability to pay damages. Again, it also suggests plugging the loopholes in anti-corruption laws like Benami Transactions (Prohibition) Act, 1988, and the Prevention of Corruption Act, 1988. Further, it proposes the establishment of Lokpals/Lokayuktas under the Constitution and State Legislations, respectively. Besides, to ensure transparency in administration, the NCRWC report recommends the passing Right of Information Act of Under this law, governments must assume a major responsibility and mobilize skills to ensure flow of information to citizens.[13]

11.2 PUBLIC GRIEVANCES IN VARIOUS SPHERES OF ADMINISTRATION

The scope of public grievances has considerably been large. It is true that bureaucratic corruption is principally visible within the ambit of public grievances against the executive organs of government. But it does not mean that this is the only element constituting corruption. "In its widest connotation, corruption includes improper or selfish exercise of power and influence attached to a public office or the special position one occupies in public life."[14] But apart from corruption, there are indifference, incompetence and insensitiveness on the part of public servants that can also become grossly harmful to the citizens.

Grievances of citizens can be of two types: general grievances and individual grievances. General grievances are normally against the governmental acts and policies and may be common to all or any section of the community. Shortage of baby food, rise in prices, over-crowding in transport services, late running of trains, etc. are some of the examples of general public grievances which may find expression in widespread disturbances occurring from time to time.[15] Individual grievances are those which the citizens, as individuals, may have against the executive organs of government. It includes both power wielding political leadership and the permanent services on account of any act or omission on their part affecting the citizens individually. We are here basically concerned with individual grievances. Due to the development of the rule of law and the evolution of a large career service, a basic change has been brought about in the public conception of integrity of public servants. Citizens now tend to believe that public officials should, by no means, use their official position to avail any kind of financial or other advantages for themselves, their friends and families. Citizens today expect the public servants to be honest, diligent, responsive, fair and competent in the discharge of their duties. These are some of the qualities which the Madhya Pradesh Administrative Reforms Commission in its report has described as "integrity and capacity in administration."

But the root of public grievances lies in the gap between people's expectation regarding public officials' attitude, on the one hand, and public officials' actual attitude and behaviour, on the other. Today, one finds a great deal of alienation between citizens and administration. The dissatisfaction of the citizens with the administrative machinery has largely grown in recent years. It is generally viewed that the administration has gradually failed to provide efficient and timely services.

Professor S.L. Goel has discussed the nature of public dissatisfaction in different sectors.[16] In the first place, he has taken up Electricity Administration. Dr. M.M. Goel, Ex-Chief Engineer, Haryana State Electricity Board, has pointed out the main grievances of the citizens regarding electricity administration in his doctoral thesis. These are as under:

- Unhelpful attitude on the part of the officials
- Inordinate delay in transacting government business
- Corruption amongst the officials
- Favouritism and nepotism in dealing with the public
- Lack of machinery for redressal of public grievances at the district level
- Delays caused by faulty procedures
- Delays caused by lack of inter-departmental and intra-departmental coordination
- Delays caused by excessive work load on government officials
- International delays.[17]

Dr. J.M. Ovasdi, IRTS, has explained the nature of public grievances in railway administration. To be more specific, in Table 11.1 given below, he has analyzed the nature of 5936 complaints received during October, November and December, 1986, from the public.[18]

Table 11.1

Sl. No.	*Nature of Complaint*	*No.*	*Percentage of total*
1.	Improper behaviour of commercial staff	548	9.2
2.	Improper behaviour of non-commercial staff	189	3.1
3.	Against reservation, enquiry and booking	960	16.1
4.	Allotment of seats/berths	323	5.4
5.	Refund of tickets	114	1.9
6.	Unauthorized passengers occupying reserved accommodation	123	2.0
7.	Against licensed porters	83	1.4
8.	Booking and carrying of luggage/parcels	222	3.7
9.	Catering and vending	306	5.1
10.	Late running of trains	650	10.9
11.	Bribery	155	2.6
12.	Cleanliness of coaches and station premises	43	0.7
13.	Maintenance of passenger coaches	197	3.3
14.	Electrical defects in coaches	174	2.9
15.	Thefts/pilferage in trains	123	2.0
16.	Improper arrangement of drinking water supply	79	1.3
17.	Miscellaneous	1647	28.4
	Total	**5936**	**100.0**

Again, Prof. S.L. Goel has explained the nature of public grievances in hospital administration. He has observed that the faith of the people in the efficiency of hospital system is decreasing because of the utter negligence and indifference on the part of hospital authorities against citizens. The patients also complain of the preferential treatment being given to VIPs and influential people. Some of the patients were of the view that big hospitals are meant only to serve the VIPs.[19] Some patients have complained that preferential treatment is given to friends and relatives of the hospital staff. Patients have also complained against the lack of coordination between supportive services and medical services. Most of the patients have complained that either their X-ray reports or other laboratory reports were totally non-available. Some have complained against the non-availability of medicines as well. Besides, in tracing patients' reports and also in referring them to other departments, an unnecessary delay is created.

Moreover, in the sphere of police administration, public grievances are no less expressed. In this context, it would perhaps not be irrelevant if we quote the observation of the National Police Commission Report (1979): "In public estimate the police appear as an agency more to implement and enforce the objectives of the government in power as distinct from enforcing law as such as an independent and impartial agency." The NPC categorically States that "the police sub-culture should take into account the fundamental rights of the people, the supremacy of laws and not of executive fiat, and our constitutional goal towards a developed and egalitarian society."[20] The NPC was absolutely aware of 'police brutality' and its cancerous corruption.

After having a look at public grievances in all the fields Stated so far, one can single out the following principal problems faced by citizens vis-à-vis administration:

- Corruption at all levels
- Inordinate delay in transacting government business
- Partiality and favouritism
- Harassment
- Discourteous and impolite behaviour of personnel
- Non-availability of personnel in their seats.

Now, we will make an attempt to find out the basic problems faced by the personnel in administration. They are:

- Political interference, resulting in low morale and motivation among employees.
- Promises by political elite to provide services without matching resources, resulting in dilution of the standard of services
- Crisis in leadership leading to organizational anarchy
- Posting, promotion and transfer based on influence and not on merit leading to gross inefficiency and mediocracy

- Outdated administrative set-up based on Acts applicable only to the colonial rule
- Lack of identity and commitment among lower-level public employees.

Now, if the society allows citizens' grievances to mount up continuously, social unrest and tensions will crop up as an endless process. It is, therefore, absolutely necessary that citizens' faith in administration should be reinforced adequately. This is of immense importance in order to ensure political stability and to preserve the social fabric.

11.3 METHODS TO PROMOTE GOOD RELATIONS BETWEEN CITIZENS AND ADMINISTRATION

Researchers of Public Administration have prescribed the following methods to promote good and close relations between citizens and administration.

11.3.1 Infusing Competence among Government Employees

The success of any administrative system depends upon the ability, intelligence and competence of personnel appointed in public organizations. It is now known to all that a large number of personnel working in such organizations occupy the positions because of political patronage, corruption and favouritism. Under such circumstances, the most crucial question perhaps is: how to ensure competence of the personnel in an organization for optimum performance? One answer is that it can be done through strict tests of recruitment, promotion based on merit and not on influence, rigorous training and refresher courses.

To quote Walter R. Sharp: "Good administration is a composite of effective organization, adequate material facilities and qualified personnel. Even poorly devised machinery may be made to work if it is manned with well-trained, intelligent, imaginative and devoted staff. On the other hand, the best planned organization may produce unsatisfactory results if it is operated by mediocre or disgruntled people."[21]

In the present context, it would probably not be irrelevant to point out the following suggestions made by Dasondha Singh Chowdhary to improve bureaucratic competence:[22]

1. Science and technology are increasingly getting important in welfare administration. Consequently, scientific attitudes, skills and outlooks should also be generated among the bureaucrats of welfare States to equip themselves a little more than mere generalists.
2. Policies framed according to the advice of inexperienced bureaucrats may be found to be somewhat unrealistic to the

requirements of the field. Similarly, field officials may remain ignorant of the spirit in which policies were made at the headquarters. Hence, a proper balance is to be maintained between the field and the Secretariat, or to be more specific, between experience and Secretariat hierarchy.

3. It is also necessary that the social background of the bureaucrat be coextensive with that of the largest segment of our citizens. The bureaucrats should also have a profound knowledge of the historical, cultural and social background of our country, specially of its rural sector.

11.3.2 Need for Administrative Improvements and Reforms

The design of an administrative system is a basic aid to the achievement of its primary goals. The administration can provide the means whereby the most effective use can be made of the knowledge and skills of the personnel engaged in different activities. The benefits of modern science and technology can reach people only if such services are properly planned and effectively implemented. An approach based on modern science and technology is an important factor in bringing about administrative efficiency.

11.3.3 Proper Matching between Expansion of Public Activities and availability of Resources

Adequate resources should be there to significantly expand governmental activities. In hospital administration, for example, problems emanate from a number of constraints on hospital authorities, e.g. shortage of staff at all levels, lack of space for providing increasing number of patients, shortage of funds, shortage of medicine and equipment, continuous political and administrative interference, etc. In order to provide satisfactory hospital services, the Union Government as well as State Governments must attend the above mentioned constraints. Citizens, too, cannot avoid responsibilities on their part in the sense that patients and their relatives must cooperate with the hospital authorities to make the best use of the available resources.

11.3.4 Proper Development of Public Relations

Public relations urge the public officials to understand the needs of the people before launching any field operations. Some of the important methods of learning about the people and the community are as follows:

1. **Discussions with the people:** Discussions can be held with formal groups of people. But informal discussions with people

in the informal places like markets, fairs, etc. can throw light as to what concerns people most. In ascertaining the health requirements of the people, CAN (Community Needs Assessment) surveys are carried out before introducing health facilities in the area.

2. **Study of newspapers, magazines and other published literature:** A public relations Department needs to study the published materials where people express their views and mention their needs including their likes and dislikes. This, definitely, is a rich source of information.
3. **Complaint and suggestion boxes:** Most of the Departments maintain complaint and suggestion boxes. The analysis of complaints and suggestions can help the organization in understanding the real requirements of the public.
4. **Surveys:** A well-designed survey, opinion poll or census can help to know the popular reactions about organizations. Researches usually take help of such surveys to understand any problem.

11.3.5 Genuine and Well-Equipped Machinery to be Set Up at All Levels to Handle Citizens' Complaints

Administrators should pay great attention to public opinion. Reorientation of officials' attitudes towards citizens is a very difficult task. Public servants of today should get rid of all the feelings of superiority in order to be close with citizens. Dr. J.M. Ovasdi suggests in the context of railway administration that the staff with maximum public contacts have to be given specialized training before dealing with the people. Commercial officers, too, have to improve the qualities of enquiries.[23]

11.3.6 Enlightened Citizenship

Citizens and their associations, on their part, need to understand their rights. Inder Jit in his article "Crusade For Clean Politics", points out that the danger to our democracy does not come only from corrupt politicians, businessmen and bureaucrats, it comes equally from the indifference of a vast majority of our people.[24] After all, in the final analysis, the only keepers of liberty are the people. Imbecility of men always invites the misuse of power.[25]

11.4 SCANDINAVIAN INFLUENCE OF OMBUDSMAN

Ombudsman is basically a Swedish word coming from the word *Ombud. Ombud*, another Swedish word, refers to a person who acts as a representative of another person. An ombudsman is generally considered as a person who is commissioned to protect citizens against any possible maladministration.[26] Sweden was the first country where the institution of ombudsman was appointed in 1809. The example was followed by Finland (1919), Denmark (1955) and Norway (1962). Inspired by these Scandinavian countries, a number of other nations of the west–including New Zealand (1962), Great Britain (1967), some Canadian provinces like Alberta, New Burnswich, Quebeck, Ontario, etc. and some of the US States like Hawaii, Nebraska, Iowa, Alaska, etc.–have appointed the institution of ombudsman. Similar institutions, sometimes with different names, have also been created by various other countries of the world.

Researchers have long been interested in answering to the question: what are the fundamental reasons for the growing popularity of this institution? Some of the factors responsible for the promotion of ombudsman are: expansion of government activities, increase of discretionary powers to the public officials, increase of citizens' expectations from the governmental sector, need for protection of individual rights against the abuse of State power, lack of legislative control over the executive, heavy burden on judicial courts, scarcity of administrative courts and the growing evils of corruption on the part of public officials. Hence, there is a strong need for an effective mechanism which can ensure the objectivity and impartiality of civil servants. An effective ombudsman system can also bring about procedural reforms in the administrative system through its fruitful recommendations to enhance administrative effectiveness.

The main criteria for an ombudsman, as identified by the UK Ombudsman Conference of 1991, are: independence from those investigated, effectiveness of the administrative machinery, fairness of the public officials, people's accessibility to the public officials, public accountability or responsiveness, right to complain without any cost, etc. This ombudsman system is not a substitute for the conventional methods of grievance–redressal, administrative reform or minimizing corruption. It is rather a device complementary to such conventional mechanisms.

The success of an ombudsman depends upon the personal charisma of the ombudsman himself, real motives of the appointing authority, the ideas and attitudes of those whose actions are supposed to be supervised by the ombudsman and the alertness and cooperation of the public whose cause is championed by the ombudsman.[27]

11.5 INDIAN EFFORTS SINCE INDEPENDENCE: SERIES OF LOK PAL BILLS IN INDIA

The problem of deficiency in the existing safeguards for citizens has attracted considerable attention in our country since Independence. The new government of independent India was not found alienated in this respect and took commendable measures in this direction. The Prevention of Corruption Act became law in 1947. A number of committees and commissions, like the Tek Chand Committee (1949), the Railways Corruption Inquiry Committee or the Kripalani Committee (1953) and the Vivian Bose Commission (1956), were set up to inquire into the problem of corruption and to make recommendations to eradicate it. The Prevention of Corruption Act (1947) was suitably amended in 1955 to make it more stringent. The Administrative Vigilance Division was established in 1955 and the vigilance units came into existence in Ministries and Departments. To improve administrative efficiency and to reduce the scope for complaints against administration, the O&M Division was set up in the Home Ministry in 1954. A Grievance Commissioner had also been appointed at the Centre to deal with public grievances. In 1962, the Government of India appointed the Committee on Prevention of Corruption under the chairmanship of K. Santhanam. Following the recommendations of the Santhanam Committee, the Central Vigilance Commission (CVC) was established in 1964.[28] Measures to check corruption were taken at the levels of the State (Anti-Corruption Department), Division (Divisional Complaints Boards) and District (District Complaints Committees) as well.

But, unfortunately, none of the above mentioned devices in various States could really solve the problem of corruption and nepotism. The reasons for their ineffectiveness were many and varied. Some of the organizations had problems in the very nature of their composition. The base of some other organizations was loosely woven. Some opine that the Vigilance Commission was too busy with solving trivial problems while others are of the view that its major imperfections lay in the reluctance on the part of public officials, lack of cooperation and indifference.

Under such circumstances of despair, the Santhanam Committee recommended for the setting up of such an institution which was patterned more or less on the office of the Parliamentary Commissioner in New Zealand. The Rajasthan Administrative Reform Commission, in its report submitted in September, 1963, recommended the appointment of an Ombudsman for the State of Rajasthan. This matter was taken up for serious and detailed consideration by the Central Administrative Reforms Commission appointed in 1966 which said categorically:

"There should be one authority dealing with complaints against the administrative acts of Ministers or Secretaries to Government at the Centre and in the States. There should be another authority in each State and at the Centre for dealing with complaints against the administrative acts of other officials. All these authorities should be independent of the executive as well as the legislature and the judiciary."[29]

The first one was to be called the Lokpal and the second one Lokayukta.

Now, there were a series of Lokpal Bills introduced in the Parliament. The Government of India accepted the recommendations of the ARC in general terms. A Bill, named the Lokpal and Lokayuktas Bill, 1968, was introduced in the Lok Sabha in May, 1968. After a consideration of the Bill by a Joint Committee of the two Houses, it was passed by the Lok Sabha on August 20, 1968 and was sent to the Rajya Sabha for consideration. The Bill, however, lapsed due to the early dissolution of the fourth Lok Sabha in December 1970.

A fresh Bill on the same subject was introduced in the Lok Sabha on August 11, 1971. But for some unknown reasons, there was a delay and, in the mean time, the entire nation faced a severe turmoil with the declaration of National Emergency in June 1975. This obviously put an end to the introduction of any such democratic institution as the Lokpal or the Lokayukta.

In March 1977, the sixth general elections took place which established an altogether new leadership under Morarji Desai who headed a combination of all opposition parties under the name of Janata Party. The Janata Party had promised to set up the Lokpal and the Lokayuktas as a major move with a view to eliminating corruption. In July 1977, the Janata Government introduced the new Lokpal Bill which, for some unknown reasons, could not be passed.

Quite a few years had passed since the Lokpal Bill was first introduced in the Lok Sabha in May, 1968. Naturally, both the Congress and the Janata governments were faced with some basic hurdles in the way of introducing such an ombudsman like institution in India. The question, likely to be raised, was whether such an institution could really accord with our system of Ministerial responsibility. By the introduction of such an institution, it began to be argued, two fundamental bases of the parliamentary form of government are directly challenged.

First, the Prime Minister and other Central Ministers are political appointees and can be held accountable only to a political body like the Parliament consisting of their "elected masters". It implies that Ministers can reasonably be expected to accept only political punishment for their official acts of commission and omission. Any investigation of their official conduct by any other institution, no matter how powerful it is, will be the negation of the principle of Ministerial responsibility. No person, not even a Minister, can remain responsible for his official conduct to two different bodies at the same time.

Secondly, the parliamentary system of government has accepted the principle of civil service anonymity and neutrality. It implies that the Minister is held responsible for the misdeeds of his subordinate, i.e. the permanent official. The public official is thus protected from public fury and attack. He is only subject to departmental investigation and punishment. Under the proposed ombudsman set-up, high officials will also be subject to investigation, condemnation and punishment if they are found guilty by the ombudsman. But this will again be a breach of civil service neutrality.

When Rajiv Gandhi became the Prime Minister in 1984 after her mother's sudden death, he revived the entire matter of Lokpal and on August 26, 1985, the Lokpal Bill was again introduced in the Lok Sabha. It was referred to a Joint Select Committee of Parliament on the 30th August of the same year where it died due to the dissolution of the Lok Sabha. But in the 1985 Lokpal Bill, the President, the Vice-President, the Prime Minister, the Speaker of the Lok Sabha and all the Chief Ministers were kept outside the purview of the Lokpal.

The matter was again revived during the Prime Ministership of V.P. Singh and the Bill, known as the Lokpal Bill, 1990, was passed in the Lok Sabha. The Bill brought all officers, including even the Prime Minister, within the ambit of the law. However, the entire matter was suddenly nullified with the fall of the National Front Government at the Centre in November 1990. The Chandra Sekhar Government was too shortlived to take up the matter. The Congress Government of P.V. Narsimha Rao did not show any special interest in the matter.

Exasperated by the delaying tactics of the parliamentarians and the political executive in creating the institution of Lokpal, H.D. Shourie, Director, Common Cause (an NGO), presented a civil writ petition in 1994 before the Supreme Court. This public interest litigation, filed under Article 32 of our Constitution, prayed for a *writ of certiorari* or any other writ, order or direction, directing the Union Government of India to specifically declare when they will bring before the Parliament an appropriately draft Bill for the enactment of the legislation for introducing the system of Lokpal in the country.

Finally, in 1998–1999, the NDA Government, under the Prime Ministership of A.B. Vajpayee, brought the Lokpal Bill. The Bill was accepted in 2001. Regarding the objective of the 1990 Lokpal Bill, it was categorically Stated that the main objective of the Lokpal Bill was "to provide for the establishment of the institution of Lokpal to enquire into allegation of corruption against public functionaries and for matters connected therewith."

11.6 MAIN FEATURES OF 1990 LOKPAL BILL

Some of the main features of the Lokpal Bill of 1990 are as under:

- The Lokpal will be a plural body with a Chairman and two other members.
- These three members will be selected from among the existing or retired judges of the Supreme Court.
- The status and emoluments of the Chairman will be similar to those of the Chief Justice of India.
- The Lokpal will have its own independent Secretariat, officials and administrative set-up and will not be dependent on the existing administration.

- Section 8(3) of the 1990 Lokpal Bill provides that the Government cannot take away any matter under the consideration of the Lokpal from its jurisdiction and hand it over to another investigating agency without the consent of the Lokpal, under the Commission of Inquiries Act.
- The Lokpal has full authority to investigate any matter concerning the misconduct and corruption of all public officials including the Prime Minister.
- The annual reports of the Lokpal will be presented to the President of India, who would place it, with his own comments, on the table of both Houses of Parliament within 90 days of its submission.

The 1990 Lokpal Bill excluded certain matters from the jurisdiction of the Lokpal like:

- Matters concerning foreign policy and international relations
- Actions taken under the 1964 Act concerning foreigners and the Extradition Act of 1962
- Matters concerning the acceptance or rejection of awards and prizes given by the government
- Actions taken concerning matters of national defence and the issuance of passports
- Decisions concerning filing a case before a court of law
- Matters concerning the appointment, salary, demotion and other conditions of service of public servants.

11.6.1 Some Recent Developments: Jan Lokpal Bill

The Jan Lokpal Bill, also known as Citizens' Ombudsman Bill, is basically an anti-corruption bill drawn up by civil society activists of India. They sought the appointment of a Jan Lokpal, an independent body, to investigate the cases of corruption. This bill also proposes to improve the Lokpal and Lokayukta Bill, 2011 (that was passed in the Lok Sabha in December, 2011).

The Jan Lokpal aims to deter corruption effectively, compensate citizens' grievances and protect whistle-blowers, i.e., persons who expose any kind of information or activity that is deemed illegal, unethical or incorrect within an organisation that is either private or public. The prefix 'Jan', meaning citizens, implies that these improvements include inputs provided by ordinary citizens of India.

To draw governmental attention, a focused campaign titled "India Against Corruption" (IAC) was launched in 2011. The first version of the Lokpal Bill drafted by the Union Government headed by the UPA in 2010 was regarded to be absolutely ineffective by anti-corruption activists from the civil society. Such activists, under the banner of IAC, came together to draft the Lokpal Bill from the citizens' viewpoint, later known as the Jan Lokpal. Public awareness drives as well as protest marches took place in support of the bill. But when Anna Hazare, a Gandhian activist, announced that he would start an indefinite fast from April 5, 2011 for the passage of the Jan Lokpal Bill, public support for the drafting of the Bill started gathering tempo. To avoid Hazare's fasting, the PMO directed the personnel and law ministers to see how the view of those social activists could be included in the bill. On April 5, 2011, the National Advisory Council rejected the Lokpal Bill drafted by the UPA government. The (then) Union HRD Minister Mr. Kapil Sibal met social activists Swami Agnivesh and Arvind Kejriwal on April 7, 2011, to find ways for bridging differences over the bill. But, on that day, no consensus could be reached owing to several differences of opinion between the social activists and the government. Anna Hazare had a huge support behind him, although political parties were particularly discouraged from participating in the movement. Hazare's fast ended on April 9, after 98 hours when the government accepted most of the demands placed by the activists. Hazare warned that if the bill could not be passed in the Parliament by August 15, 2011, he would immediately restart a hunger strike. The government agreed to set up a Joint Drafting Committee which was supposed to complete its work by the end of June, 2011.

In 2012 the Lok Sabha during the Parliament's Winter Session passed the controversial Lokpal Bill. But due to shortage of time the bill could not be passed in the Rajya Sabha. On December 13, 2013, the government tabled the Lokpal Bill in the Rajya Sabha and the debate was adjourned till December 16, 2013. The Lokpal Bill was finally passed on December 17, 2013 in the Rajya Sabha. On the next day, it was passed in the Lok Sabha.

Since 1968 the Lokpal Bill was introduced in the Parliament in the following years:

- 1971
- 1977
- 1985
- 1989
- 1996
- 2001
- 2011
- 2012
- 2013

The *Lokpal and Lokayuktas Act* was finally passed in 2013.

11.7 LOKAYUKTAS AT THE STATE LEVEL

Orissa was the first State to create the institution of Lokayukta at the State level in 1970. It was then followed by Maharashtra in 1972,

Rajasthan in 1973, Bihar in 1974, UP in 1975, Karnataka in 1979, Madhya Pradesh in 1981, Andhra Pradesh in 1983, Gujarat in 1986 and Punjab in 1995. Two other States where the institution was created are Assam and Himachal Pradesh. In 1995, the Chief Minister of the National Capital Territory of Delhi announced that his government was in the process of introducing a Bill on the subject.

In 1992, Orissa abolished its Lokpal, but the institution was again established in 1994. There are, however, some variations in the structure of the institution in different States. In a very few States like Orissa and Punjab, the official is designated as Lokpal, though it goes against the pattern as suggested by the Administrative Reforms Commission. In some States, there is a provision for Lokayukta as well as *Up* Lokayukta (for instance, in Maharashtra and Rajasthan), though the post of *Up* Lokayukta may have been lying unfilled for a long time, as is the case in Rajasthan. But there is no such provision for the appointment of *Up* Lokayukta in Himachal Pradesh, Uttar Pradesh and Bihar.

There are many States which have not yet joined the ombudsman movement. They are satisfied with their variations of the conventional models. For example, Kerala has created a three-man commission under the Kerala Public Men's Corruption (Investigation and Inquiries) Commission, 1984, whose members are all appointed by the Governor on the advice of the Chief Minister, the Chief Justice and the leader of the Opposition. By 'public man', Kerala legislation implies a wide range of people including the Chief Minister, Ministers, MLAs, members of local bodies and University syndicates, the State Transport Authority, regional transport authorities, people in the managing committees of private colleges and schools and even political party officials. Civil servants, however, are not covered by this legislation.

States like Maharashtra, Bihar and Rajasthan have not prescribed any specific qualifications for the appointment of the Lokayukta. This absence of requirement of any specific qualifications for Lokayukta follows the British, the French and the Canadian patterns where the ombudsman is not required to have a legal background or a formal training, although judges are preferred on this position in reality. On the contrary, in Andhra Pradesh, Karnataka, Himachal Pradesh, Assam, Gujarat and Uttar Pradesh, judicial qualifications are required for the appointment as ombudsman.

In Orissa, Maharashtra, Rajasthan, Uttar Pradesh and Bihar, the Chief Minister is excluded from the jurisdiction of the Lokayukta. But in Madhya Pradesh, Himachal Pradesh, Andhra Pradesh and Gujarat, the Chief Minister comes within the purview of the Lokayukta. Ministers and higher civil servants are covered in almost all the State Lokayukta legislations. In Maharashtra, even former Ministers and civil servants come within the purview of the Lokayukta. In Himachal Pradesh, Uttar Pradesh, Andhra Pradesh, Assam and Gujarat, State legislators also fall within the Lokayukta's jurisdiction. In Andhra Pradesh and

Karnataka, even the Vice-Chancellors of State Universities come within the jurisdiction of the Lokayukta. Moreover, most of such Acts cover the authorities of the local bodies, the corporations established and owned or controlled by the State Government, government companies and societies.

While Lokayuktas in Assam, Bihar, Uttar Pradesh, Maharashtra and Karnataka consider grievances as well as allegations concerning the actions of different public officials, in Andhra Pradesh, Himachal Pradesh, Gujarat and Rajasthan only complaints concerning allegations are considered for examination. Procedures of such examinations vary from State to State.[30]

The tenure of a Lokayukta in most States is five years or till he attains the age of 65 years, whichever is earlier with no provision for reappointment. In Assam, the upper age limit for the Lokayukta to continue in office is 68 years. In Assam, Bihar, Uttar Pradesh, Madhya Pradesh, Maharashtra and Rajasthan, the Lokayukta is appointed by the Governor of the State in consultation with the Chief Minister, the Chief Justice of High Court and the Leader of the Opposition in the State Assembly. In Andhra Pradesh, however, the Leader of the Opposition is not consulted on the appointment of the Lokayukta.

The Lokayukta of a State is usually responsible to the State Legislature. Its annual report is presented in the Legislature and conventionally its recommendations are accepted by the House. In case of non-acceptance, the Lokayukta may submit a special report to the State Legislature. A Lokayukta has a separate office, staff and budget, though, for conducting inquiries, he has to take the help of State investigating agencies. He is substantially empowered to call for relevant files or documents, from the State Government, necessary for his investigation. He even enjoys powers to inspect and visit government organizations being investigated. What is perhaps most important is that Lokayuktas in all States, except in Assam, Himachal Pradesh and Uttar Pradesh, have been empowered to start investigations on their own initiatives.

11.8 FUNCTIONS OF LOKAYUKTAS

Like the Lokpal, the Lokayukta is entitled to do the following:

- The Lokayukta can accept any complaint against administration from any citizen. But, obviously, such a complaint must not be against any Minister or Secretary.
- Accepting the grievance against the accused person or body of persons, the Lokayukta must inform him/them and must allow him/them to defend himself/themselves.
- The Lokayukta must investigate against the accused person/persons. In this regard, he has the full right to use independently all the facts and information necessary for the investigation.

- The Lokayukta must proceed his investigation without making these facts and information public.
- In examining the validity of the complaint, the Lokayukt a is as powerful as the civil court.
- If the Lokayukta is satisfied with the validity of the complaint, he will recommend his proposal in a written report to the State Legislature.
- If the State Legislature takes any corrective measure on the basis of the Lokayukta's recommendation, the latter will inform it to the person who has produced a written complaint and the entire matter will come to an end.

But in spite of his entitlement to performing some general functions, the Lokayukta performs his functions in various States in various ways. A few of them could make a mark during some periods only, due to the support of the State political leadership. But quite unfortunately, most of the Lokayuktas have miserably suffered as a result of the apathy of State Governments. In Andhra Pradesh, the then Governor Kumudben Joshi did not endorse the nomination for the office of Lokayukta made by the then Chief Minister N.T. Rama Rao, leading to the abolition of the institution for a while. In Orissa, her once-upon-a-time Chief Minister J.B. Patnaik's reluctance held up the appointment of Lokpal for as many as four years. There, the Lokpal took up investigation against some Ministers of the Biju Patnaik government in 1992 and as a result, the entire institution of Lokpal was abolished. In Maharashtra also, when the Lokayukta found Two Ministers of the State Government guilty of malpractice, his report was regarded to be a politically motivated one. These are all instances of executive obstruction to the proper functioning of the Lokayuktas. But sources of obstruction could as well be other than the executive. In Andhra Pradesh, for instance, when the Lokayukta made investigation against the civil servants and the existing as well as former Ministers, the High Court and the Administrative Tribunal acted as a big obstruction to awarding punishment to the accused.

But there are examples of bright pictures as well. Works done by the Lokayukta of Andhra Pradesh during the first term of N.T. Rama Rao, by the one of Karnataka during the tenures of R.K. Hegde and Birendra Patil, and by that of Madhya Pradesh deserve special praise.

It is evident from the reports of the Lokayuktas that the largest number of complaints have been launched against the Departments of public works, health, irrigation, civil supplies and those relating to municipalities and cooperative societies. A number of complaints made to the State Lokayuktas are rejected for want of jurisdiction, anonymity, pseudonymity and triviality.

On a number of occasions, government Departments do not provide sufficient information to the Lokayuktas. In Bihar, the Lokayukta was virtually forced to close a case on the conduct of a Minister because the State Government did not provide a report for as long as eight whole years.

On the whole, the performance of the Lokayuktas in Indian States is not very impressive. There is indeed much which could have been done or should have been avoided. It is somewhat disappointing that almost half of the Indian States have not yet adopted the institution while the rest are almost in the dark regarding its status.

It is suggested widely that the divergence in the patterns of the structure and role of Lokayuktas should be replaced by a uniform pattern. The initiative in this regard is to be taken by the Chief Ministers of those States which have adopted the institution of Lokayukta. This definitely is a huge task in which the Central Government should play the leading role.

A few suggestions given by experts in the field should be taken note of. They are:

- The Chief Minister should invariably come within the jurisdiction of the Lokayukta.
- Former Ministers and civil servants should also come within its jurisdiction.
- Lokayuktas should have power to start inquiries on their own initiatives.
- Lokayuktas should have their own independent investigating agencies.
- References made by the Lokayukta to the government should be accorded top priority by government officials.
- A legislative committee on the Lokayukta should be set up to monitor and follow up the implementation of the recommendation(s) made by him.
- The High Court should dispose of cases expeditiously filed before it on the recommendations of the Lokayukta.[31]

Drawn on "certain basic considerations"[32], the most significant recommendation happens to be the appointment of the Lokpal (at the Centre) and the Lokayukta (in the States). These two new instrumentalities for dealing with citizens' grievances against top functionaries in government still remain a distant dream. Corruption in many forms continues to plague the Indian public system, whose ability to successfully deal with corruption at different levels, as one scholar views,[33] has fallen short of the requirement. The other instrumentality is the 'human rights' institution at the national and State levels which is quite recent in Indian public administration. There are both international and domestic pressures to uphold human rights and ensure effective 'rights regimes' at all levels in the interest of the steady democratisation of the public sector.[34]

11.9 CENTRAL VIGILANCE COMMISSION (CVC)

The Central Vigilance Commission (CVC) was set up in 1964, as a follow-up of the recommendation of the Santhanam Committee, by an executive resolution of the Government of India. It is not a statutory body. Its functions are basically advisory but advisory in the same sense as those of the UPSC. It falls within the jurisdiction of the Ministry of Personnel. It is headed by a Central Vigilance Commissioner who is appointed by the President. He holds office for a term of six years or till he attains the age of 65 years, whichever is earlier. He cannot be removed or suspended from office except in the manner provided for the removal or suspension of the Chairman of the UPSC. After retirement he cannot accept any further employment under the Central or State Governments.

In terms of sanctioned staff strength, the CVC has remained 'lean and fit'; but it has its presence in all the Ministries, Departments and other agencies. It has a strong network culture. In processing of case-files, the CVC is highly officer-oriented.

The following bodies assist the CVC in the discharge of its duties:

- A secretariat headed by the Secretary to the CVC in the matter of examination of cases
- Commissioners for Departmental inquiries, conducting oral inquiries against suspect officers
- The Chief Technical Examiners' Organization for conducting technical audit of civil and other construction work executed by the central organizations.

The jurisdiction of the CVC is directly related to the ambit of the executive control of the Union of India. But for practical reasons, it advises on vigilance cases pertaining to certain higher categories of the public servants such as:

- Gazetted Central Government servants
- Board-level appointees in PSU
- Officers of the rank of scale III and above in the nationalized banks
- Officers of the rank of Assistant Manager and above in the insurance sector
- Officers comparable in status to the Gazetted Central Government servants in autonomous bodies or local authorities.

The CVC has powers regarding matters to which the executive power of the Central Government extends. Its jurisdiction extends to all employees of the Central Government, public undertakings, corporate bodies and other organizations dealing with any matter falling within the executive powers of the Central Government, the Delhi Metropolitan Council and the New Delhi Municipal Committee. The CVC has decided to include only gazetted officers and officers of equivalent status within its orbit. It cannot investigate cases of corruption against Ministers and Members of Parliament. Its functions may be summarized as under:

1. CVC deals with cases in which a public servant is suspected or accused to have acted in a corrupt way.
2. It asks for reports from agencies in order to control and supervise them and make an overall vigilance on them.
3. It can take over under its direct control complaints for further actions and may ask the Central Bureau of Investigation to register a regular case and investigate it.
4. It may initiate review of procedures and practices of investigation in so far as they maintain integrity in administration.

11.9.1 Vigilance Organization in Ministries/Departments

The Santhanam Committee on Prevention of Corruption made detailed recommendations for the strengthening of the vigilance organization in each Ministry/Department to make it more effective. The primary responsibility for maintaining purity, integrity and efficiency in each organization is vested in the Ministerial Secretary or the Departmental Head. In each Ministry/Department, an officer is designated as the Chief Vigilance Officer (CVO) and entrusted principally with the vigilance work. He also provides a link between the CVC, on the one hand, and the respective Ministry/Department, on the other. There is another officer, designated as Vigilance Office (VO), in each attached office and in each public undertaking. Each CVO is appointed in consultation with the CVC and the VO, in consultation with the CVO. CVOs are generally of the rank of a Deputy Secretary and VOs of the rank of an Under Secretary. In the organization under their control, CVOs undertake review of the existing arrangements in order to strengthen the existing set-up wherever necessary. But such measures are first to be referred to the CVC.

The CVC has laid down certain procedures which the various Ministries/Departments should follow if complaints are launched against them. The CVC has the responsibility for advising the Ministry/Department regarding all matters relating to administrative integrity. The CVC is also empowered to ask for reports, returns or Statements from all Ministries/Departments in order to have a general check and supervision over them to lessen corruption. It can also take over any case under its direct control.

Just after the Congress-led UPA Government came to power in the aftermath of the 14th Lok Sabha elections of 2004, Mr. P. Shankar, the Central Vigilance Commissioner, sent to the Prime Minister's Office (PMO) a detailed eighty-page report where it was categorically mentioned that the CVC, during the tenure of the just defeated NDA

Ministry, had identified at least 371 high-posted bureaucrats to be 'absolutely corrupt' and recommended their punishment. But quite unfortunately, the Vajpayee Government did not take any punitive measures against them in spite of clear charges of corruption against them were authentically verified by the CVC. After receiving such a 'blasting' report from the CVC, the PMO of the Manmohan Singh Government has asked the respective Ministries/Departments to make a thorough investigation.[35]

In the CVC report (August, 2004), the Vajpayee Government was criticized severaly where it was clearly Stated that the Government's act defending those corrupt bureaucrats, completely ignoring the CVC report, has largely astounded the Commission. The decision taken by the Vajpayee Government has not only inactivated the vigilance functions of CVC but has indeed made the entire matter a 'satire'. It was also mentioned in the report that after primarily informing the Vajpayee Government of the matter of corruption proved against at least 371 high-rank bureaucrats, the CVC in its March 3, 2003 report again alerted the Vajpayee Government that if the Government failed to commence inquiries against those bureaucrats within the next six months, the CVC would take ultimate legal steps against them. But the Government even then remained inert.

It is to be noted that the Vajpayee Government, on many earlier occasions too, was disadvantaged by the CVC reports. In such a report, just before the 14th Lok Sabha Elections, it was clearly shown how various governmental officials had misused the property of governmental undertakings. Charges of corruption wer brought against a number of bureaucrats under the NDA Government when Mr. N. Vittal was the Central Vigilance Commissioner, just before Mr. P. Shankar. Vittal was of the same opinion of the CVC report made by Mr. P. Shankar. Vittal opined that these charges of corruption against public officials should be discussed in more details and that citizens should have the full right to be informed of the actual truth. Mr. Suresh Pachaudi, the Deputy Minister of the Central Personnel Department, said that the UPA Government was putting special emphasis on the CVC report (August, 2004) from all probable angles. He added that their government would take necessary steps on the basis of that detailed report. Mr. Manmohan Singh, too, after being the Prime Minister, said on several occasions that the administration must be made transparent in order to make the system of distribution transparent. But the CVC in its eighty-page-long report has proved with data that the administrative transparency was totally ignored during the tenure of the NDA Government. While the CVC asked for replies from the NDA Government in 3942 cases, the Government neither gave the CVC any reply nor took any step in 959 cases. At least 371 bureaucrats, though marked to be 'corrupt' by the CVC, are placed in tact in service. Out of 371, at least 118 bureaucrats were of the Department of Customs. Others were of the Departments of

Central Income Tax, Central Tele-communications, Delhi Development Authority, Central Railways and Central Information and Broadcast.

After getting the detailed August 2004 CVC report, the PMO immediately informed Mr. Suresh Pachaudi all the facts contained in the report. Mr. P. Shankar has informed the Prime Minister that all the annual reports of all governmental departments are published for people's information. But the reports of the CVC are never published. He demands that from now on, all such reports be published. Mr. Lal Krishna Advani has also expressed his opinion in favour of activating the CVC report because its rights and autonomy are unquestionable.

11.9.2 Central Bureau of Investigation and the Special Police Establishment

The Central Bureau of Investigation (CBI) was created in April, 1963. Prior to 1963, the CBI was known as the Special Police Establishment, functioning under the Delhi Special Police Establishment Act, 1946. Till the creation of the Ministry of Personnel in March, 1985, the CBI functioned under the Home Ministry. After 1985, the Bureau became an attached office under the Department of Personnel and Training in the Ministry. In 1963, the functions of the CBI were enlarged significantly. The Bureau indexes criminals involved in international crimes.

The CBI through its Special Police Establishment (SPE) Division is perhaps the main investigating agency of the Central Government. It investigates cases of misconduct by public servants in the employment of the Central Government and its corporate undertakings. It also investigates cases in which the interests of the Central Government or any body or corporation financed by it, are involved, cases relating to breach of central laws in the enforcement of which the Central Government is interested, big cases of fraud, cheating etc. and other cases committed by organized gangs or professional criminals having inter-State or even international ramification. The CBI derives its power to investigate offences mentioned above from the Delhi Special Police Establishment Act, 1946.

11.10 VIGILANCE MACHINERY IN STATES

There is a State Vigilance Commission (SVC) in each State (province), which has been functioning since 1964. There is in each State a Special Police Establishment, too. The SVC is headed by a Commissioner whose status will at least be that of a High Court judge. Holding office for a term of five years, the State Vigilance Commissioner is ineligible for any further employment under the Central or State Government. Again, there is a Commissioner for departmental inquiries whose function is to conduct such inquiries under charges of corruption. The SVC submits an annual report to the State Government about its activities drawing particular attention to any recommendation made by it which has not been accepted or implemented. The SVC report is placed before the State Legislature.

There are only minor variations in the functions of the SVC from one State to another. On the whole, the SVC is empowered to discharge the following duties:

- It undertakes inquiry into any transaction in which a public servant is suspected or alleged to have acted for an improper purpose or in a corrupt way.
- It initiates review of procedure and practices of administration in so far as they relate to the maintenance of administrative integrity.
- It collects statistics and other information so as to enable it to exercise general checks and supervision over anti-corruption work.

At the divisional level, there has been constituted a Divisional Vigilance Board. It generally consists of the Divisional Commissioner, Deputy Inspector-General of Police and the Divisional Vigilance Officer.

At the district level, there is a District Vigilance Officer appointed by the Collector/Deputy Commissioner from among his gazetted assistants in consultation with the Divisional Board. Thus, there has emerged a web of vigilance agencies in the country. The Vigilance Commissioners of all States hold an annual conference presided over by the Central Vigilance Commissioner. The main aim of the conference is to ensure integrity regarding vigilance. It provides a forum for the discussion of mutual problems and exchange of experiences. It gives publicity to various efforts of vigilance on the part of both the Central and State Governments. Ultimately, it is aimed at bringing the public confidence in the government's sincerity.

11.11 CONCLUSION

It is quite unfortunate that for the prevention of political as well as administrative corruption, there is in India no effective and independent vigilance mechanism at present that is capable of inspiring public confidence. If the present government is serious to tackle problems of widespread corruption on the part of public officials, it should give due consideration to the suggestions made by U.C. Agarwal, the former Central Vigilance Commissioner of the Government of India. In brief, his suggestions are as under:[36]

- Establishment of the Lokpal institution to deal with political corruption with its own initiative against corruption-suspect Ministers and MPs.
- The Lokpal should have his own independent investigating and prosecuting agency without a necessity to depend on the CBI.

- The Lokpal should have legal powers to prosecute an accused Minister in specially designated courts after a *prima facie* case is established against him by the Lokpal's own inquiry.
- The charged Minister must compulsorily resign after filing of the charge-sheet in the trial court.
- The CVC should also be made a statutory body by a Parliamentary Law and redesignated as the Central Lokayukta.
- The Central Lokayukta could be appropriately linked to the Lokpal by making provisions of sharing or having common officers, staff, investigating and prosecuting agencies.
- The proposed Central Lokayukta should have the powers to finally decide on initiation of disciplinary action or prosecution against any public servant after a *prima facie* case is established by his own inquiry.

Unless such independent and adequately powerful vigilance bodies are established, there is no chance of preventing or controlling high-level corruption. Corruption in administration has recently taken a heavy toll of both efficiency and national morality. There are vociferous demands coming from different quarters that both politicians and bureaucrats must behave ethically.

Within this broad perspective, public administration has to do something in order to be accountable to the public.[37] In the first place, it has to be more dynamic to confront the challenges coming from different directions.

Further, public administration has to maintain, preserve and promote the constitutional order as the fundamental regulating and moral umbrella.

Again, in times of turbulence, it has to learn to manage complexities and take decisions in situations of growing uncertainty.

Moreover, it has to develop more and more technical competence and equipment support.

Further, it has to understand, and not avoid, citizens and their demands, hopes and aspirations.

Finally, it has to serve public interests without being swayed by narrow, parochial or personal interests and influences.

The success of developmental tasks depends to a significant extent upon the harmonious relations between the citizens and administration. Administration should not function in a mechanical but in a humane and purposeful way. The officials of administration should have a sense of dedication, responsiveness and alertness. Citizens, too, should meaningfully cooperate with the administrators. Under such circumstances of cooperation and coordination, it would not be difficult for administrators to implement the developmental projects and to bring about administrative modernization. Through active popular participation in the administrative process, 'democracy', in the true sense of the term, would be more and more incorporated in administration.

Questions

1. Discuss the major features of the 1990 Lokpal Bill.
2. Examine critically the Central Vigilance Commission.
3. Write short notes on:
   (a) Ombudsman
   (b) Lokayuktas
   (c) Vigilance machinery at the state level of India
   (d) Jan Lokpal Bill

Notes and References

1. Brautigam, Deborah, Governance and Economy: A Review, *Working Papers*, Policy and Review Departments, The World Bank, December, 1991.
2. UNDP, 1997: Reconceptualizing Governance, *discussion paper 2*, New York, January, 1997.
3. Robson, William, A. (Ed.), *The Civil Service in Britain and France*, Hogarth Press, 1956.
4. Goel, S.L., *Advanced Public Administration*, Sterling Publishers, 1994.
5. *ARC: Interim Report of the ARC on Problem of Redress of Citizens' Grievances*, Ministry of Home Affairs, New Delhi, 1966–1970.
6. Appu, P.S., The All-India Services: Decline, Debasement and Destruction, *Economic and Political Weekly*, Vol. XL, No. 9, 26 February–4 March, 2005.
7. *Ibid.*
8. *Vohra Committee Report*, Ministry of Home Affairs, India, Republic, 1993.
9. Vittal, N., *Corruption in India*, Academic Foundation, New Delhi, 2003.
10. *Ibid.*
11. Singh, M.P. and Rekha Saxena, *Indian Politics: Contemporary Issues and Concerns*, Prentice-Hall of India, New Delhi, 2008.
12. Aggarwal, P.K., A Survey of Bureaucracy in India, in P.K. Aggarwal and N. Vittal (Eds.), *I am Sorry: Indian Bureaucracy at Crossroads*, Manas, Delhi, 2005.
13. *NCRWC Report, Vol. 1*, Ch. 6, 2002, Chair: Justice M.N. Venkatachaliah.
14. *Report of the Committee on Prevention of Corruption, 1962*, Government of India, New Delhi, 1962.

15. *Report of the Study Team of the Central ARC on Redress of Citizens' Grievances*, Government of India, New Delhi, 1966.
16. Goel, S.L., *op. cit.*
17. Goel, M.M., *Administration and Management of Electricity in India*, Deep and Deep, New Delhi, 1987.
18. Ovasdi, J.M., *Railway Administration*, Deep and Deep, New Delhi, 1991.
19. Goel, S.L., *Public Health Administration*, Sterling, New Delhi, 1984.
20. *Eighth and Concluding Report of the National Police Commission*, Government of India, May, 1981.
21. Sharp, W.R., *Field Administration in the United Nations System*, The Carnegie Endowment for International Peace, Stevens and Sons Ltd., London, 1961.
22. Chowdhary, D. Singh, Bureaucrats: Then and Now, *The Tribune*, 17 January, 1982.
23. Ovasdi, J.M., *op. cit.*
24. Jit, Inder, Crusade for Clearn Politics, *The Tribune*, 11 May, 1982.
25. Khanna, H.R., *Making of India's Constitution*, Eastern Book Company, Lucknow, 1981.
26. *Royal Bank of Canada Monthly Newsletter*, Vol. 52, No. 11 (November, 1971). Also see, various writings of Donald C. Rowat and Walter Gellhorn.
27. Arora, R.K. and R. Goyal, *Indian Public Administration: Institutions and Issues*, Wishwa Prakashan, New Delhi, 1997.
28. The working of the CVC will be discussed in detail in Section 11.9.
29. *The Interim Report of the Central ARC on Redress of Citizens' Grievances*, Government of India, New Delhi, 1966.
30. Saxena, D.R., Ombudsman: Principles and Current Scenario in India and Rajani Ranjan Jha, Working of the Lok Ayuktas in India: Some Reflections, papers presented at the colloquium on *Ombudsman: India and World Community* at IIPA, 1995.
31. Jha, R.R., *ibid.*
32. The ARC Report, 1970, p. 8.
33. Chakrabarty, Bidyut, *Reinventing Public Administration: The Indian Experience*, Orient Longman, New Delhi, 2007.
34. *Op. cit.*
35. *The Anadabazar Patrika*, August 30, 2004.
36. Agarwal, U.C., Need for Effective Vigilance, *Indian Journal of Public Administration*, July–September, 1997.
37. Chakrabarty, Bidyut, *op. cit.*

12 Communications between the Panchayats and the Marginalized: A Development Perspective

12.1 INTRODUCTION

The Panchayati raj, as it exists in West Bengal under the Left Front rule, is more than thirty years old. Meanwhile, seven panchayat general elections were held and some very significant developments have been brought about in the approach to the Panchayati raj itself. It is, however, broadly accepted that till 2007 the 'red' panchayats of West Bengal—the principal aims of which are to widen political participation at the grassroots level and to bring about decentralized local governments at the levels of the village, block and district—are a big source of political stability in West Bengal. One of the major bases of the strength of the Panchayati raj in West Bengal lies in the absolutely changed nature of relations between the officials and the non-officials in the Panchayat bodies. The end of rock-departmentalism has resulted in enhancing the glory and glamour of the elected representatives at the local bodies. Consequently, social, economic and political power has been transferred from the pockets of the officials to those of the non-officials. Hence, it will be of immense interest to understand the relations between the political wing and the administrative wing of the panchayats. One may also be interested in knowing the relations between these two wings taken together, on the one hand, and the ruralites, on the other, for whom these wings are supposed to perform their functions. In this context, the perspective of communications becomes important because democratic decentralization—the principal philosophy behind the introduction of the panchayati raj institutions in West Bengal—widens the scope of political communication. No social organization, no matter whether it exists at a national, State (provincial) or local level, can run smoothly if its channels of communication are loosely woven. The nature of the panchayats, being a social unit, cannot be properly understood unless the patterns of communication between the political wing and the administrative wing of the panchayats and also between these two wings, on the one hand, and the millions and millions of villagers of West Bengal, on the other, are clearly explained. In this chapter, an attempt has been made in this regard.

12.2 PATTERN OF COMMUNICATIONS WITHIN PANCHAYATS

From the different studies made on the panchayati raj institutions in West Bengal, it is clear that there is a continuous flow of communications within the panchayats which is either initiated by their political members or by their administrative officials. In fact, the entire 'political team' in both the Gram Panchayats (at the village level), Panchayat Samitis (at the block level) and Zilla Parishads (at the district level) communicate in many ways with the entire 'administrative team'. On the whole, there is an incessant flow of communications between the individuals – both elected and non-elected—constituting the panchayat bodies. In fact, the net results of different dimensions of these very important communications are the birth and evolution of the relations between the elected members and the administrative staff of the Panchayats, Samitis and Parishads.

Regarding the principal pattern of such communications, it may broadly be said that it is primarily horizontal and top-down vertical. It is horizontal since the elected members at the Panchayats, Samitis and Parishads in West Bengal—apart from their Pradhans and Upa-Pradhans, Sabhapatis and Sahakari Sabhapatis, and Sabhadhipatis and Sabha Sabhadhipatis respectively—continuously communicate with each other. On the administrative side also, there is a close and constant contact between the Secretary, clerks and other administrative staff at the Panchayats, between the engineers, Secretary, field officers, Audit and Accounts Officers, Executive Officer and Additional Executive Officer at both the Samitis and the Parishads.

The flow of communications is also top-down vertical since the political members are all bound to obey the decisions of the Sabhadhipatis in the case of the Zilla Parishads, of the Sabhapatis in the case of the Panchayat Samitis, and of the Pradhans in the case of the Gram Panchayats. Similarly, all administrative personnel must obey the instructions given by their immediate superiors. In this strict chain of command, the ultimate administrative boss is the Executive Officer of the Parishad and the Samiti (DM ex-officio and BDO ex-officio, respectively). In the case of the Panchayat, the supreme most administrative power rests with the Secretary.

But it is interesting to note that sometimes this pattern of the flow of communication becomes bottom-up vertical as well. In some situations, the ordinary political members of the Panchayats or Samitis or Parishads inform their knowledge to the Pradhans/Upa-Pradhans or Sabhapatis/Sahakari-Sabhapatis or Sabhadhipatis/Saha-Sabhadhipatis, respectively. More important is that while taking decisions, the latter are somewhat influenced by such information. Among the administrative personnel also, the field officers may try to send facts and data regarding people's reactions or outputs, to their superiors like the Secretaries or the Additional Executive Officers at all three panchayat tiers.

12.3 PATTERN OF COMMUNICATIONS: PANCHAYATS AND PEOPLE

The question which haunts us is: can we see a similar pattern regarding the flow of communications between the combined political and administrative teams of the panchayati raj institutions of West Bengal, on the one hand, and the ruralites, on the other? Both the teams inform that they have regular face-to-face communications with people. But whether the poor ruralites can take 'active' roles in such communications, whether the poorest of the poor are properly informed and whether their responses are taken quite seriously are still not known. Particularly, the recent developments in some rural areas of West Bengal, viz. Singur, Nandigram and Deganga centring round the question of 'industrialization', point to an altogether different pattern of communication.

In this context, it should be kept in mind that we are repeatedly told that sacrifice is needed for this industrialization. But it is conveniently left untold that the sacrifice must be borne by those who are least capable of bearing it, viz. the poor and the most marginalized sections. The rich corporations need not sacrifice; instead they are subsidized by the government. The estimated subsidy for the Tatas in Singur in the Hughly district of West Bengal is over Rs. 850 crores for an investment of Rs. 1000 crores.[1] And the people of Singur have been kept completely in the dark. In so far as the traditional Left is concerned, first Singur and then Nandigram drove home the point that, many of the Left politicians are not that different from the 'dream team' of economic policy makers at the Centre, who favour the World Bank, the International Monetary Fund and the Asian Development Bank. The cultural nationalists of Hindutwa variety uphold violently their culture when it comes to Ram Mandir and 'Vande Mataram', but surrender willingly to foreign multinationals. The overwhelming willingness of the Gujarat Chief Minister to invite Mr. Ratan Tata for opening the Nano factory at Sanand in Gujarat reminds one of the fact.

Professor Amit Bhaduri and Ms. Medha Patkar in a joint working paper categorically mention that Indian polity with an increasingly inequitable economy thrives in the name of high growth, industrialization and development, working ruthlessly against the poor majority. Farmers with despair and anger are committing suicide in hundreds especially in Maharastra, Andhra Pradesh and Punjab because the governments want to adopt a new kind of commercial agriculture under WTO with expensive inputs supplied by the multinationals, but no subsidy, no appropriate price for their produce. In Chhattisgarh, in the name of fighting extremism, tribals are being evacuated forcibly in hundreds and thousands from their villages to be huddled in Vietnam-style concentration camps. The corporations eye greedily their mineral resource rich land. The poorest are the richest in natural resources in our country, but are kept poorest by denying them what belongs to them. In such a strange framework of "competitive federalism"[2], West Bengal is in the same rat race. The argument goes "if we in West Bengal do not do it, Uttaranchal will do it" or, "we can be more ferocious than Orissa" in pleasing the Tatas or the Jindals or some others. This has full legal and moral support of the Central Government, but the State has full constitutional power not to oblige. This results in increasing distrust and subsequent alienation on the part of the ruralites in general. Consequently, in the flow of communication the decision-makers and decision-implementers continuously play the role of the sender and the ruralites that of the recipient, thereby increasingly demeaning the value of communication. Besides, the panchayati raj institutions also gradually become the prototype of a worthless cipher.

But it should be made clear that if the flow of communication between the people, on the one hand, and the officials and non-officials of the panchayati raj institutions, on the other, is principally downward vertical, then all the new innovations and introductions are bound to go in vain in the long run.

Considering the present situations in West Bengal, it is imperative to realize that the flow of communications between the political and the administrative elite groups, on the one hand, and the ignorant ruralites, on the other, should not at all mean the blunt top-down vertical flow in which the elite groups always play the role of the transmitter while the ruralites that of the receiver. The earlier experiences, in the context of India, show that many new innovations failed to touch the mass as a result of this top-down flow of communication between the elite groups and the people. It is really difficult for the poor ruralites to easily accept, for example, the newly introduced western technology unless and until their objective conditions are properly studied, their suggestions are paid proper heed to, and they are put absolutely in an atmosphere of uncertainty and wonder instead of the one of certainty and lack of astonishment. Under these circumstances, one should rather remember Robert Chambers' argument that now the real need is to invert the relationship between the planner and the producer so that the former listens and responds to the needs and knowledge of the latter.[3]

12.4 SHIFT IN THE PATTERN OF COMMUNICATIONS SINCE THE SECOND HALF OF THE LAST CENTURY

In this context, it has to be stressed that the entire concept of the communication theorists regarding the pattern of communications has undergone a sharp change throughout the sixties and seventies of the twentieth century. In the western society, since the twenties of the twentieth century, communication began to be thought as an instrument of attaining industrial development. The industrially developed western society tried to communicate with the poorer sections of the world by showing them the gleaming end-products of the capitalist development and advertising these as the more attractive available lifestyle of the underdeveloped societies as well. Various newly invented scientific methods and technologies were encouraged to be adopted in the underdeveloped countries. Thus, the flow of communications at that time was basically 'one way vertical', or, to be more specific, 'top-down' in nature in which the industrially developed society always played the role of the addressor and the underdeveloped or developing society that of the addressee and in which the addressor never tried to know the response of the addressee.[4]

Since the fifth decade of the twentieth century, the situation began to change as a large number of underdeveloped Nation-States emerged from the colonial experience and gradually started to 'develop'. Many of these countries were newly born in the sense that they became independent from the western rule via national liberation movements. As a result, these newly independent Nation-States had some lingering distaste for the western values and culture. It seemed that the only intellectually consistent models of development which could bring about significant social change were Left-inspired.

In such a crucial situation, the West needed a somewhat new model of development to contest against the leftist outlook, a model where the western know-how would work all the magic of change. Hence, in the second half of the twentieth century, a number of western theories of communication were born and developed by Wilbur Schramm, Shannon and Weaver, Karl Deutsch and many others. But in their models of communication, communication was seen merely as a means of achieving industrial development. One should note that the very word 'development' is quite subjective since it was determined by the value patterns of the western scholars. To these scholars, development did never mean a change in individuals' attitudinal patterns or a change in the unequal environment. It was rather primarily a quantitative increase in productivity. This productivity, according to these theorists, would be increased by propagation of new techniques rather than through bringing about more humane relationships in production.

Schramm, as a communication theorist, for the first time believed that the quantitative increase in productivity could not be attained without bringing about some significant changes in the behavioural attitudes, values, beliefs, skills and norms of the people living in the underdeveloped States. He also categorically pointed out that this call for attitudinal changes should come not from 'within' the group, but from 'above'.[5]

But what Schramm categorically missed is that if only the 'above' gives this call or, in other words, if there is only the top-down flow of communication between the people and the decision-makers in the underdeveloped countries, then the right kind of attitudinal change can never be brought about. Hence, in introducing the newly invented methods of science and technology, our decision-makers, by no means, should blindly follow these western models of communication. They should realize that the kind of development which was possible in the West can be absolutely of no use in the context of the developing countries because of the difference of environment between the two. While in the western countries people had the atmosphere of 'certainty', in the context of our State, there is the atmosphere of gradual change, surprise and yet-to-be-known aims. As a result of this marked difference of atmosphere between the two set-ups, various attempts at bringing about cultural changes in India by pre-determining the "western" goals have failed miserably. Here a conflict took place between the "bottom-up" and the "top-down" flows of communication. The "bottom- up" kind of growth via the introduction of panchayati raj institutions (as imagined by Gandhi) could not go well with the "top-down" pattern of industrialization (eventually undertaken by Nehru). It must be taken note of that in the context of India, being a developing nation, the decision-makers should be influenced by the "bottom-up" kind of growth rather than by the "top-down" type. In the "top-down" type of industrialization, only the upper classes consisting of a very small section of the population are impressed by the glittering end-products of industrial development of the West and are financially able enough to change themselves according to the life-style of the Western people. The rest of the society, because of its financial backwardness, is not easily convinced of the need for changing the existing pattern of their lives. In fact, they are not so primarily because that would, by no means, benefit them. Besides, it would also invite alarmingly high rate of social inequality. The simultaneous existence of the present-day shopping malls and slums would clearly reveal the justification for such an argument.

In the metropolitan areas of India, Manhattan like world-class cities are set as our goals, when 25 per cent to 60 per cent of the city population live a subhuman existence in slums. In these areas, we need infrastructure to ensure basic amenities to the most needy. So why is this bias, and whom does it benefit? Professor Bhaduri and Ms. Patkar answer that it certainly benefits the urban elite population, and leads to uncontrolled urbanization and mega cities with growing hunger for energy, water and urban housing space. The modes of transports we are creating with more flyovers for cars (including Tata's people's car), the type of shopping or housing complex we are promoting are not merely iniquitous. The majority of our ordinary citizens, who do not consume them, also have to pay directly or indirectly for this pattern of consumption. This is why our farmers get less water and are staved of electricity in critical periods. This is why clean drinking water or hygienic sanitation is a luxury in villages. This kind of apoplexy at the top and anemia at the rest of the society should never be considered as a satisfactory sign of social health.

This situation can be clearly explained if we look back in the seventies of the twentieth century and make an attempt to analyze the pattern of modernization that took place in rural India where the rural decision-makers played the role of the addressor and the ruralites that of the addressee. The major thrust of this "top-down" persuasion technology was in the domains of family-planning, agriculture and health. But since the addressor could not try to understand the real atmosphere of the addressee, this "top-down" flow of communication miserably failed in the above mentioned domains to arouse people's consciousness of the western pattern of family size, agricultural atmosphere or health condition. This was particularly evident in the family-planning propaganda which had an almost counterproductive effect on its rural target audience.[6]

When it was felt that the poor ruralites were not inspired by the mass-media messages, considerable attempts were made again to bring about some minor improvements. Katz and Lazarsfeld's 1955 model of a "two-step flow of information" was applied. In this model new information would flow first directly from the mass-media to the opinion leaders and then from the latter to the people.[7] In fact, these opinion leaders (in the case of rural India, the grassroots level panchayat leaders), because of their personal influence, would do the actual job of convincing the common people to change their usual habits in the spheres of agriculture, health and family planning. After doing so in 1974, it was seen that in these spheres the knowledge gap between the rich and the poor had decreased while the actual adoption gap had increased. Hence, it became clear that it was not always simply a problem of faulty transmission. In other words, it is not an easy task to convince the ruralites of the underdeveloped nations since they are not ready to accept any and every radical change imposed upon them.

12.5 UNWORKABLE PARADIGM OF COMMUNICATION IN RURAL BENGAL

In the context of West Bengal also, the paradigm of a simple top-down flow of communication cannot work in the present situation. It has to be replaced by a bottom-up flow of communication in which the receiver is bound to inform his response to the transmitter. Thus, the old paradigm has failed which emphasized (a) the ability of the technical experts (who did not know the actual demands of the poorest section of the rural population and therefore had no involvement with them), (b) the attempts to solve problems without considering the actual objective conditions of developing societies, and (c) the messages full of western values and life-style (that could have no impact upon the poor mass). A brand new paradigm should emerge now which places emphasis upon (a) the ability of the ordinary rural folks, (b) the sharp distinction between the two contexts of the developed and the developing societies, and (c) new paths of change.[8] This new paradigm will have to seek paths of change only as ordinary ruralites need and demand them and always in harmony with their own sense of goodness or badness. The paradigm must not set its own course according to some "prescribed goals", but discover the course gradually by taking information from the mass through successes as well as failures.

The decision-makers in rural West Bengal must realize that while introducing newer and newer innovations, they should accept the second paradigm instead of the first. They should keep it in mind that it is the rural mass, in general, who have trusted the elected panchayat leaders instead of the earlier bureaucrats. They must not forget that people with their needs and problems usually approach the non-officials instead of their official counterparts. They must also take note of the fact that being elected elements, their ultimate source of strength is the poor rural folk. The administrative personnel, too, should have the responsibility of implementing any new project in the way suitable for the mass, of receiving the reactions of the mass on any newly implemented or yet-to-be implemented scheme and of transmitting their reactions to the decision-makers so that the latter, in their turn, can modify the scheme according to the needs of the majority. In other words, one should understand that the traditional top-down flow of communication between the political and administrative elites of rural Bengal, on the one hand, and the common ruralites, on the other, is not workable any more.

The Constitution through Article 243 provided for a Finance Commission, to support and ensure that village level local bodies become financially viable, which was to be appointed in 1993. No government, Central or State, followed this up seriously. The record of the Government of Kerala has been the best while that of the Government of West Bengal has been among the worst. Acknowledging that the Left Front played a role in getting National Rural Employment Guarantee Act enacted, it is shocking that only 14 per cent of the money allotted in the poorest district of Purulia for employment guarantee was spent until December, 2006, more than half the money of employment guarantee provided by the Centre remaining unspent in the State, and not more than 16 days of employment provided while the legal and financial provision allows for 100 days.[9]

12.6 REMARKS ON WEST BENGAL

If the Government of West Bengal had shown the same zeal in making a success of employment guarantee as it has shown in acquisitioning land from the unwilling peasants, we would have taken at least the first step towards a genuine process of development in West Bengal. Critics and scholars have raised the question that if a high rate of growth necessarily entails a certain type of industrialization touching only a certain section and completely neglecting the other, is this industrialization synonymous with development? The kind of development West Bengal is experiencing with recent high growth has three principal characteristics. First, it is led by corporations. Second, they are mostly private corporations. Third, the role that the government plays is that of a promoter, an agent of private corporations, not one of a regulator. These three features taken together can make the pattern of communication in rural West Bengal at best top-down vertical.

This top-down flow must be replaced by the bottom-up flow of communication in which the elite-groups and the people would play both the roles of the addressor and the addressee simultaneously. Only then would people accept the new innovations successfully and, consequently, would the West Bengal panchayati raj institutions reach their reputational zenith. Only then Gandhiji' s dream of local self government at the grassroots level would be properly realized here. It is not only a question of values or morality. From the practical point of view also, the Bengal decision-makers in the present context should place considerable emphasis upon the bottom-up flow of communication. In fact, the 2008 panchayati raj election in West Bengal has revealed this naked truth. After the seventh panchayat election, held in May 2008, 3220 Gram Panchayats, 329 Panchayat Samitis and 17 Zilla Parishads were formed. Data also show that while in the 2003 panchayat election Left Front controlled as many as 2303 (71.5 per cent) Gram Panchayats, 284 (86.32 per cent) Panchayat Samitis and 15 (88.23 per cent) Zilla Parishads, in the 2008 panchayat election the corresponding figures are merely 1597 (49.59 per cent), 189 (69.38 per cent) and 13 (76.47 per cent) respectively for the Gram Panchayats, Panchayat Samitis and Zilla Parishads of West Bengal.[10]

Even the pro-industrialization social scientists unhesitatingly view that the recent 2008 panchayat elections show a sharp fall in the Left seat share, which certainly has been partly associated with the recent events of land acquisition process for new industries. The unplanned and uncoordinated ways of implementing these programmes, and especially the high-handed and violent ways of meeting any popular resistance on the ground, have galvanized the opposition in the whole State, apart from causing disunity within the Left coalition and eroding its general credibility as a defender of the interests of vulnerable sections of the rural population.[11]

12.7 RURAL MARGINALISED: NATIONAL SECTOR

Dr. Mahi Pal in his paper "Decentralised Governance and Marginalised Sections" points out that the elected representatives of marginalised sections in the rural areas of India have to face a number of challenges.

The most significant of such challenges is the legal ambiguity regarding the powers and functions of the panchayats since in the Panchayat Acts most of them have not been clearly defined and demarcated.

Besides, caste and gender prejudices have become a solid block for Scheduled Castes, Scheduled Tribes and women to exercise their powers and functions boldly and effectively as members or even chairpersons of panchayat bodies.

Thirdly, a total absence of adequate information and exposure regarding their duties and responsibilities, too, acts as a hindrance to the marginalised panchayat leaders to perform their functions effectively and efficiently.

Fourthly, lack of literacy among the panchayat representatives belonging to the marginalised groups leads to an utter helplessness and consequently reluctance on their part to participate in national and international seminars, conferences and workshops of rural local self-government.

Fifthly, this illiteracy as well as lack of information and knowledge comes from their economic disability which undoubtedly is a major challenge before the marginalised panchayat members as well as the marginalised ruralites whom they are supposed to represent. If representatives themselves belong to the below poverty line, it becomes difficult for them to bring about better lifestyles to the marginalised electorates in rural India.

Last, but not the least, growth and rapid expansion of Centrally Sponsored Schemes, making District Rural Development Agency increasingly powerful, and slow pace of devolution of power to the grass-root level panchayat bodies are considered as other challenges to the marginalised panchayat leaders as well as villagers.

Questions

1. What was the main pattern of communications within panchayats? What kind of shift was seen in this pattern after the second half of the last century?
2. Discuss in brief the challenges faced by rural women of India.

Notes and References

1. Bhaduri, Amit and Medha Patkar, Industrialization: Which Way Now?, unpublished manuscript, 2007.
2. The term used by Prof. Surajit C. Mukhopadhyay, C.S.S.S.C. at a "One Day Workshop on Agriculture to Industry: The Problem of Transformation" on April 20, 2007 at C.S.S.S.C. (The name of his paper was "The Politics of Land Acquisition in West Bengal.")
3. Chambers, Robert, Rural Poverty Unperceived: Problems and Remedies, *World Development*, Vol. 9, 1981. Also see Chambers, Robert, *Rural Development: Putting the Last First*, Longman, 1983.
4. Mohan, Peggy, In Between Paradigms: Perspective On Communication Theory For India, *Economic and Political Weekly*, Vol. XXVII, No.S 15 and 16, April 11–18, 1992.
5. Schramm, Wilbur, *Mass Media and National Development—The Role of Information in the Developing Countries*, Stanford University Press, Stanford, California, 1964.
6. Mohan, Peggy, *op. cit.*
7. Katz, E. and P.F. Lazarsfeld, *Personal Influence—The Part Played by People in the Flow of Mass Communications*, The Free Press, Glencoe, III, 1956.
8. Rogers, E.M., Communication and Development: The Passing of a Dominant Paradigm, *Communication Research*, Vol. 3, 1976.
9. Bhaduri, Amit and Medha Patkar, *op. cit.*
10. *Anandabazaar Patrika,* May 22 and 23, 2008.
11. Bardhan, Pranab, Sandhip Mitra, Dilip Mookherjee, Abhirup Sarkar, Local Democracy and Clientelism: Implications for Political Stability in Rural West Bengal, *Economic and Political Weekly*, Vol. XLIV, No. 9, February 28, 2009.

13 Administrative Reforms in India Major Committees and Commissions

13.1 INTRODUCTION

Gerald Caiden has defined administrative reform as a process which involves artificial inducement of administrative transformation against resistance.[1] Basically, it tries to enhance the capacity of an administrative system to achieve its assigned goals. Administrative reform is not, by any means, confined to the narrow structural changes of an administrative system. It is, in fact, much broader in scope and includes significant improvements in structures, processes and behaviour of the administrative system and its components. Three expressions are used interchangeably in describing this process which is considered to be "a journey rather than a destination".[2] They are: administrative development, administrative modernization and administrative reform. The term 'administrative reform' has different meanings in different political systems. In most industrial and developed nations, administrative reform is a process of change in administrative structures or procedures within the public services. In the developing nations, administrative reform is often referred to as attempts to modernize and change society by using the administrative system as an instrument for social and economic transformation.[3]

One of the core issues of administrative reform is the accountability of those involved in public affairs. A lack of accountability defeats the primary goal for which governance is seen as an appropriate model in public administration. In most developing nations, this deficiency leads to misguided resource allocation, arbitrariness, governmental corruption, absence of private sector investment, slow growth rate, slow rate of eradication of poverty, etc.

The question of accountability needs to be seen in the perspective of the paradigmatic shift which has taken place in the discipline of public administration. Classical public administration, based on the western concept of bureaucracy within the framework of democracy, has so far been the main support of the accountability theory. In the practical world of the discipline today, two closely competing but contemporary paradigms seem to be prominent: one is 'new public management' and the other is known as 'good governance'. 'Reinventing government', although an innovating expression,[4] falls in line with the main current of thought, advocating quality (as against size) of governance and the entrepreneurial spirit.

13.2 ADMINISTRATIVE REFORMS IN INDIA: IMPORTANT COMMITTEES AND COMMISSIONS

In a parliamentary democracy as in India, it is the political executive which enjoys sweeping powers of introducing administrative reforms through its decisions and directives. The political executive has extensive powers by which it can appoint series of committees and commissions with a view to introducing reforms in the administrative system. Most of such committees and commissions appointed for recommending administrative reforms in India had some specific objectives involving the examination of only a few selected aspects of the administrative system. It could be civil service recruitment, training, pay structure, reorganization of the Secretariat, urban and rural local governmental structures, prevention of corruption, police administration, and so on. It was only the Administrative Reforms Commission (ARC), appointed in January 1970, which had been given the task of scrutinizing almost the entire Indian administrative system.

Besides the ARC, let us now point out some of the important individual committees and commissions appointed for introducing administrative reforms in India in a chronological order.

The Secretariat Reorganization Committee, set up under the chairmanship of Girija Shankar Bajpai, on the eve of transfer of power, reported on 10 August, 1947. It recommended certain measures for reorganizing the Secretariat Departments and also suggested certain procedural changes in the Secretariat.

The First Pay Commission, set up under the chairmanship of Vardachariar, submitted its report to the Union Government in 1947.

In 1948, the Economy Committee was set up by the Union Government. Kasturbhai Lalbhai, a well-known industrialist, was the Chairman of the Committee. Based on its recommendations, several economy committees were set up in various Ministries with a view to check governmental expenditure.

In 1949, N. Gopalaswami Ayyangar, a Union Minister, submitted reports on the reorganization of the governmental machinery. He recommended the regrouping of Ministries, improving the quality of personnel and creating an Organization and Methods Division in the Government.

In 1951, A.D. Gorwala, a retired ICS officer, submitted two reports–one on Public Administration in India and another on the Efficient Conduct of State Enterprises–to the Planning Commission. Gorwala Reports recommended strongly the introduction of organization and method procedure in various governmental organizations, efficiency and strict discipline in the civil service and promoting a kind of understanding between the politicians and the administrators. Again, in the Gorwala Reports, it was clearly Stated that the Ministries should not interfere in the working of the Heads of Departments, that recruitment methods should be reformed and that the IAS training should be made more systematic.

In 1952, R.A. Gopalaswami submitted a memorandum to the Cabinet Secretary on improving the efficiency in the Secretariat. He, too, recommended the creation of an Organization and Methods directorate.

In 1953, Paul Appleby, a Ford Foundation consultant, was invited by the Government of India to visit our country. He submitted his report entitled, 'Public Administration in India: Report of a Survey'. Appleby praised Indian administration as "among the dozen or so most advanced governments in the world" and then went on to call it "archaic, feudalistic and unimaginative." He made a number of recommendations for improving the work procedure and for enhancing the capabilities of the administrative organization. Within a year of the submission of his report, two of his recommendations were implemented. One was the setting up of the Indian Institute of Public Administration in New Delhi and another was the establishment of the Organization and Methods Division in the Cabinet Secretariat.

In 1954, Asok Chanda, in his unpublished note to the Government of India, recommended strongly the creation of more All-India Services, adoption of an officer-oriented system in government, greater delegation of powers to the lower level officials and reducing delays in the implementation of projects.

In 1955, the Railway Corruption Enquiry Committee, under the chairmanship of J.B. Kripalani, made strong recommendations to improve the standard of integrity and uniformity in the Railways, being the largest public sector enterprise. The Kripalani Report categorically mentioned the massive corruption prevalent in a major segment of Indian administration even five decades ago.

In 1956, Paul Appleby visited India again and submitted a second report, this time a brief one, entitled "Re-examination of India's Administrative System with Special Reference to Administration of Government's Industrial and Commercial Enterprises".

In the same year, the Public Services (Qualifications for Recruitment) Committee, set up under the chairmanship of A.R. Mudaliar, submitted its report.

1957 is considered to be a landmark year for Indian administration as it saw the submission of the famous Report of the Team for the Study of Community Projects and National Extension Service presented to the National Development Council by its Chairman, Balwantray G. Mehta. On the basis of the report of this Team, popularly known as the Balwantray Mehta Committee, the system of panchayati raj was introduced in India.[5]

In 1959, the Commission of Enquiry on Emoluments and Conditions of Service of Central Government Employees (Second Pay Commission), set up under the chairmanship of Jagannath Das, submitted its report. It recommended the creation of Whitley Councils, on the British pattern, for resolving the problems in employer-employee relations.

In 1962, V.T. Krishnamachari submitted to the Union Government his Report on Indian and State Administrative Services and Problems of District Administration. In this report, Krishnamachari suggested an increase in the number of direct recruits to the IAS, improvement in the system of training during the probationary period at the State level and organizing refresher courses for the IAS officers of six to seven years seniority.

In 1964, the Committee on the Prevention of Corruption, chaired by K. Santhanam, submitted its report. It favoured strengthening of vigilance organizations and adoption of a code of conduct for civil servants.

In 1965, the most comprehensive measure in administrative reforms was taken by appointing the Administrative Reforms Commission (ARC) under the chairmanship of Morarji Desai (succeeded in 1967 by K. Hanumanthaiya). The ARC presented 20 main reports which are as under:

1. Problems of Redress of Citizens' Grievances (1966)
2. Machinery of Planning (Interim) (1967)
3. Public Undertakings (1967)
4. Finance, Accounts and Audit (1968)
5. Economic Administration (1968)
6. Machinery of Government of India and its Procedures of Work (1968)
7. Life Insurance Corporation (1968)
8. Machinery for Planning (1968)
9. Central Direct Tax Administration (1969)
10. Administration of Union Territories and NEFA (1969)
11. Personnel Administration (1969)
12. Delegation of Financial and Administrative Powers (1969)
13. Centre-State Relations (1969)
14. State Administration (1969)
15. Small Scale Sector (1969)

16. Railways (1970)
17. Treasuries (1970)
18. Reserve Bank of India (1970)
19. Post and Telegraphs (1970)
20. Scientific Departments (1970)

Besides, the ARC produced 33 reports of the study teams and working groups which formed the basis of the main reports of the ARC. Out of about 580 recommendations of the ARC, a few were really significant. These included the appointment of the Lokpal at the Centre and Lok Ayuktas at the Central as well as State levels, creation of a full-fledged Department of personnel in the Central Government, uniform grade of pay structure, introduction of specialists into middle and senior management positions, special audit boards for public undertakings, etc.[6]

In 1973, the Report of the Third Pay Commission, chaired by Raghubar Dayal, was submitted. The report introduced the concept of classification of posts.

In 1975, L.P. Singh and L.K. Jha, two veteran administrators, presented to the Government of India a Note on Improving Efficiency in Administration.

In 1976, the Committee on Recruitment Policy and Selection Methods, headed by D.S. Kothari, submitted its report. Following its recommendations, a system of single examination for All-India Services was introduced.

In 1978, the Committee on Panchayati Raj Institutions, under the chairmanship of Asoka Mehta, presented its report. The Committee, popularly known as the Asoka Mehta Committee, strongly recommended the setting up of Mandal Panchayats. Because of political reasons, the Asoka Mehta Committee's recommendations were largely ignored.[7]

The National Police Commission (1977–1980), under the chairmanship of Dharam Vira, presented in 1981 its eight reports which included several recommendations on the modernization of the law enforcement machinery and on the institutional arrangements for preventing the misuse of power. In view of the growing communalisation of the police force, perhaps it is an appropriate time to have a fresh look at the 1981 report of the National Police Commission (NPC). Before the NPC was inaugurated, several police commissions were appointed by various States, of which Kerala was the pioneer in instituting a Police Reorganization Commission in 1959. Appointed in the aftermath of the 1975–1977 National Emergency, the NPC made several recommendations on police reform in its eight-volume report, submitted in 1981. Two areas that appeared to have bothered the NPC most were (a) the misuse of the police and (b) accountability and performance on the part of the police. According to the NPC, the police themselves influenced by politicians distorted their own role during the Emergency. Hence the

Commission in its 1981 report categorically States that "the police sub-culture should take into account the fundamental rights of the people, the supremacy of laws and not of executive fiat, and our constitutional goal towards a developed and egalitarian society".[8] To check the misuse of the police force, two major recommendations were made: (a) there should be a tenured office of the Chief of Police, selected by a penal drawn by a committee comprising the Chairman of the UPSC, the Union Home Secretary, the senior-most amongst the Heads of Central Police Organizations, the Chief Secretary of the State and the existing Police Chief of the State, and (b) there should be a six-member permanent State Security Commission with a fixed term of three years to annually review the performance of the police.

In the early 1980s, the Economic Reforms Commission, under the chairmanship of L.K. Jha, submitted a series of reports which advocated the rationalization and modernization of the economic administrative system and paved the way for a new economic order.

In 1984, the Commission on Centre–State Relations was set up under the chairmanship of Justice R.S. Sarkaria. It presented its report in 1988. Reiterating the sound principles of federalism, the Sarkaria Commission made several useful recommendations. One such recommendation, concerning the creation of an Inter-State Council, was implemented in 1990.[9]

In 1986, the Fourth Pay Commission, constituted in 1982 under the chairmanship of Justice Singhal, presented its report. The Commission had suggested steps to improve 'efficiency' in public administration primarily in terms of enhanced salary and other benefits.

In the same year, L.M. Singhvi Committee on Rural Development submitted its report. It put a lot of emphasis on district planning.

In 1989, the Committee on the Recruitment Policy and Selection Methods for All-India and Central Services, set up by the UPSC under the chairmanship of Satish Chandra, submitted its report. It was appointed a year ago.

With the adoption of the New Economic Policy in the early 1990s, there have been attempts at dismantling the centrally directed framework of economic development. Administrative reforms in India in the 1990s have basically been driven by the measures of economic liberalization.[10] Good governance has suddenly entered the vocabulary of public administration. From its lending experience in many developing countries, the bank came to realize that 'good governance' is central to creating and sustaining an environment which fosters strong and equitable development, and it is an essential complement to sound economic policies. The Indian response was clearly articulated in the 1996 conference of Chief Secretaries which suggested several corrective steps to arrest the drift in the civil service before it was too late. The efforts to transform an aloof, impersonal and paternalistic bureaucracy into one which is citizen-friendly and sensitive to user-needs remained the basic concern of those participating in the conference. What was suggested in the 1996 conference had its root in the arguments, put forward by Rajiv Gandhi, in favour of 'responsive administration'. He argued in 1988 that the paternalistic model of Indian administration was not suitable for a society where the main thrust of administration was on development. A more representative and more responsive administration would be better placed to relate the purposes of administration to the larger goals of our national life–democracy, socialism, secularism and non-alignment.[11]

The Fifth Pay Commission of 1997 has gone beyond the conventional bounds of a pay commission and performed the role of an administrative reform commission, touching on vital issues of Indian governance. This pay commission has set the new agenda of 'good governance' into action.[12] What is unique about the Fifth Pay Commission is its articulation of the changed role of government in response of global inputs. It clearly Stated that the government needed to be downsized and debureaucratized and that it should primarily confine itself to 'core functions' that could not be performed by the market. Everything should be left to private initiative. Thus, the Fifth Pay Commission not only suggested a new pay-structure for the civil service, but also made recommendations of a far-reaching nature, affecting its size, efficiency, morale and motivation, training and recruitment and general operation procedures.

The Sixth Pay Commission was set up by the Union Cabinet of India on October 5, 2006 for revising the salaries of Central Government employees. The Commission was set up under the chairmanship of Justice B.N. Srikrishna with a time-frame of 18 months. Other members of the Commission were Prof. Ravindra Dholakia, Mr. J.S. Mathur and Member-Secretary Smt. Sushama Nath. Justice Srikrishna submitted the report of the Commission to the Finance Minister Mr. P. Chidambaram on March 24, 2008. The Cabinet approved its recommendations with some modifications on 14th August 2008. Group-D posts were abolished to imply that only skilled and semi-skilled workers can be employed in the Central Government offices. Existing Group-D employees, who already possess the minimum qualifications recommended by the Commission, will be directly placed in Pay Band 1 designated for semi-skilled workers. Those Group-D employees who do not possess the required qualifications would have to be trained within a period of six months and only after successful re-training, they can be placed in Pay Band 1.

13.3 THE ADMINISTRATIVE REFORMS COMMISSION (ARC)

In this section, the recommendations of the report of the Administrative Reforms Commission (ARC) have been summarized.

The ARC was appointed on 5 January, 1965 "to examine the public administration in this country and to make recommendations for reforms and reorganization with a view to ensuring the highest standards of efficiency and integrity in the public services, and for making public administration a fit instrument for carrying out the social and economic policies of the Government." The following were the major areas allotted for the consideration of the Commission:

1. The machinery of the Government of India and its procedure of work
2. The machinery for planning at all levels
3. Centre-State relations
4. Financial administration
5. Personnel administration
6. Economic administration
7. Administration at the state level
8. Administration at the district level
9. Public sector undertakings
10. Redress of citizens' grievances
11. Improvement of the quality of membership of the PSC.

13.3.1 Machinery of the Government of India and its Procedure of Work

Regarding the machinery of the Government of India and its procedure of work, the ARC recommended the following:

1. The size of the Council of Ministers should be determined primarily by administrative needs. There should be national combination of subjects into ministerial portfolios.
2. A Department of Personnel should be set up under the Prime Minister and its main functions should be the formulation of personnel policies and review of their implementation, talent-hunting, development of personnel for senior management and processing of appointments to senior posts, manpower planning, training and career development, and research in personnel administration.
3. In each Department, there should be only two levels of consideration, viz. Under Secretary/Deputy Secretary, and Joint Secretary/Additional Secretary/Secretary. Work should be assigned to each of these two levels according to the 'desk-officer' system where the officer concerned will himself dispose of a substantial amount of work with the necessary staff assistance.
4. The role of the Cabinet Secretary should be that of a general coordinator and principal staff adviser to the Prime Minister, the Cabinet and the Cabinet Committees.

5. Responsibility for overall coordination within a Ministry which has more than one Department/Secretary should be specifically assigned to one of the Departments/Secretaries most appropriate for this purpose.
6. The existing Organization and Methods (O&M) units in different Ministries/Departments should be reactivised.
7. The Department of Administrative Reforms should be placed directly under the Deputy Prime Minister.

13.3.2 The Machinery for Planning at all Levels

Regarding planning, the ARC's specific recommendations are as under:

1. The Planning Commission should confine itself to the formulation of plans and evaluation of plan performance. It should have no executive function and authority.
2. The National Development Council, which is composed of the Prime Minister, the Deputy Prime Minister (if any) and the Chief Ministers of all the States, should also contain the Union Ministers of ten important Departments.

13.3.3 Centre-State Relations

Regarding the very sensitive issue of Centre-State relations, the ARC recommended the following:

1. An Inter-State Council should be constituted consisting of the Prime Minister as Chairman, the Finance Minister, the Home Minister, the Leader of the Opposition in the Lok Sabha and five representatives, one each from the five Zonal Councils. Its functions will be as Stated in Article 263 of the Constitution.
2. Powers should be delegated to the maximum extent to the States regarding their work on projects in which the Centre is directly interested or which are carried out by States as agents to the Central Government.
3. The Finance Commission may be asked to make recommendations on the principles which should govern the distribution of plan grants to the States. The appointment of the Finance Commission may be so timed that when making its recommendations, it will have before it an outline of the 5 Year Plan as prepared by the Planning Commission.

13.3.4 Financial Administration

Regarding finance, accounts and audit, the ARC's recommendations are as follows:

1. The Departments and organizations, which directly control the determination of programmes, should introduce Performance Budgeting, which would inter-relate financial outlays with physical targets and achievements. It would also present estimates and expenditure on functions, programmes, activities and projects.
2. Audit should aim at a positive and constructive approach directed towards organizational efficiency and effectiveness of financial rules and procedure.
3. Internal financial advice should be strengthened, to develop financial competence within each Ministry or Department.
4. The 1st of November should begin each Financial Year, so as to facilitate a more realistic assessment of revenue and even spread of expenditure.
5. The ARC did not consider the question of separation of audit from accounts.

13.3.5 Personnel Administration

The ARC had eleven specific recommendations on personnel administration, which are as follows:

1. The government servants should have no right to strike and their grievances should be settled through Joint Conservative Machinery and Civil Service Tribunals.
2. There should be a unified grading structure for the entire civil service.
3. The existing system of confidential reports should be replaced by performance reports in which each government servant will have an opportunity of giving a resume of his performance during the year and getting his merits properly assessed for the purpose of promotion.
4. Greater opportunities should be provided to government employees of lower ranks to rise high according to their competence and performance.
5. There should be an improvement of recruitment policies and procedures, pruning of excessive personnel, abolition of unnecessary organizations, fixation of work norms, simplification and codification of rules, limitation of overtime work and transfers.
6. The governmental functions have been greatly diversified. Posts should therefore be grouped into regularly constituted services.
7. A functional field must be carved out for the IAS.
8. In the Department of Personnel, a Central Training Division should be set up.

9. A civil servant may be allowed to retire voluntarily after completing 5 years of service; and after voluntary retirement, he/she should be given proportionate pension and gratuity.
10. Both the husband and wife should not be employed under government at the same time, to relieve the mounting problem of unemployment.
11. The quantum of pension admissible may be raised to 3/6 of the average emoluments of the last three years as against the existing 3/8.

13.3.6 Economic Administration

The ARC recommended clearly that a high-powered Commission on 'Prices, Cost and Tariff' should be set up to assist the Government in evolving rational price policies and in creating a climate of consciousness and to take over the functions of the Tariff Commission.

13.3.7 Administration at the State Level

Regarding State administration, the ARC recommended the following:

1. The Council of Ministers in a State should be compact and homogeneous. Its size should be determined by the needs of administration. In big States, the number of Ministers should vary between 8 and 12.
2. The full Cabinet should meet at least twice a month.
3. Ministers should not intervene in the day-to-day administration except in cases of grave injustice, serious default or maladministration on the part of civil servants.
4. The Standing Committees of State Legislatures may be set up in selected areas of administrative activity for promoting detailed legislative review.
5. Union Government and State Governments should take steps to reduce expenditure on Governors and Raj Bhavans in conformity with the objectives of a democratic socialist society.
6. The executive Departments should be reorganized in such a way that needless multiplicity is removed and diffusion of functions may be avoided.
7. In Departments dealing with specific subjects, two staff cells would be set up—a combined cell on planning and policy and a finance cell.
8. A Department of Personnel should be set up under the charge of the Chief Secretary. This Department should be placed under the Chief Minister.
9. There should be set up a Policy Advisory Committee in every administrative Department.

10. The proliferation of personnel under the State Governments must be checked.

13.3.8 Administration at the District Level

ARC's recommendations on district administration are as under:

1. The judicial work of the Collector should be transferred to the judiciary.
2. The district administration should be divided into two sectors– one concerned with 'regulatory' functions and the other with 'development' functions. The District Collector should be the head of the first sector while the Panchayati Raj administrator (i.e. the Secretary of the Zilla Parishad) should be the head of the second one.
3. Only two administrative units in the district should permit their heads to make decisions regarding district administration. One should have its headquarters in the tehsil taluka and the other should have it at the district.
4. The district level officers in charge of the development Department should be transferred to the jurisdiction of the Zilla Parishad.
5. A senior officer, designated as the District Development Officer, should be appointed as the Chief Executive Officer of the Zilla Parishad.
6. A District Tribunal, consisting of the Collector and a Subordinate Judge, should hold enquiries in cases where removal of members of the panchayati raj institutions is involved.

13.3.9 Public Sector Undertakings

On public sector undertakings, the ARC specifically mentioned the following:

(a) The practice of deputing Government officers in public sector undertakings temporarily should be stopped.

(b) 'Sector corporations' should be set up with the main function of promotion and development of each major area of enterprise.

(c) The Bureau of Public Enterprises should be reorganized so as to make it a more effective service agency for the Ministries and the public sector undertakings.

(d) Four or five Audit Boards should be constituted, each for a specific section of public enterprises, for conducting efficiency audit and appraisal of performance.

13.3.10 Redress of Citizens' Grievances

ARC's specific recommendations on the redress of citizen's grievances are as under:

1. Special officers should be appointed for the redress of citizens' grievances. There should be one authority—Lok Pal—dealing with complaints against the administrative acts of Ministers or Secretaries to Government at the Centre and in the States.
2. There should be another authority—Lok Ayukt—in each State and at the Centre for dealing with complaints against the administrative acts of other officials.

13.3.11 Improvement of the Quality of Membership of the PSC

The recommendations of the ARC in respect of improving the quality of membership of the Public Service Commission are as follows:

1. In making appointments to a State Public Service Commission, the Governor of each State should consult the Chairman of the Union Public Service Commission and the Chairman of the State Public Service Commission. The latter may be consulted also with regard to the appointment of his own successor.
2. In making appointments to the Union Public Service Commission, the Chairman of the Union Public Service Commission should be consulted (even regarding the appointment of his own successor).
3. Not less than two-thirds of the members of the Union Public Service Commission should be drawn from among the Chairmen and members of the State Public Service Commissions.
4. At least one of the members of a State Public Service Commission should belong to a different State.
5. The minimum academic qualification for membership of a commission (UPSC or SPSC) should be a University degree.
6. A member selected from among government officers should have held office under a State Government or the Central Government for at least ten years.
7. Members selected from non-officials should have practised at least for ten years in any of the recognized professions like teaching, law, medicine, engineering, science, technology, accountancy or administration.

13.4 THE SARKARIA COMMISSION ON CENTRE–STATE RELATIONS

13.4.1 Appointment of the Commission

The Constitution of India speaks basically of two tiers of government—

one at the level of the Union, and the other at the level of the States or Provinces. The dynamism of the federal system has given birth to some problems and conflicts in the working of Union-State relations. Stresses, strains and irritations generated by such problems affect the working of the federal system, endangering the unity and integrity of India. Under such circumstances, the late Prime Minister Mrs. Indira Gandhi made a parliamentary announcement in March, 1983, to appoint a Commission, under the chairmanship of R.S. Sarkaria, a retired judge of the Supreme Court. It was declared that the Commission would review the existing arrangements between the Centre and the States while keeping in view the socio-economic developments that had already taken place. Mrs. Gandhi added that the Commission's review would take into account the importance of unity and integrity of our country for promoting the welfare of the Indians. She also made it absolutely clear that the Commission would examine the working of the existing arrangements between the Centre and the States and would recommend such changes in the said arrangements as might be appropriate within the present constitutional framework.

The Sarkaria Commission was formally constituted according to the Government of India, Ministry of Home Affairs Notification No. IV/11017/1/83-CSR, dated June 9, 1983. Subsequently, two more members were inducted. Sri B. Shivaraman was appointed on July 7, 1983 and Dr. S.N. Sen on July 27, 1983.

13.4.2 Main Contents of the Report of the Sarkaria Commission

The report of the Sarkaria Commission was published in 1988. It consists principally of two parts. The first part contains the main report and the second one consists of the memoranda received from the State Governments and political parties. The report covers issues which have a direct impact on inter-governmental relations in administrative and legislative spheres. It felt the need for establishing a standing Inter-Governmental Council under Article 263, to ensure inter-governmental coordination. The report also includes some related matters like the role of the Governor, Emergency Provisions, Deployment of the Union's armed forces in a State to help maintain public order, etc. The report further covers intergovernmental relations germane to socio-economic development, namely, Financial Relations, Economic and Social Planning, National Economic and Development Council, and some miscellaneous items like agriculture, industry, mines and minerals, inter-State trade and commerce, inter-State river disputes, forests, food and civil supplies, mass-media, etc. Finally, language, Union Territories and general observations and conclusions were contained in the report.

13.4.3 Main Issues in Union and State Relations

The main issues in Union-State relations are as under:

1. A study of the memoranda submitted to the Sarkaria Commission by various State Governments as well as political parties shows a wide variation of views. Many opine that the basic structure of the Constitution is sound and should not be disturbed. On the contrary, there are some who are of the view that it requires drastic changes so as to bring it according to their own perception of an ideal federal system.
2. The second group of people points out that the actions of the Union Government have led to a large degree of over centralization in all aspects where the States are reduced to mere administrative agencies of the Union.
3. They also allege that the Union has occupied most of the concurrent field, leaving little for the States. They point out that legislation in these fields is undertaken with no or inadequate prior consultation with the State.
4. The institution of the Governor was conceived of as an effective link between the two levels of government. It is alleged that this instrument has been misused to destabilize the State Governments run by parties different from that in power in the Union.
5. It is complained that the resources of the States have not grown satisfactorily according to the growth in their responsibilities. On this ground, it is demanded that more resources should be included in the States' share, if necessary by amending the Constitution.
6. Another point raised is that the emergence of planned development has concentrated all powers in the hands of the Union where the Planning Commission acts as a limb of the Union Government. It is emphasized that the central interference is significantly noticed in all matters which lie within the exclusive competence of the States. Hence, it is suggested that the Planning Commission should be restructured to limit the scope of the Union's interference in the area reserved for the States.
7. The system of controls, licenses and permits has proliferated greatly to the central dominance over States. This has led to a vast expansion in the power of the Union Government at the cost of the State Governments and local bodies. This unhealthy centralization needs to be revised.
8. It is finally pointed out that institutions or forums specially envisaged in the Constitution for sorting out problems arising in the working of inter-governmental relations (for instance, the

setting up of a permanent Inter-State Council, as contemplated in Article 263) have not at all been created. It is urged that in matters of dispute between the Union Government and the State Governments, an independent assessor should be appointed to examine the case, before a decision is taken.

13.4.4 Main Recommendations of the Sarkaria Commission

1. **Administrative Relations between Centre and States:** In its recommendations, the Sarkaria Commission has kept it in mind that the critics of the existing Union-State relations have serious objections to three main Articles—Article 256, Article 257 and Article 365. Article 256 lays down that the executive power of every State shall be so exercised as to ensure compliance with the laws made by the Parliament. Article 257 States that the executive power of every State shall be so exercised as not to impede or prejudice the exercise of the executive power of the Union. Again, according to Article 365, if a State fails to comply with, or give effect to, any directions given by the Union Government, it shall be lawful for the President to hold that a situation has arisen in which the Government of the State cannot be carried on in accordance with the provisions of the Constitution.

   The Sarkaria Commission categorically States that a direction, under Articles 256 and 257 and the application of sanctions under Article 365 in the event of non-compliance, is a measure of last resort and hence before issuing directions to a State or application of sanctions under Article 365, utmost caution should be exercised and all possibilities should be explored for settling points of conflict by all other available means.
2. **Legislative Relations between Centre and States:** Regarding legislative relations between the Union Government and State Governments, the Sarkaria Commission clearly recommends that residuary powers regarding taxation should continue to remain exclusively in the Concurrent List. The residuary field other than that of taxation should also be placed in the Concurrent List. To give effect to this recommendation, the Constitution may be suitably amended. Ordinarily, the Union should occupy only that much field of concurrent subjects on which uniformity of policy and action is essential in the larger interest of the Indian Nation.

   Further, whenever the Union proposes to undertake legislation with respect to a matter in the Concurrent List, there should be prior consultation not only with the State Governments individually, but also collectively with the Inter-Governmental Council. In fact, when the Bill is to be introduced in the Parliament, a resume of the views of the various State Governments and the comments of the Inter-State Council should accompany the Bill.

Again, when a resolution, passed by the Legislative Assembly of a State, for the abolition or creation of a Legislative Council in the State is received, the President must place the resolution before the Parliament, within a reasonable time, together with the comments of the Union Government.

3. **Role of the Governor:** Regarding the ideal position and role of the Governor, the Commission has clearly Stated in its report that it is desirable that a politician from the ruling party at the Union level is not appointed as Governor of a State which is being run by some other party or a combination of other parties.

   In order to ensure effective consultation with the State's Chief Minister in the selection of a person to be appointed as Governor of that State, the procedure of consultation should clearly be prescribed in our Constitution itself by amending Article 155.

   The Vice-President of India and the Speaker of the Lok Sabha may be consulted by the Prime Minister in selecting a Governor.

   The Governor's visual tenure of office of five years in a State should not be disturbed except very rarely and that, too, for some extremely compelling reasons.

   The Governor should not be eligible for any other appointment or office of profit under the Union Government or any State Government except for a second term as Governor or election as Vice-President or President of India.

   In choosing a Chief Minister, the Governor should be guided by the two following principles:

   (a) The party or combination of parties which commands the widest support in the Legislative Assembly should be called upon to form the Government.

   (b) The Governor's task is to see that a government is formed. He should never try to form a government which will pursue policies that the Governor approves.

   The Governor should not risk to determine the issue of majority support, on his own, outside the Assembly. The prudent course for him would be to cause the rival claims to be tested on the floor of the House.

   The Governor can by no means dismiss his Council of Ministers so long as they continue to command a majority in the Legislative Assembly. Conversely, he is bound to dismiss them if they lose the majority and yet do not resign.

   The discretionary powers of the Governor, as Stated in Article 163, should be left untouched.

4. **Reservation of Bills by Governors for President's Consideration:** Article 200 empowers the Governor to reserve the Bills for the consideration of the President. The Sarkaria Commission recommends in this regard that in dealing with a State Bill presented to the Governor under Article 200, he should not act contrary to the advice of his Council of Ministers merely because he does not like the policy embodied in the Bill. Needless reservation of Bills for President's consideration should strictly be avoided. Bills should be reserved only in exceptional circumstances.

   If a Bill is reserved for the consideration of the President, his assent should not ordinarily be withheld on the ground that the Union is contemplating a comprehensive law in future on the same subject. If a Bill reserved for the consideration of the President clearly tends to subvert the constitutional system of the State, the Union Government may advise the President to withhold his assent to the Bill.

5. **Promulgation of Ordinances:** The Sarkaria Commission recommends that State Governments should avoid the wrong practice of mechanical and repeated promulgation of an Ordinance without caring to get it replaced by an Act of the Legislature.

   A decision to promulgate or repromulgate an Ordinance should be taken only on the basis of Stated facts necessitating immediate action collectively taken by the State Council of Ministers.

6. **Emergency Provisions:** Critics of the Centre–State relations tend to argue that Article 356 is quite often abused by the Union Government to topple State Governments which are controlled by parties different from that ruling at the Centre. Article 356 States that if the President, after receiving any report from the Governor of a State or otherwise, is satisfied that a situation has arisen in which the government of the State cannot be carried on according to constitutional provisions, the President may by proclamation assume to himself all or any of the functions of the State Government or any of the powers vested in or exercisable by the Governor.

   On this issue, the Sarkaria Commission categorically recommends that Article 356 should be used very sparingly, in extreme cases, as a measure of last resort. It may be used only when all available alternatives fail to prevent or rectify a breakdown of constitutional machinery in the State.

   In a situation of political breakdown, the Governor should explore all possibilities of having a government enjoying a majority support in the Assembly. If it is not possible for such a government to be installed and if fresh elections can be held without avoidable delay, the Governor should ask the outgoing Ministry to continue as a caretaker government. The Governor should then dissolve the Legislative Assembly leaving the resolution of the constitutional crisis to the electorate of that State.

7. **Deployment of Union's Armed Forces in a State:** The Sarkaria Commission views that the existing relations between the Union's armed forces and the State's civil authorities as prescribed in the relevant Union Laws and Procedures need not be changed.

   However, before the Union Government deploys its armed and other forces in a State in aid of its civil power, otherwise than on request from the State Government, or declares an area within a State as "disturbed", it is desirable that the State Government should be consulted wherever feasible, and the State Government's cooperation should be sought, even though prior consultation with the State Government is not obligatory.

8. **All-India Services:** Regarding the All-India Services, the Sarkaria Commission States that they are as much necessary today as they were when the Constitution was framed.

   Any move to disband the All-India Services or to permit a State Government to opt out of the scheme must be regarded as harmful to the larger interests of the country. Such a step is sure to encourage parochial tendencies and undermine the integrity, cohesion, efficiency and coordination in Indian administration.

   The All-India Services should further be strengthened and greater emphasis should be placed on their roles.

   The Commission has made a number of recommendations for improving the efficiency and morale of these All-India Services.

9. **Inter-Governmental Council:** Article 263 empowers the President to establish an Inter State Council, and to define its duties along with its organization and procedure. Critics tend to complain that such a forum has not been established.

   The Sarkaria Commission strongly recommends that a permanent Inter-State Council, called the Inter-Governmental Council (IGC), should be set up under Article 263. The IGC should investigate and discuss subjects in which all or some or any of the States have a common interest. It should further make recommendations upon any such subject for the better coordination of policy and action regarding that subject.

   The IGC will consist of a General Body assisted by a smaller Standing Committee. The Prime Minister will be the Chairman of the General Body as well as of the Standing Committee.

   The Sarkaria Commission also recommends that the Zonal Councils[13] which were constituted under the State Reorganization

Act, 1956, should be constituted in a fresh manner under Article 263.

10. **Financial Relations and Socio-economic Planning:** To improve the existing financial relations between the Centre and the States, the Sarkaria Commission recommends that the question of raising resources from agricultural source would require an in-depth and comprehensive consideration in the National Economic and Development Council.

    Another important recommendation of the Sarkaria Commission is that by an appropriate amendment of the Constitution, the net proceeds of corporation tax may be made permissibly sharable with the States, if and as the Parliament by law so provides. This would have the advantage of enlarging the base of devolution so that in the revenues of the States, there would be greater stability and 'predictability' in future.

    The Commission also recommends that the surcharge on income tax should not be levied by the Union Government except for a specific purpose and for a strictly limited period only.

    The Commission has made several recommendations for the improvement of the working of the Finance Commission, the Planning Commission and the National Development Council. In its view, the present division of responsibilities between the Finance Commission and the Planning Commission is sound and hence may continue.

    The Commission further emphasizes the need for decentralization of the planning process. It clearly says that since there is a general tendency towards greater centralization of power, there is a special need in a country like India for a conscious and purposive effort to counter it all the time. "Indeed, centralization does not solve but aggravates the problems of the people", comments the Commission in its report.

11. **No Drastic Change in Constitution:** There has been a demand in our country from several quarters that the Constitution should be drastically altered. On this issue, the Sarkaria Commission observes:

    "In our view, it is neither advisable nor necessary to make any drastic changes in the basic character of the Constitution."

"But there is certainly scope for improvement and reform in a number of aspects. The actual working of the Constitution leaves much to be desired."

13.5 PUNCHHI COMMISSION (2007)

The second commission on Centre–State Relations was set up by the Union Government in April 2007 under the chairmanship of Madan

Mohan Punchhi, former Chief Justice of India. It was a 3-member Commission. The Commission made the following recommendations:

1. **Appointment of Governor:** While selecting Governors, the Union Government should adopt the following strict guidelines as recommended in the Report of the Sarkaria Commission and follow its mandates in letter and spirit:
   - (i) He should be eminent in some walk of life.
   - (ii) He should be a person from outside the state.
   - (iii) He should be a detached figure and not too intimately connected with the local politics of the state.
   - (iv) He should be a person who has not taken too great a part in politics generally and particularly in the recent past.
   - (v) Governors should be given a fixed tenure of five years and their removal should not be at the sweet will of the Government at the Centre. The procedure laid down for the impeachment of the Indian President can be made applicable for the impeachment of our Governors as well.
2. **Role of Governor:**
   - (a) The convention of Governors acting as Chancellors of Universities and holding other statutory positions should be done away with. His role should be confined to the constitutional provisions only.
   - (b) On the question of dismissal of a Chief Minister, the Governor should invariably insist on the Chief Minister proving his majority on the floor of the House for which he should prescribe a time limit.
   - (c) The Governor should have the right to sanction for prosecution of a state minister against the advice of the Council of Ministers, if motivated by bias in the face of overwhelming material.
   - (d) Article 163 does not give the Governor a general discretionary power to act against or without the advice of his Council of Ministers.
3. **In Case of Hung Assembly:** On the question of Governor's role in the appointment of Chief Minister in the case of a Hung Assembly, it is necessary to lay down certain clear guidelines to be followed as Constitutional conventions. These are as under:
   - (i) The party or combination of parties which command the widest support in the Legislative Assembly should be called upon to form the Government.
   - (ii) If there is a pre-poll alliance or coalition, it should be treated as one political party and if such coalition obtains a majority, the leader of such coalition shall be called by the Governor to form the Government.

(iii) In case no party or pre-poll coalition has a clear majority, the Governor should select the Chief Minister in the order of preferences indicated here. These are as under:

  (a) The group of parties which had pre-poll alliance commanding the largest number
  (b) The largest single party staking a claim to form the government with the support of others
  (c) A post-electoral coalition with all partners joining the government
  (d) A post-electoral alliance with some parties joining the government and the rest including independents supporting the government from outside.

4. **Legislative:**

  (a) To facilitate effective implementation of the laws on List III subjects, it is necessary that some broad agreement is reached between the Union and states before introducing legislation in Parliament on matters in the Concurrent List.
  (b) The Union should occupy only that many of subjects in concurrent or overlapping jurisdiction which are absolutely necessary to achieve uniformity of policy in national interest.
  (c) The period of six months prescribed in Article 201 for State Legislature to act when the bill is returned by the President can be made applicable for the President also to decide on assenting or withholding assent to a state bill reserved for consideration of the President.
  (d) Parliament should make a law on the subject of Entry 14 of List I (treaty making and implementing it through Parliamentary legislation) to streamline the procedures involved. The exercise of the power obviously cannot be absolute or unchartered in view of the federal structure of legislative and executive powers.
  (e) In respect of bills passed by the Legislative Assembly of a state, the Governor should take the decision with six months whether to grant assent or to reserve it for consideration of the President.

5. **Failure of the Constitutional Machinery:**

  (a) When an external aggression or internal disturbance paralyses the state administration creating a situation of a potential break-down of the Constitutional machinery of the state, all alternative courses available to the Union for discharging its paramount responsibility under Article 355 should be exhausted to contain the situation and the exercise of the power under Article 356 should be limited strictly to rectifying a "failure of the Constitutional machinery in the state".

(b) On the question of invoking Article 356 in case of failure of Constitutional machinery in states, suitable amendments are required to incorporate the guidelines set forth in the land-mark judgement of the Supreme Court in *S.R. Bommai* vs. *Union of India* (1994). This would remove possible misgivings in this regard on the part of states and help in smoothening Centre–State relations.

6. **Emergency Provisions:** Given the strict parameters now set for invoking the emergency provisions under Articles 352 and 356 to be used only as a measure of "last resort", and the duty of the Union to protect states under Article 355, it is necessary to provide a Constitutional or legal framework to deal with situations which require Central intervention but do not warrant invoking the extreme steps under Articles 352 and 356.

7. **Inter State Council:**

   (a) Suitable amendments to Article 263 are required to make the Inter State Council a credible, powerful and fair mechanism for the management of inter-state and Centre-state differences.

   (b) There should be a continuing auditing role for the inter-state Council in the management of matters in concurrent or overlapping jurisdiction.

8. **Zonal Council:** The Zonal Councils should meet at least twice a year with an agenda proposed by states concerned to maximise coordination and promote harmonisation of policies and actions having inter-state ramification. The Secretariat of a strengthened Inter-State Council can function as the Secretariat of the Zonal Councils as well.

9. **Fiscal Matters:**

   (a) The Empowered Committee of Finance Ministers of States proved to be a successful experiment in inter-state co-ordination on fiscal matters. There is a need to institutionalise similar models in other sectors as well. A forum of Chief Ministers, chaired by one of the Chief Ministers by rotation can be similarly thought about particularly to co-ordinate policies of sectors like energy, food, education, environment and health.

   (b) All future Central legislations involving states' involvement should provide for cost sharing as in the case of the RTE Act. Existing Central legislations where the states are entrusted with the responsibility of implementation should be suitably amended providing for sharing of costs by the Central Government.

(c) To bring greater responsibility, all fiscal legislations should provide for an annual assessment by an independent body and the reports of these bodies should be laid in both Houses of Parliament/State Legislature.

10. **All India Services:** New all-India services in sectors like health, education, engineering and judiciary should be created.
11. **Rajya Sabha:** A balance of power between states *inter se* is desirable and possible by equality of representation in the Rajya Sabha. This requires amendment of the relevant provisions to give equality of seats to states in the Rajya Sabha, irrespective of their population size.
12. **Local Bodies:** The scope of devolution of powers to local bodies to act as institutions of self-government should be constitutionally defined through appropriate amendments.
13. **Royalty Issue:** The royalty rates on major minerals should be revised at least every three years without any delay. States should be properly compensated for any delay in the revision of royalty beyond three years.
14. **Tax Issues:** The scope for raising more revenue from the taxes mentioned in Article 268 should be examined afresh. This issue may either be referred to the next Finance Commission or an Expert Committee which is to be appointed to look into the matter.
15. **Finance Commission:** The Finance Commission Division in the Ministry of Finance should be converted into a full-fledged department, serving as the permanent secretariat for the Finance Commissions.
16. **Inter-State Trade and Commerce Commission:** Steps should be taken for the setting up of an Inter-State Trade and Commerce Commission under Article 307. This Commission should be vested with both advisory and executive roles with decision making functions.

The Punchhi Commission made 273 recommendations in its seven-volume Report presented to the Union Government on March 30, 2010.

In general, the Commission, set up in 2007, came to the conclusion that 'cooperative federalism' will be the key for sustaining India's unity, integrity and socio-economic development in future. Thus, the principles of cooperative federalism may have to act as a practical guide for Indian polity and governance.

13.6 CONCLUSION

In the concluding section, we discuss some of the drawbacks of the Administrative Reforms Commission (ARC). ARC is very often compared with the Hoover Commission in the USA (1953–1955) and the Royal Commission on Government Organization in Canada (1960–1963). Both the Commissions focused on the federal government level in their respective countries. The ARC in India surveyed the administrative system at all the vertical levels and its range encompassed a whole host of functional areas. Some observers feel that the scope of the ARC should have been restricted to the federal sphere alone.[14] This probably might be a reason that it gave up its mission midway and left its task incomplete. Out of about 580 recommendations of the ARC, some have not been implemented even more than thirty eight years after they were made. Notwithstanding this procrastination, the value of these recommendations remains undisputed.[15]

Just as in the aftermath of the Second World War the Hoover Commission, appointed in 1953, made a series of recommendations in 1955 to improve the US administrative system, in India also the most comprehensive enquiry, ever undertaken in the aftermath of decolonization, was the ARC that came into being in 1966 under the stewardship of Morarji Desai. Two important ideas seemed to have governed the constitution of the ARC. The first was the changing nature of administration–from a mere law and order maintenance agency to an apparatus responsible for development. This radically altered the traditional conception of administration. The second was the ideological goal of a socialist pattern of society which called for a drastic overhauling of the machinery of government that so far discharged the responsibility in a very stereotyped way. Hence, the ARC was given a wide mandate and was entrusted with the task of "giving consideration to the need for ensuring the highest standard of efficiency and integrity in the public services and for making public administration a fit instrument for carrying out the social and economic goals of development as also one which is responsive to the public."[16]

While pointing out the limitations of the ARC, B.S. Narula observes that there was a virtual absence of any strategy of selecting the key points on the part of the ARC. It paid inadequate attention to improving the administrative capacity of field agencies and to the application of an appropriate information system and the use of modern management tools. ARC ignored the behavioural aspects of administration. It was not futuristic in orientation. It failed to evolve any clear conceptual and comprehensive framework for dealing with problems of development administration.[17] The unplanned winding up of the ARC also left a number of important issues in the lurch. Several subjects, on which the Study Teams and Working Groups had submitted reports, could not be examined by the ARC. This included agricultural administration, relations between the media and the administration, defence, police, medical and health administration, cooperatives, company law administration, developmental policy and regulatory administration, customs and central excise administration, and so on.

Thus, the ARC's untimely dissolution left a noticeable lacuna which has not even been attempted to be filled. The Department of Administrative Reforms, which was asked to complete the unfinished task of the ARC, did not perform the function. Even the final report of the ARC could not be produced in a systematic manner. The damage done to the administrative reforms movement is Stated to be irreparable.

But there are some who love to see the bright side of anything. They have always emphasized the monumental tasks of the ARC. Just like the 1953–1955 Hoover Commission which believed that "the government cannot be any better than the men and women who make it function", the ARC also insisted that "the road to the top must be open to every competent and qualified government servant [and] to higher management in the Secretariat, talent must be drawn from every cadre and class of government servants." Based on this philosophy, the ARC has been successful in articulating its suggestions in four different ways:

1. A rational system needs to be devised for recruitment to policy making positions of personnel possessing the required qualifications and competence.
2. Senior management personnel must be selected from all relevant fields–generalists and specialists–and for this purpose, talent needs to be discovered and developed in all the services.
3. A rational pay structure requires to be introduced so as to truly reflect the actual responsibilities associated with each job finally.
4. To boost morale in the civil service, talented lower rank personnel should be given greater scope than what exists now to move up in the hierarchy on the basis of competence and performance.[18]

No wonder, Prof. Amareshwar Avasthi and Prof. Anand Prakash Avasthi were in favour of the immense contributions made by the ARC. Some of the recommendations of the Commission, as they have concluded, have been accepted by the Government while others are receiving serious attention. There is no doubt that when all the recommendations are fully considered and final decisions are taken, there will be a considerable change in the administrative machinery of the country; and administration will be an instrument for realizing the goals enshrined in the Preamble to our Constitution.[19]

Questions

1. Examine the purposes of major committees and commissions in post-independence India.
2. What were the major areas of Indian administration where the Administrative Reforms Commission (ARC) made its recommendations?

3. Discuss the role played by the Sarkaria Commission.
4. Write short notes on:
   (a) Any two important committees in post-independence India and their recommendations
   (b) Sarkaria Commission
   (c) Any two major recommendations of the ARC.
5. Discuss the major recommendations of the Punchhi Commission (2007).

Notes and References

1. Caiden, Gerald, *Administrative Reforms*, Chicago, Aldine, 1969.
2. *Governance in Transition: Public Management in Reforms in OECD Countries*, OECD, Paris, 1995.
3. Farazmand, Ali, Administrative Reform in Global Perspective: A Symposium, *International Journal of Public Administration*, Vol. 22, No. 6, 1999.
4. Chakrabarty, Bidyut, *Reinventing Public Administration: The Indian Experience*, Orient Longman, New Delhi, 2007.
5. *Balwantray Mehta Committee Report* has been discussed in detail in Chapter 7 of this book.
6. Recommendations of the *ARC Report* will be summarised in Section 13.3.
7. *Asoka Mehta Committee Report* has been discussed in detail in Chapter 7 of this book.
8. *Eighth and Concluding Report of the National Police Commission*, Government of India, May 1981.
9. Recommendations of the *Sarkaria Commission Report* will be discussed in Section 13.4.
10. Bhagwati, J. and T.N. Srinivasan, *Indian Economic Reforms*, Ministry of Finance, Government of India, New Delhi, July 1993; Also see, Bhaduri, Amit and Deepak Nayyar, *The Intelligent Person's Guide to Liberalization*, Penguin, New Delhi, 1996.
11. Gandhi, Rajiv, Responsive Administration, (speech on 18 June, 1988, at Coimbatore), *The Times of India*, 19 June, 1988.
12. Chakrabarty, Bidyut, *op. cit.*
13. Discussion of Zonal Councils has been made in Section 10.6 of Chapter 10.
14. Bhaumik, Dhrubhjyoti, Administrative Reforms in India: A Critique, in Arora, R.K. and S.L. Kaushik (Eds.), *The Universe of Public Administration: Essays in Honour of Professor Sudesh K. Sharma*, Associated, New Delhi, 1994.

15. Arora, Ramesh K. and Rajni Goyal, *Indian Public Administration: Institutions and Issues*, Wishwa Prakashan, New Delhi, 1997.
16. *Administrative Reforms Commission's Report*, Ministry of Home Affairs, New Delhi, 1966–1970.
17. Narula, B.S., Administrative Reforms Commission: Perspectives and Findings, *Indian Journal of Public Administration*, Vol. XVII, 1971.
18. Maheshwari, S.R., *Indian Administration*, Orient Longman, New Delhi, 1999.
19. Avasthi, A. and A.P. Avasthi, *Public Administration in India*, Lakshmi Narain Agarwal, Agra, 2003.

14 Welfare Administration

14.1 MEANING: HISTORICAL BACKGROUND AND CONSTITUTIONAL SUPPORT

A 'Welfare State' is very often distinguished from a 'Law and Order State'. A broad difference between the two is that the first one is concerned more with the general development of the people, particularly that of the backward sections, i.e. the depressed and the disabled groups of the broader society, while the second one is concerned more and more with maintaining the country's internal peace and law and order and also the defence of the country. For India, the concept of welfare State and administration, though seems to have a liberal democratic influence of Great Britain, is not out and out a foreign concept. It is, in fact, an amazing continuity of history. If we look back in the past, it is evident that Indian history is full of the attempts of our ancient and medieval rulers to provide amenities for the welfare of their subjects.

Indian administration has the heritage of Kautilya, Ashoka, Sher Shah, Akbar, and the British colonial administration, the last one having the deepest impact upon Indian administration. The Kautilyan model of welfare administration talked of taking up some public work. Kautilya used to exhort the king to pay attention to the welfare of his subjects. Ashoka's paternalistic attitude is expressed in the remark: *Sabe Munishe Poja Moma* (all men are my children). He regarded the welfare of his subjects as his primary responsibility. He was always in personal contact with his subject to secure greater welfare for them. This partially accounts for his undertaking of extensive tours throughout his empire. His edicts depict that new developments in administration for the well-being of his people were undertaken. In ordering punishment, Ashoka abolished discrimination of caste and position.[1] His administration, ingrained in *Dharma*, could be regarded as a programme of social welfare, which, in the 20th century parlance, is known as 'welfare administration'.[2] In the administrative reforms introduced by Sher Shah and Akbar, there were both regulatory and welfare considerations. Making of roads, planting of trees on both sides of the roads, arrangements for the temporary stay of travellers, arrangements for carrying *dak* (mail) were some examples of the benevolent steps of welfare administration in ancient India.

Yet, it is observed by scholars that with a minor exception of the said rulers in India, the ancient and medieval rulers were, by and large, more concerned with defence of the country and maintaining internal peace and law and order rather than with the welfare of the backward sections of the population.[3]

The birth of the New Deal in the USA, birth and development of the liberal spirit in Britain, emergence of socialism in the (then) Soviet Union, the Great Economic Depression of 1929 and the subsequent recession of the entire thirties of the last century led to a rethinking; and eventually a new concept of welfare State and administration was born. After World War II, even the so-called capitalist countries also began to adopt some special welfare measures. The inevitable result was the birth of socialist and even communist thinking.

Though the nineties of the last century witnessed the death and destruction of communist regimes in Russia and East European States, the concept of a welfare State and administration has still remained alive.

Social security and social welfare are twin concepts that are very intimately related to each other. These twin concepts after combination constitute the broader concept of welfare State and administration. Under social security can be included Employees' State Insurance Scheme, Family Pension, Labour Legislation, Workers' Safety, etc. Under social welfare come more positive schemes for helping the depressed and disabled groups like the Scheduled Castes, Scheduled Tribes, Backward Classes, Minorities, Physically and otherwise Handicapped, Pensioners, Prisoners, and other schemes for Prohibition and Rehabilitation.

Immediately before our independence (1947), the Indian Constituent Assembly met in 1946 for the first time. The ruling Congress party and its leadership was firmly committed to the inauguration of a liberal democratic and welfare State in India. As a result, our new Constitution (1950) categorically speaks of ensuring justice and equality of status and of opportunity to every citizen. The Constitution includes one full chapter on Fundamental Rights and another full chapter on Directive Principles. By the 42nd Constitutional Amendment Act of 1976, the term "socialist" was added to the Preamble of our Constitution, and Directive Principles were made justiciable and mandatory. By the 42nd Amendment in Article 39 of our Constitution, Clause (f) has been added which is as follows: "that the children are given opportunities and facilities to develop in a healthy manner and in condition of freedom and dignity and that childhood and youth are protected against exploitation and against moral and material abandonment". Article 38 mentions: "that the State shall strive to promote the welfare of the people by securing and protecting, as effectively as it may, a social order in which justice, social, economic and political, shall inform all the institutions of the national life."

Our Constitution, influenced by the concept of welfare State and administration, is thus based on the principle of social justice and social equity for all sections of the population. Article 46 requires that the State shall promote with special care the educational and economic interests of the weaker sections of the people in general and the Scheduled Castes (SC) and the Scheduled Tribes (ST) in particular. The rights of the religious and linguistic minorities are also specifically mentioned. The Constitution emphatically provides for the welfare of the women and children. It does not even forget to provide special safeguards for the handicapped and the disabled.

14.2 ADMINISTRATIVE PROVISION

Subsequently, the welfare of the weaker sections of the Indian society was entrusted to a number of Ministries or Departments. In order to provide an integrated thrust to the development and welfare of these sections of our population, a new Ministry of Welfare was constituted on the 25th September, 1985 by integrating the following subjects:

1. Welfare of the SC and ST and socially and economically Backward Classes, Other Backward Classes (OBCs), religious and linguistic minorities earlier dealt with within the Home Ministry.
2. The work relating to the welfare of the disabled and the handicapped, and programmes on social defence connected with the victims of alcoholism, drug addiction, juvenile maladjustments, welfare of the aged, all dealt with earlier by the erstwhile Ministry of Social and Women's Welfare.
3. Matters relating to the administration of welfare.

The Ministry of Welfare is today reorganized into the Department of Welfare and the Department of Women and Child Development. This new Ministry of Welfare is the nodal agency for overall policy planning and coordination of programmes and each Central Ministry and Department is the nodal agency concerning its sector. The Ministry also maintains liaison with the Central Ministries and State Governments.

States and Union Territories at the governmental level have separate departments of their own for the purpose. Administrative provisions for the welfare of the SCs, STs, OBCs and women, however, vary from State to State. In Bihar, Madhya Pradesh and Orissa, separate Ministers have been appointed to look after tribal welfare (Article 164). Some other States have set up committees of members of the State Legislatures on the pattern of the Central Parliamentary Committee. All the States including West Bengal and Tamil Nadu have constituted

Tribal Advisory Councils as per the provision in the Fifth Schedule to advise on matters pertaining to the welfare and advancement of the STs.

It is to be mentioned that the responsibility for implementation of welfare schemes is being shared between the Centre and the States. The Centre is responsible for formulating welfare policies and programmes besides coordinating, guiding and promoting implementation of welfare services by States.

14.3 WELFARE ADMINISTRATION: A CASE STUDY OF A CIVIL SERVANT

The quality of welfare administration depends, to a significant extent, upon the real intention of the civil servant. Thus, Sankaran's model of civil service, basically a product of welfare administration, touched innumerable poor citizens of Nellore in Andhra Pradesh. In the present section, such a model of civil service, viewed as an exceptional style thrown by indigenous culture going beyond the Weberian model of bureaucracy, is sought to be discussed.

S.R. Sankaran, as a civil servant, from the very beginning of his career, rejected the elitist and status-oriented administrative culture. That culture, as inherited by the ICS and eventually the IAS, distanced them from the masses. On the contrary, Sankaran's intentional rejection of this culture and the adoption of his own indigenous culture responded to the poorest of the poor.[4] He enriched every office he occupied and in his three and half decades of administrative service, he was closely associated with the welfare of the poor. Even after his retirement in 1992, he was vigorously involved in addressing the problem of poverty and deprivation in the country and also initiated the formation of the Committee of Concerned Citizens. The Committee of Concerned Citizens (CCC) is an independent group with a self-imposed moral responsibility of establishing an egalitarian social order and enhancing the democratic space. Even after a span of twenty five to thirty years, the beneficiaries still recall the bright memories of Sankaran's pro-poor activities with intense emotions and gratitude. His name has become a household name in Nellore district where Sankaran worked as the Joint Collector (1963) and the District Magistrate (1968–69). The beneficiaries had their deep sense of zeal, respect and affection towards Sankaran's administration. During his tenure in various capacities, Sankaran brought a paradigmatic shift in the administrative work-ethics.

The way Sankaran looked at the administrative system was absolutely unique. When a large number of civil servants entered the service because of its 'pomp and power' providing a comfortable living, good pay and prestige, Sankaran entered the government service as it was identified with service to the people. "The civil service", says Sankaran, "forms an important part of the institution of the State and plays a crucial role in the administration of the country. It was to carry out tasks in terms of the constitutional mandate and the legal framework. A stable body of experienced and competent permanent officials in diverse fields, it constitutes an elite corps, with the vast authority vested in it, to be exercised in public interest for achieving public policy objectives."

He upheld the constitutional obligations to implement various Acts and policies both in letter and spirit, for the amelioration of the deprived sections of the society. Through his pro-poor intervention and pioneering work in designing and delivering anti-poverty programmes, he brought about striking changes in the lives of the poor that came under his ambit. One of the measures initiated by the government soon after Independence was the programme of land reforms. Sankaran motivated the administrative personnel to identify the types of land and involved them in the proper distribution of land. In his approach towards the implementation of land reforms, he was totally uncompromising. Resistance from the landlords was met with police force and Sankaran ensured that it was occupied by the allottee. Whenever the tribals were harassed by the district forest officers, their illegal command was met with a humble response: "This is government land allotted by Sankaraiah (that is how he was called by the local poor), please send him, he will show us the boundaries." Large tracts of land were distributed to the scheduled castes and scheduled tribes in almost all the villages; cultivable lands were not only distributed but irrigated by various means. Wells were dug and bores were sunk. Many pipelines and water supply channels were connected to the fields. Canals were dug, lift irrigation appliances like oil engines and motors were also supplied.

Sankaran also helped the nomadic tribes (Yanadies–Erukula) in shifting their settlements. These settlements were also connected by the roads. Sankaran's model of welfare administration laboured hard on matters of concern like human dignity, accessibility to basic amenities like food, shelter and drinking water. Harijans and Girijans were provided vocational training in driving and mechanics. Loans were given to educated unemployed youths to start some petty trades. Rickshaws were provided to rickshaw pullers to eke out a living, and some students were sent for higher education out of Sankaran's own resources.

Since time immemorial, Harijans and Girijans had been prohibited from entering the Jonnawada Kamakshamma Temple, a very famous temple in Nellore. Sankaran's interference eventually lifted up the taboo and the right to enter the temple was finally ensured. In Sriharikota, Mudalliars used to forbid the entry of Harijans into temples and public places. Sankaran convened 'Harijan Day' and taught them the value of human dignity.

Because of all these welfare oriented administrative endeavours,

Sankaran earned the reputation of being the 'poor man's collector'. Accessibility is one of the remarkable features of Sankaran's model. Hundreds and hundreds of poor people met him every day at the collectorate, his bungalow or at the places of his visit. He encouraged the people who approached him and listened to each one's problem. There were no specific timings or appointments to meet him. One could just walk into his chamber. To the less privileged, he was more of a friend or a relative than a collector. This unusual accessibility enabled him to organize the depressed and the disabled on a mass-scale. This led the political leaders to go along with him to tap this mass base. He, thus, could also involve the political leaders in helping the poor. He was thoroughly brave in the sense transfers and postings (swords in the hands of the politicians to punish the unobliging administrators) did not at all matter to him. His intensive and extensive touring and the personal attention which he paid to solve the problems of the poor, attracted young and old, politicians and officials alike. Above all, his welfare administrations emphasized the uplift of the scheduled castes, scheduled tribes and economically backward sections in the developmental agenda of the nation.

14.4 WELFARE OF SCHEDULED CASTES AND SCHEDULED TRIBES

Our Constitution has prescribed protection for the citizens belonging to scheduled castes and scheduled tribes either specially or by way of insisting on their general rights as citizens. The Constitution tries to protect their educational and economic interests and remove the social disabilities they are subjected to. Successive Five Year Plans have also regarded their progress as a major objective of national policy. There is no doubt about the fact that, on the whole, these sections are, economically speaking the most depressed and backward sections of society. Hence, all general measures to eradicate poverty in our country are bound to affect them most. Socially, too, these sections are most exploited and ill-treated. The people belonging to scheduled castes and tribes are continued to be vulnerable since atrocities are continued to be committed against them in one form or the other. In order to protect them from such atrocities, the Government has enacted the SC and ST (Prevention of Atrocities) Act, 1989. The Act came into force on 30th January, 1990.

14.4.1 Machinery for Safeguards of Such Deprived Sections

The machinery for safeguarding the interests of the deprived sections can be discussed under the following three heads:

1. **Parliamentary Committees:** The Central Government had set up three Parliamentary Committees in 1966, 1971 and 1973,

respectively, to examine the implementation of development programmes for the Scheduled Castes and Scheduled Tribes. Each of these committees has since been constituted as a Standing Committee of the Parliament, the tenure of its members being one year.

2. **National Commission:** By virtue of the Constitution (Sixty-Fifth) Amendment Act, 1990, the Special Officer's post under Article 338 has been substituted by the National Commission for SCs and STs. The Commission consists of a Chairman, a Vice-Chairman and five other members appointed by the President. The National Commission has the power to regulate its own procedure. The Commission has the powers of a Civil Court trying a suit. In brief, the functions of the Commission are:
   - To investigate and monitor all matters relating to the safeguards for the Scheduled castes and scheduled tribes provided by law and to evaluate the working of such safeguards.
   - To enquire into specific complaints regarding the deprivation of rights and safeguards of the Scheduled Castes and Tribes.
   - To participate in and advise on the planning process of socio-economic development of the Scheduled Castes and Tribes and to evaluate the progress of their development.
   - To present to the President annually and otherwise the reports on the working of the safeguards of the Scheduled Castes and Tribes.
   - To perform some other functions relating to the protection, welfare, development and advancement of the Scheduled Castes and Tribes.
   - To be consulted by the Union Government and every State Government on all major policy matters affecting the Scheduled Castes and Tribes.
3. **Voluntary Organizations:** A number of voluntary organizations also promote the welfare and overall progress of these sections of our population. The government provides grants-in-aid to the non-official voluntary organizations.

14.4.2 Centrally Sponsored Schemes

Here, we discuss two principal schemes of such type: reservation of seats in Legislatures and reservation of seats in public services.

Reservation of Seats in Legislatures

Under Articles 350 and 352 of our Constitution, seats are to be reserved for the Scheduled Castes and Tribes in the Lok Sabha and State

Legislatures in proportion to their population. Initially, this provision for reservation was for a period of ten years. But, subsequently, it has been extended through amendments. There is no reservation of seats in the Upper House of the Indian Parliament, i.e. the Rajya Sabha and the Upper House of the State Legislature, i.e. the State Legislative Councils. Out of 543 seats in the Lok Sabha, 79 are reserved for the Scheduled Castes and 41 for the Scheduled Tribes. In the largest (from the point of view of population) State of Uttar Pradesh, out of the total of 425 members in the Legislative Assembly, Scheduled Castes have 92 seats and Scheduled Tribes have only 1 seat. In Madhya Pradesh (the largest State in India from the point of view of area), out of 320 seats in the Legislative Assembly, Scheduled Castes have 44 seats and Scheduled Tribes have as many as 75 seats. The total for all the Indian States is 4047 seats, out of which 2963 seats are general, 557 seats are reserved for Scheduled Castes and 527 seats are reserved fro the Scheduled Tribes.[5]

Reservation of Seats in Public Services

Article 335 provides that the claims of Scheduled Castes and Scheduled Tribes in public services shall be taken into consideration consistent with the maintenance of administrative efficiency. In making appointments to posts and services in connection with the affairs of the Union Government, the State Governments have also framed rules under the powers given to them by item 41 of the State List of the Seventh Schedule for reservation of posts for Scheduled Castes and Tribes and have taken steps to increase their representation in State services. Reservation in State Government services, however, is under the exclusive jurisdiction of State Governments.

In all the educational institutions led by the Union Government or State Governments, some seats are reserved for Scheduled Castes and Tribes.

14.5 WELFARE OF OTHER BACKWARD CLASSES

From time immemorial, the Hindu society in India has been a hierarchical society, divided into innumerable castes organized in a descending order. Our society includes within its ranks millions of people occupying the lowest strata and doing jobs considered to be 'mean' and 'inferior'. These groups have always remained the most exploited and oppressed section of the population and are regarded as "untouchables". Consequently, there have occurred many rebellions against the existing social order leading to the birth of many sects and religions like Jainism, Buddhism, Sikhism, etc. A common feature of all such rebellions has been anti-cesteism. Subsequently, we got such leaders as Mahatma Gandhi, Baba Sabeb Ambedkar who were agitated against such tyranny and exploitation. In the southern part of India, where high caste domination was significantly prominent, a number of movements arose to remedy the situation. One such movement was the "Vaikom Satyagraha" in the then princely State of Travancore in 1924–1925, which aimed at social justice and removal of caste-based discrimination. It was the first struggle in the twentieth century in India which led to the victory for the oppressed sections. The leader of this movement was E.V. Ramaswamy Naicker. Untouchability reached its peak in the twenties of the last century in the then Madras Presidency embracing the present States of Tamil Nadu, Andhra Pradesh, Karnataka and Kerala. As a result, there arose the Justice Party in Madras which launched a movement against such high-caste oppression. It succeeded both in gaining entry into Hindu temples and in reserving high government positions for the non-Brahmins. The movement eventually became a movement against the Brahmins as a caste, Hindi and Sanskrit languages, Ayanism and took shape of an anti-north domination. In due course, the Justice Party first took the form of Dravid Kazgham, then Dravid Munetra Kazgham and, finally, All India Dravid Munetra Kazgham.

From its birth, the Indian National Congress fought for the cause of the depressed sections. The return of M.K. Gandhi from South Africa gave a boost to such causes and he appeared to be the leader in the crusade against untouchability. Our Constitution, as a result, contains provisions against such system. Coming into force on the 26 January, 1950, it, in its Preamble resolves to constitute India into a "sovereign, socialist, secular, democratic republic" and to "secure to all its citizens justice, liberty, equality and fraternity". The Constitution includes a separate Part III on Fundamental Rights guaranteeing to all its citizens right to equality (Articles 14–18)[6] and right against exploitation (Articles 23 and 24) along with some other rights. The Constitution also devotes Part IV (Articles 36–51) to Directive Principles of State Policy. Article 45 specifically mentions that the State shall promote with special care the educational and economic interests of the weaker sections of the people. The same Article also puts stress on free and compulsory education for all children up to the age of 14 years. The Constitution goes further to make some special provisions for the weaker sections of society (Article 46).

In the Hindu society in India, just above the so-called "untouchable" castes, come various socially and educationally backward castes. These castes have been aptly described as the intermediate "castes" by M.N. Srinivas. *Yadavas* and *Kurmis* belong to these castes in Bihar and Uttar Pradesh. These are prosperous agricultural castes and by no means can be described as economically weak. But these castes are undoubtedly weak from the point of view of education and, hence, social status. With the passage of time, these castes have come up the social caste hierarchy and are forming the present-day ruling class. This is particularly true of the Yadavas.

These castes in India have been pressurizing the Union Government for quite some time for reservation in public services. Our Constitution has indirectly agreed to this demand and has added Clause (4) to Article 16 which provides for equality of opportunity in public employment. Clause (4) provides, "Nothing in this Article shall prevent the State from making any provision for the reservation of appointments and posts in favour of any backward classes of citizens which, in the opinion of the State, is not adequately represented in the services of the State." These castes have also demanded protection under Article 46 which promises promotional, educational and economic interests of the weaker sections of the population.

Besides reservation in public services, these castes have also demanded reservation in technical and educational institutions run by the Union and/or State Governments. Incidentally, many State Governments have announced such steps. The Janata Government, during its short tenure, appointed a Commission under the chairmanship of B.P. Mandal, a leader from Bihar. The Mandal Commission submitted its report to the Congress Government. But the Congress Party delayed with the report for nearly a decade and did nothing to implement the Commission's recommendations. All of a sudden, the Janata Government under the Prime Ministership of Mr. V.P. Singh announced in August 1990 the implementation of the major recommendations of the Mandal Commission to reserve 27 per cent to 49.5 per cent of all posts in Central Government and Public Sector Undertakings for all the backward classes (including Schedules Castes, Scheduled Tribes and Other Backward Classes) in India. This decision was resisted by the affected (belonging to general castes) castes, leading to 'gheraos', 'pitaos', violence and riots. This violence stopped only after the Supreme Court had given a stay order prohibiting the implementation of the government notification and resignation of the V.P. Singh Ministry. After it, the minority government of Chandra Shekhar was formed which remained in power only for a few months. Then the President dissolved the Lok Sabha and announced for fresh elections.

In the ensuing elections, both the Janata Dal and the Samajwadi Janata Party lost in spite of their loud fight for the cause of the so-called backward and weaker sections. V.P. Singh's slogan of "social equity" and the massive Mandal Ratha Yatra through the areas populated by the backward classes in Bihar and UP, led by Sharad Yadav, a prominent leader of the Janata Dal, went in vain. Their cry for social justice for the backward classes did not attract the general public and eventually alienated them significantly from the people belonging to the general castes. It appears that Mandalization failed to remain the main demand of both the Janata Dal and the Samajwadi Janata Party.

14.6 WELFARE OF WOMEN

The erstwhile Ministry of Social and Women's Welfare became the Department of Women and Child Development since April, 1990. It was shifted to the Ministry of Welfare as a full-fledged Department. The Women's Development Bureau of this Department is responsible for the welfare and development of women in our country. Its activities extend to the formulation of policies, plans and programmes, enacting and implementing legislation relating to the overall progress of women and implementing certain welfare and development programmes for women.

There are three main areas where some of the important achievements have been identified regarding women's development and welfare:

1. Legislative measures for women's welfare
2. Activities of the Central Social Welfare Board
3. Other important women's welfare programmes by some other organizations.

Legislative measures for women's welfare

A number of laws were enacted or amended to ameliorate women's conditions such as Immoral Traffic (Prevention) Act, 1956 (the original Suppression of Women and Girls Act, 1956 was amended in 1978 and again in 1986); the Dowry Prohibition Act, 1961, as amended in 1984; the Indecent Representation of Women (Prohibition) Act, 1986 seeking to prevent indecent display of women through advertisements, books, posters, etc.; the Commission of Sati (Prevention) Act, 1987; and amendments to various criminal laws to make penal provisions against the offence of rape and other such crimes against women more stringent and also to make a new provision in the Indian Penal Code to make cruelty against women by husband and other relations punishable.

Activities of the Central Social Welfare Board

The Central Social Welfare Board is basically a company under the Indian Companies Act, 1956. It has evolved various programmes in the area of welfare of women, children and the handicapped by harnessing the services of hundreds of voluntary agencies. The Department of Women and Child Development gives financial assistance to the Board for its multi-faceted programme, which provides financial assistance to many voluntary organizations for rendering welfare services, particularly to women.

Besides, the Central Social Welfare Board encompasses activities like field counselling and inspection, evaluation and statistics, construction of housing complexes and quarters for the staff, strengthening of the State Social Welfare Advisory Boards, etc. The Board implements its socio-economic programmes with a view to providing needy women, including the economically backward, the destitute, the widowed, the deserted, etc. with opportunities for work and wages. Financial assistance is also given to voluntary organizations to take up a wide variety of income generating activities by the target group of needy women.

Other important women's welfare programmes by some other organizations

Some important Women's Welfare Organizations like Women's Development Corporation, Hostels for Working Women, Employment-cum-Income Generating Production Units, Training Centres for Rehabilitation, Short-Stay Homes, etc. were set up to bring about women's welfare. A National Commission for Women was also set up to ensure due representation of women in all spheres, to check discrimination against women and to take proper actions according to their grievances. The National Commission for Women Act, 1990 has become a part of the statute book. Its main task is to study and monitor all matters relating to the Constitution and legal safeguards provided for women. It also looks into the complaints and takes actions on the cases involving women's deprivation of rights.

14.6.1 Welfare of Rural Women

In December 1992, the Parliament of India passed a new amendment to the Indian Constitution in order to revive and revitalize the Panchayati Raj—the rural local self- government in India. This 73rd amendment gave a constitutional mandate for democratically elected panchayats at the village, block and district levels in the whole country with provisions (a) for their regular elections, powers, resources and (b) for representation of the hitherto socially and politically marginalized sections of the Scheduled Castes, Scheduled Tribes and women. It has thus become a watershed in deepening democracy and evolution of a third tier of constitutionally guaranteed stratum of government. Nirmala Buch in her study of women in panchayats after the amendment in 1992 (Buch: 1999) mandating a minimum one-third representation to women in all panchayats in the country had found that rural women had a remarkable extent of representation in all the tiers of panchayats. Her study captures the impact of rural women's participation in decision-making at the grass-roots level government in the three northern States of Madhya Pradesh, Rajasthan and Uttar Pradesh.

Some basic myths about women's participation in panchayats have been identified by Buch. These are as under:

- Women's passivity and disinterest in political institutions ——— i.e. they have contested elections not on their own initiative, but being forced by outsiders.
- Only the well-to-do, upper strata women will come through reservations.
- Representing women have significant political connectivity ——— i.e. only privileged relatives of powerful politicians will enter these institutions to keep the seats for them.

- Women who have entered the panchayats as a result of 33 per cent reservation are only proxy and namesake members, who do not actively participate in the panchayat activities.

The study by Buch (1999) questioned these myths and explored the experience of women in these three most difficult Indian States–Madhya Pradesh, Rajasthan and Uttar Pradesh–in terms of grass roots democracy and gender. These three States together account for 31 per cent of India's rural population. These States also account for one-third of India's population living below the poverty line. These three States are low on indicators of human development as well as of gender. Three districts were selected in each State giving regional representation along with variations of literacy, socio-economic development and population profile, including those of weaker sections. Similarly, in each district four blocks were selected and in each block, five gram panchayats were selected for the study area, with a purposive selection of panchayats with women chairpersons. Finally, a sample of 1199 respondents were selected for interview, which included elected representatives of village level panchayats, district level panchayats and intermediate or block level panchayats including chairpersons and members. These included 843 women, 176 men, besides 180 members of the village community.

Their data explored the myths and brought out the emerging leadership of rural women in the new political space created for them by the constitutional amendment. They have found that the panchayat elections shattered the first myth of women's passivity in politics. It was clear from their study that women contested elections sometimes on their own initiative, but mostly on the initiative of their family members. The constitutional amendment, by making it mandatory for one-third positions to be contested only by women, gave a legitimacy and respect leading to the emergence of families motivating women to contest, taking the new position as a point of entry for the entire family and not only for the individual woman. 95 per cent women in these three States had contested panchayat elections for the first time against only 69 per cent in the case of their male counterpart.

The study also explored the basis of the second myth and found that their socio-economic profile had indicated the entry of a large number of women from families without any land or from families of small landholders who had low assets holding and whose family incomes were also quite low.

The third myth that only the female relatives of the privileged have entered panchayats is also not borne out if we look at the previous political experience and political affiliations of women representatives' family members in the affinal and natal families. Only 3.7 per cent and 6.2 per cent elected women had family members on the natal and affinal family side who had any previous experience in panchayats. Majority of women were first time entrants in panchayats as well as in similar institutions.

The fourth myth was that women member had lack of awareness and knowledge about panchayat related matters. The study explored that aspect and looked at their knowledge about reservations, panchayat's powers and responsibilities, panchayat meetings, attendance of elected representatives, resources of panchayats, their views about raising resources and also about the level of success of development schemes. It has clearly been evident from the study of Buch that a majority of women have good awareness level about panchayat related matters.

Expectedly, the chairpersons have higher level of awareness and knowledge than the ordinary members.

14.7 PROGRAMMES UNDERTAKEN RECENTLY FOR THE WELFARE OF SCs/STs/OBCs AND WOMEN

14.7.1 Welfare of SC/ST/OBCs

SC/ST Cell

In accordance with the policy of the Government of India, an SC/ST cell is functioning in the Department of Commerce. A Liaison Officer is nominated in the Department and in each of the organizations under the Department. So far as services and posts in the Department and organizations under its administrative control are concerned, one of the posts has been exempted from the purview of the reservation orders. The Liaison Officer examines and rectifies, whether necessary, the roster maintained by the various organizations for ensuring representation to SC/ST/OBCs. The Liaison Officer also provides relevant guidelines of the officers in the Department of Commerce, its attached and subordinate officers and the Public Sector Undertakings, in accordance with the instructions issued by the Department of Personnel and Training (DOP&T) from time to time. The Cell is also looking after the work regarding the implementation of the Government Orders in respect of 27 per cent reservation in direct recruitment.

A statement showing total number of government employees and the number of SC/ST/OBCs as on 31-12-2006 in the Department of Commerce, its subordinate offices, Public Sector Undertakings, semi-autonomous bodies, etc. is attached at Appendix-III.

The Commodity Boards under the administrative control of the Department of Commerce have certain specific schemes under special tribal plans, which are operated with a view to supplementing the efforts of the government in improving the socio-economic conditions of the SC/ST in the non-traditional areas. The welfare activities undertaken by different organizations attached to this department are given below:

1. **Rubber board:** The various schemes operated/activities undertaken by the Rubber Board for the welfare of SC/ST category of growers during the year 2006–2007 include:

- An amount of Rs. 7.35 lakh was disbursed to 94 SC/ST tappers employed in the unorganized sectors under the housing and sanitary assistance scheme.
- Cash assistance of Rs. 35.75 lakh was disbursed to 1507 beneficiaries under Rubber Plantation Development Scheme. A total amount of Rs. 11.84 lakh was disbursed to 460 beneficiaries as reimbursement of cost for high yielding planting material.
- Assistance of Rs. 4.98 lakh was provided to 349 beneficiaries for boundary protection fencing material for rubber plantation.
- 466 persons were given free training in rubber cultivation, tapping, processing and manufacturing.
- Total area of 14.79 hectares was planted for the benefit of tribal communities in traditional area.

2. **Projects and Equipment Corporation (PEC) Limited**
   - There is a welfare scheme in PEC under which merit scholarship is given to the wards of the employees securing certain percentage of marks in the annual examination. In the case of the wards of SC/ST employees, the merit scholarship is given with relaxed standard.
   - There exists a Time Scale Promotion Scheme for staff cadre. Qualifying period for promotion for employees belonging to SC and ST categories is relaxed by one year in each stage of promotion.
3. **State Trading Corporation (STC) of India Limited**
   - One-year relaxation is given to SC/ST employees in the qualifying period of service at each stage of promotion under the Time Bound Promotion Policy in the unionized cadres.
   - A relaxation of 5 per cent in marks is allowed to the wards of SC/ST employees while considering the grant of merit scholarship.
   - Reservation for SC/ST employees is kept in allotment of residential apartments maintained by the Corporation at New Delhi.
   - Nomination of SC/ST employees to various training programmes (including awareness programmes) held both in-house and outside.
4. **India Trade Promotion Organisation (ITPO):** In every Departmental Promotion/Selection Committee meeting, an officer of the appropriate level belonging to SC/ST category is being associated to look after the interest of SCs/STs.
5. **Agricultural and Processed Food Products Export Development Authority (APEDA):** Training programmes are conducted for SC/ST personnel in India and abroad.

6. **Indian Institute of Foreign Trade (IIFT):** During the year 2006-07, all the three faculty members belonging to OBC category were nominated to participate in seminars/workshops to upgrade their knowledge. Three SC/ST employees on administrative side were also nominated to attend English/Hindi shorthand classes, as also training programmes organized by DOPT.
7. **Export Credit Guarantee Corporation (ECGC) of India Limited:** Housing loan, residential accommodation and financial assistance for higher studies are provided to SC/ST/OBC employees.
8. **Minerals and Metals Trading Corporation (MMTC) Limited**
    - Training in various functional areas of work was imparted to 1226 employees out of whom 240 employees belonged to SC/ST categories. In-house training programme was organized on "Reservation for SC/ST/OBC Categories in Employment" for the benefit of Liaison Officers, SC/ST Cell members, Office Bearers of the SC/ST Associations with the help of external faculty.
    - Under the MMTC Employees' Welfare Scheme, a relaxation of 5 per cent in marks is allowed to the wards of SC/ST employees while considering grant of merit scholarships. There is a provision for reservation in the allotment of residential quarters to SC/ST employees.

14.7.2 Welfare of Women

Women Cell

An independent 'Women Cell' has been set up in the Department of Commerce with the following broad functions:

- Prevention and redressal of sexual harassment at workplace, constitution of Complaints Committee in the Department of Commerce, its attached and subordinate offices, PSUs, autonomous bodies, etc. monitoring their performance and providing necessary help and guidance.
- Coordination with the Department of Women and Child Development, National Commission for Women and other concerned agencies in respect of the matters connected with the welfare and economic empowerment of women and other related issues.
- Review of plan schemes and other programmes of the Department of Commerce to ensure that various aspects of women welfare, development and empowerment are promoted through the programmes and schemes of the Department.

- Preparation of Action plan pertaining to the Department of Commerce for the overall development of women in line with the National Policy for empowerment of women.
- Other incidental matters pertaining to the subject.

The Women Cell actively participated in the various workshops/ seminars on gender issues organized by National Commission for Women. During the year 2006, no complaint of sexual harassment at workplace was received.

Women in Public Sector (WIPS)

The Women In Public Sector (WIPS) activities within the MMTC aim at networking, experience sharing, interacting with various organizations and other PSUs and women bodies like National Commission, Women and Child Development Ministry, ILO, DPE, NGOs and other such institutes, etc. seeking to enhance women's role at the workplace. Women employees from different organizations participate in the regional meet and national meet for discussions on the various developments. A Committee headed by a senior female officer of the rank of CGM, duly assisted by two other senior female officers of GM and DGM level, is in force at Corporate Office to handle grievances and cases of sexual harassment of women at workplace. Similar committees are functioning at various regional offices also.

14.8 ARGUMENT FOR PRIVATE SECTOR RESERVATION

India has made explicit use of multiple remedies against discrimination (in the form of legal measures and reservation policy) in employment, education, and political and civil spheres. But this policy of 'reservation' remained confined to a tiny government and public sector only, and the vast private sector (comprising agriculture, industry and service sectors), in which more than 90 per cent of SC and ST are employed, remained outside the purview of the reservation policy. In other countries such a policy has either to begin with or been started already both for public and private sectors.

In social science literature, the concept of social exclusion is defined as "the process through which individuals belonging to some groups are wholly or partially excluded from full participation in the society in which they live" (Arjan De Hann, 1997). Hann argued that this definition focuses on the process responsible for deprivation, in relation to the means that exist within a society.

Amartya Sen draws attention to the various meanings and manifestations of the concept of social exclusion (Sen, 2000). Among them, Sen draws distinction between the situations where some people are being kept out (or at least left out) and where some people are being included (may even be forced to be included) in deeply unfavourable terms, and described the two situations as "unfavourable exclusion" and "unfavourable inclusion". The "unfavourable inclusion," with unequal treatment, may carry the same adverse effects as "unfavourable exclusion."

Sukhadeo Thorat presents some empirical evidences on the continuing discrimination at present in economic and social spheres. His focus is particularly on market discrimination. From the massive literature on the practice of discrimination and untouchability, he has picked the study by Action Aid conducted in 2000–2001 in about 550 villages from eleven States of India.

The study reveals that the discrimination in labour markets operates through exclusion in hiring and lower wages. In about 36 per cent of the villages, the SCs were denied casual employment in agriculture. In about 25 per cent of the villages, the SCs faced discrimination in terms of wage payments. In about one-third of the villages, the SCs were excluded from employment in construction of houses.

In the case of other markets as well, the study observes discriminatory treatment upon SCs in access to irrigation water as well as public and private services. In little more than one-third of the villages, the SCs were denied access to irrigation water for agriculture. In the case of access to common property resources like grazing land, fishing pond and the like, the SCs faced exclusion in about one-fifth of the sample villages (about 21per cent).

In 35 per cent of the villages, the SCs were not allowed to sell any kind of goods at village level markets, wherein the identity of the SC person was known. In about 47 per cent of the villages, the SCs were not allowed to sell milk to village cooperatives and private buyers.

Similar to India, one also finds a number of remedies against discrimination have been used in different countries like the USA, Northern Ireland, South Africa and Malaysia, to provide legal and other safeguards against market and non-market discrimination and to correct the imbalances in access to resources, employment, education, etc. But it will be too simplistic to put the remedies used in these countries in uniform pattern.

There are some possible consequences of the methods used in ensuring fair access to employment to discriminated groups. It is argued that relaxations in qualifications for appointment may supposedly hamper the productivity of firms. But according to the propounders of reservation like Thorat, this argument has less support in economic theory and in empirical literature on discrimination. The fallacy of the argument becomes evident considering the fact that recruitment in public sector under reservation in India and elsewhere is based on the required qualification, and that the norms of appointment and those of qualification are not relaxed. Therefore, as Thorat argues, the question of compromising productive efficiency does not arise. Some firms take necessary steps in the initial stages of recruitment through proper screening, orientation and also through mid-service training of minority employees. But that apart, there are no studies whatsoever on the relative work efficiency of those recruited with reservation and without in India. Similarly, there is no evidence elsewhere in the world.

14.9 CRITICISM OF RESERVATION

But there are some strong critics[7] who believe that the really backward sections of our community can gain nothing from the reservation in the educational sphere. A study was conducted by the National Sample Survey in 1999–2000 regarding the educational attainment in India. From that study, it is evident that in the rural and urban sectors of India less than 4 per cent SCs, almost 5.5 per cent STs and a little more than 6.5 per cent OBCs have passed the Higher Secondary Examination. Now, in order to have an access to higher education, only 5 per cent–6 per cent of the backward sections are benefitted. The 'advantages' of reservation cannot even reach the vast 94 per cent–95 per cent of the cursed sections. As a result, 22.5 per cent to 49.5 per cent seats reserved for the SCs, STs and OBCs are likely to remain vacant for the most part. NSS study shows that only 7 per cent SCs and 3.5 per cent STs can have the opportunity to get admitted to the IITs. In fact, only the creamy layer of the SCs, STs and OBCs can have access to higher education and only to that layer the benefits of reservation are available. Hence, the primary task of our government is to extend and expand education thoroughly at the primary, secondary and higher secondary levels if it is really concerned with the welfare of the 'backward classes' in the truest sense of the term.

14.10 CITIZEN AND SOCIAL WELFARE

From time to time since independence till recent years various useful schemes related to the social welfare of the vulnerable sections of our citizens have been made and dealt with by a number of Ministries of the Government of India. Such schemes are principally of three types: (a) National Schemes, (b) State-specific schemes, and (c) Schemes in joint collaboration between the Centre and the State/States. The schemes are as under:

Sl. No.	*Schemes*	*Year of Launching*	*Sectors*
1.	Atal Pension Yojana	2015	Pension
2.	Bachat Lamp Yojana	2009	Electrification
3.	Central Government Health Scheme	1954	Health
4.	Deendayal Disabled Rehabilitation Scheme	2003	Social Justice

Sl. No.	Schemes	Year of Launching	Sectors
5.	Deen Dayal Upadhyay Gram Jyoti Yojana	2015	Rural Power Supply
6.	Deen Dayal Upadhyay Grameen Kaushalya Yojana	2015	Rural Development
7.	Digital India Programme	2015	Digitally Empowered Nation (Technology)
8.	Grameen Bhandaran Yojana	2007	Agriculture
9.	Pradhan Mantri Grameen Awaas Yojana	1985	Housing (Rural)
10.	Indira Gandhi Matritva Sahyog Yojana	2010	Mother Care
11.	Integrated Child Development Services	1975	Child Development
12.	Integrated Rural Development Programme	1978	Rural Development
13.	Janani Suraksha Yojana	2005	Mother Care
14.	Jawaharlal Nehru National Urban Renewal Mission (JNNURM)	2005	Urban Development
15.	Kasturba Gandhi Balika Vidyalaya	2004	Education
16.	INSPIRE Programme	2008	Science and Technology
17.	Kishore Vaigyanik Protsahan Yojana	1999	Science and Technology
18.	Livestock Insurance Scheme	2005 (pilot basis) and 2008 (regular basis)	Education
19.	Mahatma Gandhi National Rural Employment Guarantee Act	2006	Rural Wage Employment
20.	Members of Parliament Local Area Development Scheme	1993	Statistics and Programme Implementation
21.	Midday Meal Scheme	1995	Health, Education
22.	Namami Gange Programme	1995	Clean and Protect Ganga River
23.	Nation Literacy Mission Programme	1988	Education
24.	National Pension Scheme	2004	Pension
25.	National Scheme on Welfare of Fishermen	1991	Agriculture

Sl. No.	*Schemes*	*Year of Launching*	*Sectors*
26.	National Service Scheme	1969	Personality Development through Social Service
27.	National Social Assistance Scheme	1995	Pension
28.	Pooled Finance Development Fund Scheme	2006	Finance
29.	Pradhan Mantri Adarsh Gram Yojana	2010	Model Village
30.	Pradhan Mantri Kaushal Vikas Yojana	2015	Skill Development Initiative Scheme
31.	Pradhan Mantri Suraksha Bima Yojana	2015	Insurance
32.	Pradhan Mantri Jeevan Jyoti Bima Yojana	2015	Insurance
33.	Pradhan Mantri Jan Dhan Yojana	2014	Financial Inclusion
34.	Pradhan Mantri Gram Sadak Yojana	2000	Rural Development
35.	Rajiv Awas Yojana	2013	Urban Housing
36.	Rajiv Gandhi Grameen Vidyutikaran Yojana	2005	Rural Electrification
37.	Rashtriya Krishi Vikas Yojana	2007	Agriculture
38.	Rashtriya Swasthya Bima Yojana	2008	Insurance
39.	RNTCP (Revised National Tuberculosis Control Programme)	1997	Health
40.	Rajiv Gandhi Scheme for Empowerment of Adolescent Boys	2014	Skill Development
41.	Sabla or Rajiv Gandhi Scheme for Empowerment of Adolescent Girls	2011	Skill Development
42.	Sampoorna Grameen Rozgar Yojana	2001	Rural Self Employment
43.	Swabhiman	2011	Financial Inclusion
44.	Swarnajayanti Gram Swarozgar Yojana	1999	Rural Employment
45.	Swavalamban	2010	Pension
46.	Udisha	1999	Child Care
47.	Voluntary Disclosure of Income Scheme	1997 (closed in 1998)	Income Tax
48.	National Rural Livelihood Mission	2011	Rural Development

Sl. No.	Schemes	Year of Launching	Sectors
49.	National Urban Livelihood Mission	2013	Urban Planning
50.	HRIDAY—Heritage City Development and Augmentation Yojana	2015	Urban Development
51.	Sukanya Samridhi Yojana (Girl Child Prosperity Scheme)	2015	Child Welfare
52.	Smart Cities Mission	2015	Urban Development
53.	AMRUT	2015	Urban Development
54.	Pradhan Mantri Awas Yojana (PMAY)	2015	Housing
55.	National Child Labour Projects (NCLP)	1987	Labour and Employment
56.	National Career Service	2015	Employment
57.	Antyodaya Anna Yojana	2000	Public Distribution
58.	Pradhan Mantri Kaushal Vikas Yojana	2015	Skill Development
59.	National Food Security Mission	2007 (for 5 years)	Agriculture
60.	Pradhan Mantri Ujjwala Yojana	2016	Poverty Alleviation

In spite of such schemes launched in order to do good to our citizens, critics opine that people have not sufficiently been benefitted by them. In 2015 Anumeha Yadav in her article questioned the utility of such welfare schemes and Acts.[8] She has clearly pointed out that in spite of the existence of Article 41 and Article 42 to our Constitution, which ask the State to make effective provision for securing the right to work, education and public assistance in cases of unemployment, old age, sickness and disability and in other cases of undeserved want (Article 41) and also to make provisions for securing just and humane conditions of work and for maternity benefits (Article 42), India "does not yet explicitly recognize a national minimum social security cover. In recent years, with an intervention by the Supreme Court in the Right to Food case, the government has moved forward to providing nutrition and employment support with a legal guarantee through the MGNREGA."

Prof. Amartya Sen and Prof. Jean Dreze distinguish between two aspects of social security, namely "protection" and "promotion". "Protection" means preservation against a fall in living conditions through ill-health, accidents etc. On the other hand, "promotion" implies improvement of living conditions, helping everyone overcome consistent and continuous deprivation of capabilities. In India, unfortunately only a fraction of citizens enjoy any "protection" at all and provisions aimed at "promotion" are also being threatened with continuous fund shrinking.

In 2004 the UPA government appointed the National Commission for Enterprises in the Unorganised Sector (NCEUS) to look into the livelihood conditions and social security for workers in the unorganised sector. The NCEUS found that 79 per cent of workers in that sector lived on an income of less than ₹20 a day. It made quite clear that the gains of growth were bypassing the majority of the working class. India under the NDA also fails to protect and promote bulk of its population. It spends only 1.4 per cent of its GDP on social protection, among the lowest in Asia, far lower than China, Sri Lanka, Thailand, and even Nepal. The present government has not yet been able to indicate any support to the idea of legally guaranteed social protection for all workers. The question which haunts us is: Can the issuing of smart cards to the unorganised sector workers really uplift their socio-economic conditions and benefit them in the truest sense of the term? Under such circumstances, we shall make an attempt to examine such social welfare schemes as MGNREGA, SSA and NRHM, respectively

14.10.1 Mahatma Gandhi National Rural Employment Guarantee Act (MGNREGA)

To alleviate poverty in the rural areas of our Country, employment should be guaranteed to the ruralites. National Rural Employment Guarantee Act (NREGA), later renamed as the Mahatma Gandhi National Rural Employment Guarantee Act (MGNREGA), is an Indian labour law and a potent measure of social security, aiming to guarantee the right to work to the Indian ruralites. The goal of this Act is to increase livelihood security in rural areas of India by providing a minimum 100 days of wage employment in a financial year to every rural family whose adult members volunteer to do unskilled physical work. Employment is to be provided within 5 km of an applicant's residence. Minimum wages are to be paid to the worker. If work is not provided within a period of 15 days of application, the applicants are entitled to an unemployment allowance. Hence, employment under MGNREGA is a legal entitlement.

Another very significant aim of MGNREGA is to create durable assets (such as roads, canals, ponds, wells etc.).

Protection of the environment, empowerment of rural womenfolk, reduction of rural to urban migration and strengthening socio-economic equality are four more important goals of MGNREGA.

The ninth Prime Minister of India, P.V. Narasimha Rao initially proposed this Act for the first time in 1991. Finally, after a long gap of 15 years, our Parliament accepted the Act in 2006 and it started to be implemented in 200 districts of India. Later, from April 1, 2008, MGNREGA aimed to cover all the Indian districts. The Government of India describes the Act as "the largest and the most ambitious social security and public works programme in the world." The World Bank has termed the statute in 1914 as a "steller example of rural development."

In MGNREGA contractors' involvement is totally banned. The scheme is to be implemented mainly by Gram Panchayats. Labour-intensive tasks such as creating infrastructure for water harvesting, drought relief and flood control are preferred.

Quite a few safeguards to promote the effective management and fruitful implementation of MGNREGA are provided by the law. The Act clearly mentions the principles of and agencies for implementation, the list of allowed works, the financing pattern, monitoring and evaluation and also the detailed measures to ensure and guarantee transparency and accountability.

There have been a long list of predecessors of MGNREGA, including Rural Manpower Programme, Crash Scheme for Rural Employment, Pilot Intensive Rural Employment Programme, Drought Prone Area Programme, Marginal Farmers and Agricultural Labourers Scheme, Food for Work Programme, National Rural Employment Programme, Rural Landless Employment Guarantee Programme, etc. The total government allocation to such predecessors of MGNREGA had been about three quarters of ₹1 trillion.

The UPA Government had planned to increase the number of guaranteed working days from 100 to 150 before the 2014 Lok Sabha Elections of India, but in vain.

The NDA Government has decided to provide 150 days of working to the ruralites living in rain-hit areas.

MGNREGA lists the following works as permissible:

- Water conservation
- Water harvesting
- Drought proofing including afforestation
- Irrigation works
- Restoration of traditional water bodies
- Land development
- Flood control
- Rural connectivity
- Other works notified by the Government

The provision of accredited engineers needed to implement the Act, worksite facilities and a weekly report on worksites are all mandated by the Act. Besides, in the MGNREGA there is a minimum limit to the wages either on a time-rate basis or on a piece-rate basis. Honoring gender equality, wages are to be paid. MGNREGA stipulates Gram Panchayats to have a single bank account for NREGA works which will be subjected to public scrutiny. The Act mandates 'monthly squaring of accounts' to promote transparency. To establish public vigilance, the MGNREGA designates 'social audits' as key to its implementation.

The most detailed part of MGNREGA (as stated in Chapters 10 and 11) deals with transparency and accountability. Here, the role of the state, the public vigilance and the social audits are all laid out. MGNREGA requires the following for a correct evaluation of outcomes:

- Management of data
- Maintenance of records
- Maintenance of employment registers
- Maintenance of job cards, assets etc.

All the above-mentioned data and records are maintained by the implementing agencies at the village, block and district levels.

The law allows convergence of MGNREGA with other programmes. As MGNREGA intends to create 'additional' employment, such convergence should not affect employment provided by other programmes.

There have been quite a few studies on some of the aspects of MGNREGA. These aspects are as under:

- Improvement of the economic conditions of labourers
- Potential for women's empowerment
- Asset creation
- Environmental effects
- Corruption related to the scheme
- Link between electoral gains and implementation of MGNREGA

Researchers have attempted to study *whether and to what extent the economic conditions of the labourers have been improved as a result of the implementation of MGNREGA*. Particularly they have seen whether the bargaining power of labourers has improved or not. Several studies have concluded that agricultural wages have increased remarkably, especially for women, since the introduction of the scheme. Some more extensive researches highlight that the principal benefit of the scheme lies in the reduction of wage volatility. Such studies view that MGNREGA may be an effective insurance scheme. Overall welfare effects of the scheme have been sought to be evaluated by some researchers. Some others try to understand specifically whether the scheme has reduced rural to urban migration of labourers searching for casual work.

A second group of researchers are more interested in studying the *potentiality of the scheme for women's empowerment*. They have identified three very important provisions for women in MGNREGA. They are as follows:

- One-third of all employment related to the Act is reserved for women only.
- There is a significant provision for equal wages for men and women in the Act. This would eradicate gender disparity to a great extent.

- In MGNREGA there is a provision for child care facilities at the worksite.

Some more recent studies have concluded that women's participation has become higher as a result of the inception of the scheme, though the figure varies from one state to another.

A third group of researchers have attempted to analyse the *potential for asset creation under the MGNREGA.* But there have not been too many detailed studies on it so far. The researchers have made some common conclusions:

(a) The potential for asset creation under the scheme is substantial.
(b) In some places of India it is being realised.
(c) Lack of staff, particularly technical staff, rather than lack of material is the primary cause for poor realisation of this potential.

A fourth group of researchers are interested in studying the *environmental effects related to the introduction of MGNREGA.* Some of them have pointed out that water harvesting and soil conservation works promoted to MGNREGA could have higher positive results on environmental security and biodiversity and the conservation of the environment. Some researchers of the Indian Institute of Science have conducted a study where they have tried to quantify and measure the environmental and socio-economic benefits of works done through MGNREGA.

A fifth group of researchers are concerned with the *aspect of corruption related to MGNREGA.* Studies reveal that wage corruption in MGNREGA has declined from about 50 per cent in 2007–08 to between 4–30 per cent in 2009–10. Much of this improvement, as the researchers have found, is due to the fact that MGNREGA wages are paid through bank and post office accounts. Some of the success in battling corruption can also be attributed to the strong existence of community monitoring.

A sixth group of researchers focus on the *link between electoral gains and the implementation of MGNREGA.* They find that politics may influence programme expenditure in some places of India. Such studies have been made in Andhra Pradesh, West Bengal and Rajasthan. Some local studies are still being conducted to see the impacts of MGNREGA.

The principal quantitative achievements of MGNREGA, as identified by the Congress Minister of Rural Development, Mr. Jairam Ramesh, are as under:

- Since its inception in 2006, around ₹110,000 crore has gone directly as wage payment to rural households. 1200 crore person-days of employment has been generated. On an average, 5 crore households have been provided employment every year since 2008.

- 80 per cent of households are being paid directly through bank or post office accounts. As a result, 10 crore new bank or post office accounts have been opened.
- The average wage per person-day has gone up by 81 per cent since the introduction of the scheme, with state-level variations. The notified wage today varies from a minimum of ₹122 in Bihar and Jharkhand to ₹191 in Haryana.
- Scheduled Castes and Scheduled Tribes have accounted for 51 per cent of the total person-days generated and women for 47 per cent—well above the mandatory 33 per cent as required by the Act.
- 146 lakh works have been taken up since the beginning of the programme, of which about 60 per cent have been completed.
- 12 crores Job Cards have been provided and uploaded on the Management Information System (MIS), available for public scrutiny. Since 2010–11, all details regarding the expenditure of the MGNREGA are available on the MIS in the public domain.

A number of drawbacks are still labelled against the scheme. They are as follows:

1. A major flaw of MGNREGA is that a lot of money disbursed by the government gets siphoned off by middlemen, thus leaving a huge number of MGNREGA workers either unpaid or paid less than the standard wages or are given 5 kg of rice by private contractors, as workers in Mahuadand in Jharkhand have been paid.
2. Landholders quite often oppose the scheme because landless labourers are more interested in giving labour to the MGNREGA worksites rather than in agricultural farms as the minimum wage rate in the former is usually higher than the latter. Hence, to attract such labourers, the big farmers are bound to raise the daily wage rate in the agricultural farms as well. Thus, as a result of the introduction of MGNREGA, agriculture has undoubtedly become less profitable.
3. Economists like Jagdish Bhagwati and Arvind Panagariya have labelled MGNREGA as "an inefficient instrument of shifting income to the poor" for it takes five rupees to transfer one rupee to MGNREGA workers. Economists like Surjit Bhalla have termed it as unsuccessful, saying that any scheme with 85 per cent leakages cannot be proclaimed to be "working successfully."
4. Besides, the scheme has also been criticised for leakages and corrupt implementation. It is alleged that individuals have received benefits and wages for work not done by them at all, or have done only on paper, or are not poor at all. In 2014–15,

only 28 per cent of the payments were made on time to workers. Following the allegations of corruption in MGNREGA, the NDA Government ordered a re-evaluation of the scheme in 2015.

Nitin Gadkari, the Union Rural Development Minister under the BJP Government, proposed to limit MGNREGA programmes within tribal and poor areas. He also wanted to change the labour: material ratio from 60:40 to 51:49. According to his modified proposal, the programme would be implemented in 2500 backward blocks coming under Intensive Participatory Planning Exercise. But this new proposal was sharply criticized. A number of economists with varying views opposed the idea of "focussing" implementation in a few blocks or districts only. In November 2014 Birender Singh replaced Nitin Gadkari as the Rural Development Minister. Just after being the Minister Mr. Singh assured that MGNREGA would continue in all the Indian districts. But unfortunately around the same time MGNREGA budget saw a sharp cut, and in the name of "focussing" on a few backward blocks MGNREGA has been in reality limited to those blocks only.

As a result, a new set of demands known as "Save MGNREGA" became very popular and they were proposed during the joint meeting of the national leaders of the CITU, AIAWU, AIDWA and AIKS in New Delhi. They strongly criticised the dilution of the scheme of MGNREGA by the newly formed BJP Government. Following demands were placed by them:

- Government of India should increase the Central allocation for MGNREGA so that the number of workdays can be increased to 200 and per day wage can be increased to ₹300.
- Job Card should be issued to everyone who would demand a job, failing which, after 15 days of placing the demand for a job, employment benefits are to be provided.
- Minimum 100 days of work should be ensured to all cardholders.
- Minimum Wage Act must be implemented strictly. Delay in wage payment should not be made.
- MGNREGA should be extended to urban areas as well.
- For checking corruption and smooth implementation of MGNREGA, Gram Sabhas should be strengthened.

As a part of 2017 Union budget of India, the Finance Minister Arun Jaitley announced that ₹48,000 crore would be allocated to the MGNREGA. For the financial year 2018–19, he further allocated ₹55,000 crore for MGNREGA.

14.10.2 Sarva Shiksha Abhiyan (SSA)

Sarva Shiksha Abhiyan (SSA) or the Movement of Education for All is a programme launched by the Government of India aiming at the universalisation of elementary education "in a time bound manner".

It is mandated by the 86th Amendment to the Constitution of India (December, 2002), making free and compulsory education to children between the ages of 6 and 14 years (estimated to be 205 million children in 2001).

In fact, Article 21A has been made a new Fundamental Right known as Right to Education in which it is clearly stated that "The State shall provide free and compulsory education to all children of the age of six to fourteen years in such a manner as the State may, by law, determine."

Secondly, for Article 45 to the Indian Constitution a new Article has been substituted, namely, "Provision for early childhood care and education to children below the age of six years."

Thirdly, in Article 51A to the Indian Constitution, after clause (J), the following clause shall be added, namely "(K) who is a parent or guardian to provide opportunities for education to his child or, as the case may be, ward between the age of six and fourteen years."

The programme was pioneered by Shri Atal Behari Vajpayee, the former Indian Prime Minister.

SSA is not only a programme for Universal Elementary Education. It is also an attempt to provide to all children community-owned quality education with a missionary zeal. In other words, it is a response to the demand for quality basic education all over the country. The basic features of SSA are as under:

(a) SSA is a programme with a clear time frame for universal elementary education.
(b) SSA is a response to the demand for quality basic education all over India.
(c) SSA is an opportunity for promoting social justice to our children through basic education.
(d) SSA is an expression of political will for universal elementary education across the country.
(e) SSA is a partnership between the Central, State and Local governments.
(f) SSA is an opportunity for states to develop their own visions of elementary education.
(g) SSA is a constructive effort at effectively involving the panchayati raj institutions, parents–teachers associations, school management committees, rural and urban slum level education committees, tribal autonomous councils and other grassroots level structures in the management of primary and secondary schools.

SSA has the following objectives:

1. To provide useful and elementary education for all children of 6 to 14 years of age.
2. To bridge social, regional and gender gaps with the active participation of community in the management of schools.

3. To permit children to know and master their natural environment for the development of their spiritual and material potential.
4. To inculcate value-based education which gives children an opportunity to work for each other's well-being rather than to become more selfish in their thoughts and activities.
5. To place emphasis on Early Childhood Care and education.

The following are the specific future visions of the SSA.

- All children are in school. By 2003 Education Guarantee Centres, Alternate Schools and Back-to-School Camps should be completed.
- Five years of primary schooling for all children should be completed by 2007.
- By 2010 all children should complete elementary schooling.
- Focus would be on elementary education of satisfactory quality with special emphasis on education for life.
- Bridging all gender and social category gaps at primary stage by 2007 and at elementary education level by 2010.
- Universal retention would be completed by 2010.
- Quality education for all is of crucial importance.

SSA has been guided by the following principles:

- Holistic view of education, as interpreted in the National Curriculum Framework 2005, with significant implications for curriculum, teacher education, educational planning and management.
- Equity, to mean not only equal opportunity, but also creation of conditions in which the various disadvantaged sections of the society—children of SC, ST, Muslim minority, landless agricultural labourers and children with special needs etc.— can avail of the opportunity.
- Access to education should be ensured to all children not only within specified distance, but also belonging to all traditionally excluded categories like those of the SC, ST and other sections of the most disadvantaged groups, the Muslim minority, girls in general and children with special needs.
- Gender concern, implying not only an effort to enable girls to keep pace with boys but to view education in the perspective spelt out in the National Policy on Education (1986–92), i.e., a decisive intervention to bring about a basic change in the women's status.
- Centrality of teachers, to motivate them to innovate and create a culture in and beyond the classroom that might produce an inclusive environment for children, specially for girls from the marginalised backgrounds.

- Moral compulsion is imposed through the Right to Information Act on parents, teachers, educational administrators and other stakeholders.
- Convergent and integrated system of educational management is a pre-requisite for the implementation of the RTE Act. All states must move in that direction as speedily as possible.

Two broad outcomes of SSA are as follows:

1. SSA provides a wide framework for the implementation of Elementary Education schemes.
2. SSA is a programme with budget provision for strengthening vital areas to achieve universalisation of elementary education.

Moreover, SSA interventions include opening of new schools and alternate schooling facilities, construction of school buildings and additional classrooms, toilets and deep tube wells for drinking water, provision for more teachers, regular teachers in service training and academic resource support, free textbooks and uniforms, and support for improving learning achievement levels. Changes have, however, been incorporated into the SSA approach, strategies and norms, with the passage of the RTE Act.

Important schemes under SSA are discussed below:

Mahila Samakhya Programme (MSP)

This programme was initially started as early as in 1988 for empowering women, of the remotest corners of rural areas of India, belonging to the socio-economically downtrodden sections. When SSA was officially started, a committee was established to try to find out the programme of empowering rural women who were among the poorest of the poor. The committee was formed to see meticulously how the programme was working even in the remotest corners of the rural areas of India and whether possible new changes suitable for the incumbents of the said areas could be recommended properly.

Kasturba Gandhi Balika Vidyalaya (KGBV) Scheme

This scheme was launched in July 2004, to provide education to girls at primary level. It is primarily, though not exclusively, for the girls of the underprivileged sections and belonging to rural areas where the literacy level for females is extremely low. Schools that were set up under this scheme have 100 per cent reservation—75 per cent for female students belonging to backward classes and 25 per cent for BPL (Below Poverty Line) female students.

[*Source:* Revised Guidelines for Implementation of Kasturba Gandhi Balika Vidyalayas (KGBVs)]

National Programme for Education of Girls at Elementary Level (NPEGEL)

This programme was launched in July, 2003. It was an incentive to reach out to the girls whom SSA was not able to reach through other schemes. Through this programme of NPEGEL, SSA tried to benefit the "hardest to reach girls". This scheme has covered 24 states of India. Under the NPEGEL, a number of "model schools" have been set up to provide better opportunities to girls.

[*Source:* www.ssa.mp.gov.in>NPEGEL]

Padhe Bharat Badhe Bharat (PBBB)

This is a nationwide sub-programme of SSA. Children who fail to read in early education lag behind in other subjects. This programme (PBBB) is designed to improve comprehensive early reading, writing and early mathematics programme for children in Classes I and II. Under this programme a sum of ₹762 crore was approved to the states of India. The programme is aimed at providing print-rich environment, timely distribution of books and introducing a teacher mentoring and appraisal system.

Since 2015 SSA has made the following goals:

1. SSA seeks to open new schools in those areas which do not have schooling facilities and to strengthen the existing school infrastructure through maintenance grant and school improvement grants.
2. Existing schools with inadequate teacher strength are provided with additional teachers. Again, the capacity of existing teachers is being strengthened by extensive training, providing more useful materials and strengthening the academic support structure.
    - SSA puts particular stress on educating girls, educating children with special needs and on computer skill and training.

      There are several Non-Governmental Organisations (NGOs) which are also significantly working in the direction of the development and upliftment of children, specially in the fields of health and education. To name a few of such organisations, *Smile India, Plan India, Childhood Enhancement Through Training and Action* (CHETNA) etc. Such organisations are all taking active measures on a regular basis to motivate the underprivileged and deprived children of the society towards education and consequently towards a better life.

14.10.3 National Rural Health Mission (NRHM)

National Rural Health Mission (NRHM), now under National Health Mission (NHM), is an initiative taken by the Government of India to address the health needs of our rural areas which for a long time has been under-served. It was launched by our former Prime Minister, Mr. Manmohan Singh, on April 12, 2005. The initial target area of NRHM was composed of 18 Indian states that had been identified as having weak public health indicators. Hence, basically the goal of NRHM is to provide accessible, affordable and quality health care to the ruralites of our country, specially the vulnerable groups. Under the NRHM, the Empowered Action Group (EAG) states, North–Eastern states, Jammu and Kashmir and Himachal Pradesh have been given particular emphasis. The principal aim of NRHM is to establish a fully functional, community owned, decentralised health delivery system with inter-sectoral convergence at all levels. The ultimate objective is to ensure simultaneous action on a wide range of determinants of health, such as water, sanitation, education, nutrition, social and gender equality.

NRHM focuses on Reproductive, Maternal, Newborn, Child Health and Adolescent Services. The main focus here is to make suitable strategies so as to improve maternal and child health through intensive care and also the life cycle approach. It envalues a direct link between adolescent health, family planning, maternal health and child survival. Besides, there is also a clear focus on the linking of community and facility-based care and on strengthening referrals between various levels of health care system so that a continuous care pathway is created in our rural areas.

As per the 12th Plan document of the Planning Commission, the programme of NRHM is aimed to be strengthened under the umbrella of National Health Mission. The focus on covering rural areas and ruralites will continue along with up-scaling of NRHM to include non communicable diseases and expanding health coverage to urban areas. The Union Cabinet headed by the (then) Prime Minister Dr. Manmohan Singh, vide a decision dated May 1, 2013, has approved the launch of National Urban Health Mission (NUHM) as a sub-mission of National Health Mission (NHM), with NRHM being the other sub-mission of NHM.

The NRHM was launched as a framework of partnership among Government of India, related Departments of the Government, particularly the Departments of Women and Child Development, Drinking Water Supply, Panchayati Raj and Development of North Eastern Region State Governments. The Mission Steering Group under the Chairmanship of the Union Minister for Health and Family Welfare provides policy guidance and operational oversight at the central level. The State Governments have been part of the Stakeholder Consultations for finalising the strategy of NRHM. The Mission was started to achieve the following goals set under the National Health Policy (2002) and the Millennium Development Goals (that are to be achieved in a time-bound manner):

- NRHM aims to facilitate the access and utilisation of quality health services by all.
- NRHM aims to forge a partnership between three tiers of government—National, State and Local.
- NRHM aims to set up a platform for involving the panchayats and the community in the management of primary health programmes and infrastructure.
- NRHM aims to provide an opportunity for promoting equity and social justice.
- NRHM aims to establish a mechanism to provide flexibility to the states and the community to promote local initiatives.

The Indian public health system is characterised by serious regional and social disparity. The curative services are essentially anti-poor in the sense that for every ₹1 spent on the poorest 20 per cent population, a sum of ₹3 is spent on the richest population. Impacts of public health programmes are significantly inefficient, unaccountable and ineffective. Issues of sanitation, hygiene, nutrition and drinking water are not properly integrated. On 10 per cent of Indians have some form of health insurance and over 25 per cent of hospitalised Indians fall below poverty line.

To overcome the hindrances in public health system the Government of India, recognising the crucial importance of good health in the process of socio-economic development, has launched NRHM. The Mission is aimed to make the Government raise public expenditure on health from 0.9 per cent of GDP to 2–3 per cent of GDP.

NRHM is different from its predecessor schemes as the focus on NRHM is on holistic health system at all levels, from the village to the district with active participation of panchayats as well as the community. NRHM also subsumes the key national programmes, namely, the Reproductive and Child Health II Project (RCH II), the National Disease Control Programmes (NDCP) and the Integrated Disease Surveillance Project (IDSP), thus making it an umbrella initiative of the Government.

Principal strategies of NRHM are as under:

- Training and enhancing capacity of panchayats to own, control and manage public health services.
- Promoting access to improved healthcare at household level through the female health activists.
- Making health plan for each village through the Village Health Committee of the panchayat.

- Strengthening sub-centre through an united fund to enable local planning and action and more Multi-Purpose Workers (MPWs).
- Strengthening existing Public Health Centres and Community Health Centres.
- Preparing and implementing an inter-sectoral District Health Plan prepared by the District Health Mission.
- Integrating vertical Health and Family Welfare programmes at National, State, District and Block levels.
- Providing technical support to National, State and District Health Missions.
- Strengthening capacities for data collection, assessment and review for evidence-based planning, monitoring and supervising.
- Formulating transparent policies for deployment and career development of Human Resources for health.
- Developing capacities for preventive health care at all levels for promoting healthy life styles, reducing consumption of tobacco, alcohol etc.
- Promoting non-profit sector, particularly in under-served areas.

Features of implementation framework in NRHM are as follows:

1. Public health delivery system to be made fully functional and accountable to the community.
2. Human resource management to be made.
3. Community involvement to be made more effective.
4. Decentralisation to be emphasised.
5. Rigorous monitoring and evaluation of schemes to be made continuously.
6. Convergence of health and related programmes make villages modern.
7. Innovations and flexibility in financing to be stressed.
8. Interventions for improving the health indicators to be made.

The NRHM has the ability to initiate things independently. Some of the significant trump cards under NRHM are as under: [*Sources:* (1) http://www.thehindu.com/news/national/nrhm-to-be-national-health-mission-soon/article 2988618.ece. (2) Singh, Pavneet, *India Year Book, 2014*, Pearson, 2014, Ch. 16].

ASHA or Accredited Social Health Activists

For introducing a connection between the health system, on the one hand, and ruralites, on the other, Community Health Volunteers have been engaged actively and the latter are known as Accredited Social Health Activists or ASHAs. Poor people of the remotest corners of rural areas, specially women and children, cannot get help from the rural health services easily and hence they are forced to place their medical demands before the ASHA. ASHA, being an immensely popular health programme, has made the public health system in rural areas of India grossly successful, and in a number of Indian states such volunteers are providing health-related services to the deprived sections of the rural community. Through ASHAs outpatient services, inpatient care, diagnostic facilities and institutional deliveries have remarkably been increased both qualitatively and quantitatively.

Patient Welfare Committee or Hospital Management Society

In a management type structure, such a committee consists of a group of trustees who manage the hospital-related functions. Such committees do a lot of works for the development of the patients in rural areas. An untied fund provides financial support to these committees.

Untied Grants to Sub-Centres

Such financial assistance is absolutely necessary for the lowest level developments in rural health care system of India like antenatal care and children's health. Two important areas of such grants are as under:

- Efficiency of Auxiliary Nurse Midwives (ANMs) is sought to be increased from this grant so that they can provide better and more improved antenatal and postnatal care.
- Untied grants have also been significantly utilised by the Village Health Sanitation and Nutrition Committees (VHSNCs) who can now pay more attention to address the health-related demands of poor families, in general, and poor children, in particular.

Health Care Contractors

As a part of NRHM, such contractors have largely been appointed in the remotest corners of rural India where health-related services have not yet been available. Under this scheme, capacity building of nursing staff and auxiliary workers is remarkably being emphasised which deserves special mention.

Janani Suraksha Yojana (JSY)

By encouraging pregnant women of rural areas to deliver in government health centres, the scheme's primary objective is to minimise maternal mortality. For this, such women are also provided financial aid so that they can go to public hospitals during the time of delivery. The scheme has witnessed the light of unprecedented success.

National Mobile Medical Units (NMMUs)

Through such units, people of a number of under-served or unserved areas of rural India have immensely been benefited regarding health facilities.

National Ambulance Services (NASs)

Free ambulance services are available in every remote corner of Indian villages within 30 minutes of the calls from rural patients or families. This undoubtedly is a great achievement under NRHM.

Janani Shishu Suraksha Karyakram (JSSK)

Pregnant women who come to public institutions for delivery and sick infants up to one year of age, under this scheme, are regularly provided the following benefits:

- free diagnostic practices
- free medicines
- free blood
- free to and fro transport
- free food to pregnant women and sick infants (up to one year old).

Rashtriya Bal Swasthya Karyakram (RBSK)

This scheme is related specifically to child health. Accordingly, a Child Health Screening and Early Intervention Service was introduced in rural India in February, 2013. Its main objective was to identify the undiagnosed diseases related to children health, like developmental delays, disability, birth defects, deficiencies etc. This was undertaken to cover about 27 crore children up to 18 years of age in rural areas of India. Those, having health problems diagnosed under this scheme, have been sought to be identified and provided with free treatment and even surgery, if required.

Mother and Child Health Wings (MCH Wings)

Reduction of maternal and child mortality was the primary aim of this scheme. In extremely busy and congested district hospitals and community health centres extra beds have been created for ailing mothers and children. In such institutions MCH wings with the capacity of 100/50/30 beds have been sanctioned to cover more and more mothers and children of rural India.

Free Drugs and Free Diagnostic Service

It is an innovative initiative on the part of NRHM to provide drugs and diagnostic service to the ruralites free of cost. This automatically decreases their health-related expenditure.

District Hospital and Knowledge Centre (DHKC)

This is another new effort of the NRHM to strengthen district hospitals and introduce multi-speciality health care units in the rural areas of our country. Such care units include dialysis care units, intensive cardiac care units, cancer treatment units, mental illness units, emergency medical units and trauma care units.

National Iron Plus Initiative

India is one of the nations in the world with very high prevalence of anaemia. Nutritional anaemia is a major public health problem in India, which is primarily due to iron deficiency. The National Family Health Survey-3 data suggest that 80 per cent of anaemia is prevalent among children under 3 years of age and 70 per cent among children below 5 years of age. Under this scheme, irrespective of their Iron or Hb status, patients are meticulously provided with iron and folic acid supplements. Pregnant women, lactating mothers and infants belonging to the age group of 6–60 months are supposed to be the primary target group of this scheme.

Tribal TB Eradication Project

A number of medical studies show that tuberculosis is widely prevalent among the Indian tribals. Shri Faggan Singh Kulaste, Minister of Social Health, launched this project on January, 20, 2017 at Mandla in Maharashtra. The primary aim of this project was to eradicate the disease. Indian Council of Medical Research (ICMR) has conducted a research to find out that some tribes in Madhya Pradesh are genetically predisposed to tuberculosis. The focus of the medical programme has basically been on the detection and cure of the disease among the unreached tribals.

Chiranjeevi Yojna (CY)

Under this scheme, institutional deliveries were sought to largely replace home deliveries. Private practitioners were also encouraged to help in the deliveries in remoted corners of the Indian villages in general and those in Gujarat in particular. Infant and maternal mortality rates can thus be reduced.

Panchamrit

This programme was launched in Rajasthan to improve the general health of rural mothers and babies. Poorest areas and poorest of the poor villagers of Rajasthan, who could not find any sort of medical help so far, were the main targets of the scheme. The areas that received particular emphasis under Panchamrit are as under:

- Vaccine for preventable diseases
- Elimination of micronutrient deficiency
- Family welfare
- Safe motherhood
- Ensuring healthy new-born babies.

Emphasising these areas of medical support, poor mothers and their children of rural India have been sought to be benefited.

In Odisha, some NGOs have been managing Public Health Centres efficiently. They are usefully taking help of various participatory techniques to understand the genuine needs of the community, methods of developing local resources and meeting the health needs of the poorest of the poor. Hence, health centres which were lying defunct for a long time have now become vibrant, dispensing basic needs to the marginalised.

NRHM has significantly contributed to *capacity building*. There are now more than 1200 Programme Management, Finance Management and Data Management professionals who have in recent years joined the system at State and District levels. The introduction of these skills has immensely improved programming, monitoring, evaluating, financial reporting and record keeping. A special kind of training for management of neonatal and childhood illness has been introduced in more than 25 States. Assam Government has initiated a radio programme for Accredited Social Health Activists (ASHAs) with All India Radio, Assam, to develop the knowledge and skills of trainers.

Regarding *evaluation* of NRHM, it may be said that NRHM has set up effective systems of monitoring and evaluation. Disaggregated figures about the performance of the scheme regarding vulnerable social groups like SCs and STs have now been operationalised. An effective Financial Management Reporting System has become functional with quarterly reports from states. In collaboration with NGOs a pilot survey on community monitoring is being initiated. The Institute of Public Auditors of India are working in five states, viz., Assam, Bihar, Kerala, Tamil Nadu and U.P. The assessment of ASHA programme in Bihar, M.P., Odisha, Rajasthan and U.P. is being done with support of some international organisations like the UNICEF. A system of independent assessment of performance of states by institutions of excellence is almost finalised. After being introduced, NRHM has gradually made commendable achievements. Lots of local initiatives are enjoying good success both in terms of popularity and effectiveness. Thus NRHM has been made a sustainable practice of the government. Besides, since a number of schemes do not have any budgetary implications tied to them, health centres under NRHM are relatively free of financial constraints.

NRHM can reasonably be considered as a best practice since the community and peripheral health staff partners are progressing towards achieving significantly better changes in the sector of health. For a long time it was a challenge for the Nation to devise a mechanism that reaches the socio-economically deprived sector, particularly in rural areas of India. This challenge in the health sector has been successfully met by the NRHM. The principal aspects of its success are as under:

- NRHM is implemented through a decentralised administrative system in which local bodies have full rights in designing and implementing health schemes according to local needs.
- NRHM significantly improves the availability of health services to ordinary ruralites.
- NRHM directly links health services to community participation and decisions.
- NRHM strengthens entrepreneurial energy and initiative of the people in creative outcomes.

Questions

1. Critically discuss the welfare programmes undertaken recently for the SCs, STs, OBCs and women.
2. Write short notes on:
   (a) Argument for private sector reservation
   (b) Critique of reservation
   (c) Welfare of SCs/STs/OBCs/Women.
3. Write critical notes on:
   (a) MGNREGA (b) SSA
   (c) NRHM (d) ASHA

Notes and References

1. Thapar, Romila, *Ashoka and Decline of Mauryas*, Oxford University Press, Delhi, 1992.
2. Sowjanya, P.M. and G. Haragopal, From Legal-Rational to Moral-Legal-Rational Bureaucracy: A Case Study of a Civil Servant, in Dhameja, A. (Ed.), *Contemporary Debates in Public Administration*, Prentice-Hall of India, New Delhi, 2003.
3. Avasthi, A.P., *Indian Government and Politics*, Lakshmi Narain Agarwal, Agra, 2004.
4. Sowjanya, P.M. and G. Haragopal, *op. cit.*
5. Avasthi, A.P., *op. cit.*
6. See Articles 15, 16 and 17 in particular of our Constitution.
7. Sarkar, Abhirup, editorial article, *The Anandabazar Patrika*, June 28, 2006.
8. Yadav, Anumeha, "How effective are social security and welfare in India", *The Hindu*, January 26, 2015.

15 Issue Areas in Indian Administration

15.1 INTRODUCTION

In this chapter, we deal with some major issue areas in Indian administration. The areas are as under:

- Constitutional framework
- Personnel administration
- Administration of law and order
- Public sector administration
- Information technology and its impact on administration
- Human rights
- Globalization and civil society.

India has opted for a parliamentary system of democracy. The ideas of democracy—progress, prosperity and protection of the common mass—can be attained only through a workable and well conceived document of Constitution, an impartial personnel administration, a proper maintenance of law and order, a thorough and honest public sector administration, etc. L.D. White has clearly stated that administration is a moral act and an administrator is a moral agent. Such a thinking forms the very base of public administration if it really wants to be an effective weapon for bringing about a democratic welfare State.

Again, one cannot probably deny the massive change in public administration that has reached its height in the newly emergent phenomenon of the 'structural adjustment programme'. It is facilitated, to a great extent, by the new Information Technology (IT) revolution (Internet, fax and web-based communication).

Similarly, globalization is considered to be an important input in the search for appropriate explanatory models of governance. It cannot be denied that following the onset of globalization, the traditional bureaucratic model appears to have lost its significance principally because of the growing importance of the non-State actors in administration.

One of the recent public administrative instrumentalities is the 'human rights' institution at the National and State levels. This is somewhat recent in Indian public administration. There are both international and domestic pressures to uphold human rights and ensure effective 'rights regimes' at all levels in the interest of the steady democratization of the public sphere.[1]

In the following sections, all these seven major areas of polity and administration are discussed.

15.2 CONSTITUTIONAL FRAMEWORK

The prominent leaders of the Indian National Congress started to contemplate about the framework of the Constitution of independent India just after the attainment of Independence in August, 1947. A Drafting Committee was constituted to draft the Constitution under the able chairmanship of Dr. B.R. Ambedkar. The Committee took 141 days to frame the draft. After its presentation to the Constituent Assembly, more than 2 years were taken by the Assembly to give the finishing touches to the Constitution. Nehru and Patel were rightly called the founding fathers of the Constitution. Dr. Ambedkar, on the contrary, was called the mother of the Constitution, for he "had to bear in fact other ideas and nurture them and bring them out as his own and he did remarkably well."[2]

The Constitution of India was drafted after going through many Constitutions of the world and hence it is a blend of good features of prominent Constitutions of the USA, UK, Ireland, Canada, Soviet Union (now Russia), etc. Following are the salient features of our Constitution.

1. **Written and Lengthy:** Initially, the Constitution of India comprised 395 Articles and 12 Schedules. Presently, it is the lengthiest document consisting of 444 Articles and 12 Schedules. The Constitution makes provision for the administrative machinery both at the Centre and at the States and Union Territories. The Federal Scheme adds to its volume. Enough space has been devoted to the Union and State relations. The details of the Fundamental Rights and later the inclusion of Fundamental Duties by the 42nd amendment add to its length. Provision for the chapter on Directive Principles of State Policy, special provision for the constitutional safeguards for the minorities and inclusion of Articles on three types of Emergencies–national, State and financial–undoubtedly make the Constitution vaster. Again, provisions concerning citizenship, national and regional languages, elections, the services, trade, contracts, etc. are also responsible for the huge size of our Constitution.

2. **Sovereign Democratic Republic:** In the Preamble to the Indian Constitution, India is stated to be a sovereign democratic republic. Sovereignty is reflected through our internal independence and avoidance of any external control on us.

   Besides, the free, fair and impartial periodical general elections for Parliament, State Legislatures and the local bodies ensure the democratic spirit of our nation.

   Unlike that of the UK, Nepal, etc., which have hereditary monarchs as the heads of the States, India has opted for an elected functionary as head of the State. As he is elected by the people of India, the 'republican' spirit of our State is ensured since the ultimate sovereign power is in the hands of the people.
3. **Secular State:** The Preamble to the Indian Constitution as well as the right to religion clearly reflects that secularism is the cardinal principle of our Constitution. Being a secular State, India does not have any State religion. It allows freedom of faith, conscience and worship to all without any discrimination. Our nation believes in complete religious neutrality and does not accept any man-made barrier on the basis of religion. It is, as observes H.V. Kamath, neither a godless State nor an irreligious nor an anti-religious State.
4. **Quasi-Federal:** It is interesting to note that our Constitution has opted for federalism and yet the word 'federal' has not been used. Instead, India is called a 'Union of States'. Dr. K.C. Wheare holds that the Indian Constitution establishes a system of government which is at the most quasi-federal. It is a unitary State with subsidiary federal features rather than a federal State with unitary features. Dr. B.R. Ambedkar has also confessed that our Constitution has not been set in a tight mould of federation.
5. **Parliamentary Form of Government:** Like Great Britain, India, too, has opted for the parliamentary form of government. Here the Prime Minister–the real head of the State or the head of the government—along with the Council of Ministers is collectively responsible to the Lok Sabha, i.e. the Lower House of the Parliament. The President, like the British monarch, is the Constitutional Head of the State equipped with only ornamental authority. The ultimate control over legislation lies with the Lower House. Besides, a healthy and effective opposition is the prerequisite of parliamentary democracy.
6. **A Separate Chapter on Fundamental Rights and Fundamental Duties:** Part III of our Constitution incorporates a separate chapter on Fundamental Rights. In the initial stages, seven rights were embodied in the Constitution, namely, right to equality, right to freedom, right against exploitation, right to freedom of religion, cultural and educational right, right to

property and right to constitutional remedies. At a later stage, the 44th Amendment Act (1978) deleted right to property from the list of Fundamental Rights.

The provision of Fundamental Duties did not exist prior to the passage of the 42nd Amendment Act (1976). These duties, though called fundamental, are not enforceable. Some of the important fundamental duties are:

(a) To uphold the sovereignty and protect the unity and integrity of our country
(b) To promote harmony and the spirit of common brotherhood amongst all the people of India
(c) To abide by the Constitution and respect its ideals
(d) To defend the country and render national service when called upon to do so
(e) To protect and improve the national environment including forests, lakes, rivers and wildlife
(f) To safeguard public property and avoid violence
(g) To develop the scientific temper, humanism, spirit of enquiry and reform.

7. **Directive Principles of State Policy:** Part IV of our Constitution deals with the Directive Principles which are non-justiciable but considered to be fundamental in the governance of our nation. These principles are Gandhian, socialistic, liberal-intellectual and of general category.

   Gandhian principles include prohibition of intoxicating drinks, establishment of the Panchayati Raj, etc. Socialistic principles include avoidance of concentration of wealth, ensuring adequate means of livelihood to the citizens, assistance in cases of unemployment, old age, sickness, etc. and right to work. Liberal-intellectual principles comprise the preservation of ancient monuments and articles of historical interest, the separation between the executive and the judiciary, promotion of cottage industries, etc.

8. **Semi-rigid and Semi-flexible Constitution:** Our Constitution is a mixture of rigidity and flexibility. Article 368 explains its rigidity. Some of the matters, viz. Fundamental Rights, Directive Principles, etc. require support of the majority of the total membership of Parliament and two/thirds of the members present and voting. Again, some of the provisions, like the extent of executive powers of the Union and the States, manner of election of the Indian President, High Courts of Union Territories etc., necessitate the ratification of each House of Parliament by majority of total members of both the Houses and two/thirds majority of the members present and voting.

On the other hand, about two dozen Articles can be amended by our Parliament by a simple majority. The Articles pertain to (a) qualifications of citizenship, (b) creation of new States, changing of their names and boundaries, (c) creation and abolition of Upper Chambers in the States, and (d) salaries of the judges of the Supreme Court and High Courts.

Keeping in view these two methods of amendment, one can conclude that ours is a rigid-cum-flexible Constitution.

9. **Bicameral Legislature:** The Indian Parliament has two Houses. The Lok Sabha, i.e. the Lower House, is a directly elected chamber. The Rajya Sabha, i.e. the Upper House, is an indirectly elected chamber. Presently, there are 545 members in the Lower Chamber and 245 members in the Upper Chamber. The Lower House is undoubtedly more powerful than the Upper House like its counterpart in Great Britain. The Lower House controls the purse and can oust the Council of Ministers by a vote of no-confidence.
10. **Impartial and Independent Judiciary:** The Indian judiciary has been accorded supremacy. The fact that the Supreme Court enjoys the power of judicial review necessitates the existence of an impartial and independent judiciary. The method of appointment of the Supreme Court and High Court judges, their high qualifications, security of tenure, their handsome emoluments chargeable on the Consolidated Fund of India and the debarring of Court judges from practising after retirement reflect that sincere efforts have been made to make the Indian judiciary absolutely impartial and independent.
11. **Single Citizenship:** The Constitutions of the USA and Switzerland cater to double citizenship. But in the case of India, an Indian, residing in any part of our country, is known as an Indian citizen and not as a citizen of West Bengal or Bihar or Orissa. This single citizenship has been established to inculcate the spirit of true nationalism and solidarity amongst the people of India belonging to different castes, tribes, sects, religions, having various food and dress habits, languages, etc. who witnessed partition of the country and the drama of barbarism emerging out of narrow parochial interests.
12. **Language Provisions:** India being a multi-linguistic State, language posed a special problem to the makers of our Constitution. In India, there are more than 1018 spoken languages, including 63 non-Indian languages. Language is a very sensitive issue and hence it is needed that the problem of language should be solved carefully. It is due to such a sensitive character of the problem that the Indian Constitution incorporates an entire chapter containing the linguistic provisions.

13. **Popular Sovereignty:** The Preamble to the Indian Constitution states that India is a land of the people of India who are truly the authors of constitutional law. The Union Government cannot claim sovereignty because its authority is derived out of the Constitution which can, through its amending process, deprive it of its powers. The same is the case with the individual States. The Constitution itself is not sovereign either, as its provisions can be amended by the constitutional process of amendments.

    The Preamble highlights the sources of the Constitution–the people of India. Sovereignty resides in them and consequently, the real authority emanates from them. They have enacted the Constitution and only they can unmake it. Organized in the Parliament and State Legislatures, only the people are empowered to amend the Constitution.

14. **Welfare State:** The ideals as enshrined in the Preamble to the Indian Constitution constitute the cornerstone of a welfare State. The Constitution prohibits artificial barriers and man-made inequalities. Interests of backward classes and minority communities have been properly looked after. Article 15 authorizes the State to make special provisions for the advancement of socially and educationally backward classes of citizens, the Scheduled Castes and Scheduled Tribes, etc.[3]

Considering all the salient features of our Constitution as stated above, it may be said that the Indian Constitution is neither 'a bag of borrowings' nor a 'hotch potch Constitution'. It should not be categorized as a mere glorified edition of the 1935 Act. It is rather a wise conglomeration of good points of various Constitutions of the world, duly adapted to circumstances, congenial to the Indian environment and in consonance with national heritage. The basic postulates of our Constitution are federalism, secularism, democratic socialism, parliamentary democracy and independent judiciary.

15.3 PERSONNEL ADMINISTRATION

Personnel administration is the totality of concern with the human resources of an organization. It is one of the organization's major linkages with its environment. Personnel administration is basically an attitude comprising the understanding of both the forces which shape manpower needs, supply and problems and, at the same time, the importance of human will and personality. It is a kind of an ongoing educational process for the employer and the employee alike.

The term 'personnel' means the body of employees, officers or servants who fill the various positions in an organization. Hence, it is a collective name given to the employees who man the various posts in an organization. Thus, personnel administration is the administration of human beings in an organization.

Personnel administration is also known as 'personnel management' besides other terms such as 'labour management', 'manpower management', 'industrial relations', and so on. The Indian Institute of Personnel Management defines that Personnel Management, Labour Management or Staff Management means quite simply the task of dealing with human relationship within an organization.

The Institute of Personnel Management (UK) defines personnel management as that part of management concerned with people at work and with their relationship within an enterprise. Its aim is to bring together the men and women who make up an enterprise and, having regard for the well-being of the individual and of working groups, to enable them to make their best contribution to its success. In this definition, three objectives of personnel management are clearly expressed: (a) to maintain good and healthy relations within an organization, (b) to enable each person to make his maximum personal contribution to the organization as a member of a working group, and (c) to achieve these things through a clear respect for human personality and the well-being of the individual.

Broadly speaking, there are three distinct types of personnel administrative system, namely, bureaucratic, aristocratic, and democratic.

15.3.1 Bureaucratic System

In a broader sense, the term 'bureaucratic system' is used "to describe any personnel system where the employees are classified in a system of administration composed of a hierarchy of sections, divisions, bureaus, departments and the like."[4] The Prussian Civil Service System is termed *bureaucratic* whose characteristic features are as under:

1. The services owe their appointment to the King and are responsible to him. The King recruits them and prescribes the conditions of their services.
2. Being responsible to the King Alone, the services consider themselves to be superior to the people. Thus, a master-servant relation is likely to be grown between the services and the public.
3. Public services not only perform executive but also legislative and judicial functions.

15.3.2 Aristocratic System

The aristocratic system began and developed in England and was later adopted by other Western countries. The characteristics of this system are as follows:

1. Under this system, a distinction is made between different grades of personnel, and promotion from the lower grade to the

higher one is highly restricted. Secretaries, Joint Secretaries, etc. occupy the higher class whose appointment depends upon the discretion of the Chief Executive.

2. Next to the higher class is the administrative class which includes all those who occupy all the important positions in public administration, e.g. heads of divisions and districts. In India, they generally belong to the IAS cadre. This class is recruited through a competitive examination held by the Union Public Service Commission.
3. Below the administrative class come the technical and supervisory classes. They are also appointed through competitive examinations.
4. These two classes of public services are kept in watertight compartments and there is no possibility that employees of technical and supervisory classes get promoted to the administrative class.
5. Public service is made a permanent career. This introduces pure professionalism in public services.
6. General mental ability and knowledge of the candidates rather than any specialized expert knowledge is required for qualifying such posts.

15.3.3 Democratic System

The United States has opted for this new type of system. Its main characteristic features are:

1. The system is immune from class division. An employee originally joining at the lowest category may ultimately attain the highest position.
2. The age requirements (18–45 years) enable persons to enter public services throughout their active life-span.
3. Highly specialized educational qualifications are required for such jobs.
4. Public service is not a life-long career. An individual can enter the public service at any stage and leave it whenever he likes.

15.3.4 Functions

Personnel administrative functions involve POSDCORB, i.e. Planning, Organizing, Staffing, Directing, Coordinating, Reporting and Budgeting. As far as specific activities are concerned, personnel administration consists of many functions, such as:

1. To bring new employees into the organization (selection)
2. To administer day-to-day operations involving current public employees (in-service operation)

3. To assess the capabilities of existing personnel and plan for future requirements (monitoring analysis and planning)
4. To link the personnel with the budgetary system so as to control public programmes (programme and budget control)
5. To provide information essential for labour management negotiations and relations (labour-management relations)
6. To support other related functions such as pay and employee benefits (support to other system).

Examining all the above functions, it may be said that the importance of personnel administration cannot be ignored. In a country like India, where modern technological methods have been adopted to foster its socio-economic developments, the complex duties of the government cannot be left in incompetent hands. As a result, the functions of personnel administration have assumed an added importance in the administrative system.

15.4 ADMINISTRATION OF LAW AND ORDER

Maintenance of law and order is the primary condition for the socio-economic development and successful working of the administrative system of any country. For the past few years, there has been a disturbing trend regarding the law and order situation in India. Large-scale mass violence and anti-authority agitations have become the order of the day. A saddening aspect of the affair is that even the guardians of law and protectors of the public order do not hesitate in disturbing the maintenance of law and order through massive agitative demonstrations. The police in many States have on various occasions defied laws and started vigorous unrest to seek redressal of their grievances. Of late, group clashes, political unrest, industrial strikes, peasants' uprisings and students' agitative protests have reached their height. Besides, there are the problems of terrorism, insurgency, extremism and caste wars. Religious intolerance, too, is on the increase in various States of India, and gradually the secular character of our nation is strictly threatened.

India has developed a complex network of police organization for the maintenance of public order. 'Public order' and 'police' are State subjects. The Union Government is not empowered to raise any police force. The Border Security Force (BSF), the Central Reserve Police Force (CRPF), the Rapid Action Force (RAF), Railway Protection Force (RPF), Central Industrial Security Force (CISF) and the Indo-Tibetan Border Police (ITBP) fall in the category of "other armed forces of the Union". The word 'police' in the title of CRPF and the ITBP is a misnomer. These "other armed forces of the Union" are more commonly known as paramilitary forces.

The 42nd Constitutional Amendment in 1976 has inserted a new Article (257A) authorizing the Union Government to "deploy any armed force of the Union or any other force subject to the control of the Union for dealing with any grave situation of law and order in any State." The police administration of the Union Territories is an exclusive responsibility and concern of the Union Government.

A brief descriptive profile of the paramilitary forces, the management of which is the responsibility of the Ministry of Home Affairs, is given below.

1. **CRPF:** The CRPF had its beginning in 1939 as "Crown Representative Police". Its main task was to help the Princely States to maintain law and order. After Independence, it was renamed as CRPF by a Parliamentary Act.

   The RAF was formed in 1992 by conversion of 10 standard battalions of the CRPF to deal specially with riots and riot-like situations.

   CRPF is a reserve establishment for emergencies. It is sent by the Government of India to those troubled areas where the Central Government has a special responsibility to discharge. The State administration also can in times of special crisis seek its services. It has today become the most hard-worked force of the land. It has to rush about from place to place–fighting communalism, rushing to help any State which sends an S.O.S. to the Centre, helping during various natural calamities, fighting terrorism, assisting election authorities in the peaceful conduct of polls, etc.
2. **BSF:** The BSF was raised in 1965 to check incidents of crime on the borders. It patrols the borders between India and various States and gives a high sense of security to the people living in border areas by providing special protection to their persons and property. It also deals effectively on the spot with incidents of minor intrusions, illegal infiltrations and trans-border smuggling. The BSF coordinates the activities of various law and order agencies involved in the detection and prevention of crime in the border areas.

   The BSF is headed by a Director-General.
3. **RPF:** The Railway Police are divided into Government Railway Police (GRP) and Railway Protection Force (RPF). The GRP is a special branch of State Police, while the RPF is a Central Government Force to guard and protect railway property. It is headed by an independent Director-General in the Railway Board.
4. **CISF:** CISF was created in 1969 to provide security in the major industrial undertakings of the Government of India in the public sector. It is meant to prevent violence and labour unrest which sabotage work and retard production in public sector units. It is headed by a Director-General of Industrial Security.

5. **ITBP:** The ITBP's functions are more or less similar with those of BSF. It checks crime on the Indo-Tibetan Borders and illegal infiltrations from across the border and provides security to the people living in the border areas.

Administration of law and order is a complex phenomenon which includes many activities, such as protection of life and property, enforcement of multifarious laws, internal security, detection and prevention of crime, etc.

Public order and police are principally State subjects. Therefore, the primary responsibility for the maintenance of peace and order falls on the State Governments. To perform their responsibility, the States maintain a police department which consists of both line and staff agencies.

15.5 PUBLIC SECTOR ADMINISTRATION

There are four key elements of good governance:

- Public sector administration or public sector management
- Accountability
- The legal framework for development
- Information and transparency.

Kettl and Milward (1996) have argued that New Public Management is neither a traditional public administration concept nor it belongs to policy analysis in its accepted meaning.[5] This new trend of administration or management was most noticeable in N. Flynn's book *Public Sector Management* published in 1993 from the UK. The main tenets of public sector administration, which have been categorically stated by Osborne and McLaughlin,[6] are as under:

- A focus on **hands-on and entrepreneurial management** in contrast with traditional bureaucracy
- Explicit **standards and measures of performance**
- Emphasis on **output controls**
- Importance of **disaggregation and decentralization** of public services
- A shift to the **promotion of competition** in the provision of public services
- Stressing on **private sector styles of management** and their superiority
- Promotion of **discipline and parsimony** in resource allocation.

A need is widely felt for creating more accountable and resonant public institutions rather than for simply efficient markets. Some basic commitments of the democratic State can be protected by building up a public sector enterprise for the following[7]:

1. Devolution and decentralization for the empowerment of local communities and not simply consumers.
2. Contracting out, deregulating and privatizing should take place only through proper feasibility studies within the constitutional framework.
3. Rightsizing bureaucracy should give priority to employees' rights, labour laws and the status of women's employment in every country.
4. Citizens' Charters should be effectively implemented and legal reforms should be undertaken to strengthen service delivery systems.
5. Taxation reforms, labour laws reform, and property rights are areas of immediate concern.
6. Technological advancement including e-governance reforms should address the requirements of people and help them in the exercise of their democratic rights.

In the context of India, public sector administration basically implies governmental bureaucracy.[8]

The public sector in India has had a chequered career. It has played a useful role in many critical areas of nation-building and development. But in many functional areas, its performance has been absolutely unsatisfactory. Its inefficiency and high costs need no elaboration. Under the changed situation of liberal economic policy, great concern has been shown for shedding its extra weight and subsequently increasing its efficiency and economy.

The government's response to the demand for public sector reforms is taking shape only gradually and half-heartedly. There has not been any comprehensive plan for revitalizing the public sector. The latter suffers as usual from complacency and conventional rigidity. The Rangarajan Committee on the reforms of public sector undertakings had recommended that the government must divest 74 per cent in all areas and 26 per cent in reserve areas. In a few Central Public Enterprises, the process of disinvestment has been undertaken in practice. But the outcome has not been much encouraging. The government now believes that the ownership of public enterprises should be diluted. In the first four years following the initiation of economic reforms in mid-1991, the Central Government put in more money into public sector companies as budgetary resources than what it earned through disinvestment.

The Board for Industrial and Financial Reconstruction (BIFR), designed to tackle the problems of industrial sickness, has failed to deliver because of its insistence or functioning in the way of "a court-cum-tribunal rather than an agency for conciliation and facilitation." [Quoted from P. Chidambaram's remarks as printed in the *Times of India*, July 19, 1995.]

With a view to making jobs in the public sector a little more lucrative, the Government of India periodically announces for the employees of the public sector undertakings new pay scales. It is made clear that the new pay scales are funded through the internal resources of public sector undertakings themselves and that no budgetary support is provided by the government for this purpose. Again, the government has also given these enterprises the flexibility to accept or reject the new pay scales.

A series of reforms for PSUs are awaiting. Yet, the problems of inefficiency, overstaffing, high costs, etc. continue to affect these undertakings adversely. The issue of ensuring greater accountability and balancing it with the enormous needs of autonomy remains unresolved. Regarding professionalization and modernization of the public sector management, some urgent steps are required to be taken.

15.6 INFORMATION TECHNOLOGY AND ITS IMPACT ON ADMINISTRATION

The Information Technology revolution (Internet, fax and web-based communication) brought about a radical change in the field of administration. The recent conceptualization of 'e-governance or digital governance' is significant in administrative reforms. Drawn on the latest information technology, the aim of e-governance is to open up government processes and enable greater public access to information. Digital/e-governance refers to the use of emerging IT like the internet, web sites and mobile phones to deliver information and services to citizens. It includes the publication of information about government services on web sites from where citizens can download application forms for these services. IT in administration also includes filling of a tax form, the renewal of a license and processing on-line payments. Scholars believe[9] that the appropriate use of various techniques of IT will usher in a new era in public administration by making governmental functioning and processes more and more transparent and accessible. Thus, e-governance, though a technological innovation, 'has changed the basic character of governance—its operational methodology, functional style, ideological orientation, even the spirit, heart and soul.'[10]

In India, digital governance has been legalized by the Information Technology Act of 2000. The Act provides legal recognition for transactions carried out by means of electronic data interchange and other means of electronic communication, commonly referred to as 'electronic commerce'. The latter involve the use of alternatives to paper-based methods of communication and storage of information, to facilitate the electronic filling of documents with government agencies.[11]

More importantly, e-governance is certainly an attack on bureaucratic red-tapism causing unnecessarily excessive delay and corruption. Besides, it also creates a space for the regular involvement of citizens who, as customers of public services, in the changed situation have direct access to governmental activities through the IT. As a result, governmental activities not only become more transparent before the citizens, the latter can also provide significant inputs to the government through e-mails and electronic devices.

The IT-based e-governance has ushered in a new era in government innovations with capacities to reduce the cost of government, increase citizens' input into government, improve public decision-making and increase the transparency of government transactions. Considering these functional characteristics, e-governance is regarded to be a very meaningful step in combating corruption. E-government empowers the citizens by making their intervention in the transactions of governmental business regular through the IT.[12]

Thus, e-governance takes public administration in an absolutely new path. But its application is somewhat limited in the public sector simply because e-governance threatens the mass retrenchment of workers involved in government. So, the public sector cannot opt for e-governance to replace people for two basic reasons:

- The access to the Internet is still limited even in developed countries. The government has to maintain both the old and new systems to sustain its 'public' character. Otherwise, a large number of people will remain outside governmental transactions.
- Reducing public sector employment in many countries would result in economic hardship to those employees losing jobs. For obvious reasons, this has severe political repercussions. This definitely is not a desirable option unless there is no other option available.[13]

15.7 HUMAN RIGHTS

An important challenge to the Indian administrative system emanates from the growing awareness of and concern for human rights in India. It emerged as a direct consequence of the international movement for the protection of human rights and dignity and for the reinforcement of equality among human beings. Regarding their rights, Indian public opinion is also becoming more and more vigilant. Yet, the voices supporting this movement are still few and feeble.

The National Human Rights Commission (NHRC), set up in October 1993, in its annual reports has pointed out a number of cases of alleged custodial deaths, rapes, atrocities against women, police atrocities, disappearance of persons, torture on prisoners, and so on. Side by side with pursuing various cases with the governmental authorities, the Commission has also made general as well as specific recommendations and directives to the State Governments. For example, the Commission has asked all the State and Union Territory Governments to direct all the District Magistrates and Superintendents of Police to report to the

Commission all cases of custodial deaths and rapes within 24 hours of their occurrence or the receipt of news about their occurrence.[14]

In the subsequent years, the National Human Rights Commission has called for the restoration of the authority of Magistrates and the judiciary over the police, reorganizing the police with a view to improving their skills and standards of integrity and also a nation-wide reform of prisons.

In November 1995, the Commission took a decision of far-reaching significance. It directed the Bihar Police to prosecute an IPS Officer under Section 302 of the IPC for his involvement in a 'fake encounter' in 1994, when the officer was an SP of a particular district. Four other officers also faced similar indictment.[15] In December 1995, the Commission declared its programme to train policemen in human rights and even to systematically introduce the subject of human rights in school textbooks. Thus, the NHRC is sincerely trying to go beyond the domain of theory and enter the realm of action.

Within a very short span of time, the Commission has expressed its concern to cover socio-economic issues of national importance. For instance, it has categorically recommended the adoption of appropriate legislation on compulsory primary education, matched with the resources required for this purpose. Hence, it is suggested that the Commission, in order to cope with its increased functions and enhanced responsibilities, should be provided with extensive staff and infrastructure.

In January 1995, first ever public enquiry into crimes against women was initiated by the National Commission for Women. Almost 65 cases were brought before the Commission of which 26 cases were heard and the rest were referred to the authorities concerned. Such commissions and other human rights organizations make the administrative system increasingly accountable to public opinion.

Thus, the administrative system in India, more particularly its law and order subsystem, has made an honest attempt to reorient itself to the requirements of the protection of human rights. It may not be very difficult to change laws and rules for this purpose. What is most urgently needed is a judicious, positive as well as sympathetic outlook and attitude on the part of the government functionaries at all levels, but most importantly at the cutting-edge level. It is conceded that training people at the lower rungs of administration in attitudinal transformation is a highly difficult task. Broad-based moral understanding between people and management, safeguarded by legal and constitutional guarantee, can make the system work smoothly. Both the individual freedom and governmental imperatives can be attained simultaneously.

15.8 GLOBALIZATION AND CIVIL SOCIETY

Issues arising out of globalization have radically changed the nature and scope of public administration. The discipline in the changed environment has to respond to the challenges of the 'new economic order' which appear to have significantly influenced public administration. In the context of globalization, national economies tend to become more and more open and subject to supra-national economic influences. As economies lose their discrete, self-contained character and become enmeshed in global networks and processes, they become less amenable to national control and management. In short, the ideology as well as practice of globalization privileges voluntarism and the market as the underpinnings of the new economic order.[16]

Under the changed circumstances, the discipline of public administration has gone through a few models. The *market model* of governance has been holding central position since the late eighties of the twentieth century. Drawing upon the basic thrust of this model, several new models were constructed to articulate emerging trends in governance.[17] For example, the *participatory model* that concentrates on the participation of the lower echelons of workers. In this model, even the clients and citizens are expected to participate directly to displace the traditional hierarchic bureaucratic structure of administration. Similarly, the idea of *flexible government* goes against the conventional model of permanent employment. Public organizations with much less full-time employment and an increasing level of part-time and temporary workers have steadily come into existence at many places, depending upon the nature of labour market.

With the introduction of liberal economies in the greater part of the world, competitiveness has emerged as the key propeller of change in the administrative world. The old rule-bound, rigid, slow, conservative and unresponsive bureaucratic systems are more and more viewed as archaic. The winds, or rather storms, of change are affecting not only the structures, processes and functions, but also the behavioural or attitudinal patterns of the governmental system throughout the world. Some of the strikingly visible trends of globalization and its effects on civil society are mentioned below:[18]

1. The arrival of a post-industrial, knowledge-based global economy has undermined old realities throughout the world and has created enormous opportunities for governments at all levels to respond positively and meaningfully to these realities.
2. Governments have to be "re-invented" making them more entrepreneurial and assuming that they should "run like a business".
3. In order to "re-invent" governments, old, obsolete and inappropriate ideas and initiatives have to be discarded. Newer ideas are to be absorbed and willingness is to be shown to do more with less.
4. A need is strongly felt to shape "catalytic government" that

would inspire, guide and help communities, the private sector and the mass to run their own affairs independently.

5. Governments ought to become "competitive" in nature. There should be more and more competitions between the government and the private sector and also between the government agencies themselves. Only thus the delivery system may be improved significantly.
6. Rule-bound public organizations should be replaced by a mission-driven government whose employees will find themselves to be free to pursue the organizational mission.
7. Through rigorous performance-orientation mechanisms, increasing emphasis should be laid on result-orientation.
8. Public organizations must be conscious of the quality of their outcome.
9. Continuous innovations and reforms in governments should be evolved to modernize the public sector.
10. Governments need to become more and more consumer-friendly. Needs of the customers should be considered to be of utmost importance.
11. Governments should explore newer avenues of revenue generation by developing profit centres and curbing wastage.
12. Governments should be more proactive and anticipatory rather than only reactive and curative.
13. Emphasis should be placed on participation and team work and promoting decentralized government replacing a rigid hierarchical government.
14. Governments and the public sector should become market-oriented and they must seek to strike a balance between markets and the community.

Examining all the above mentioned features of administration as a result of globalization, it is almost clear that under the changed circumstances of liberalization and globalization, the traditional concept of public administration revolving round a sheltered bureaucracy is no longer viable. For example, in the 'public choice' perspective, the question is: why the bureaucratic form of organization should enjoy the monopoly over providing public goods and services. It is alleged that bureaucratic failures affect the society adversely both immediately and in the long run. It is not necessary that governments should always assume the role of a direct provider of goods and services. Instead, they can operate indirectly as 'enablers' allowing non-government agencies to operate directly in a wider social perspective. Contracting out on the part of the public sector and introducing 'privatization' in many forms are the present hallmarks of what is commonly known as 'the New Right' philosophy of governance.

15.9 GENDER AND ADMINISTRATION

Over the course of history in the area of public administration gender has played a crucial role. Now it has become almost impossible to look at public administration without properly taking note of the feminine masculine dichotomy. In fact, gender and diversity are two essential themes in the study of public administration. As a result of the existence of these two themes, the discipline of public administration does not forget to welcome "otherness" and to know thoroughly the effects of "otherness" in policies and programmes. When public administration was not quite matured as a discipline, the literature significantly ignored the question of women as such. Their experiences and contributions did not find a place in the textbooks or curriculum of public administration till the 19th and the early part of the 20th centuries. With the introduction of Civil Rights Acts of 1964 and 1968 and consequently with several movements for equal opportunities between sexes and job protection laws, the gender issue was given emphasis in public administration. As a result, women's views and voices came to the forefront in administration and the influence of men was somewhat decreased who wanted to control the discipline of public administration as an 'academic discipline'.

Till the second half of the 20th century, there were a number of gender discriminatory laws and customs even in the United States. For example, by virtue of a declaration of the US Government, women government employees were paid one-half of the salary of men government employees for doing the exactly same job. The Equal Pay Act of 1963, however, changed this ugly discrimination and thus helped the womenfolk. Yet, inequality in payment between sexes still persists implicitly because US women at present earn 77.8 cents for each dollar earned by a man. Domonic A. Bearfield of A&M University emphasises the aspect of gender discrimination in administrative jobs and observes that this is especially true of female federal employees. Again, Hsieh and Winslow's study (2006) indicates that though women's conditions regarding payment and representation have on the whole improved, yet women of various racial and ethnic groups still suffer from inequality.

There are two different and contradictory viewpoints regarding gender roles in public administration. The first one focuses on efficiency and objectivity in administration and is known as the 'Masculine' approach. The second viewpoint emphasises the aspect of social justice in administration and is known as the 'Feminine' approach. Quite interestingly till the outbreak of The First World War, there was a peaceful harmony and co-existence of these two contradictory approaches. Both men and women till that period used to work together in the field of administration, devote in implementing policies unitedly and efficiently and jointly emphasise the principle of classical pragmatism. But since the war started, there was a significant shift in the field of public administration regarding gender roles. The entire public administrative system and machinery became more and more dependent on male-dominated organisations such as the *Social Science Research Council's Advisory Committee of Public Administration*. The approach of efficiency or objectivity started to be stressed. In other words, the 'Masculine' approach dominated the 'Feminine' approach in the discipline of public administration where significantly increased dependence on 'Masculine' principles started to be noticed.

On the contrary, the American society's approach influenced the area of administration in a new way. Their emphasis was increasingly upon the aspect of social justice. Thus the 'Feminine' approach in administration was emphasised by the US society.

As a result of this dichotomy, men started to control the areas of finance and other science-based organisations, while women started to control the areas of social work, social justice etc.

In recent years the aspect of 'difference' in public services has started to be encouraged and appreciated. It is said that to establish democratic governance, the discipline of public administration has to place more emphasis upon inclusiveness. In this respect the gender question in administration is particularly welcomed, while established public administration emphasised the matter of technical implementation of policies as efficiently and effectively as possible. Hence, the principles of efficiency and effectiveness only were given priority, while those of social equality, protection of minority rights and opportunity, social justice etc. were emphatically neglected. No wonder, the 'gender' question at that time took a back seat in administration. The goal of truly integrating women into the administrative system can be achieved only when a depolarised workplace of administration is established where both women and men's worth is equally recognised and appreciated. Women's proper representation in and contribution to the administrative milieu, as observed by Mrs. T.J. Bowlker long ago, would definitely mean a distinctiveness in views, perspectives and skills in the work of policy execution or implementation. This would ultimately make the work of administration increasingly inclusive and hence democratic in nature. Women's representation and participation can replace a partial representation with a complementary and enriched representation in the administrative field.

Slowly but gradually there has been a remarkable increase of women among students as well as faculty members of public administration. Consequently, the supply and demand for gender-related scholarships have significantly increased. Number of female administrators, too, have been on the rise. But the administrative systems in most of the cases were not women-friendly. Most of the administrative organisations lacked nursing rooms at the office (for pregnant or lactating women) or facilities like maternity leave or early afternoon hours (in order to pick up children after schools and take care of them) etc., because for a long time there were not adequate female administrators. Eventually, the presence of the marginalised sections of the community, viz., women, members of the religious minority, ethnic groups etc. is largely noticed in various public administrative organisations. More and more articles on subjects like same sex marriage, workplace benefits for women workers, transgender nondiscriminatory policies etc. are now published in journals of public administration. With the introduction of such new policies and developments, women's conditions in the administrative sector have improved, but not been made at par with men. Scholars observe that discrimination still persists.

Some notable figures of marginalised identities in public administration are as follows:

- Mary Anderson (1866–1953)
- M.P. Follett (1868–1933)
- Camilla Stivers (1938–)
- Martha Nussbaum (1947–)
- Susan Stanton (1959–)

Mary Anderson (1866–1953)

As feminism started in the United States during the late 19th century and early 20th century, a significant number of women entered the public sphere and started struggling for women's labour legislation and more socio-economic equality. Mary Anderson made continued efforts to create equality between sexes in government and bureaucracy. In the mid-1880s she migrated to the United States from Sweden and by 1910s she earned considerable reputation as an active member of the labour movement. In 1911, after a very prominent garment workers' strike, she took a leading role in drafting an agreement between the labourers and the management. To include a women's division in the labour department of America, she created an extensive lobbying campaign in which she was not successful. Yet she became quite well-known for her genuine efforts and when the 20th Amendment to the US Constitution was passed in 1920 and the Women's Bureau was formally established as a permanent organisation, Mary Anderson became the Head of the Bureau.

M.P. Follett (1868–1933)

Mary Parker Follett emerged as a forerunner to the trend of feminist perspective in administrative studies. In 1927 she clearly wrote: "It seems to me that whereas power usually means power-over, the power of some person or group over some other person or group, it is possible to develop the conception of power-with, a jointly developed power, a co-active, not a coercive power."[19] The concept of "power-over" versus "power-with" became a recurring theme in feminism since the 1970s, and even now it remains in active and conscious use.

Follett was not only an American social worker, management consultant and philosopher, but a notable pioneer in the fields of organisational theory and organisational behaviour. Along with Lillian Gilbreth, Follett was indeed one of the two great female management theorists in the early days of Classical Management Theory. She authored a number of books and essays, articles and speeches on democracy, human relations, political philosophy, psychology, organisational behaviour and conflict resolution. Her ideas gained great influence after Chester Barnard published his seminal work *The Functions of the Executive*. Her emphasis on such soft factors as 'communication', 'informal processes' in organisations etc. inspired Elton Mayo and many other management theorists like Abraham Maslow, Kurt Lewin, Douglas McGregor, Chris Argyris etc. She innovated a totally new concept of leadership in the following way:

"Moreover, we have now to lay somewhat less stress than formerly on this matter of the leader influencing his group because we now think of the leader as also being influenced by his group."[20]

Camilla Stivers (1938–)

Feminist administrative theories have to be traced back to Camilla Stivers and her very influential work—*Gender Images in Public Administration* (1993). She emphasises on developing a gender–neutral management. She sees the historical exclusion of women from business and politics and their directed confinement to homemaking and housekeeping may neither be natural nor intentional. This view addresses the pre-existing dichotomy in gender positions by seeking to change it to a certain extent.

Along with a number of well-known books and articles she is the author of *Gender Images in Public Administration: Legitimacy and the Administrative State*, for which she has received the Distinguished Research Award from the Section on Women in Public Administration. The reviewer of this book Hugh T. Miller believes that the book informs and engages while simultaneously focusing on the major aspects of public administration. Her contributions to the fields of Urban Studies and Public Service are reflected in her influential work *Bureau Men, Settlement Women: Constructing Public Administration in the Progressive Era*. Though partially retired, Dr. Stivers currently serves as a professor at Cleveland State University.

Martha Nussbaum (1947–)

Martha Nussbaum is an American philosopher. Her work on capabilities has often focused on the unequal freedoms and opportunities of women. She has developed a distinctive type of feminism, inspired by the liberal tradition and at the same time emphasising that liberalism, at its best, involves radical rethinking of gender relations as well as relations within the family.

Nussbaum's *Sex and Social Justice* (1998) demonstrates that sex and sexuality are morally irrelevant distinctions that have artificially been enforced as sources of social hierarchy. Thus, as she observes, feminism and social justice have common concerns.

At present, Martha Nussbaum is the Ernst Freund Distinguished Service Professor of Law and Ethics at the University of Chicago. She is here jointly appointed in the Law School and the Department of Philosophy. She has a special interest in political philosophy, feminism and ethics. She also holds associate appointments in classics, divinity and political science.

Susan Stanton (1959–)

Susan Ashley Stanton is a transgender woman and active city manager of Greenfield, California. She decided to transform her gender (from male to female) while acting as the city manager of Largo, Florida. A month after she declared her decision, Stanton was fired from her work and was forced to find work somewhere else. The board that fired her claim that the decision of firing was not related to her transition to a new gender, but the board could not trust her ability to manage the city any more. Stanton, though served the city of Largo for 17 years, was fired and had to remain jobless for two years. Ultimately she found a position as city manager of Lake Worth, Florida, in 2009. She left Lake Worth for Greenfield, California, where she became the city manager and served there for four years. Then she became the Chief Operating Officer of Administrative Services of the Santa Clara Valley Water District in San Jose, California in 2017.

Postmodern writers like Simone de Beauvoir, Judith Butler etc. wrote on the social construction of the 'masculine' and 'feminine'. This construction looked at the 'hard' approach of traditional public administration which conflicts with the ideas referred to as 'soft' approach. Post-modern feminism created a synthesis, a wise blending between the 'hard' and the 'soft' styles of public administration.

There is also a recognisable orthodoxy apparent in the works of a number of other public administration scholars. They are known as Equity Feminists. Equity Feminism demands the elimination of the problems arising out of socio-economic discriminations between genders. Their concern is basically to establish social equity and justice for women and fair conduct in the way women are treated in employment. In fact, in conventional studies of public administration, the feminist approaches in general have been concerned with the two following issues:

- Identifying and reducing gender-based inequalities
- Promoting a more egalitarian workplace

At present, one has to understand the fact that gender division in public administration or creating obstructions for women to participate effectively in public organisations is a serious denial of social justice. This is bound to detrimental to the progress and development of the nation, its people and ultimately the world at large. In order to promote women's ability to systematically contribute to the decision-making forum, different areas of interventions are necessary.

Questions

1. Discuss the salient features of the Indian Constitution.
2. What is meant by Personnel Administration? Discuss its role in the Indian administrative system.
3. What is Public Sector Administration? Discuss its role in Indian administration.
4. Explain the effects of globalization on the civil society in India.
5. Write short notes on:
   (a) Human Rights in Indian administration
   (b) Impact of IT on administration
   (c) Some important law and order agencies in India and their functions.
6. Write a note on the relations between administration and gender issues.

Notes and References

1. Chakrabarty, Bidyut, *Reinventing Public Administration: The Indian Experience*, Orient Longman, New Delhi, 2007.
2. Rao, K.V., *Parliamentary Democracy in India*, World Press Ltd., Calcutta, 1961.
3. This has been dealt in detail in Chapter 14 of this book.
4. Willoughby, W.F., *Principles of Public Administration*, Brookings Institution, Washington, 1927.
5. Kitt, D.F. and H.B. Milward (Eds.), *The State of Public Management*, Johns Hopkins University Press, Baltimore, 1996.
6. Osborne, Stephen P. and Kate McLaughlin, The New Public Management in Context, in Kate McLaughlin, Stephen P. Osborne and Evan Ferlie (Eds.), *New Public Management: Current Trends and Future Prospects*, Routledge, London, 2002.
7. Singh, Amita, Marketing Public Administration: The New Public Management Approach, in Dhameja, Alka (Ed.), *Contemporary Debates in Public Administration*, Prentice-Hall of India, New Delhi, 2003.

8. Governmental bureaucracy in India has been discussed in detail in Chapter 2 of this book.
9. Chakrabarty, Bidyut, *op. cit.*
10. Dey, B.K., E-Governance in India: Problems, Challenges and Opportunities–A Future Vision, *Indian Journal of Public Administration*, Vol. XLVI(3), July–September 2000.
11. *The Information Technology Act, 2000,* Government of India, New Delhi, 2000, Ch. 1.
12. Bhatnagar, Subhas, Administrative Corruption: How Does E-Government Help? *Global Corruption Report, 2003,* Transparency International, New York, 2003.
13. Kamarck, Elaine, Government Innovations Around the World, *Faculty Research Working Paper,* John F. Kennedy School of Government, Harvard University, 2004.
14. Letters of the Commission to the Chief Secretaries of all States and Union Territories, No. 66/SG/NHRC/93 dated 14 December, 1993, National Human Rights Commission, *Annual Report, 1993–1994,* New Delhi, 1994.
15. *The Pioneer* (Delhi), November 26, 1995.
16. Chakrabarty, Bidyut, *op. cit.*
17. Peters, B. Guy, Models of Governance for the 1990s, in Kitt, D.F. and H.B. Milward (Eds.), *The State of Public Management,* The Johns Hopkins University Press, Baltimore, 1996.
18. Osborne, D. and T. Gaebler, *Reinventing Government: How the Entrepreneurial Spirit is Transforming the Public Sector,* Prentice-Hall of India, New Delhi, 1992.
19. Follett, M.P., *Dynamic Administration*, Harper & Brothers Publishers, New York, 1927, Reprint 1942.
20. Follett, M.P., "Dynamic Administration: The Collected Papers of Mary Parker Follett", Ed. by E.M. Fox and L. Urwick, Pitman Publishing, London, 1940.

16 Some Recent Developments in the Concept of Administration

16.1 INTRODUCTION

In this chapter some recent developments centering round the concept of administration, in general, and Indian administration, in particular, are sought to be explained. Three such significant developments of the relatively recent times are as under:

- Public Administration in the era of Globalisation, Liberalisation and Privatisation
- Governance and Government
- Right to Information

First, we will try to explain how in an era of globalisation, liberalisation and privatisation, both public administration as a concept and public sector administrative organisations as bodies are being affected structurally and functionally. [For the relation between globalisation and public administration, see Chapter 15, Section 15.8].

16.2 LIBERALISATION AND PRIVATISATION

Normally, globalisation brings with it *liberalisation* which basically means the whole-hearted efforts to be free from the restrictions on production, expansion and following of rigid and rigorous governmental rules and regulations. Several impacts of liberalisation are:[1]

- Flexibility in policies
- Increase in production
- Reducing the burden of work on administration
- Increase in creativity and innovation
- Newer experiments
- Lessening the administrative control on economic and commercial activities

Under the impact of economic liberalisation, new inputs from the contemporary socio-economic sectors have brought about significant changes in the Indian administrative system. Under this changed situation the public sector is forced to compete with a number of private sector organisations in cases of cost, quality and span of production in order to survive physically. Indian financial matters under the impact of liberslisation, are no longer determined solely by the Indian administrative system. Such matters, related to banks, inflation, monetary and fiscal policy, budget etc., are nowadays being finalised to a great extent by the international financial market. Liberalisation has largely encouraged the entry in our country of foreign investors in the sectors of roads, telecommunications, airports, health, education, insurance, IT etc. Powers and functions of the governmental bureaucracy have been enormously reduced and hence the scope of the Indian public sector is consequently being curtailed.

Numbers of public sector employees are remarkably reduced for removing dysfunctional and sick units. As a result, job security, which is definitely a major feature of Indian administrative system, is drastically being crushed. The principles of New Public Management tend to control Indian administration to a large extent so that the latter can easily face the challenges of liberalisation. The principle of quality management is given particular stress so that the domestic economy, by maintaining stability, can cope with the global economy.

With IT sector developments, the work culture and the entire work environment have been changed in the public sector as well. Traditional methods and pace of work have been replaced with modern ones as an impact of liberalisation on the public administrative sector.

Due to the continuous use of advanced means of communication and increasing access to print as well as electronic media, common citizens are now encouraged to put their grievances and opinions before the government and administration. As a result, transparency in administration is smoothly brought about, defeating secrecy and the hidden faces of administration. Thus ethical values and responsiveness of the public sector are also being increased.

With liberalisation, significant efforts have been made by different departments to improve the structural, financial, personnel and managerial positions by introducing structural and policy changes. Such changes can easily attract foreign investments and consequently bring about organisational stability to a great extent.[2]

After facing liberalisation, Indian public administrative system tends to play the role of a motivator and a developer to motivate and develop the unemployed and untrained citizens by encouraging grass root level organisations, NGOs and Self Help Groups to participate in welfare programmes.

As a result of liberalisation, Indian administration in general has become more efficient, productive and customer-friendly due to the enforcement of transparency in administration.

Liberalisation also encourages market-oriented structures and policies in Indian administration. Reduction of the rigorous hierarchical structures, downsizing of the bureaucracy and decentralisation of policy formulation are significantly being encouraged.[3]

As globalisation encourages and increasingly introduces IT advancements in the administrative sector, liberalisation puts emphasis on e-governance, right to information and a gross administrative transparency—all likely to be preferred by the citizens in general.

With liberalisation, cost and time bound techniques have been applied to increase production. In other words, administrative efficiency and effectiveness can be produced. Liberal policies have paved the way for greater coordination and cooperation between Indian administration and multiple other organisations.[4]

But liberalisation, though trying to make administration adoptable to varied situations, tends to pose problems for national integrity because collective decisions are made in a context in which the national government has practically no control.

Moreover, the global meltdown has also adversely affected the Indian market and economy. In a situation of economic depression, each and every country tends to prioritise its own economy, instead of being 'global' in a true sense. In short, the negative effects of liberalisation are as under:

- Loss of job-security
- Adverse impacts of global meltdown on Indian industry
- Increase in the number of frauds and cyber crimes
- Increase in internal and external security problems.

Like liberalisation, globalisation brings with it *privatisation* as well. *Privatisation* is a rather indistinct concept, covering a wide range of ideas, policies and programmes. Broadly speaking the term implies a roll-back of the state in the lives and activities of citizens and strengthening the role of markets. In its narrow sense, the term is meant by a transfer of ownership from the public to the private sector. This transfer is made as it is expected to help lead to efficiency and encourage investment which will eventually help in the development of infrastructure. Globalisation tends to open up the world trade, thus transforming the entire world into a small global village or global market. Under these new circumstances of privatisation, public administration has to play the role of an enabler, collaborator, facilitator and co-operator. It is expected to partner (through public-private partnership in various sectors like telecom, airlines, electricity, etc.), regulate the market and handle sensitive departments directly (such as defence, law and order, atomic energy and foreign policy). Regarding social programmes and effective implementation of social policies, public administration is likely to partner up with various NGOs and welfare organisations.

With the introduction of privatisation, a period of stress as well as development can be seen in the field of public administration both as a discipline and an activity. Such impacts of privatisation on the administrative sector are as follows:

(a) **Public–Private Partnership (PPP):** Though there are differences between the two sectors, public and private, yet if they join hands, their respective strength can be increased and the joint venture can prove to be successful in the administrative sphere. On social issues and policies, public administrative sector can offer better expertise while regarding management, private administration can bring in its specialisation as well as efficiency.

(b) **Public Administration in Policy Making:** Policy implementation and policy formulation can never be separated in a sensible way. Under privatisation, public administration's task is not only to implement policies but to frame them as well. Through their exercise of choice and judgement in administering policies, administrators can efficiently implement policies. Besides, they take active part in formulating policies through their analytical, suggestive and interpretative roles.

(c) **Movement towards Political Economy:** In recent years economists, under the influence of globalisation and privatisation, have developed new methods of analyzing the cost and benefits of various governmental programmes. On the other hand, administrators tend to choose economics more as a base of public administrative issues.

(d) **Changing Goals of Administration:** Technical efficiency and effectiveness are the ultimate goals of public administration under the changed situation.

(e) **Coordination, not Antagonism, between Staff and Line:** Staff units are the technically specialised coordinating and facilitating agencies between upper strata of management from where decisions are taken and the line units are those who implement such decisions. So, line units are basically field work units. Under the impact of privatisation, staff agencies and line agencies are in good relations.

(f) **Human Relations Approach in Public Administration:** As administrative organisations in the public sector in an age of privatisation change structurally and functionally, a change is significantly noticeable in their values and attitudes as well. Such organisations are nowadays more friendly towards the underprivileged like minority groups, women and the poor. Bureaucrats are now more concerned with issues like socio-economic equality, sensitivity to human sufferings, social needs etc.

Globalisation as an ideology had been dominating the world scenario since the breakdown of the Soviet Union (1988–89). China and some South East Asian Countries had adopted globalisation even earlier. The wave of globalisation reached India in its nascent form during the regime of Rajiv Gandhi, but became a compulsion since 1991 when the country did not have any option but to take a loan from the IMF to tide over its foreign exchange crisis. Globalisation along with liberalisation and privatisation was imposed on India as a condition of taking the loan. Since then, the country has been practising globalisation, albeit in varying degrees across various political regimes.

Globalisation literally means free international trade. It involves not only free movement of goods across countries, but that of services and capital as well. Privatisation requires the replacement of government-run enterprises by private entrepreneurship. Liberalisation entails an economic environment free from inefficient government intervention, in general and 'licence-raj', in particular. Under the strict vigilance of the IMF all the three practices were adopted in India since the early 1990s. But even after the IMF loan was repaid and monitoring by the Fund had ended, the practice continued.

Globalisation as an economic ideology is close to that of 'laissez faire'. It puts emphasis on private endeavours and argues that an economic fabric based primarily on private enterprises is more efficient than a system principally governed by the State.

But this does not mean that the State has no role to play in a globalised, liberalised and privatised economy. This is particularly true of a less developed economy like India. In the pre-globalisation era, India witnessed government intervention almost in every sphere of business. The government had decided to take up producing not only basic commodities like petroleum and steel, but indulge into the manufacturing of a wide variety of consumer products with breads and wristwatches at one end of the spectrum and computers, televisions and automobiles at the other. Clearly, this was unnecessary and inefficient. More important, since the government's energy was mostly spent in running sectors where it should not have intervened, it spent little time, energy and resources in sectors where its presence was absolutely necessary. The drive towards globalisation led the government to mobilise its resources more towards sectors where private enterprise cannot give the best results, leaving the rest in the hands of individual entrepreneurs.

Private enterprises cannot yield the socially optimum results for sectors with externalities. By 'externality' we mean a situation where the benefit or the cost of consuming a commodity is not restricted to the consumer alone. An example of positive externality is education. Not only the educated person herself is benefited by the education she is getting, but also her family and immediate neighbourhood can get a benefit of her education if she helps others in her vicinity to take informed decisions. An example of negative externality is pollution. When a person is polluting the environment, it is not only costly for him, but also for others living in his neighbourhood. In both cases the government has to intervene. It has to intervene in the educational sector by providing subsidies and in the environmental sector by restricting the consumption of commodities which pollute the environment through taxation. Other important examples of sectors with positive externalities are health, transport and physical infrastructures like roads, dams and bridges, etc.

There is yet another reason why governments have to intervene in sectors like health and education in a less-developed economy like India. In India, a large section of population lives below the poverty line and cannot reach their full potential. From the point of view of the society, it is necessary to develop the human capital in this underprivileged section. For this, too, government intervention is absolutely necessary. In other words, even in an era of globalisation, government machineries are to be geared towards developing education, health and physical infrastructures and regulating social evils like deterioration of the environment and emergence of monopolistic practices.

16.3 GOVERNANCE AND GOVERNMENT

Governance, the emergence and types of the concept and the difference between the two concepts, viz., Governance and Government, are going to be explained in this section.

By 'governance' we usually mean the making and establishment of policies and continuous monitoring of their proper implementation, by the members of the governing body of an organisation. It includes the mechanisms which are required to balance the powers as well as accountability of these members and the principal duty of increasing the development and sustenance of the organisation. Thus governance is basically "all of the processes of governing, whether undertaken by a government, market or network, whether over a family, tribe, formal or informal organisation or territory and whether through the laws, norms, power or language of an organized society".[5] According to scholars like Hufty, governance relates to "the processes of interaction and decision-making among the actors involved in a collective problem that lead to the creation, reinforcement, or reproduction of social norms and institutions."[6]

Thus, by 'governance' we generally mean the way in which rules, norms and actions of an organisation are structured, controlled, maintained and remained responsible. Both the internal rules of the given organisation and the external rules regarding the relation between the organisation and its business partners determine the degree of formality of the said organisation. Determined by different aims and results, governance may be of various types like public governance, private governance, global governance, non-profit governance, corporate governance, project governance, environmental governance, IT governance, participatory governance, regulatory governance, contract governance, metagovernance, collaborative governance, security sector governance, etc.

Public Governance

Generally, public governance is that kind of governance that occurs in three broad ways. *First*, through networks involving public–private partnerships (PPP) or in collaboration with community organisations.

Second, through the use of market mechanisms in which market principles of competition serve to allocate resources while operating under government control.

Third, through top-down methods that principally involve governments and the state bureaucracy.

Private Governance

Private governance is that kind of governance in which private entities make public policies. It occurs when non-governmental entities, including private organisations, dispute resolving organisations or other third party groups make rules that have immense impacts upon the quality of life of the larger public.

Global Governance

Global governance is defined as the complex of formal and informal institutions, mechanisms, relationships and processes between and among states, markets, citizens and organisations through which collective interests on the global plane are articulated, rights and obligations are established, and differences are mediated.[7]

Non-Profit Governance

Non-profit governance is that kind of governance which emphasises two things simultaneously.

First, it stresses upon achieving the organisation's social mission.

Second, it ensures that the organisation is viable.

Corporate Governance

Corporate governance is that kind of governance which primarily includes two things.

First, the way in which boards or similar bodies of corporate organisations direct the organisations.

Second, the laws, customs, rules etc. applying to that direction. The first documented use of the term 'corporate governance' was by Richard Eells, who in 1960 used the term to denote the "structure and functioning of the corporate polity."

Project Governance

Project governance is that sort of governance which describes the processes that need to exist for a successful project. This term is used in industry, particularly in the IT sector.

Environmental Governance

Environmental governance is that kind of governance which advocates sustainable development as the supreme consideration for managing all human activities—political, social and economic. Environmental governance is basically a concept used in political ecology and environmental policy.

IT Governance

IT governance is that sort of governance which principally deals with the relations between business focus and the management of the Information Technology. The aim of a clear governance includes an assurance that the investment in the IT sector generates business value and reduces the risks associated with IT projects.

Participatory Governance

Participatory governance is that kind of governance which puts significant emphasis upon deep democratic engagement through participation of all citizens in the process of governance of their state. Thus such governance ensures people's direct role in the decision making process or at least their whole-hearted engagement with political issues of their own nation.

Regulatory Governance

Regulatory governance is that kind of governance which is found in a controlling state. It reflects the emergence of decentered and mutually adaptive policy regimes that rest on control or regulation rather than service provision.

Contract Governance

Contract governance is that sort of governance which focuses on creating a structure of governance in which the contractual parties have a vested interest in managing contractual arrangements in a more collaborative, aligned, flexible and credible way. Since contracts are bound to be varied and complex, contract governance structures, too, vary with the nature of the transaction.

Metagovernance

Metagovernance is that sort of governance which represents the established ethical principles or 'norms' which shape and steer the entire governing process. Hence, it can be defined as the "governing of governing."[8]

Collaborative Governance

Collaborative governance is that sort of governance the framework of which uses a relationship between management structure, joint performance and transformation of management processes. It also uses an exit management plan as controlling mechanisms to encourage the organisations to make ethical, proactive changes so that all parties are mutually benefited.

Security Sector Governance

Security sector governance is a sub-category or framework of security governance. Its focus is particularly on decisions about security and their implementation within the security sector of a single state.

Quality wise, governance can be of various types: *Weak Governance, Fair Governance, Good Governance*, etc.

Weak Governance

Weak governance is that kind of governance in which public sector actors are unable or unwilling to assume their roles and responsibilities in protecting rights, providing basic services and amenities and ensuring the public in general that public sector management is efficient, effective and responsible. Such failures on the part of the government lead to broader failures in political, economic and civic institutions as well. On the whole, what is produced can be referred to as weak governance. Poverty, inequality, poorly planned urban development etc. are the features of a weak governance in which governments, the private sector and public institutions all work weakly. There is a slight difference between poor governance and weak governance. Poor governance implies the governmental inability to provide services and amenities to citizens. On the other hand, weak governance means not the inability but the unwillingness on the part of the government to provide such basic services and amenities. When the government has little control over the country, corruption and lawlessness are created. Such situations are termed as weak governance.

Good Governance

The concept of good governance emerges as a model to compare ineffective or inefficient economies or political organisations with viable economies and political organisations. When people in general instead of selected groups of population in a society are happy with the governmental performance regarding the fulfilment of their needs and demands, it may be said that the government is responsible giving birth to 'good governance'. Since primarily the liberal democratic states of the west like the United States and the European states are referred to as 'most successful', good governance standards quite often measure other state institutions against these states. In good governance, people's basic services and amenities are provided by governments at all levels. Basically, good governance is an indeterminate term used in the literature of international development to describe how public institutions and organisations perform functions related to public affairs and manage public resources. The World Bank puts emphasis on economic dimensions including five key principles related to 'good governance'. They are as under:

- Public Sector Management,
- Organisational Accountability,
- The Rule of Law,
- Transparency, and
- Citizens' Access to Information

Academia and civil society focus on the social dimension related to 'good governance'. It is:

- Active and Meaningful Participation by Citizens in the Affairs of the State.

UNDP, OECD, EU etc. give emphasis upon political dimension, adding some other principles related to 'good governance'. They are:

- Governmental Legitimacy
- Downward Accountability
- Protection of Human Rights
- Responsiveness of the Government
- Equality and Fairness

Some political thinkers believe that 'fair governance' connects with society and fights with inequality more than 'good governance'. Governments need to change their mindset to bridge the gap between governance and practice, while most governments have short-term focus, primarily concerned with the victory in the next election. The only way to fight inequality and injustice in society is through 'fair governance'. In 2013, the Norwegian Deputy Minister for International Development Arvinn Eikeland Gadgil stressed on the difference between good governance and fair governance. To him, the first is a very technical concept while the second understands the society in a much better way. Fair governance is about political choices and choosing to understand why social inequality is increasing. "It is an abstract concept but needs to seep into policymakers' mind." His view of 'fair governance' is that the government of which is able to understand plight of the poorest section of the society and to make sure that the poor should not become relatively poorer and that they should have a voice.

The concept of 'governance' is not quite new. Over the years it has gained momentum and a wider meaning. Nowadays it is not merely an instrument of public affairs management, or a gauge of political development. It has also become a useful mechanism to increase the legitimacy of the public realm. Moreover, it has become an analytical framework or approach to comparative politics. The general definition of 'governance' as provided by Webster's Third New International Dictionary (1986) indicates that governance is a synonym for government. But the working definition used by the British Council emphasises that governance is a much broader notion than government. 'Governance' encompasses the related concepts like the state, government, regime and good government. Many of the elements and principles underlying 'good government' have become integral parts of the meaning of governance.

The World Bank's emphasis on 'governance' reflects the worldwide thrust towards political and economic liberalisation. Such a governance-oriented approach highlights issues of greater state responsiveness and accountability, and also the impacts of these factors on political stability and economic development.

It is also necessary to refer to academic literature on the term 'governance'. Scholars working with international development and donor agencies mostly use the term. Most of these scholars have concentrated almost exclusively on the issue of political legitimacy, which, in fact, is the dependent variable produced by effective governance. In academic literature, governance is defined as the conscious management of regime structures, with a view to enhancing the public realm.

Goran Hyden's contribution to bring greater clarity to the concept of governance needs to be mentioned. To him governance is an "umbrella concept to define an approach to comparative politics, an approach which fills analytical gaps left by others. His views on governance include the following:[9]

- Governance is a conceptual approach that can frame a comparative analysis of macro-politics.
- Governance concerns 'big' questions of a 'constitutional' nature that establish the rules of political conduct.
- Governance involves creative intervention by political actors to change structures that inhibit the expression of human potential.
- Governance is a rational concept, emphasising the nature of interactions between state and social actors, and among social actors themselves.
- Governance refers to particular types of relationships among political actors.

Key components of 'governance' are as under:

- Governance refers to the activity or process of decision-making and implementation of decisions.
- Governance is broader than 'government'.

- Governance articulates how interests are accommodated and power is exercised in a society.
- Governance includes formal and informal rules.
- Governance has some quality principles like accountability, participation, transparency, rule of law etc.
- Governance is contextual.

The differences between the two terms 'government' and 'governance' may be explained if one looks at the respective definitions. Governance is the act of governing or ruling. It is the set of rules which are made or framed by the government. Such rules are to be implemented through the representatives of the state.

- Government is a group of people who rule or run the administration of a nation. It is basically the body of representatives who govern or control the state at a given time. Thus, government is the medium through which the power of the state is employed.

  But, governance is the function of ruling the people of the state via the representatives in the government. Simply put, governance is what governments do.
- Government may be of different types or forms. It may be a democratic or an autocratic form of government, though most modern governments are democratic in nature.

  Governance is a concept that can be followed in an organisation of any size or dimension. Governance may be of various types like global governance, corporate governance, project governance, IT governance, non-profit governance, participatory governance etc.
- Government is a body through which the physical exercise of the polity is done.

  Governance is itself the physical activity of the polity.
- Government being the nucleus of the state is a body of elected representatives. It is always headed by a single person.

  Such a body is supposed to make use of established rules to run the affairs of the state smoothly and efficiently in favour of the people of the state. Such an activity is known as governance.

  Thus, members of a *government* are engaged in the task of *governance*.

16.4 RIGHT TO INFORMATION

Right to Information (RTI) is an Act of the Parliament of India to provide for setting out the practical regime of right to information for citizens and replaces the erstwhile Freedom of Information Act, 2002. This RTI law was passed by our Parliament on 15 June, 2005 and came into force fully on 12 October, 2005.[10]

The RTI Act (2005) is basically a timely response to citizens' requests for government information. It is an initiative taken by the Department of Personnel and Training, Ministry of Personnel, Public Grievances and Pensions. The Act principally provides an RTI portal gateway to the citizens for quick search of information on the details of first Appellate Authorities, Public Information Officers (PIOs) etc. and also an access to RTI-related information published on the website by various public authorities under the Government of India and State Governments.

The basic objective of the RTI Act is to enable Indian citizens to know the working and activities of the government and thus to empower them more, to promote transparency and accountability in the working of the government, to reduce governmental corruption and also to make our democracy meaningful in a true sense. It is known to all that when citizens are more aware and informed, they are better equipped to keep necessary watch on the governmental instruments and thus to make the government more and more accountable to its citizenry. The RTI Act (2005) is undoubtedly a significant step towards making the citizens more and more aware and informed of the governmental activities. The Act requires that every public authority should computerise their records for a wide dissemination so that the citizens can have ready access to any and every information (regarding the working in the public sector) formally. Information disclosure in India was restricted by the Official Secrets Act (1923) and various other special laws. The new RTI Act (2005) relaxes such restrictions. Hence, it codifies a fundamental right of our citizens.

The first RTI application was submitted by Shahid Raza Burney to a Police Station in Pune, Maharashtra, on October 12, 2005.

The RTI Act (2005) covers the whole of India except Jammu and Kashmir, where a separate Jammu and Kashmir RTI Act is applicable. The RTI Act (2005) covers all constitutional authorities, including the executive, legislature, and judiciary, anybody or organisation established or constituted by a Parliamentary Act or a State Legislative Act, and any body owned, controlled or substantially funded by the Government or any NGO. Private bodies, strictly speaking, are not within the ambit of the Act. But in a decision of *Sarbjit Roy* vs. *Delhi Electricity Regulatory Commission*, the Central Information Commission stated that privatised public utility companies also fall within the purview of the RTI Act (2005). Till 2014, private institutions and NGOs receiving over 95 per cent of the infrastructure funds from the government have come under this Act.

A citizen who wishes to get an access to some information from a public authority is required to send, along with the application, a Postal Order or a Demand Draft or a Banker's Cheque payable to the Accounts Officer of the public authority as fee prescribed for seeking information. The applicant may be required to pay additional fees towards the cost of providing the exact information, details of which are to be intimated to the applicant by the Public Information Officer as prescribed by the RTI Act (2005). Persons from disadvantaged communities need not pay any fee.

16.4.1 RTI Act (2005) and Intellectual Property Rights

A number of civil society members have recently complained against the dilution of the RTI Act (2005) by the occasional citation of Intellectual Property Rights argument by the governmental agencies. Most notable among such dilutions are as under:

(a) The Right to Information denied by the Reserve Bank of India citing Intellectual Property Laws.

(b) The Right to Information denied by the Department of Irrigation, UP, after more than eight months of an RTI appeal regarding the construction of the Gomti Riverfront Development Project by a group of environmental researchers. They were eager to know about some environmentally adverse impacts of the project and whether they were or were not stated in the project report. Citing Intellectual Property Rights, this RTI application was denied.

16.4.2 Citizen's Charter

Following Great Britain, India, too, has introduced Citizen's Charter by which the public bodies have been able to improve their functioning over the years. They refer to the principles and timelines, enshrined through these charters, tend to promote good governance and greater satisfactions to citizens in general. Citizen's charter is a document published by an organisation for public reference. It provides details of the nature, working and functions of the organisation and incorporates the service quality as well as the time period for providing different services which citizens can expect from the organisation.

Citizen's Charter is significantly important in public administration or public management on the following grounds:

- It makes the government and other public organisations open and transparent.
- It promotes good governance.
- It incentivises accountability in administration.
- It is citizen-friendly in nature, prioritising citizens' needs and demands.
- It ensures better service quality and grievance redressal of the government and other public organisations.
- It emphasises the 'public' element of public administration, thus making the government more democratic in a true sense.

Being a British political initiative, Citizen's Charter was first launched by the (then) Prime Minister of Great Britain, John Major, on July 22, 1991. Its principal aim was to improve the quality of British public services by taking following steps:

(a) Making administration accountable and citizen-friendly.
(b) Ensuring to citizens administrative transparency and their right to information.
(c) Taking measures to cleanse and motivate the civil service.
(d) Adopting clearly a stakeholder approach.
(e) Saving time of both the administrators as well as the clientele.
(f) Ensuring stability as well as quantification and documentation of public organisational works.

It was specifically mentioned that all public services would have to be published with clear targets. Dozens of such services, following Citizen's Charter, did so—from hospitals to prison services, from local government offices to fire services. A significant part of this citizen-friendly public administrative initiative was the granting of 'Charter Marks' to those public bodies who had successfully met defined standards.

In India the Citizen's Charter Bill or the Right to Citizens for the Time-Bound Delivery of Goods and Services and Redressal of their Grievances Bill was passed in the year 2011. This is known as Citizens' Charter. The Bill *firstly* makes it mandatory for every public authority to publish a Citizens' Charter within six months of the commencements of the Act. *Secondly*, it specifically states that every citizen is given the right to get time-bound delivery of goods and services. *Thirdly*, it also indicates that if they are not delivered to the people in time, there must be redressal mechanism in people's hands.

According to the bill, citizens' charters should be applied in the following format:

Name of service	Designated officer	Time limit for service	First appellant officer	Time limit for disposal	Second appellant authority

The appeal must contain the following contents:

- List of details of the goods and services provided by a public authority.
- Name of the person or agency responsible for providing the goods or services.
- Time-frame within which such goods or services have to be provided.
- Category of people entitled to the goods or services.
- Details of the complain redressal mechanism.

This bill aims to establish Public Grievance Redressal Commissions at the Centre as well as the states. Any such Commission would comprise of a Chief Commissioner and a maximum number of ten Commissioners. Persons from the present or former Supreme Court Judges or Chief Justices of High Courts, High Court Judges or District Court Judges, the present or former Secretaries to the Central Government or State Governments, and eminent persons with at least 20 years of experience in social sectors with a post-graduate degree in the relevant sector are to be chosen as Public Grievance Redressal Commissioners. In a Public Grievance Redressal Commission at the Centre, the Chief Commissioner and other Commissioners are to be appointed by the President of India, while the Chief Commissioner and other Commissioners at the state level are to be appointed by the Governor of the respective state. But, the recommending authority is in the hands of a Select Committee, which at the Union level will comprise of the Prime Minister of India, Leader of the Opposition in Lok Sabha and the sitting Chief Justice of the Supreme Court and at the state level will comprise of the Chief Minister, Leader of the Opposition in the State Legislative Assembly and the sitting Chief Justice of the High Court.

Under certain conditions, the Commissioners may be removed by an order of the Indian President or Governor (of the respective state).

In Great Britain, the Citizen's Charter initiative was immensely criticised on the ground that such initiatives could only claim to improve the quality of public services, while in reality public services were not at all improved qualitatively. Money available to the public organisations, too, was drastically curtailed. Private methods of management were increasingly introduced in the public sector, and such introductions were the targets of criticism. The result of a "box-ticking mentality", it was also alleged, failed to understand the actual grievances of individual users regarding the quality of public goods and services.

In India also it is criticised on the ground that while the Citizens' Charter Bill provides for Grievance Commissions both at the Central and state levels, only the state legislatures have jurisdiction to make laws regarding state public services. But the Parliament does not have any jurisdiction to enact such laws. The states of Bihar, Delhi, Jammu and Kashmir, Madhya Pradesh, Rajasthan, Uttar Pradesh, Punjab, Uttarakhand and Himachal Pradesh have their own laws in place. Many of such state laws have much better provisions than those proposed in the Citizens' Charter Bill.

Questions

1. How administration is affected by liberalisation and privatisation?
2. What is meant by 'governance'? What are its various kinds?
3. Write a critical note on Right to Information.

4. Write short notes on:
   (a) Citizen's Charter
   (b) Differences between Governance and Government
   (c) Impacts of privatisation
   (d) Good governance.

Notes and References

1. Dr. Meenu, "Impact of Globalisation and Liberalisation on Indian Administration", *International Journal of Marketing, Financial Services and Management Research*, Vol. 2, No. 9, September, 2013.
2. Goyal, Krishan A., "Impact of Globalisation on Developing Countries with Special Reference to India", *International Research Journal of Finance and Commerce*, Issue 5, 2007.
3. Crafts, N., "Globalization and Growth in the Twentieth Century", IMF Working Paper, IMF, Washington DC, 2000.
4. Gill, S. and Law, D., *The Global Political Economy: Perspectives, Problems and Policies*, Johns Hopkins University Press, Baltimore, 1988.
5. Bevir, Mark, *Governance: A Very Short Introduction*, Oxford University Press, Oxford, UK, 2013.
6. Hufty, Marc, "Investigating Policy Processes: The Governance Analytical Framework (GAF)" in Wiesmann, U., Hurni, H. et al., Eds., *Research for Sustainable Development: Foundations, Experiences and Perspectives*, Geographica Bernensia, Bern, 2011.
7. Thakur, Ramesh, Van Langenhove, Luk, "Enhancing Global Governance through Regional Integration", *Global Governance*, No. 12, 2006.
8. Kooiman, J., *Governing as Governance*, Sage Publications, 2003.
9. "Governance Barometer: Policy Guidelines for Good Governance", Website of South Africa's National Party.
10. Act No. 22 of The RTI Act 2005.

Name Index

Abul Kasem Fazlul Haque, 163
Adarkar, B.P., 279
Akbar, 10, 11, 12, 13, 14, 369
Ambedkar, B.R., 114, 376, 410, 411
Amte, Baba, 215
Anderson, Mary, 428
Appleby, Paul H., 35, 43, 53, 127, 292, 343
Appu, P.S., 303
Ashoka, 369
Avasthi, Amareshwar, 366
Avasthi, Anand Prakash, 366
Ayyangar, N. Gopalaswami, 35, 65, 66, 342

Bandyopadhyay, Debabrata, 204, 212
Banerjee, Surendranath, 163
Bardhan, Pranab, 225
Beaman, Lori, 234
Bhaduri, Amit, 204, 332
Bhalerao, C.N., 46
Bharadwaj, 7
Bhattacharya, Mohit, 27
Box, Richard C., 28
Bryce, Lord, 142, 143
Buch, Nirmala, 232, 380

Caiden, Gerald, 341
Canning, Lord, 18
Canton, 151
Chakraborty, Biswanath, 225
Chakravarti, Sukhomoy, 244
Chambers, Robert, 333
Chanda, Asok, 64, 65, 287, 290–292, 343
Chandra, Satish, 43, 346
Chandrasekhar, 75
Chapman, Brian, 151
Chatterjee, Sovan, 163
Chattopadhyay, Raghav, 224, 235
Chaturvedi, B.K., 76
Chaturvedi, T.N., 130, 292
Chaudhury, Benoy, 202, 212
Cornwallis, Lord, 17, 62

Das, Dwarka, 127
Desai, Morarji, 36, 74, 88, 344, 365
Deutsch, Karl, 334
Dhar, P.N., 74
Duflo, Esther, 224, 235

Fayol, Henri, 241
Follett, M.P., 428

Gandhi, Indira, 27, 36, 37, 74, 88, 304, 354
Gandhi, Mahatma, 30, 201, 376
Gandhi, Rajiv, 37, 75, 78, 183, 194, 228, 249, 258, 315, 347, 437
Gandhi, Sanjay, 74
Goel, M.M., 306
Goel, S.L., 306
Gopalaswami, R.A., 343
Gorwala, A.D., 42, 343
Gowda, Deve, 75, 88
Gujral, I.K., 88

Hankey, Maurice, 80

Hanumantha Rao, C.H., 270
Hastings, Warren, 16, 17
Hawkins, 10
Hazare, Anna, 317
Hoare, Sir Samuel, 45
Hooja, Rakesh, 269
Hudson, Cyril L., 241
Hyden, Goran, 443

Iyer, Lakshmi, 235

Jean, Dreze, 210, 390
Jha, L.K., 73, 74, 345, 346
Jones, 287
Joshi, Kumudben, 320

Kashyap, Subhash, 284
Katz, 336
Kautilya, 6, 7, 8, 11, 275, 369
Khera, S.S., 121, 128
Kothari, D.S., 345
Krishnamachari, T.T., 35
Krishnamachari, V.T., 249, 265, 344
Kulkarni, Sudheendra, 76
Kumar, Santosh, 235
Kunzru, H.N., 279

Lazarsfeld, 336
Lenin, 180
Lieten, G.K., 219

MacIver, 143
Maheshwari, S.R., 53, 68, 80, 91, 172, 254
Major, John, 447
Marks, Charter, 447
Mathur, Kuldeep, 27
Maurya, Chandragupta, 3, 4
Mayo, Lord, 154
Mehta, Balwantray G., 344
Mies, Maria, 210
Millikan, Max, 242
Mill, John Stuart, 142, 143, 144
Mishra, Brajesh, 76
Mitra, Sandip, 225
Mitra, Sanjay, 76
Modi, Narendra, 76
Mookherjee, Dilip, 225
Morris–Jones, W.H., 287, 290
Mudaliar, A.R., 343
Mukherjee, Nirmal, 204
Mukherjee, Pranab, 246, 249, 296

Nair, T.K.A., 76
Narasimha Rao, P.V., 75, 391
Narayan, Jayprakash, 216, 305
Nehru, B.K., 279
Nehru, Jawaharlal, 73, 88, 155, 244, 248, 257, 266
Neogi, K.C., 261
Niemeyer, Sir Otto, 278
Nishith Prakash, 235
Nussbaum, Martha, 429

O'Malley, 130

Panagariya, Arvind, 260
Parashar, 7
Parra Torrado, M.L., 225
Patkar, Medha, 204, 215, 332, 335
Patnaik, Biju, 320
Patnaik, J.B., 320
Pfiffner, J.M., 1
Pillai, N.R., 80
Pradhan, Girish, 34
Prasad, Beni, 11

Rama Rao, N.T., 320
Rao, V.K.R.V., 269
Ripon, Lord, 18
Robson, William A., 143, 162, 303
Roy, Bidhan Chandra, 163

Saikia, Ashok, 76
Santhanam, K., 35, 313, 344
Sarkar, Abhirup, 204, 225
Sarkar, Nalini Ranjan, 163
Sathe, Vasant, 256
Schramm, Wilbur, 334
Sekhar, Chandra, 88
Sen, Amartya, 210, 385, 390
Sengupta, Jatindra Mohan, 163
Shah, Sher, 10, 369
Shankar, V., 74

Shannon, 334
Sharp, Walter R., 309
Shastri, Lal Bahadur, 73, 88, 130
Sibal, Kapil, 317
Simon, Herbert, 28
Singh, Charan, 88
Singh, L.P., 345
Singh, Manmohan, 76
Singh, V.P., 88
Singhvi, L.M., 183, 346
Sivaraman, B., 136
Spear, Percival, 10
Srinivas, M.N., 377
Stanton, Susan, 430
Stivers, Camilla, 429

Thahane, T.T., 242
Thorat, Sukhadeo, 386
Tottenham, Richard, 66

Vajpayee, Atal Behari, 75, 76, 88, 281, 315, 397
Vira, Dharam, 345
Vishalaksha, 7
Visvesvaraya, M., 248
Vittal, N., 305, 324
Vohra, N.N., 304

Webster, Neil, 219
Weidner, Edward, 26
Weiner, Myron, 109
Wellesley, Lord, 17, 62
Wheare, K.C., 411
White, L.D., 1, 33, 181, 409
Wilson, Woodrow, 1

Subject Index

73rd Constitutional Amendment, 193

Accredited Social Health Activists (ASHA), 403
Administration, 1, 302, 303
Administrative reform, 341
Administrative Reforms Commission (ARC), 36, 49, 66, 262, 303, 342, 344, 347, 364
Ahors, 120
Ain-i-Akbari, 10, 12, 13
Amatya, 6, 7
Aitchison Commission, 19
All India Services, 303, 304
American local government, 144
Anchalik panchayat, 189
Appointment committee, 95
Aristocratic system, 415
Arrondisement, 151
Arthasastra, 8
Asian Development Bank, 332
Asoka Mehta Committee, 181–183, 198, 217, 345
Association of Regional Cooperation, 138
Audit department, 276
Ayyangar Report, 80

Balvantrai Mehta Committee, 181, 182, 183, 217
Bihar panchayats, 235
Biographies, 10
Board for Industrial and Financial Reconstruction, 420
Bombay Plan, 244
Border Security Force (BSF), 417, 418
British administration, 4, 16, 20, 155
British Local Government, 148
Broomfield, 218
Buddha period, 6
Bureaucratic system, 415
Bureau of Public Enterprises, 36, 352

Cabinet Committees, 95
Cabinet Secretariat, 77, 78
  role of, 78
Cabinet Secretary, 79
Cantonment Board, 170
Central Bureau of Investigation (CBI), 325
Central Industrial Security Force (CISF), 417, 418
Central Reserve Police Force (CRPF), 417, 418
Central Secretariat, 62, 63
  meaning, nature, functions and role of, 63
  structure of, 64
Central Social Welfare Board, 379
Central Vigilance Commission (CVC), 322
Centralization, 181
Centre–State relations, 23, 91, 135, 280, 346, 349, 353, 358, 360, 363
Chakla, 15
Charter marks, 447
Chief Executive Officer (CEO), 132
Chief Minister, 115
Chief Secretary, 102
Chipko Movement, 214
Chiranjeevi Yojna (CY), 406

Citizens, 303
Citizen's Charter, 38, 446
Citizens' Charter Bill, 448
City-manager plan, 147
Civil service, 33
Civil Service Day, 59
Civil Service Tribunals, 350
Civil society, 409, 423, 442, 446
Clientele, 447
Collaborative Governance, 441
Collector, 120, 124
  changing role of, 126
  duties of, 125
Commission, 146
Commissioners, 146
Commission plan, 146
Committee on parliamentary affairs, 95
Commune, 151
Communications, 334
Community development, 181
Community Development Programme (CDP), 181
Composition of the Planning Commission, 249
Composition of the Union Public Service Commission (UPSC), 44
Comptroller and Auditor General (CAG), 285, 286, 290
Contract governance, 440
Corporate governance, 439
Corruption, 141
Councillors, 161
Council of Ministers, 86, 115, 117
Crisis administration, 130

Decentralization, 180
Dehradun-brigade, 75
Democracy, 142, 155, 180
Democratic decentralization, 180
Demonetisation, 30
Departmental Commission, 151
Department of Economic Affairs, 90
Department of Expenditure, 89
Departments/Directorates, 105
Deshmukh Study Team, 80
Developing countries, 2, 141, 241, 335, 346
Development, 229, 334
  officer, 131
  planning, 242
Development Programme (IRDP), 131
Diplomacy, 8
Directive principles of state policy, 412
Discretionary powers of the Governor, 112
District administration, 120, 121
  function of, 121
  organisation of, 122
District Development Council, 192
District Magistrate, 128
District planning, 269
District Rural Development Agency (DRDA), 131, 339
Dravid Munetra Kazgham, 377
Dyarchy, 19

East India Company (EIC), 16, 50, 124
Economic administration, 351
Economic Affairs Committee, 95
Economic Reforms Commission, 346
Election Commission, 293
Electoral Quota, 83
Electors' Photo Identity Cards (EPICs), 297
Electronic Voting Machines or EVMs, 297
Environmental governance, 440
Epic period, 5
Estimates Committee (EC), 276, 284, 285, 288
Evaluation of the working of the Union Public Service Commission, 46
Externality, 437

Fair governance, 441, 442
Finance Commission, 276, 277
Financial administration, 275, 348, 349
Flexible government, 424
Fort William College, 17
Franchise, 161, 217
French Local Government, 150
Fulton Committee, 46

Gandhian plan, 244
Gandhian principles, 412
Gender and administration, 426
General grievances, 306
Global governance, 439
Globalisation, 423, 424, 435
Good governance, 28, 441, 442
Goods and Services Tax (GST), 30

Gorwala Report, 35, 343
Governance, 28
Governance and government, 438
Government of India Act (1919), 154
Government of India Act (1935), 154
Government Railway Police (GRP), 418
Governor, 110
    dxecutive powers, 111
    financial powers of, 112
    legislative powers, 111
Governor-General's Council, 18
Gram Sabha, 184
Grievance redressal, 446
Gupta Period, 9

Hanumantha Rao Group, 270
Hierarchy, 4
Human Rights, 422
Hung Assembly, 361

Illahi gaz, 13
India Development Report, 1997, 214
Indian administration, 4, 5, 18–20, 22, 23, 26–28, 34, 36, 55, 156, 343, 344, 347, 369, 409, 433–435
Indian administration, 3, 53, 359
Indian Enterprise Development Service, 59
Indian Skill Development Service, 59
Indira Mahila Block Kendras (IMBKs), 223
Indira Mahila Kendras (IMKs), 223
Indira Mahila Yojana (IMY), 223
Individual grievances, 306
Indo-Tibetan Border Police (ITBP), 417, 419
Indus Valley Civilization, 5
Infant mortality rate, 24
Information Technology, 421, 440
Integrated Rural Development Programme (IRDP), 131
Intellectual Property Laws, 446
Intellectual Property Rights, 446
International Monetary Fund (IMF), 332, 437
Inter-State Council, 346
Islam, 11
IT governance, 440

Janani Shishu Suraksha Karyakram (JSSK), 405
Janani Suraksha Yojana (JSY), 404
Janapada panchayat, 190
Jan Lokpal Bill, 316
Janpad, 7
Japanese local government, 152
Jimmis, 11
Jizia tax, 11
Judicial Powers, 112

Kasturba Gandhi Balika Vidyalaya (KGBV) Scheme, 399
Kautilya's Arthasastra, 3
Kolkata Municipal Corporation (KMC), 163
Kothari Committee, 40, 42, 43
Kotpal, 14
Kumaramatya, 4

Law and order, 369, 417
Lee Commission, 19, 43, 46
Legislative Councils, 18, 19
Liberalisation, 435
Licence-raj, 437
Life expectancy, 24
Local government, 155
    constitutional status of, 156
Local Self Government, 155
    characteristics of, 139
    success of, 140
Local Self Government, 138
Lokayukta, 305, 313, 314, 316–321, 327
    functions of, 319
Lokpal, 305, 313
Lokpal Bill, 1990, 315

Macaulay Committee, 17
Mahabharata, 3, 6
Mahalanobis, 245
Mahalanobis model of planning, 244
Mahamatya, 4
Mahatma Gandhi National Rural Employment Guarantee Act (MGNREGA), 391
Mahila Samakhya Programme (MSP), 399
Maitreesh Ghatak and Maitreya Ghatak (2002), 224
Mandalas, 120
Mandal Commission, 378
Manikyamba, 228

Mann Ki Baat, 29
Mansabdari system, 12, 14
Market model, 424
Mauryan Period, 6
Mayor, 161
Mayor-council plan, 146
Metagovernance, 440
Ministry, 99
  of external affairs, 93
  of finance, 89
  of home affairs, 91
Modi government, 29
Mohkuma Parishad, 192
Monopolistic practices, 438
Montague–Chelmsford reforms, 62
Morley Minto Reforms, 19
Mughal administration, 4, 10
Mukarji–Bandyopadhyay Report (1993), 219
Mukhia, 186
Mukhyamatya, 5
Municipal Commissioner, 162
Municipal Corporation, 159
  discretionary functions of, 160
  obligatory functions of, 159
Municipal Council, 167
Municipality, 167

Narmada Bachao Andolan (NBA), 215
National Commission, 375, 385, 391
National Commission for Women (NCW), 216, 221, 223, 380, 384, 385, 423
National Development Council (NDC), 261
  committees of, 263
  composition of, 262
  evaluation of, 265
  functions of, 264
National Election Study (NES), 305
National Human Rights Commission (NHRC), 422
National Iron Plus Initiative, 406
National Police Commission, 345
National Police Commission Report (1979), 308
National Population Policy, 263
National Programme for Education of Girls at Elementary Level (NPEGEL), 400
National Rural Health Mission (NRHM), 401
Nehru-Mahalanobis, 245
New Economic Policy, 346
New Public Management (NPM), 27, 434
NITI Aayog, 257
Non-profit governance, 439
None Of The Above (NOTA), 297
Notified Area Committee, 169
NREGA, 392

Ombudsman, 311
Operation Barga, 212
Organization of the Planning Commission, 253

Padhe Bharat Badhe Bharat (PBBB), 400
Padshah, 11
Panchamrit, 406
Panchas, 186
Panchayati raj, 330
Panchayat or Gram Panchayat, 186
Panchayat Samiti, 189
Panchayat union council, 190
Parliamentary Committees, 284, 285, 374
Participatory governance, 440
Participatory model, 424
People's Plan, 244
Personnel, 414
Personnel administration, 350, 409, 414
Plan, 241
Planning, 241
Planning Commission, 244, 246, 247, 248, 249, 252
  composition of, 249
  evaluation of, 256
  functions and responsibilities of, 252
  organization of, 253
PMO, 71, 72, 73
  functions, 72
  role of, 73
Political affairs committee, 95
Poor governance, 441
Post-Vedic period, 5
Prabhat Datta and Chandan Datta (1999), 224
Pradesas, 120
President, 82

Prime Minister, 86
Prime Minister's Secretariat (PMS), 70
Private governance, 439
Privatisation, 435
Project governance, 440
Prussian Civil Service, 415
Public, 1
Public Accounts Committee (PAC), 276, 284, 285, 287, 290
Public administration, 1
Public governance, 306, 439
Public Grievance Redressal Commissioners, 448
Public Grievance Redressal Commissions, 447
Public Information Officer, 446
Public–Private Partnership (PPP), 436
Public Sector, 419
Public Sector Undertakings, 352
Public Service Commission, 353
Punchhi Commission (2007), 360

Railway Protection Force (RPF), 417, 418
Rajasthan Administrative Reforms Committee Report, 104
Rajput administration, 4, 9
Ramayana, 3, 5
Rapid Action Force (RAF), 417, 418
Regulatory governance, 440
Responsive Administration Conference, 38
Revenue Collector, 128
Revenue department, 89
Right to Information (RTI), 38, 399, 433, 435, 444, 445
Rigvedic period, 5
Rock departmentalism, 202
Royal Commission, 19, 43, 365
RTI Act (2005), 445
RTI portal, 445
Rural-Urban Relationship Committee, 168, 172, 173

Sabha, 5
Samiti, 5
Sandwich course, 51
Santhanam Committee, 313, 322, 323
Sardar Vallabhbhai Patel National Police Academy, 54
Sarkar, 120
Sarkaria Commission, 23, 267, 346, 353–356, 358–361
Sarpanch, 186
Sarva Shiksha Abhiyan (SSA), 396
Satish Chandra Committee, 40
Secretariat, 63
Secretariat Reorganization Committee, 342
Security sector governance, 441
Self Employed Women's Association (SEWA), 216
Self Help Groups, 434
Sepoy Mutiny of 1857, 17
Seventy-Fourth Constitutional Amendment, 173
Sex ratio, 25
Shah Commission, 36
Shikdar, 10
Shikos, 10
Simon Commission, 43, 105
Singhvi L.M., Committee, 183
Single citizenship, 413
South Asian, 138
Special Police Establishment (SPE), 325
SPSC, 48
Stakeholder, 447
State Planning Boards, 268
State Planning Department, 267, 268
State Public Service Commission, 46, 106, 112, 116, 353
  composition, 47
  evaluation of the working, 49
  functions, 48
State Reorganization Commission, 35
State Secretariat, 99, 100
  appointment of, 102
  functions of, 100, 103
  structure, 100
  tenure, 103
State Vigilance Commission (SVC), 325
Structure of Civil Services, 34
Subahs, 120
Sultanate administration, 4, 9

Taluk development board, 190
Taluk panchayat, 190
Tariff Commission, 351
Tarikh-i-Shahjahani, 10
Tebhaga movement, 211
The Constitution (73rd Amendment) Act, 1993, 193

Tirthas, 7
Town Area Committee, 170
Township, 172
  training, 46
Training, 50
  institutes, 52
  kinds of, 51
  need for, 50
  origin and development of, 50
  shortcomings or imperfections, 55
Treasury, 7
Tribal TB Eradication Project, 406
Tujuk-i-Jahangiri, 10

UNDP Human Development Reports, 208
Union Government, 81
Union Public Service Commission, 23, 42–44, 46, 96, 277, 353, 416
  composition, 44
  evaluation of the working, 46
  functions, 44
Union Public Service Commission (UPSC), 44, 55, 346
United Nations, 138
UPSC Jobs, terms and conditions of, 39
Urbanization, 157, 158
Urban Local Self Government, 157

Vice-President, 85
Vishays, 120
Voluntary Retirement Scheme (VRS), 38
Voter Verified Paper Audit Trail (VVPAT), 297

Wazir, 9
Weak governance, 441
Weaver, 334
Welfare administration, 369
Welfare state, 369–371, 409, 414
Women cell, 384
Women's participation, 207
World Bank, 443

Zilla Parishad, 132, 192
Zonal Councils, 297